CODEX NEW YORK

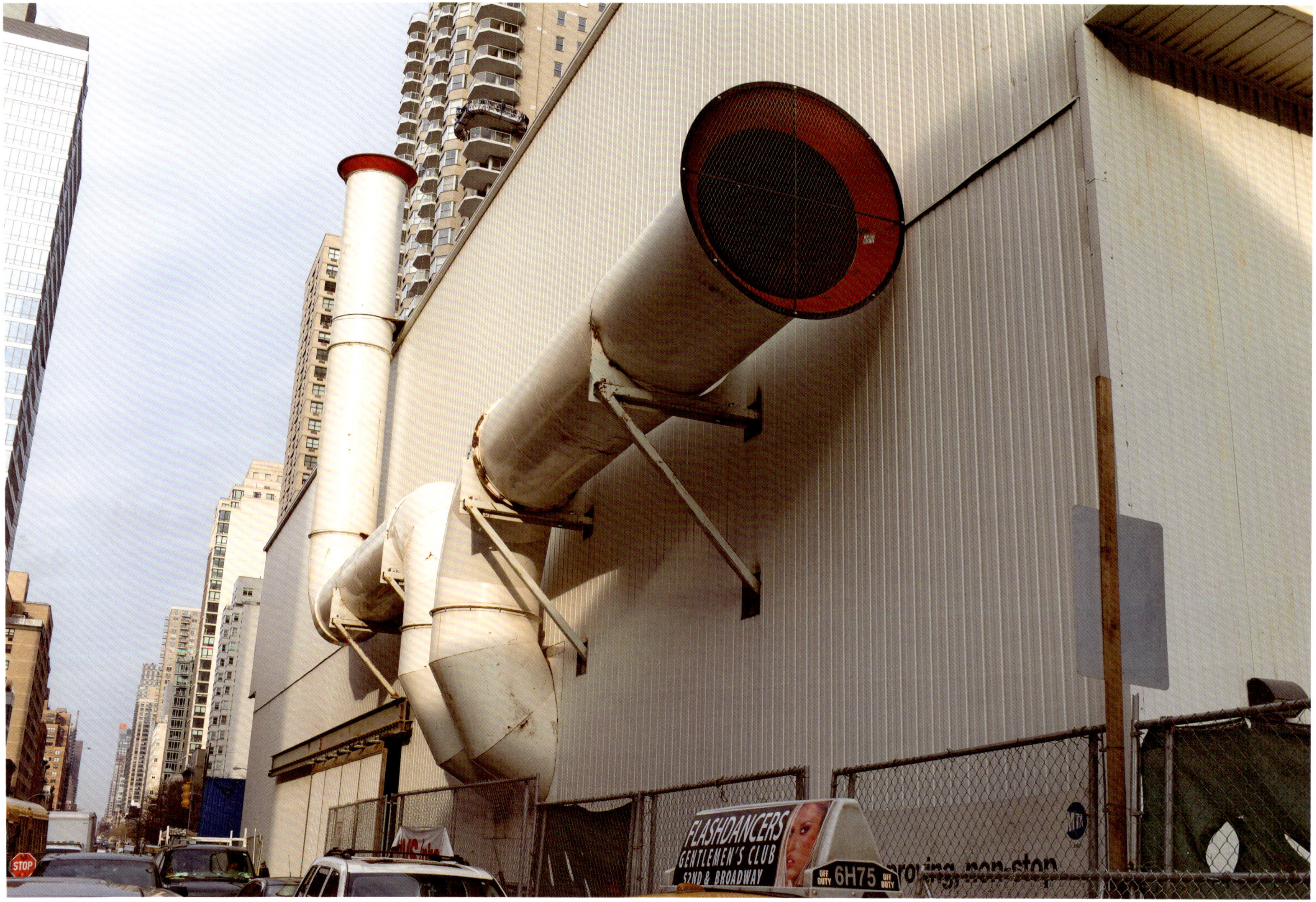
FLASHDANCERS
GENTLEMEN'S CLUB
52ND & BROADWAY
OFF DUTY
6H75
OFF DUTY
STOP

CODEX NEW YORK

TYPOLOGIES OF THE CITY

STANLEY GREENBERG

FOREWORD BY KARRIE JACOBS THE MONACELLI PRESS

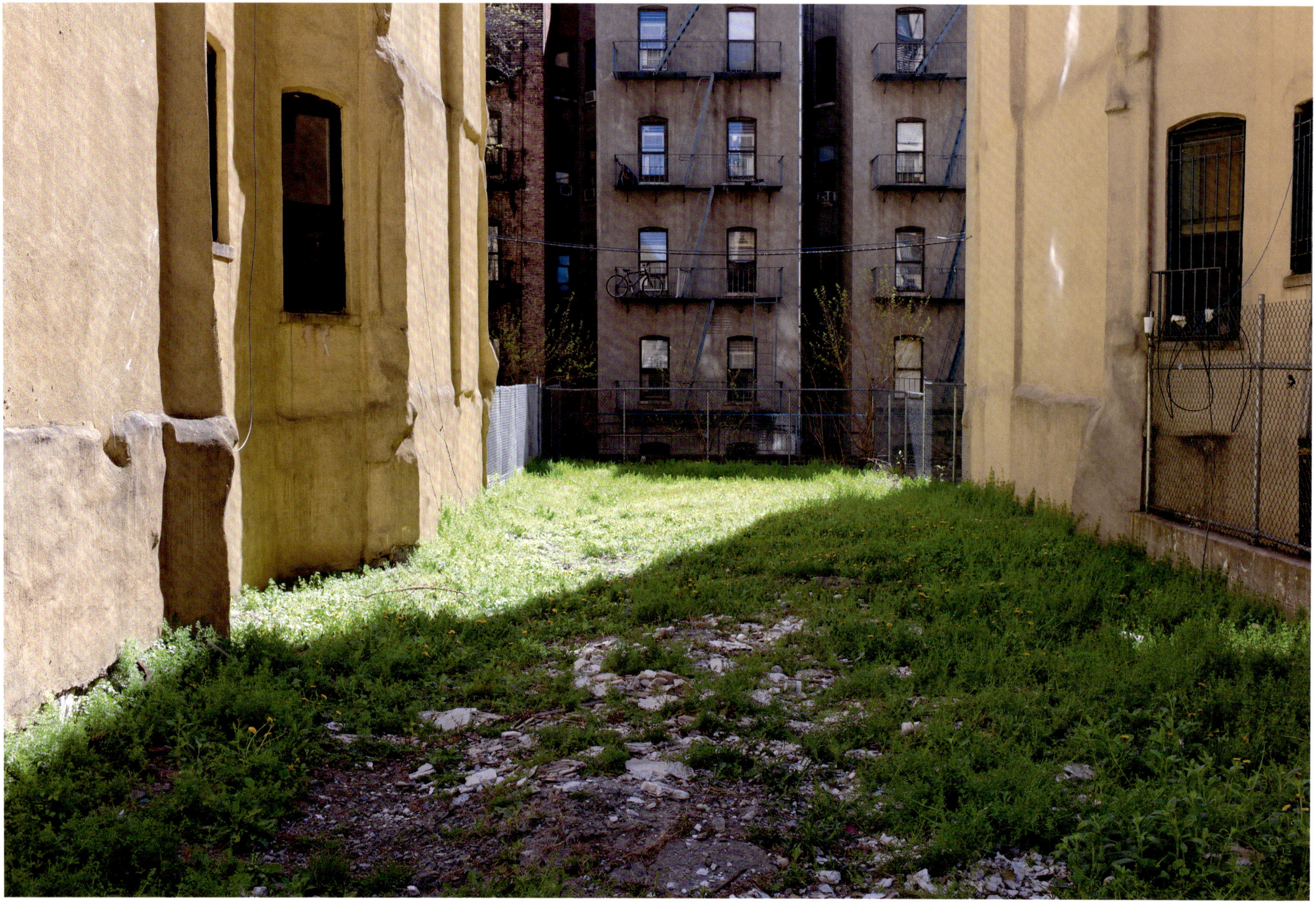

CONTENTS

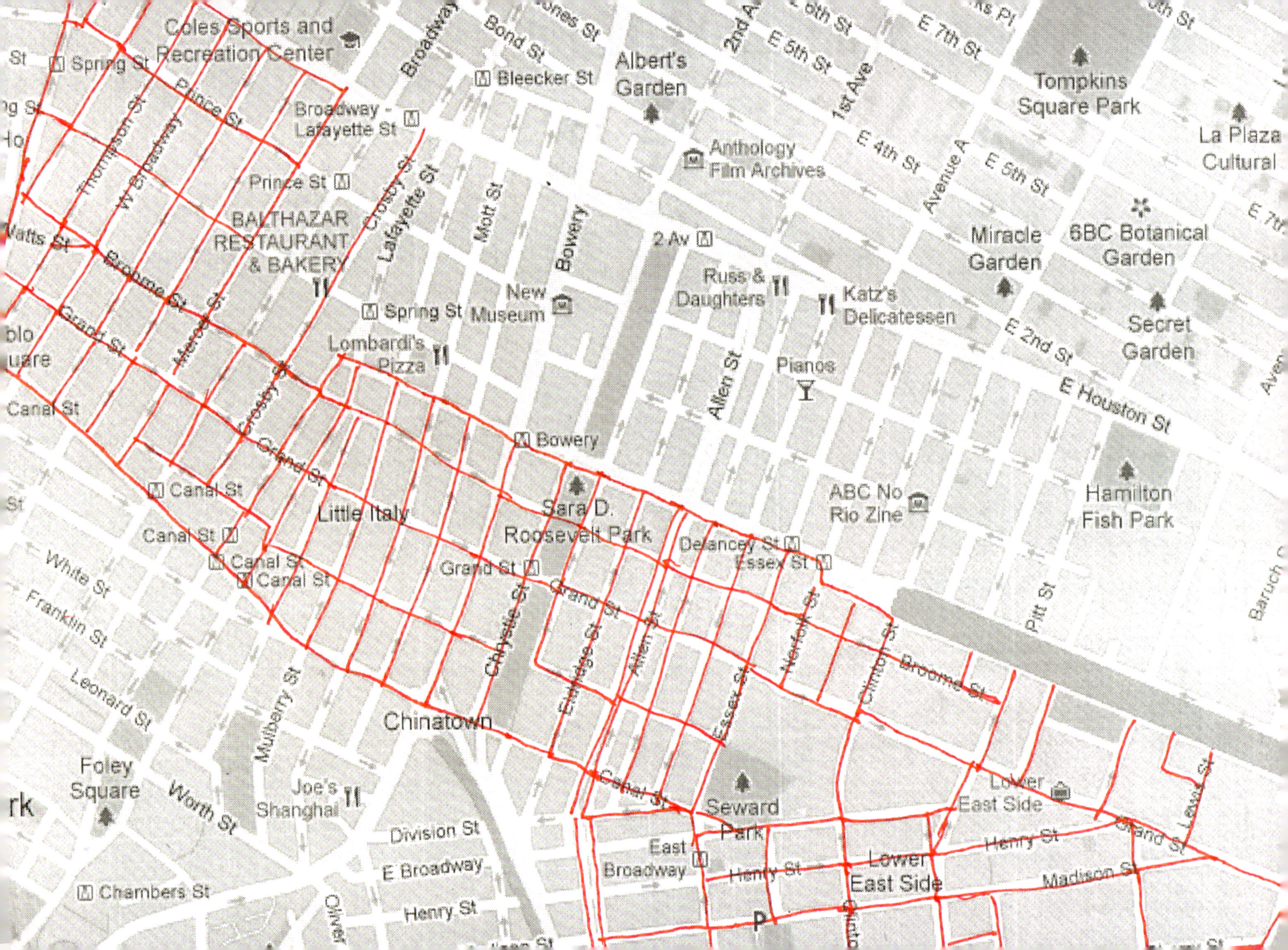
Coles Sports and Recreation Center
Spring St
Prince St
Broadway - Lafayette St
Prince St
Thompson St
W Broadway
BALTHAZAR RESTAURANT & BAKERY
Watts St
Broome St
Grand St
Mercer St
Crosby St
Lafayette St
Canal St
Canal St
Canal St
Canal St
Canal St
Broadway
Bond St
Bleecker St
Albert's Garden
2nd Av
E 5th St
1st Ave
E 7th St
Tompkins Square Park
La Plaza Cultural
Anthology Film Archives
E 4th St
Avenue A
E 5th St
Mott St
Bowery
2 Av
Miracle Garden
6BC Botanical Garden
Russ & Daughters
Katz's Delicatessen
Secret Garden
E 2nd St
New Museum
Spring St
Lombardi's Pizza
Allen St
Pianos
E Houston St
Bowery
ABC No Rio Zine
Hamilton Fish Park
Little Italy
Sara D. Roosevelt Park
Delancey St
Essex St
Grand St
Grand St
Chrystie St
Eldridge St
Allen St
Essex St
Norfolk St
Clinton St
Broome St
Pitt St
Baruch
White St
Franklin St
Leonard St
Mulberry St
Chinatown
Foley Square
Worth St
Joe's Shanghai
Canal St
Seward Park
Lower East Side
East Broadway
Henry St
Lower East Side
Henry St
Grand St
Madison St
Lewis St
Division St
E Broadway
Henry St
Chambers St
Oliver

FOREWORD KARRIE JACOBS

The moment I sit down in Stanley Greenberg's Gowanus, Brooklyn studio, he hands me a copy of a magazine that's sitting near his computer. The cover story is, "The Death of a Once Great City." It's a multi-thousand word screed arguing that New York is being remade exclusively for the rich and that everyone and everything that once made the city creative and exciting has been driven out or soon will be.

While I can't much argue with the premise, I find it impossible to read the entire article. For one thing, I've heard it all before, and, for another, aside from some policy suggestions (stop subsidizing the real estate industry) the story fails to offer up much help to fix what's broken. The whole problem with gentrification is intractable and frustratingly paradoxical because it turns out anything you do to make the city less dull somehow winds up attracting more rich people whose presence will eventually drive up the overhead on your enterprise until it reaches an unsustainable level. In other words, everything you do to make the city less dull ultimately makes it more dull.

But here's a thought: maybe Greenberg himself is the antidote to this, or, at least, his photography is. No, I don't expect that he has the power to halt the onslaught of glass towers for billionaires, but his work is a powerful counterpoint to the notion that New York City could ever be dull. His methodology is a simple one: he walks around with his eyes open and he notices the things that are right in front of him, things that most of us are too distracted to see. Greenberg's photos, for example, document the fact that myriad older New York buildings tend to lean on their neighbors and, when those adjacent buildings are demolished, require shockingly primitive-looking buttresses to forestall structural failure. And he compulsively documents Manhattan's irregularities, the spots where the borough's defining grid—a smooth plain marked by streets crossing at right angles—becomes unexpectedly sharp-cornered or hilly.

I'm sympathetic to this strategy because I practice it myself. As a writer and as a teacher, I spend a lot of my time urging people to look at the city around them. In particular, I like to send graduate students out into the streets to search for examples of ephemeral qualities like truth or beauty. Why? Because the muzzy, conceptual nature of the assignment focuses their awareness on the streetscape. It forces the students to look harder at absolutely everything. And the city isn't dull at all, if you pay attention.

Additionally, it increasingly seems pretty obvious that the dullness of the city is commensurate to the interestingness of the glowing rectangle we habitually hold in front of our faces. The smart phone is a mind-suck of historic proportions and as we focus on it, checking the analytics of our most recent selfie or tracking the whereabouts of an ex-boyfriend, the city around us fades. It loses definition. It becomes a sketchily articulated background to the brilliant electronic foreground. It's not just that the city somehow turned into a gilded habitat for rich people (who don't even truly live here) when we weren't paying attention; the transformation happened specifically *because* we weren't paying attention.

Cause and effect become obvious when you read pre-iPhone narratives about the streetscape. The classic example is Ian Frazier's 1990 *New Yorker* essay about Canal Street. "Near the corner of Canal and Broadway is a store that used to sell luggage, jewelry, and takeout Chinese food but now just sells luggage. Another store sells plastic sheeting and imitation classical statues made of fiberglass. The nymphs and dryads and goddesses are displayed out front, chained to a security gate with bicycle locks around their necks." Frazier was observing closely and the city responded by yielding a mother lode of specificity. Today, many of the blocks he described almost three decades ago have been methodically scrubbed by what the real estate industry thinks of as "highest and best use."

While there are economic and political reasons that kind of thing happens, an important and rarely considered cause is that we've averted our eyes. As philosopher George Berkeley once said, "To be is to be perceived." And, presumably, the inverse is true. What is no longer perceived ceases, in any meaningful way, to be.

As his fundamental philosophy as a photographer, Greenberg perceives. It's what he does. His photography is about being deeply aware of the city around us, even noticing and documenting those things that lay beneath the city's surface or outside its boundaries that, nonetheless, allow New York City to exist.

When I first came across Greenberg's photography, he'd recently completed his 2003 book *Waterworks*, in which he documented the components of the system that transports New York City's water, some 1.3 billion gallons a day, from reservoirs in the Catskills to faucets and toilets in the Five Boroughs. The photos, in black and white, are both quotidian and epic, documenting infrastructure—dams, pumping stations, tunnels—that tell the story of a far-sighted nineteenth-century scheme that guaranteed New York City's future growth and prosperity (at the expense of Catskills farming communities that were flooded when a half dozen reservoirs were built). Greenberg's portraits of the water system were not just photos of a massive engineering project but showed the basic support system that allows 8.5 million people to live cheek-by-jowl at a density of 27,000 per square mile.

Codex New York is a much broader project, an attempt to create a visual taxonomy of the city, an effort to isolate and appreciate some of its component parts. Because the word *codex* usually describes an ancient manuscript, a loosely bound stack of vellum, the title could imply that Greenberg's work is somehow archaeological, that, like the protagonist of a W.G. Sebald novel, Greenberg is on the trail of memories and meaning that are retained by

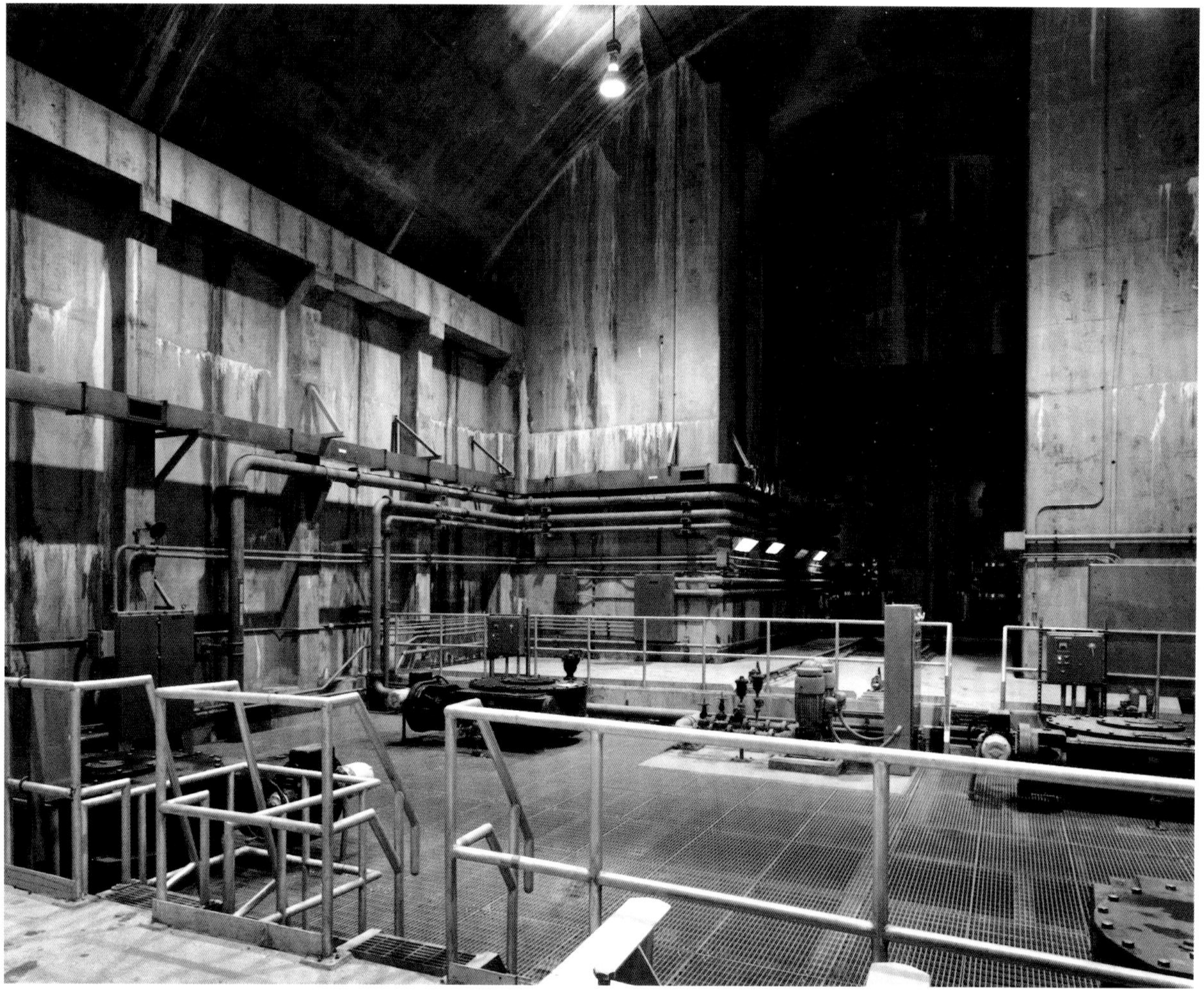

10 *Shaft 13b, City Tunnel No. 3, New York, New York, 1994*

certain works of architecture. Greenberg, however, uses the word to mean something less weighty. For him, a codex is more like a guidebook or a sketchbook: "The book is also about all the things I know about New York, and then all the things I don't know about it. And all the things I discovered while walking." Indeed, the knowledge Greenberg brings to the surface about New York City's characteristic infrastructural language isn't particularly lost. It's not buried in the Catskills or beneath the skins of buildings. The knowledge is in plain view, where anyone could see it if they would just look up. The operative word here is *attention.*

Actually, *Codex* emerged from a completely different project. Greenberg was searching for "big empty spaces where buildings had been torn down." If you know New York—or any city, really—you understand that demolition can be revelatory. The denser the setting, the more things appear when a building suddenly vanishes. At minimum, razing one building uncovers the walls from the adjoining buildings that had been obscured for decades, perhaps centuries. Particularly in midtown Manhattan, the removal of a building creates something that works like a plaza. Where you can suddenly gain a perspective—maybe something as simple as the sun hitting the sidewalk at a new angle—that didn't exist before.

Greenberg originally set out to find and document those absences that we usually come upon by chance. He started at the Battery and began working his way north from there. "I took the train in from Brooklyn, got out at the Customs House and started walking." His idea was that he'd document the gaps with a digital camera and return later to frame his shots with a large-format camera. "I had a Google map of the neighborhood in hand, ready to mark the empty spaces. Within a half hour knew I was going to walk every block on the island."

What was truly captivating, however, as Greenberg covered the map, street by street, was "building typologies and infrastructure." He soon realized that "it was a different project than I originally thought it was." Sticking with the smaller, more versatile digital camera he set out to document features that explain "what the city is made of and what it takes to make it work. . . . I thought about what made up the city, the history, the layers, the unseen, places I had been that were restricted."

Some features, he noticed, were everywhere—like playgrounds and parking lots—and others were concentrated in just one area. For example, his depictions of "visible geology and topography," in which familiar urban objects, like subway station entrances, coexist with startling rock formations, are mostly way uptown in the northern reaches of Manhattan.

The quality of Greenberg's perception is such that even if you think you know Manhattan, his photos will reveal new aspects of the city. Alleys, for example, turn out to come in two types, those designed for cars, smooth and blandly industrial, and those designed for people or, more commonly, garbage. Some of the latter type are neglected and others are landscaped like suburban front yards. Among the alleys, there's one in the West Village in which there's a tree hung with Christmas decorations accompanied by a birdbath. Another, unpaved and lined with garages, looks like it belongs in a different city, or someplace far less urban. The vast majority of the alleys have the best qualities of in-between spaces: under-designed, unplanned, and unselfconscious. Occasionally, they reveal moments of strange beauty. In one photo shot on the Upper West Side, an alley frames a neo-Gothic style garage bathed in sunlight.

A section called "Bridges, Tunnels, Tracks," by contrast, looks at some of the most conspicuous and admired objects in the urban landscape. There are beauty shots of certain bridges, like a long view of the George Washington Bridge, its gray steel blending into an overcast sky and a cloud-colored river. But mostly Greenberg focuses on the less appreciated aspects of these heroic structures. For example, there are photos of the rarely noticed undersides of bridges revealing the elegance of the supporting columns and arches, and many photos show the awkward ways that bridges and tunnels connect to the city, how a monumental stone anchorage drops into the streetscape like an uninvited dinner guest, or tunnel entrances that open unexpectedly, like portals to another dimension.

Examples of this awkwardness, a syntax of strange adjacencies, is a dominant theme in *Codex New York.* One section of the book focuses on the places that are beyond the reach of Manhattan's grid, any place below Houston Street or above 155th, or those spots where the rectilinear approach simply falls apart, triangular lots created where avenues converge. One of the loveliest photos in the book is of an anonymous pre-war apartment building at the confluence of two hilly, curving uptown streets, Fairview Avenue and Wadsworth Terrace. It is Edward Steichen's *The Flatiron*, without the mystique. It is an unsung moment in an out-of-the-way neighborhood that is—all by itself, if you stop to contemplate it—an argument against the death of greatness.

Of course, there is nothing prescriptive about this book. Greenberg makes no recommendations for the places he closely observes. He doesn't claim to be fixing anything. He simply looks and allows us to look with him. He is quietly advancing the notion that we can make the city better by observing it closely and responding to what we find. This isn't a novel idea or an untested one. It's implicit in Jane Jacobs' advocacy of close-grained detail. It's what

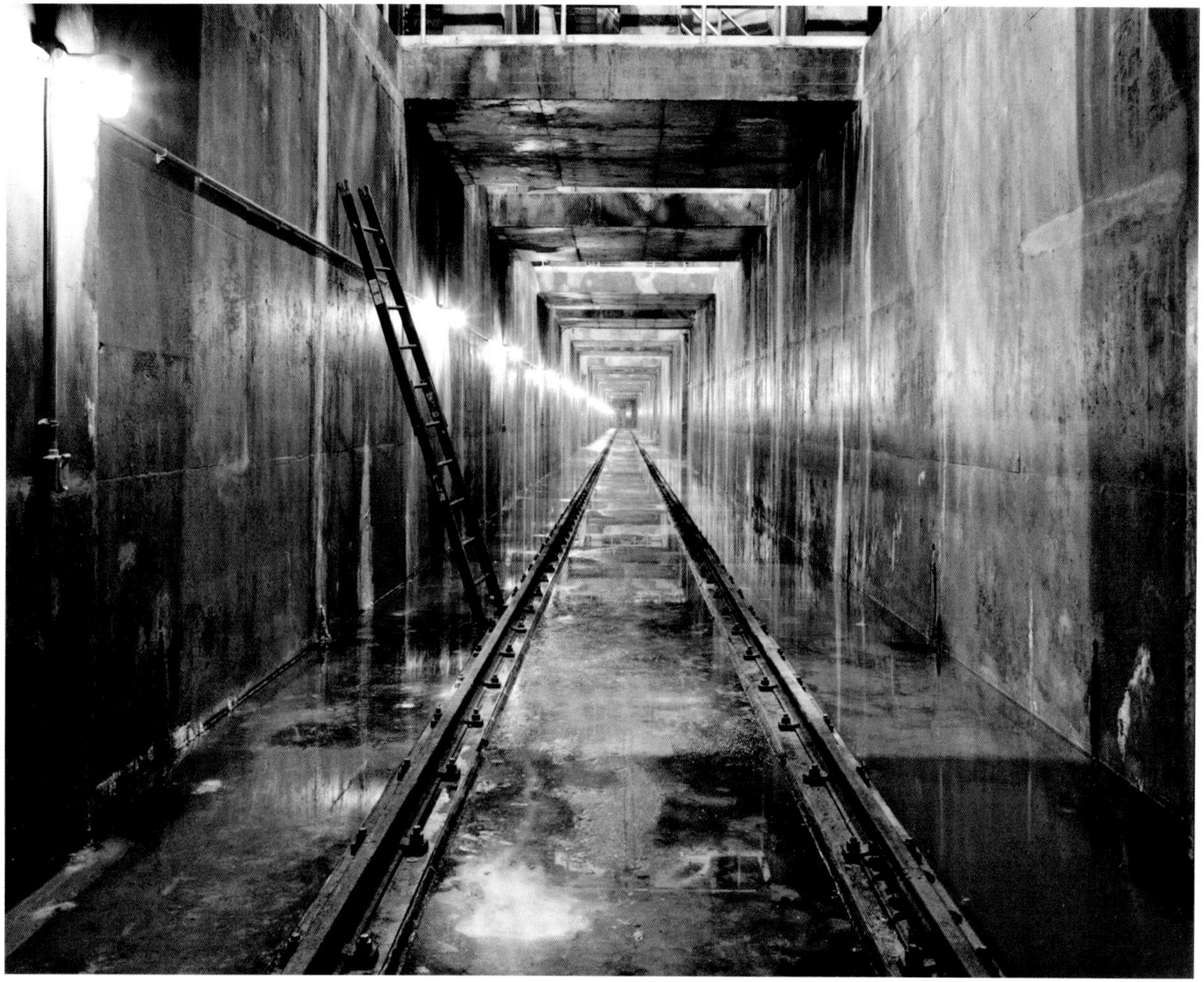

14 *Shaft 2b, City tunnel No. 3, Bronx, New York, 1992*

the designer George Nelson was advocating in his book, *How to See,* when he asked, "Does anyone ever notice a street corner, judge it in terms of decency, effectiveness, amenity? . . . Have you ever looked at one?" It is the motivation, I think, for Robert Venturi's *Complexity and Contradiction in Architecture,* in which he declared his allegiance to "messy vitality over obvious unity. . . ."

However, from these moments of heightened awareness, in which we recognize the extraordinary nature of an urban tableau we generally take for granted, can emerge small acts of civic engagement or inspired reconsiderations of the entire man-made environment. But even if it doesn't lead to a minor revolution or a major paradigm shift, the simple act of regarding what's right in front of us, of contemplating our workaday habitat, has therapeutic value; it's a surprisingly powerful corrective for the state of buzzing preoccupation in which most of us spend our days. Harvard psychologist Ellen Langer, a leading proponent of "mindfulness," insists this is scientific fact. "The very simple process of actively noticing new things," she says, is "literally, not just figuratively, enlivening."

Greenberg isn't just speaking to architects, planners, or designers, or even photographers or the authors of long, dispirited assessments of the fate of the city. His audience is more universal. His message is more catholic. What *Codex New York* reveals isn't mysterious at all. His photos are an argument for seeing with determination, for seeking out what makes New York City unique, for understanding that we are surrounded by a work of boundless ingenuity, passion, messy vitality, and, sometimes, genius. It's a collection of photographs that states unequivocally that our job, as human beings, is to see what's in front of us, and to consciously, willfully, observe.

CODEX NEW YORK

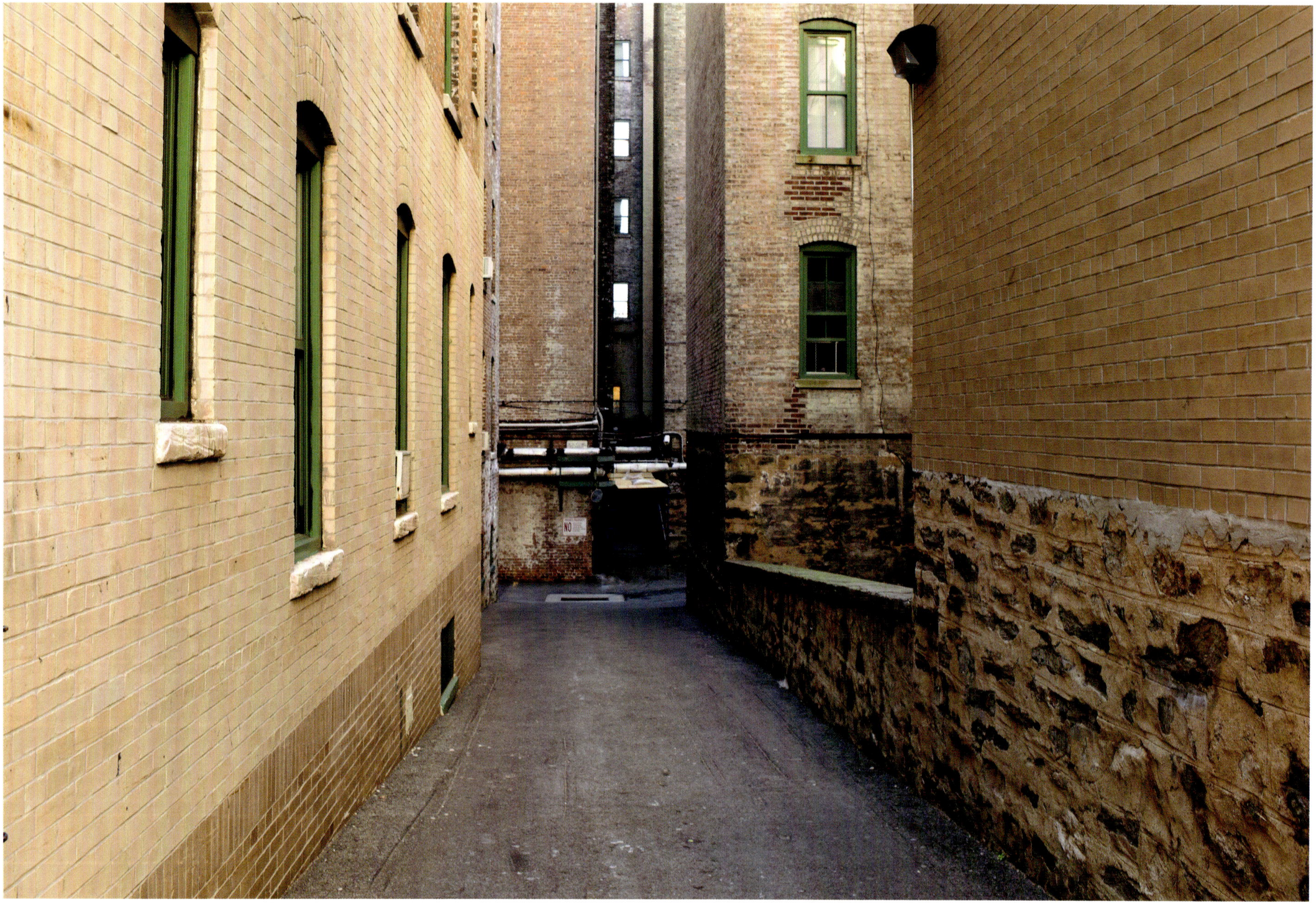

ALLEYS

Here the term is used to also include mews, maintenance spaces, and parking entrances. Many cities have alleys to accommodate trash pickups, vehicles, and other storage needs, but there are only a few like that in Manhattan. Most of Manhattan has no alleys because the commissioners of the 1811 Grid Plan didn't include them, in line with the pervasive idea of the era that they were unclean and unsafe. The ironic result is that much of the city has to put all the things that other cities put in alleys—trash, utility meters, gas access panels—out on the sidewalk for everyone to see, or trip over.

Much more prevalent in Manhattan are the spaces either between apartment buildings or within a single building—as when parents say, "Go play in the alley" (or, "Don't play in *that* alley"). They range from completely designed and manicured—some have been turned into play or green areas, and bicycle parking—to barren expanses of concrete. In some parts of the city they accommodate angular, pre-Grid spaces; in Upper Manhattan they also accommodate elevation changes. Alley-facing windows on these buildings allow for views, if only of the facing building ten feet away.

1 Upper East Side
2 Harlem
3 Striver's Row
4 Gramercy Park
5 Gramercy Park
6 Upper West Side
7 Union Square
8 Gramercy Park
9 Upper East Side
10 West Village
11 Upper West Side
12 Inwood
13 Upper East Side
14 Upper East Side
15 West Village
16 West Village
17 Upper East Side
17 Upper West Side
19 Upper West Side
20 Upper West Side
21 Upper West Side
22 West Village
23 Upper East Side
24 West Village
25 Upper West Side
26 Upper West Side
27 Upper West Side
28 Gramercy Park
29 Upper West Side
30 Hudson Heights
31 Harlem
32 Washington Heights
33 Upper West Side
34 Washington Heights
35 West Village
36 Upper East Side

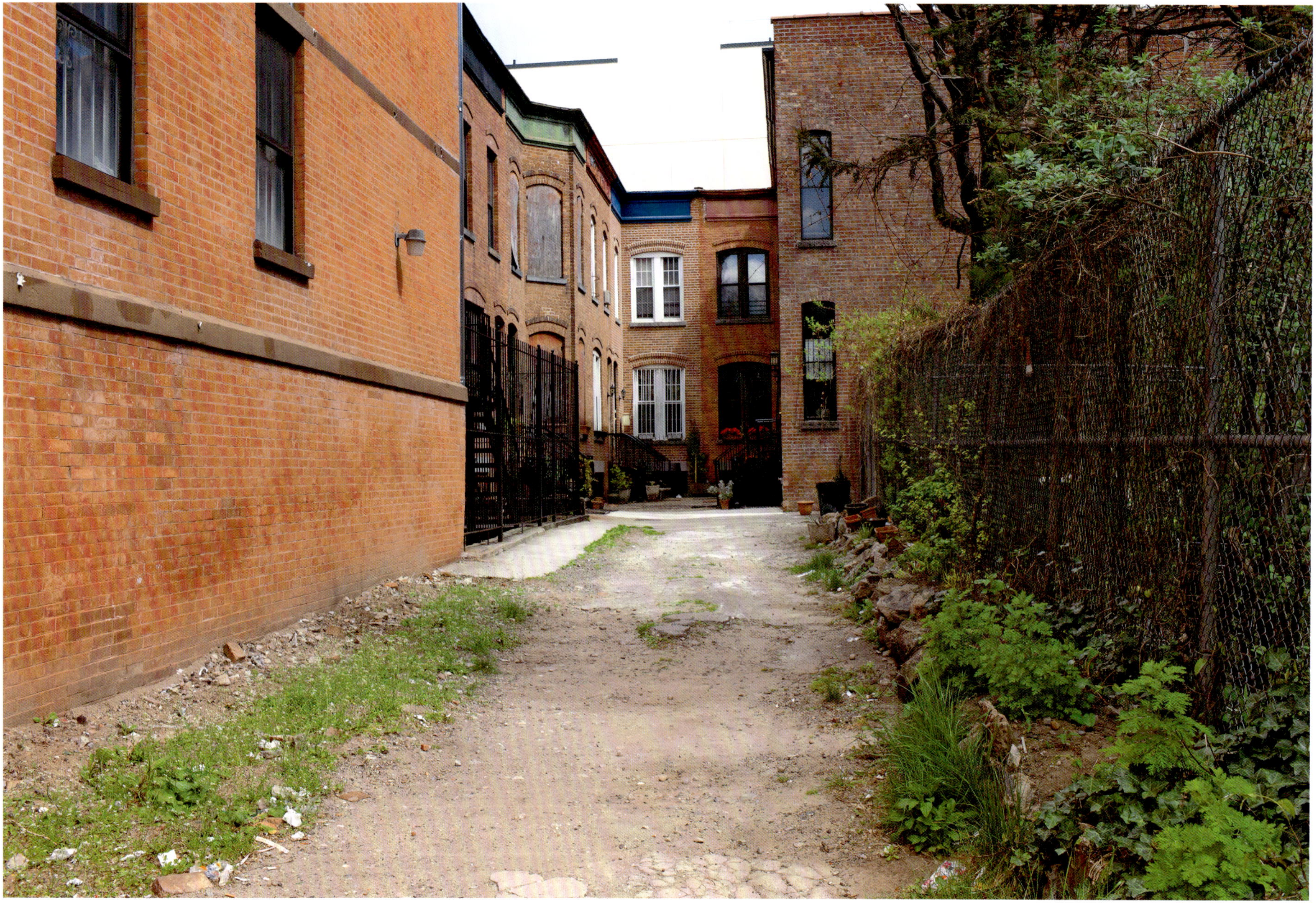

2

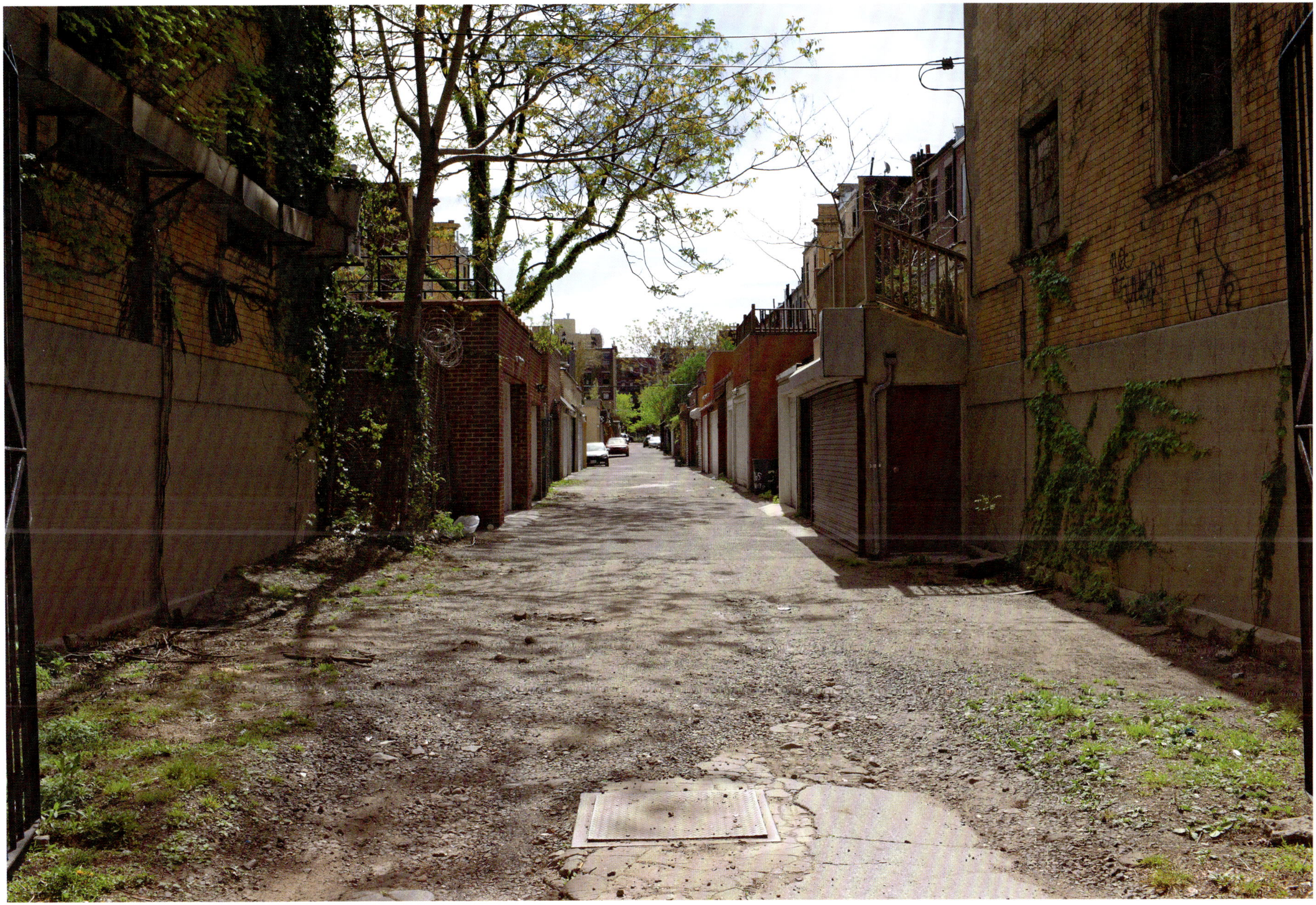

3

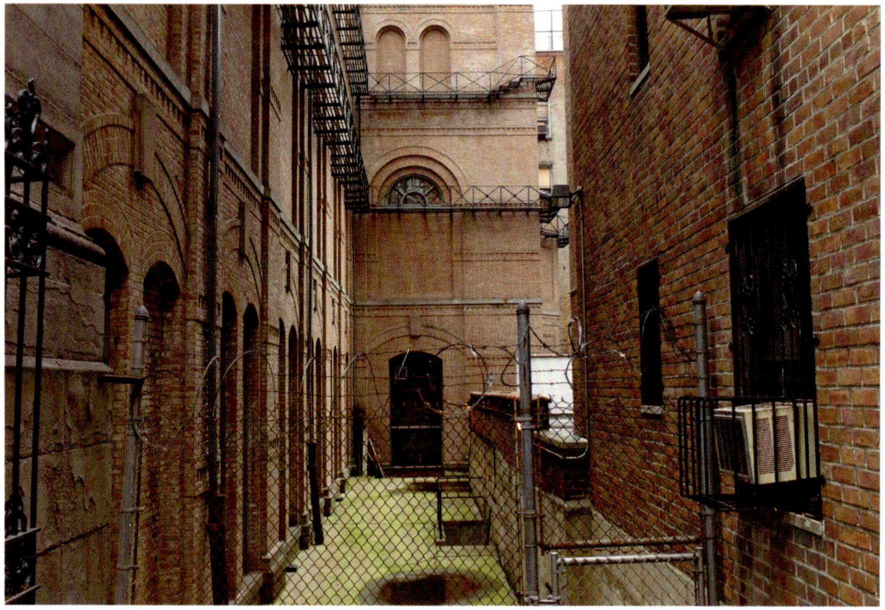

4

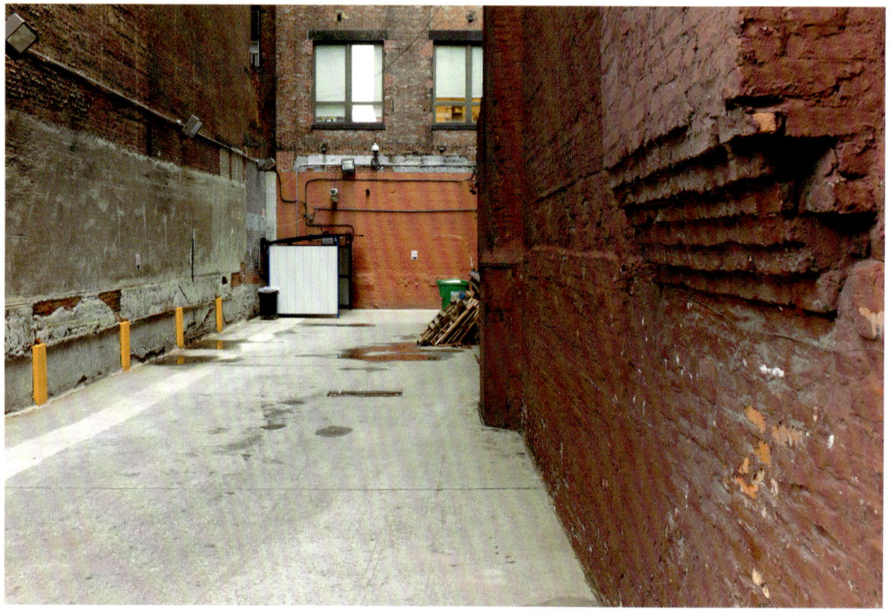

5

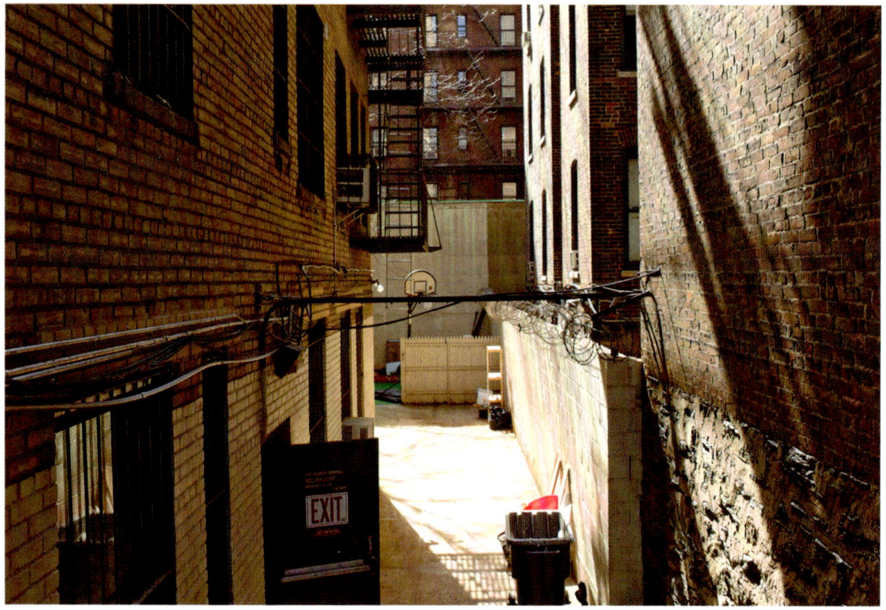

6

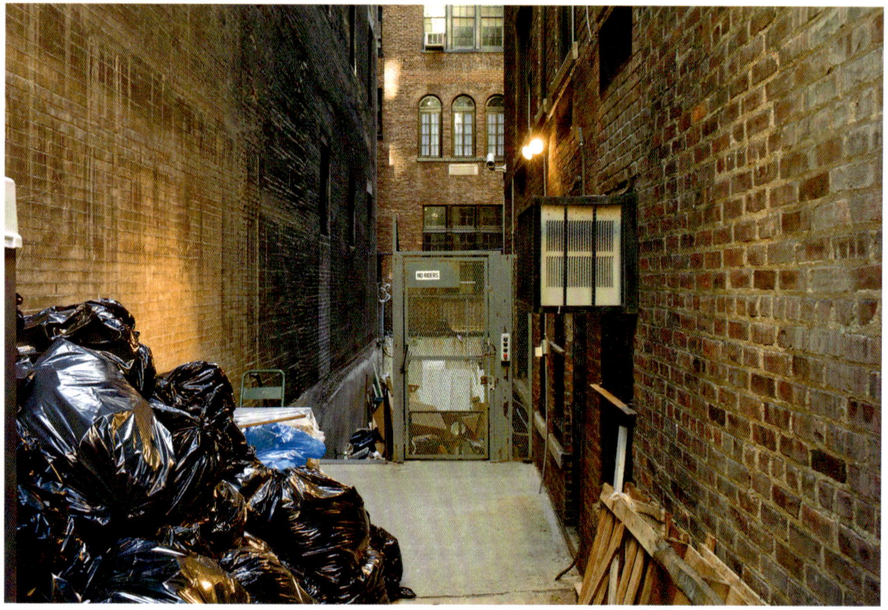

7

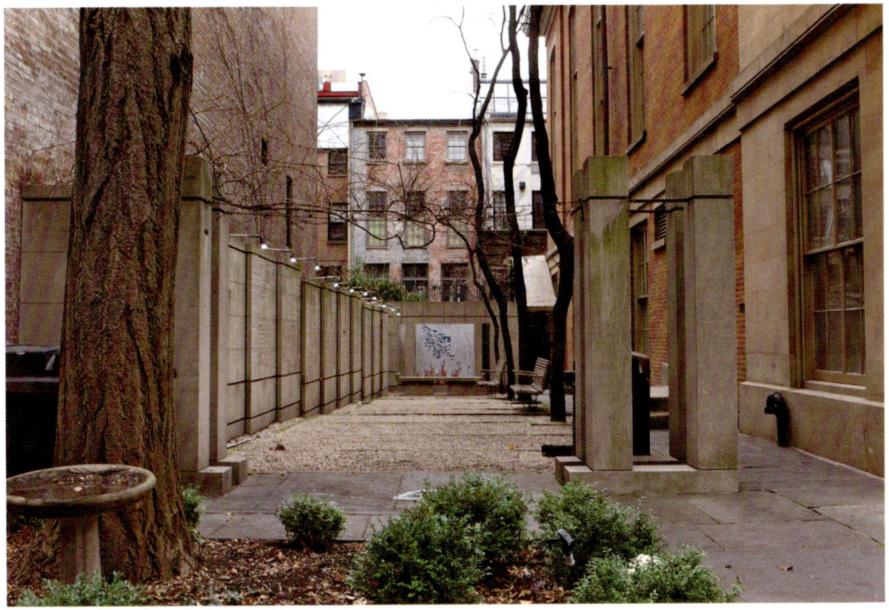
8

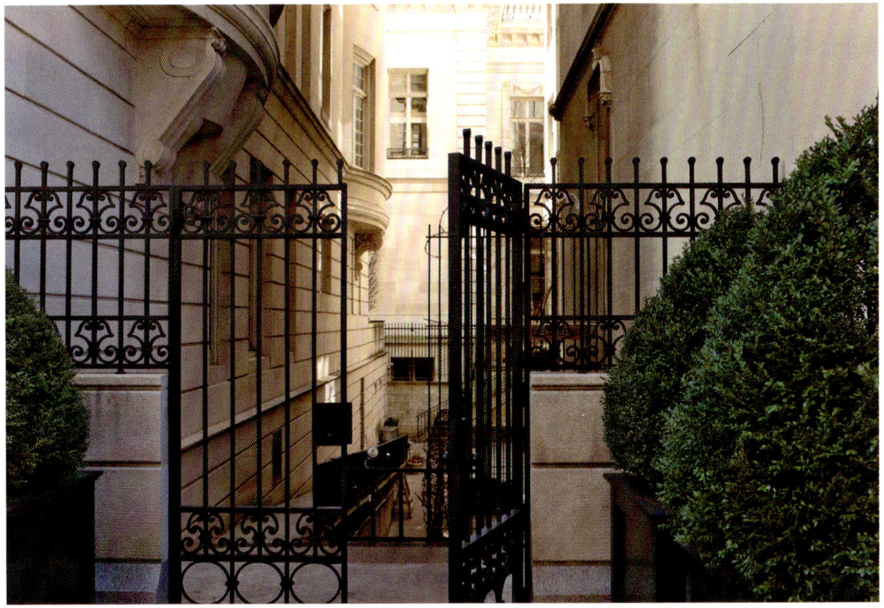
9

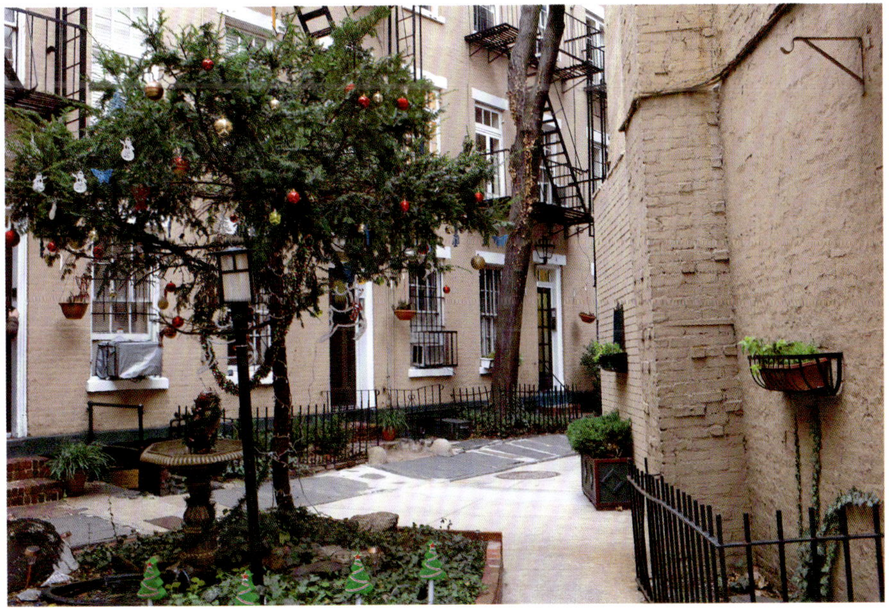
10

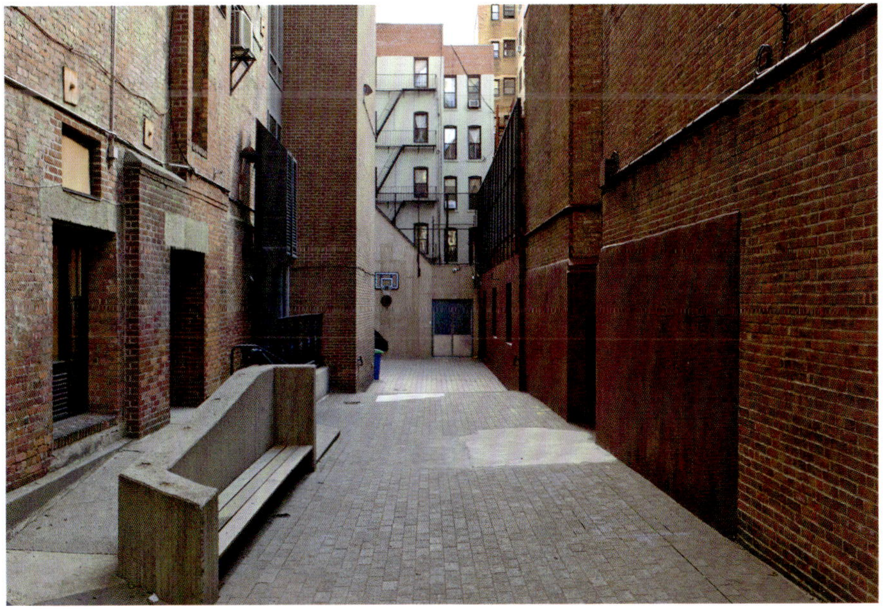
11

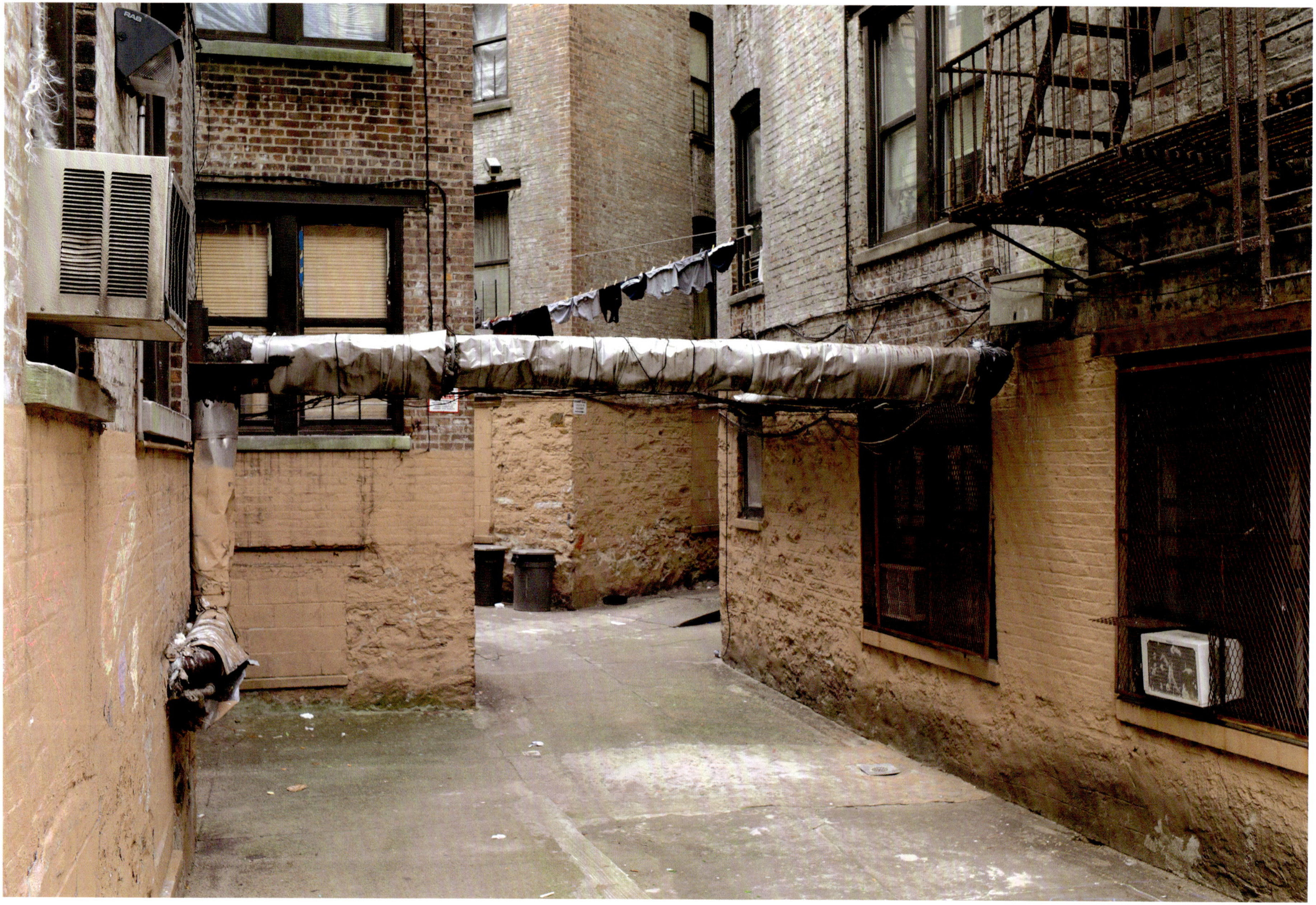

12

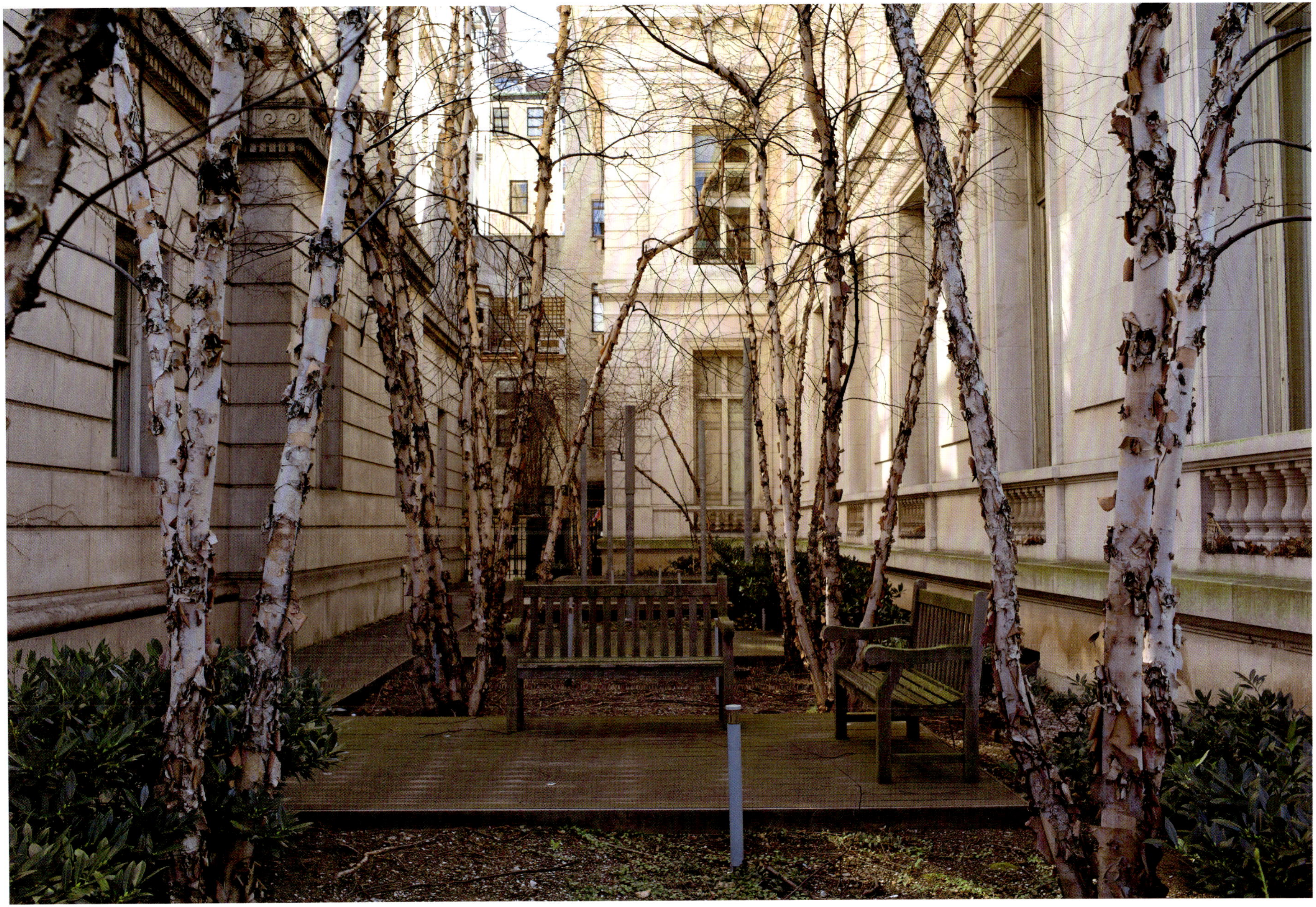

13

26

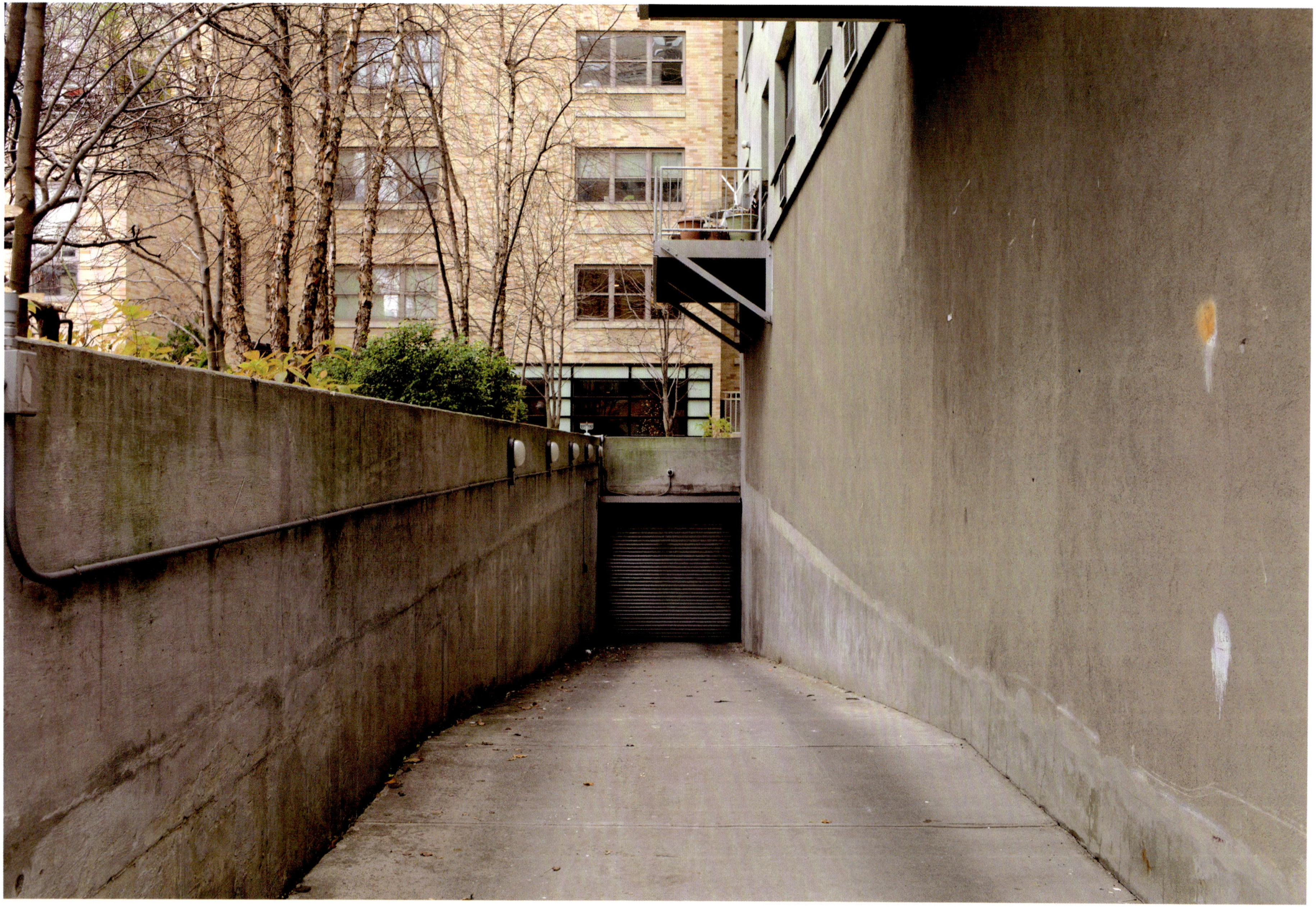

14

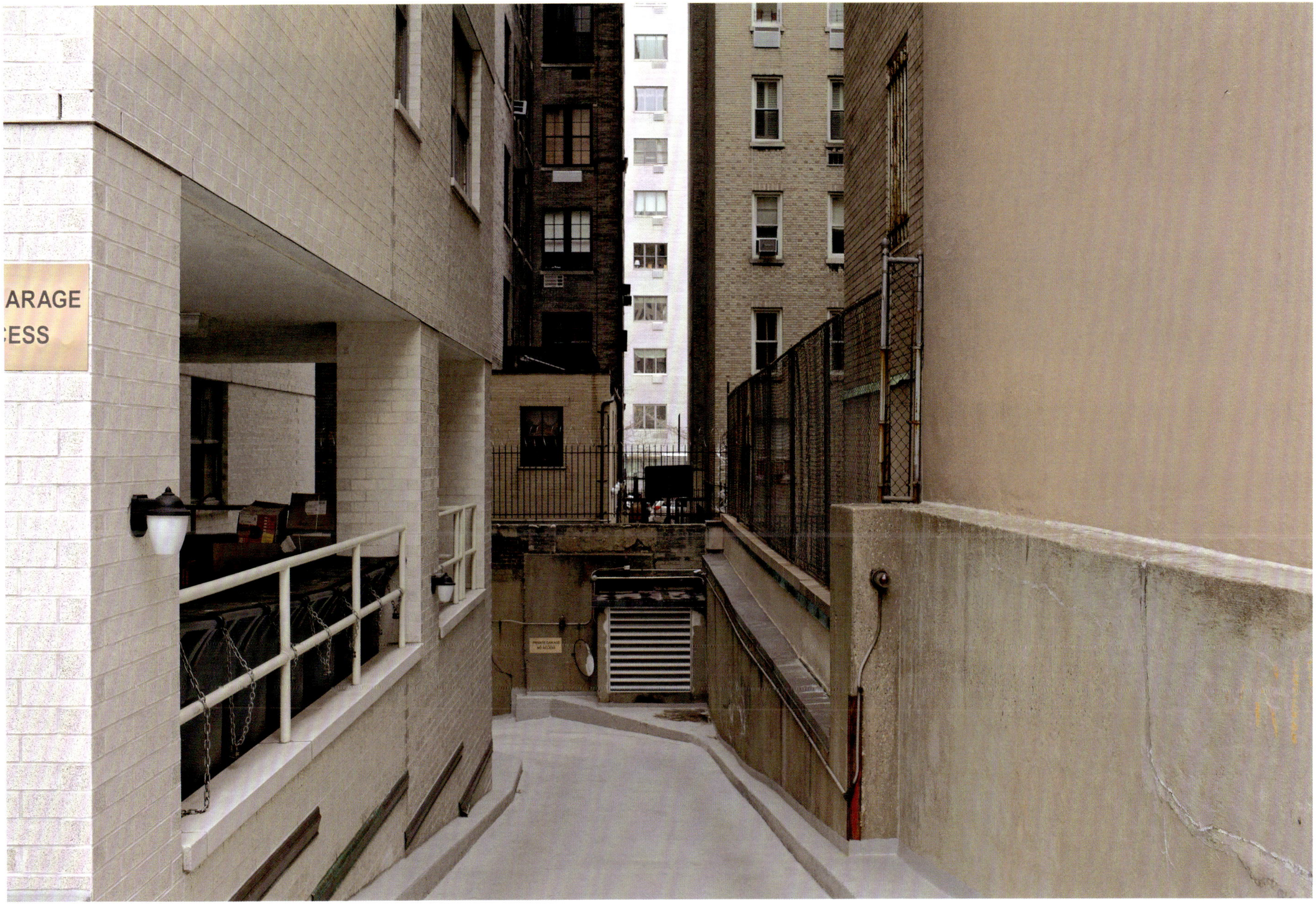

27

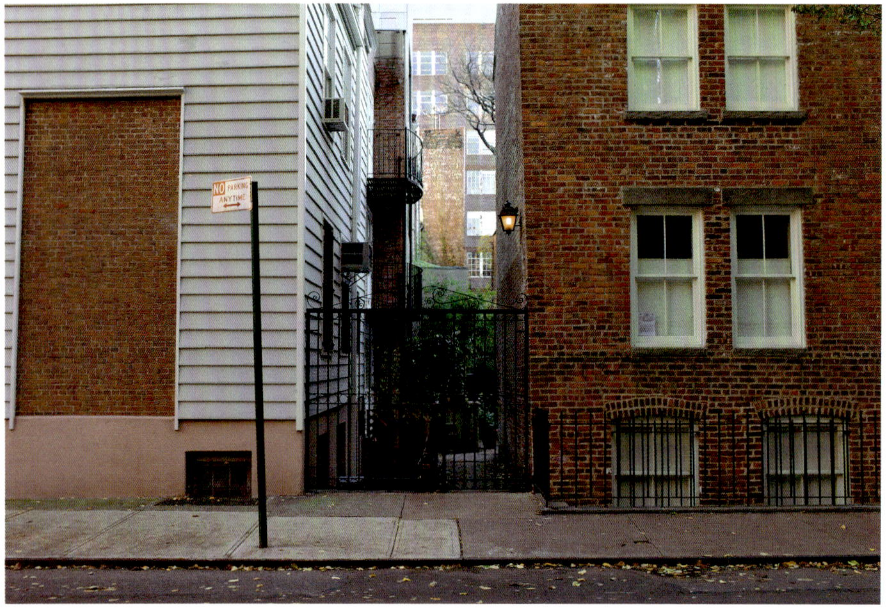

16

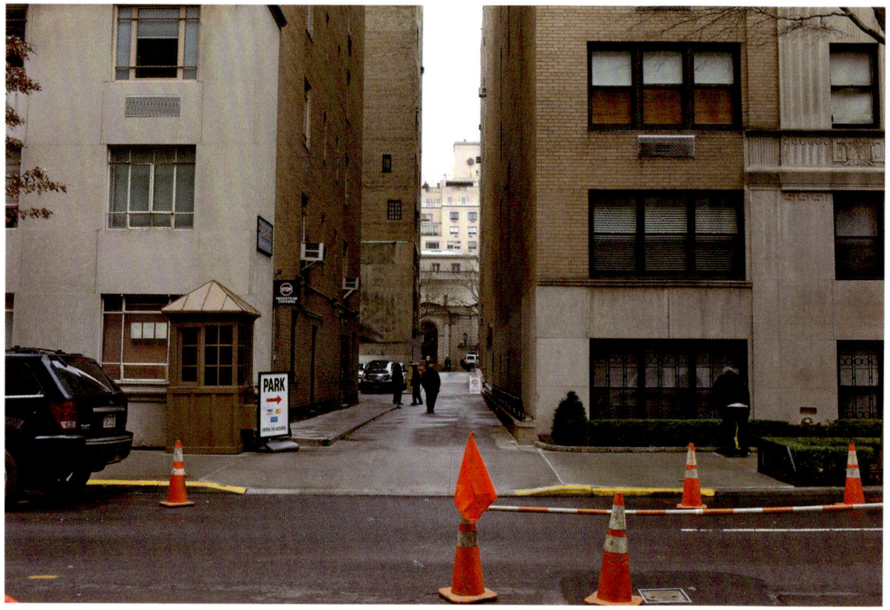

17

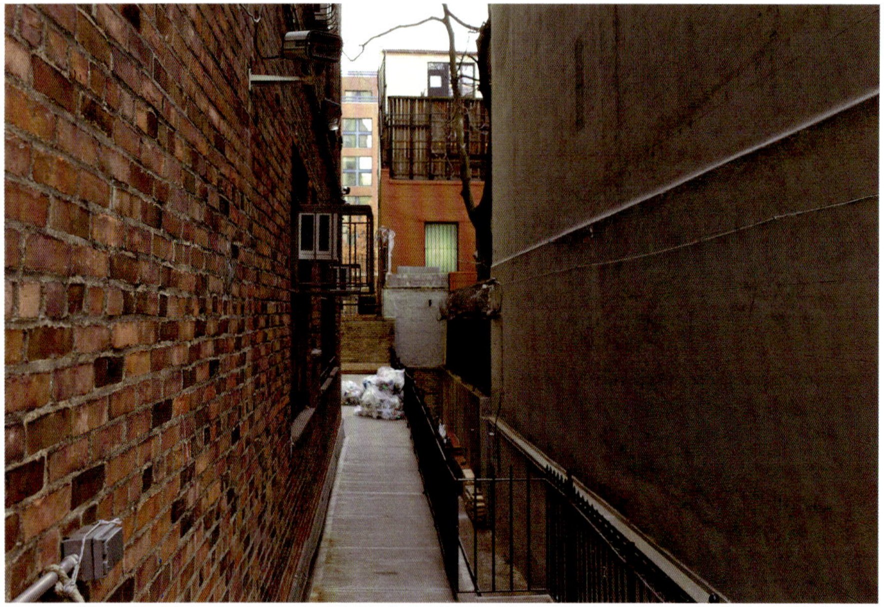

18

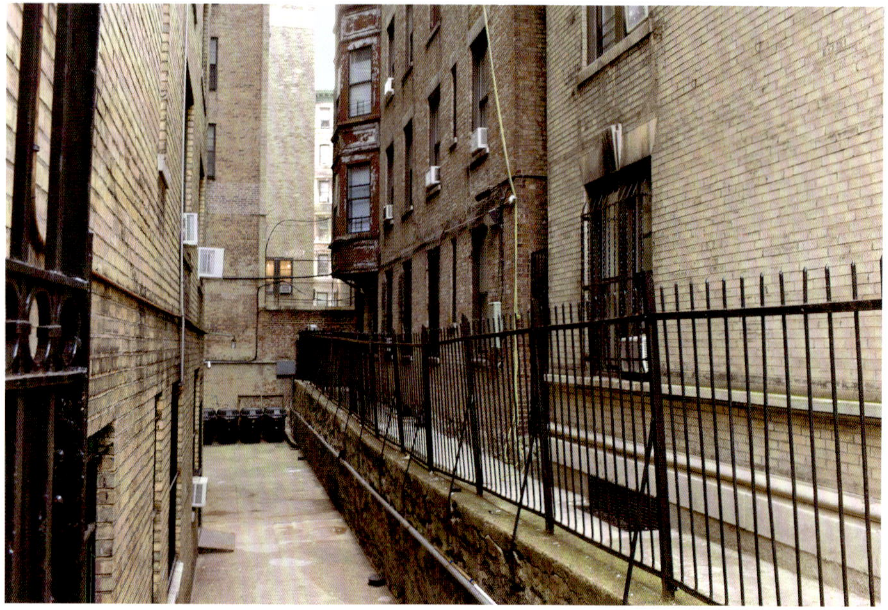

19

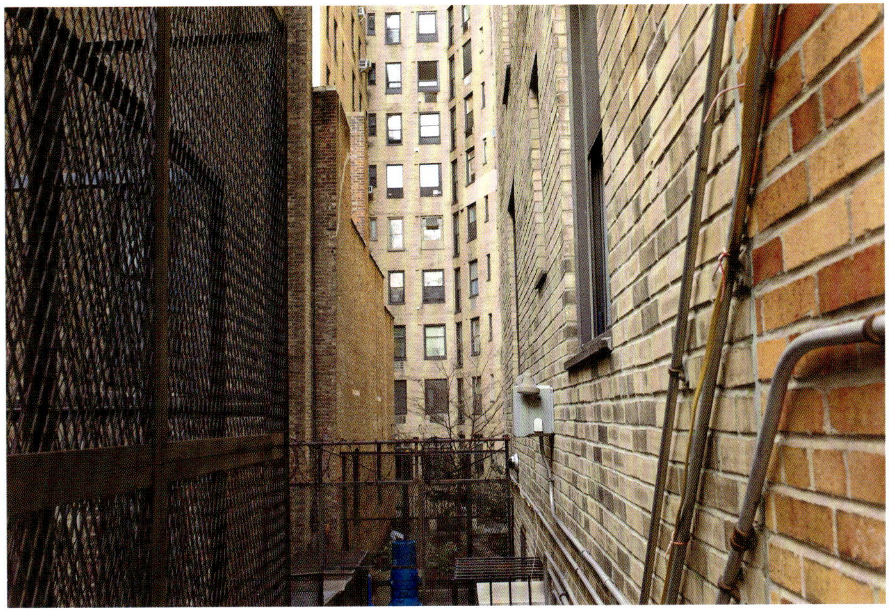

20

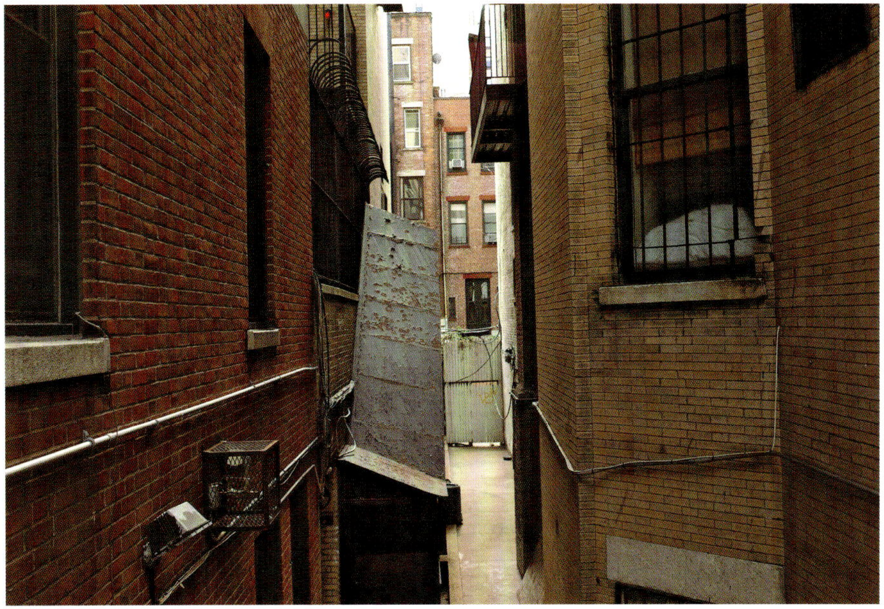

21

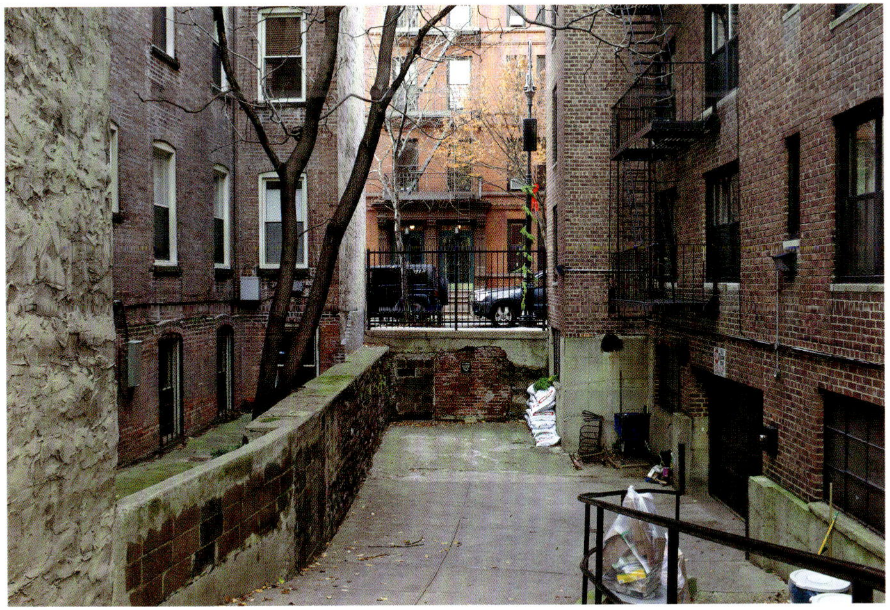

22

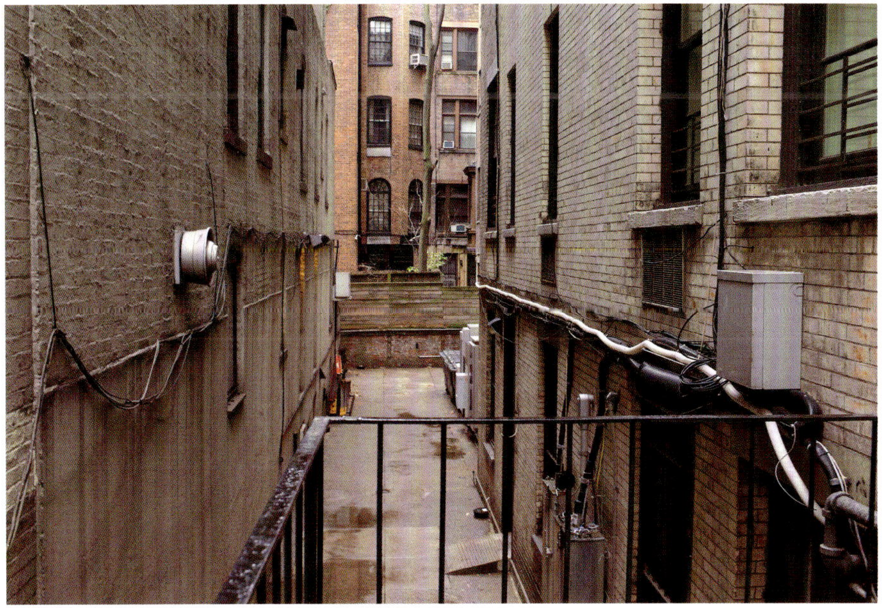

23

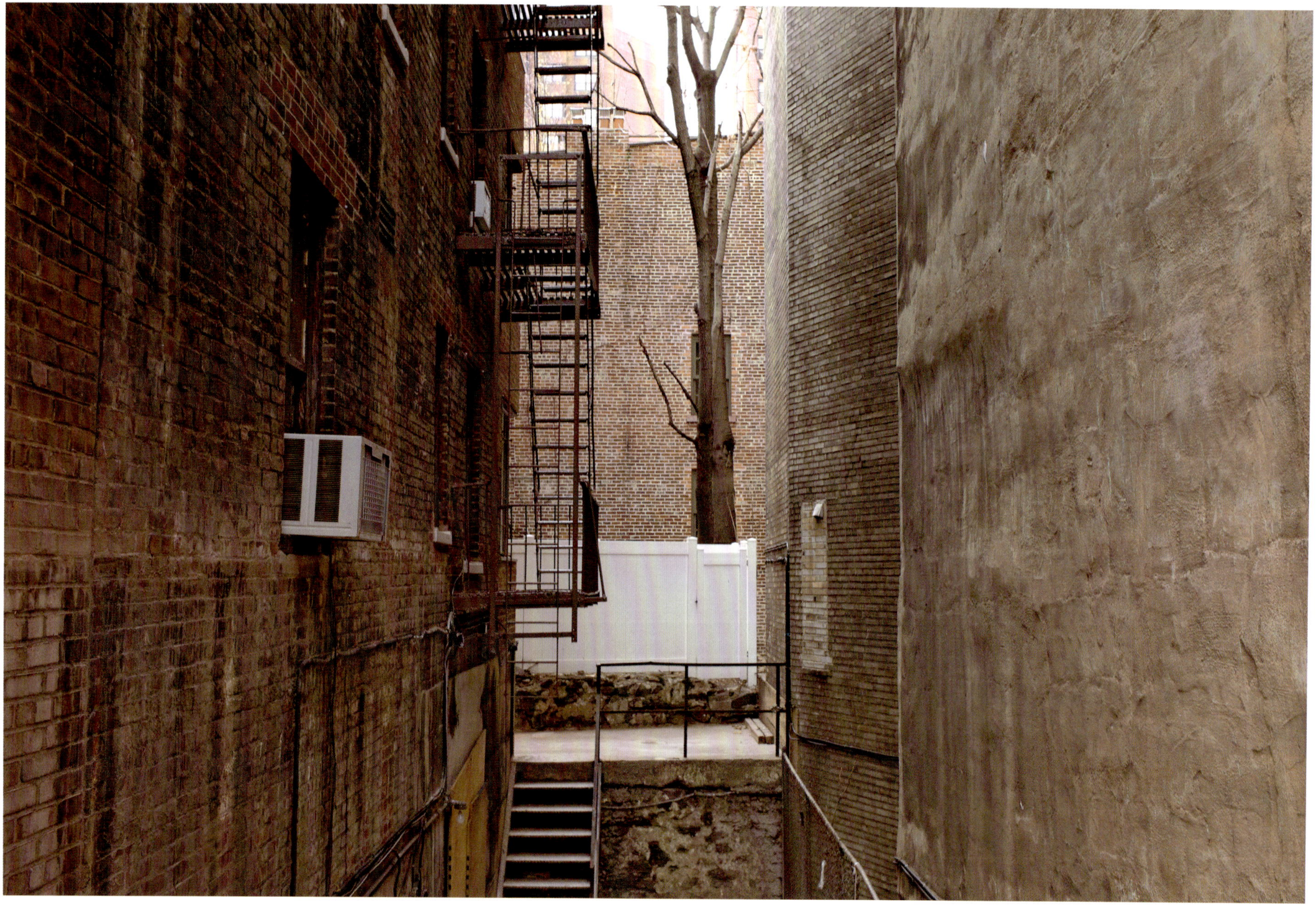

24

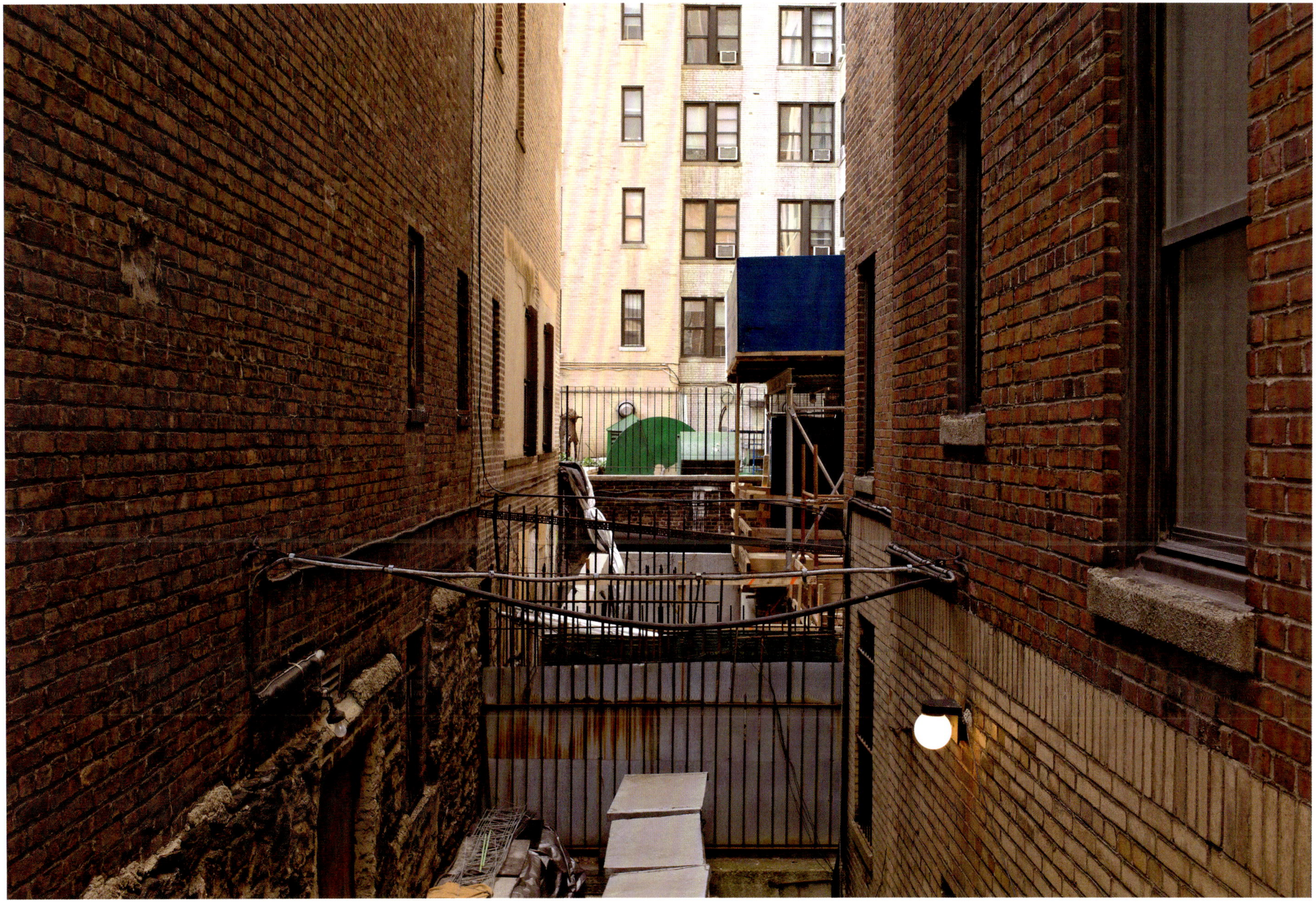

31

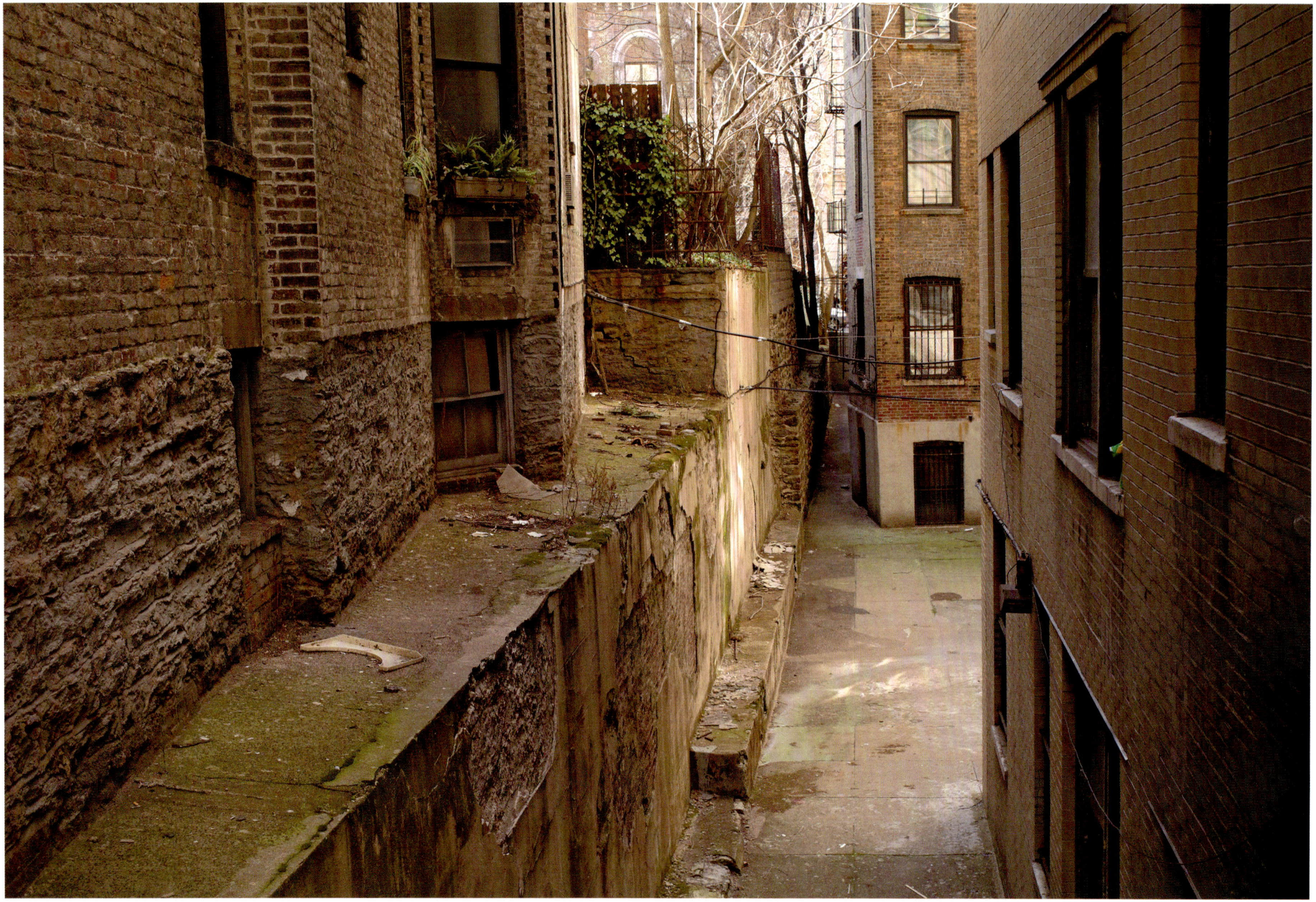

26

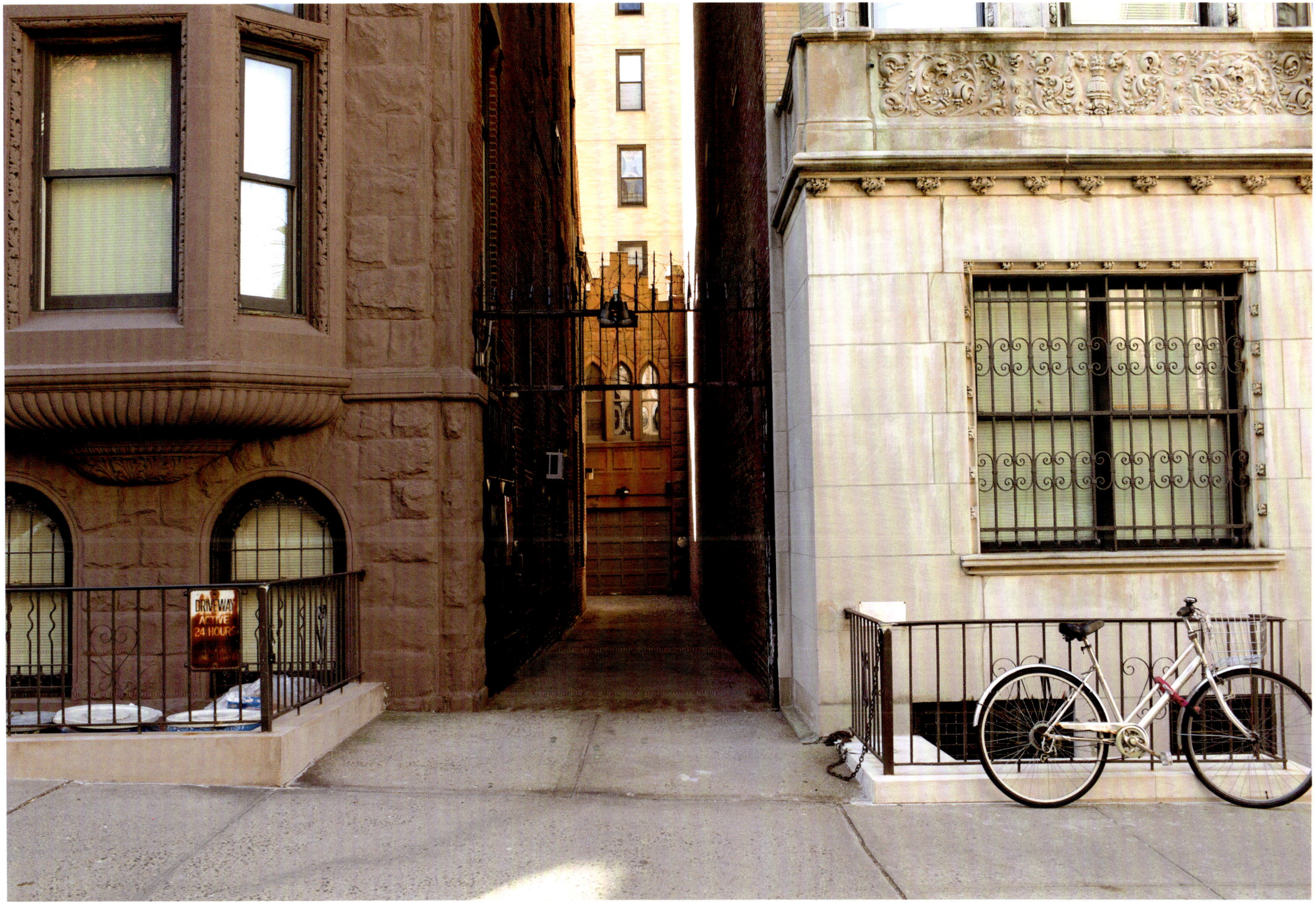

27

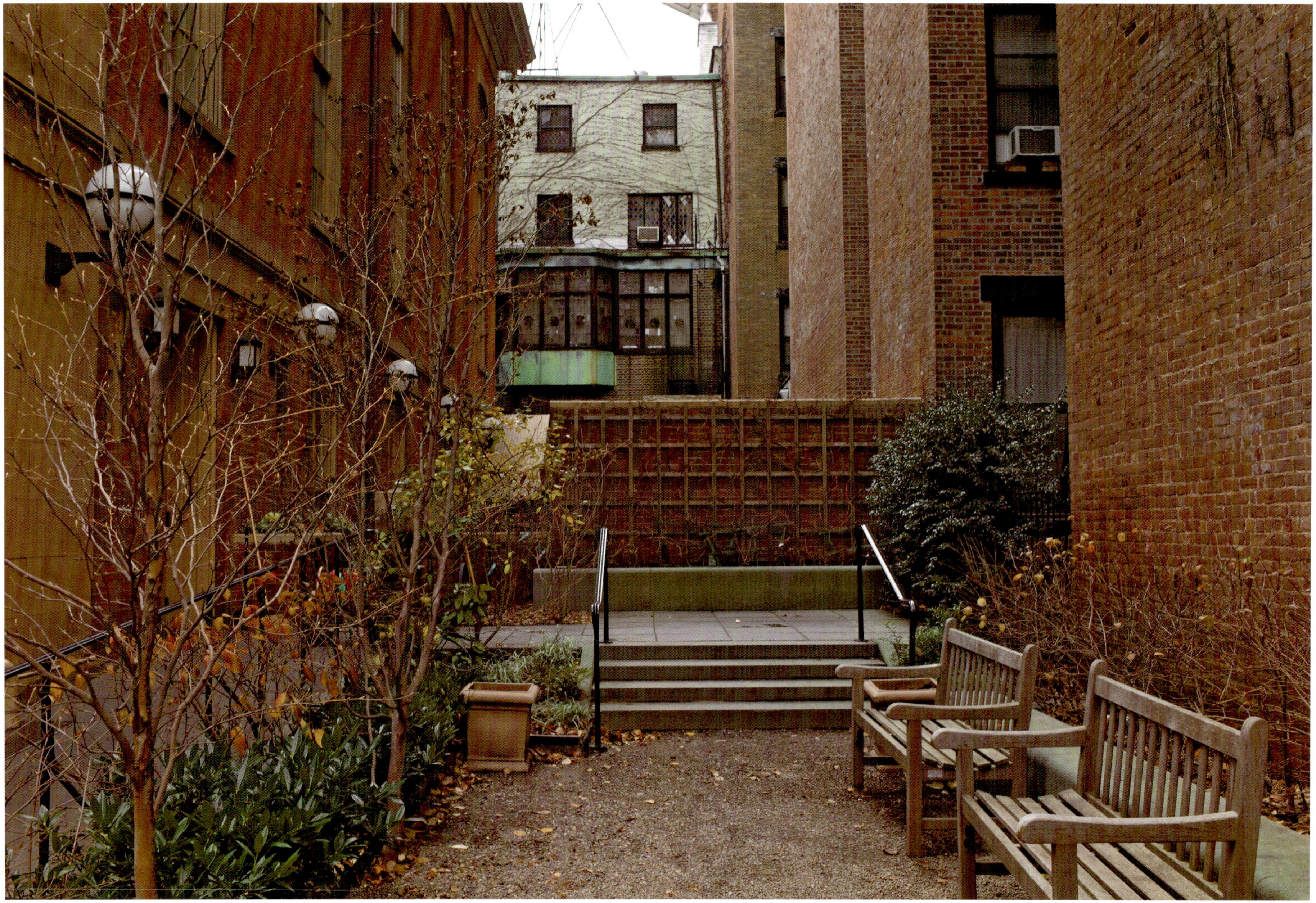

28

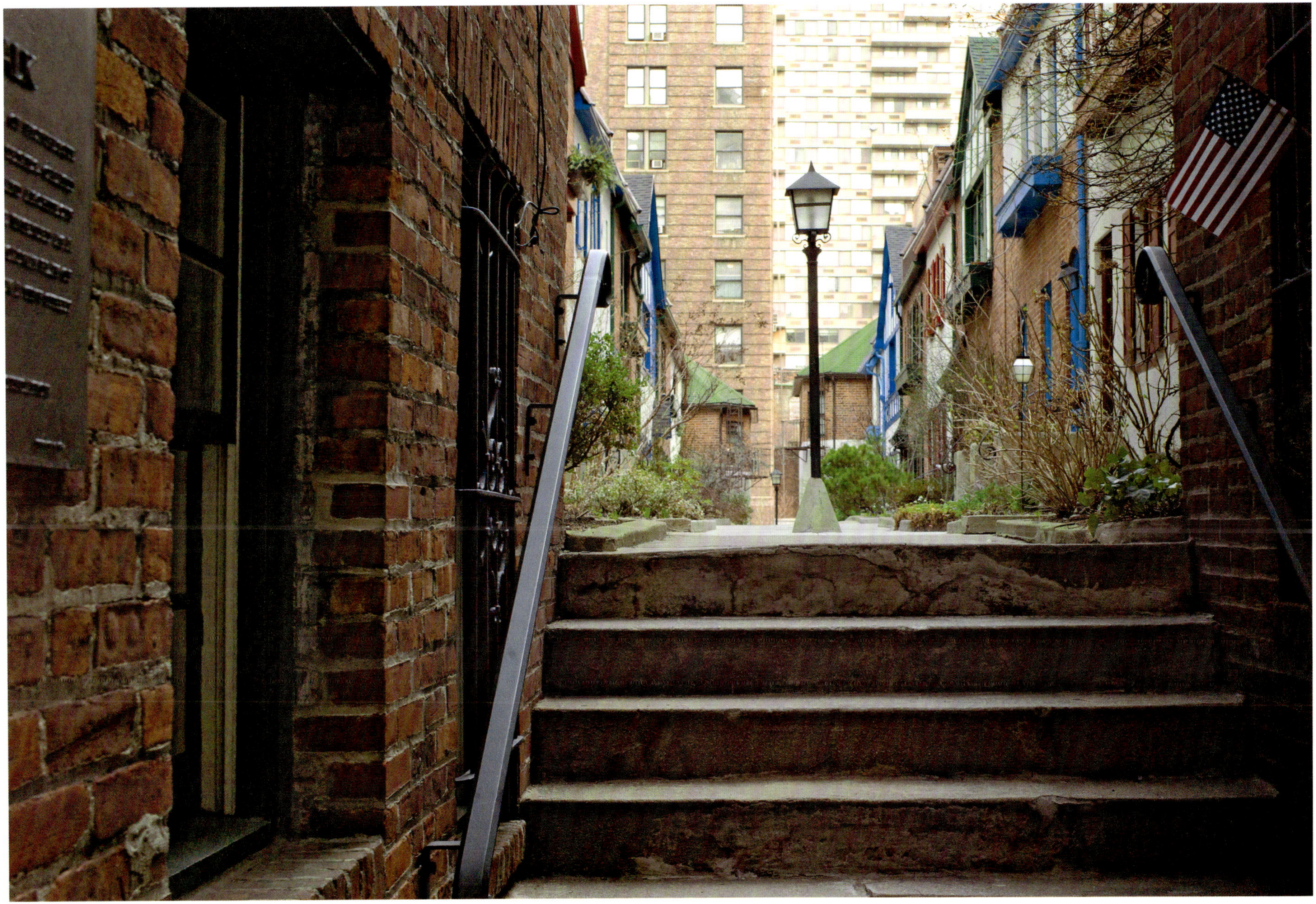

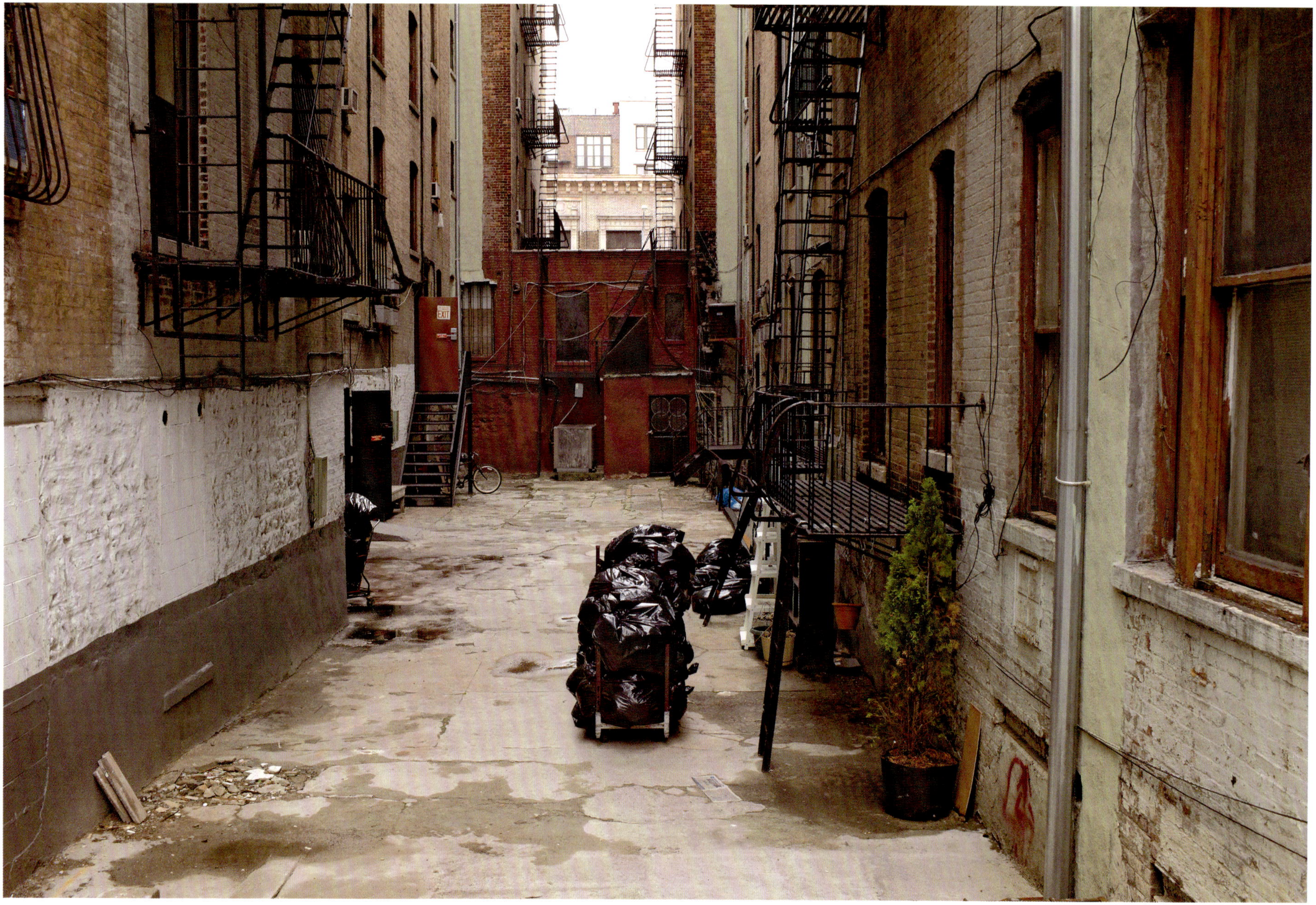

30

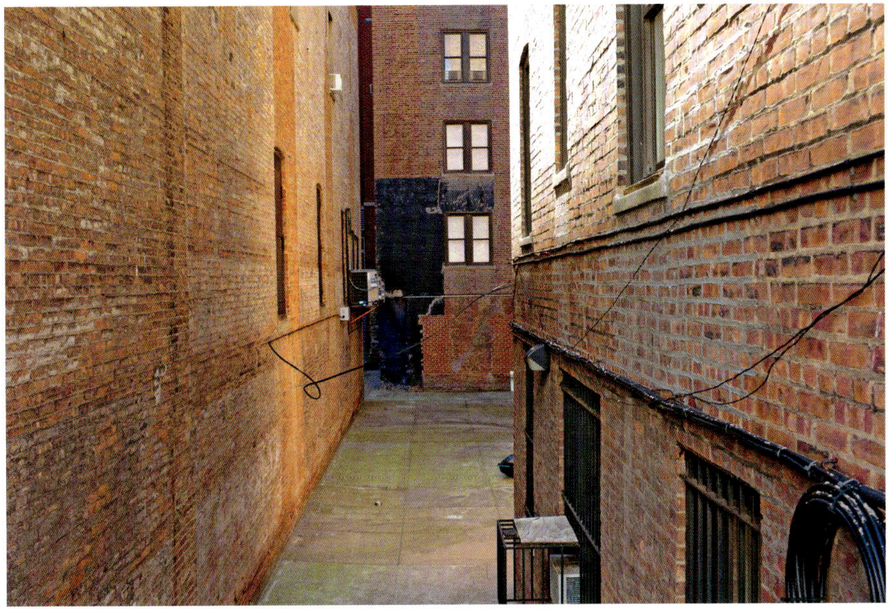
31

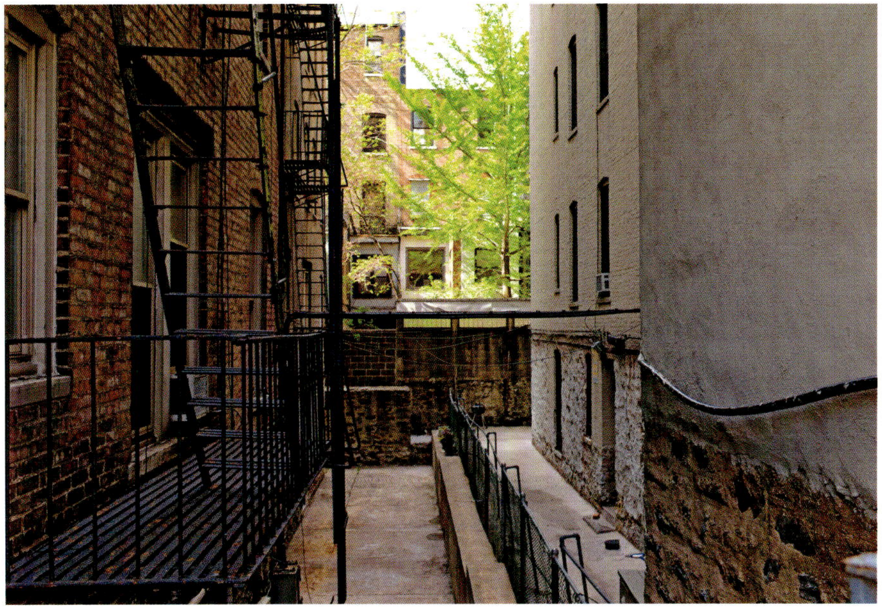
32

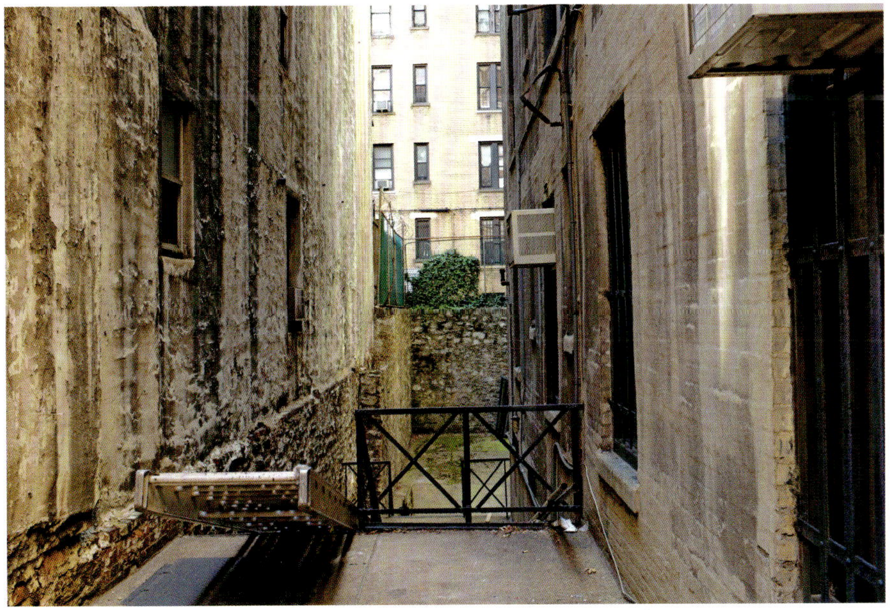
33

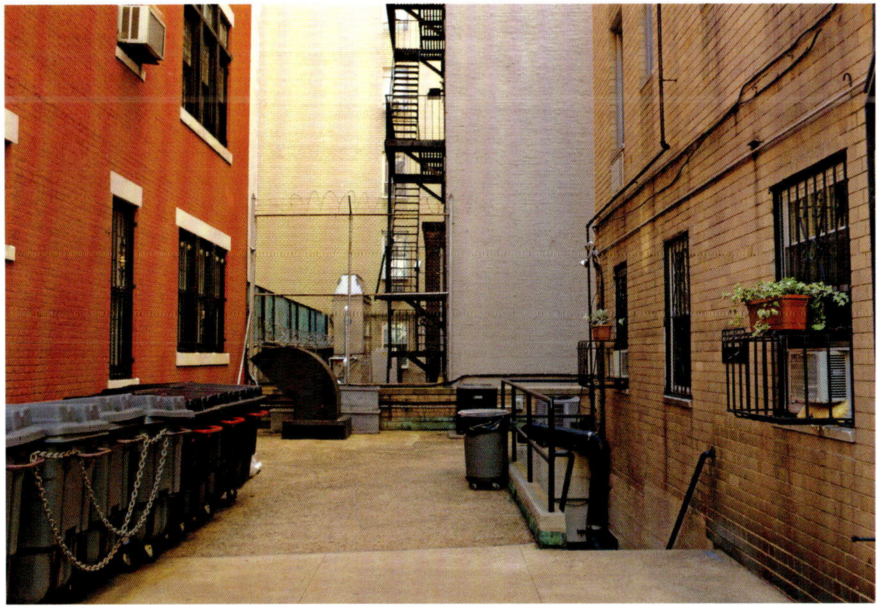
34

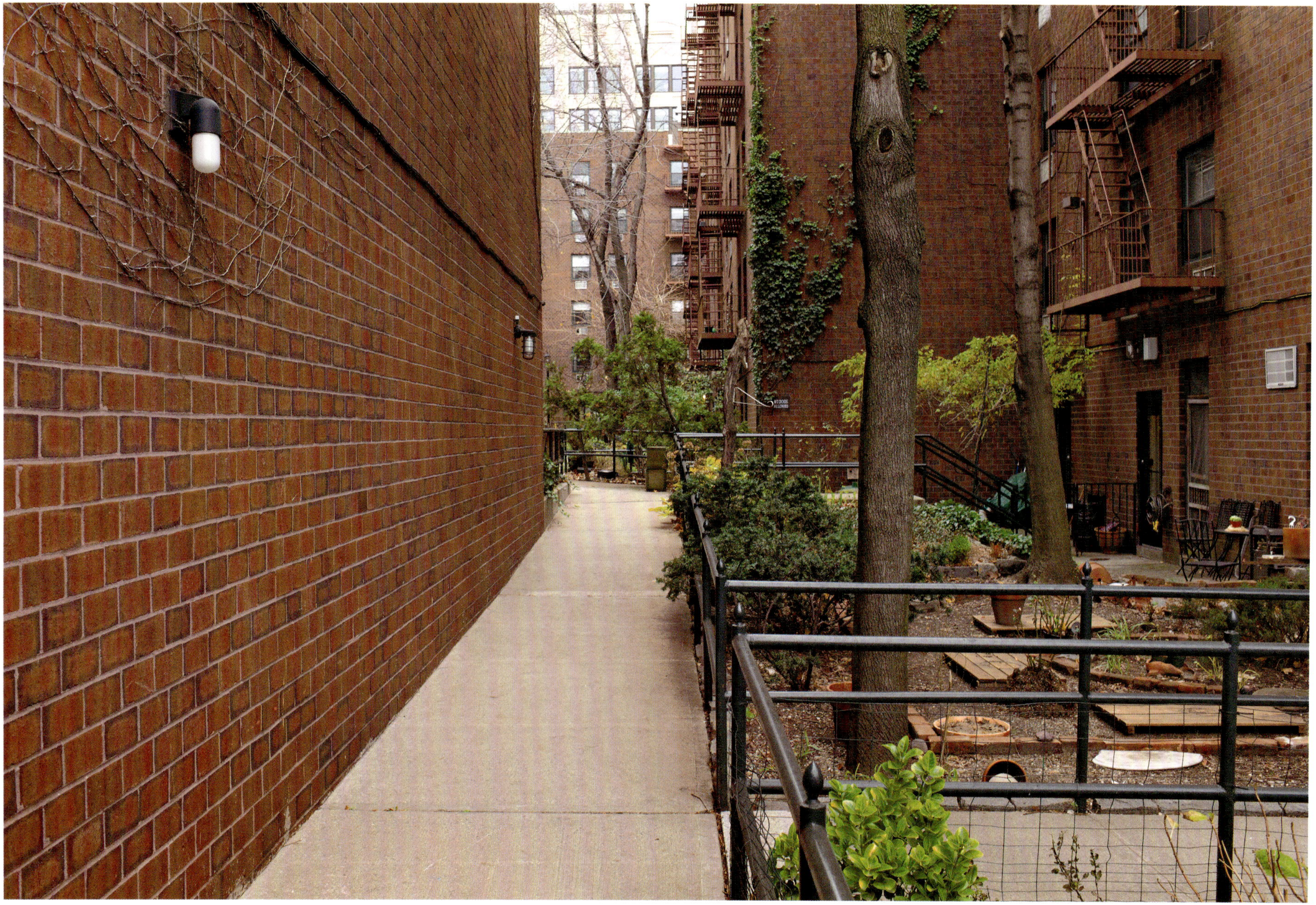

35

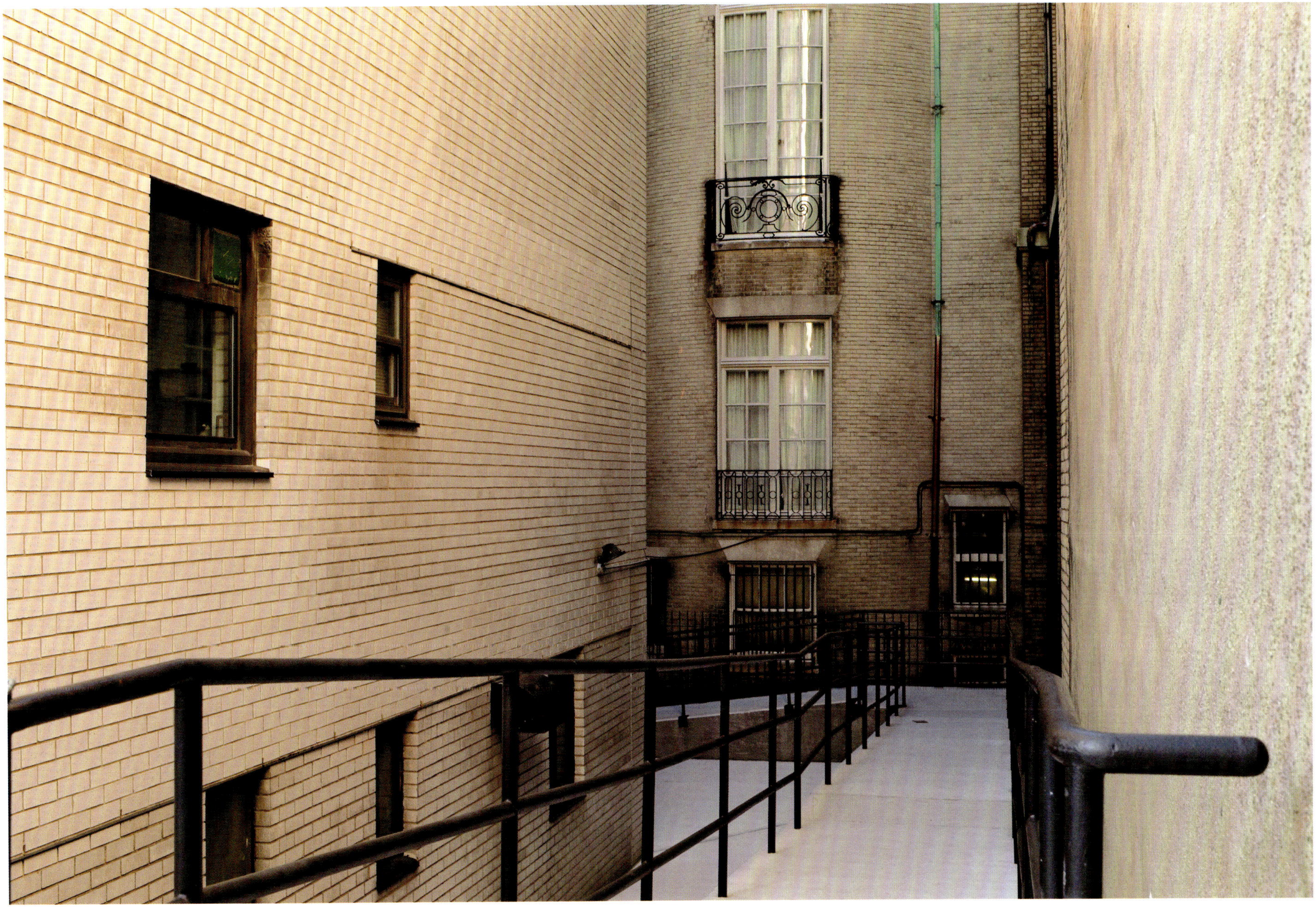

39

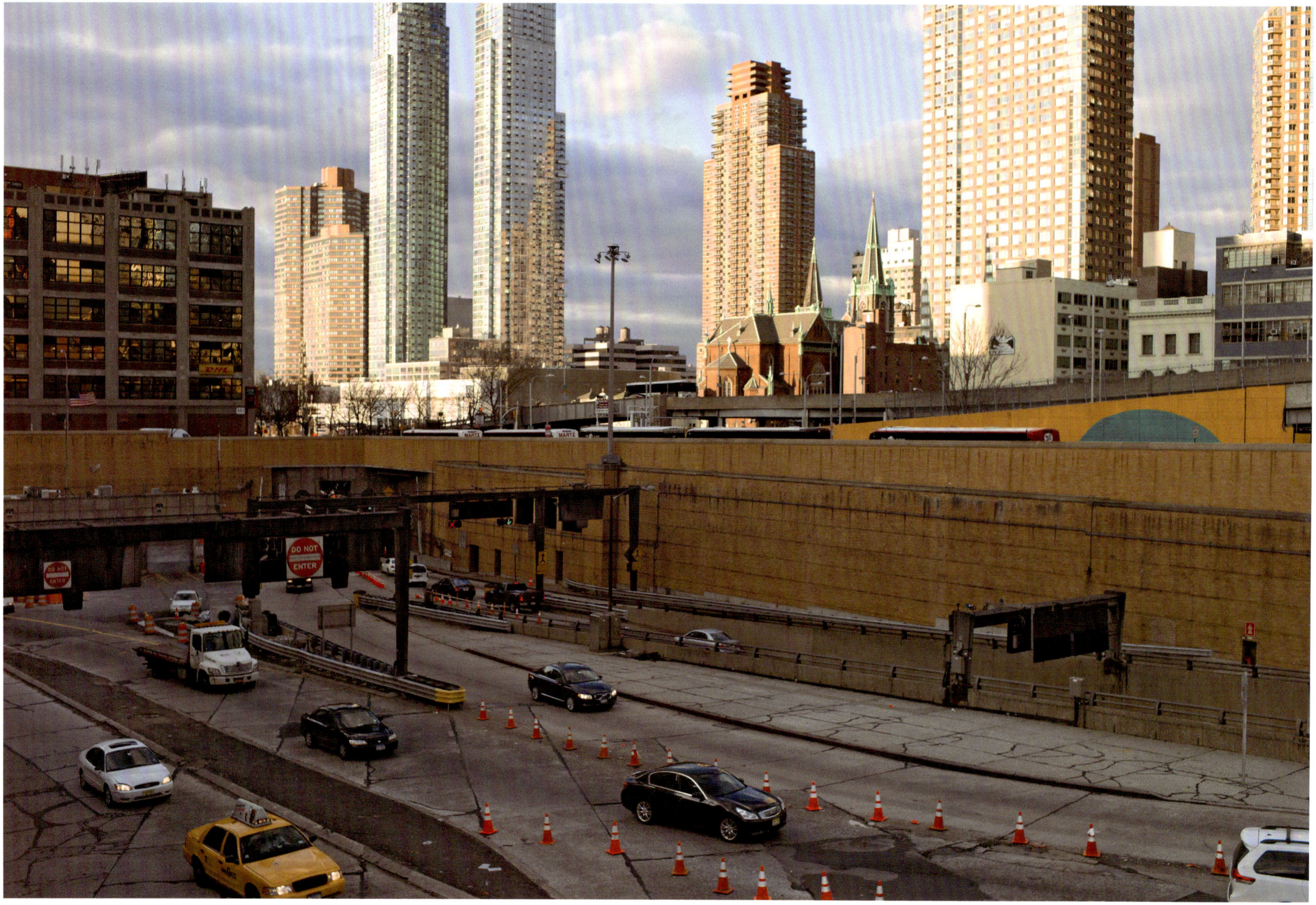
DO NOT
ENTER

BRIDGE/TUNNEL/TRACK

The only ways in and out of Manhattan are by bridge, tunnel, or boat. There are also tunnels for water, electricity, gas, and steam. Two bridges are for pedestrians only (the High Bridge, the city's oldest extant bridge and recently reopened, and the Ward's Island Bridge to Randall's Island, politically part of Manhattan). Entrances to the older and smaller bridges (Macombs Dam, 145th Street, Madison Avenue, etc.) are more integrated into the city's existing street grid.

The tunnels take huge chunks out of the city. Their intake and outflow lanes take over the neighborhoods they burrow into, distorting the spaces around them. These places are often unfriendly to pedestrians, creating forbidding zones consisting of series of bumper-to-bumper traffic lanes, or vast expanses punctuated by pedestrian islands for anyone who might want to venture across. Places where the new grid meets the old organic streetscape can also be dangerous, though some are helped with later interventions. The oldest parts of the city are more pedestrian-centric.

Tracks on the west side are largely hidden, until they reach far north. On the east side, tracks from Grand Central Terminal travel underground until they resurface and perch on a stone median on Park Avenue that divides the neighborhood. In Harlem they rise high enough onto steel supports to create an "El" system with open space underneath.

1 Lincoln Tunnel
2 Williamsburg Bridge
3 Madison Avenue Bridge
4 Brooklyn Bridge
5 Queens-Midtown Tunnel
6 Brooklyn Bridge
7 Riverside Drive Viaduct
8 155th Street Viaduct
9 Henry Hudson Bridge
10 Harlem River Speedway, Alexander Hamilton Bridge, and Washington Bridge
11 Wards Island Bridge
12 Macombs Dam Bridge
13 Amtrak, Hell's Kitchen
14 Manhattan Bridge
15 High Bridge
16 Amtrak, Inwood
17 Manhattan Bridge
18 Metro-North Viaduct, East Harlem
19 Holland Tunnel
20 Holland Tunnel
21 Queensborough Bridge
22 Macombs Dam Bridge
23 Lincoln Tunnel
24 Lincoln Tunnel
25 Lincoln Tunnel
26 Holland Tunnel
27 Lincoln Tunnel
28 Queens-Midtown Tunnel
29 Lincoln Tunnel
30 Lincoln Tunnel
31 Queens-Midtown Tunnel
32 Triborough Bridge
33 Willis Avenue Bridge
34 Queens-Midtown Tunnel
35 Holland Tunnel
36 Lincoln Tunnel
37 Williamsburg Bridge
38 59th Street Bridge
39 Queens-Midtown Tunnel
40 Metro-North, Upper East Side
41 Kips Bay
42 Williamsburg Bridge
43 Henry Hudson Parkway
44 Macombs Dam Bridge
45 Brooklyn Bridge
46 Brooklyn Bridge
47 Manhattan Bridge
48 Triborough Bridge
49 George Washington Bridge
50 Holland Tunnel

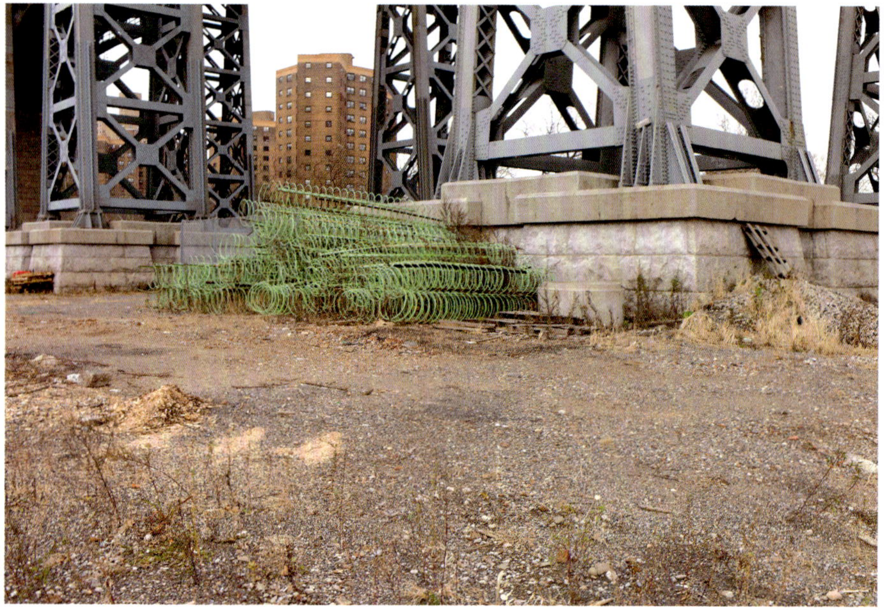

2

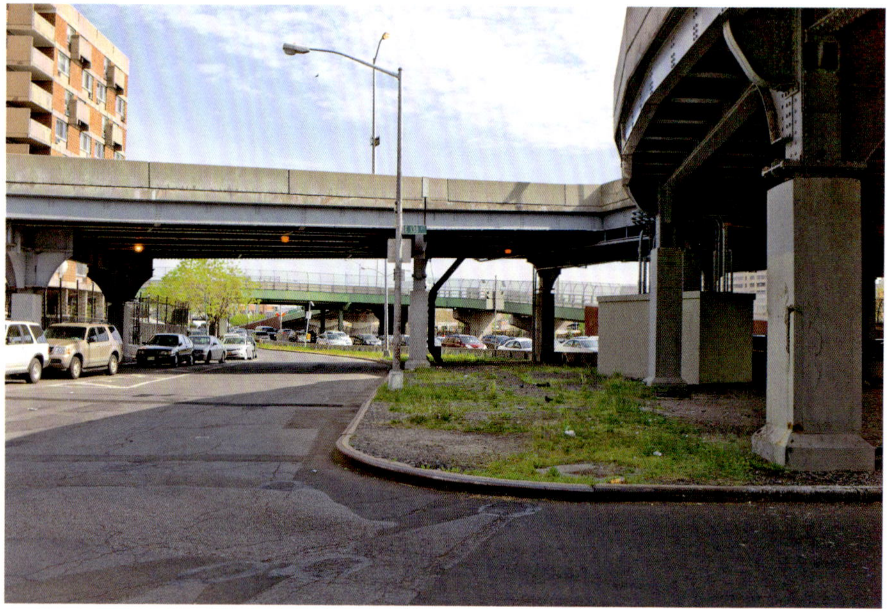

3

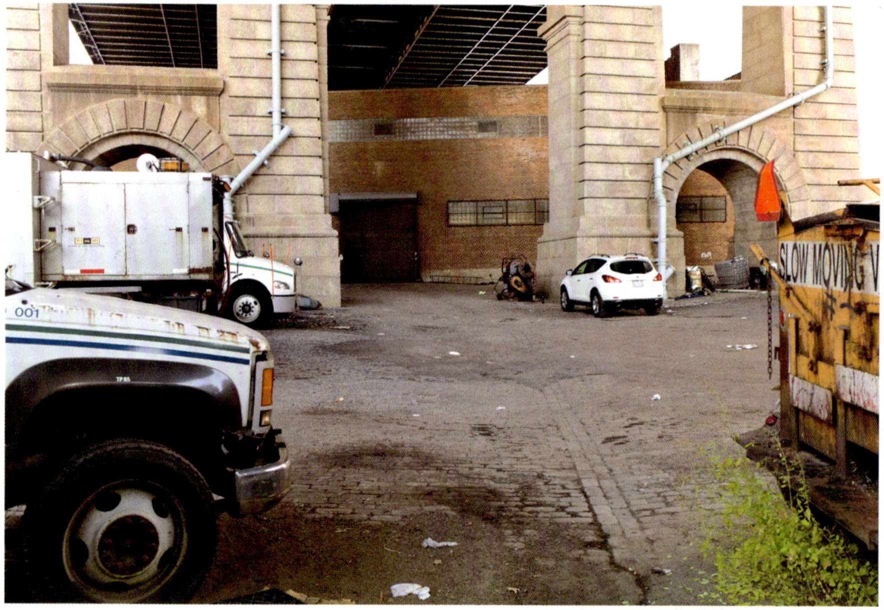

4

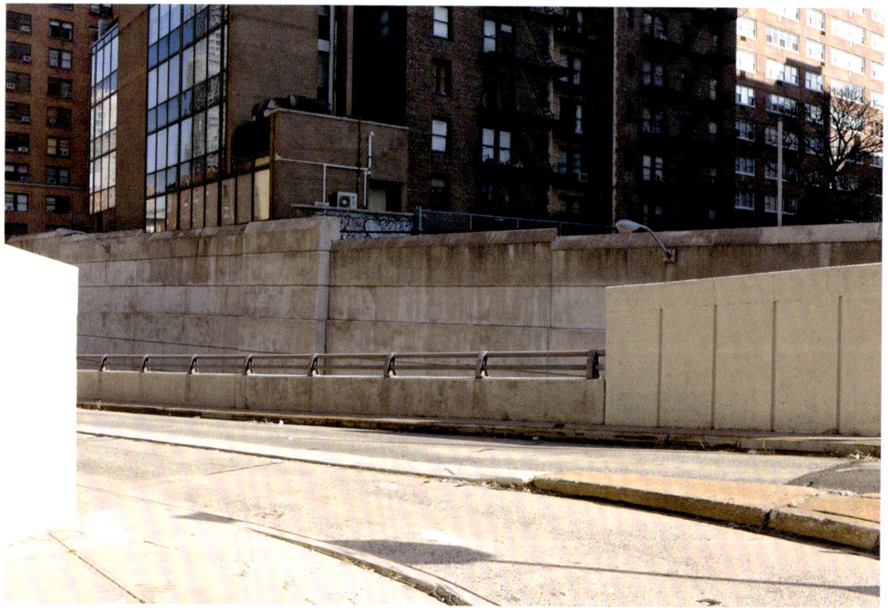

5

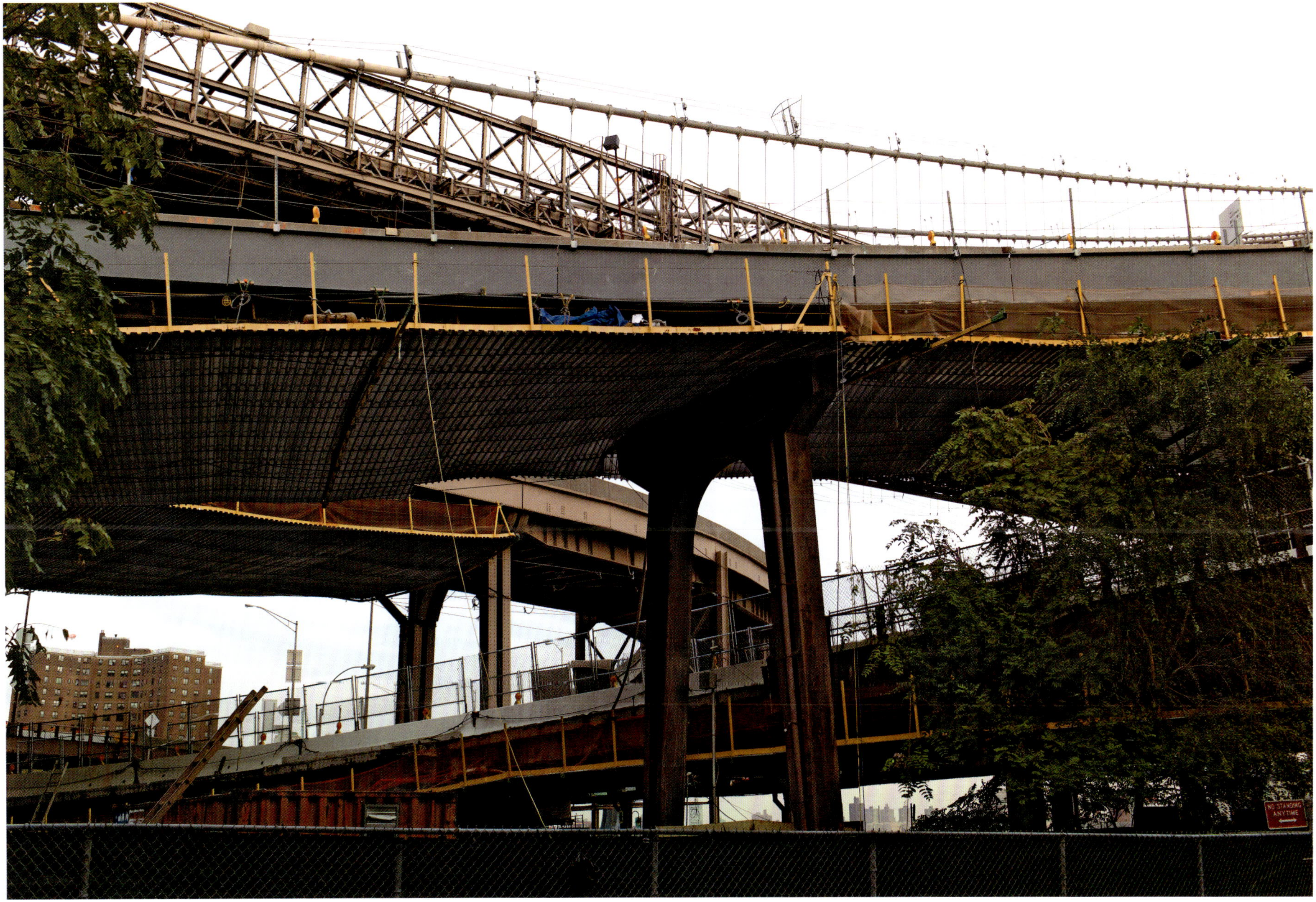

43

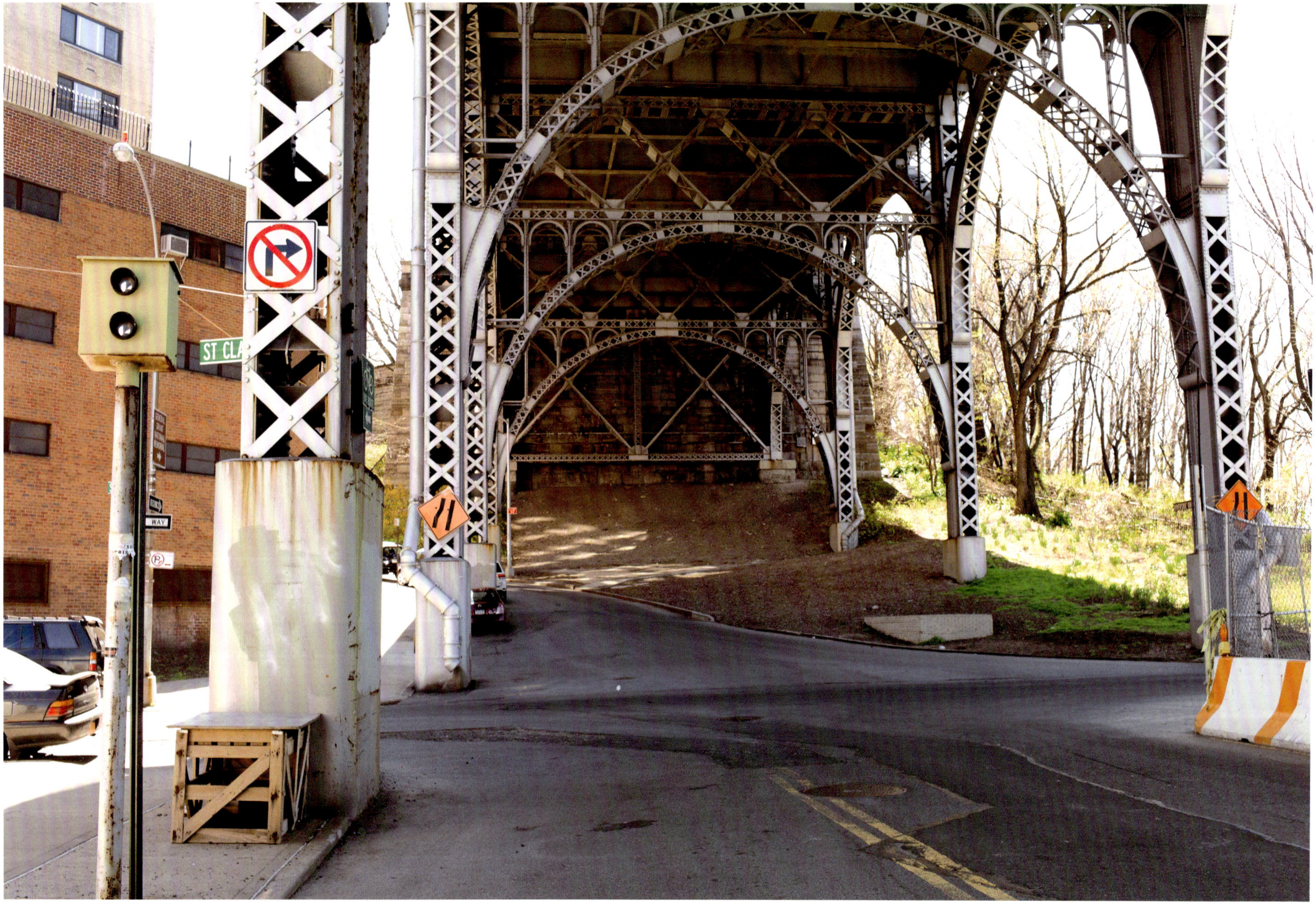

7

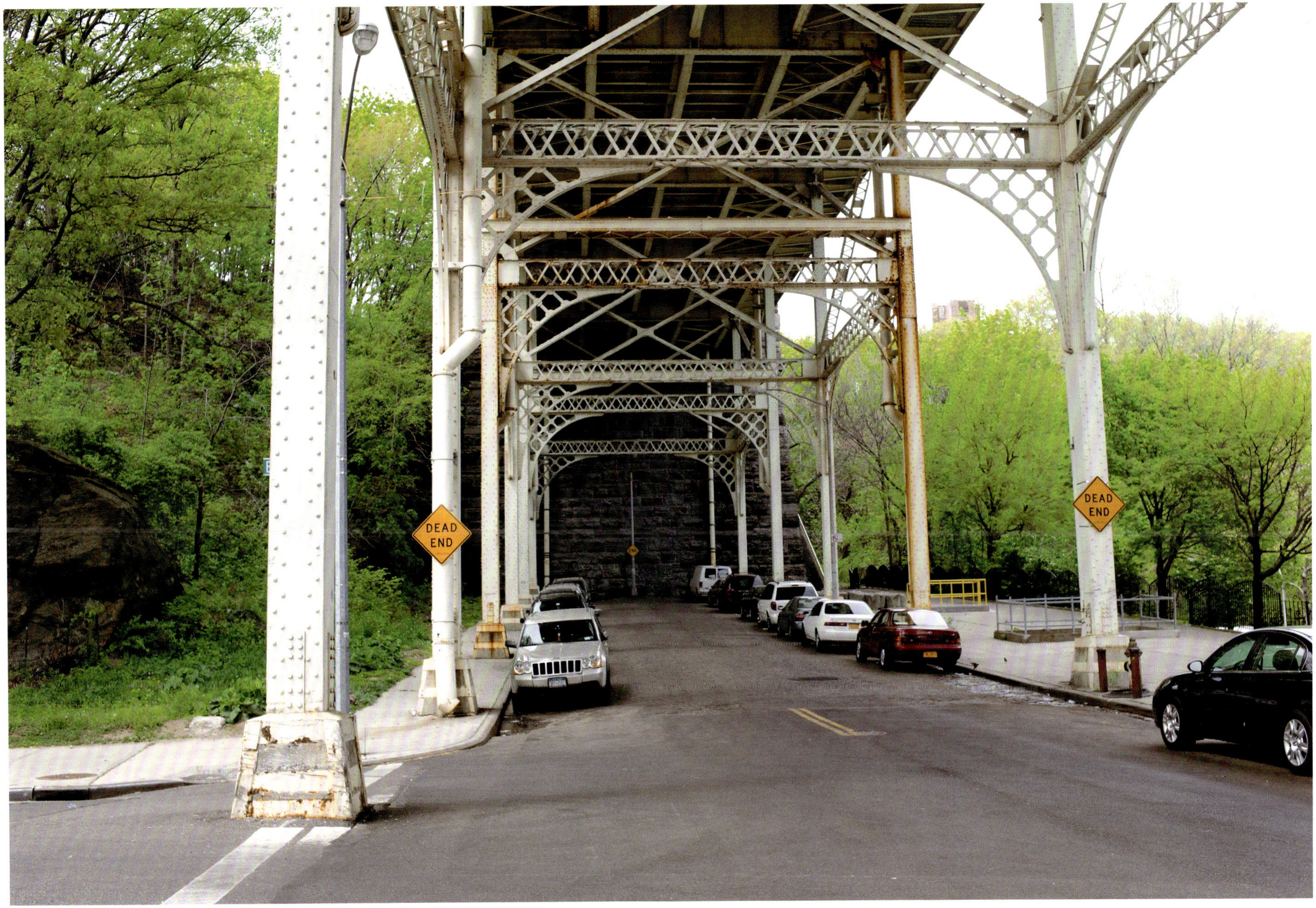

8

46

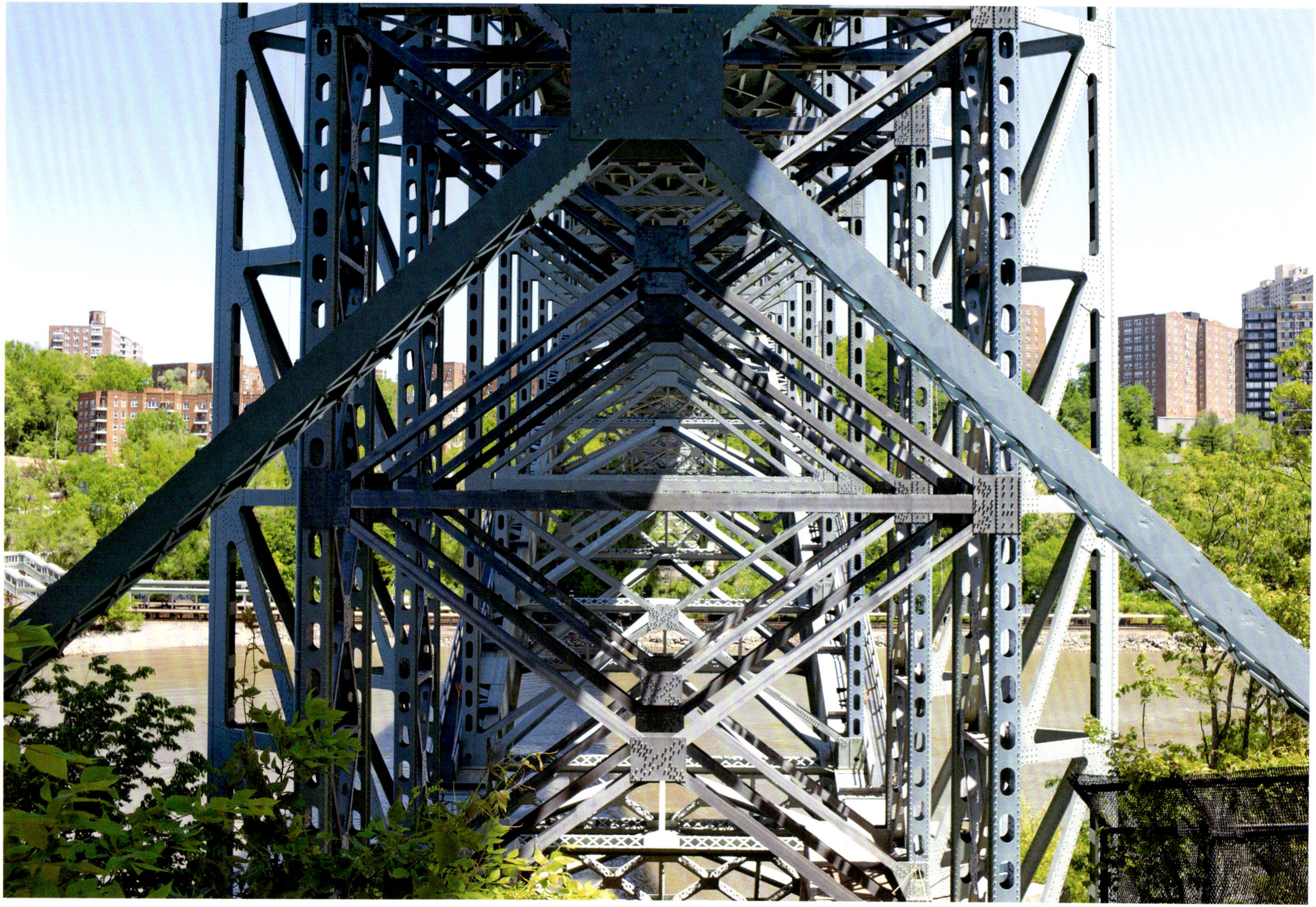

9

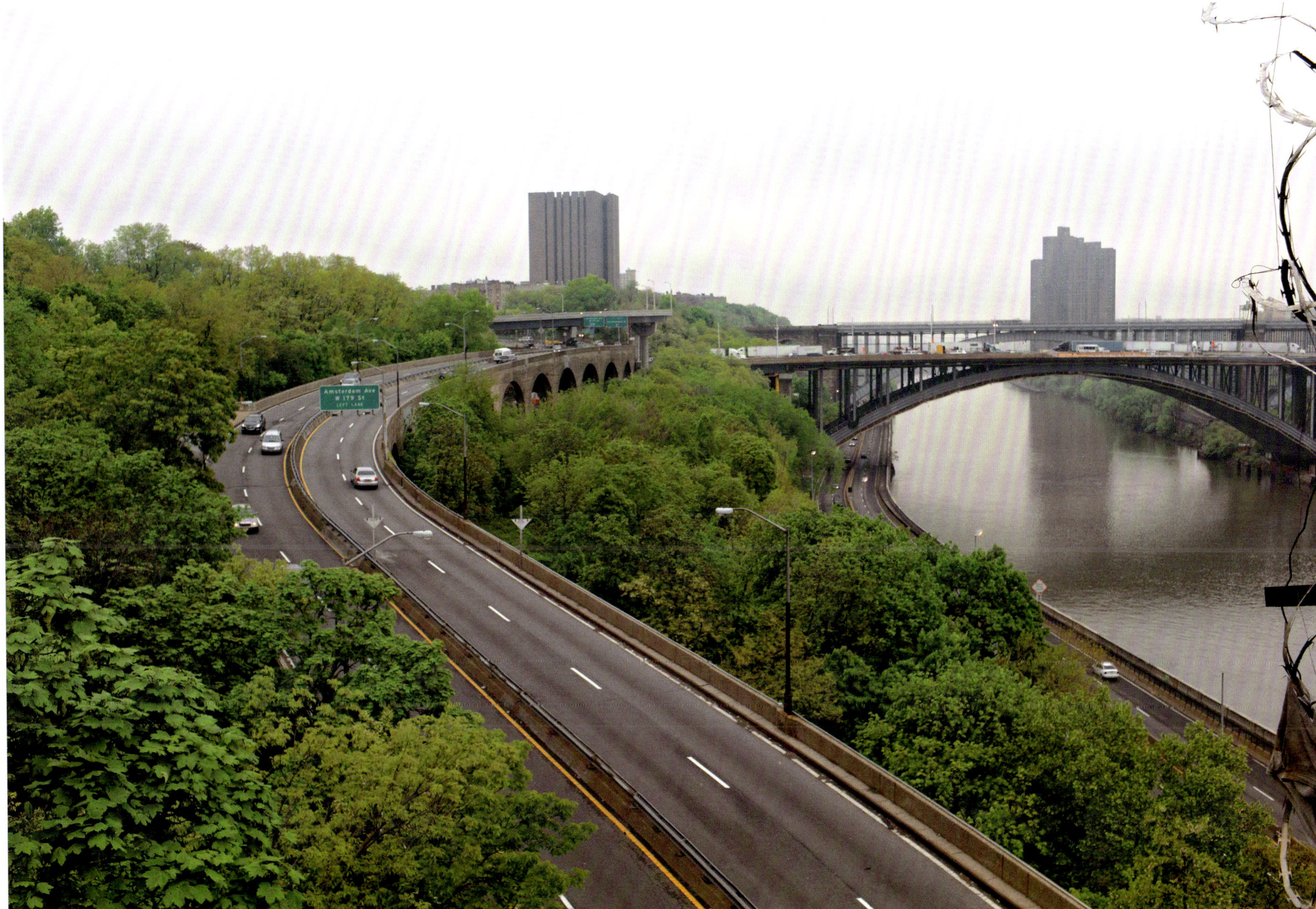

10

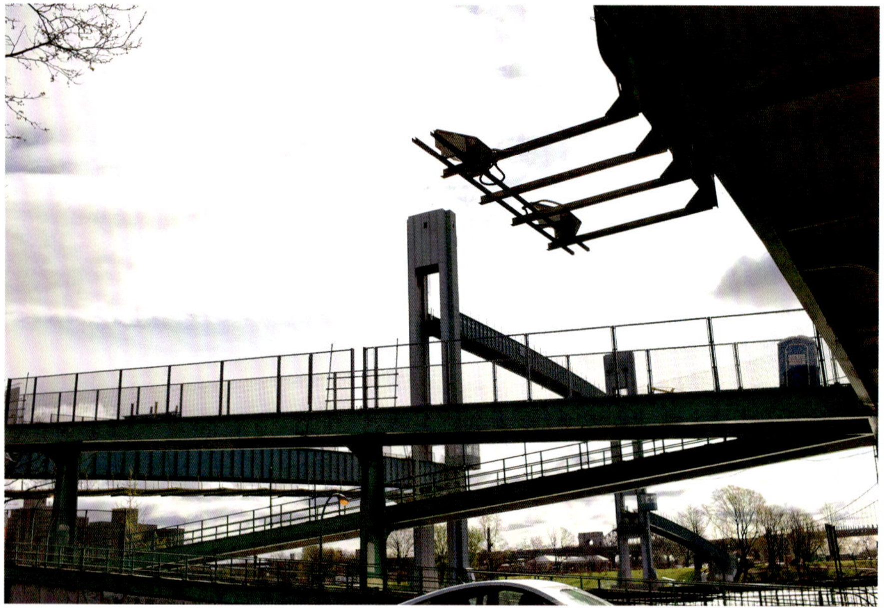

11

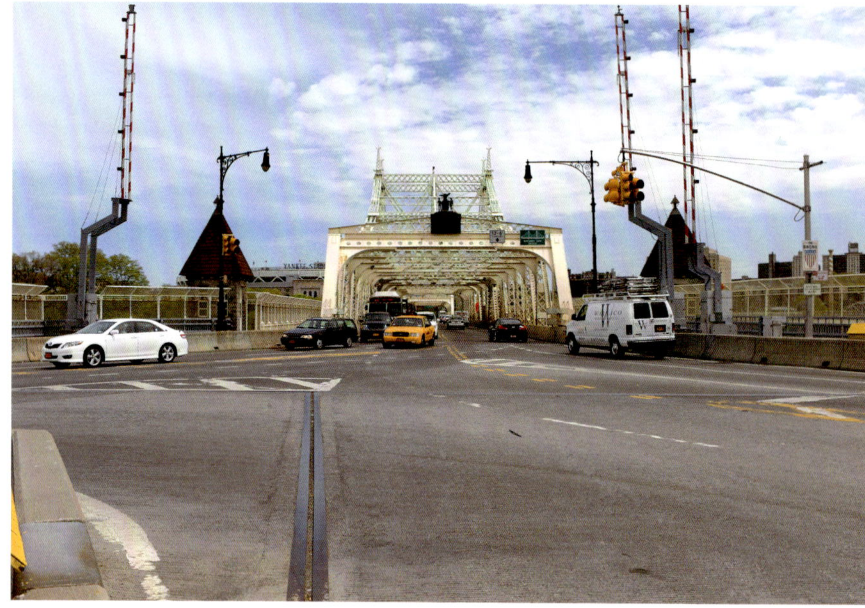

12

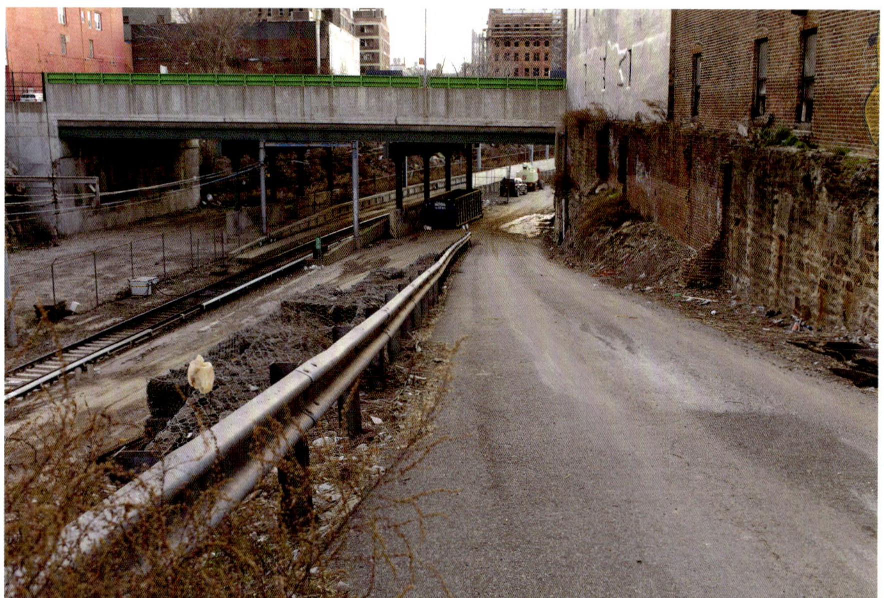

13

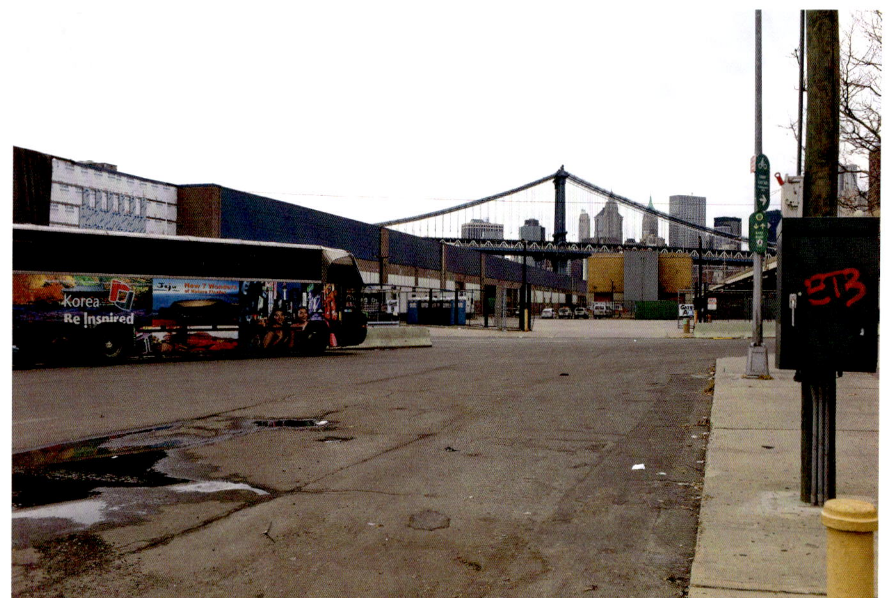

14

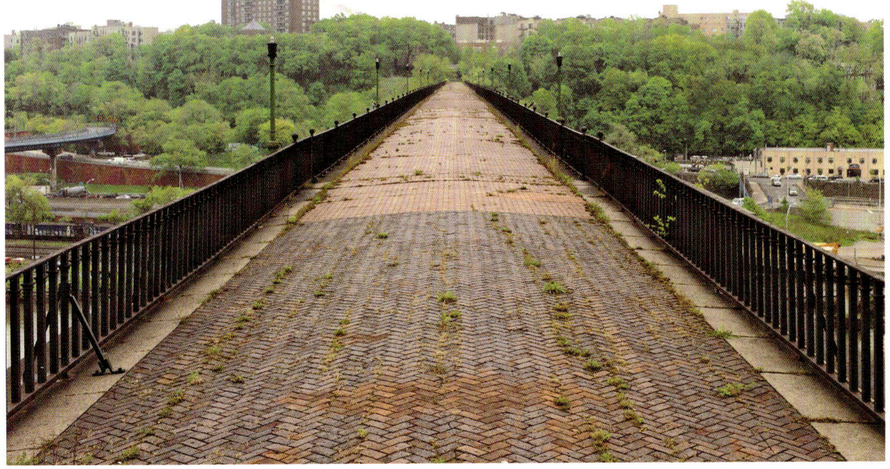

15

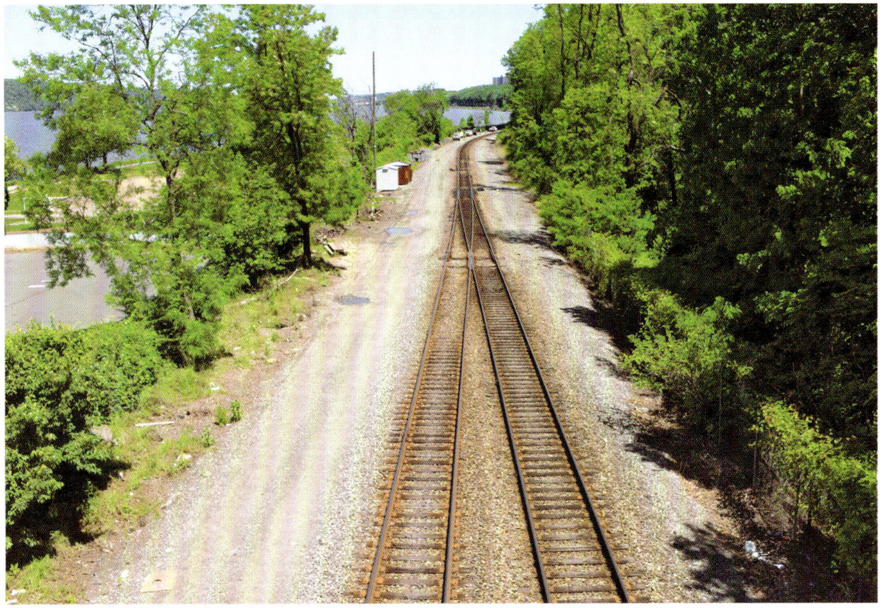

16

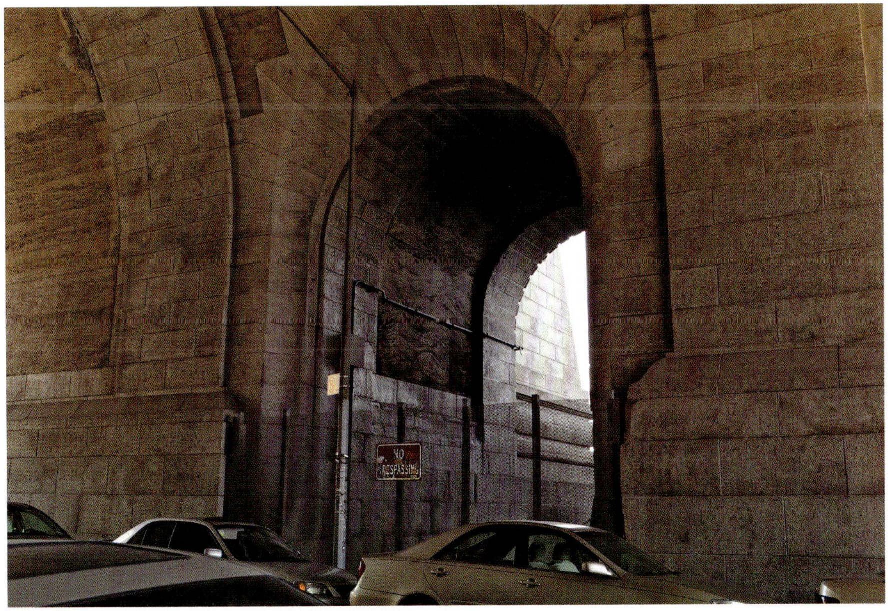

17

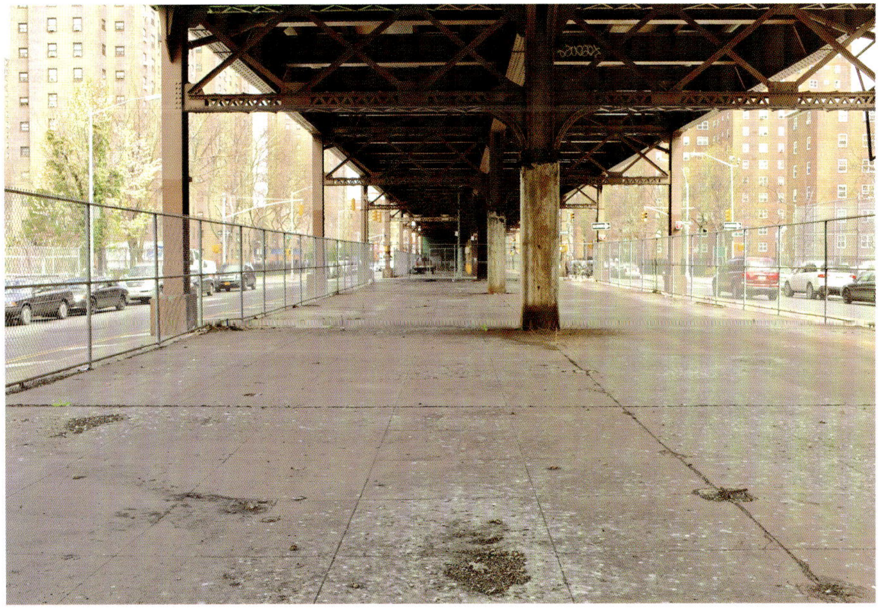

18

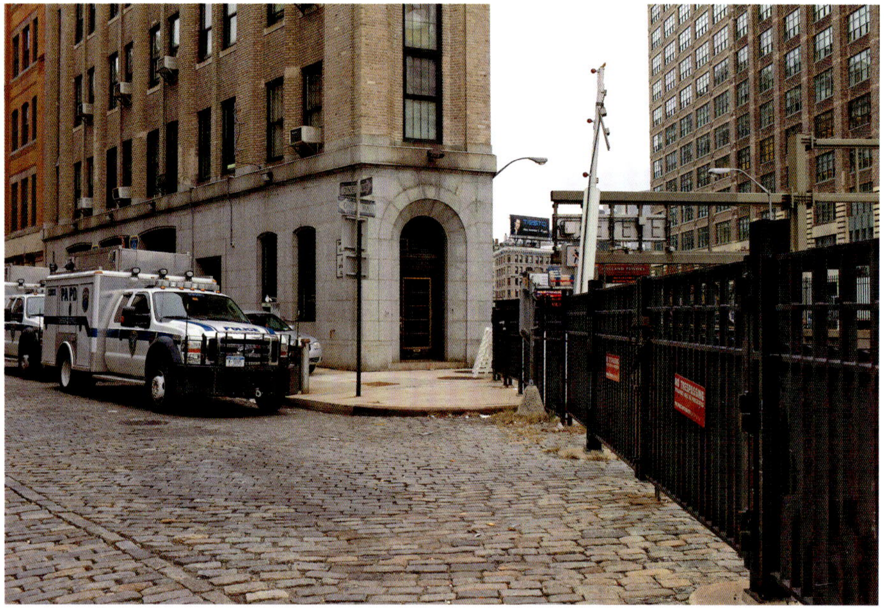

19

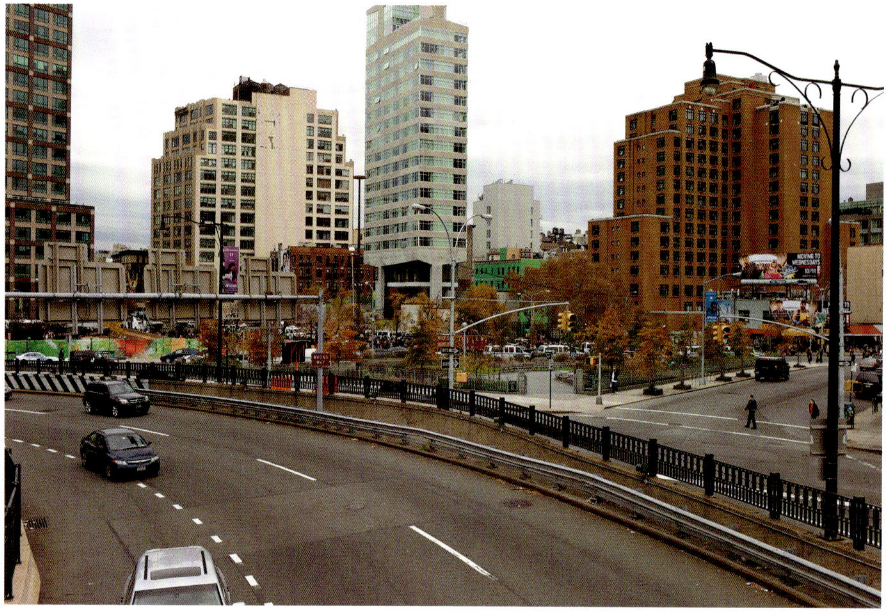

20

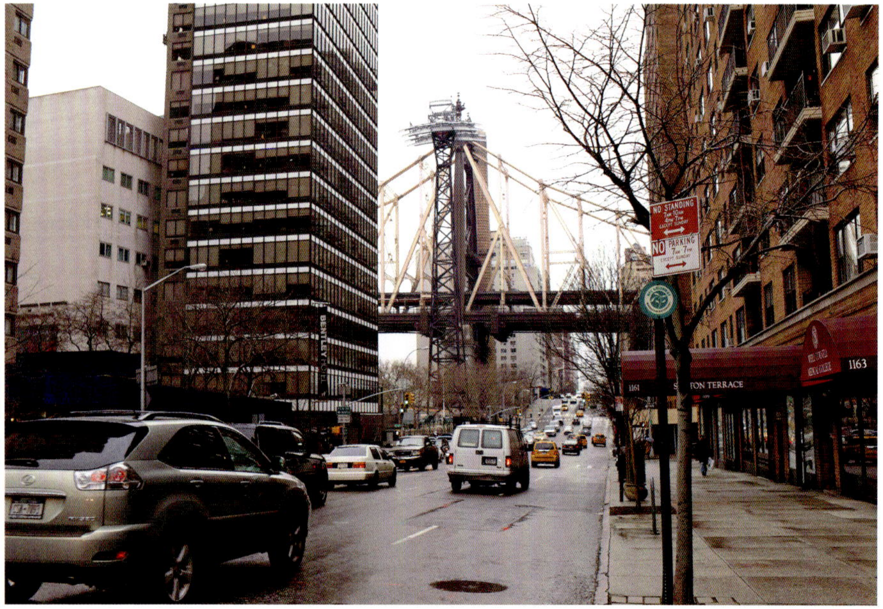

21

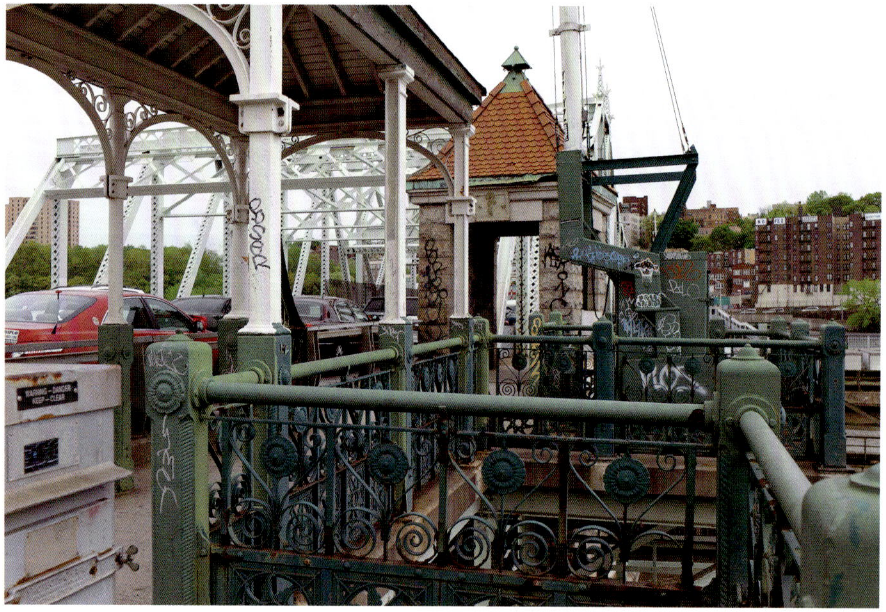

22

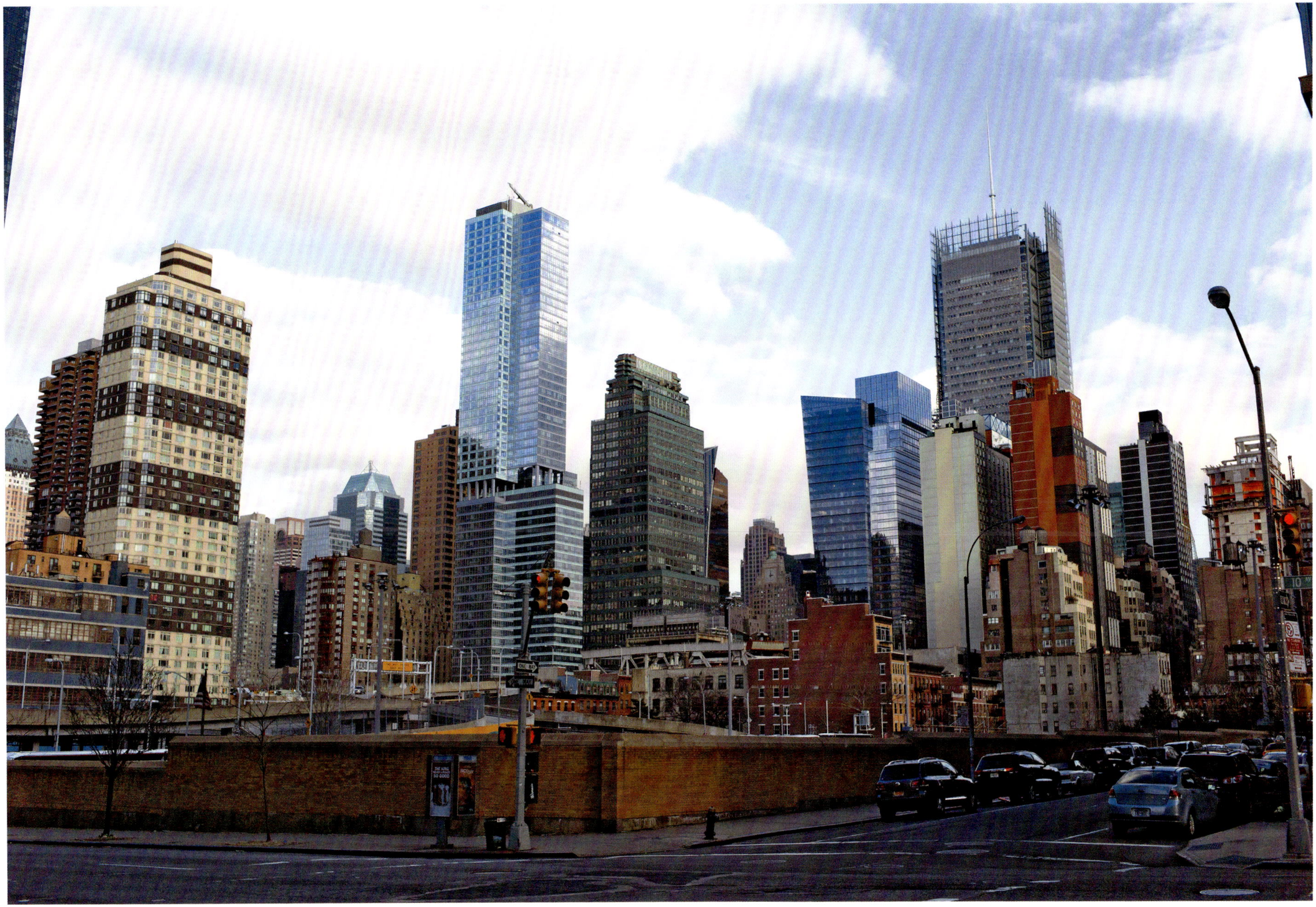

23

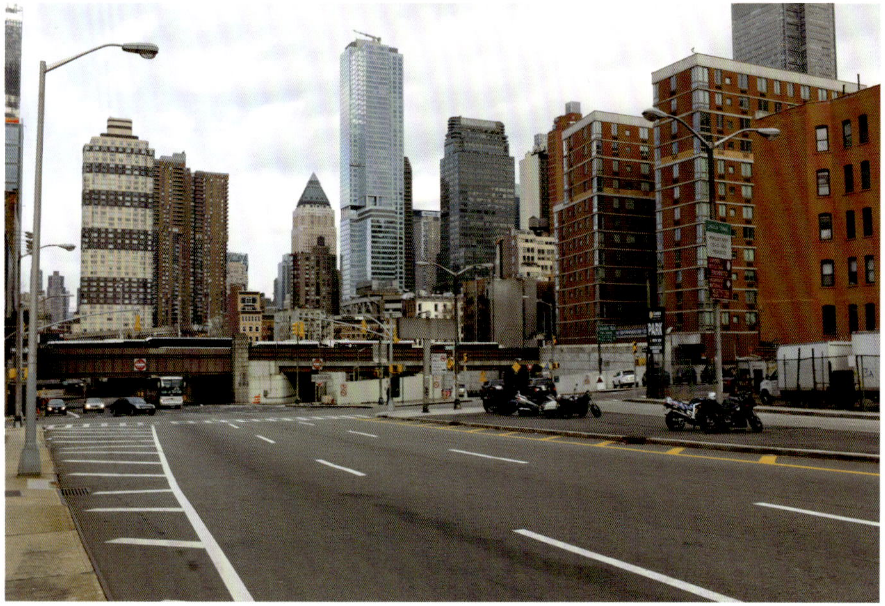

24

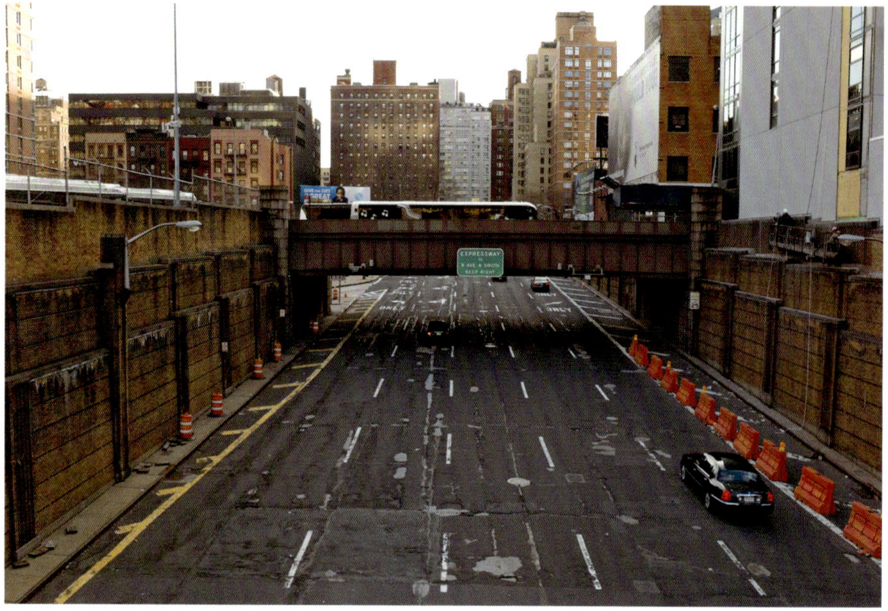

25

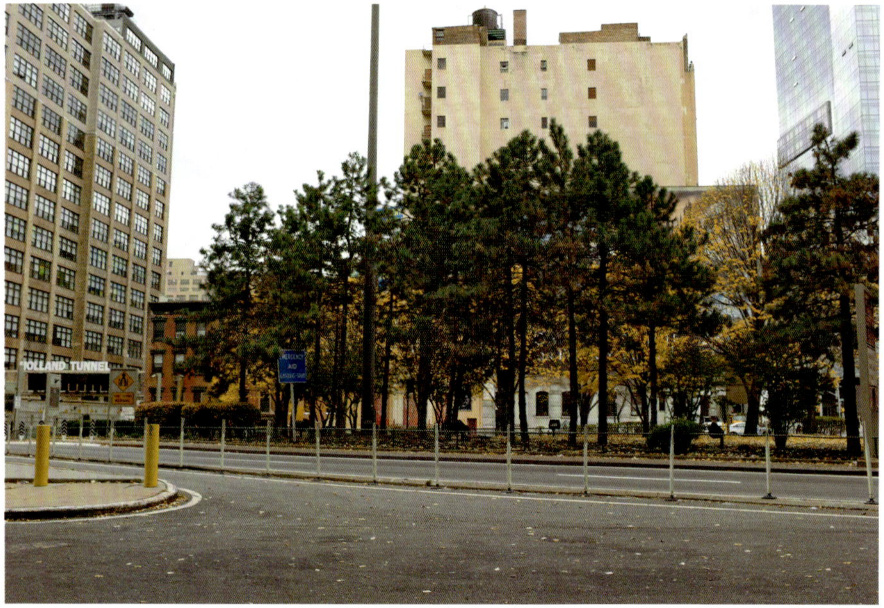

26

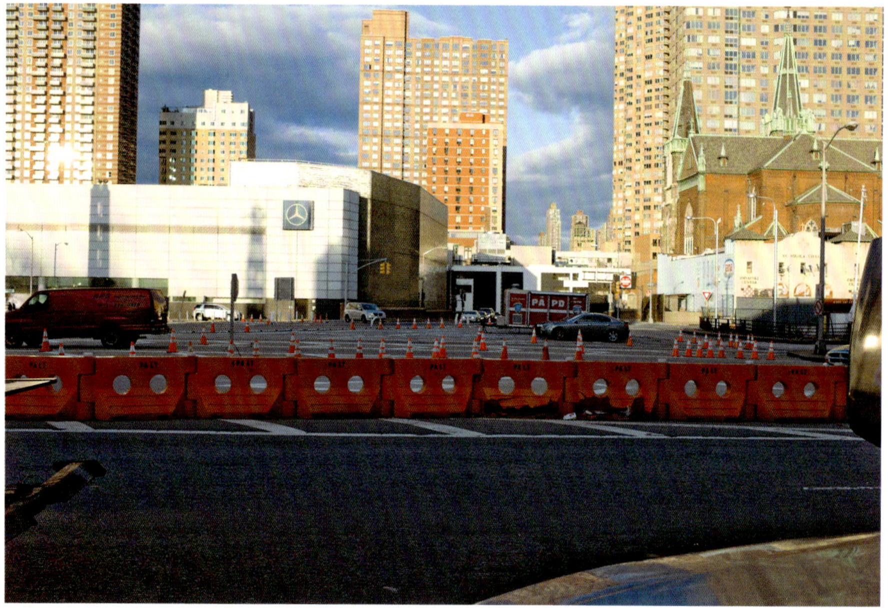

27

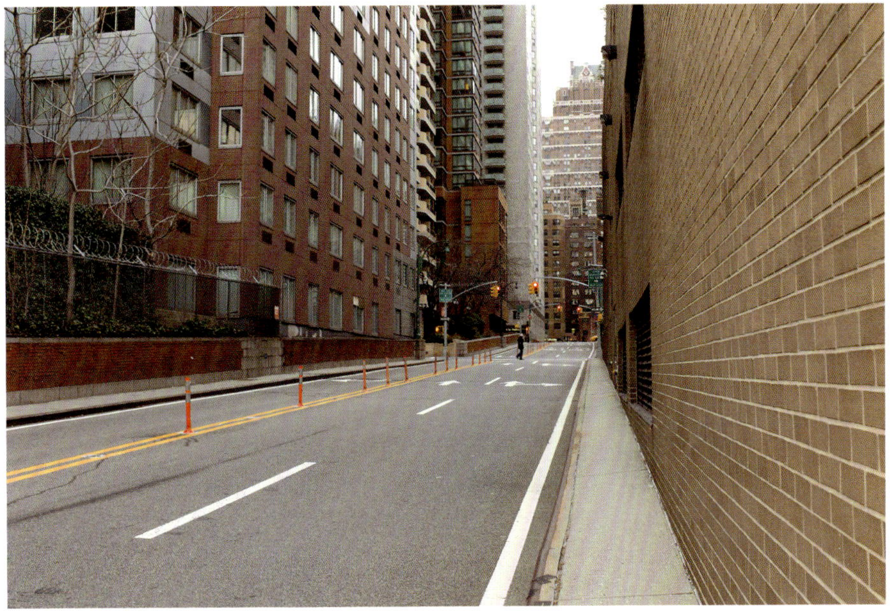

28

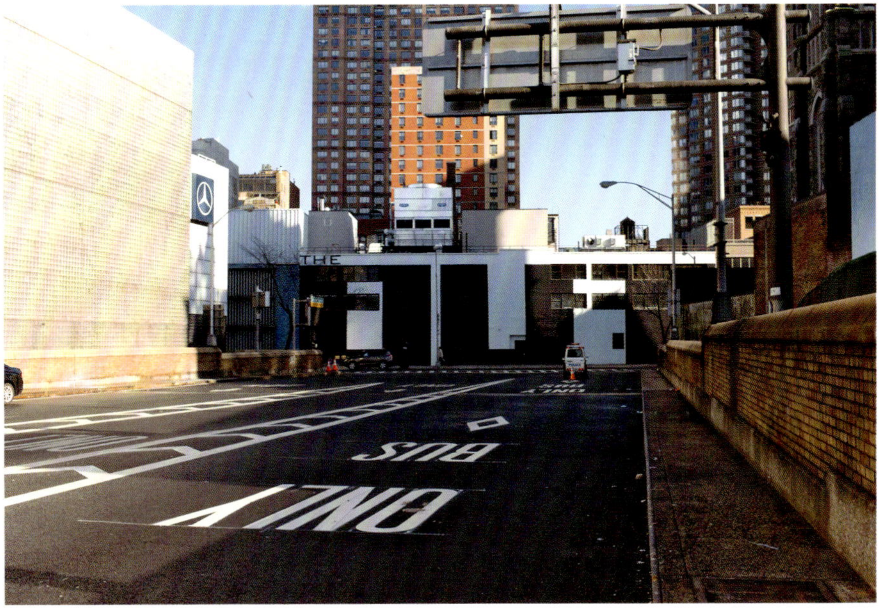

29

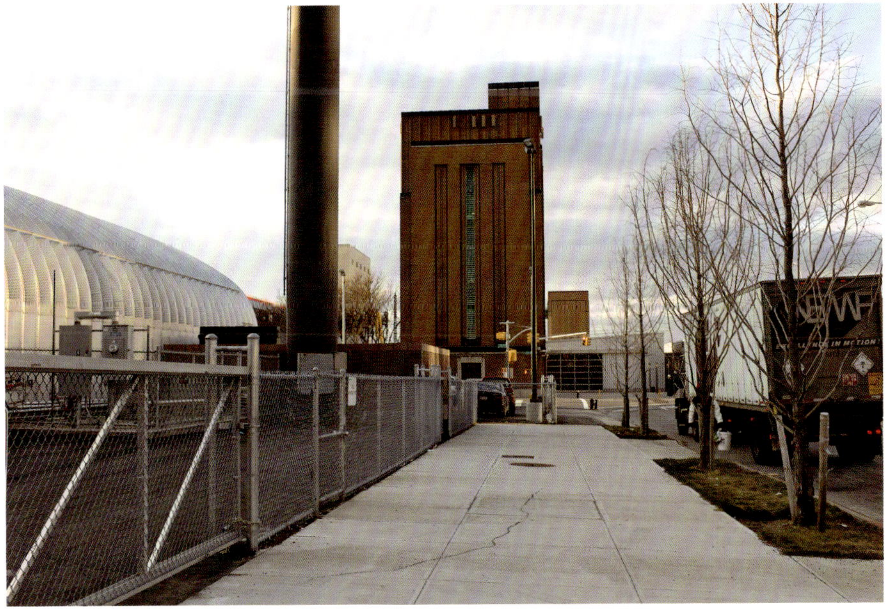

30

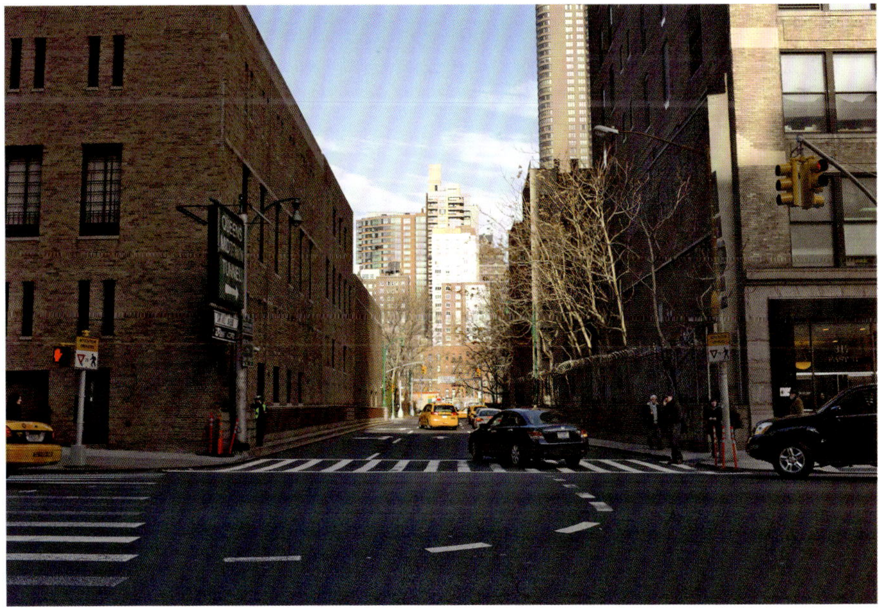

31

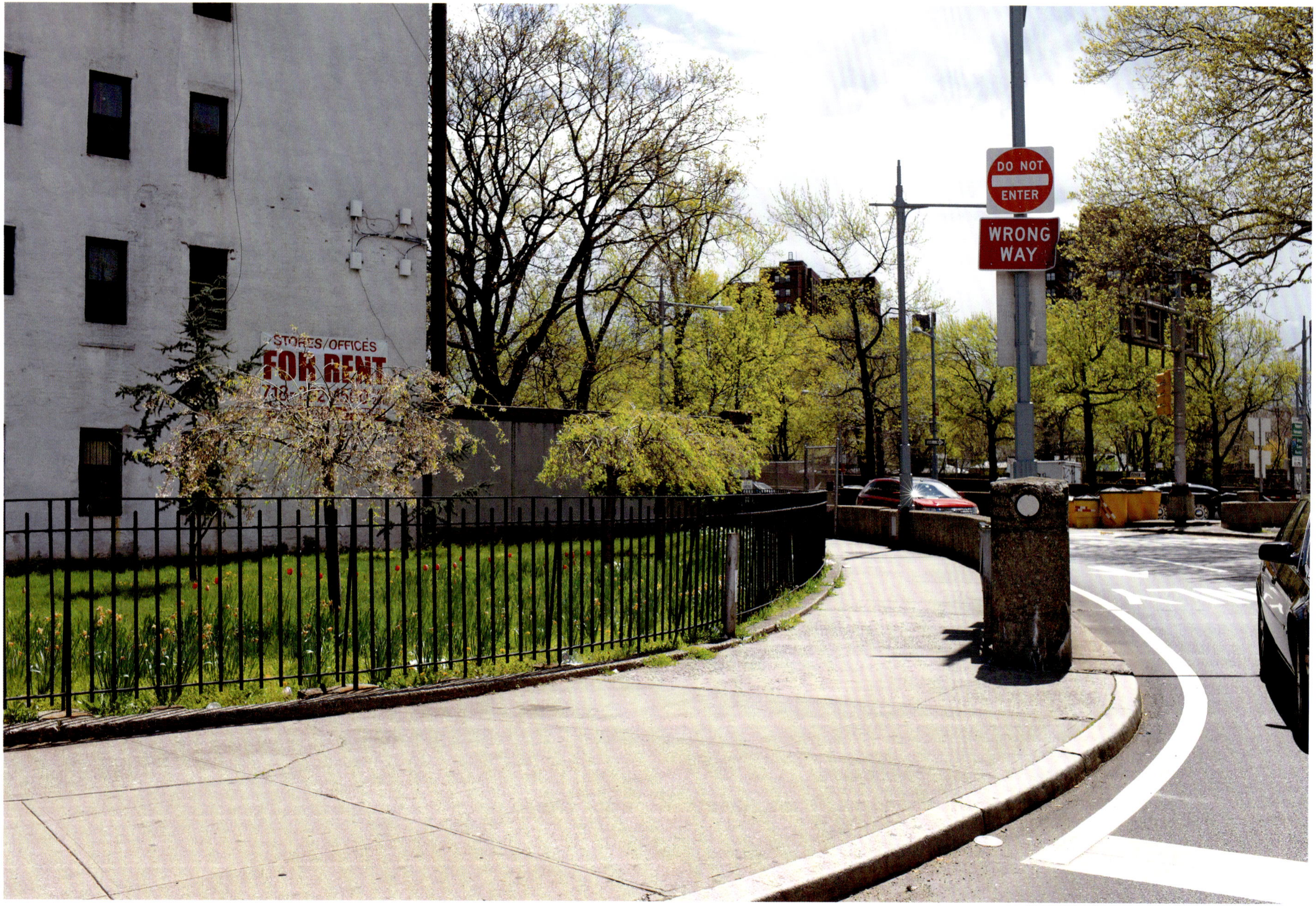

32

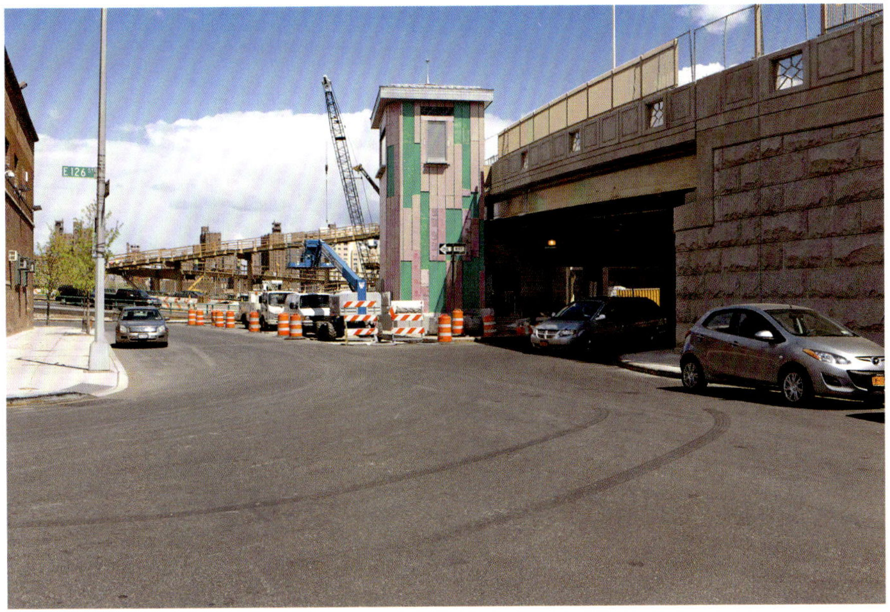

33

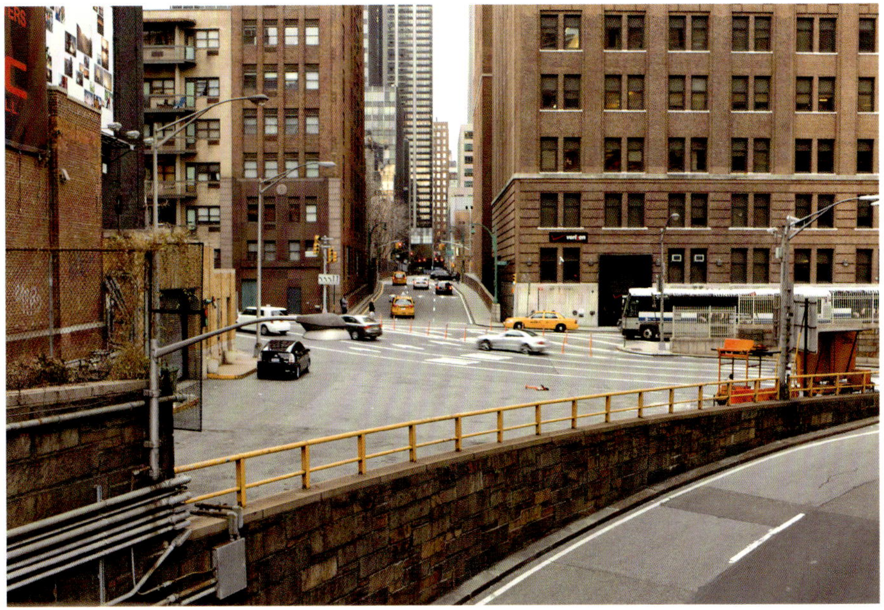

34

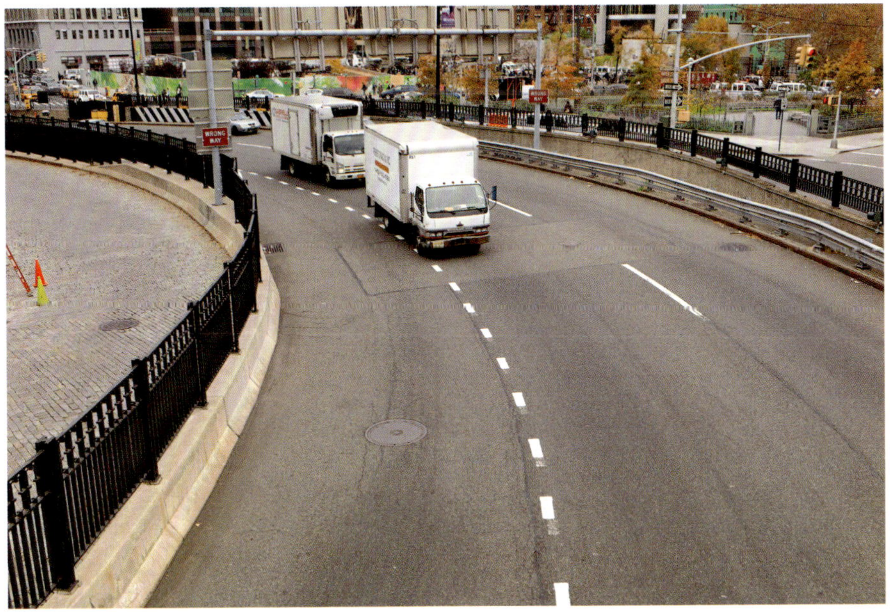

35

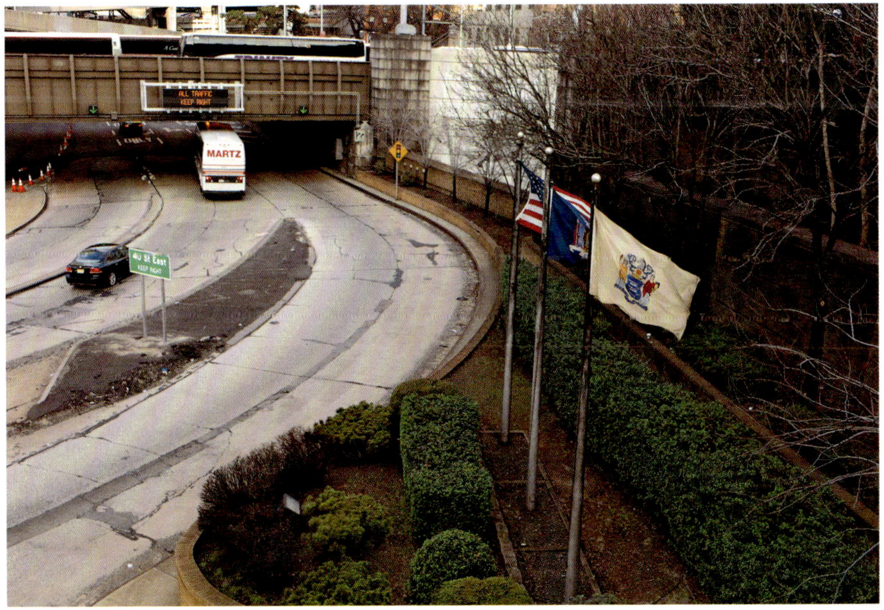

36

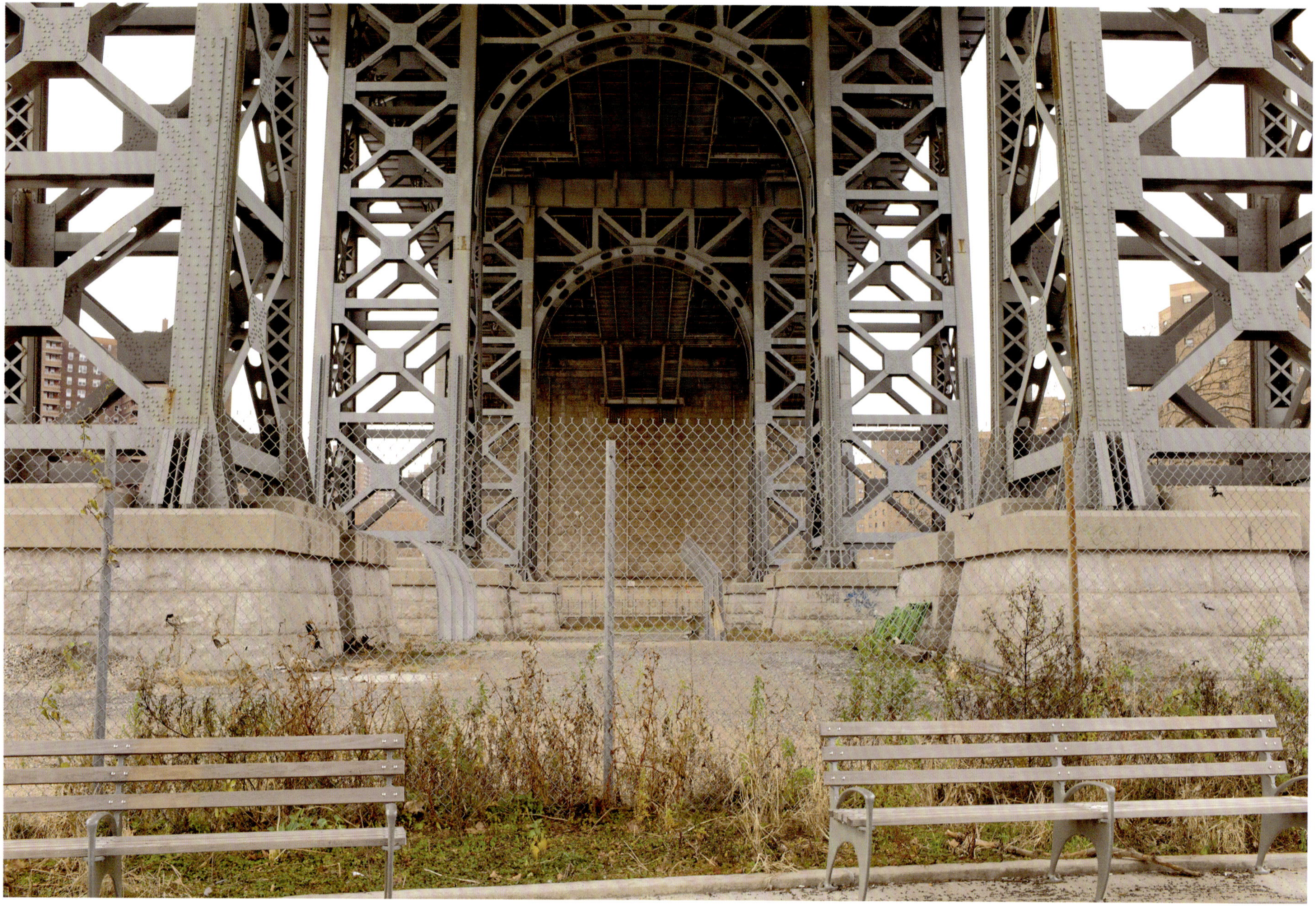

56

37

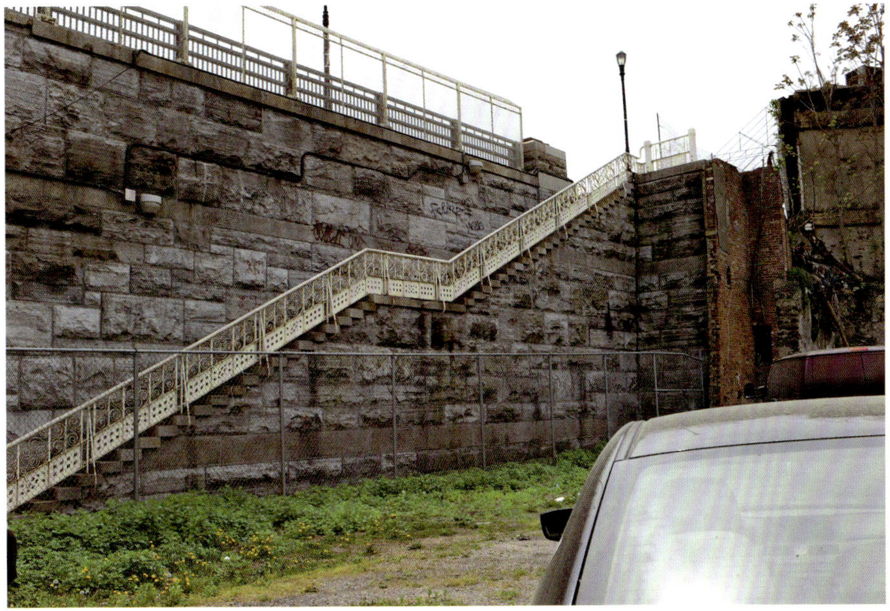

38

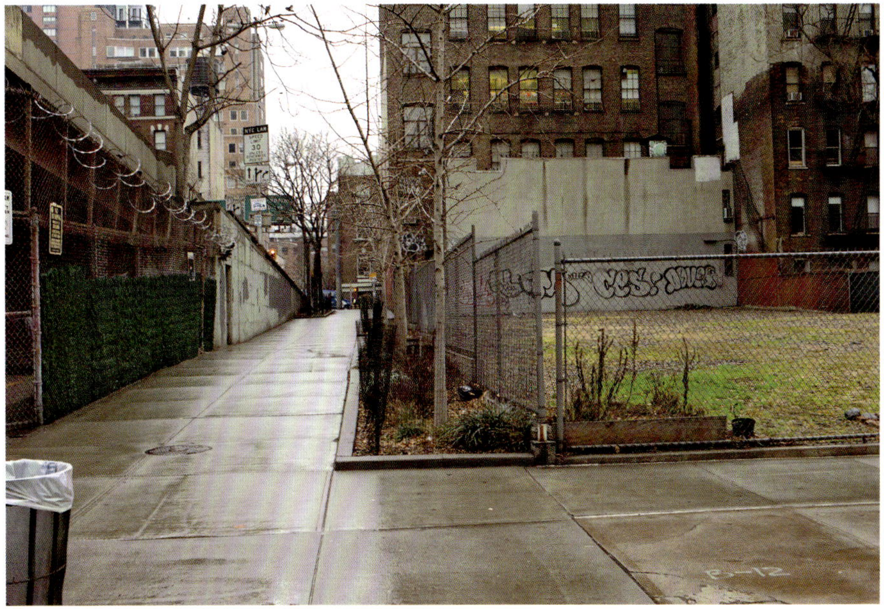

39

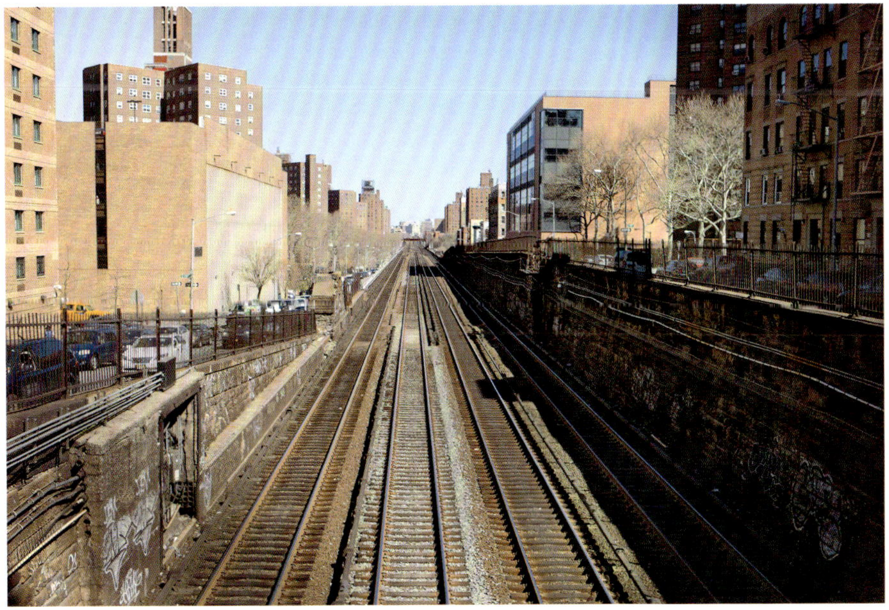

40

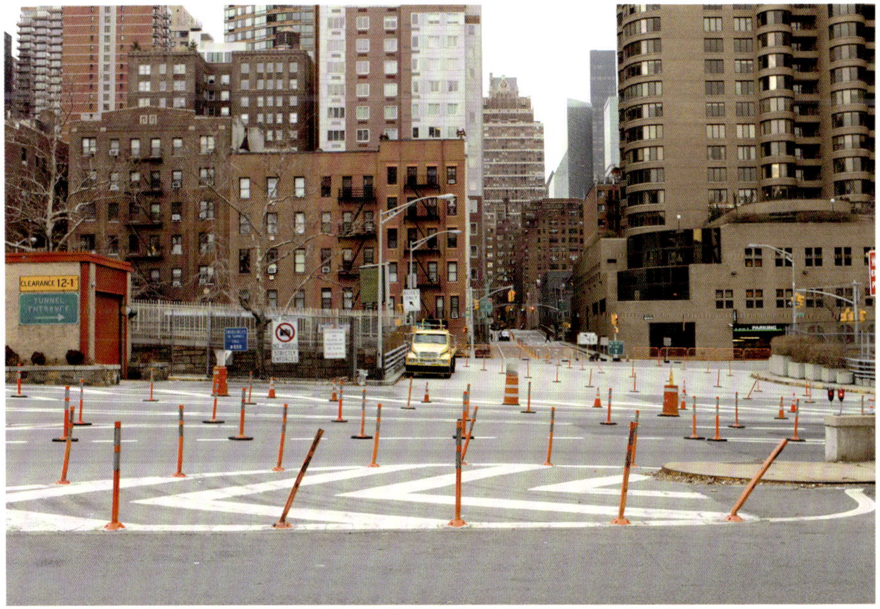

41

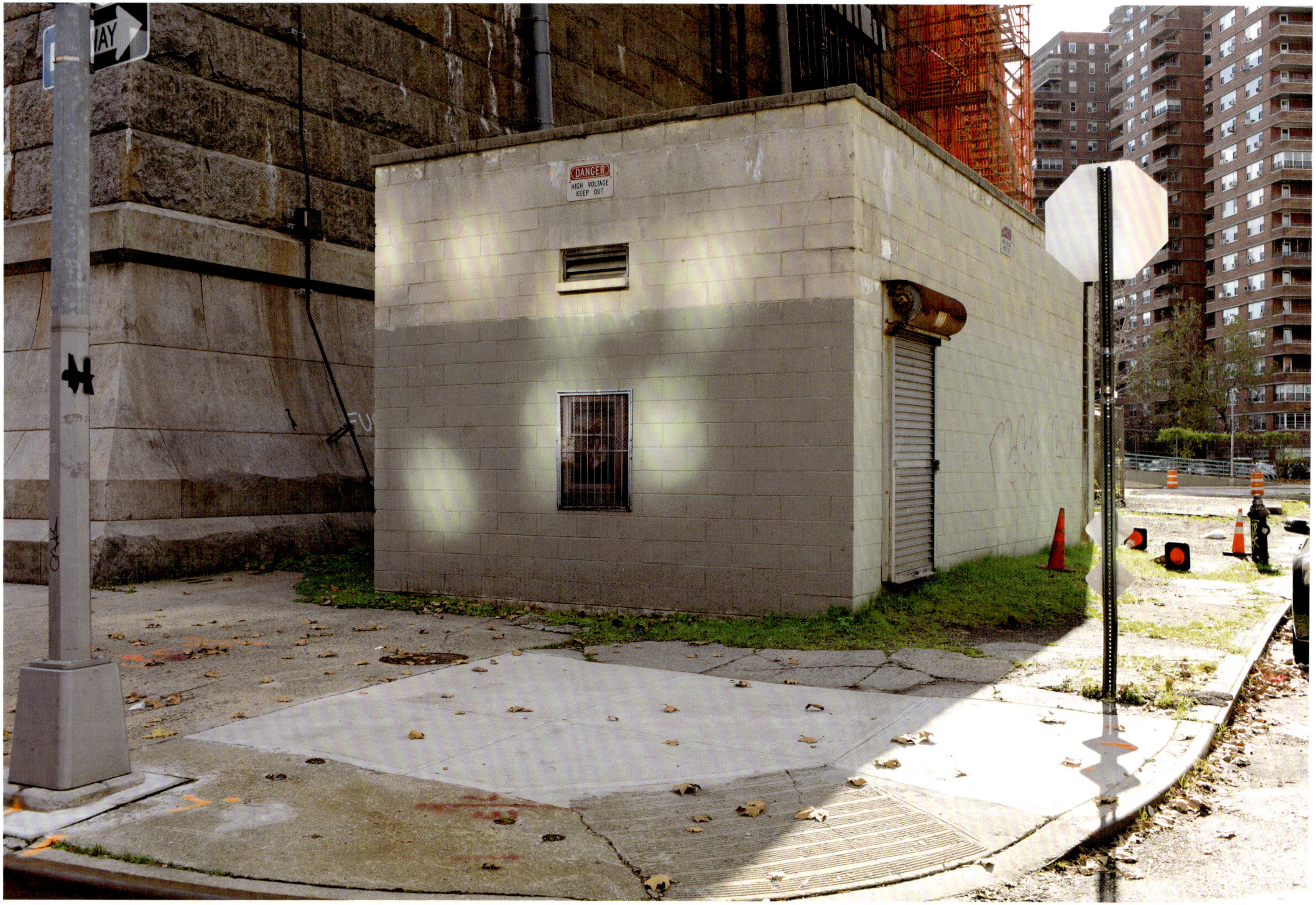

42

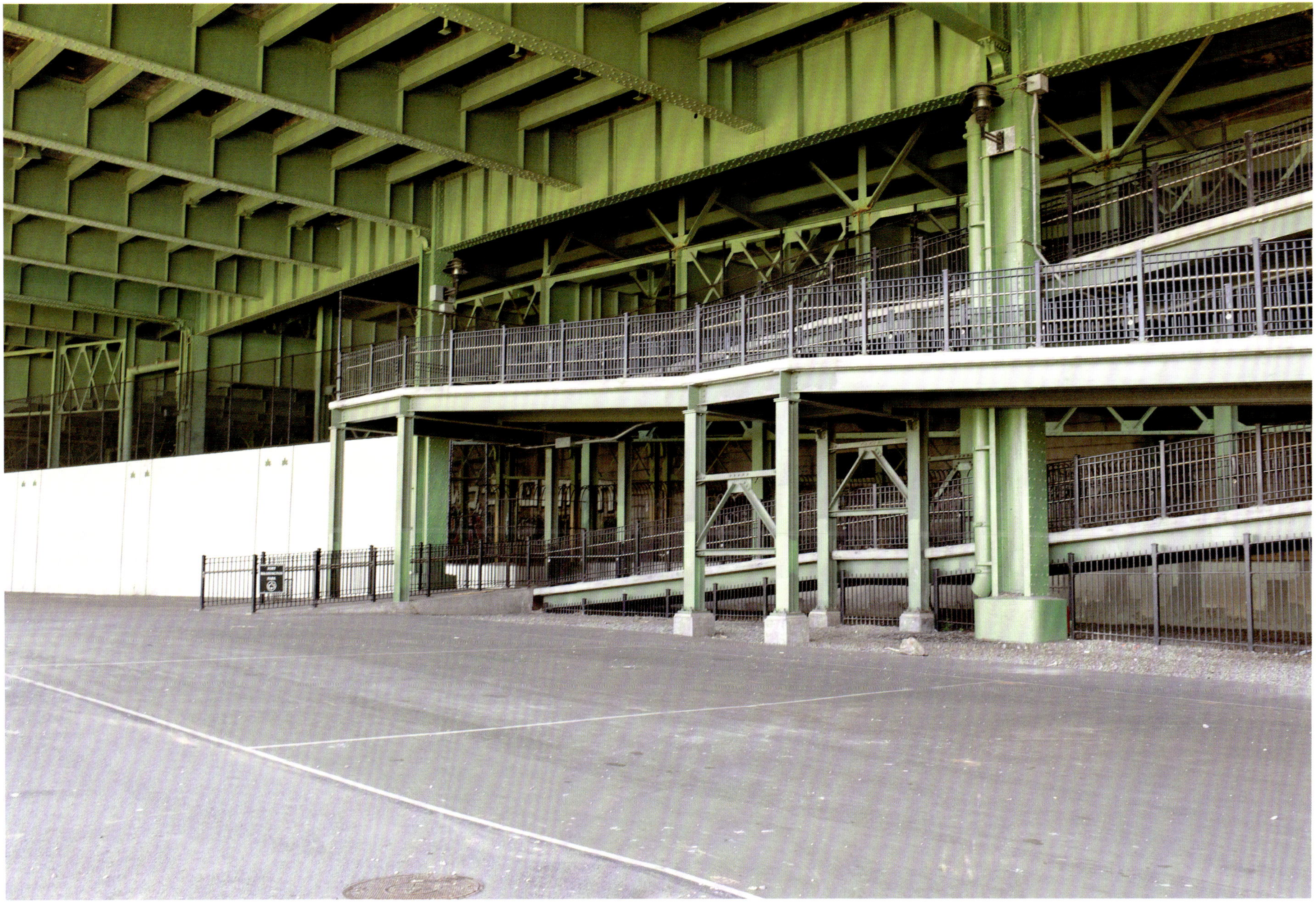

59

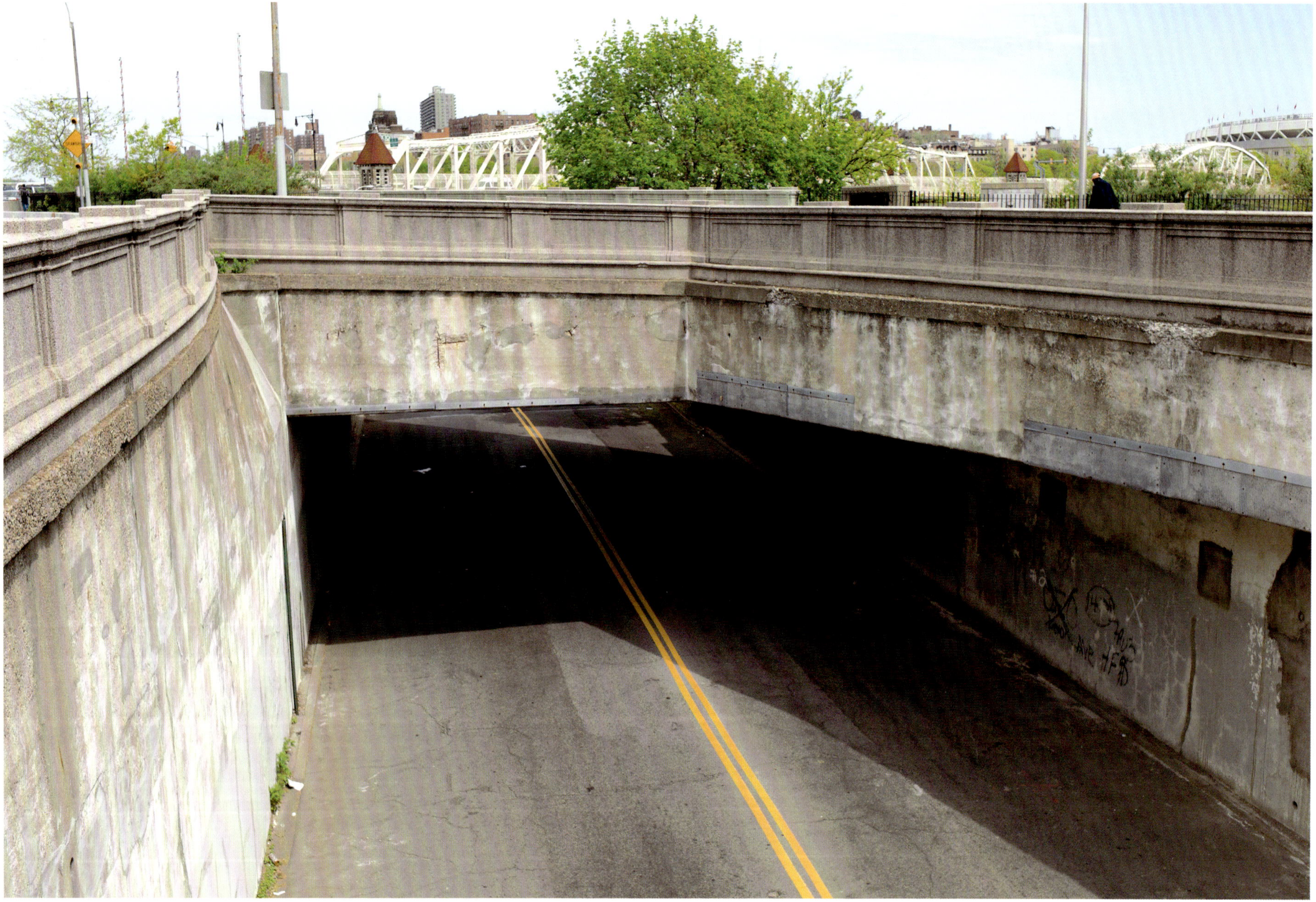

44

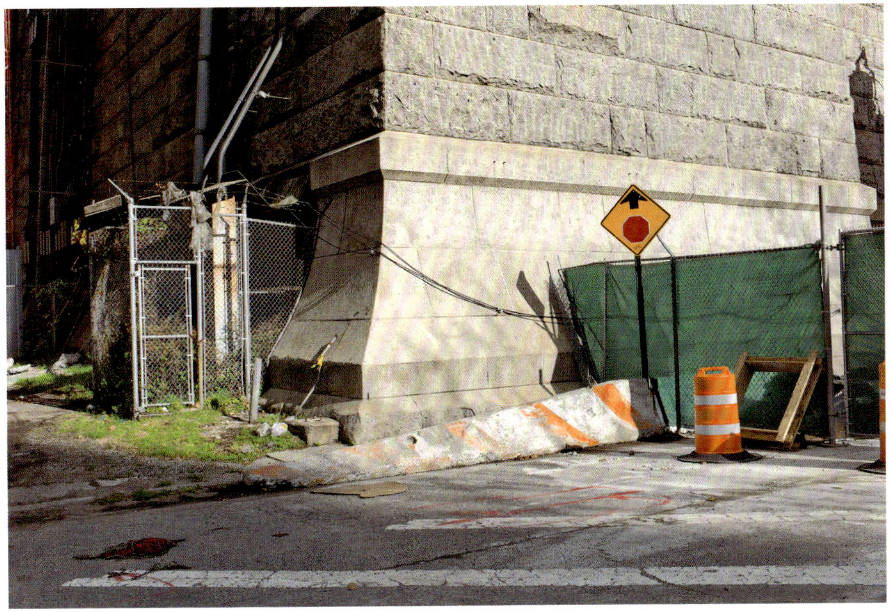

45

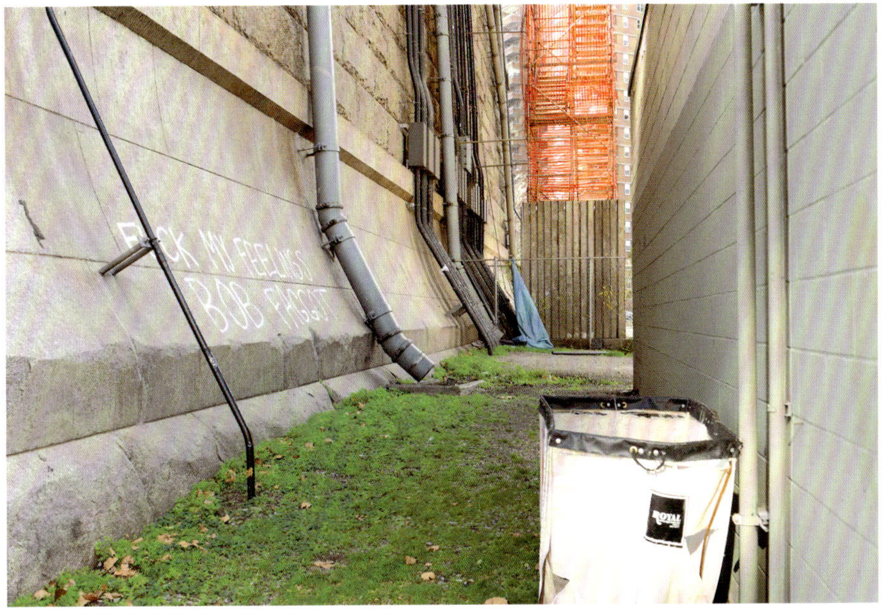

46

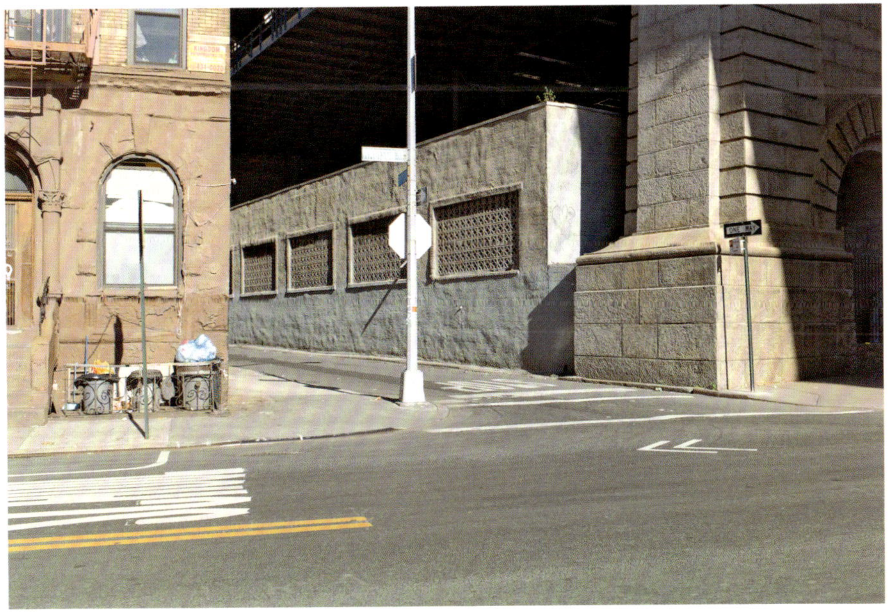

47

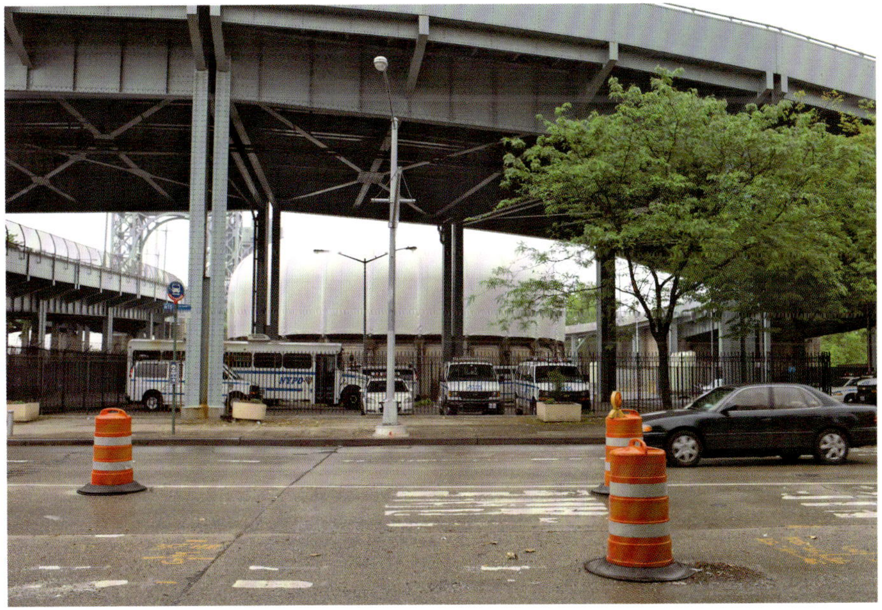

48

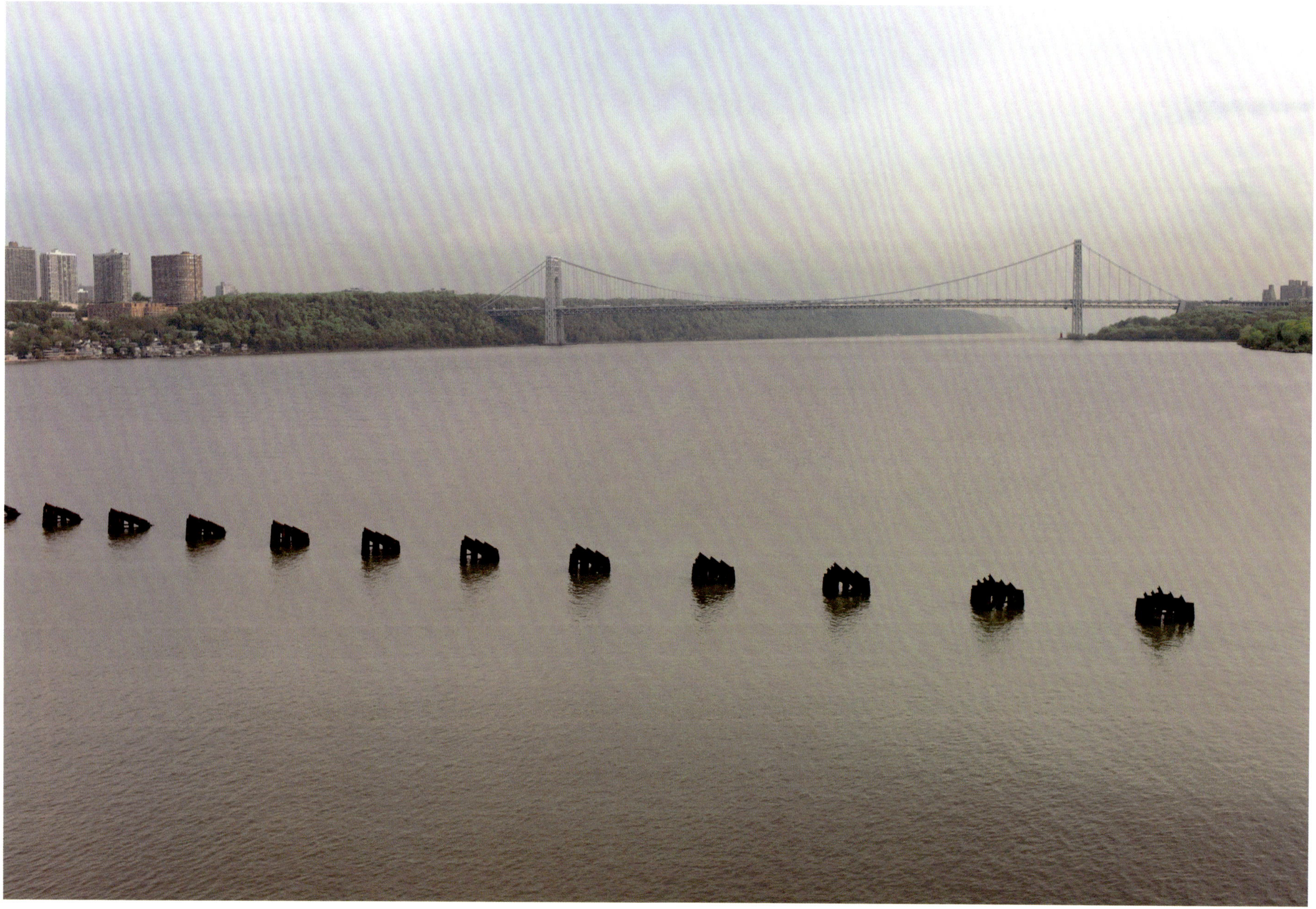

62

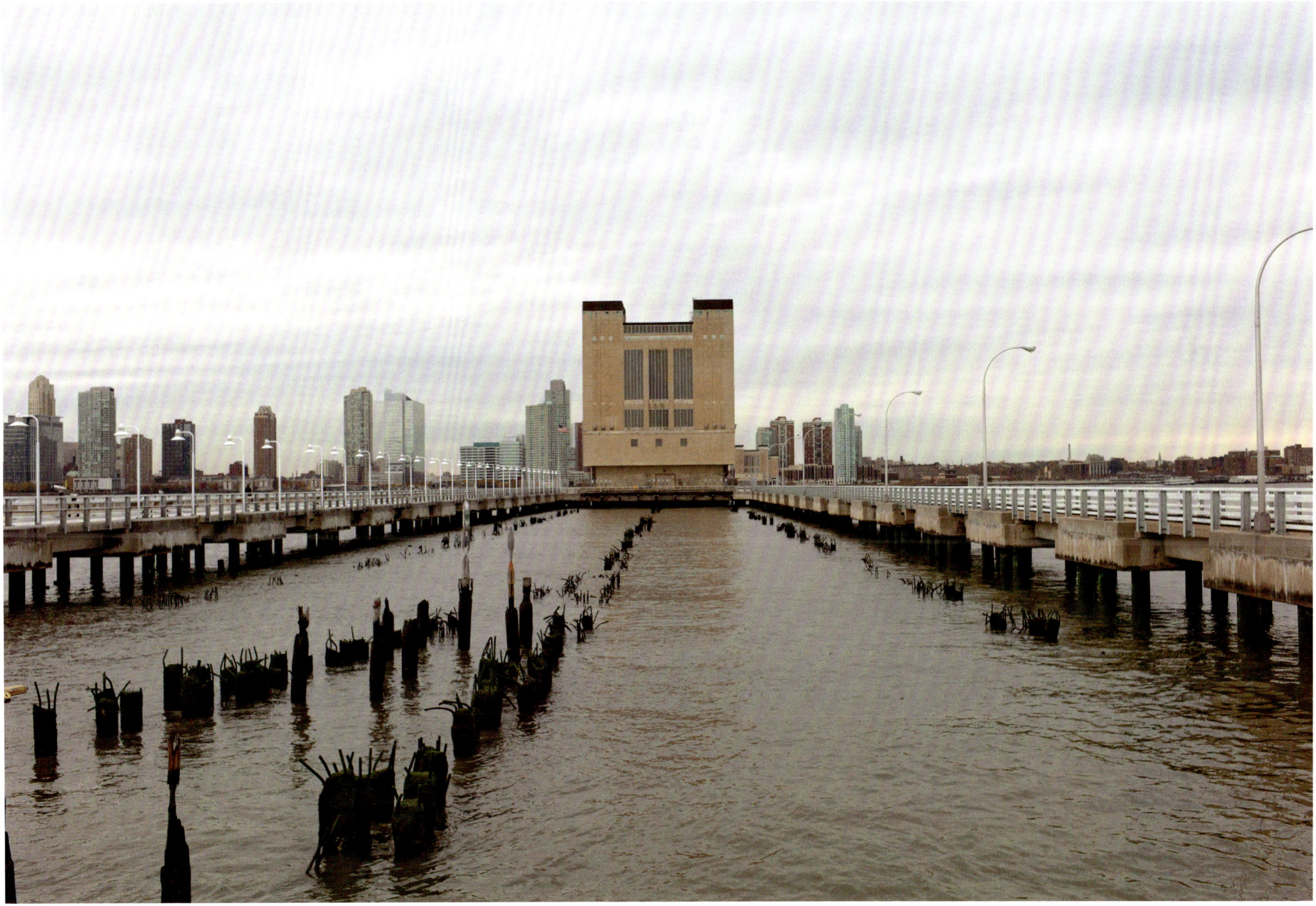

63

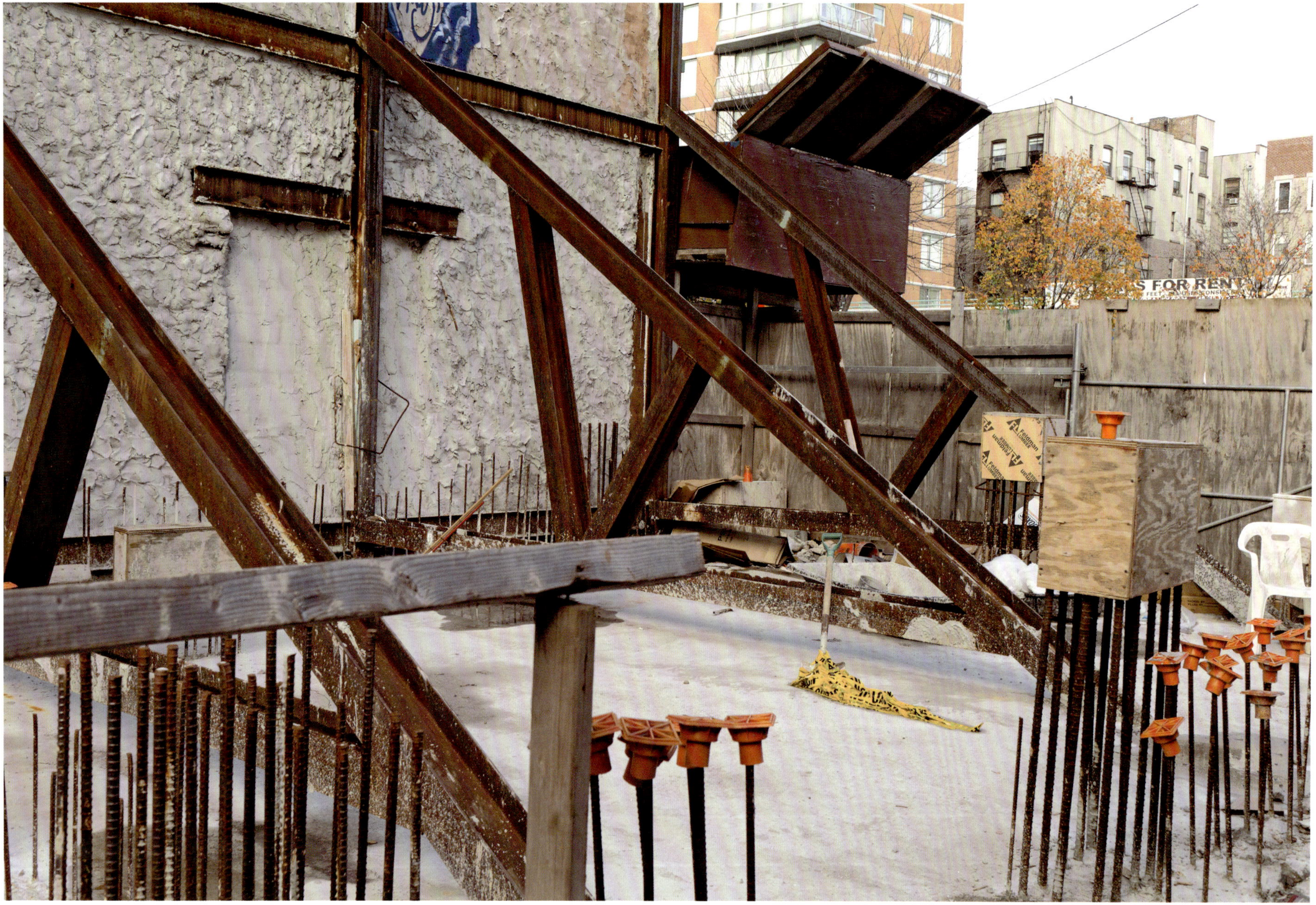

BUTTRESSES

Many Manhattan buildings, especially townhouse rows, at least partly depend on next-door buildings for their structural strength. When one building is removed, it can lead to instability in neighboring buildings, and sometimes the process of demolition of an adjacent building can damage the surrounding structures. So steel supports are often installed to help brace those buildings until the adjacent space is filled. Larger buildings require extensive structures designed by engineers.

Unlike those on Gothic cathedrals, these buttresses are never intended to be permanent, but some are in place for years. Smaller arrangements are often required when there are other structural problems with buildings; they seem almost handmade, only put in place as a stopgap when it is apparent that a part of the building—wall, bay window, terrace—has become unstable.

1 Lower East Side
2 Upper West Side
3 Lower East Side
4 Tribeca
5 Murray Hill
6 Sugar Hill
7 Chelsea
8 Chelsea
9 East Village
10 SoHo

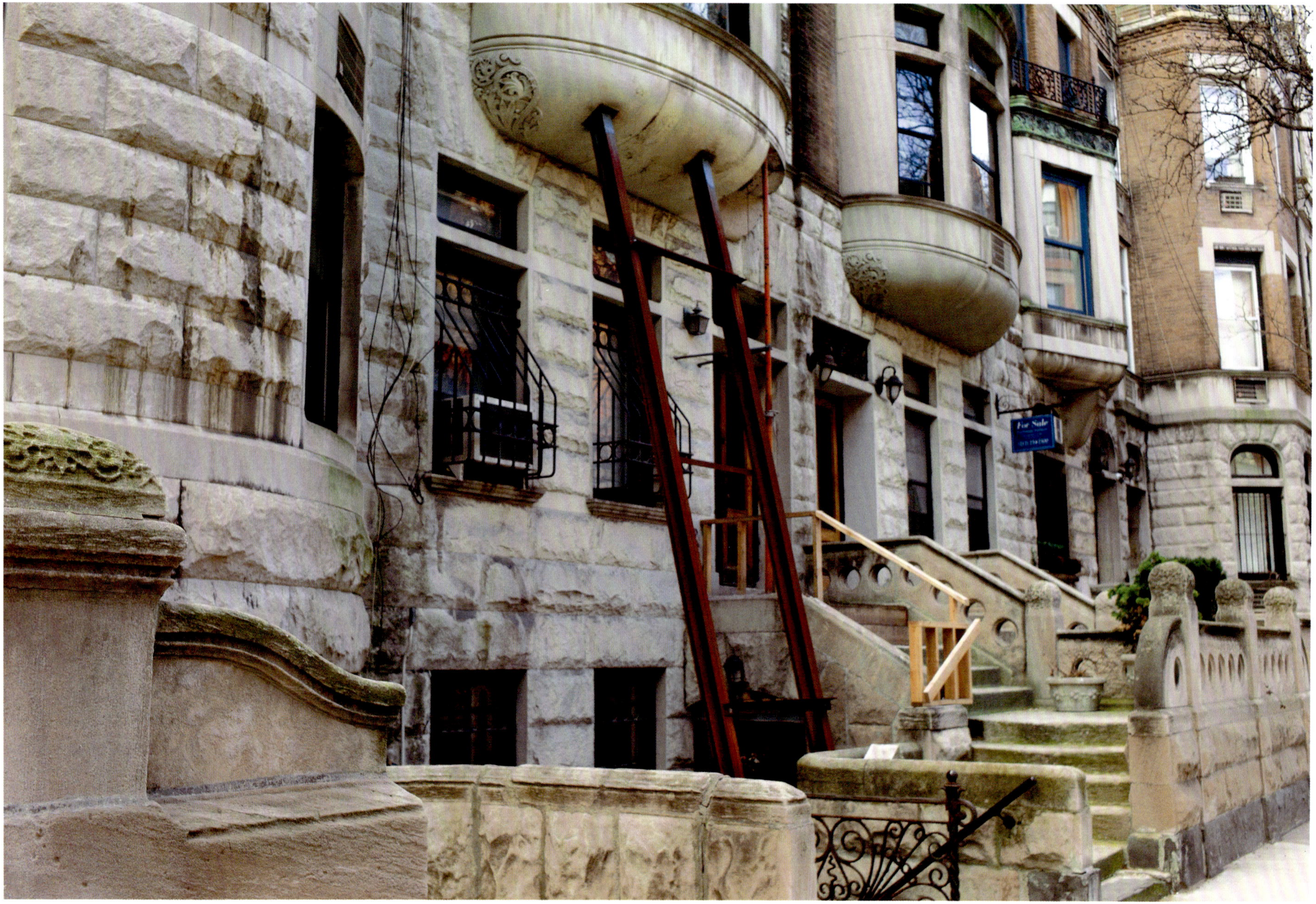

2

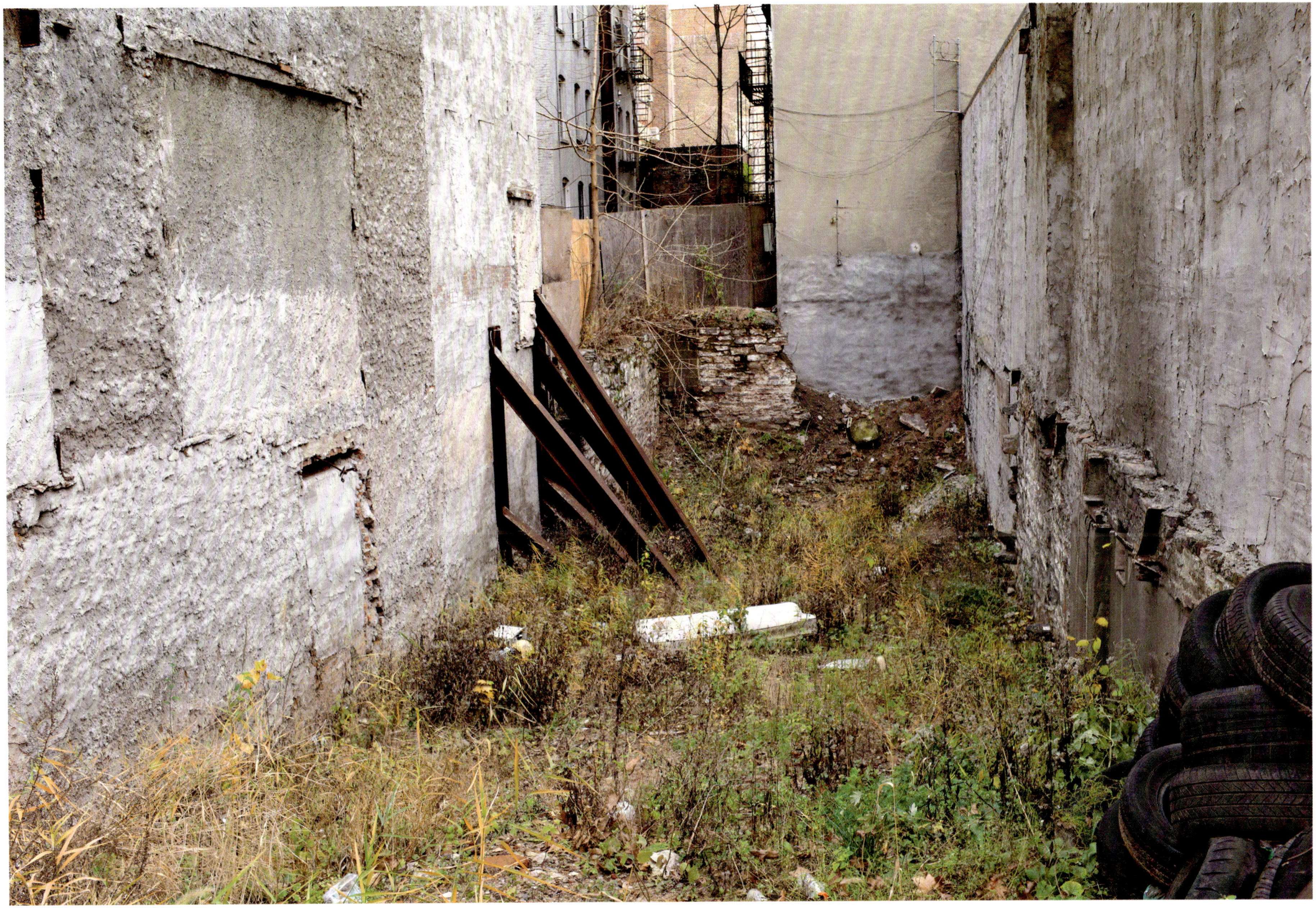

3

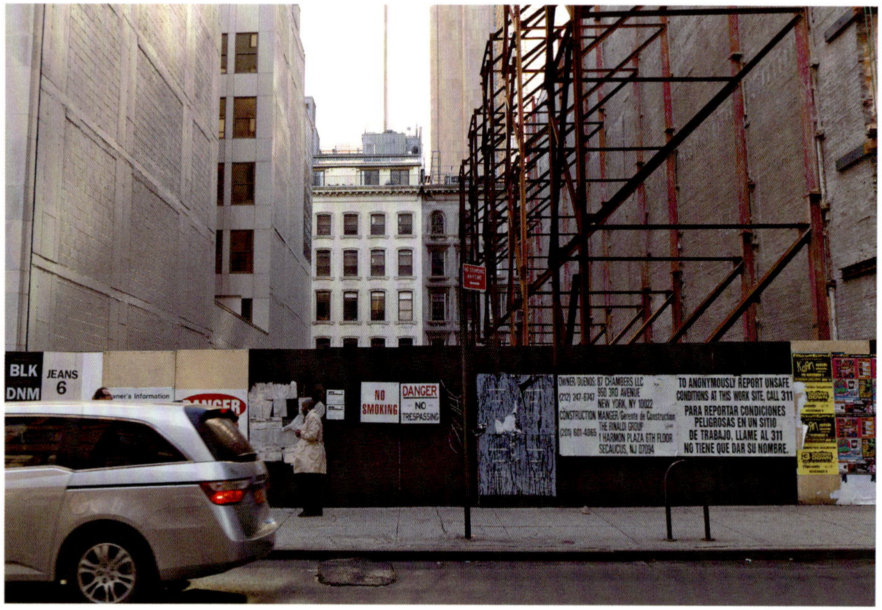
BLK DNM
JEANS 6
NO SMOKING
DANGER NO TRESPASSING
OWNER/DUENOS: 87 CHAMBERS LLC
(212) 247-6747 950 3RD AVENUE
NEW YORK, NY 10022
CONSTRUCTION MANGER/Gerente de Construction
THE RINALDI GROUP
(201) 601-4065 1 HARMON PLAZA 6TH FLOOR
SECAUCUS, NJ 07094
TO ANONYMOUSLY REPORT UNSAFE CONDITIONS AT THIS WORK SITE, CALL 311
PARA REPORTAR CONDICIONES PELIGROSAS EN UN SITIO DE TRABAJO, LLAME AL 311
NO TIENE QUE DAR SU NOMBRE.

4

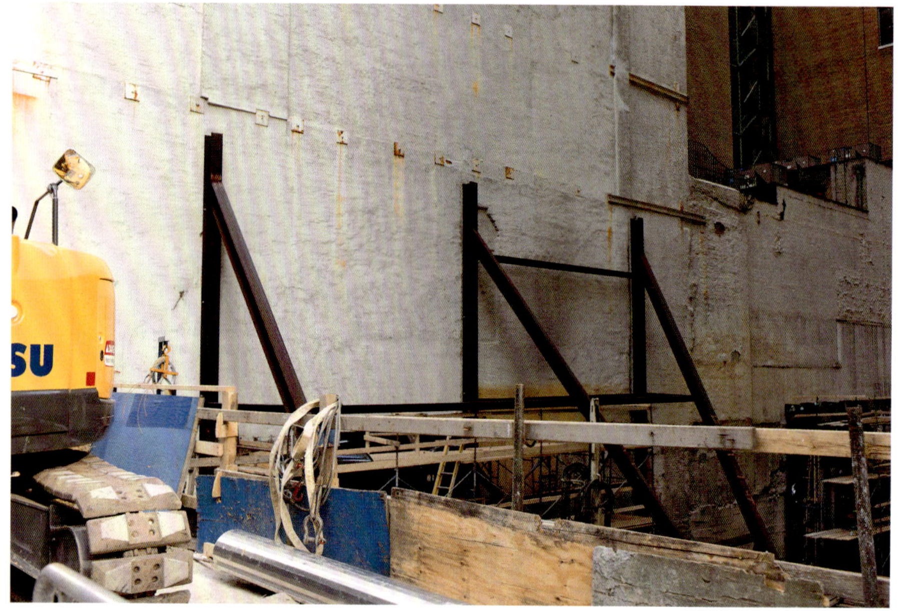

5

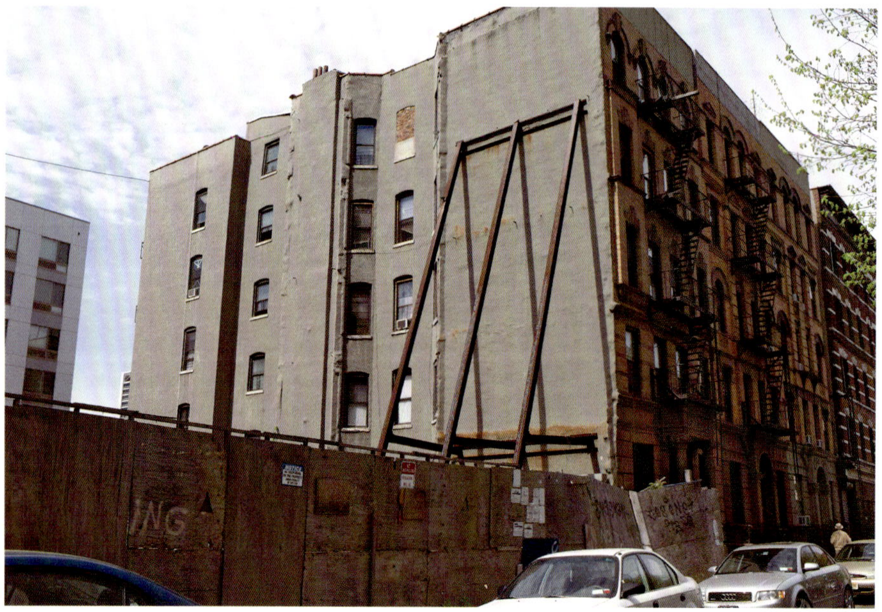

6

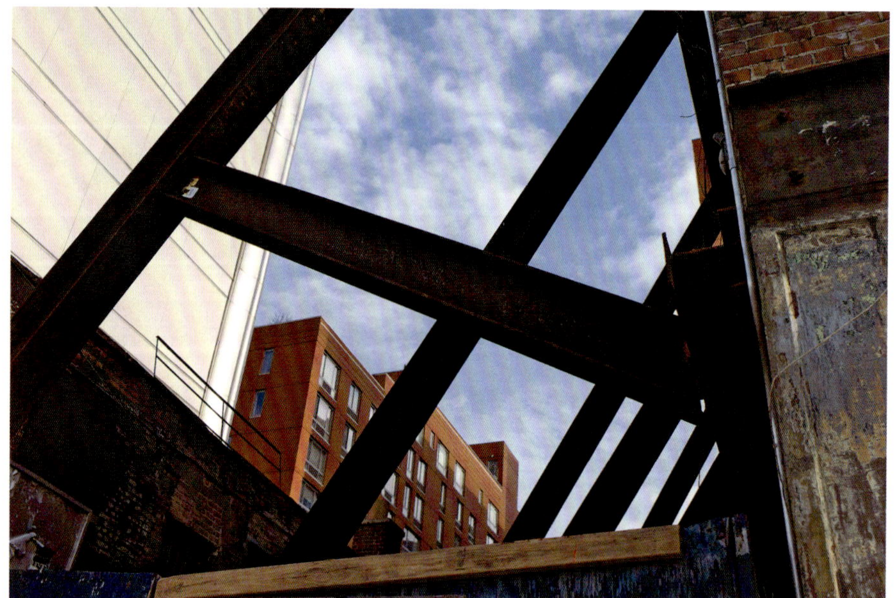

7

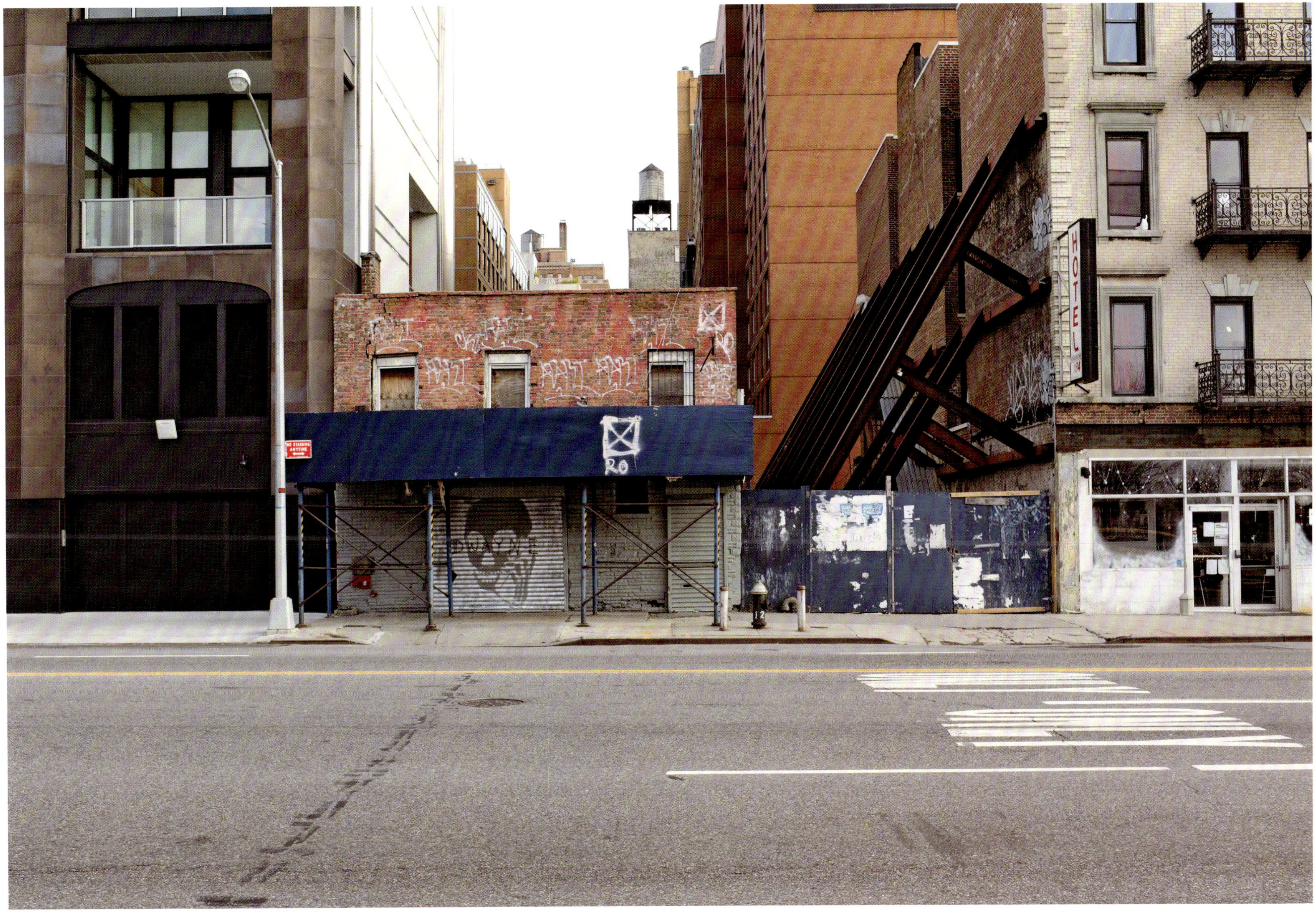

69

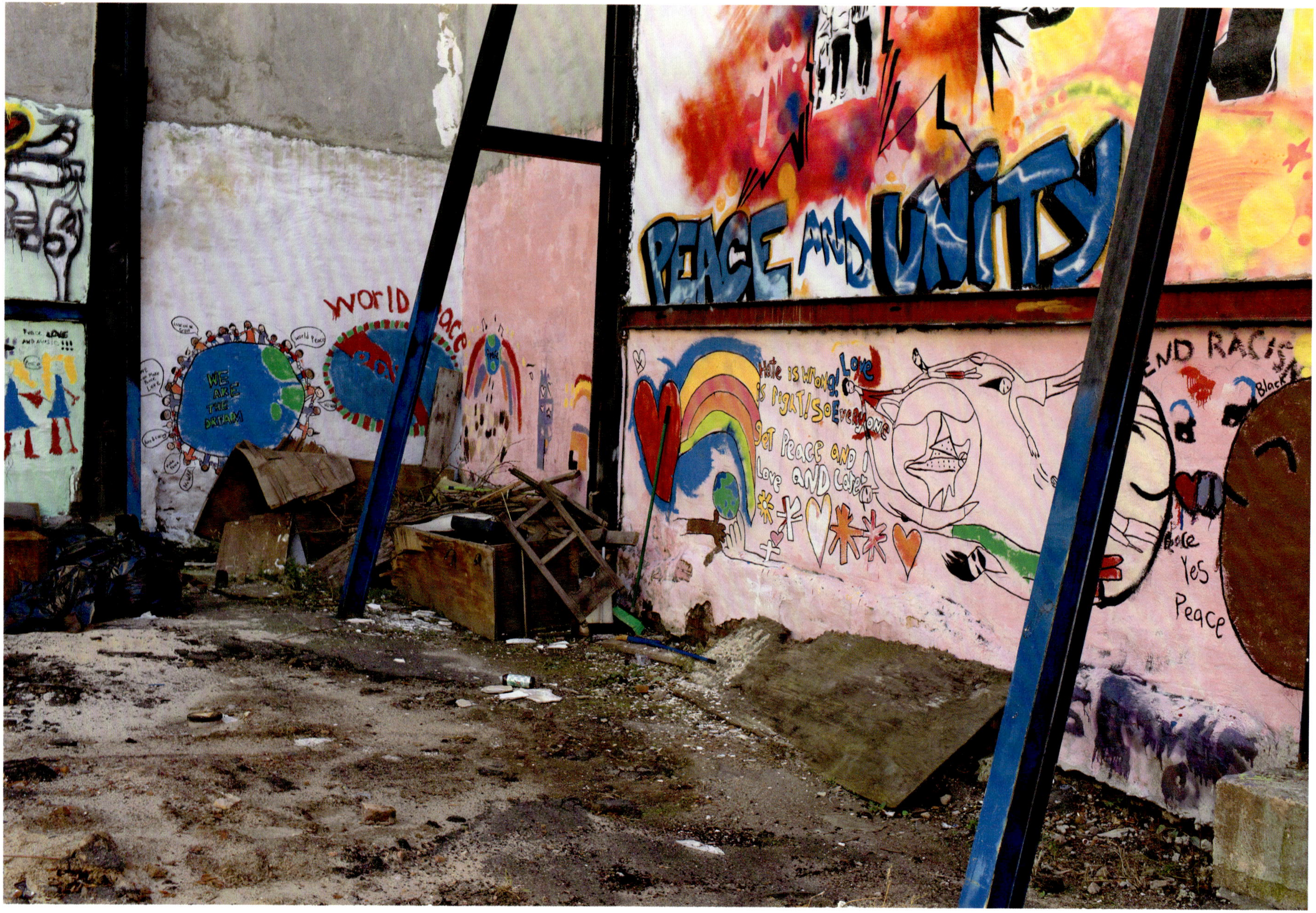
PEACE AND UNITY
World
WE ARE THE DREAM
Hate is wrong! Love is right! So everyone got peace and love and care
END RACIS
Yes
Peace

9

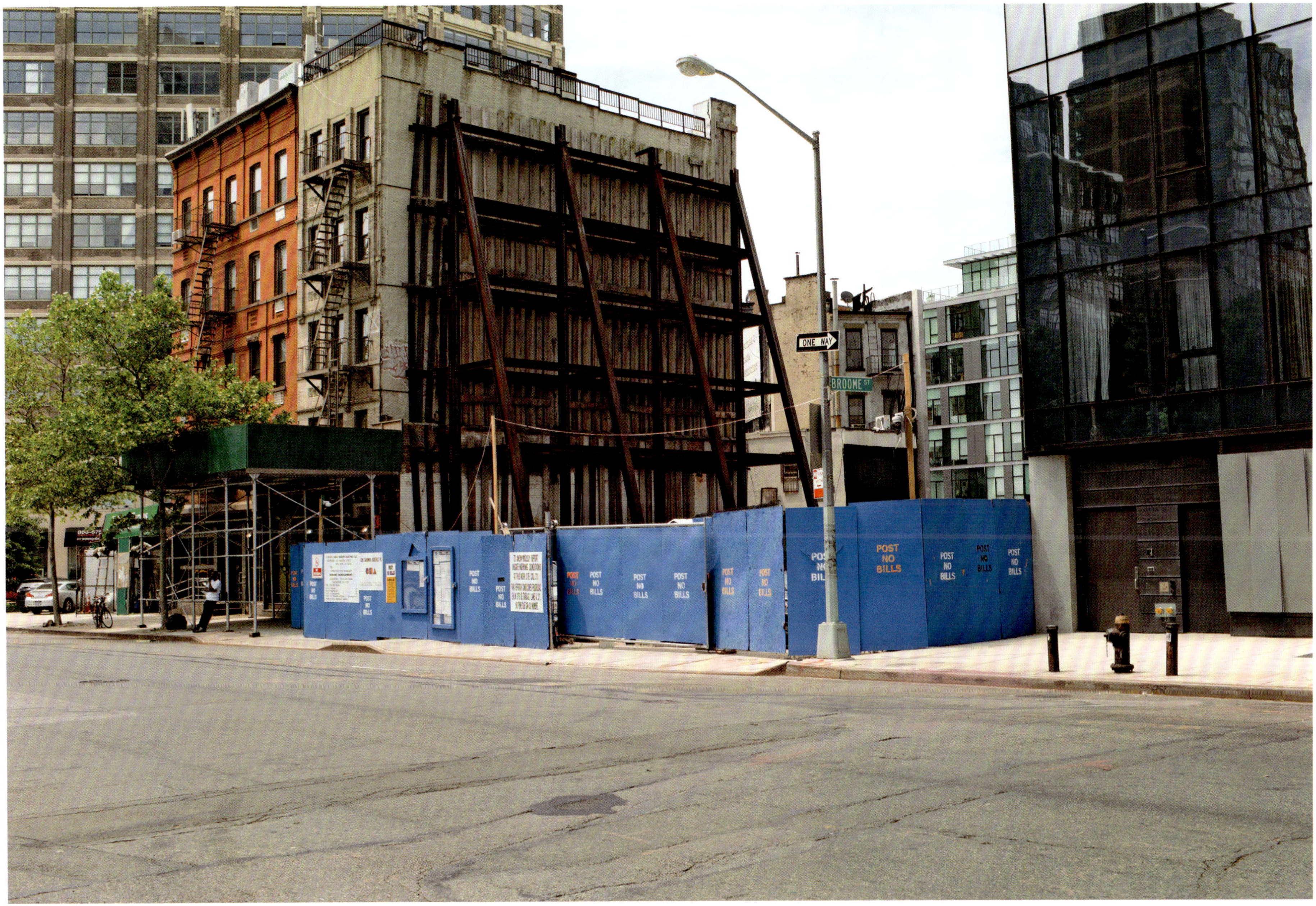

71

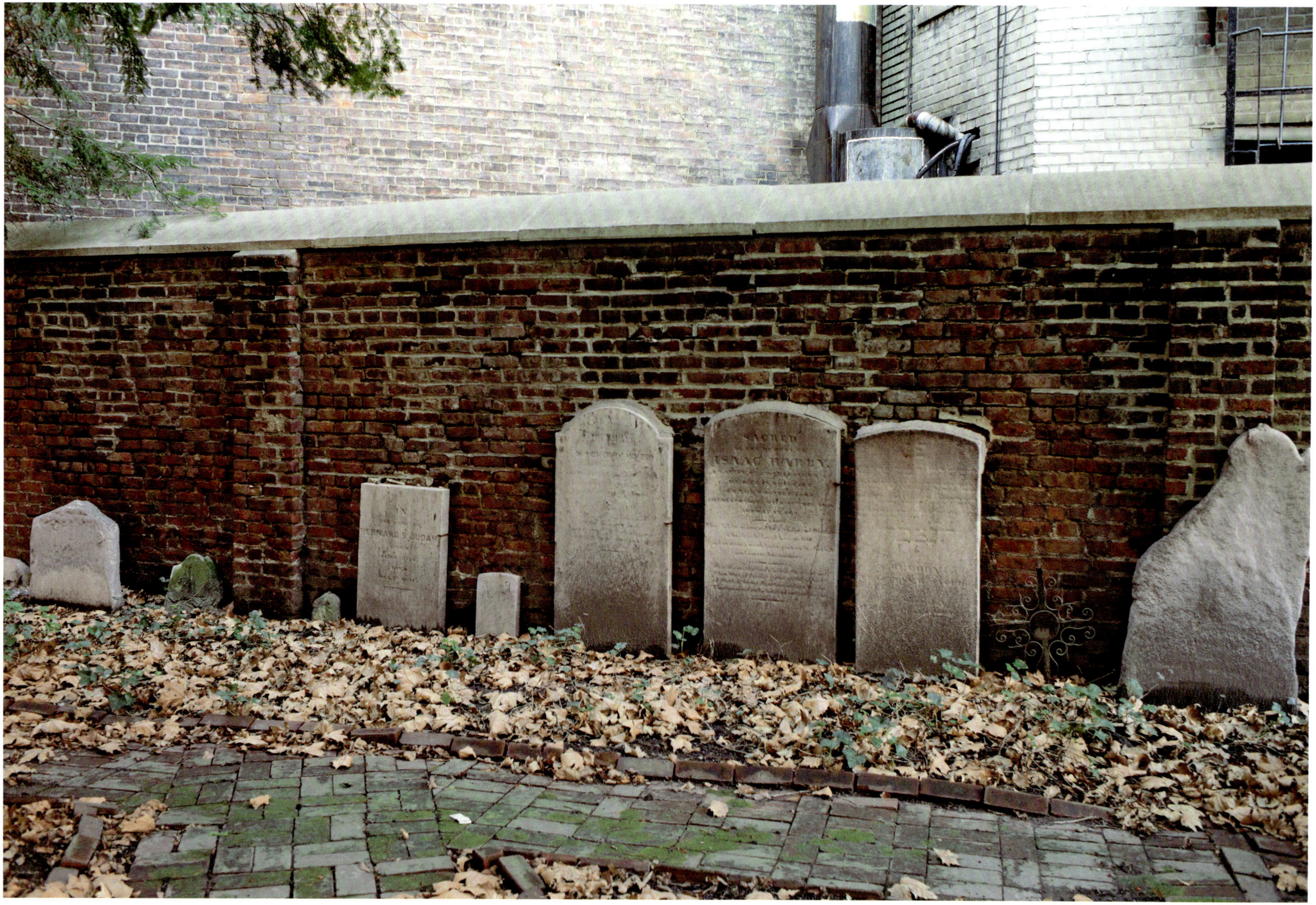

CEMETERIES

Many cemeteries and potter's fields in Manhattan were made into parks in the nineteenth century (Washington Square Park, Union Square, Bryant Park), but the bodies were not always exhumed. More often than not, African American cemeteries were just bulldozed for development. Trinity Church owns three cemeteries, two downtown (where you can find the Hamiltons and Schuylers) and one uptown (where the Astors and John James Audubon, who lived nearby, rest).

The first nonsectarian cemeteries were built around 1830, both near Houston Street. There are a few individual burial sites around the island, including Grant's Tomb in Riverside Park and the nearby Amiable Child. You can trace the expansion of the city by following the three Shearith Israel cemeteries as they moved uptown, from Chinatown to the West Village, then over to Chelsea. The Chinatown site, on St. James Place, was on a hill just overlooking the East River. So much land has been added to Manhattan since then that it is now about 1500 feet from the shore.

The African Burial Ground near City Hall was rediscovered in 1991 during excavation for a new federal building. The earliest and largest site of its type, the cemetery had been clearly visible on early maps, but unknown in modern times. Activists and scholars fought to preserve the burial ground and Congress eventually agreed. It is now a US National Monument.

1 West Village
2 East Village
3 Chelsea
4 Madison Square
5 Manhattanville
6 Financial District
7 West Village
8 Two Bridges
9 Financial District
10 East Village
11 Manhattanville
12 Hamilton Heights
13 Chelsea
14 Hamilton Heights
15 Chelsea
16 East Village
17 West Village
18 Hamilton Heights
19 Hamilton Heights
20 Lower Manhattan

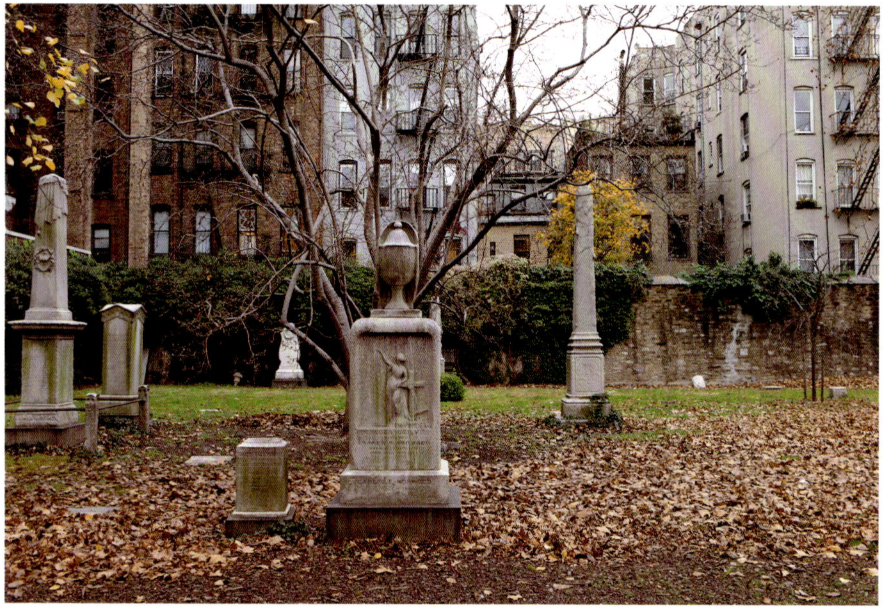

2

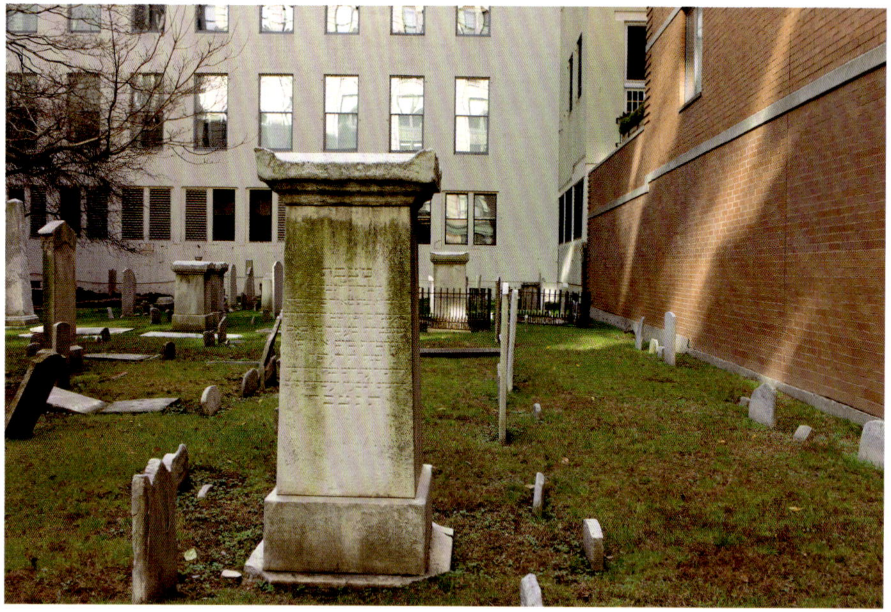

3

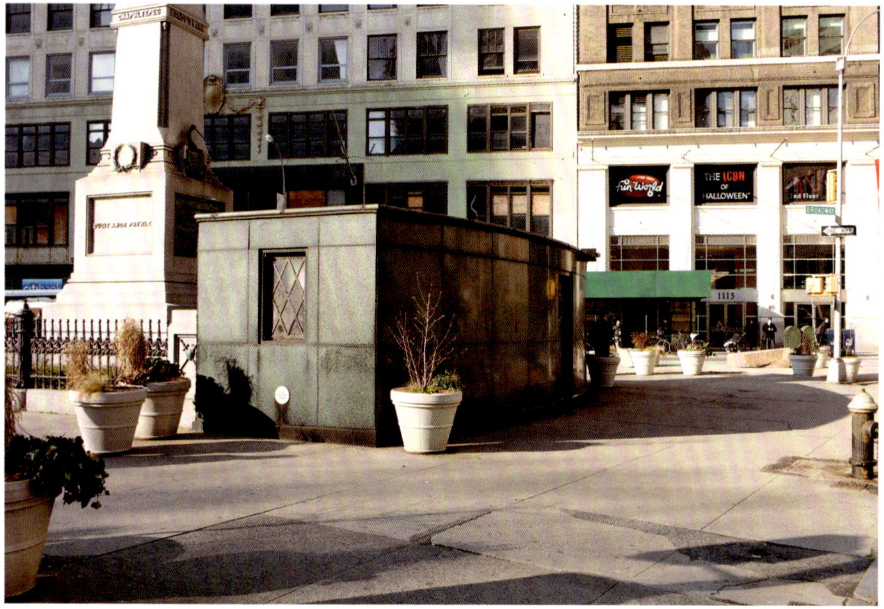

4

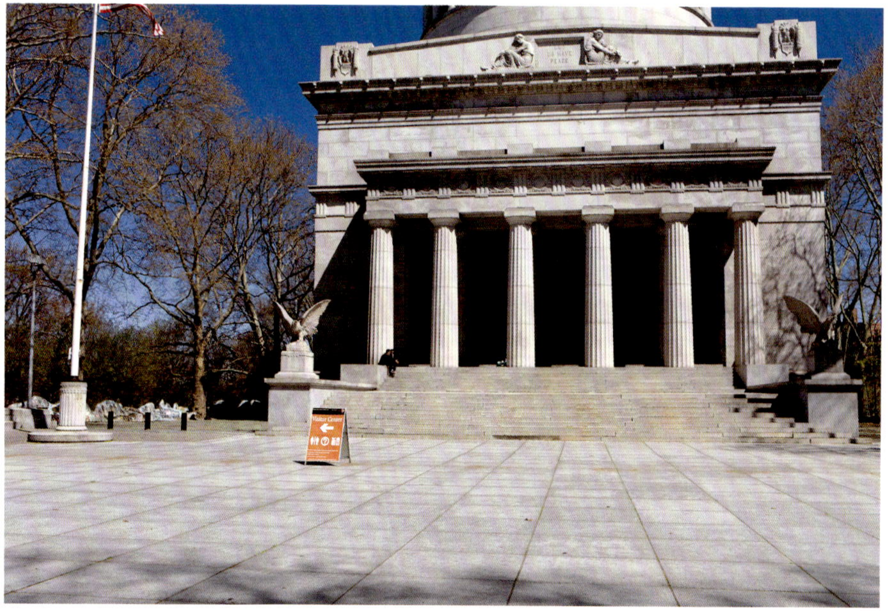

5

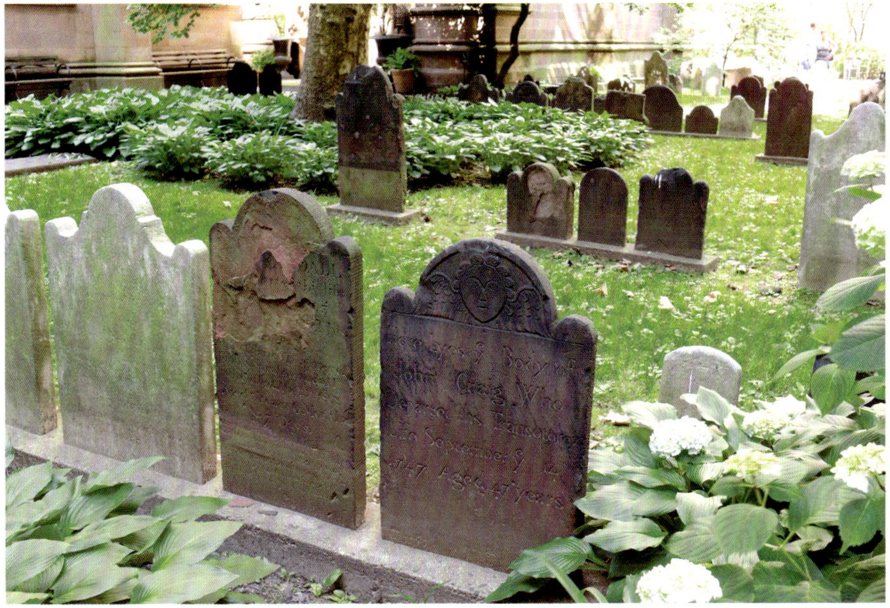

6

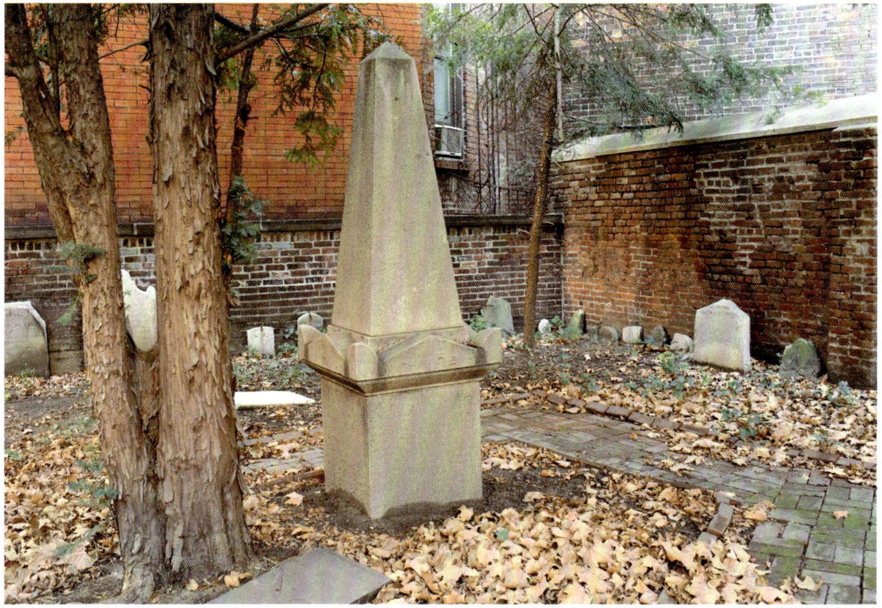

7

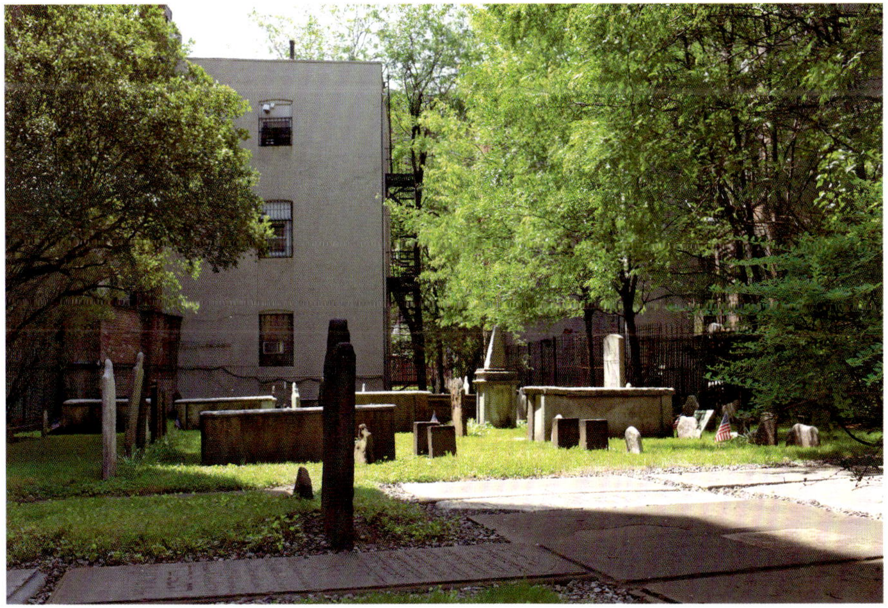

8

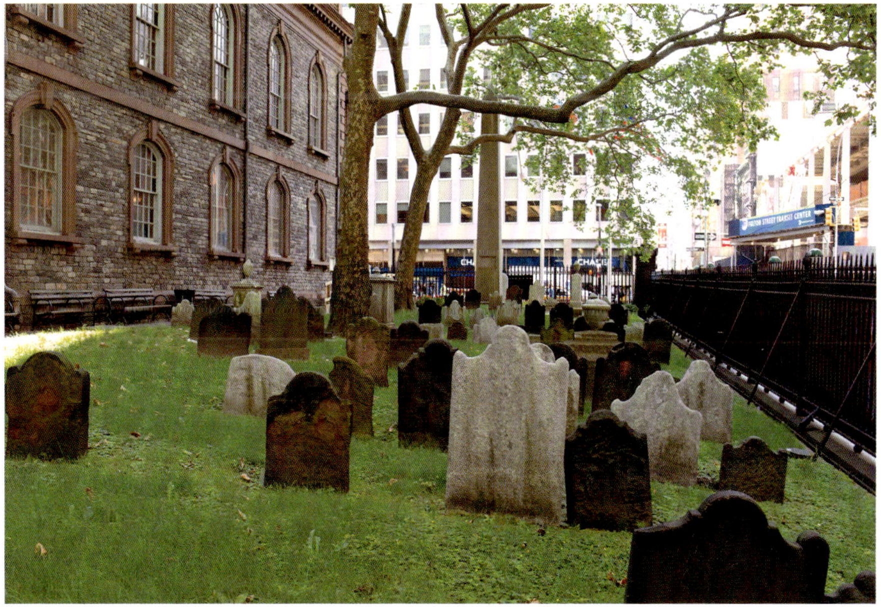

9

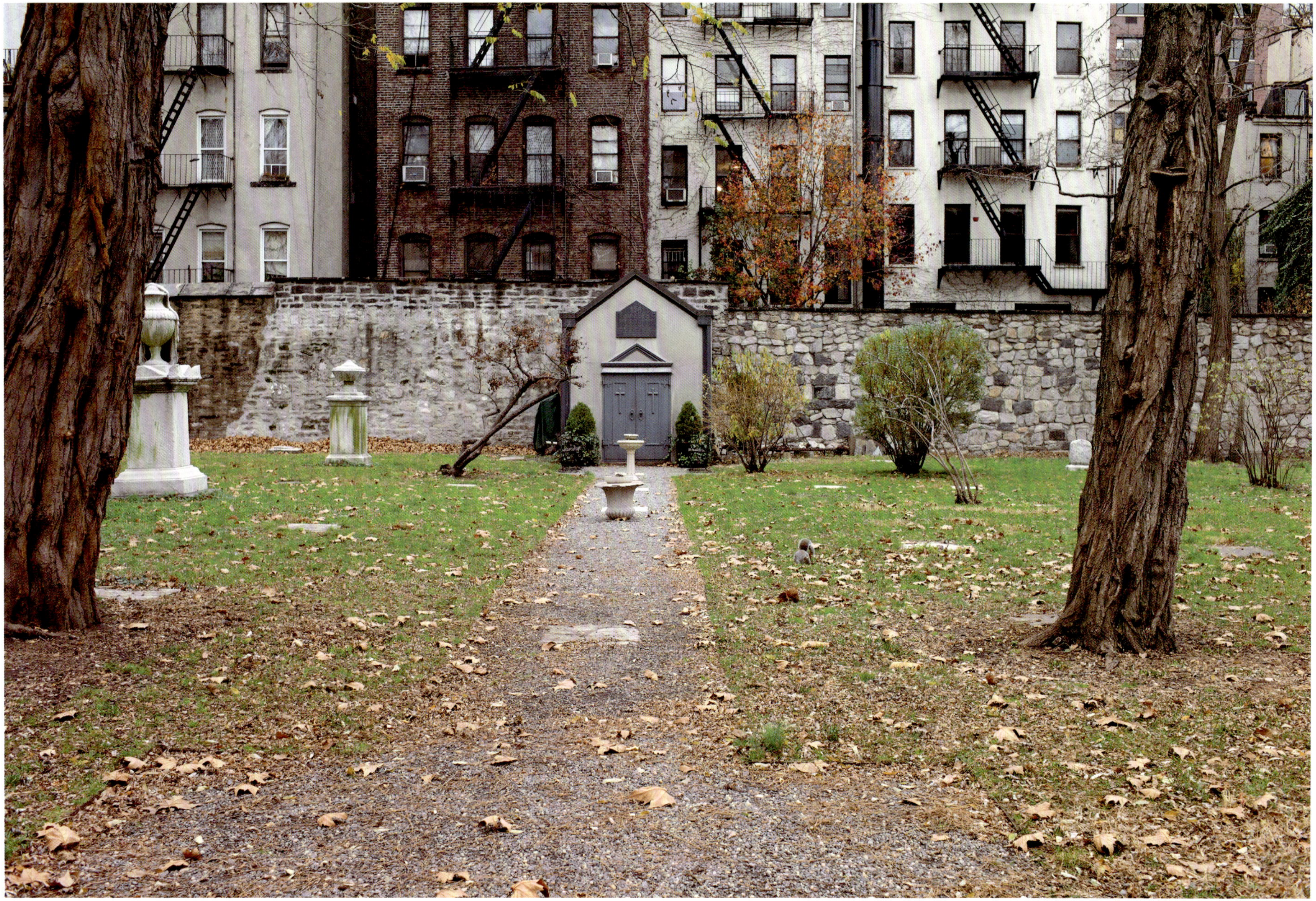

10

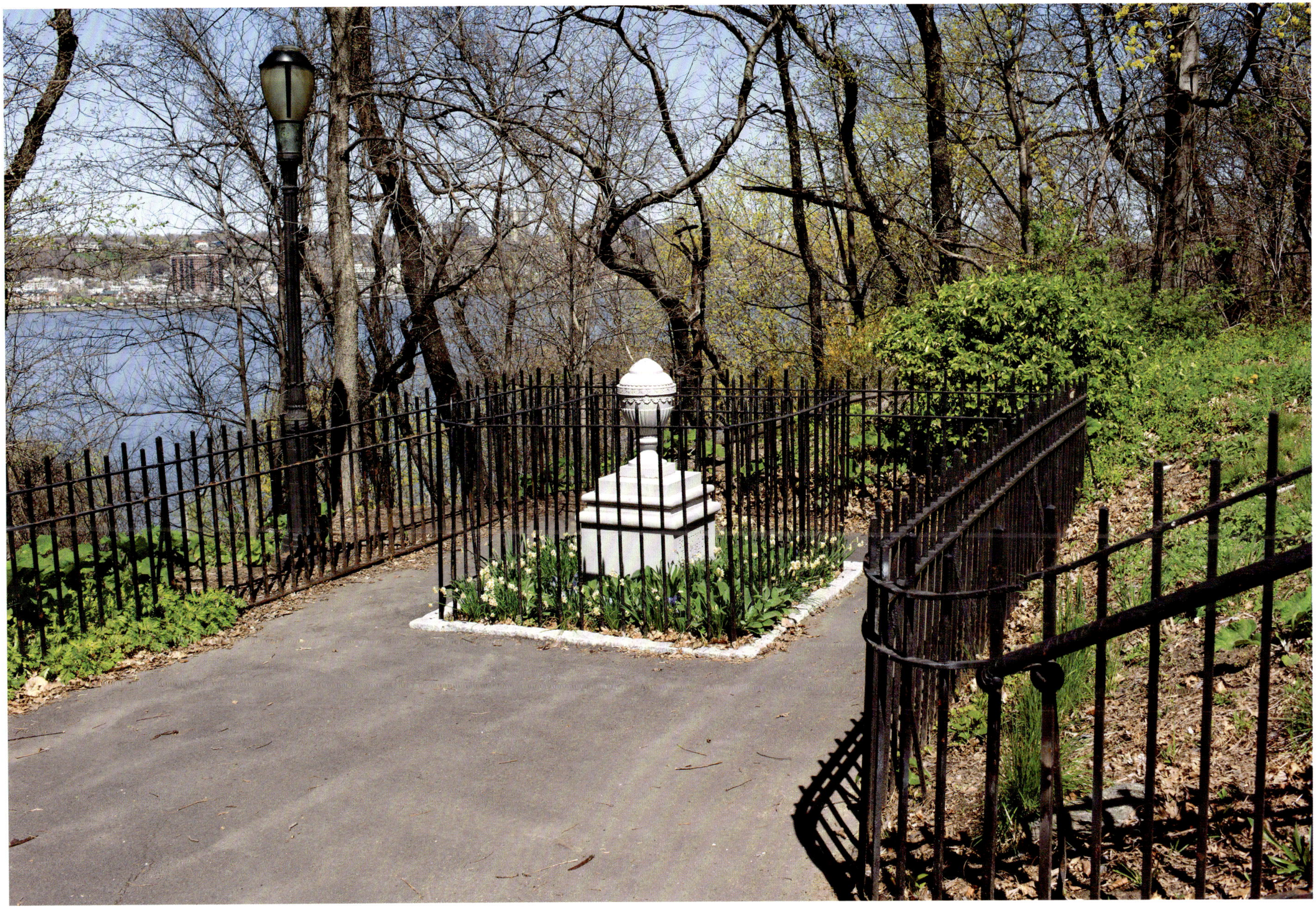

11

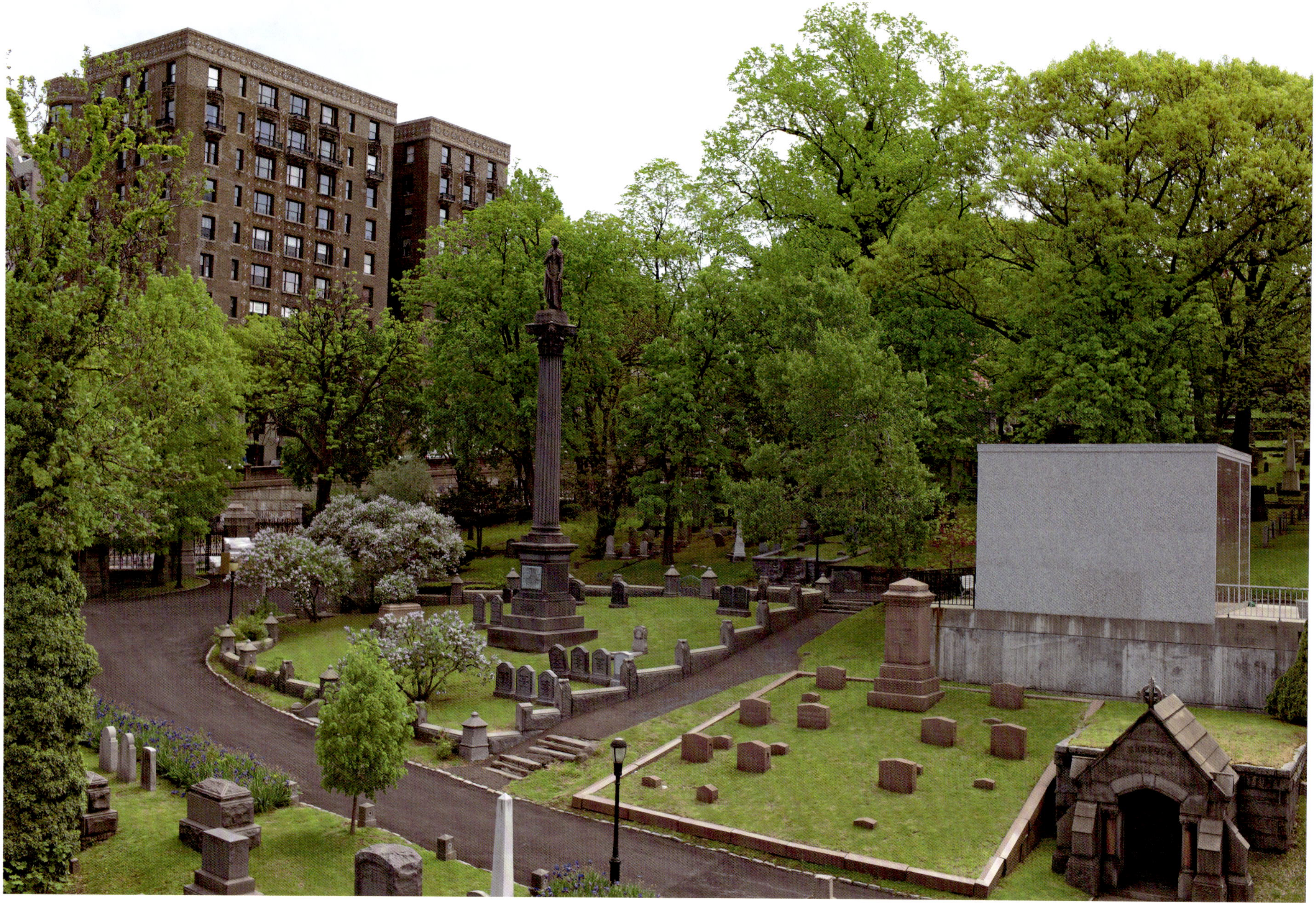

12

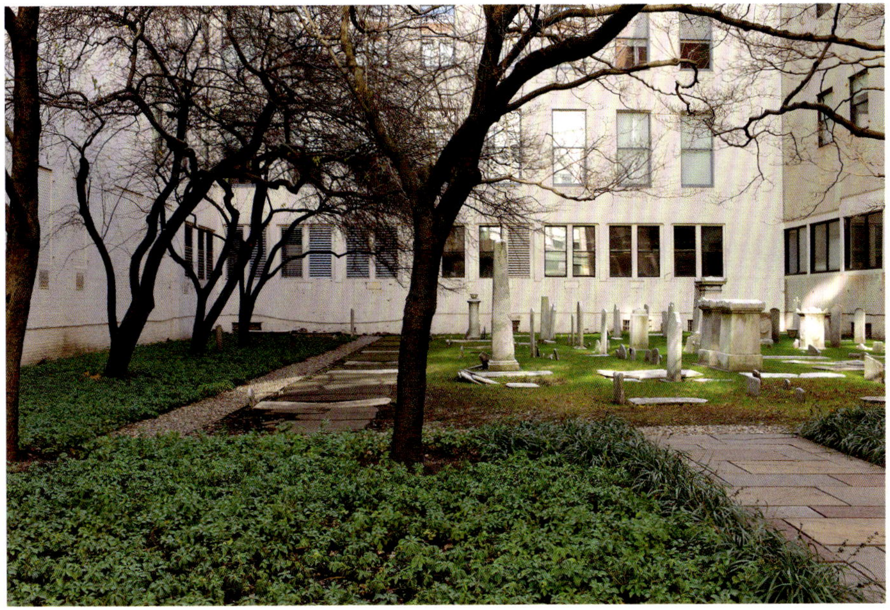

13

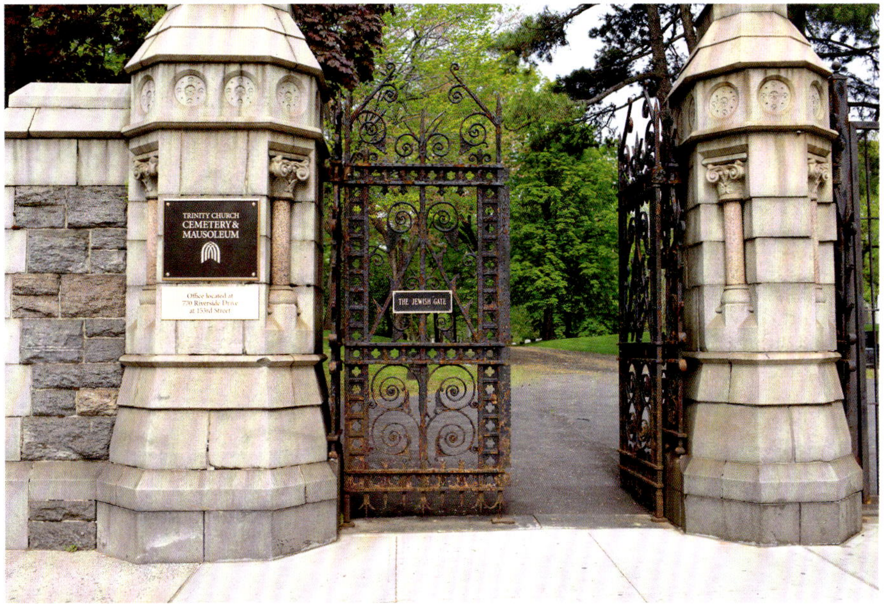
TRINITY CHURCH
CEMETERY &
MAUSOLEUM
Office located at
770 Riverside Drive
at 153rd Street
THE JEWISH GATE

14

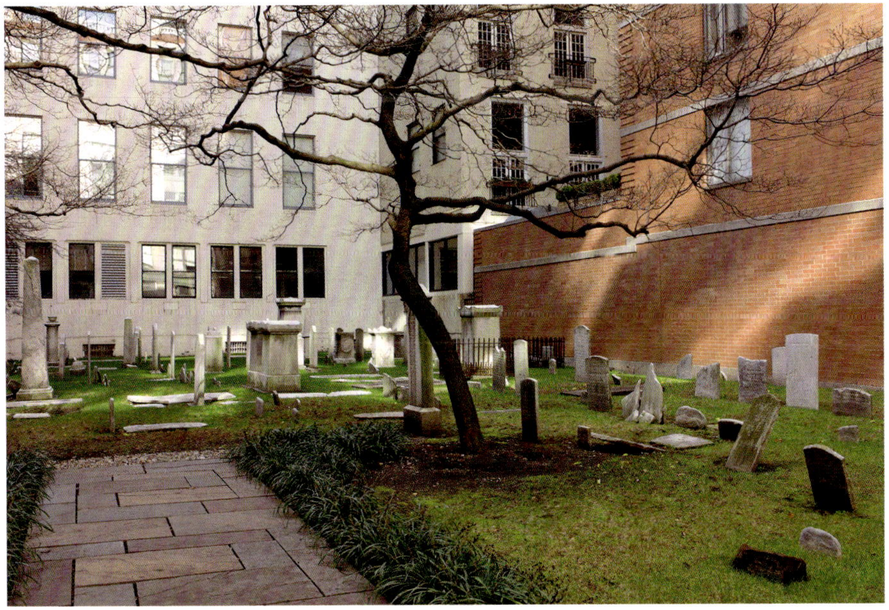

15

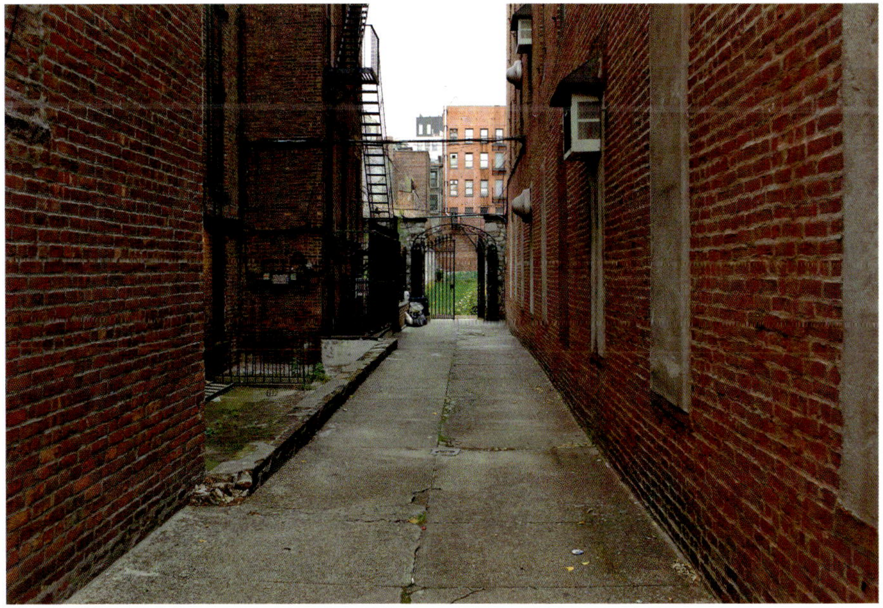

16

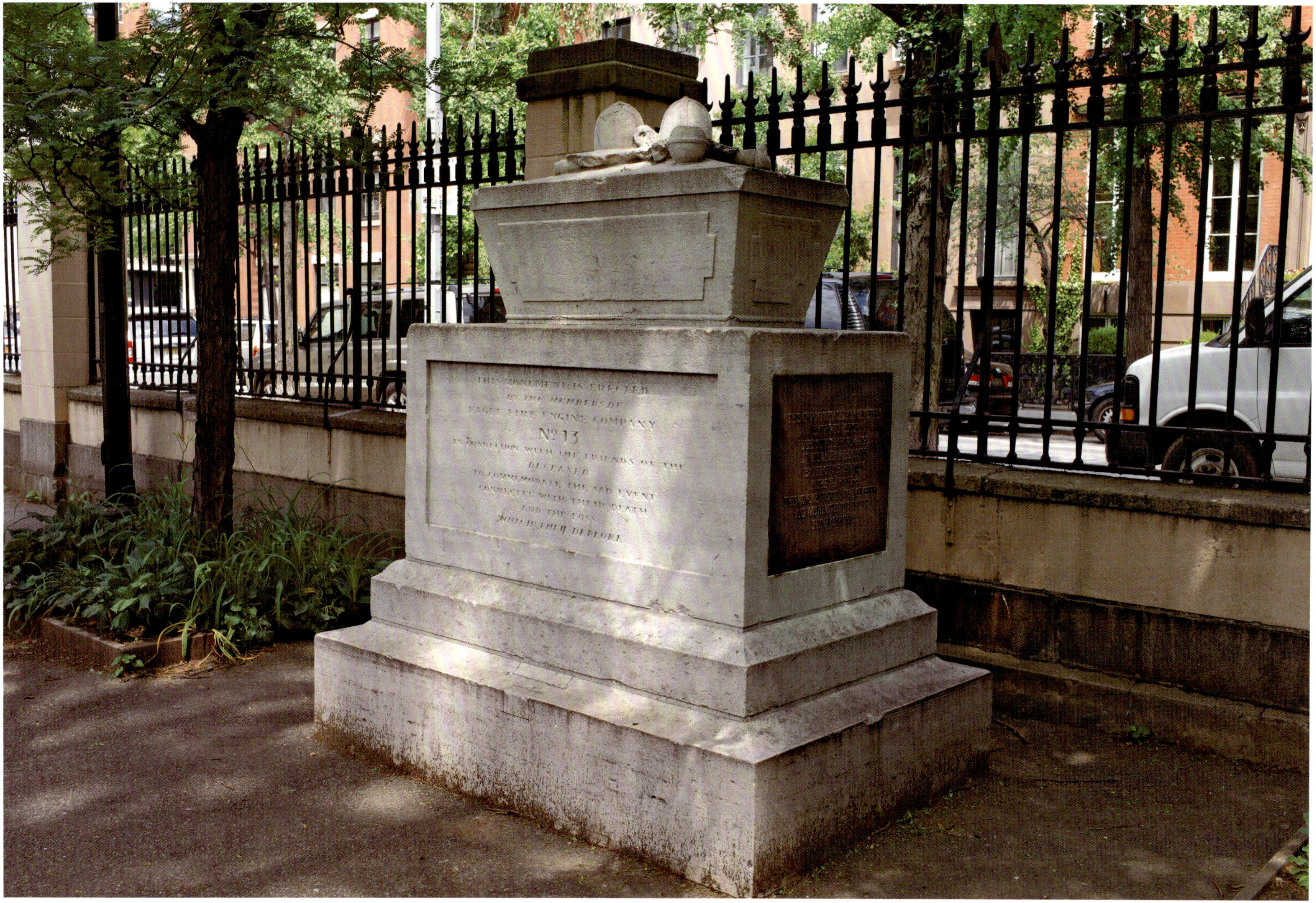

17

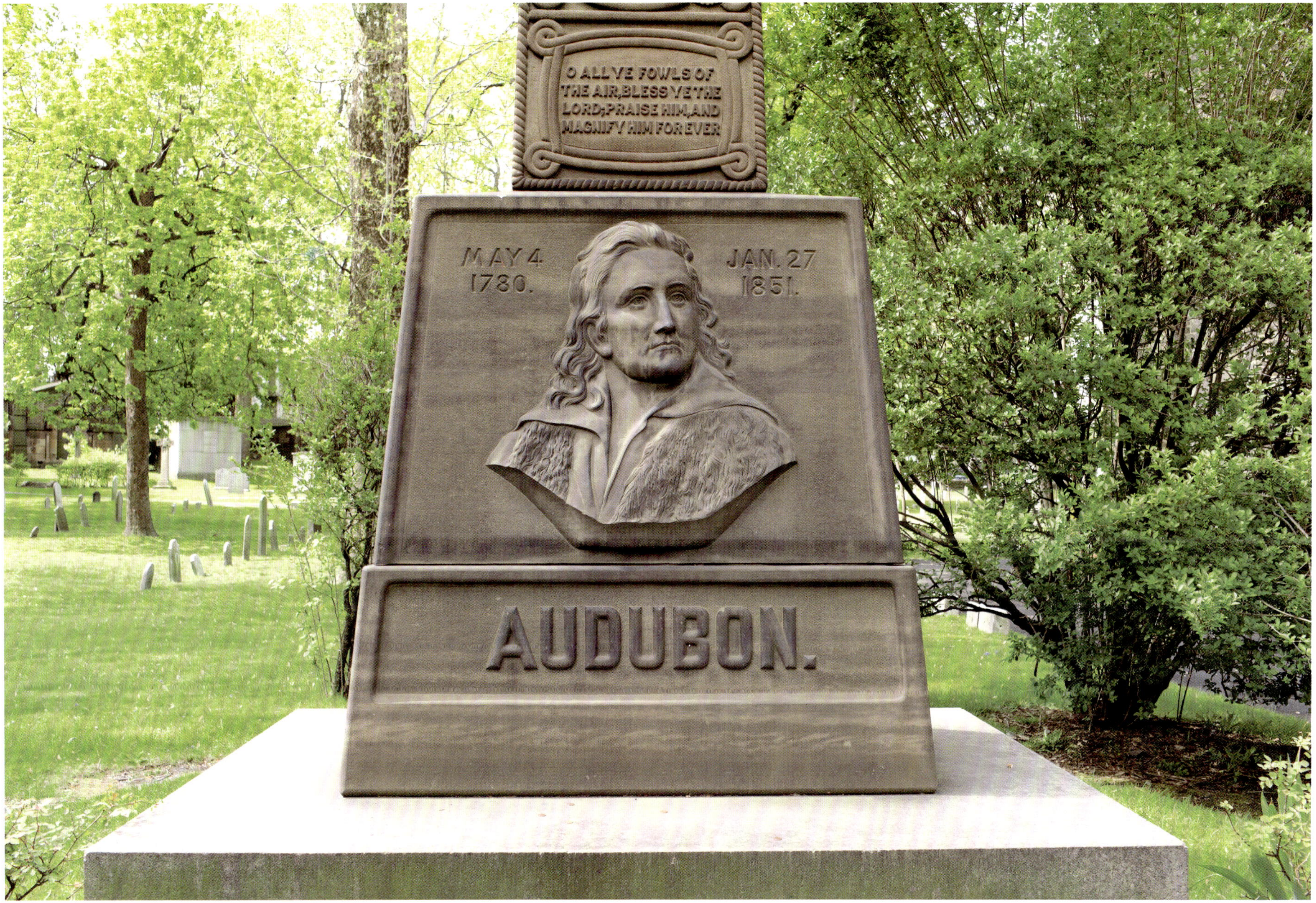
O ALL YE FOWLS OF
THE AIR, BLESS YE THE
LORD; PRAISE HIM, AND
MAGNIFY HIM FOR EVER
MAY 4
1780.
JAN. 27
1851.
AUDUBON.

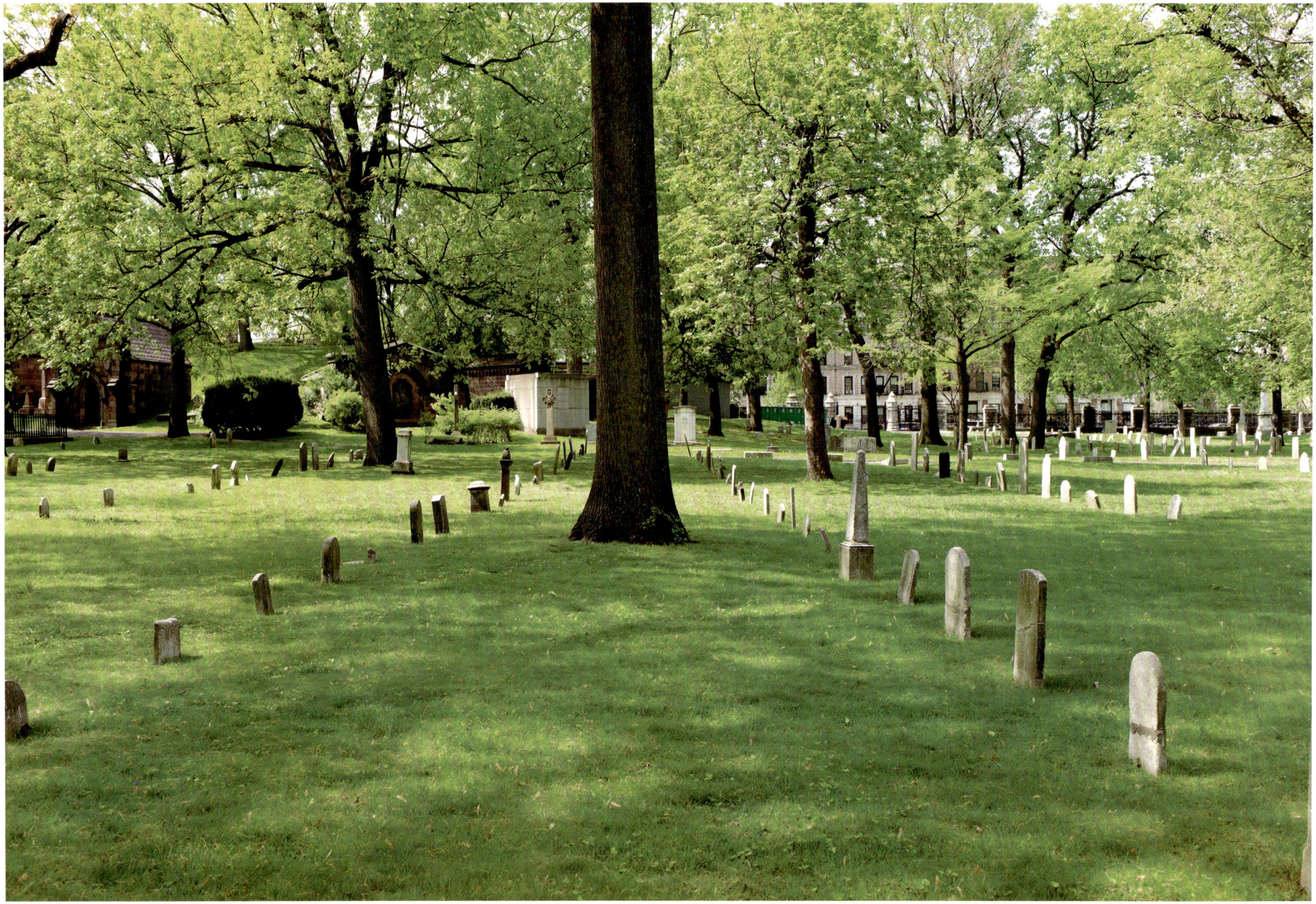

82

19

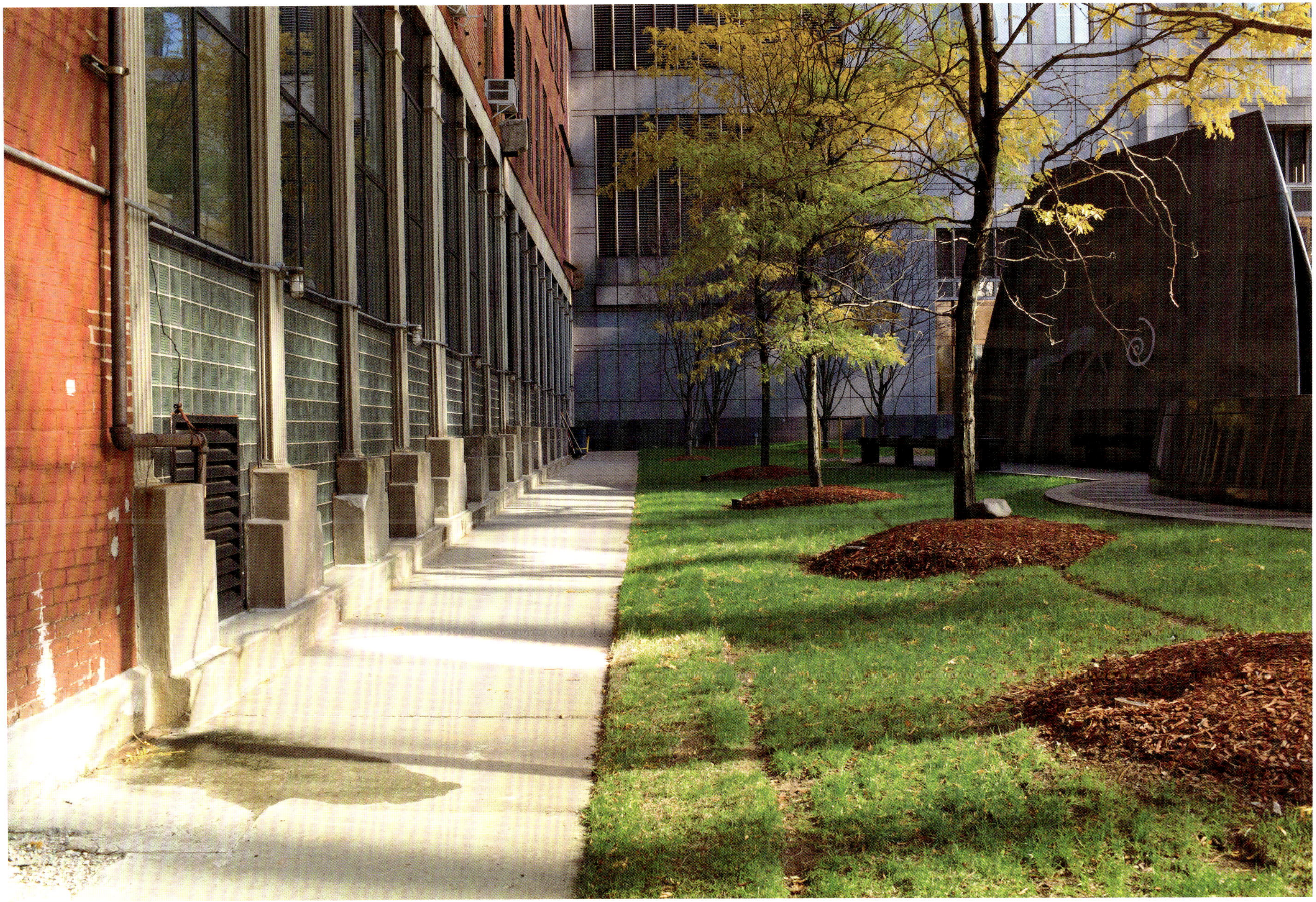

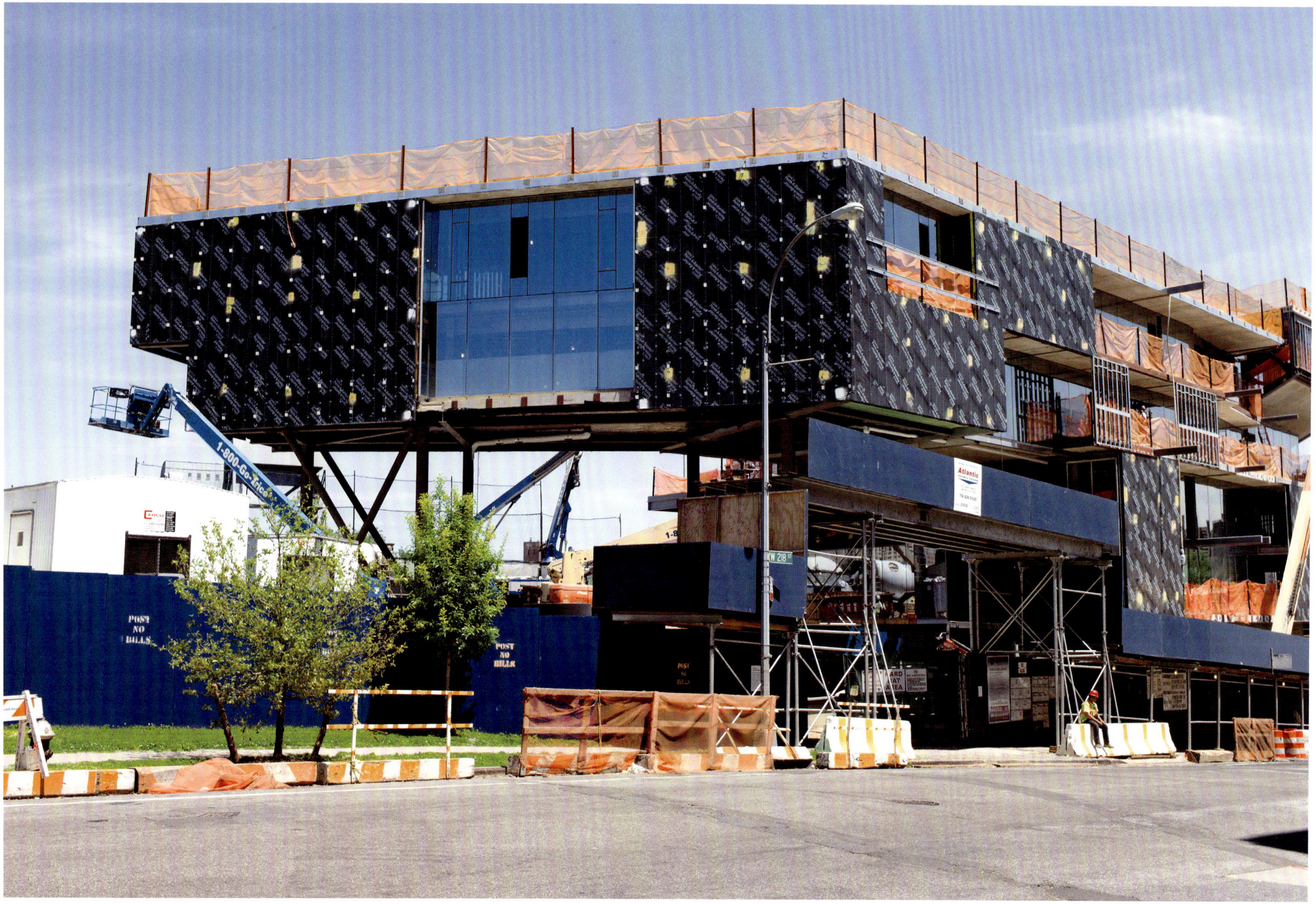

1

CONSTRUCTION

Manhattan has been under constant construction for the past 400 years. Marshes were filled in and the island's square mileage also increased with fill at the shorelines. Now that those practices have largely ended, buildings can go up only where others come down (or where engineering creates new buildable space, like over the West Side Yard).

Many small projects happen right in front of you; there's just not enough space to contain them. For larger buildings, the sites are often so closed off it's difficult to figure out what's going on until the building comes out of the ground and clears the fencing. But nothing remains secret that long; gates open for vehicles and workers, there are holes to peer through, or we figure out another way to look over the top.

Some of the more interesting projects are deep underground, but even these need large aboveground staging areas and construction zones; long stretches of Second Avenue were overtaken by ventilation and staging equipment for the new subway line during the time I walked this part of Manhattan. Other infrastructure improvements were also underway at the time: connections to the new water tunnel, the 7 subway line extension, an additional gas pipeline, and installation of electrical conduits from across the Hudson.

1 **Inwood**
2 **World Trade Center**
3 **Chelsea**
4 **Chelsea**
5 **Chelsea**
6 **West Village**
7 **World Trade Center**
8 **Hell's Kitchen**
9 **West Village**
10 **Hudson Yards**
11 **World Trade Center**
12 **Tribeca**
13 **Tribeca**
14 **East Harlem**
15 **Upper West Side**
16 **Upper East Side**
17 **Upper East Side**
18 **Chelsea**

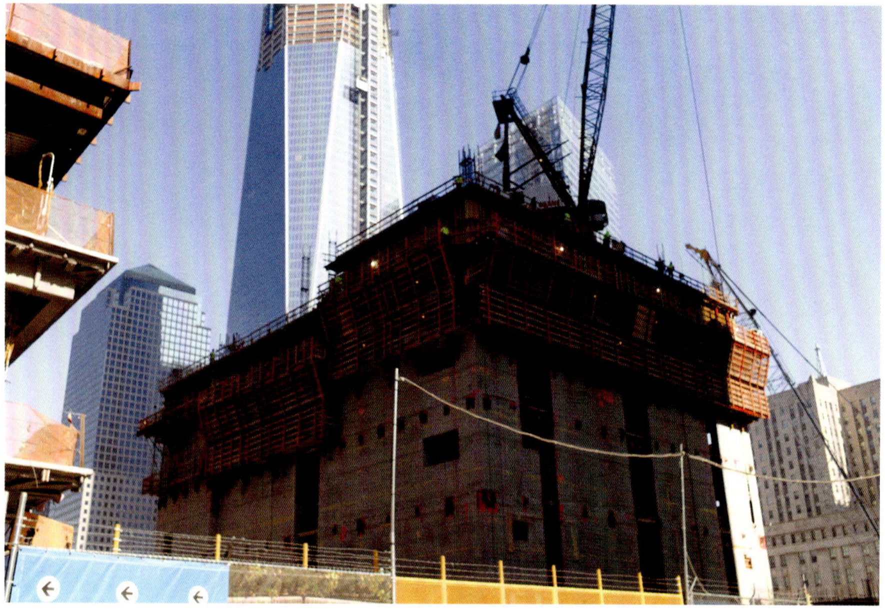

2

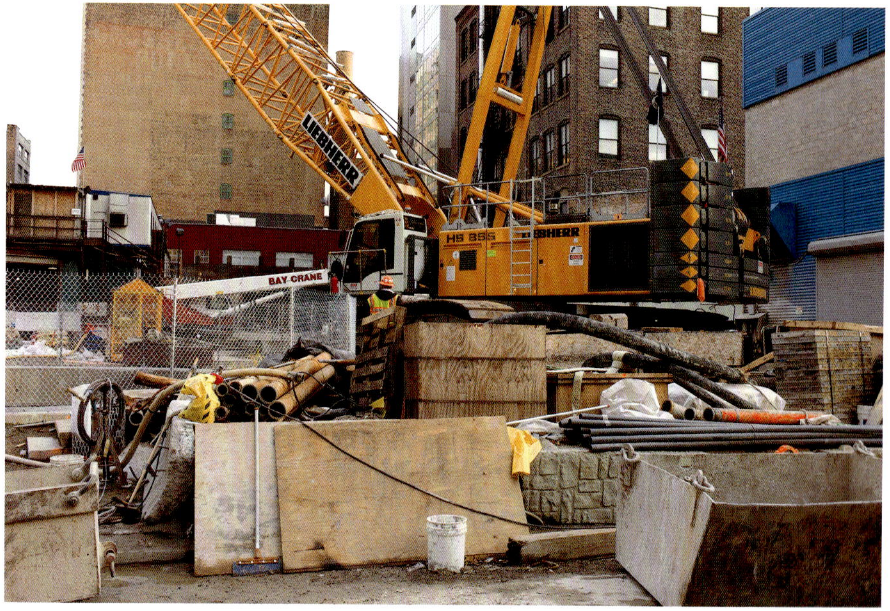

3

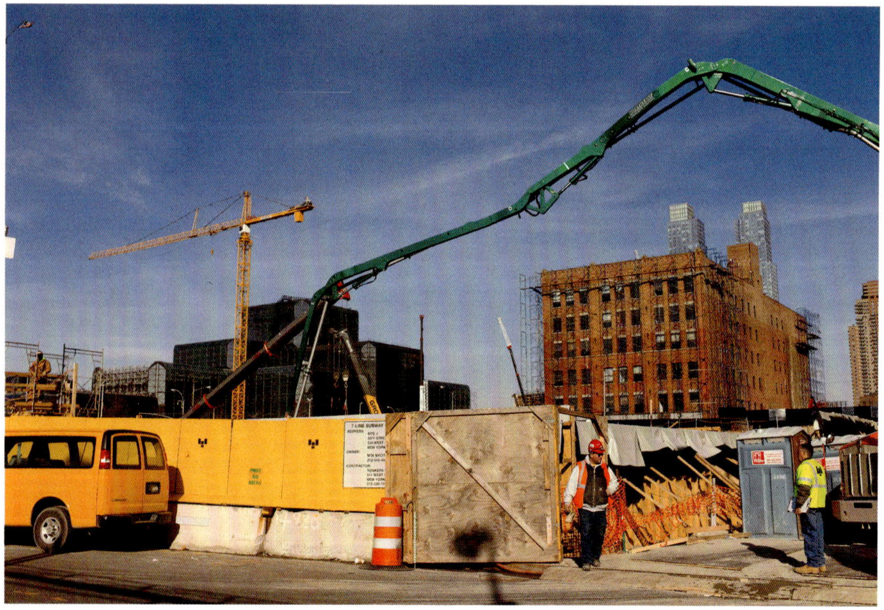

4

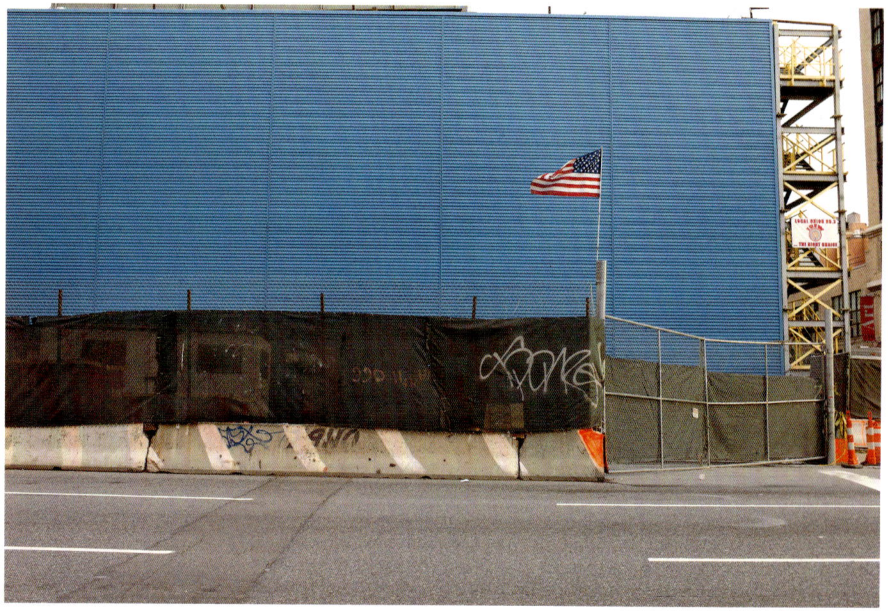

5

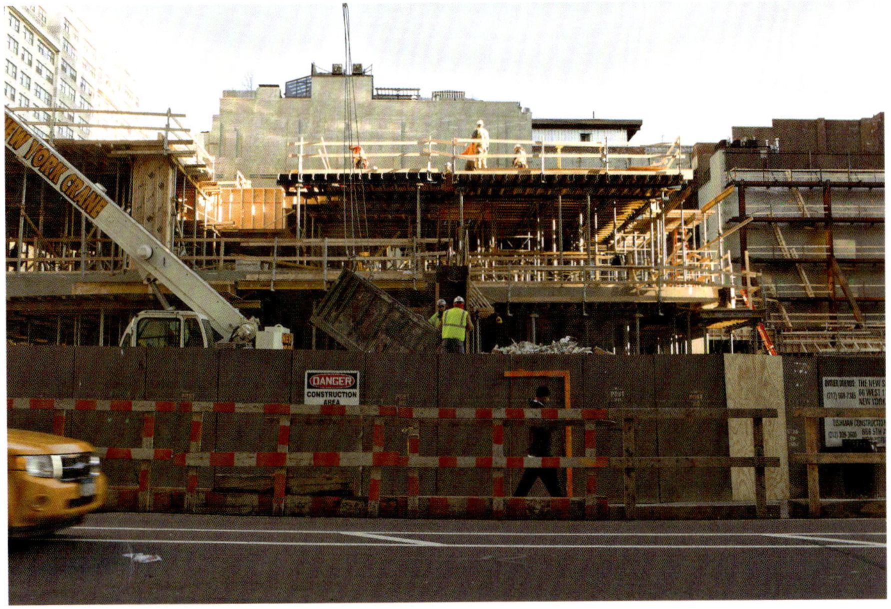
NEW YORK CRANE
DANGER
CONSTRUCTION AREA

6

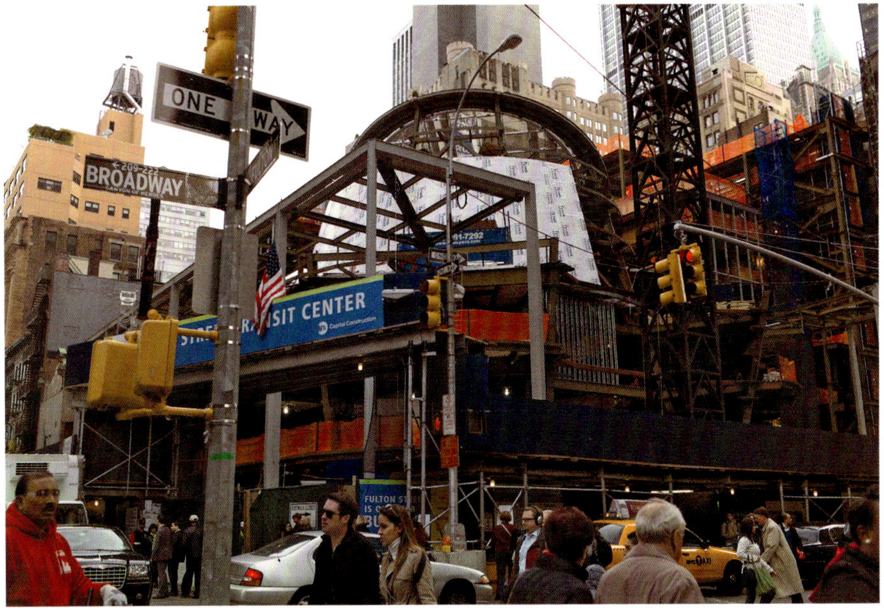
ONE WAY
BROADWAY

7

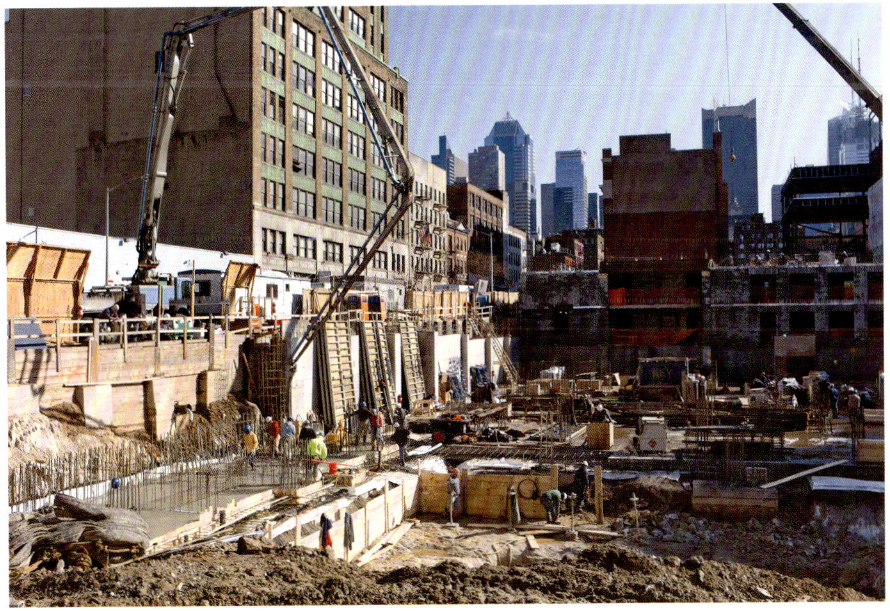

8

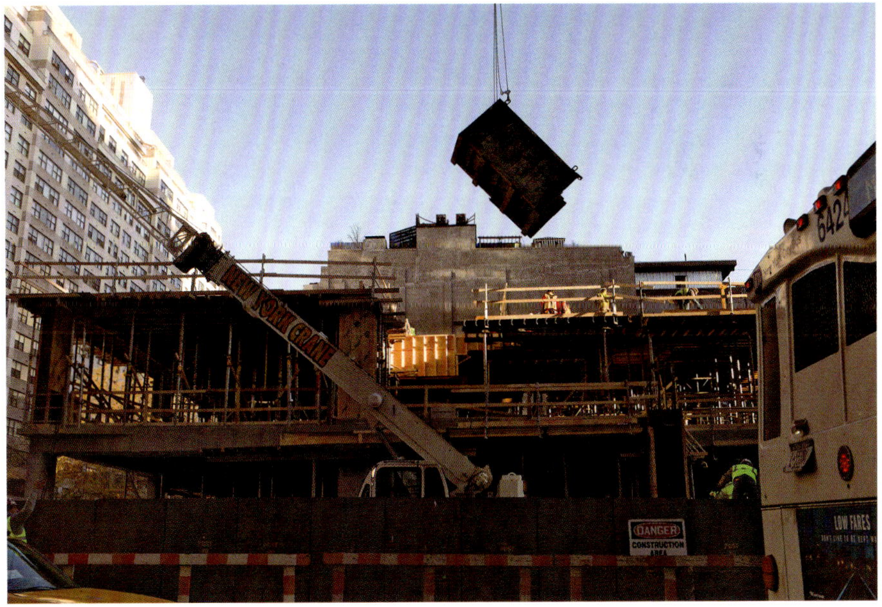
NEW YORK CRANE
DANGER
CONSTRUCTION AREA
LOW FARES

9

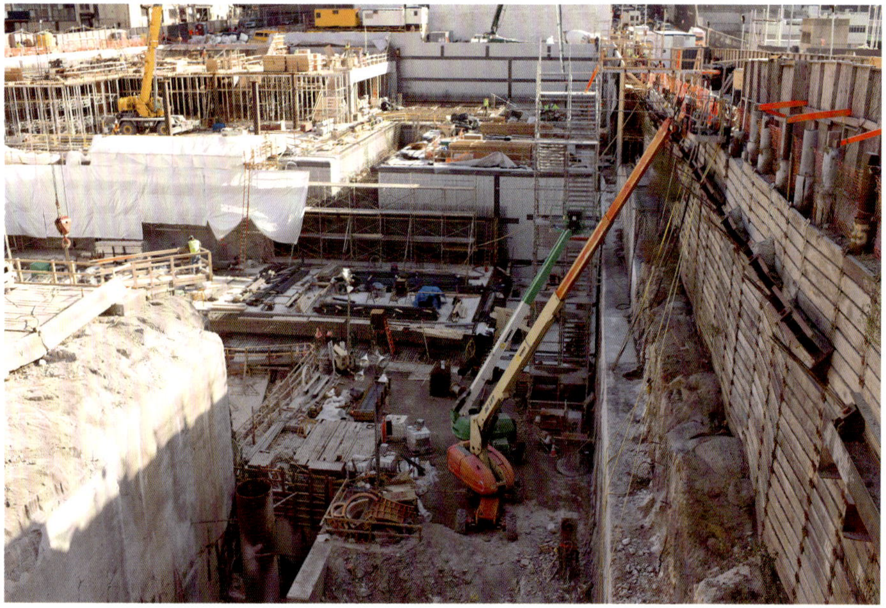

10

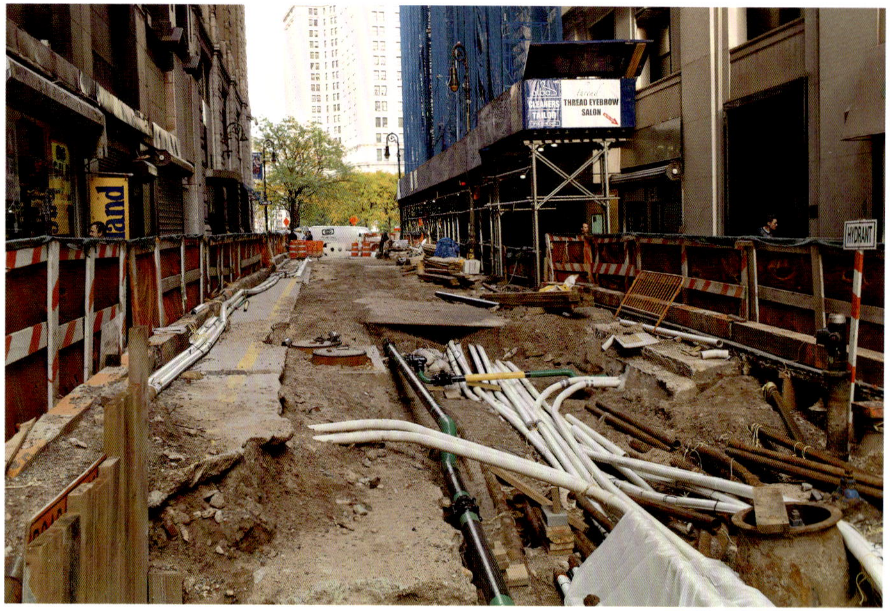

11

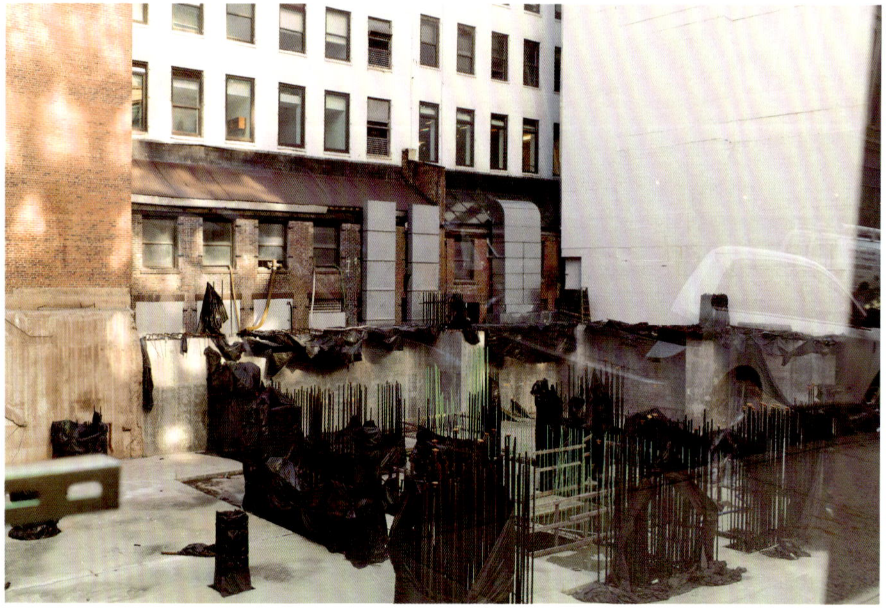

12

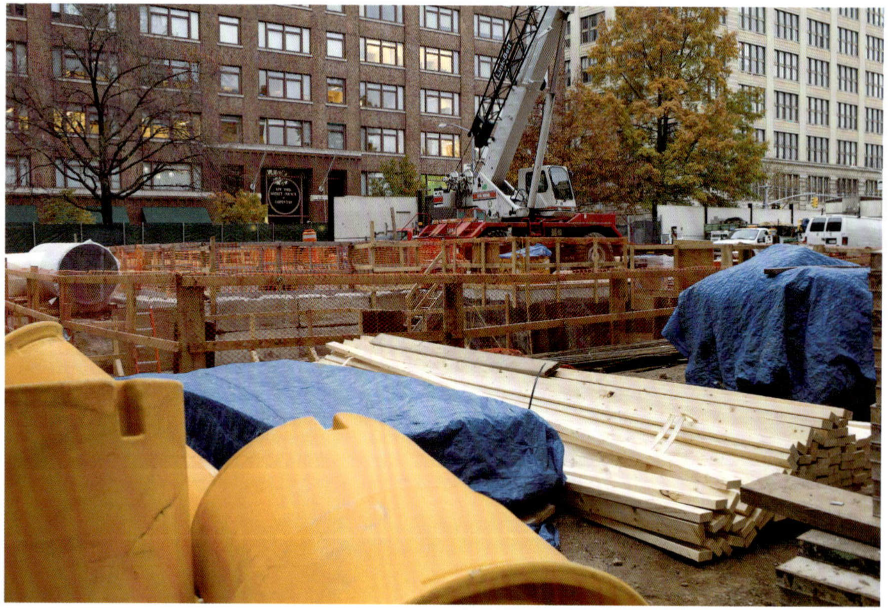

13

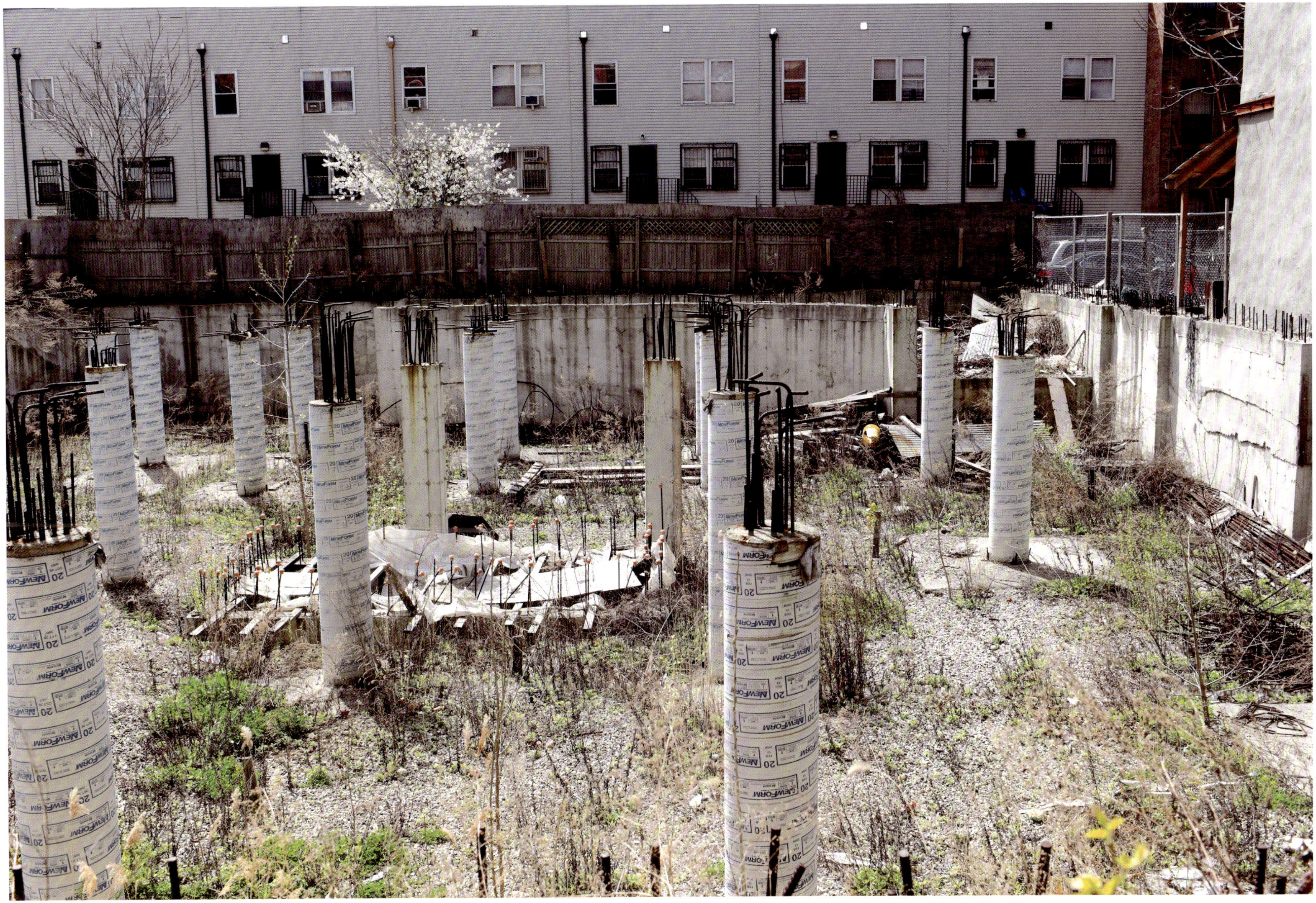
NEWFORM

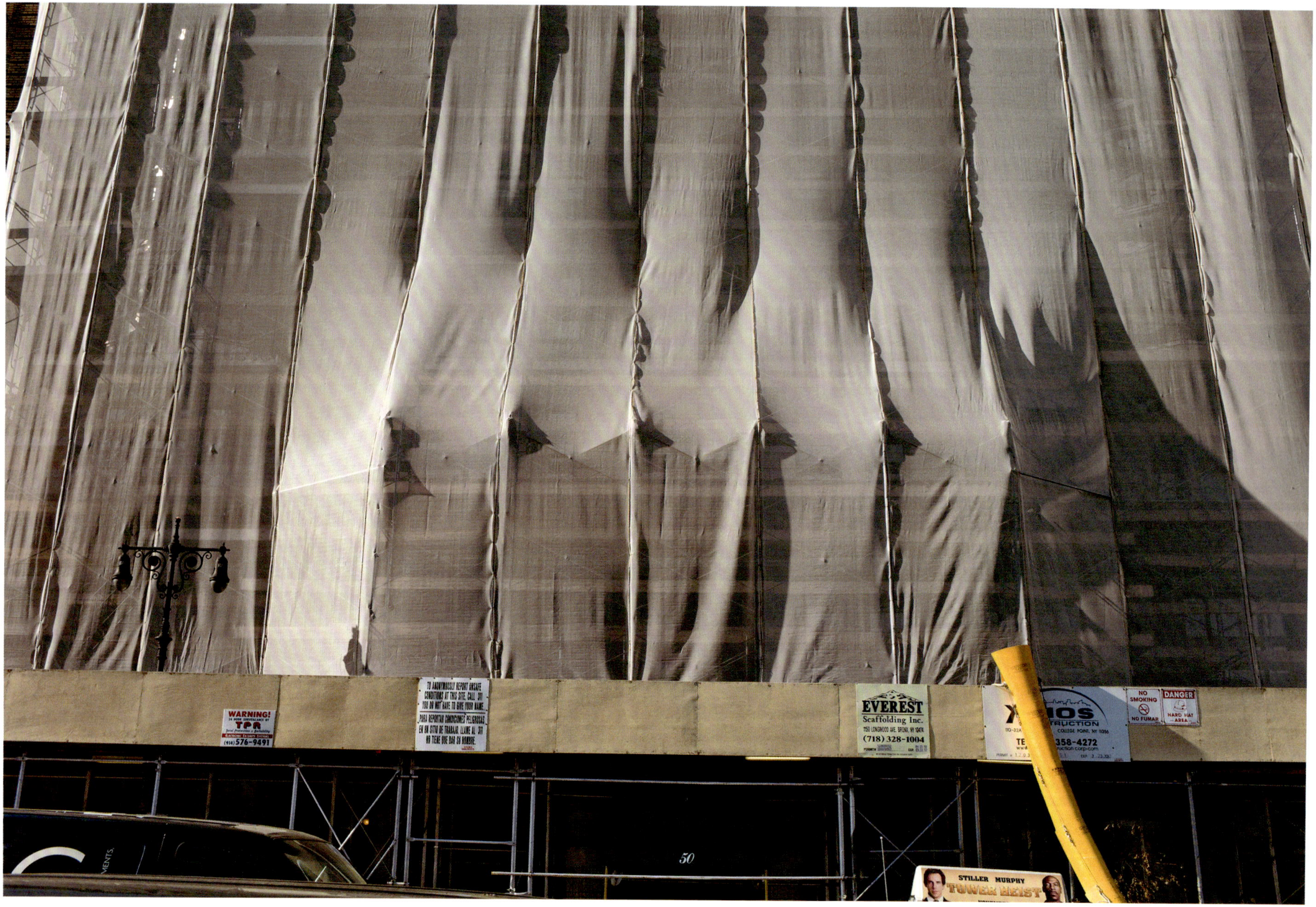
WARNING!
TPR
(914) 576-9491
TO ANONYMOUSLY REPORT UNSAFE
CONDITIONS AT THIS SITE, CALL 311
YOU DO NOT HAVE TO GIVE YOUR NAME.
PARA REPORTAR CONDICIONES PELIGROSAS
EN UN SITIO DE TRABAJO, LLAME AL 311
NO TIENE QUE DAR SU NOMBRE.
EVEREST
Scaffolding Inc.
(718) 328-1004
358-4272
NO SMOKING
NO FUMAR
DANGER
HARD HAT AREA
50
STILLER MURPHY
TOWER HEIST

15

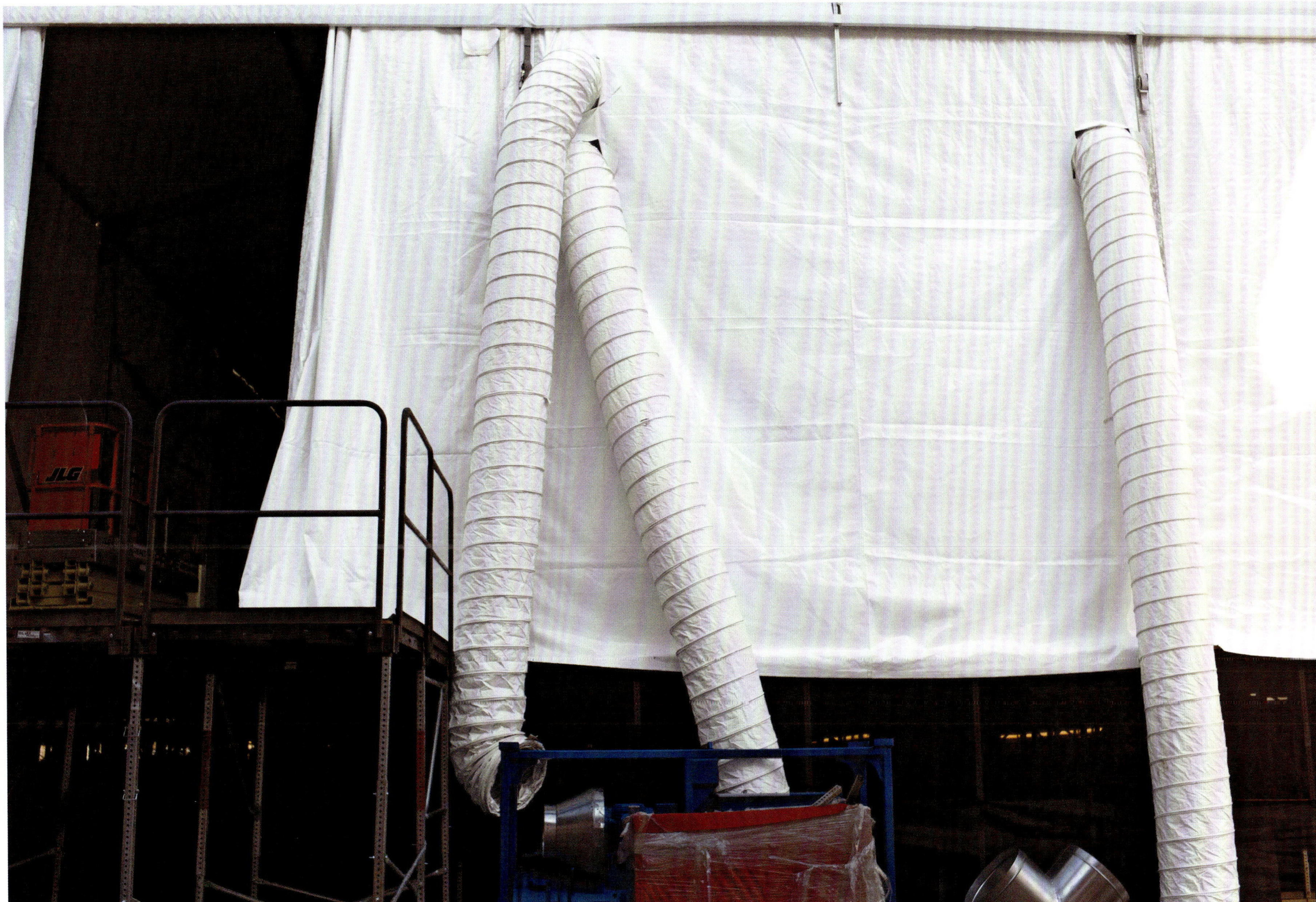

91

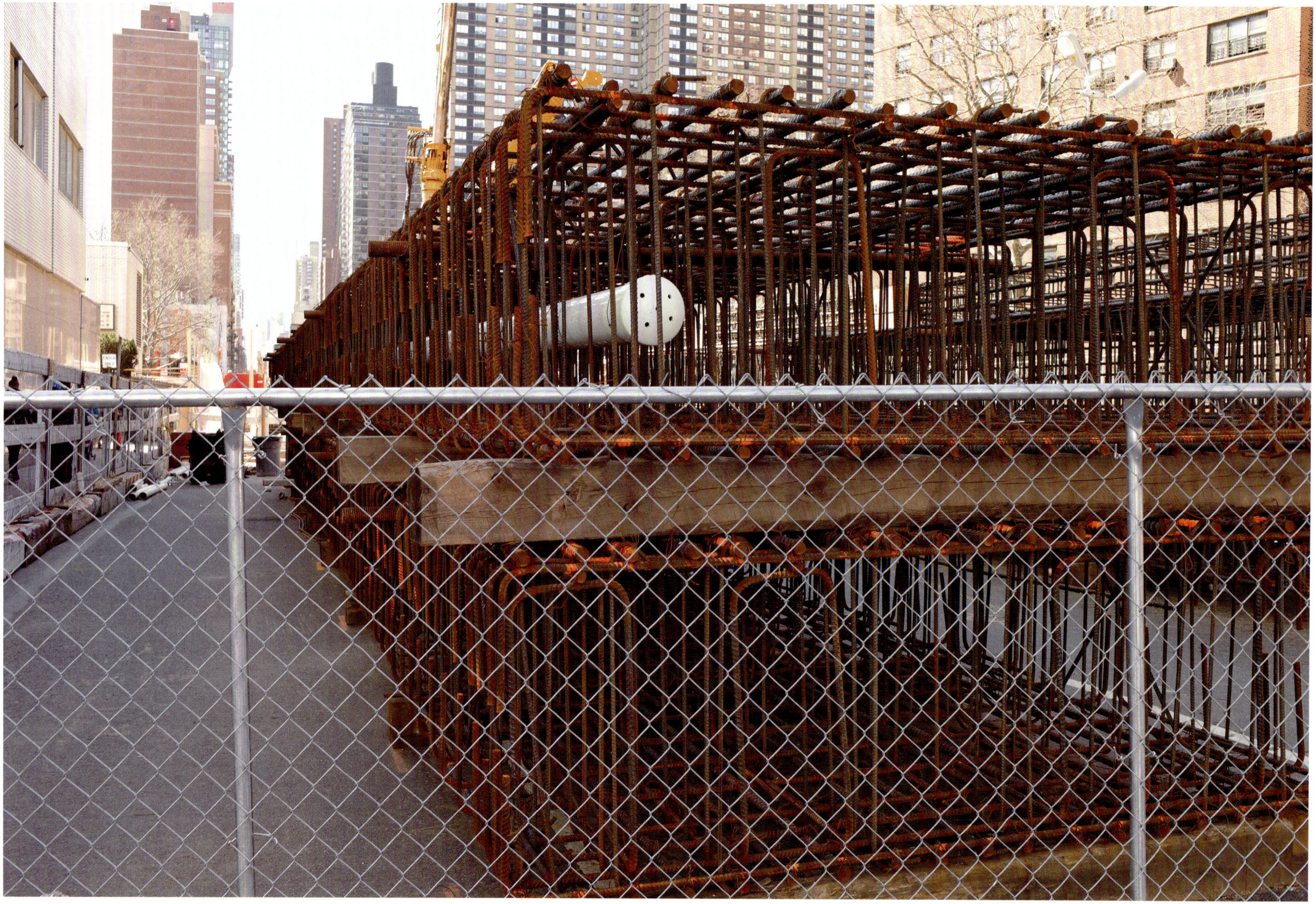

17

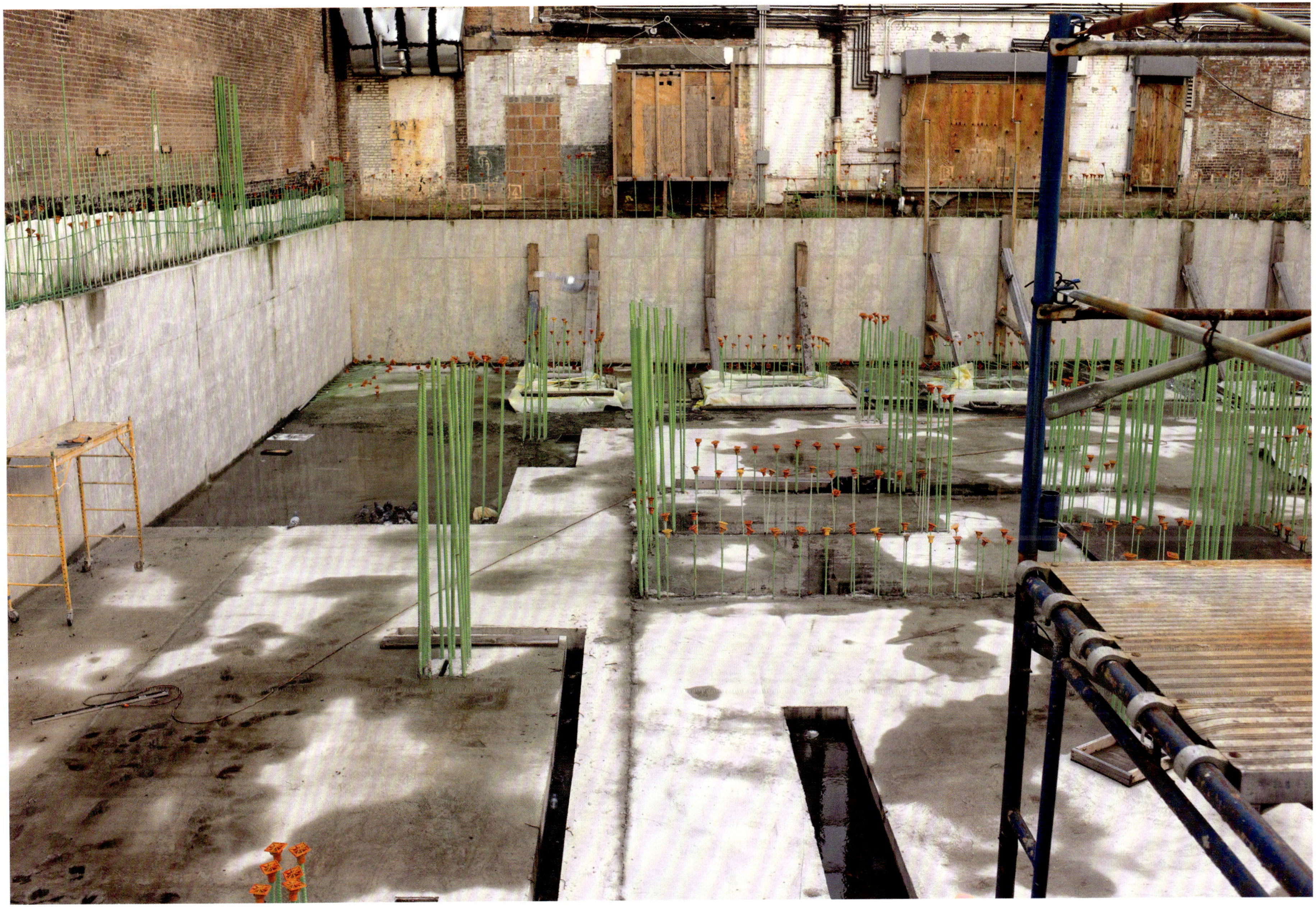

93

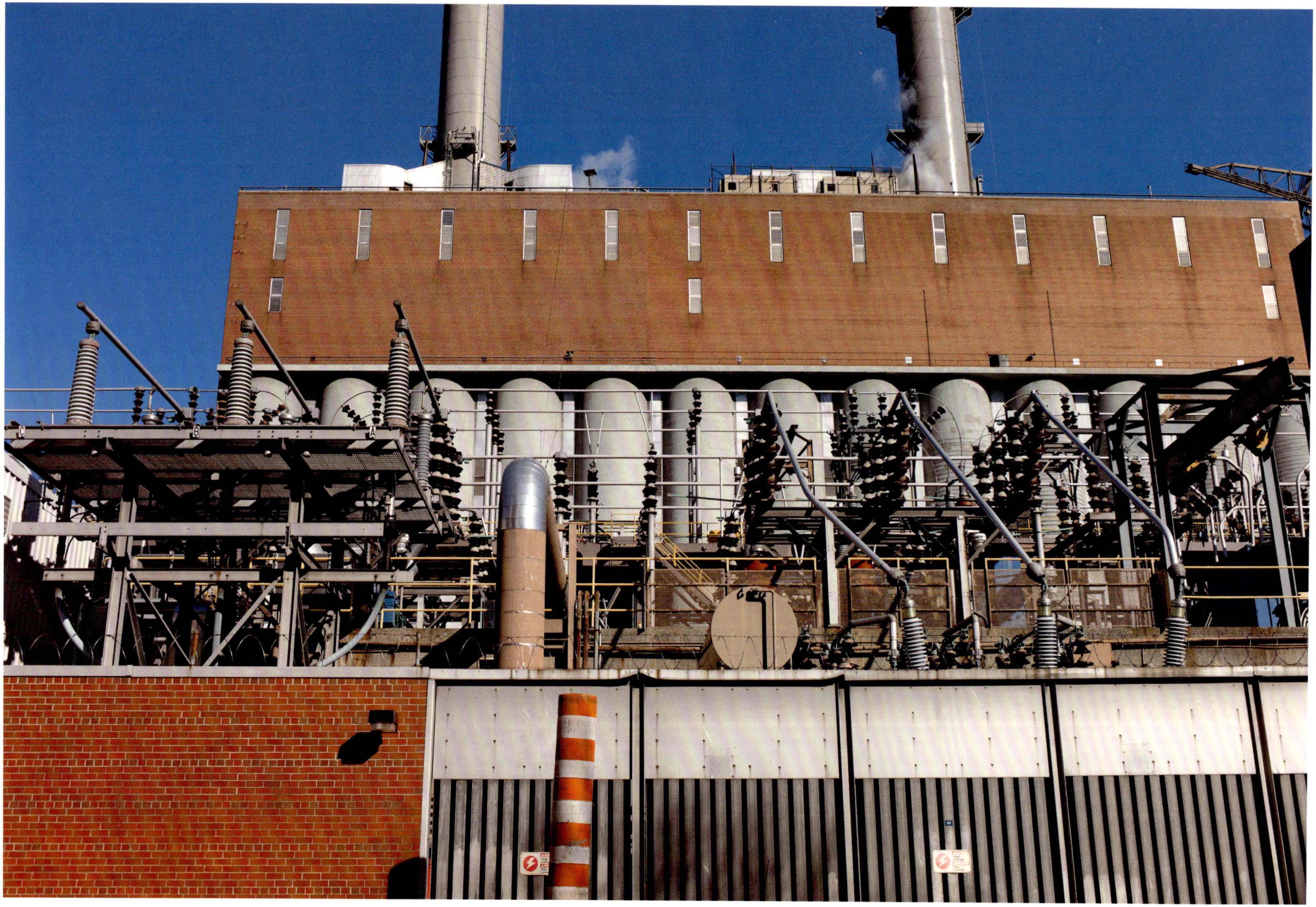

GAS/ELECTRIC

The city's power is administered by Consolidated Edison, which was formed by the merger of several gas-light companies in the late nineteenth century. Gradually steam and gas companies increasingly consolidated, and in 1936, after electricity demand and supply outpaced both, the name was changed to Consolidated Edison Company of New York. In 1998 the utilities were deregulated, and by 2001 most of the power stations had been sold to other operators. Substations, located all over the city, are still managed by Con Ed.

For some reason (security or a misguided attempt to match neighborhood context) many of the substations are sheathed to look like buildings from earlier time periods, before there was an electrical supply. Facades with false doors and windows hide these essential pieces of infrastructure from the public. The only large power station left in Manhattan is on 14th Street. The rest of the city's electricity comes from stations in the other boroughs or from hydro, nuclear, and other sources much further away, transmitted by cables underground and under the rivers.

1 Alphabet City
2 Upper East Side
3 Upper East Side
4 Hell's Kitchen
5 Upper West Side
6 Inwood
7 Hell's Kitchen
8 Manhattanville
9 Alphabet City
10 Lower East Side
11 Alphabet City
12 Inwood
13 Harlem
14 East Harlem

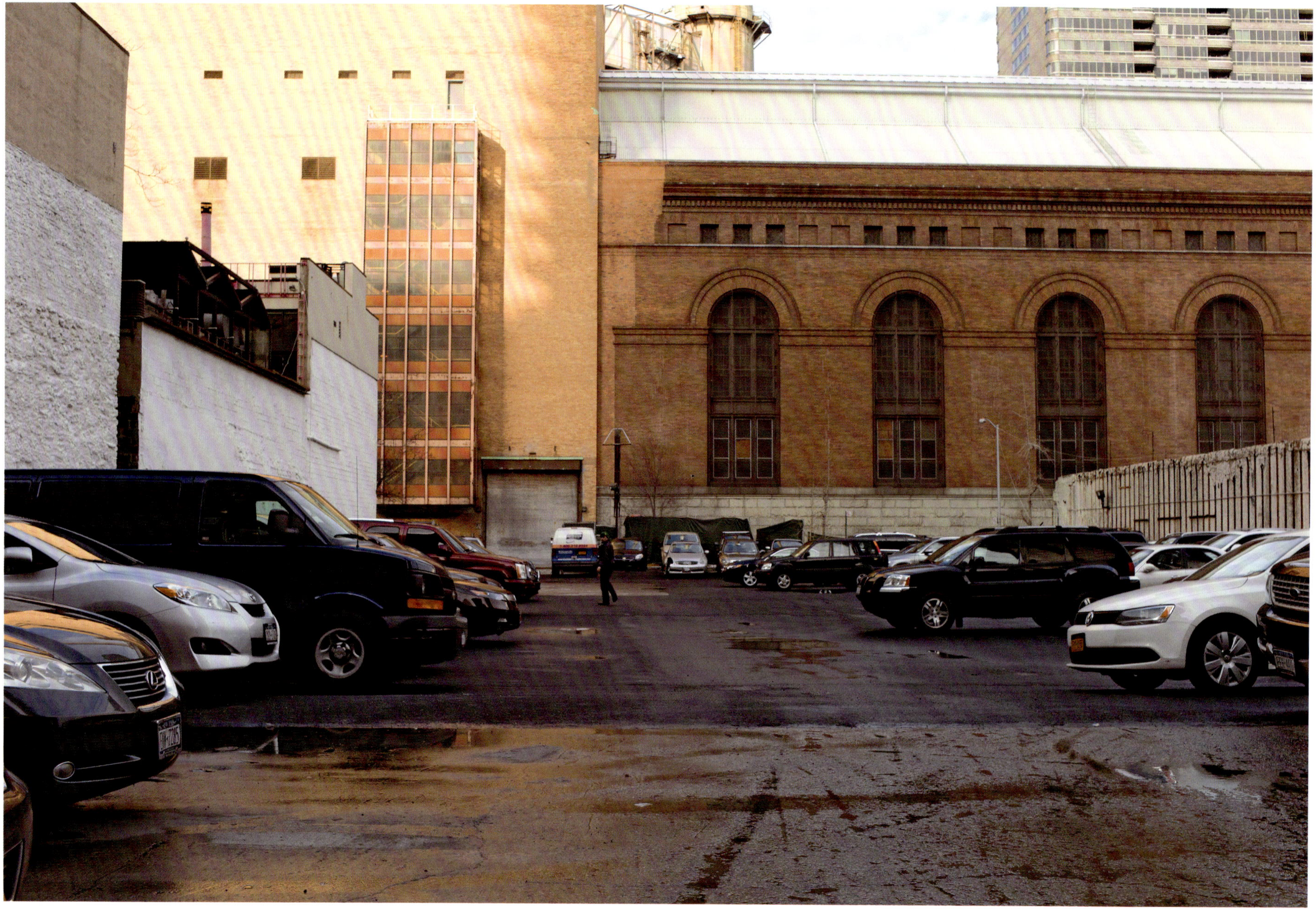

2

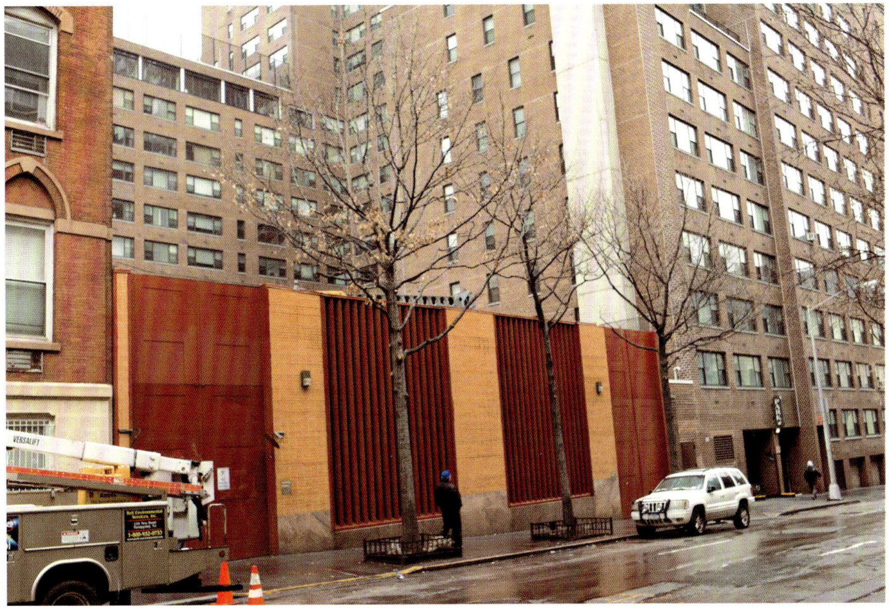

3

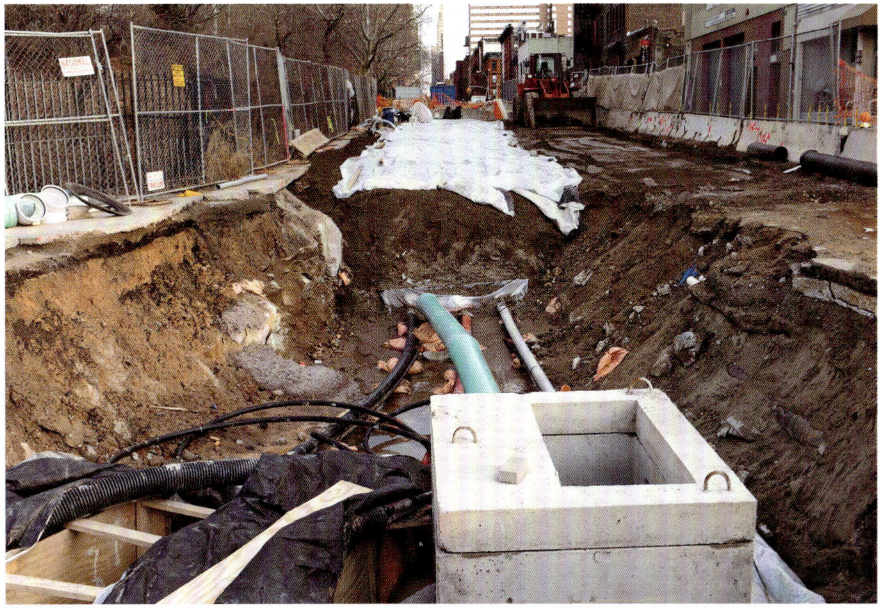

4

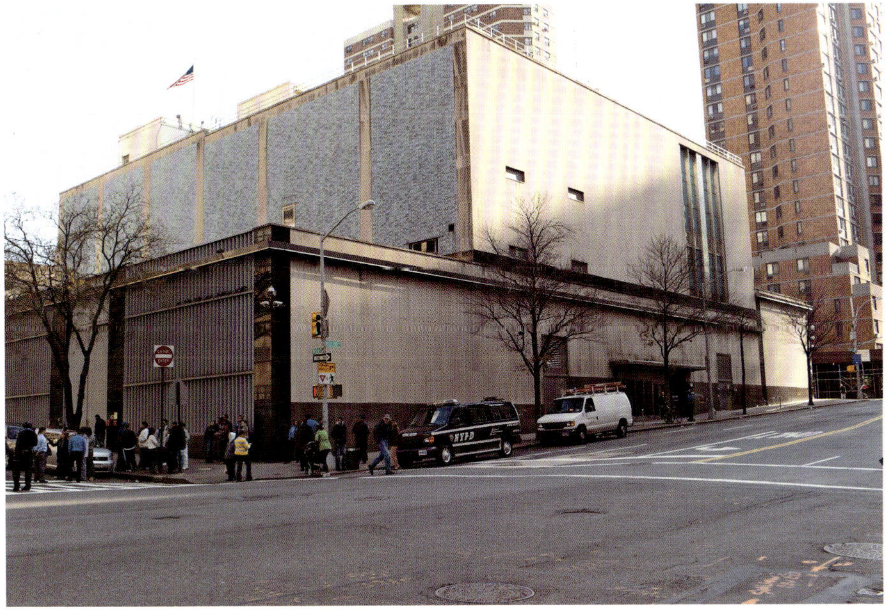

5

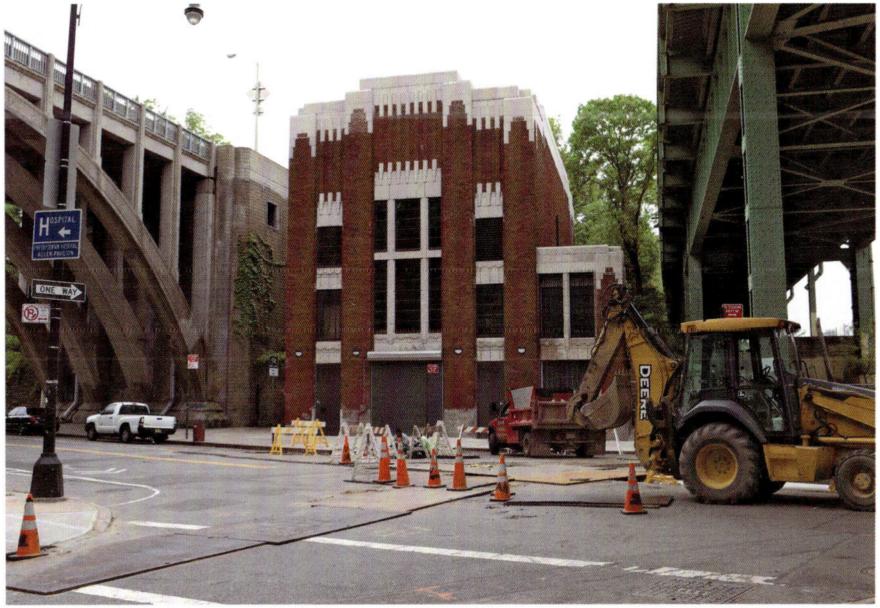

6

98

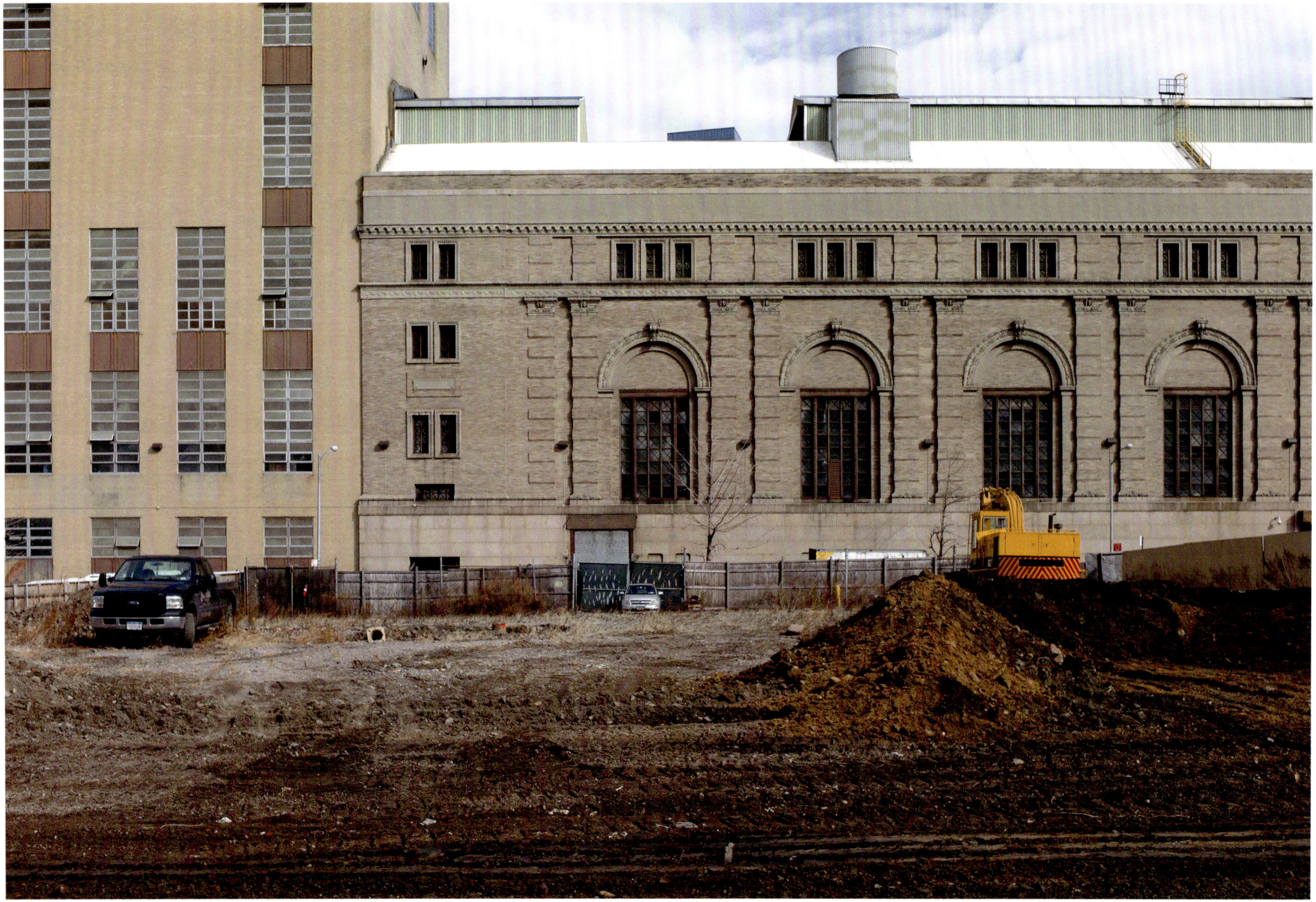

7

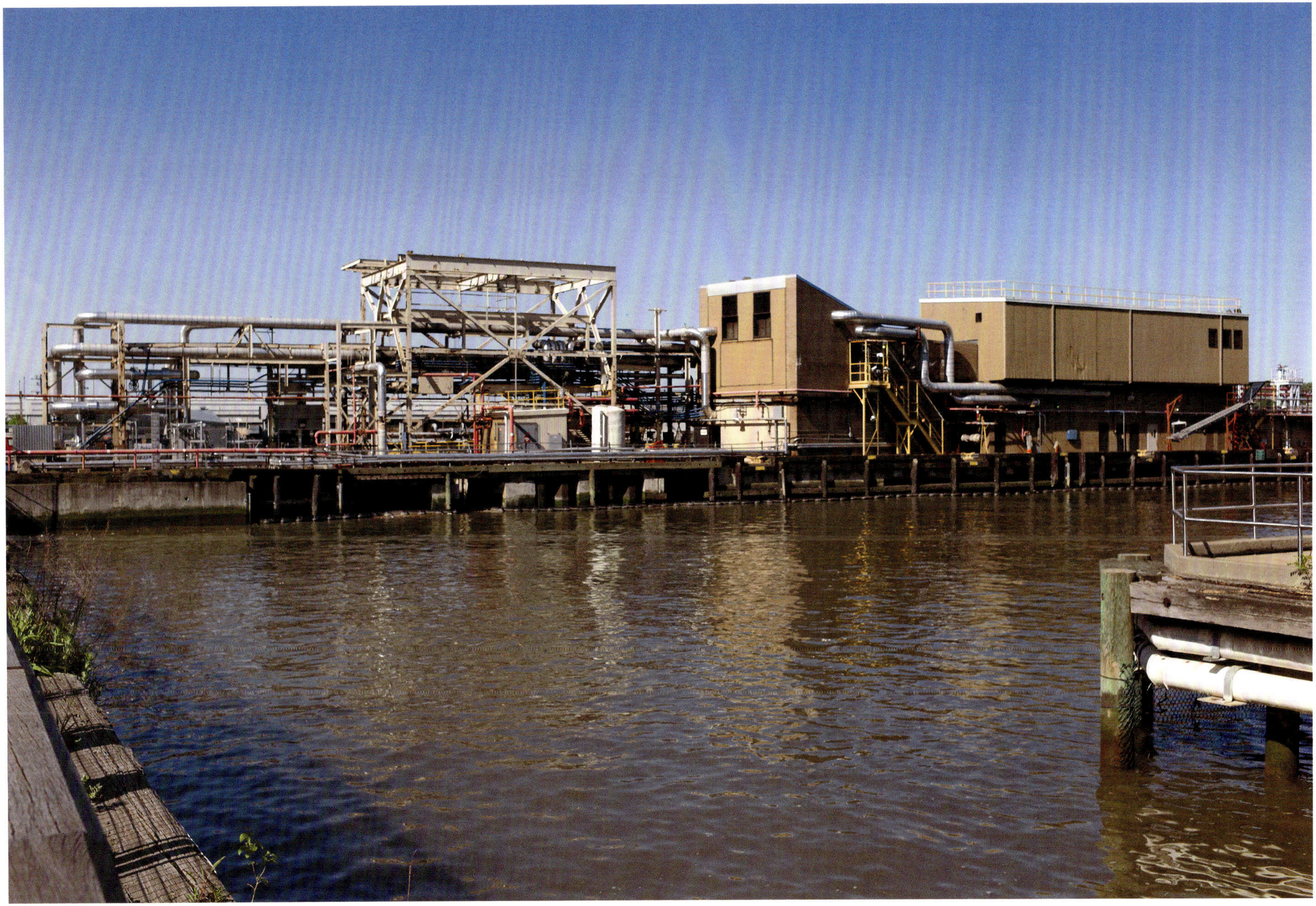

99

100

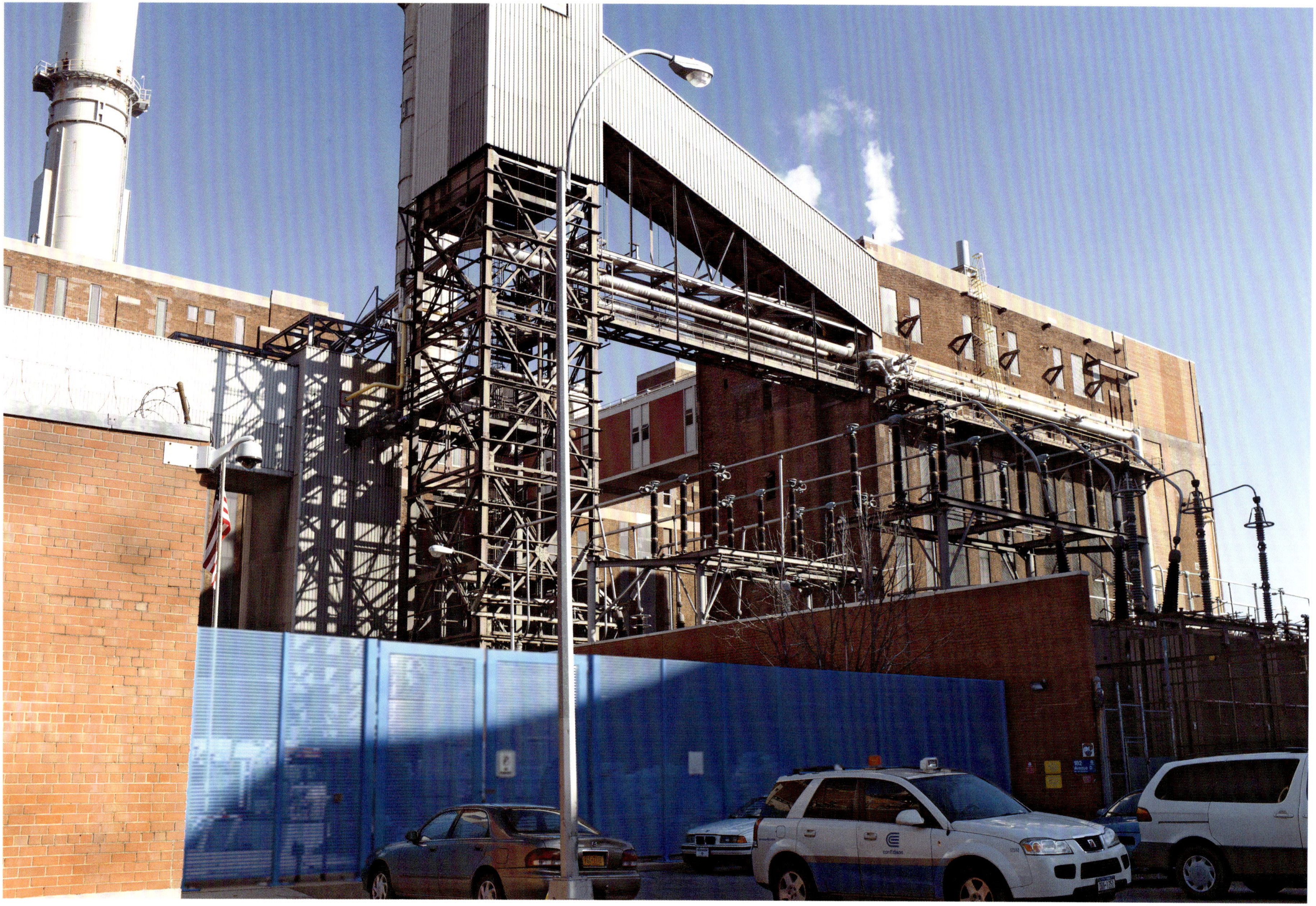

9

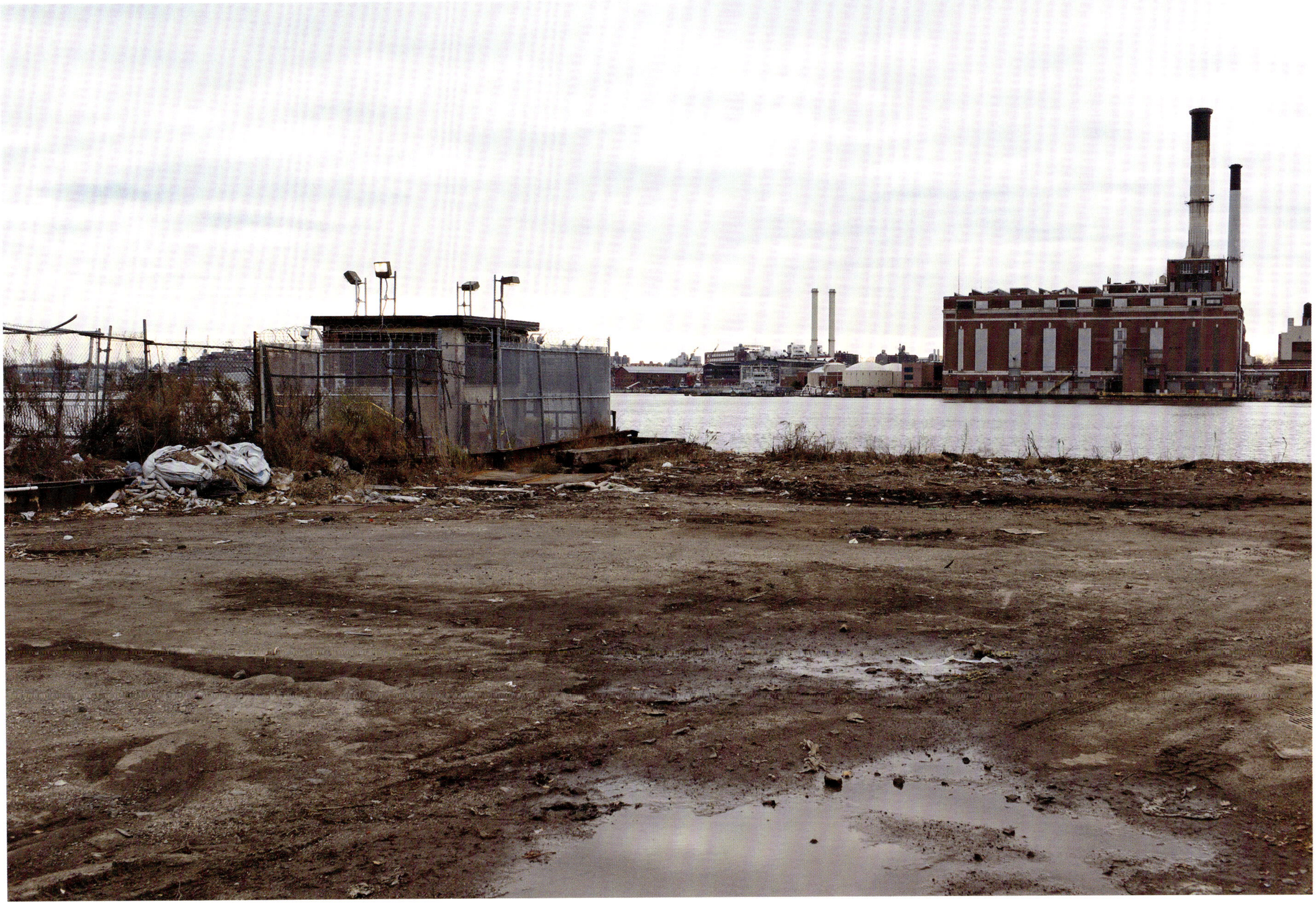

101

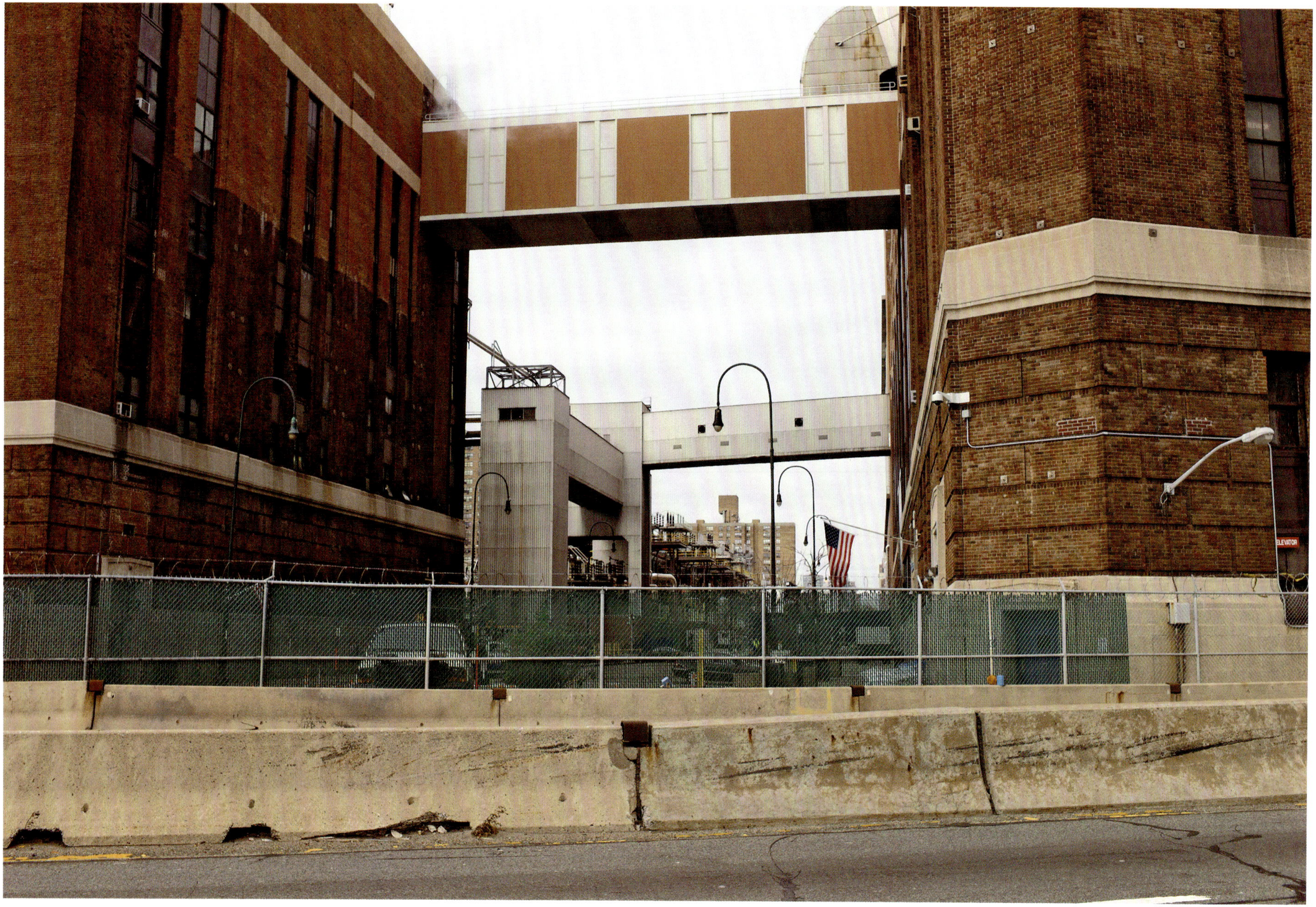
ELEVATOR

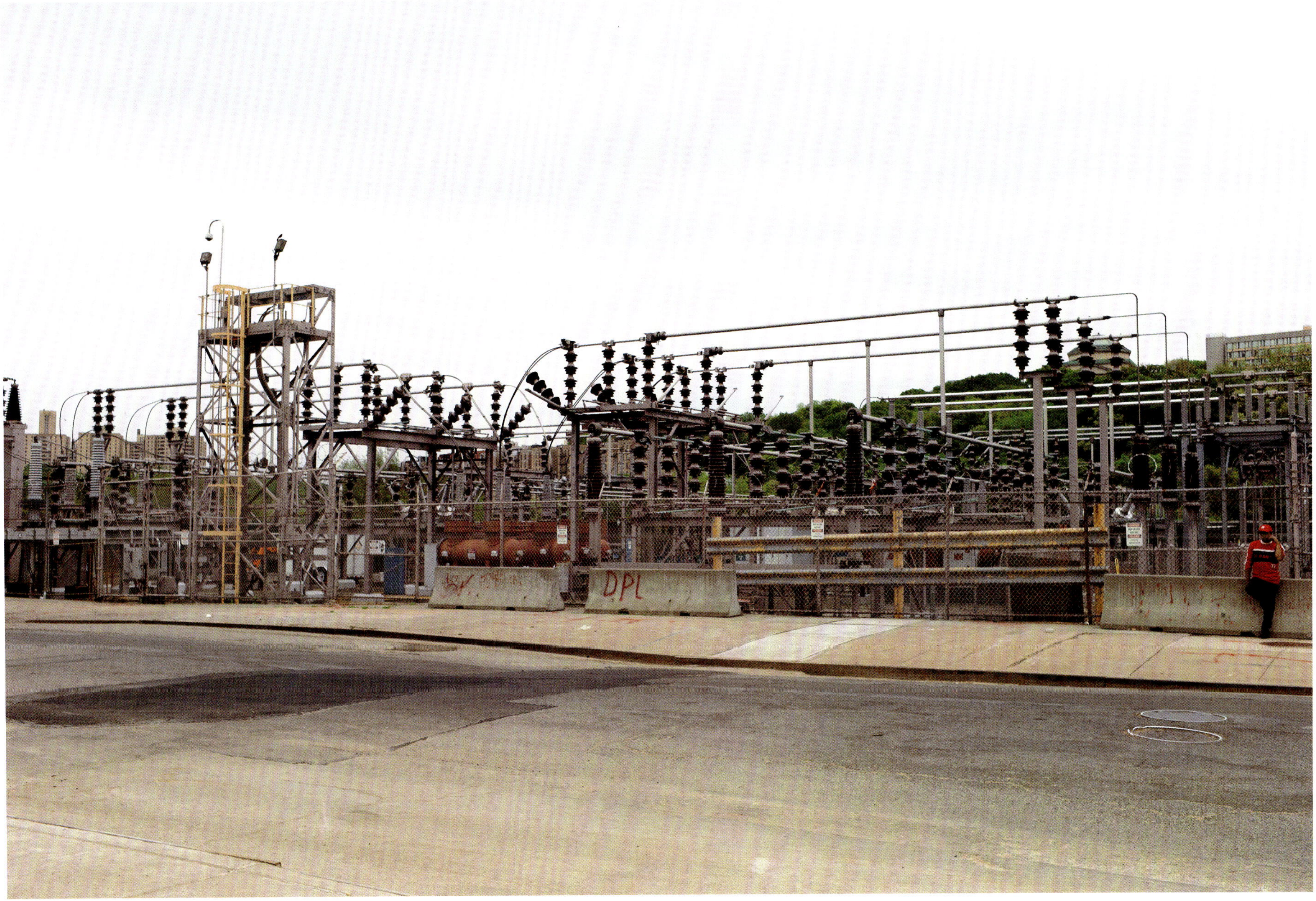

12

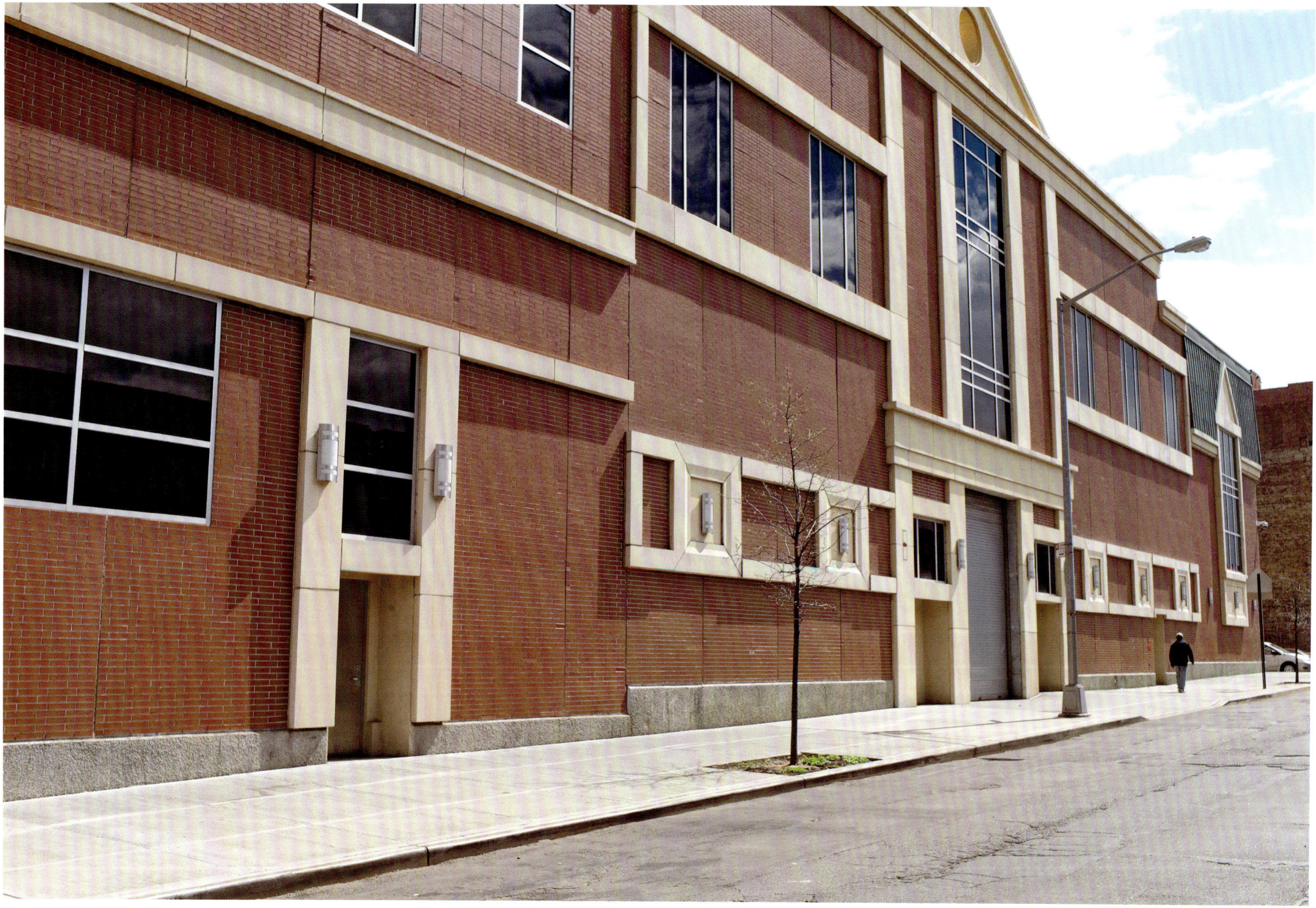

13

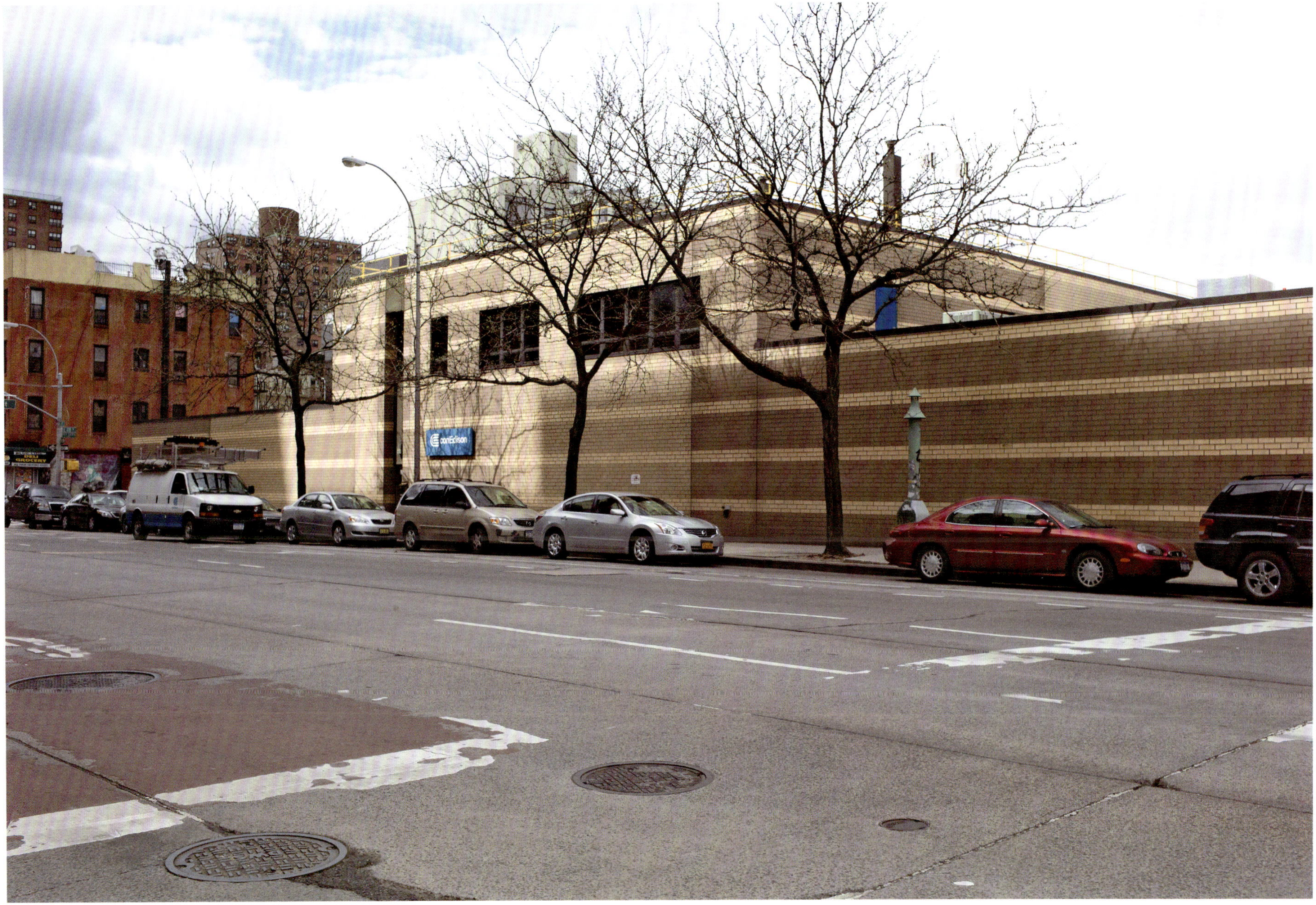

14

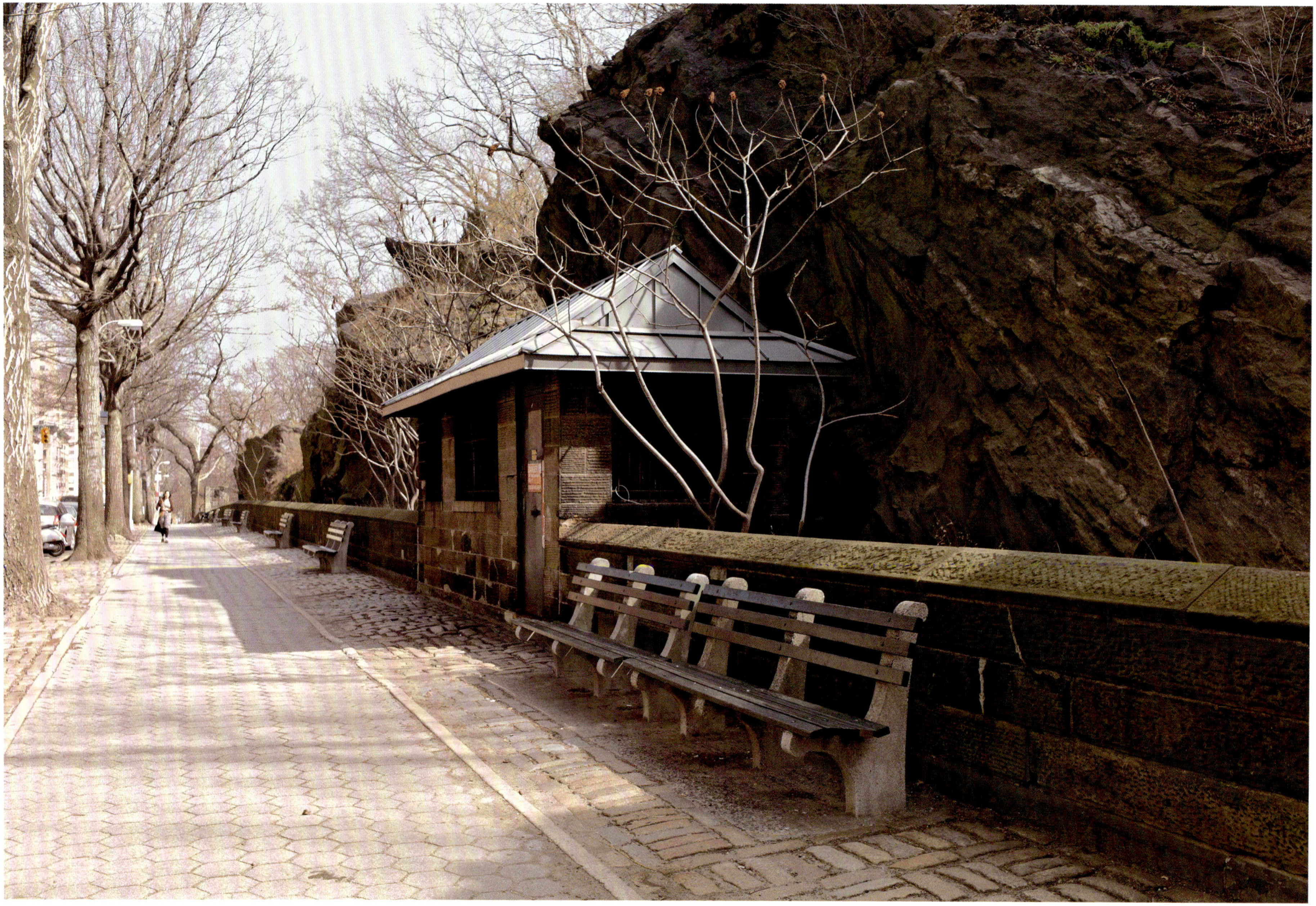

1

GEOLOGY/TOPOGRAPHY

Manhattan is built largely on schist. Most of it is deep underground, providing a stable underpinning for all the tall towers. Many parts of Manhattan were hillier (and wetter) than they are now. Geology is more evident in parks and at the northern tip of Manhattan on the Hudson shore, where Inwood Hill Park is located. Stair streets connect adjacent variable elevations, and a single subway station may have both high and low entrances.

Originally there were marshes, streams, and springs all over Manhattan, some of which are memorialized in place names, like Canal Street or Minetta Street. Some of the waterways nearly crossed the entire island. Here again the northern extremity of Inwood holds a few of the last aboveground springs to be found in Manhattan; with a couple exceptions, the rest have been buried under concrete. And every so often you can find outcroppings that somehow survived the bulldozer and dynamite, mostly on the Upper West Side, in a few apartment courtyards and interstitial spaces between buildings.

1 Upper West Side
2 Hudson Heights
3 Fort George
4 Sugar Hill
5 Highbridge Park
6 Hudson Heights
7 East Harlem
8 Hudson Heights
9 Washington Heights
10 Sugar Hill
11 Sugar Hill
12 Manhattanville
13 Hudson Heights
14 Hudson Heights
15 Washington Heights
16 Hamilton Heights
17 Inwood
18 Fort George
19 Washington Heights
20 Washington Heights

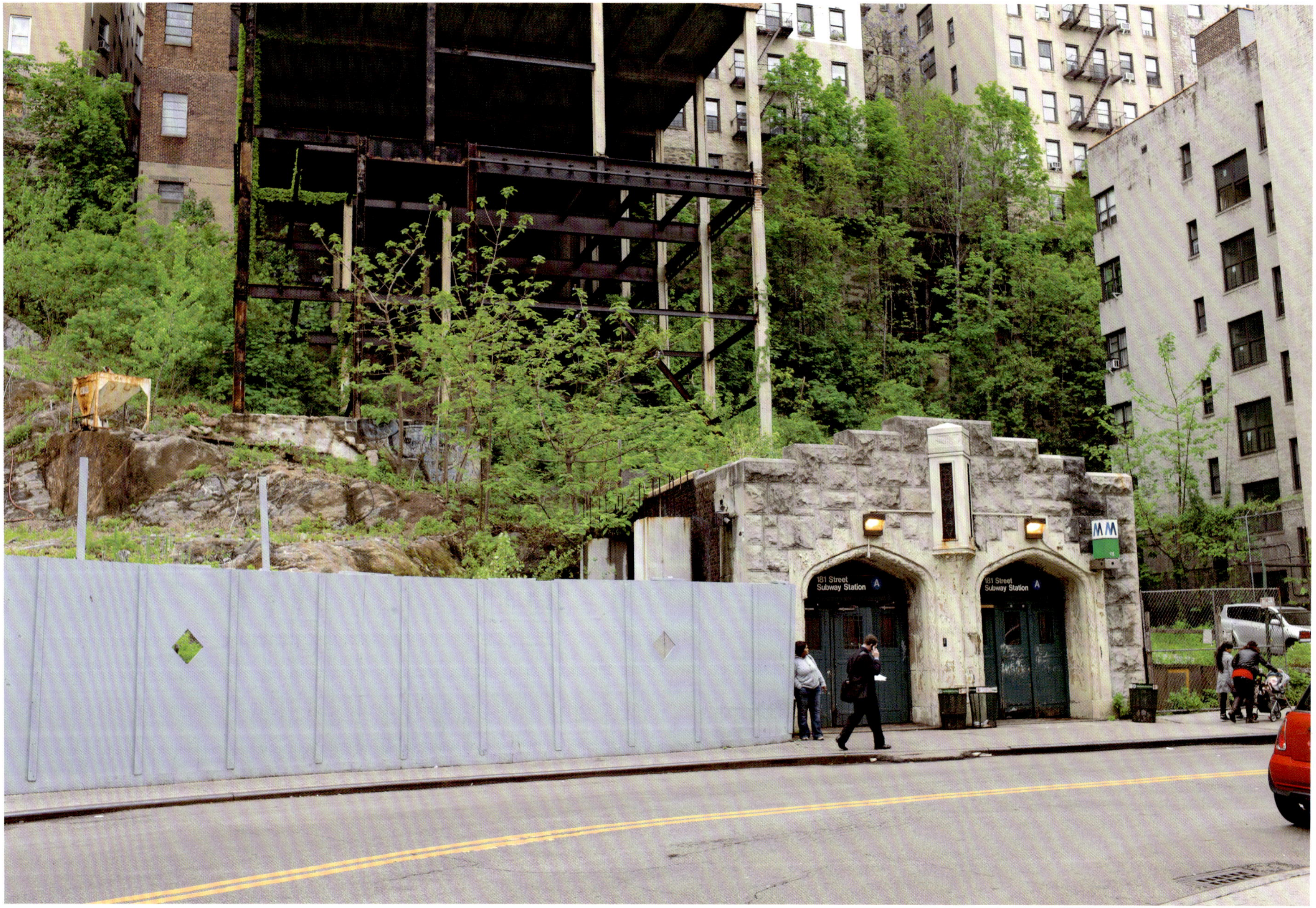

2

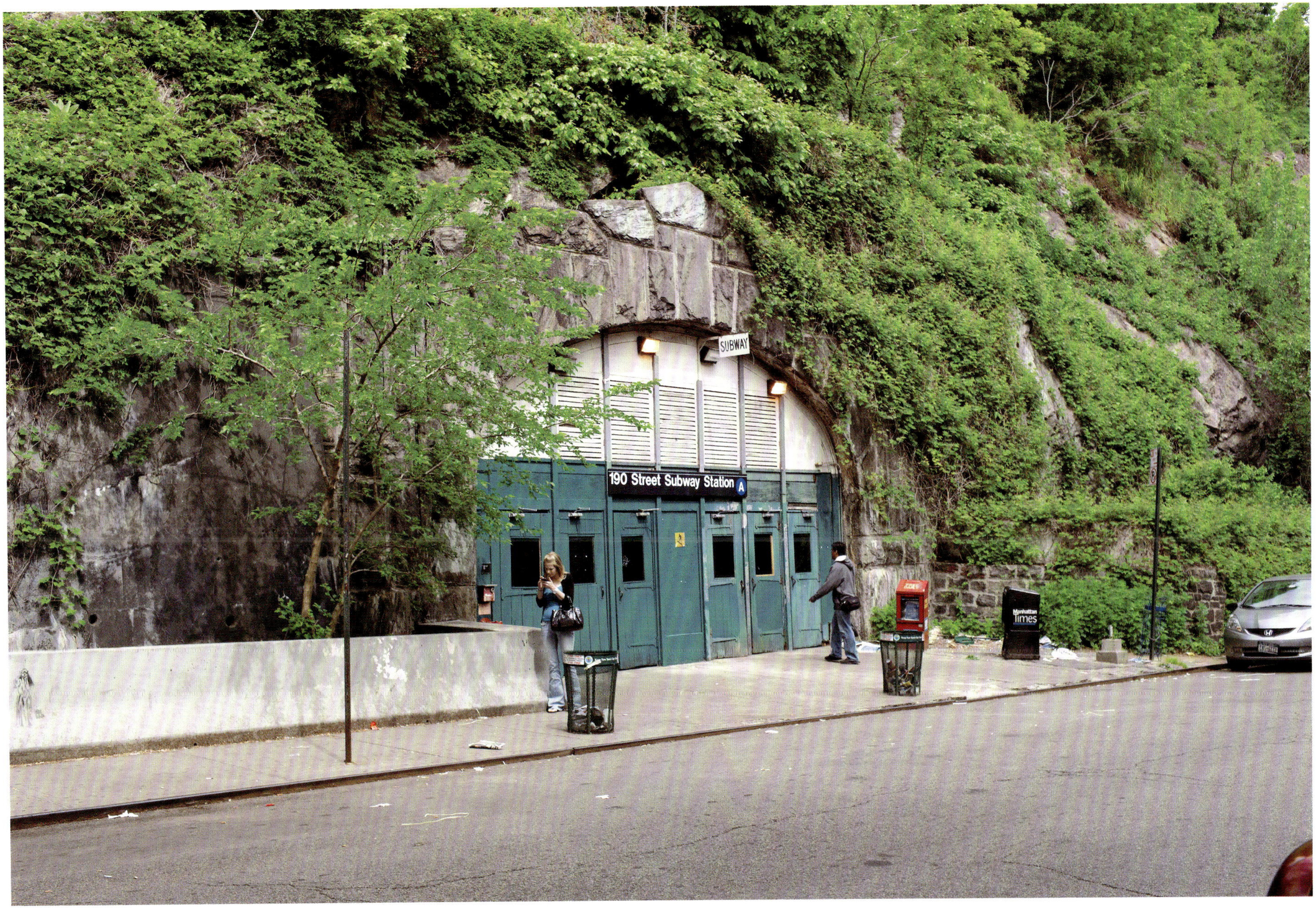

3

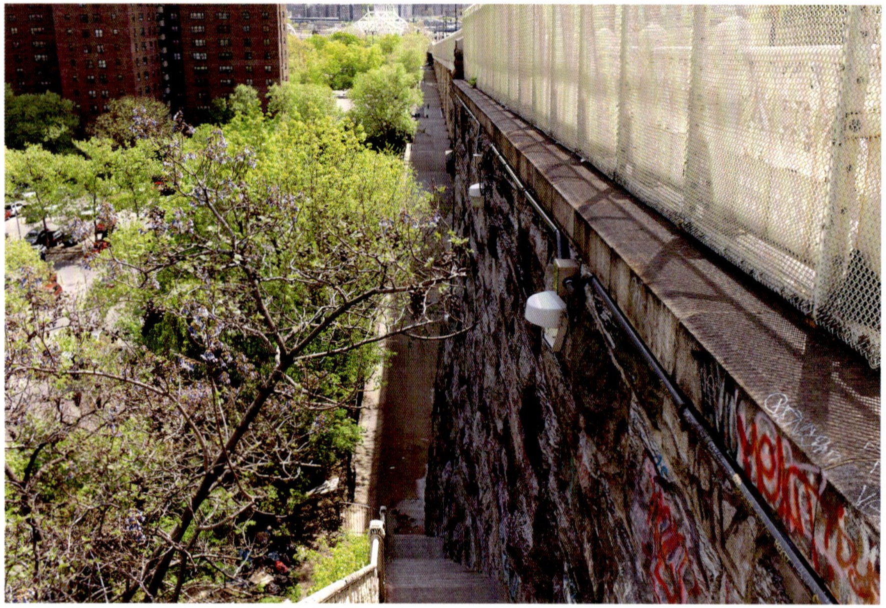

4

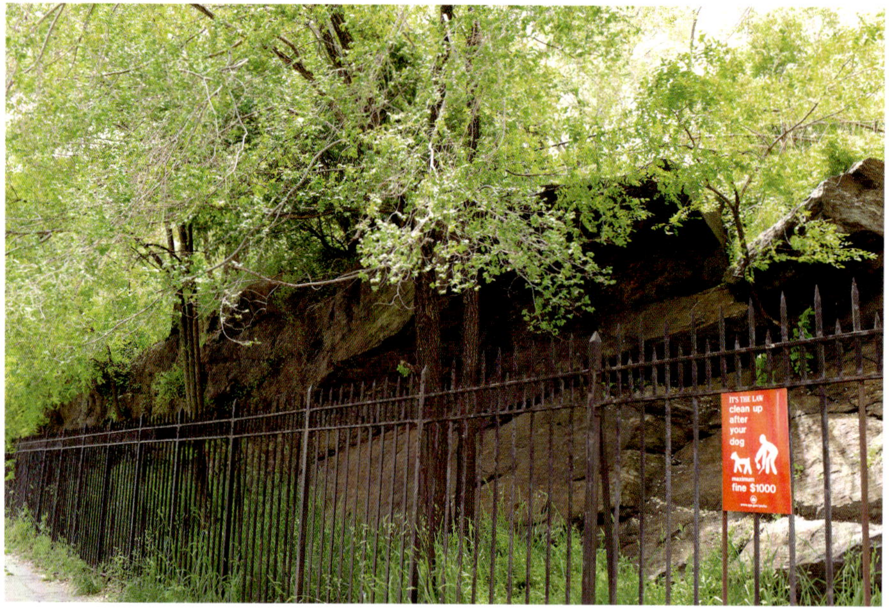

5

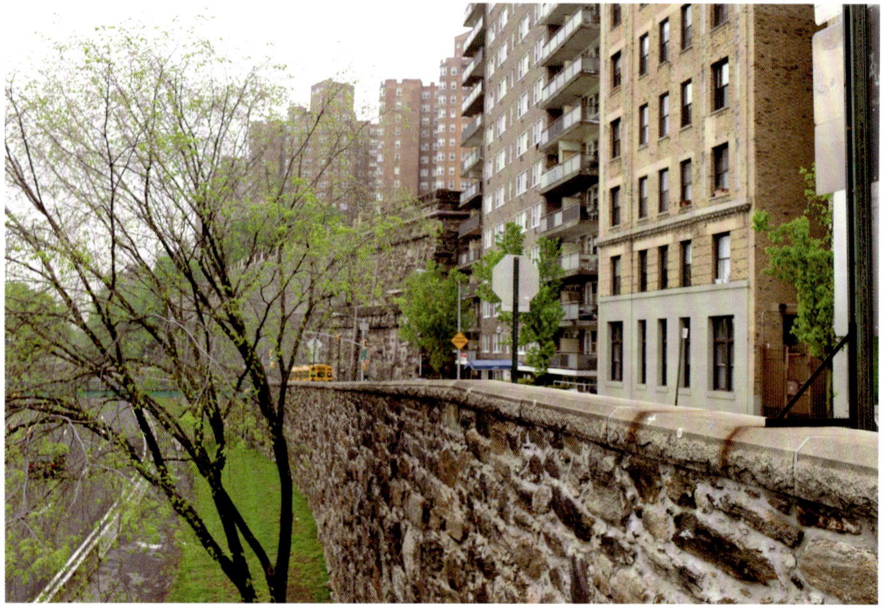

6

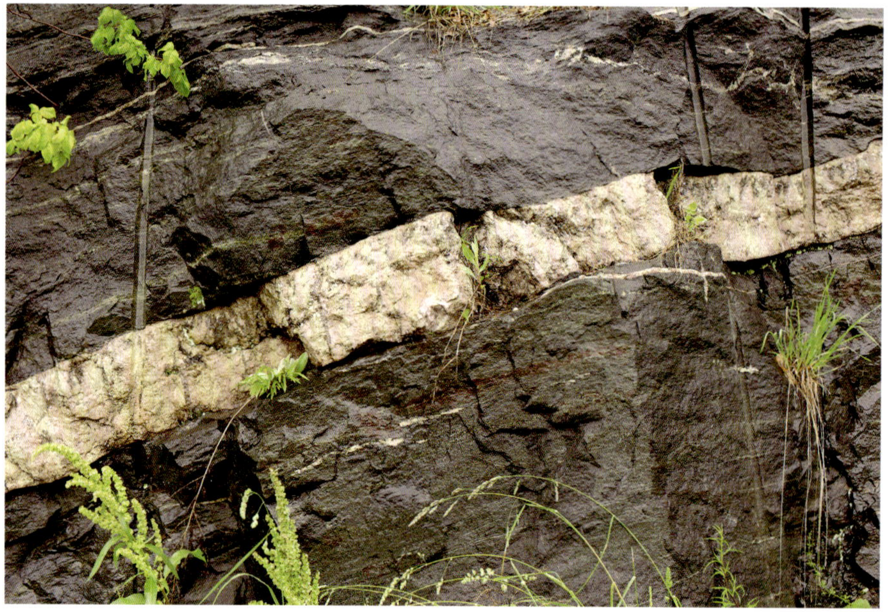

7

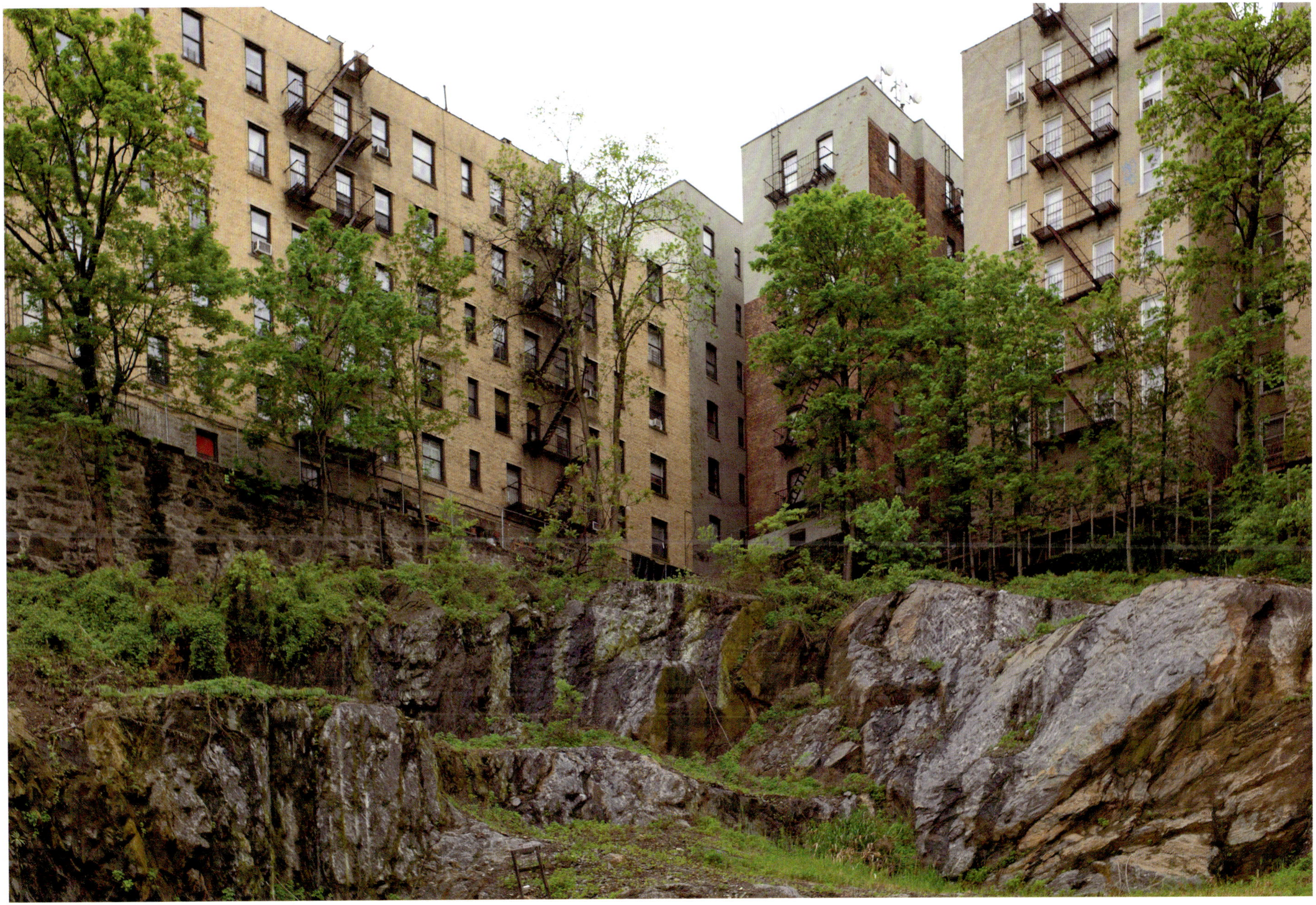

111

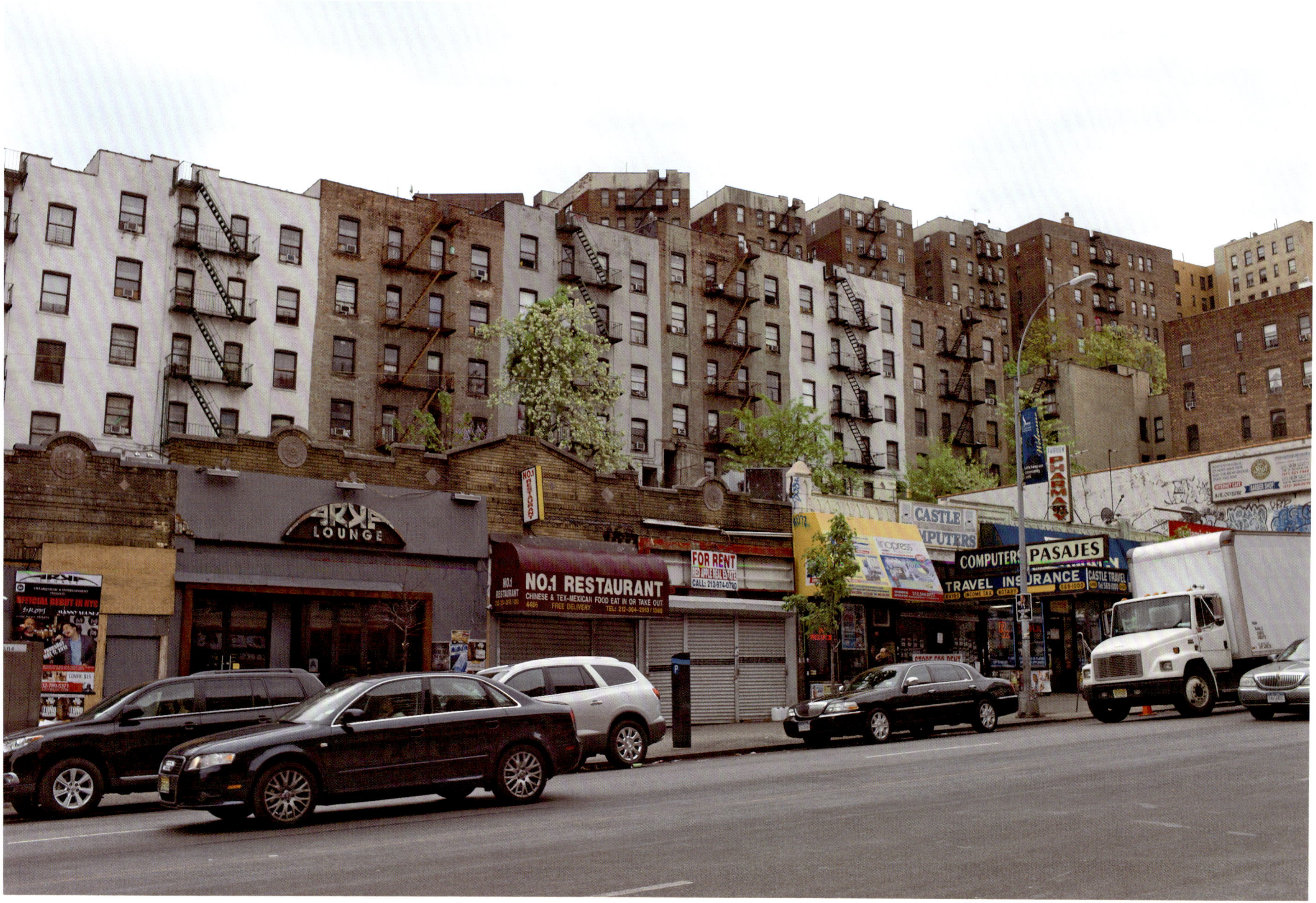
LOUNGE
NO.1 RESTAURANT
CHINESE & TEX-MEXICAN FOOD EAT IN OR TAKE OUT
FREE DELIVERY
FOR RENT
CASTLE
COMPUTERS
PASAJES
TRAVEL INSURANCE
PHARMACY

9

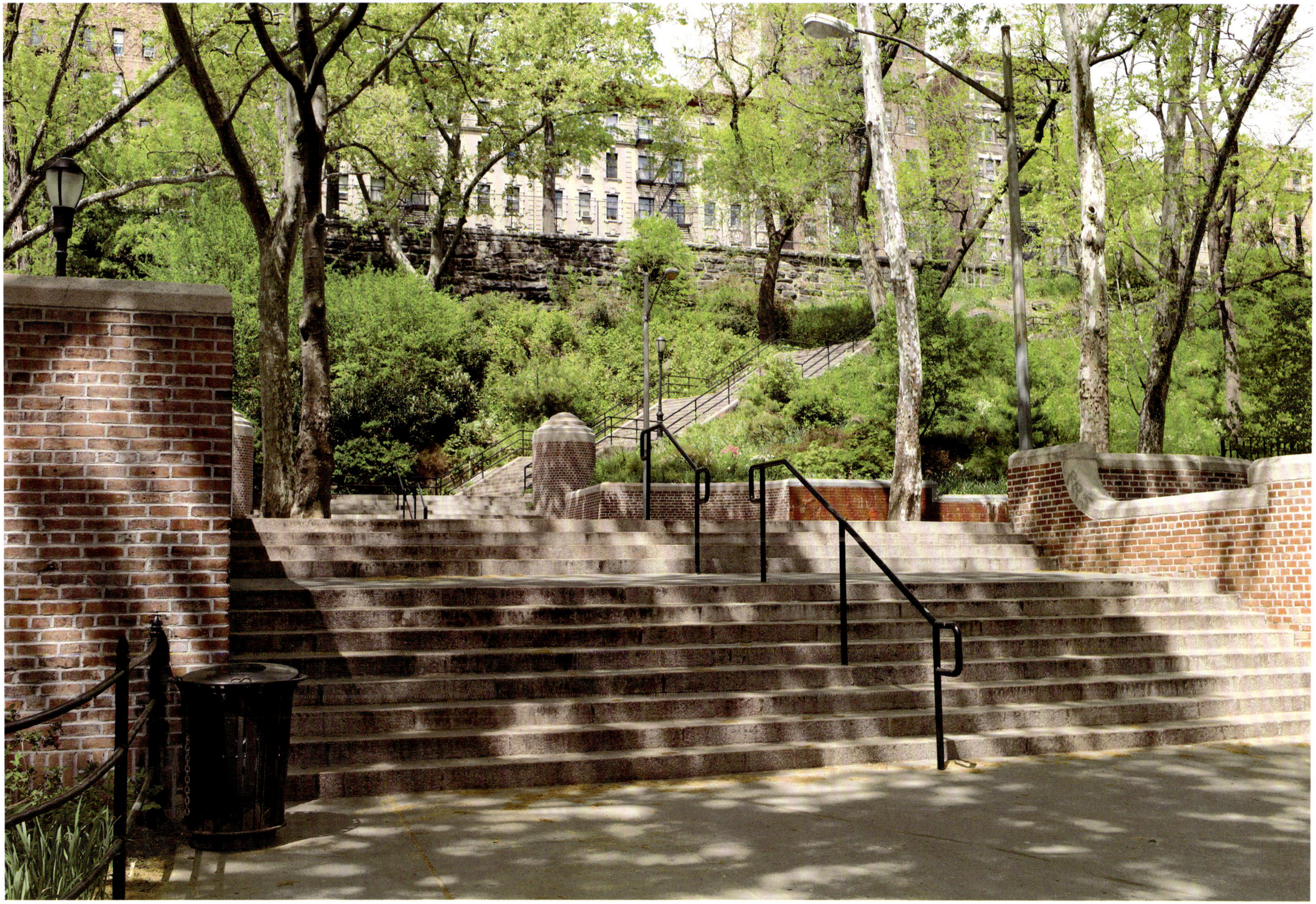

113

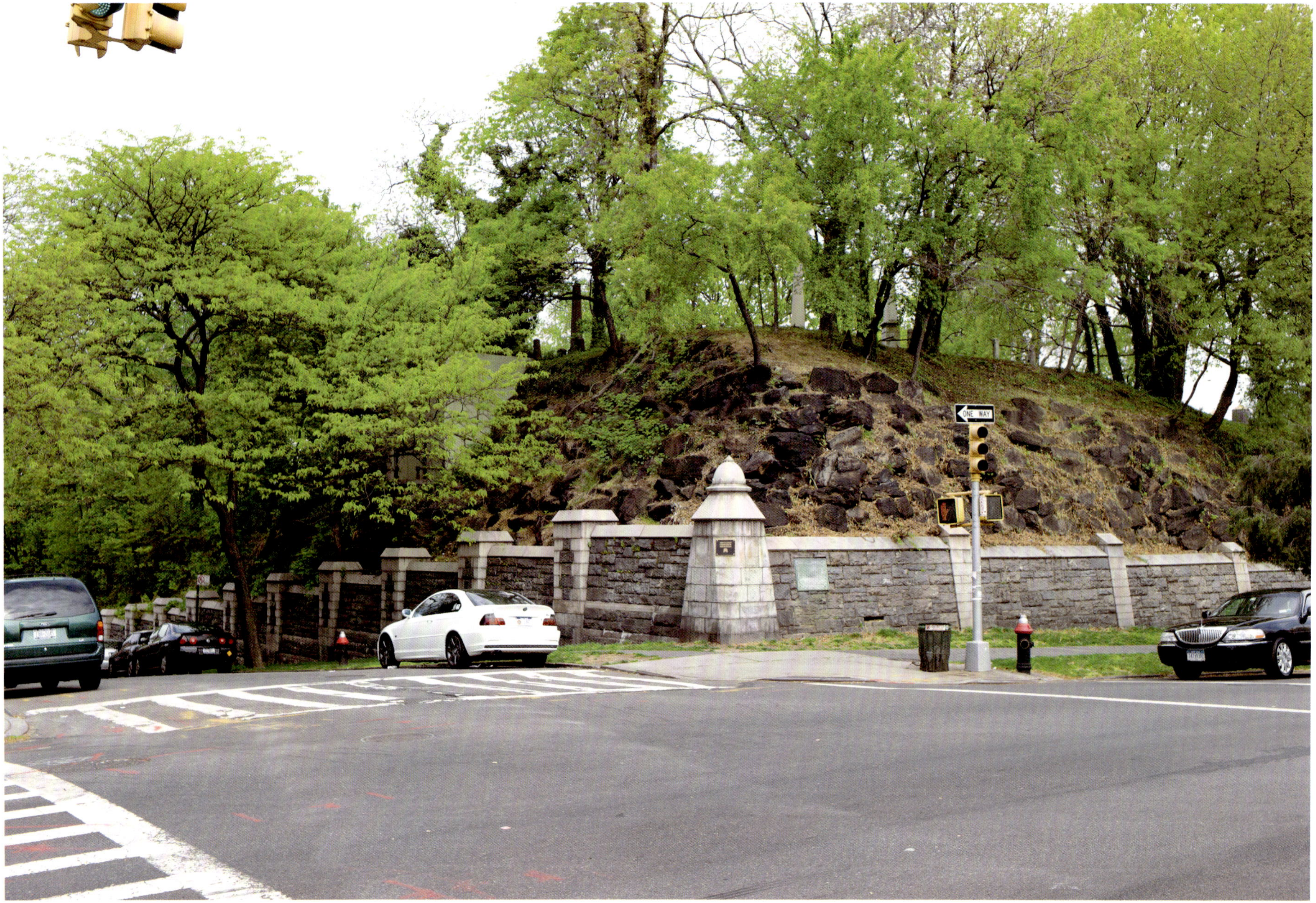

11

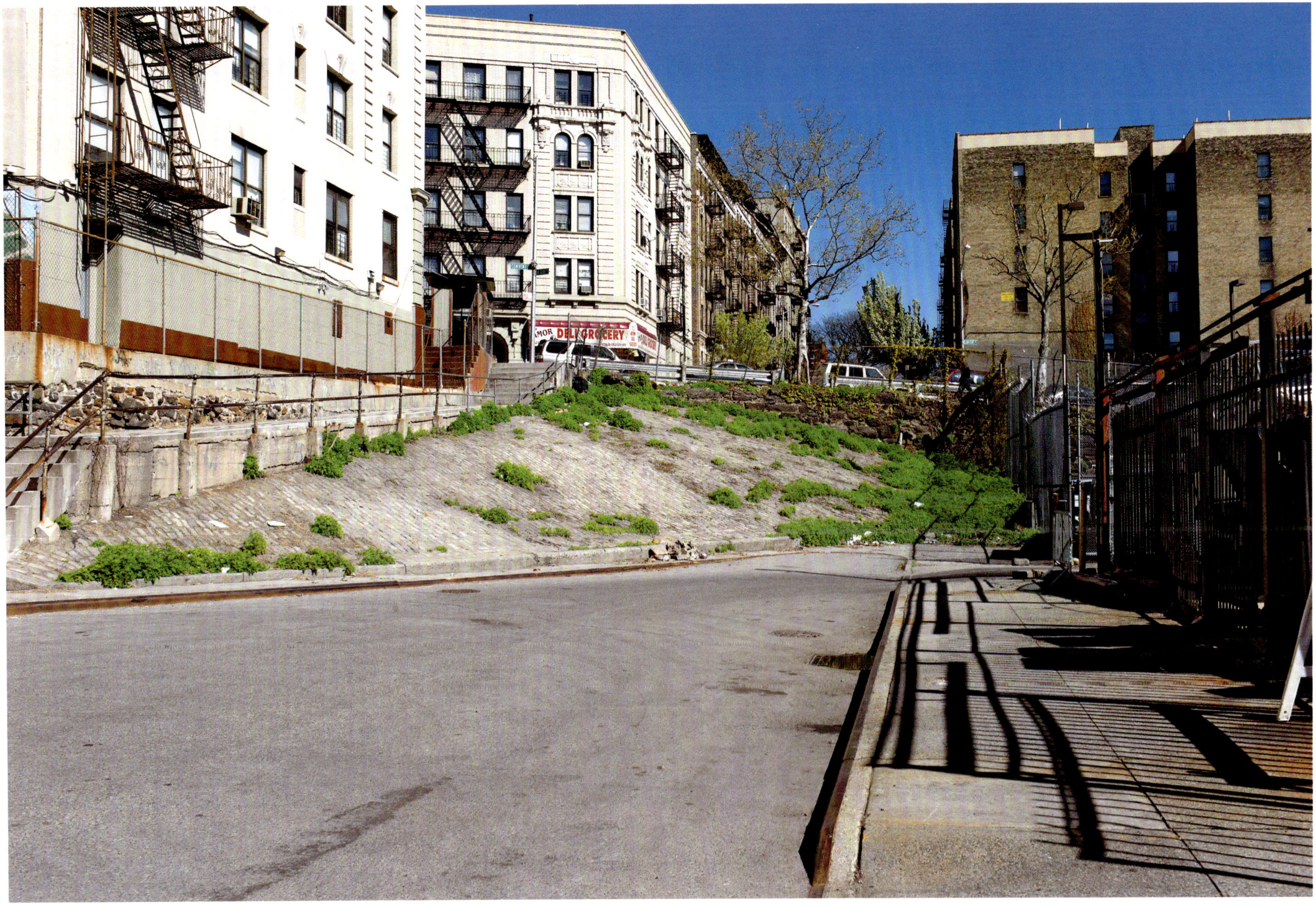

115

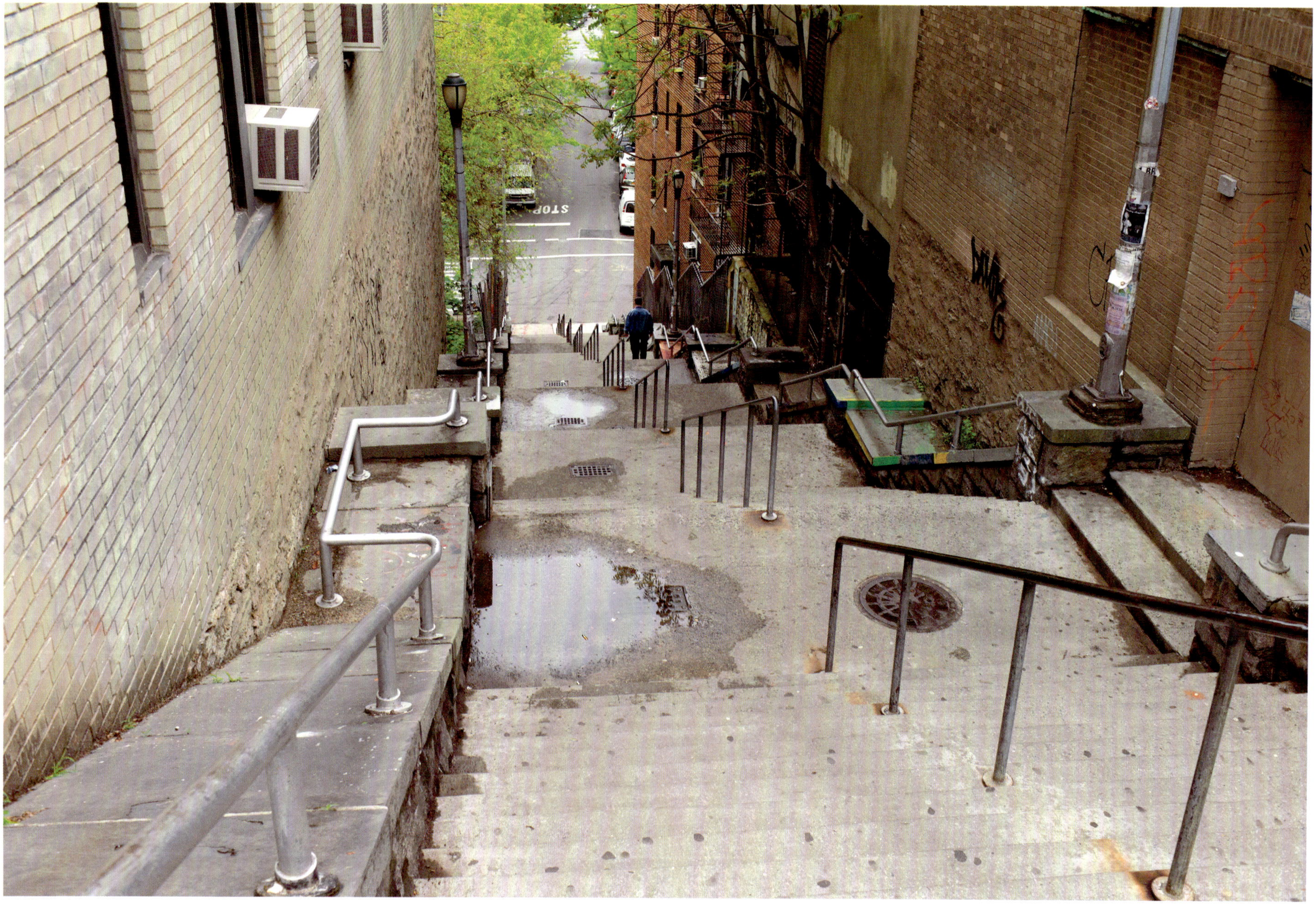

13

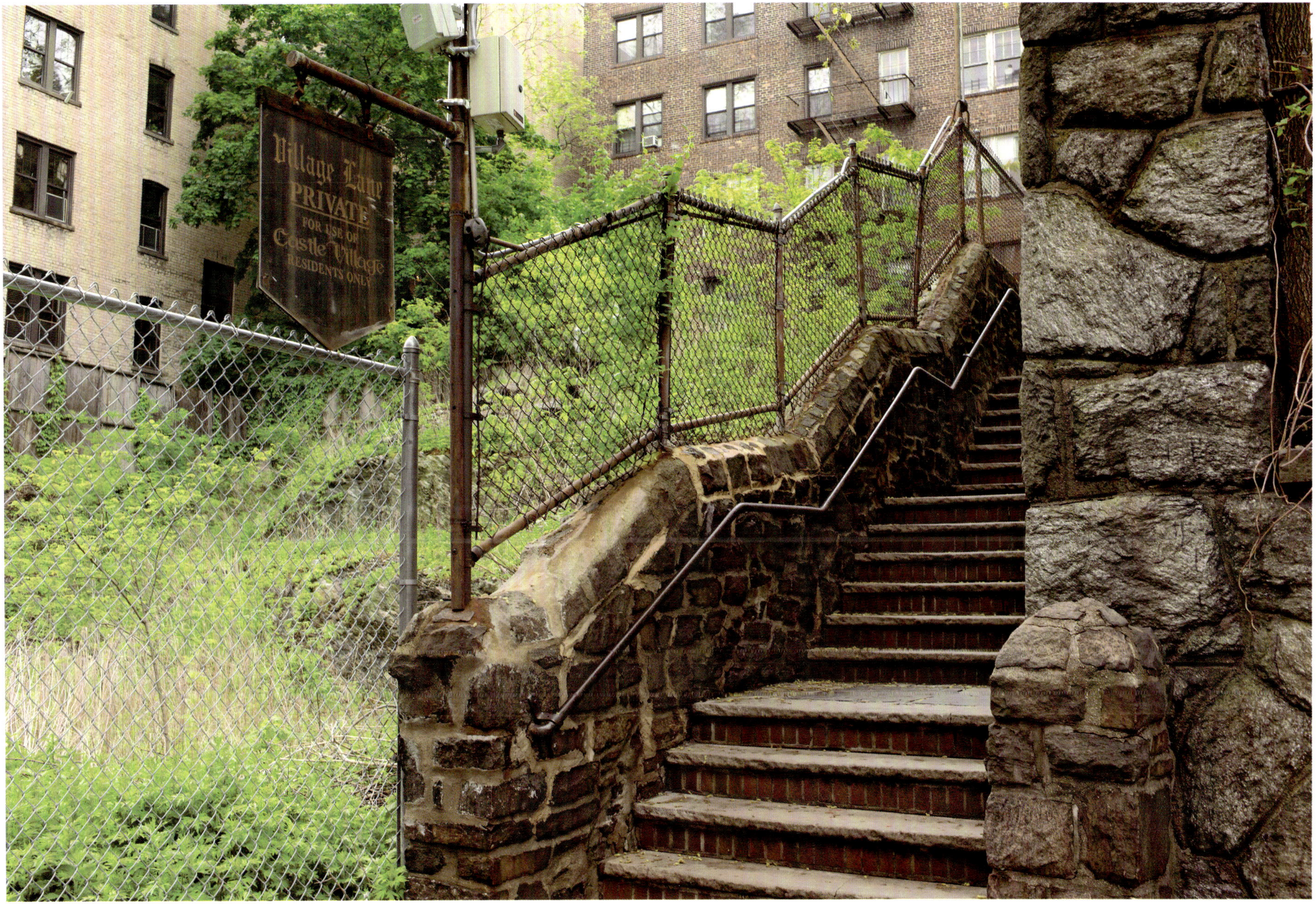
Village Lane
PRIVATE
FOR USE OF
Castle Village
RESIDENTS ONLY

117

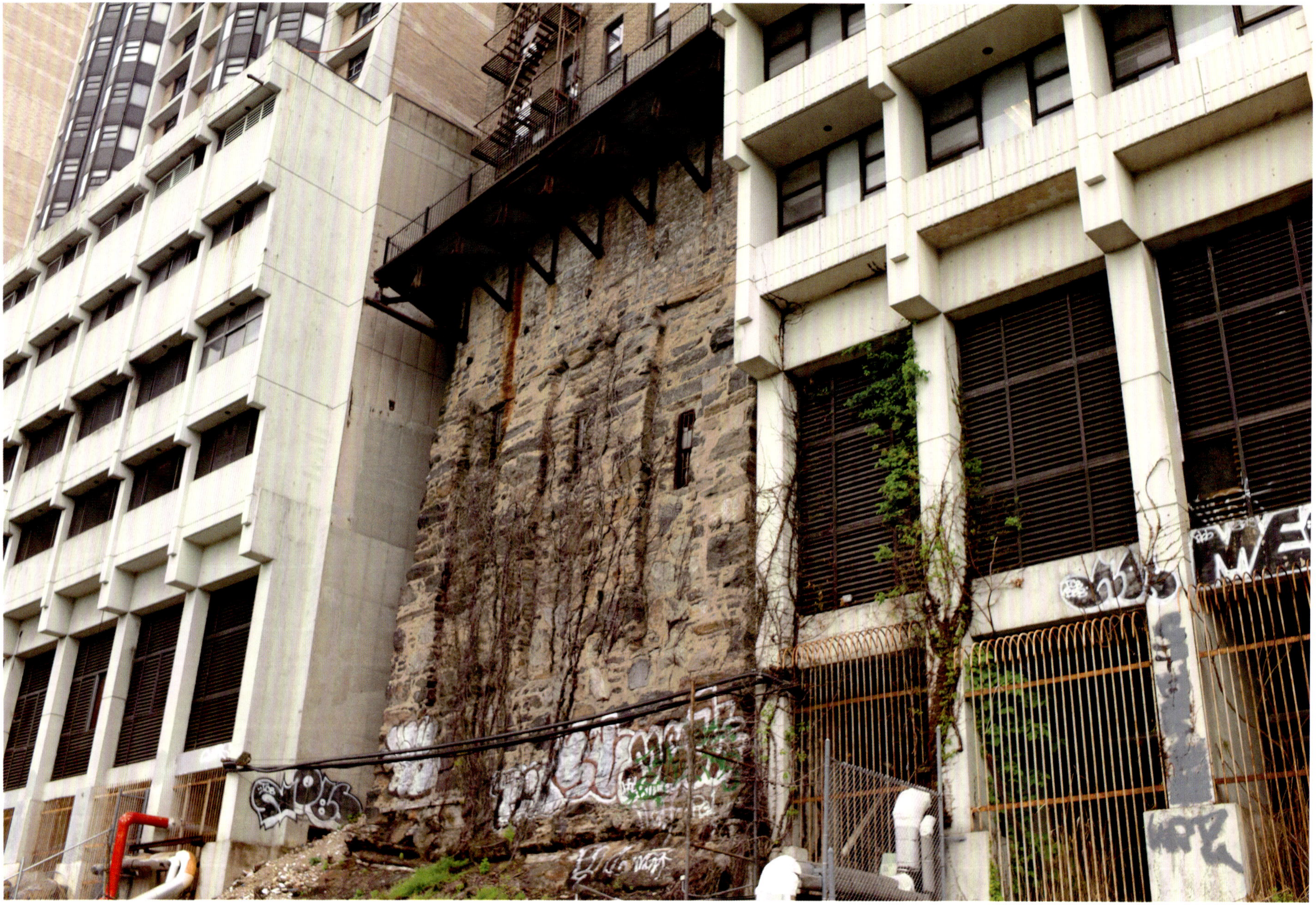

15

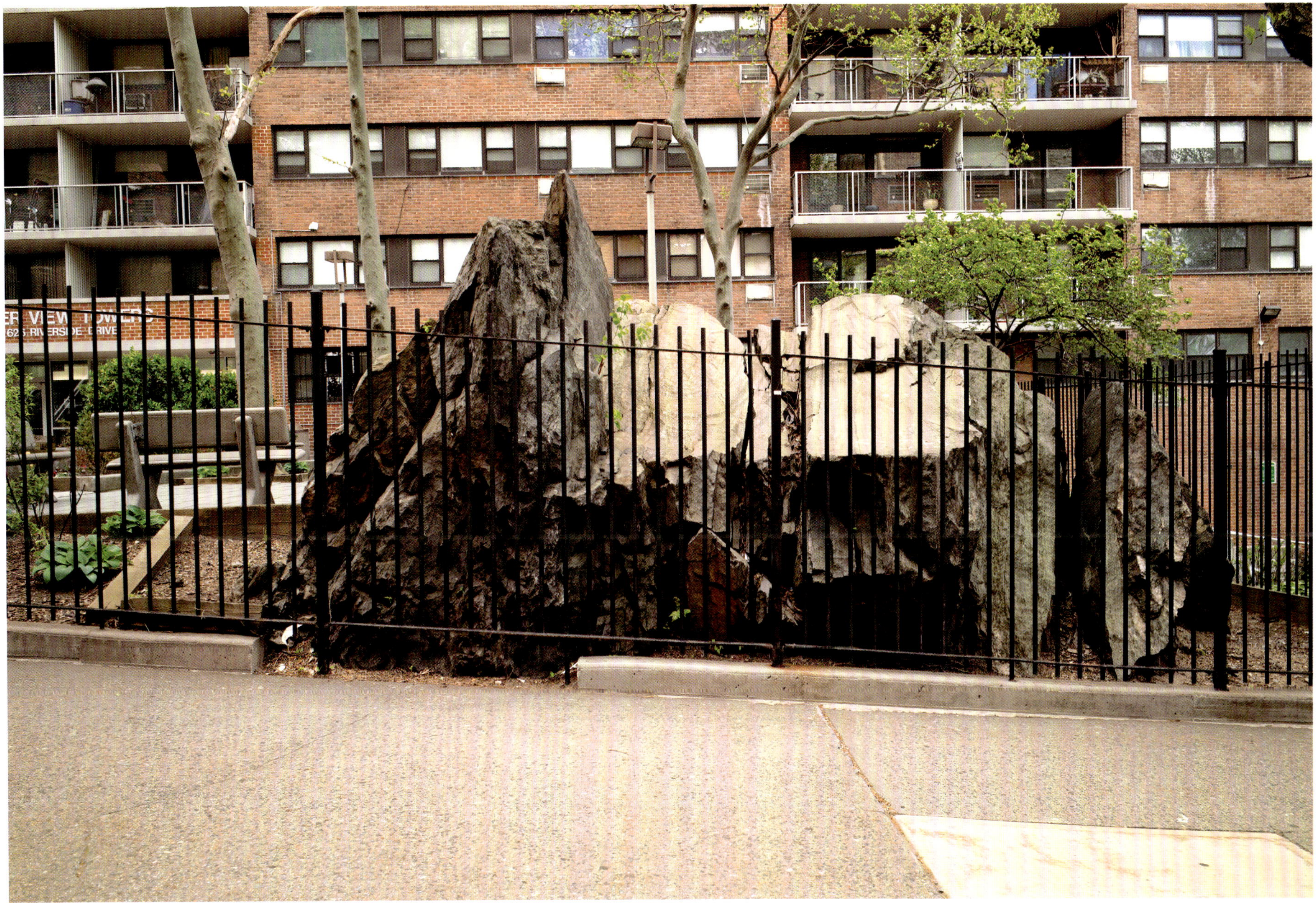

119

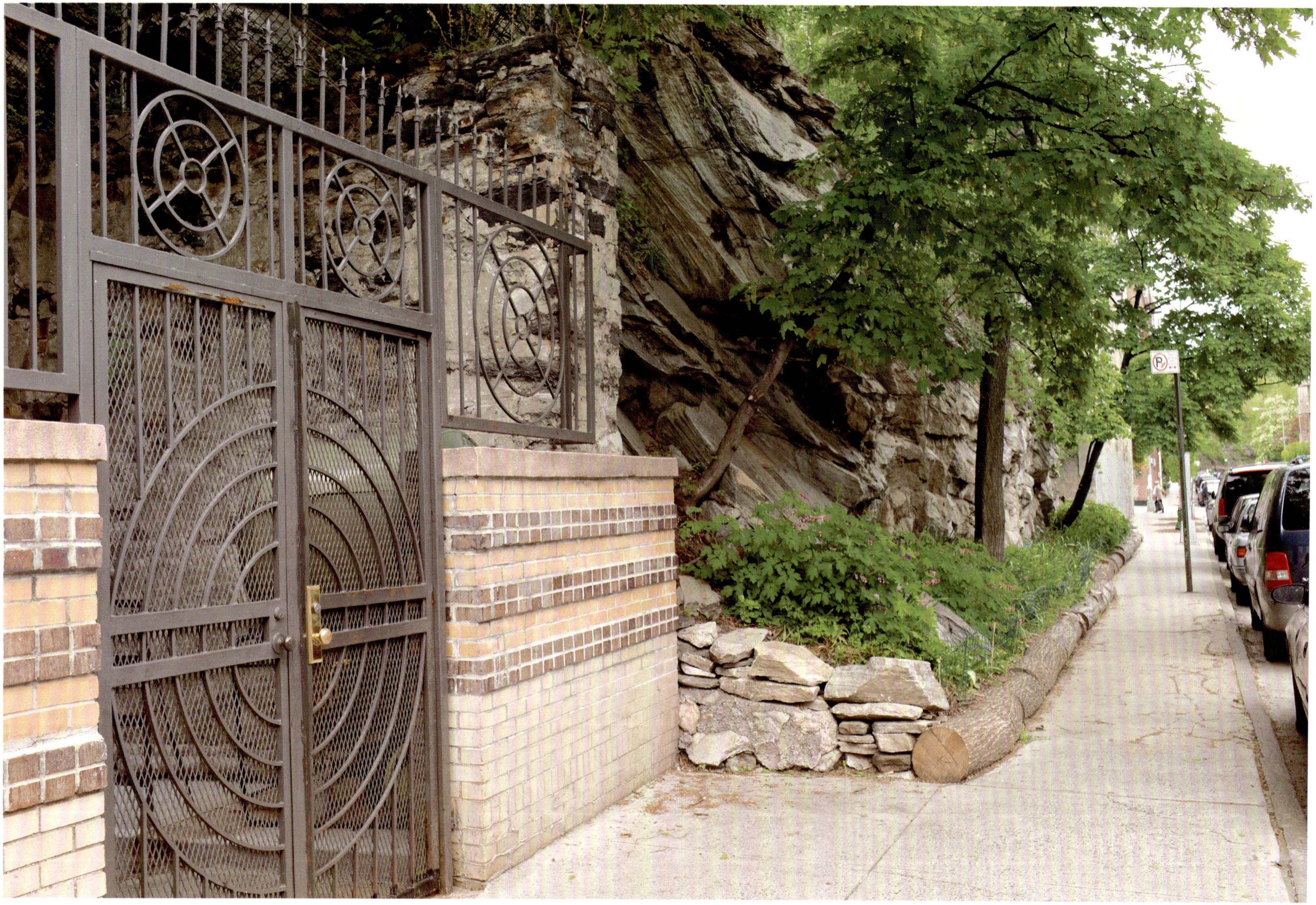

17

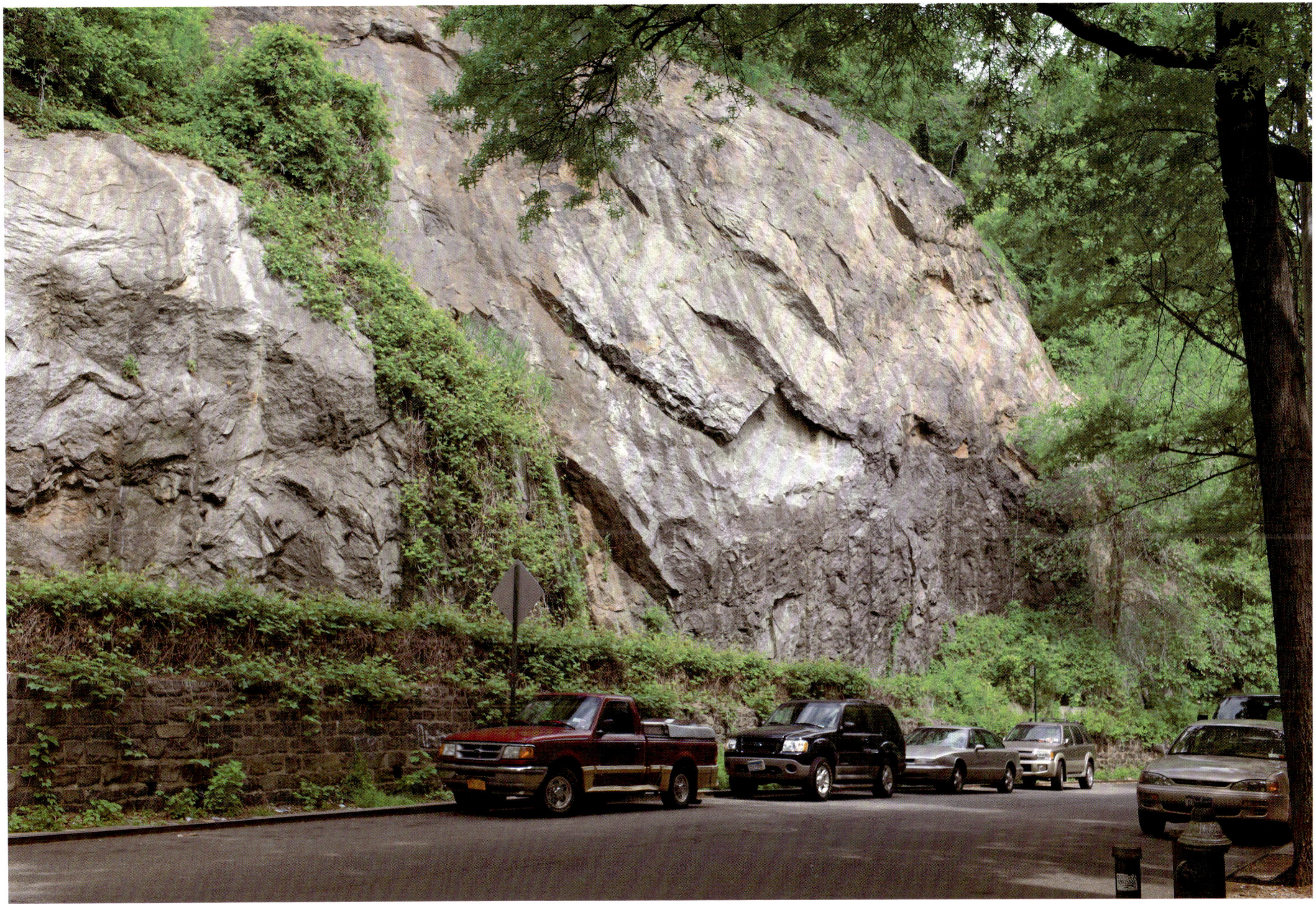

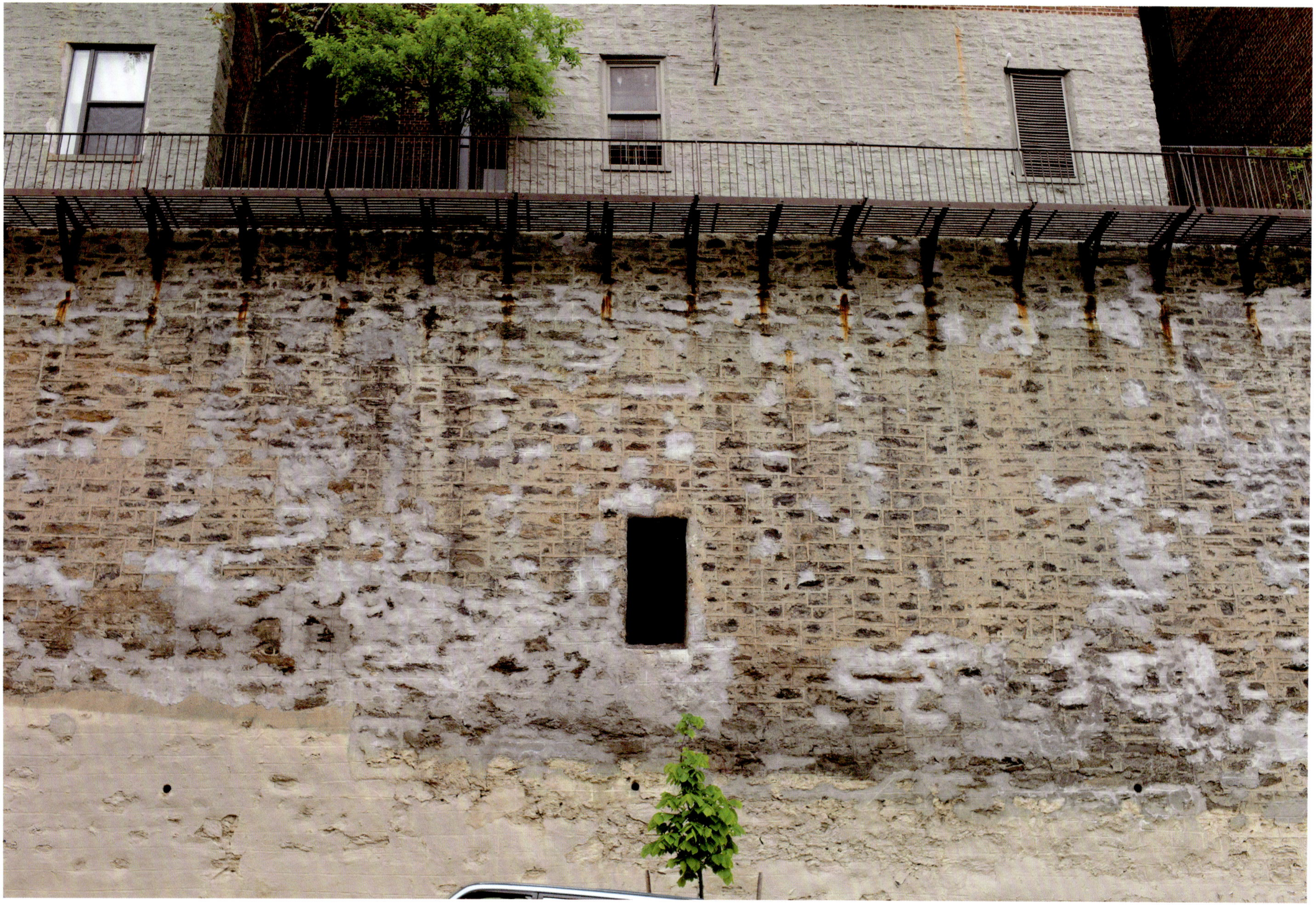

19

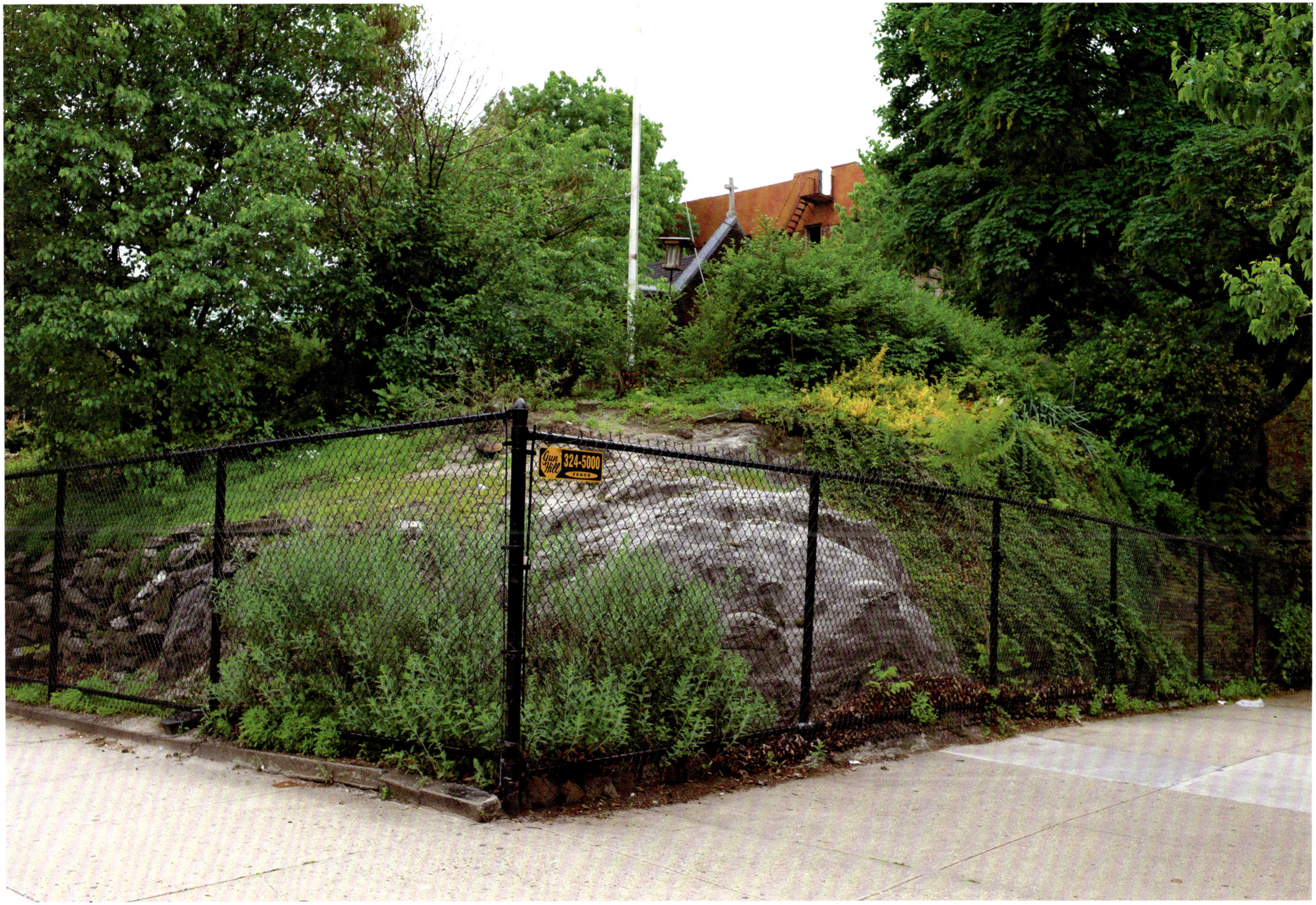

123

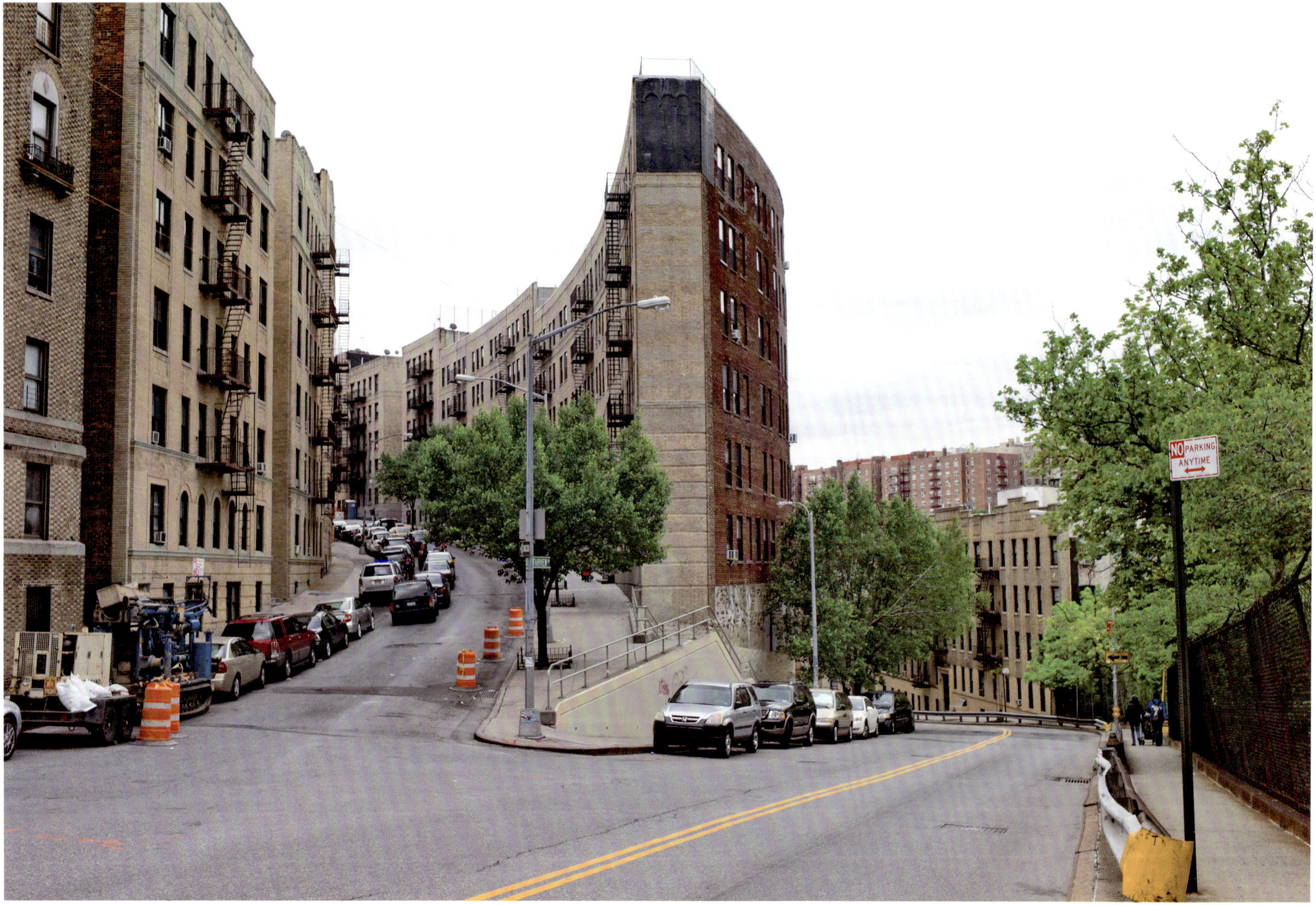

1

GRID/NON-GRID

When the city agreed to use John Randel Jr.'s grid plan in 1811, much of Lower Manhattan had already been laid out and built up; streets either followed existing Indian paths or grew organically, largely guided by private estate boundaries and the locations of ports and warehouses. The new plan would cover the area from Houston Street to 155th Street, resulting in numerous junctures of the newer grid and the streets that existed before, occasionally leading to odd intersections, such as where West 4th and West 11th Streets cross. The plan also called for the elimination of Broadway, which of course never happened.

The area uptown beyond where the 1811 grid stops has its own character, with bigger and steeper hills, stair streets, and outcroppings of rock not seen anywhere else on the island, except in a few parks (see *Geology/Topography*). Streets curve around hills and parks, huge supporting structures are required for buildings on hillsides; the landscape is more varied here and neighborhoods often adapted their layout around these features, instead of leveling the topography and imposing a strict rectilinear hierarchy.

1 Fort George
2 Lower East Side
3 Manhattanville
4 West Village
5 East Village
6 East Village
7 Astor Place
8 West Village
9 West Village
10 West Village
11 Chelsea
12 Central Harlem
13 Central Harlem
14 Hudson Heights
15 Financial District
16 Lower East Side
17 Chinatown
18 West Village
19 West Village
20 West Village
21 Washington Heights
22 West Village
23 Inwood
24 Washington Heights
25 Tribeca

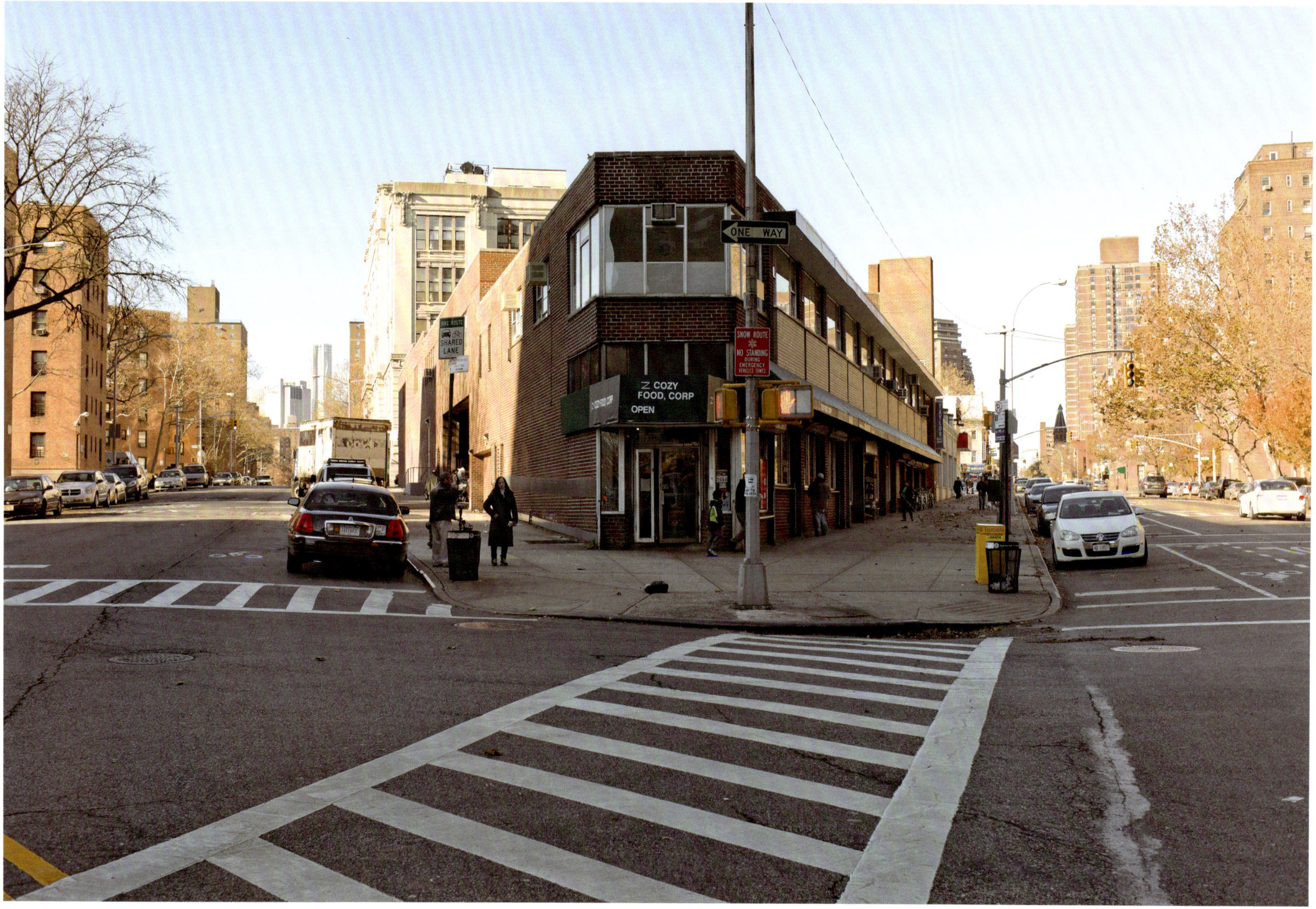
ONE WAY
SNOW ROUTE
NO STANDING
Z COZY
FOOD, CORP
OPEN
SHARED
LANE

2

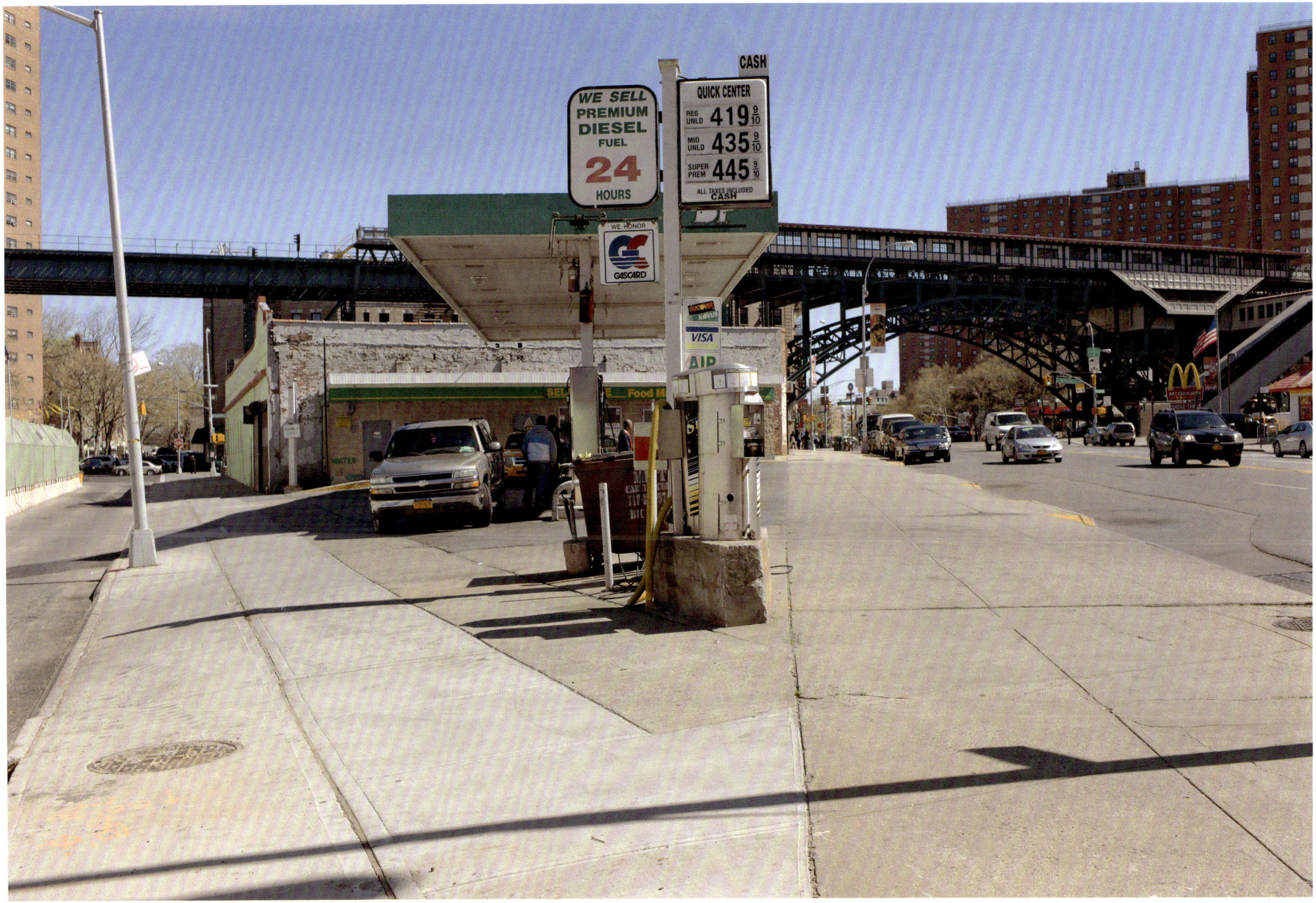
CASH
QUICK CENTER
REG UNLD 419 9/10
MID UNLD 435 9/10
SUPER PREM 445 9/10
ALL TAXES INCLUDED
CASH
WE SELL
PREMIUM
DIESEL
FUEL
24
HOURS
WE HONOR
GASCARD
VISA
AIR

3

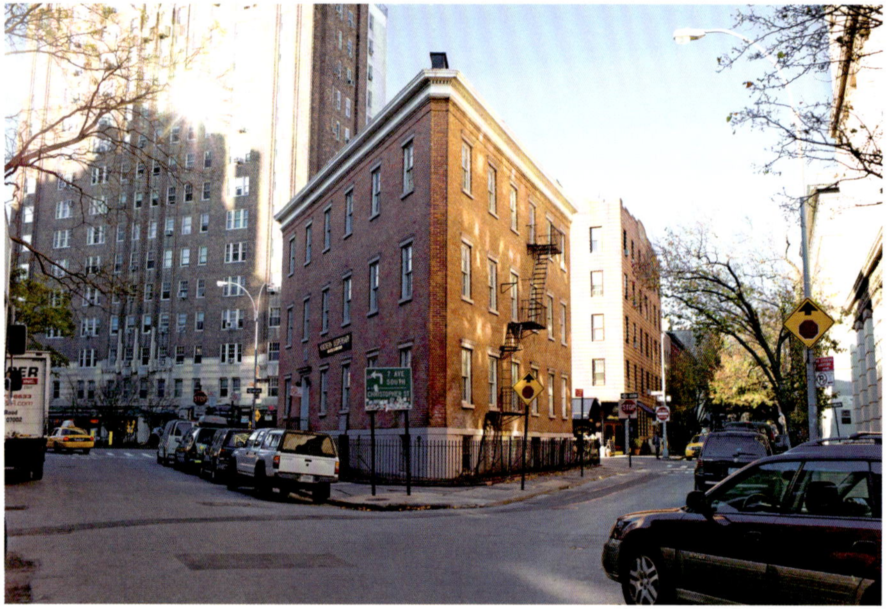

4

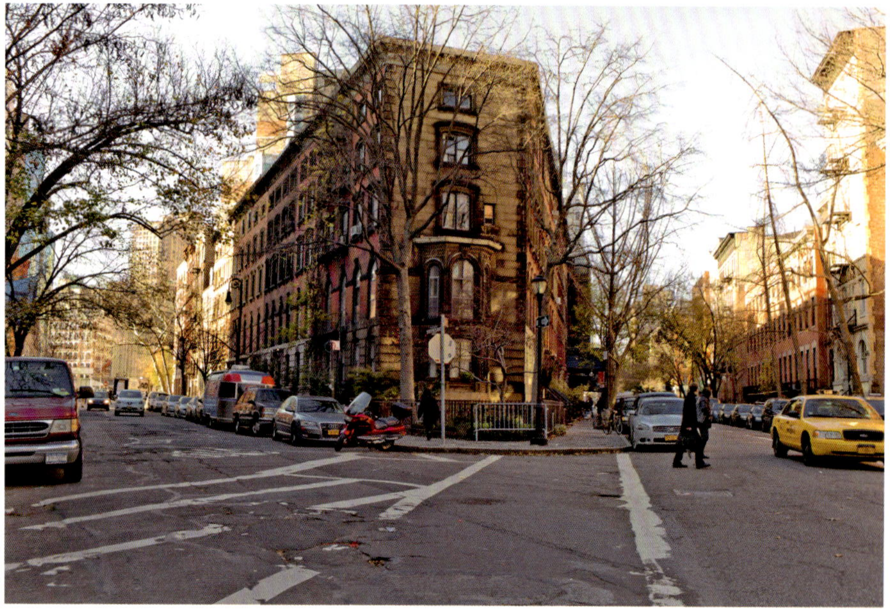

5

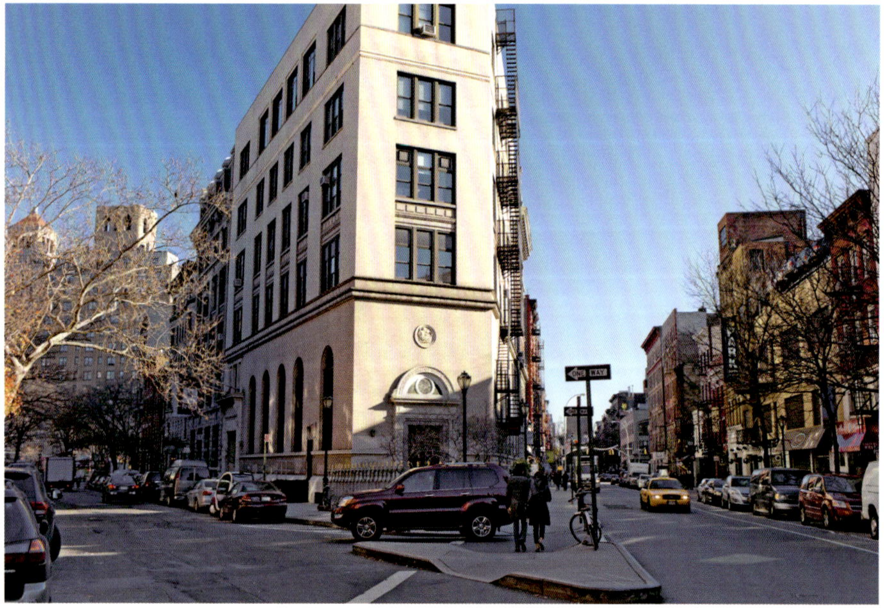

6

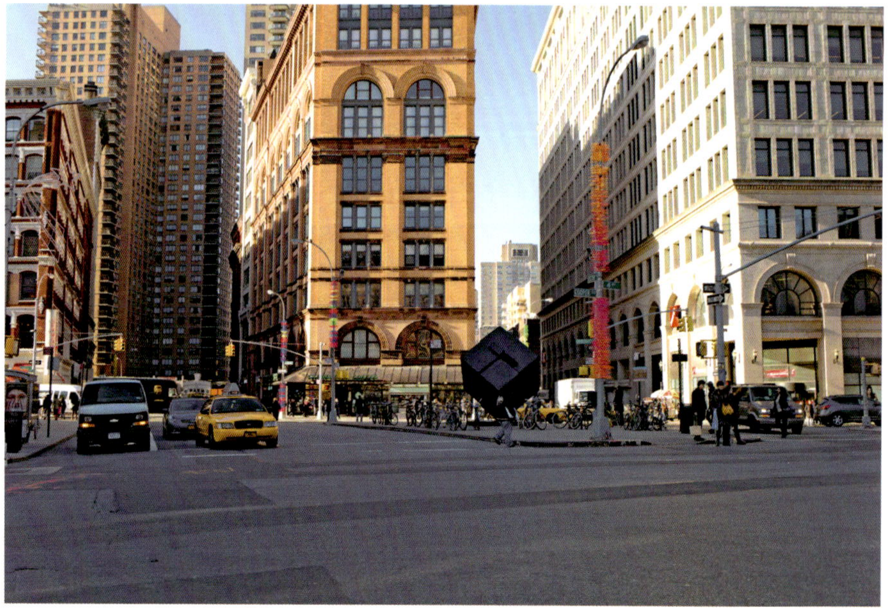

7

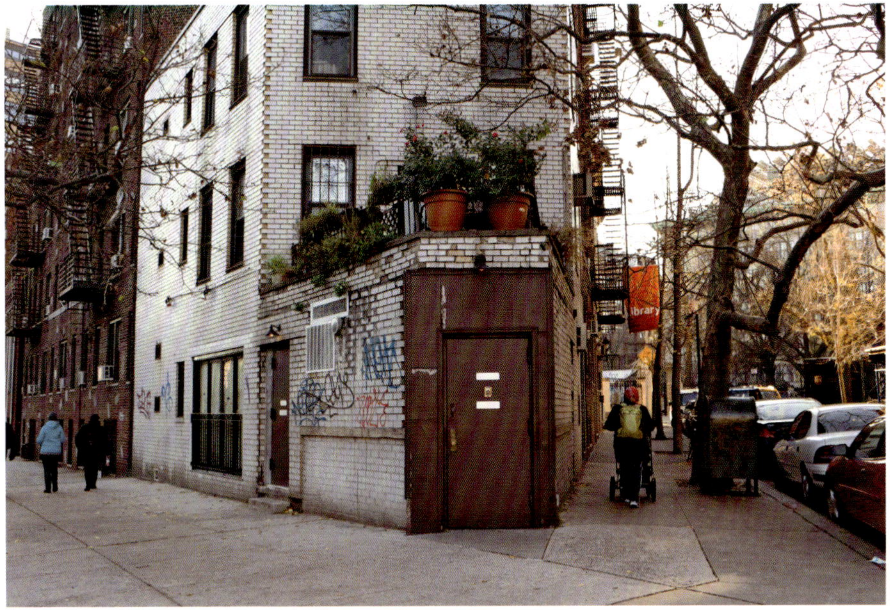

8

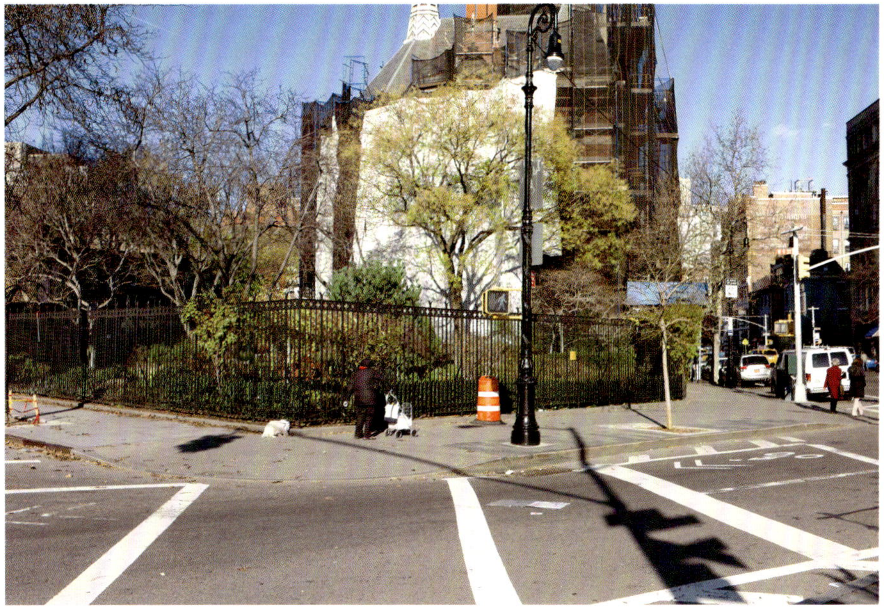

9

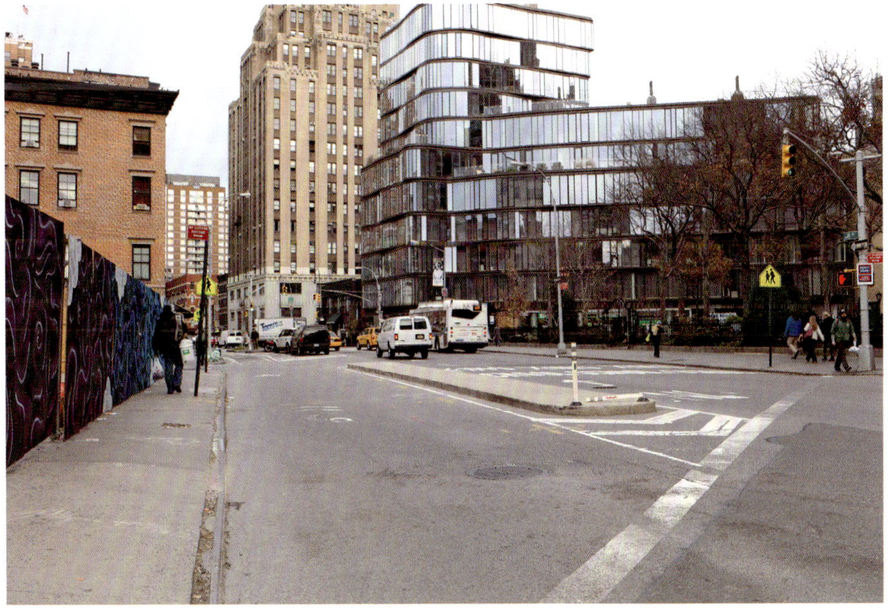

10

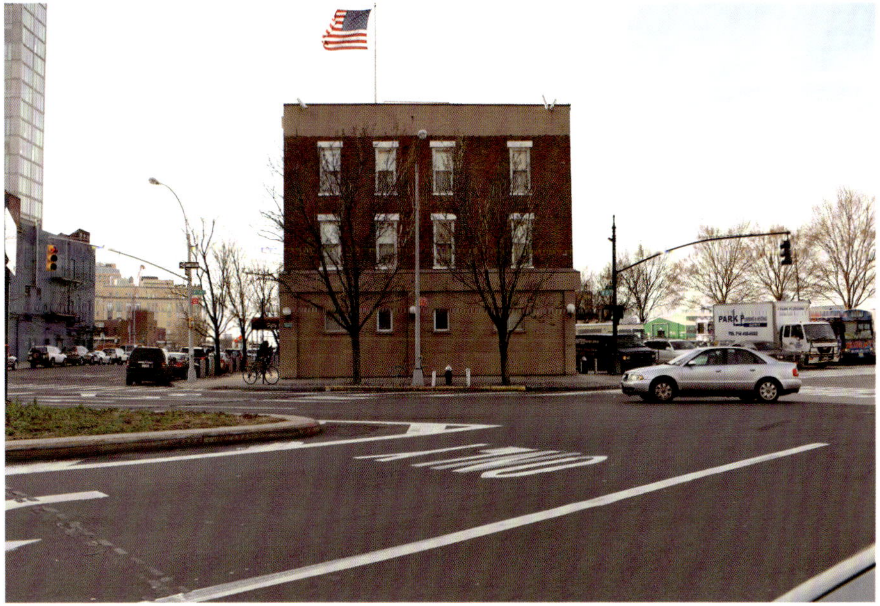

11

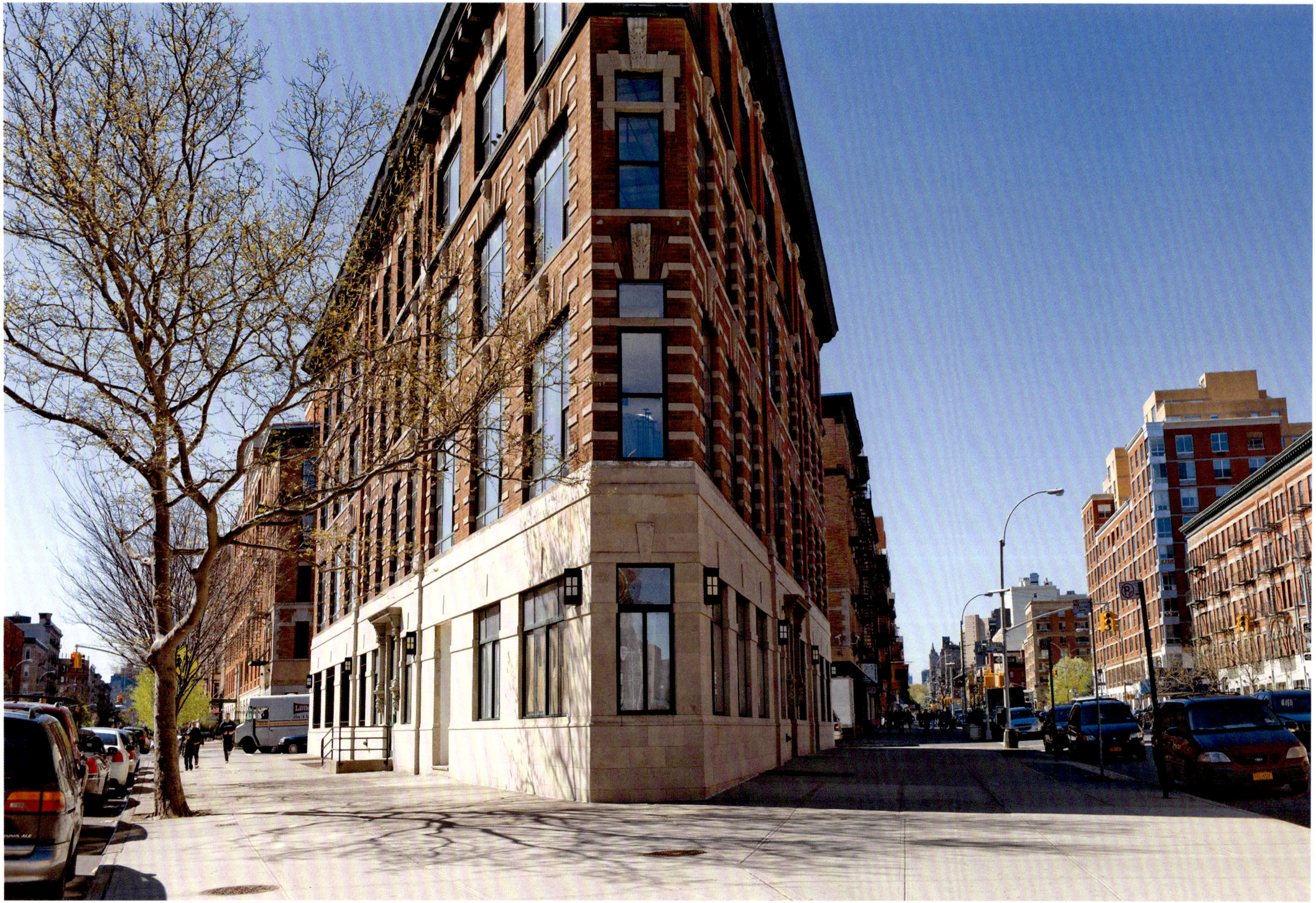

12

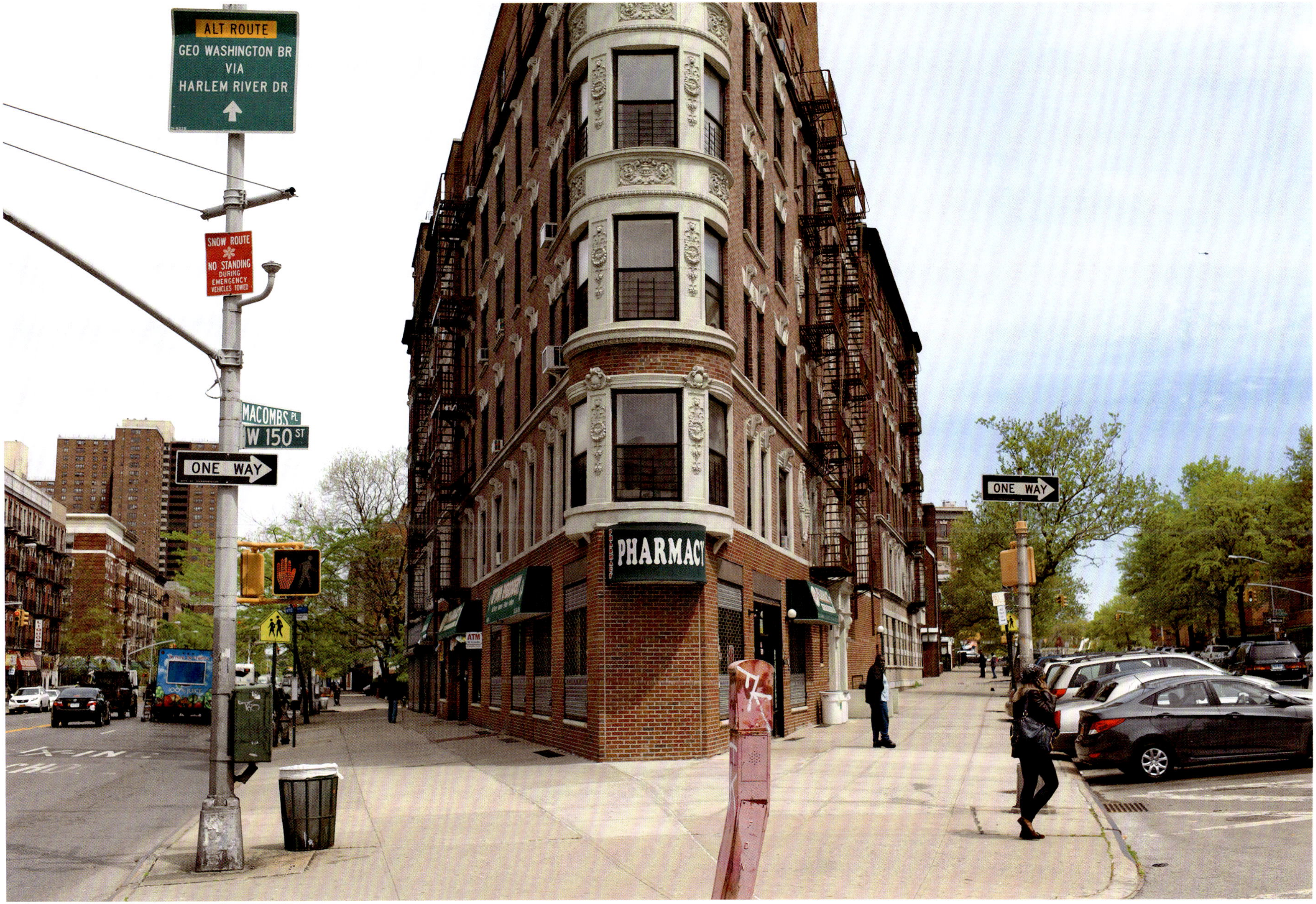
ALT ROUTE
GEO WASHINGTON BR
VIA
HARLEM RIVER DR
SNOW ROUTE
NO STANDING
DURING
EMERGENCY
VEHICLES TOWED
MACOMBS PL
W 150 ST
ONE WAY
PHARMACY
ONE WAY

13

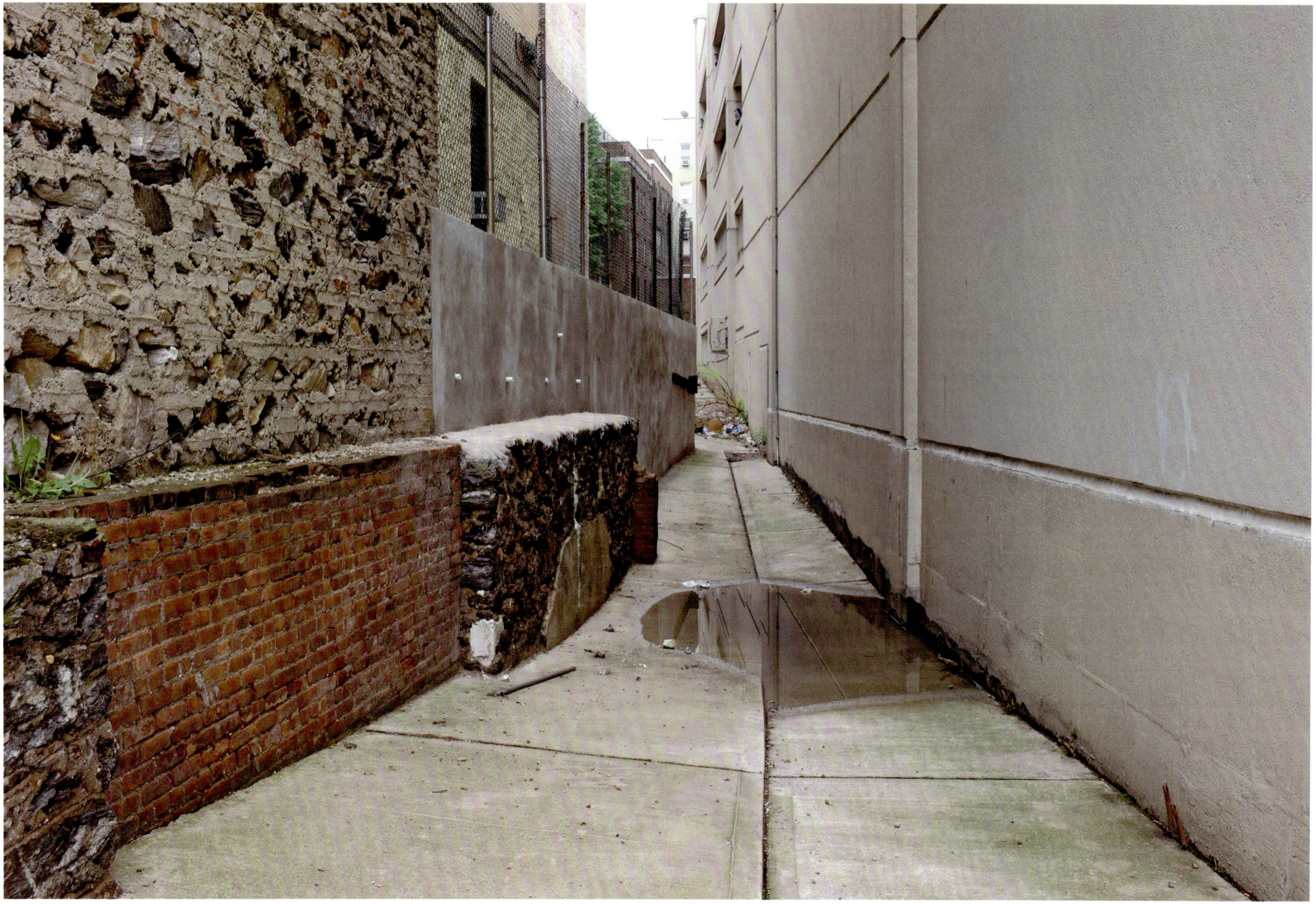

14

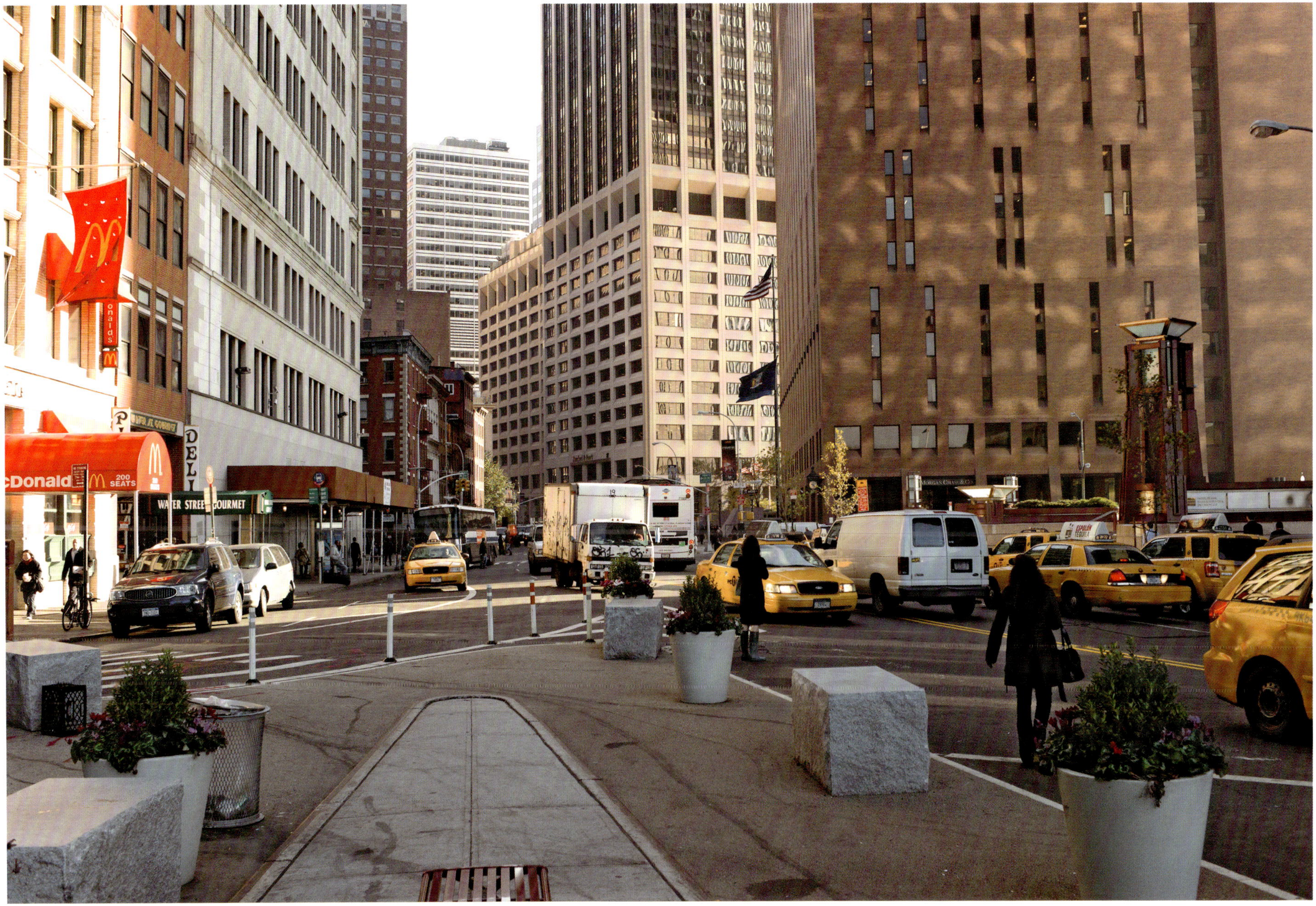

15

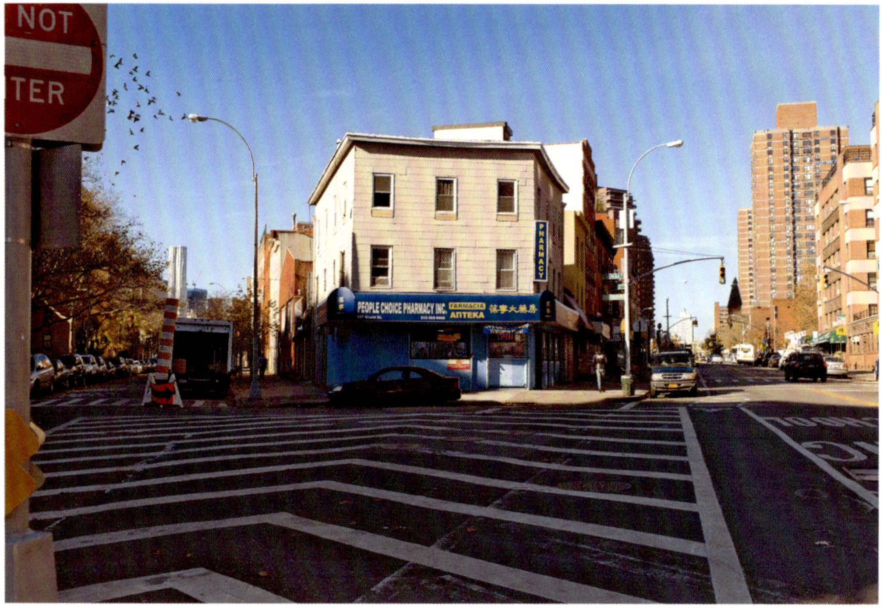
NOT
TER
PHARMACY
PEOPLE CHOICE PHARMACY INC.
FARMACIA
АПТЕКА

16

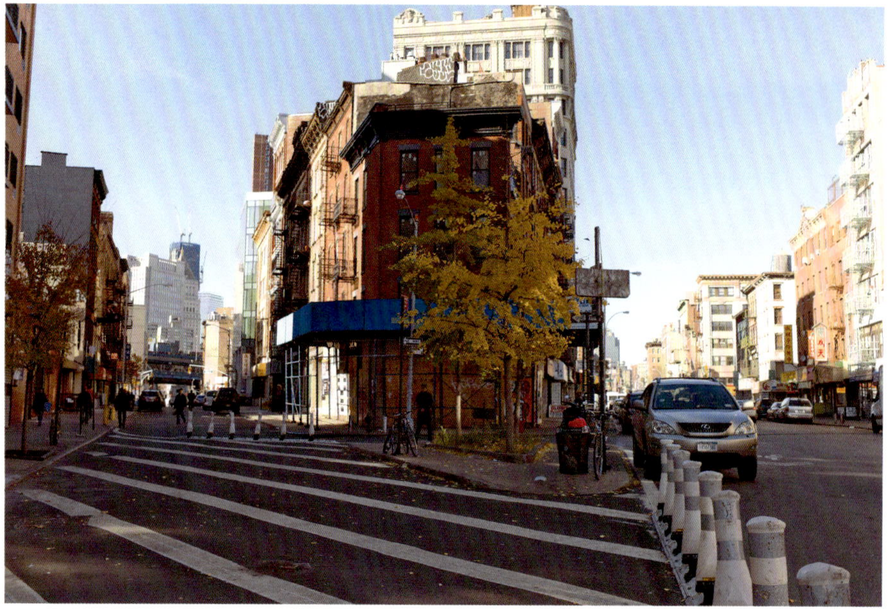

17

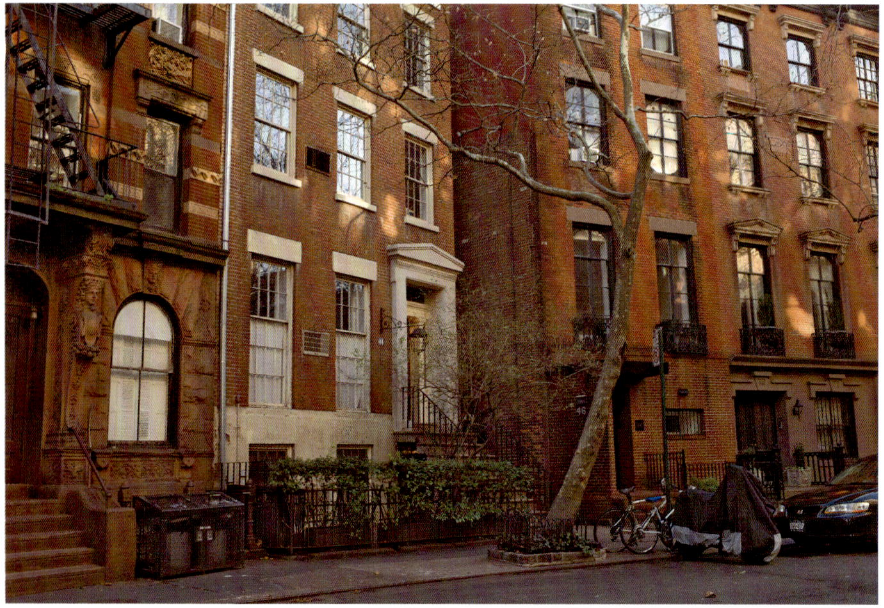

18

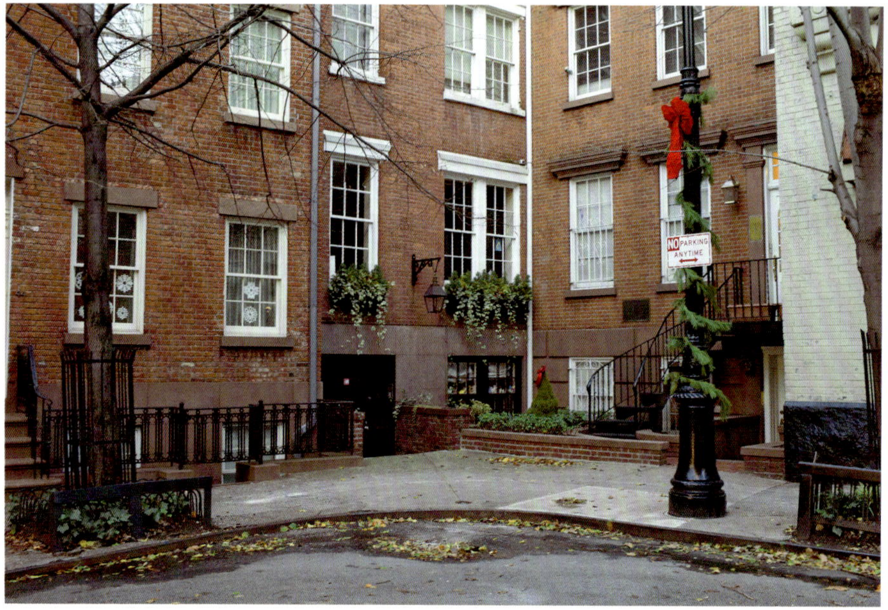
NO PARKING
ANYTIME

19

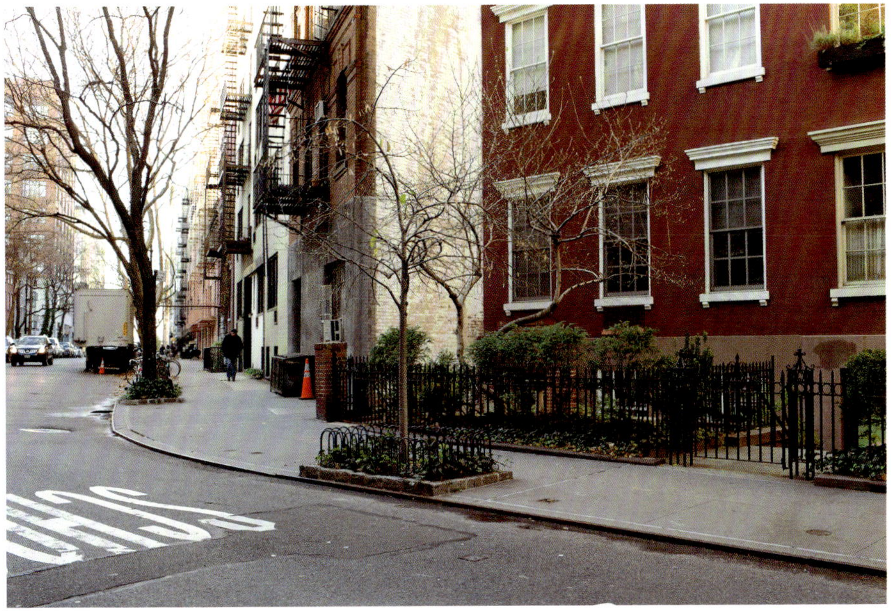

20

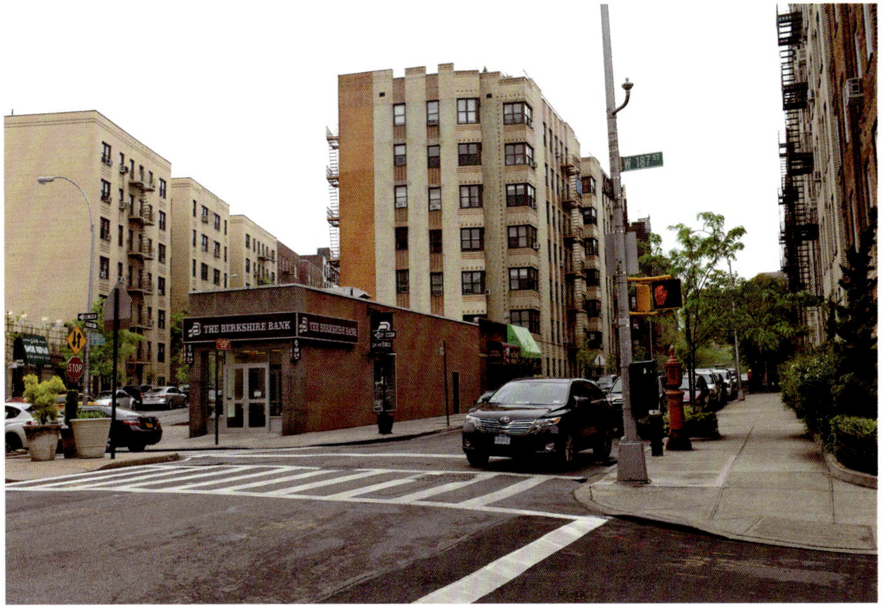

21

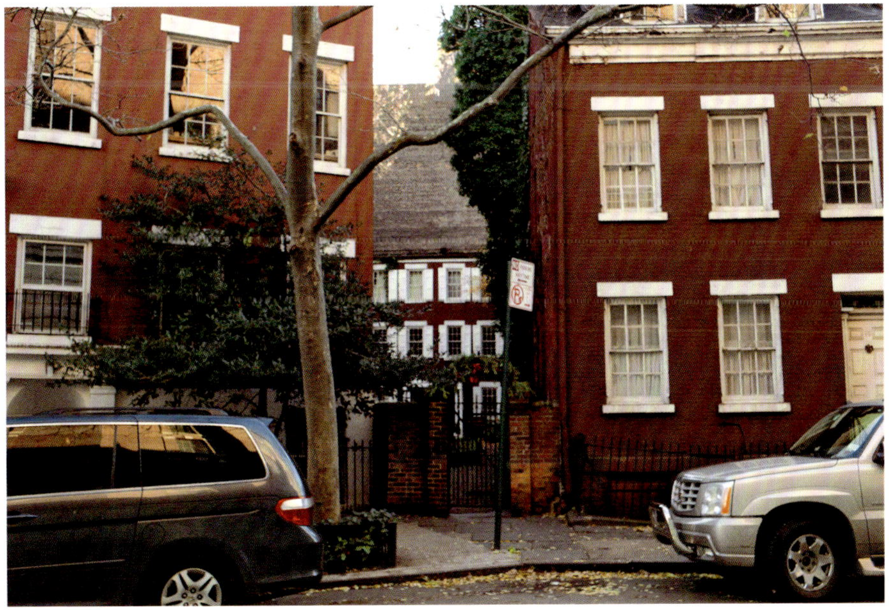

22

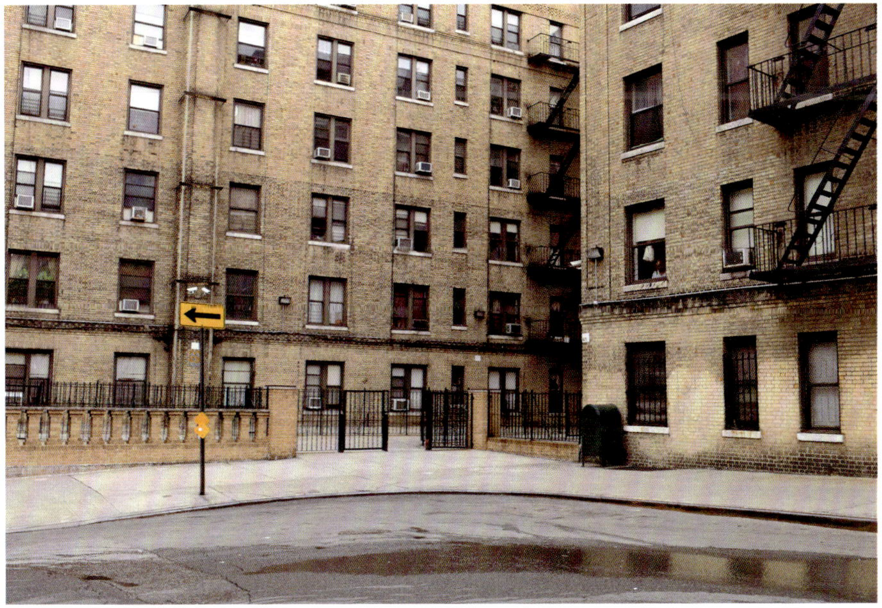

23

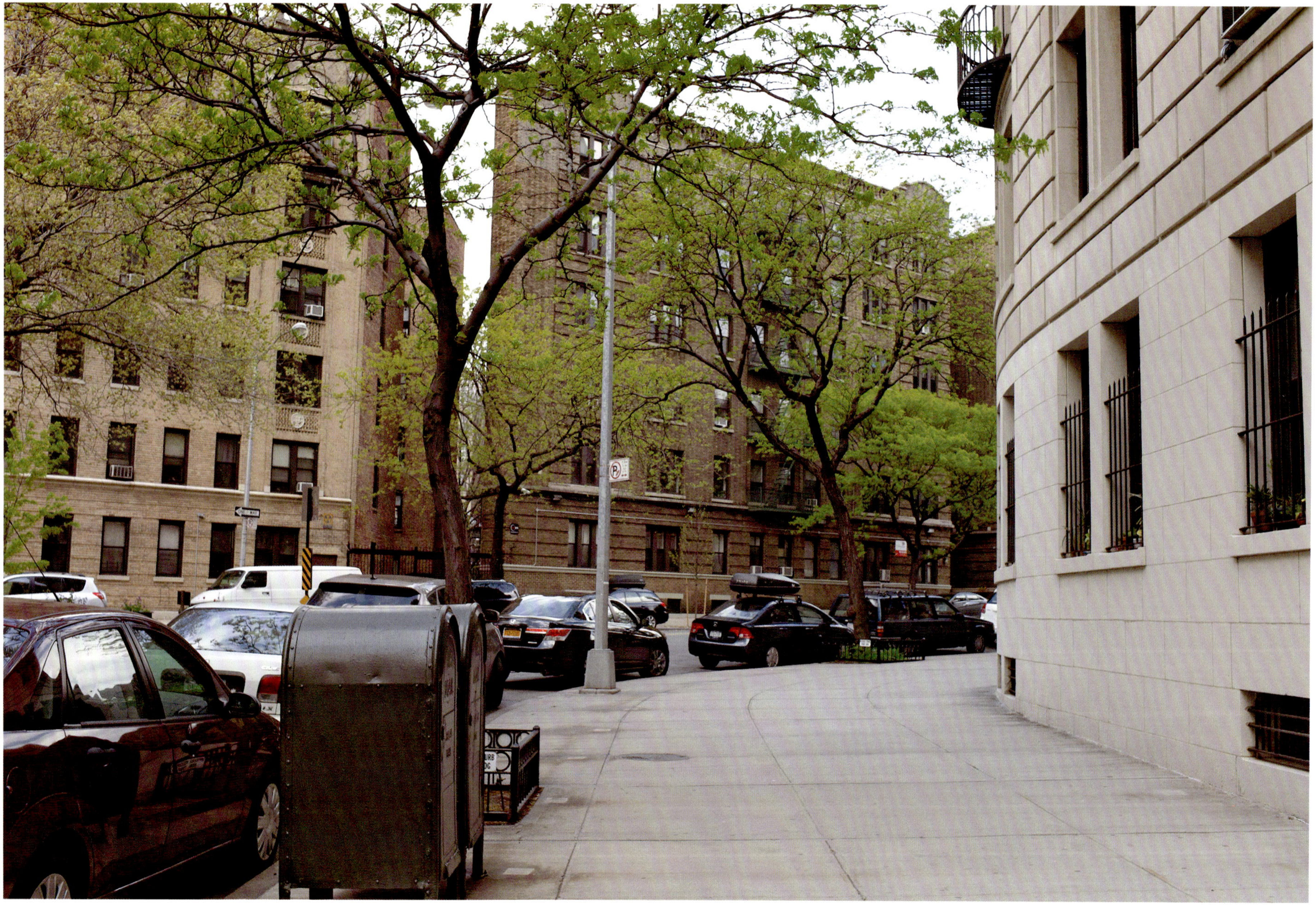

24

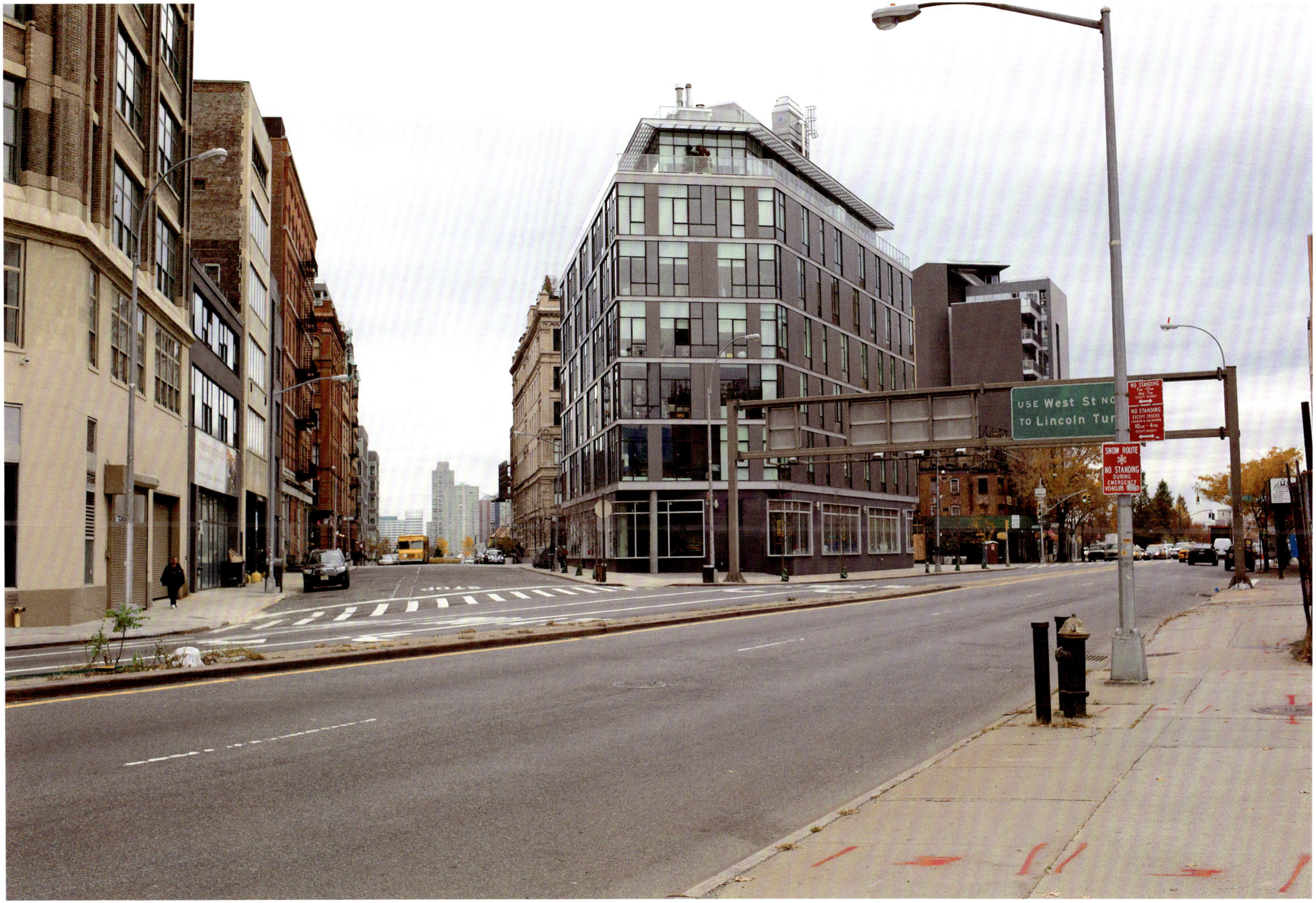

25

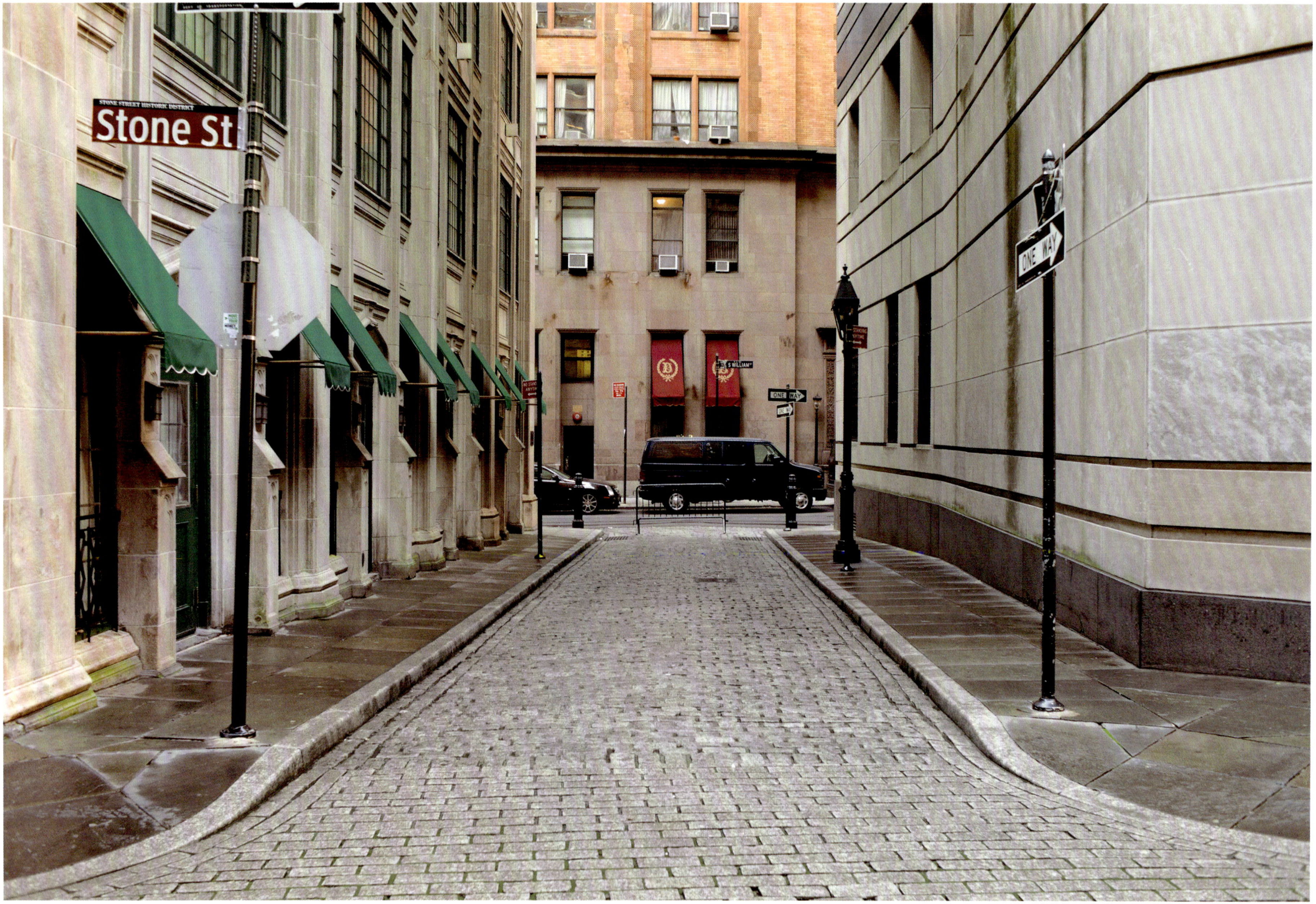
STONE STREET HISTORIC DISTRICT
Stone St
ONE WAY

LITTLE STREETS

Most of these streets are in lower Manhattan, remnants of early New Amsterdam. Walking through some of them calls to mind the layouts of medieval European cities; it's easy to forget where you are. The rest of the city falls away from the narrow warrens and horizon lines disappear, especially on the curved streets. The older streets came about more organically, and often delineated various private properties.

Several streets have retained their original, or at least older, buildings, like Sylvan Terrace uptown. Most of the other short streets uptown were further truncated by later incursions (bridges, highways, tunnels, etc.). And they often feel just like that: cut off from their destination.

1 Financial District
2 West Village
3 Tribeca
4 Lower Manhattan
5 Lower Manhattan
6 Tribeca
7 West Village
8 Chinatown
9 Tribeca
10 Tribeca
11 Tribeca
12 NoHo
13 Washington Heights
14 Tribeca
15 NoHo
16 West Village
17 West Village
18 East Village
19 Jumel Terrace
20 SoHo
21 Yorkville
22 West Village
23 West Village

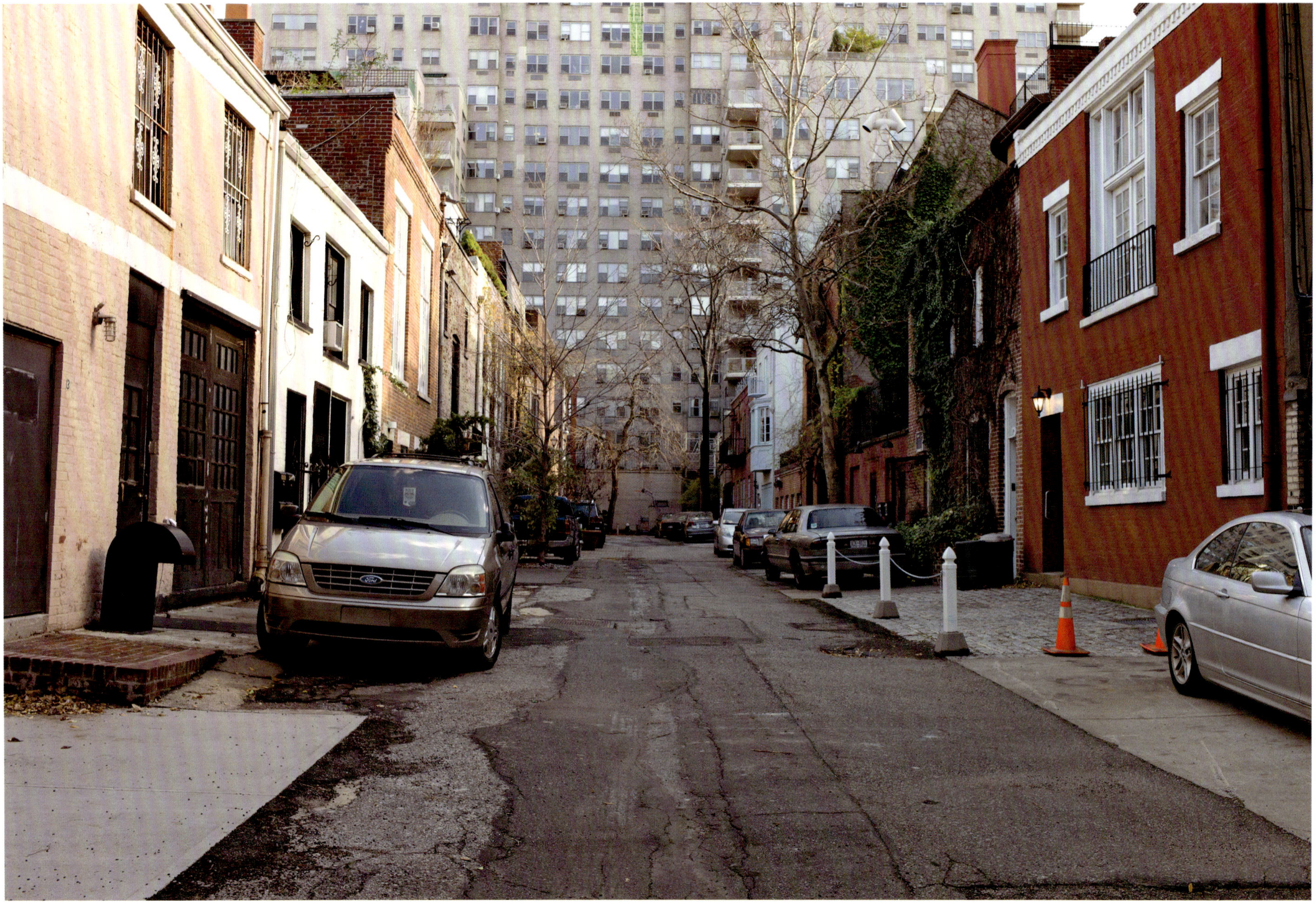

2

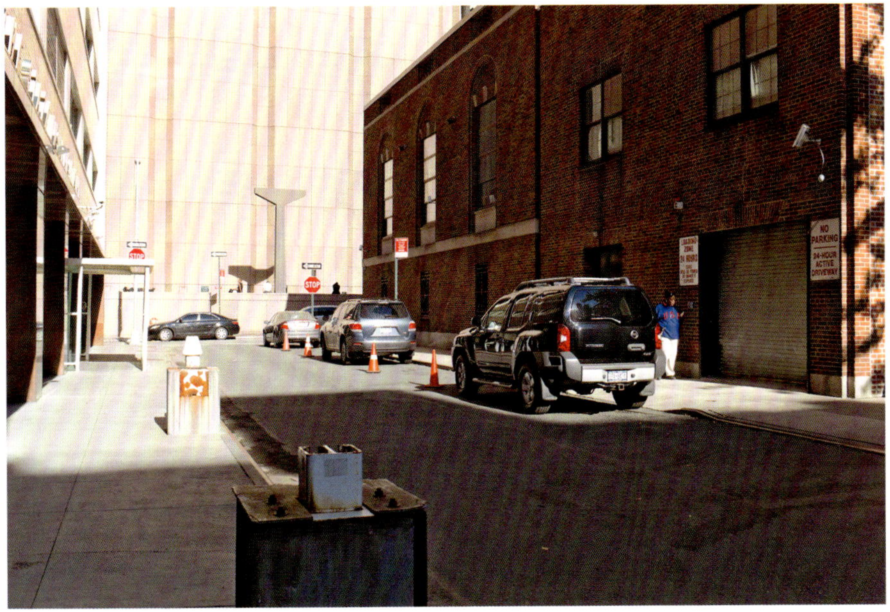

3

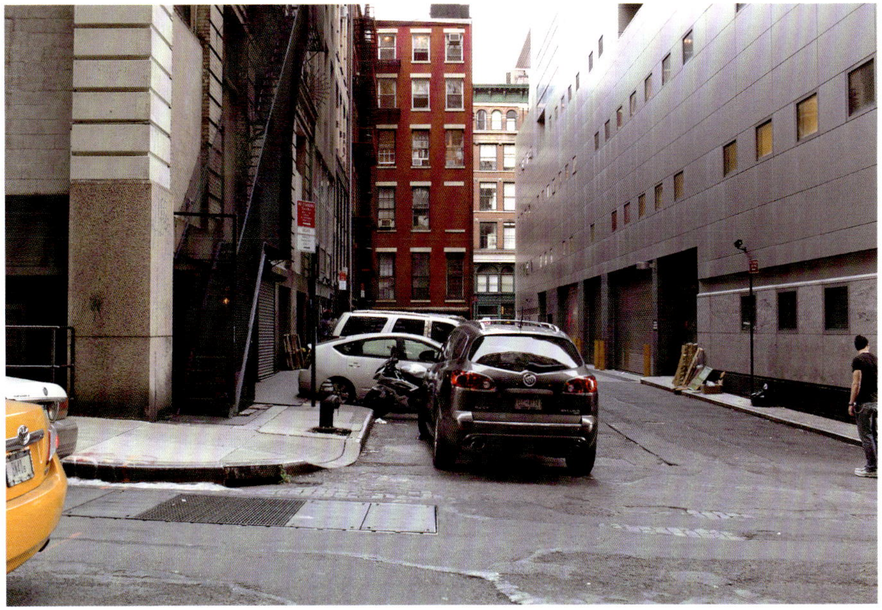

4

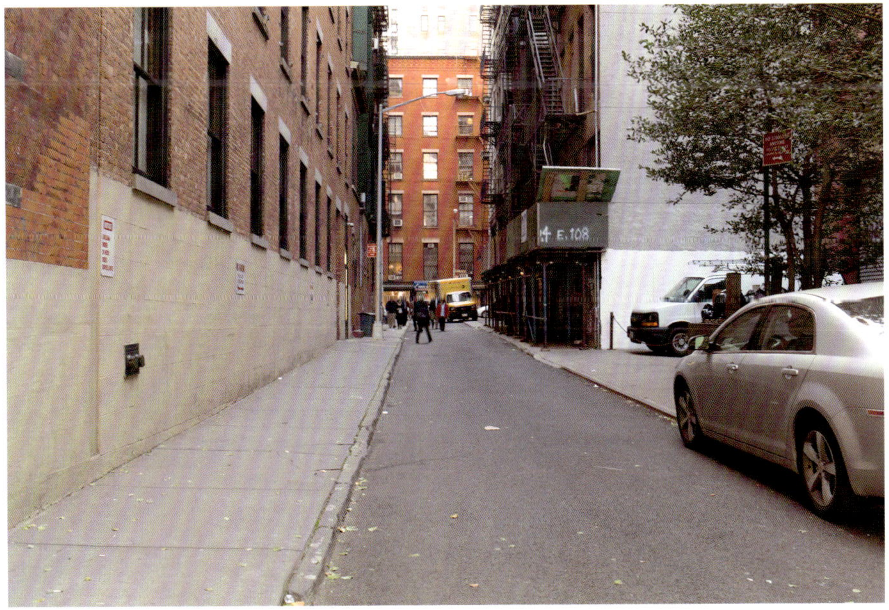

5

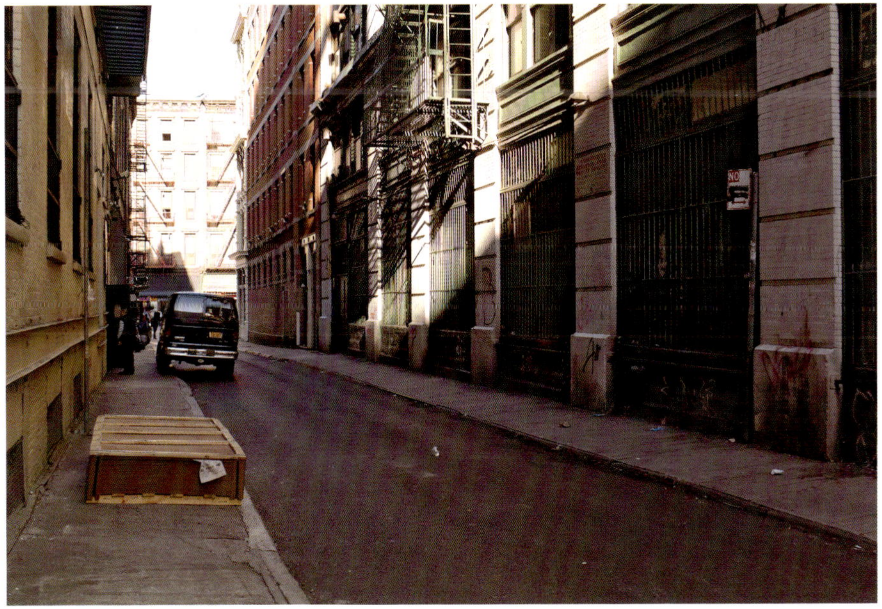

6

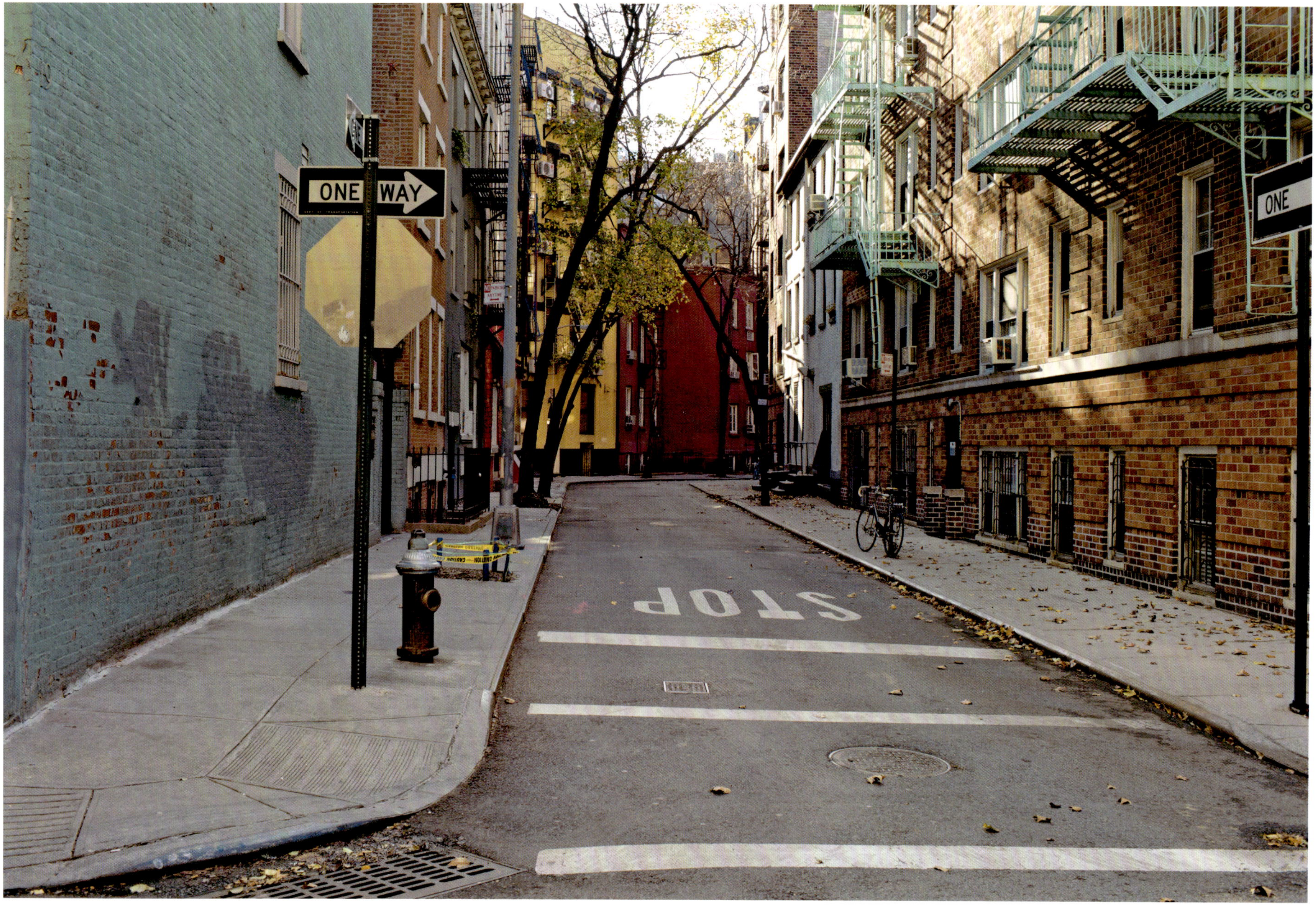

7

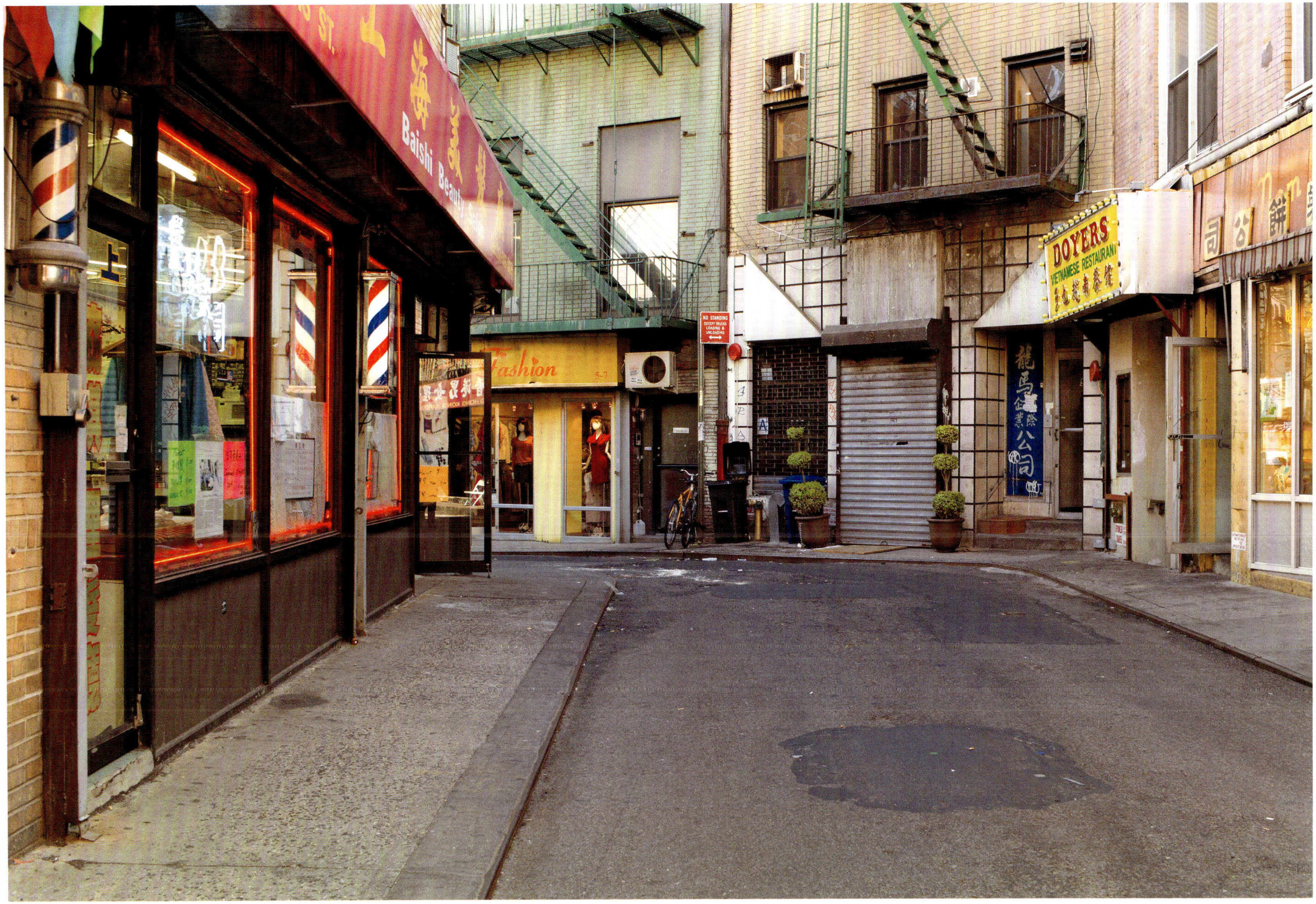

8

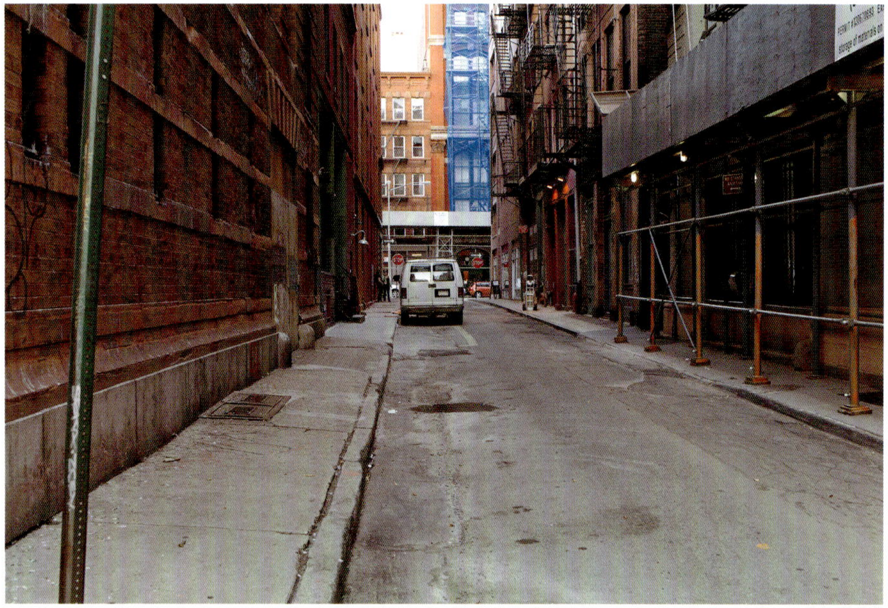

9

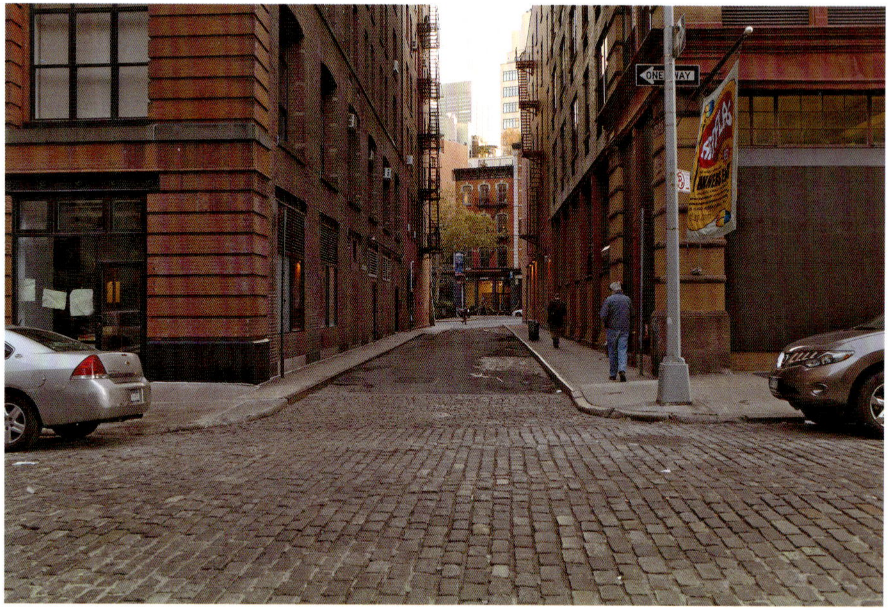

10

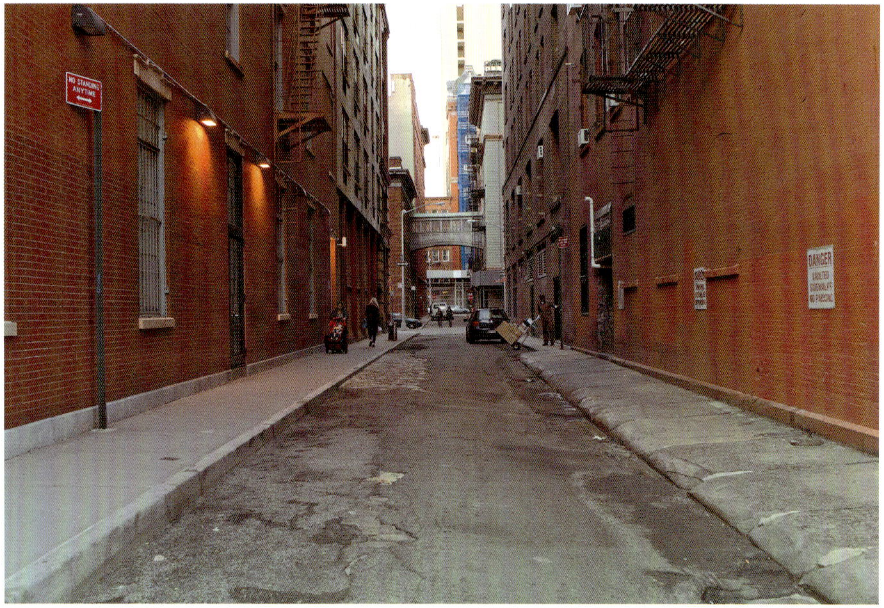

11

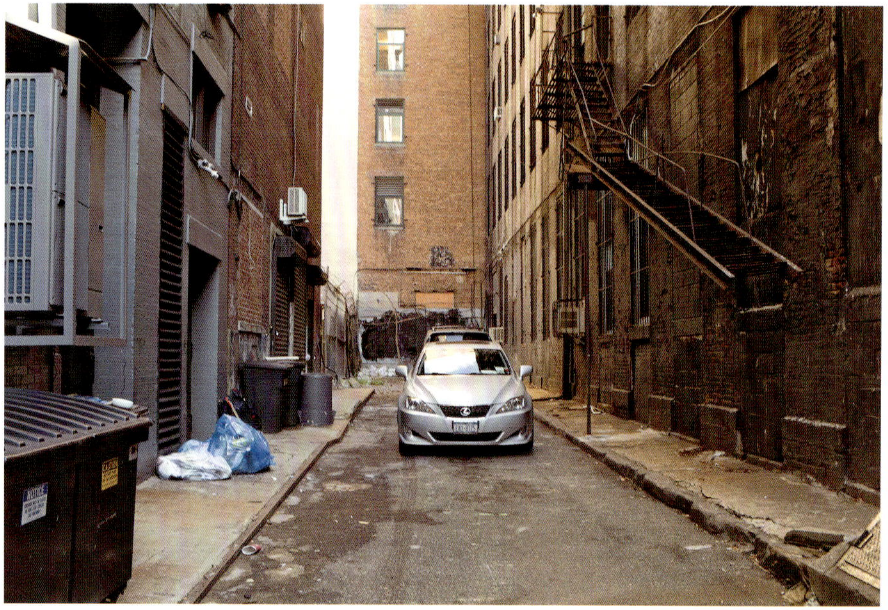

12

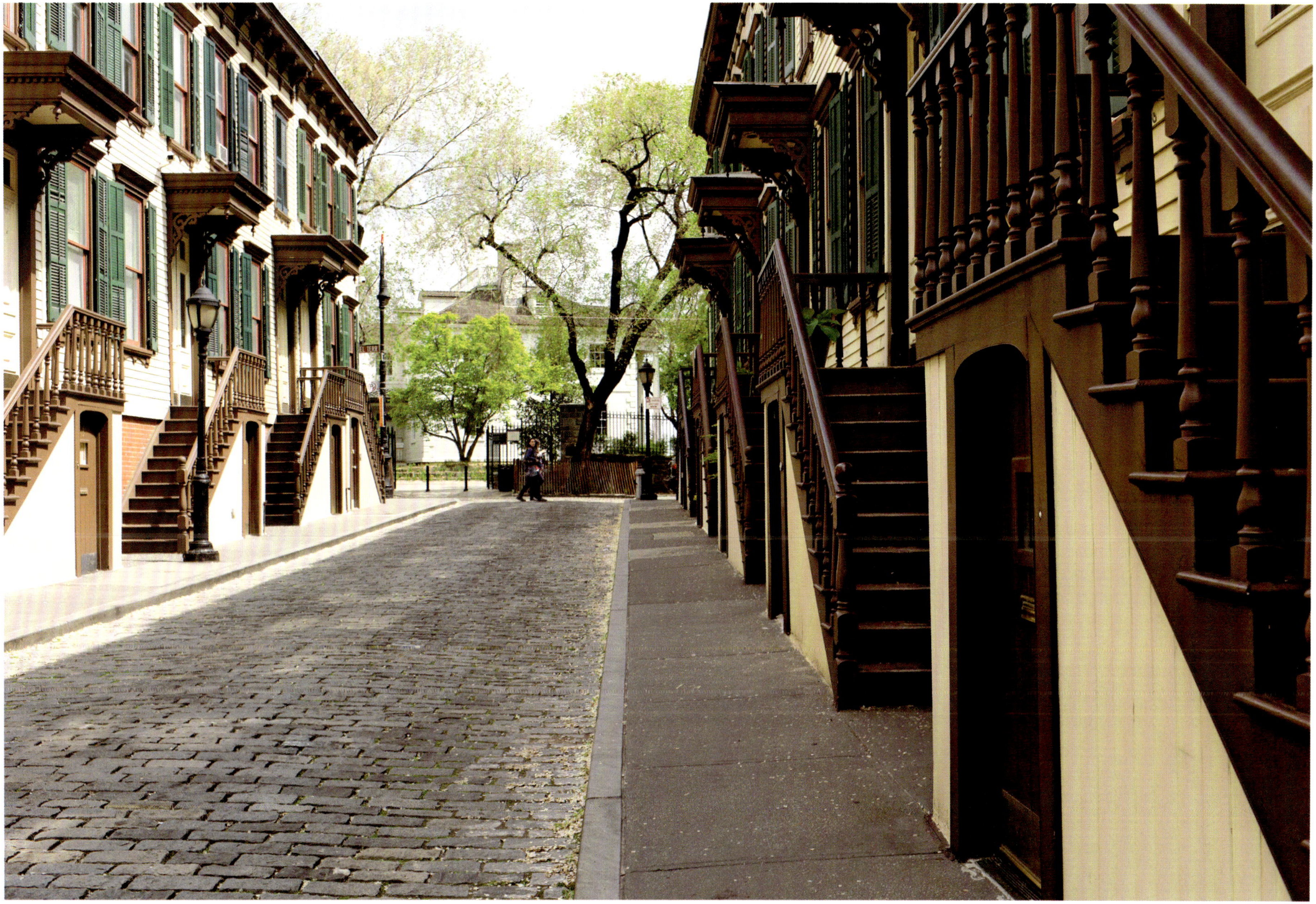

13

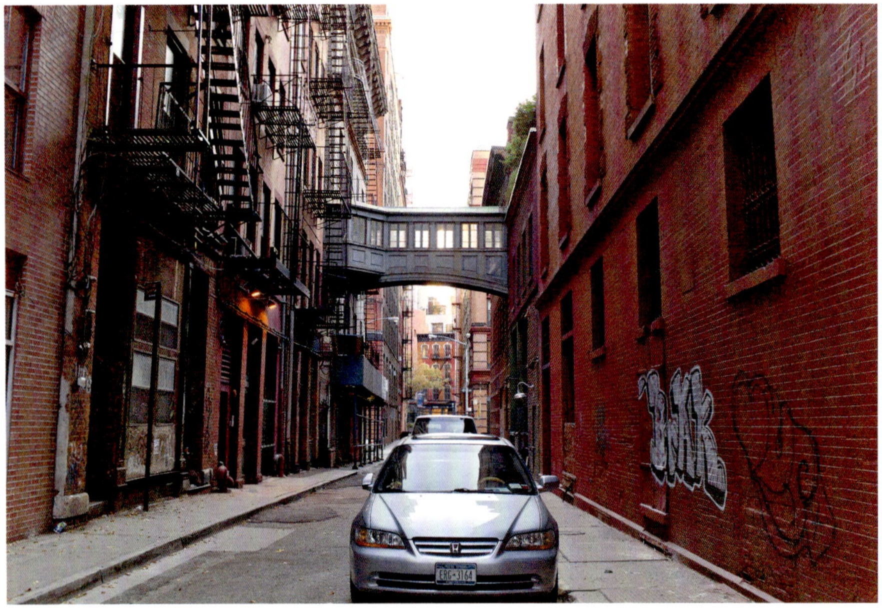

14

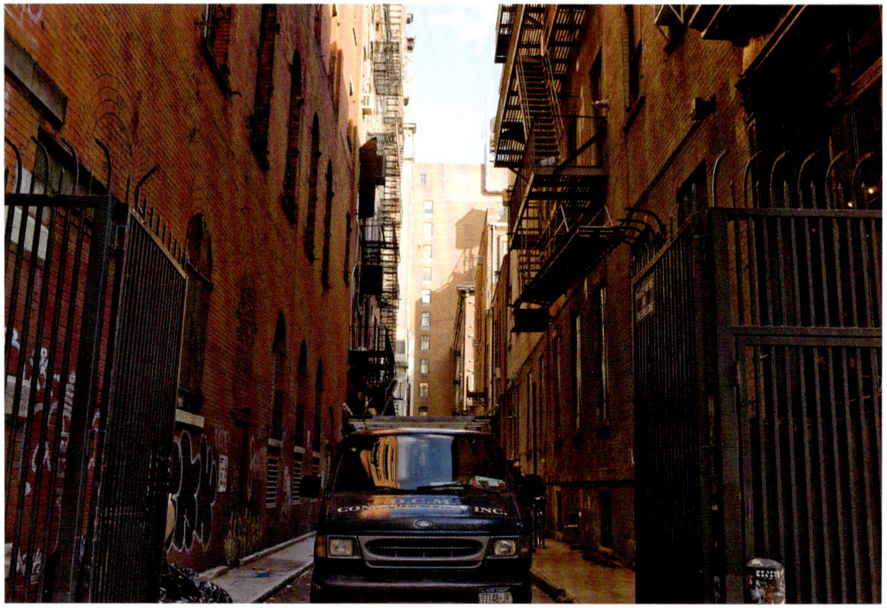

15

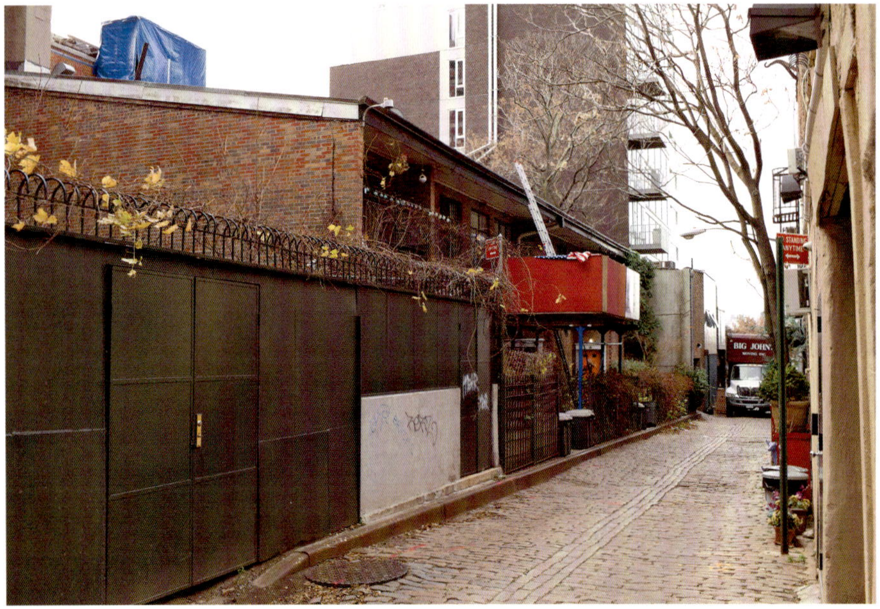

16

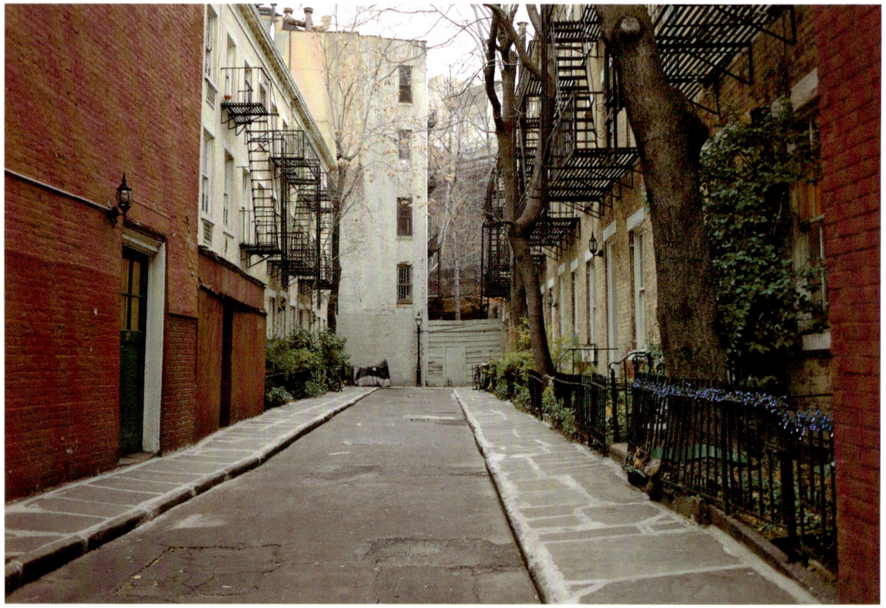

17

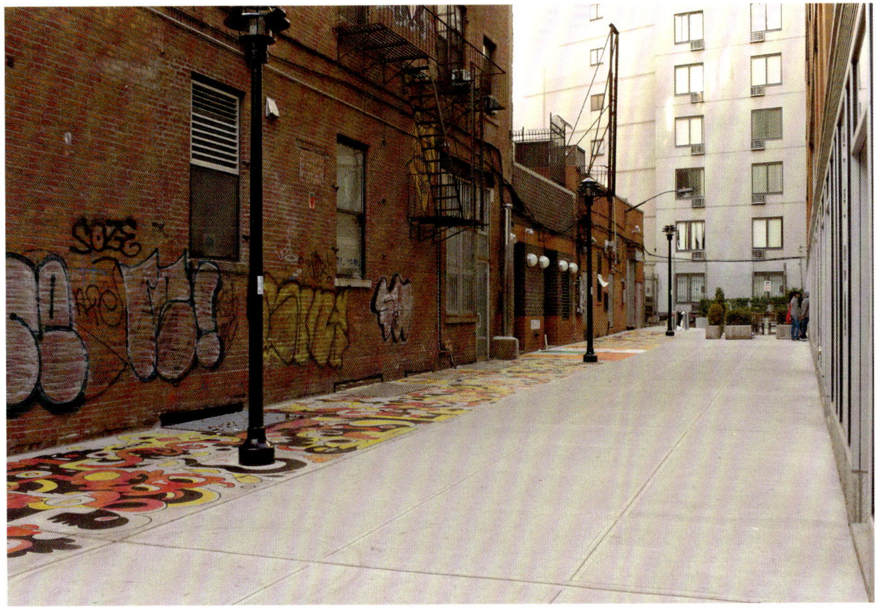

18

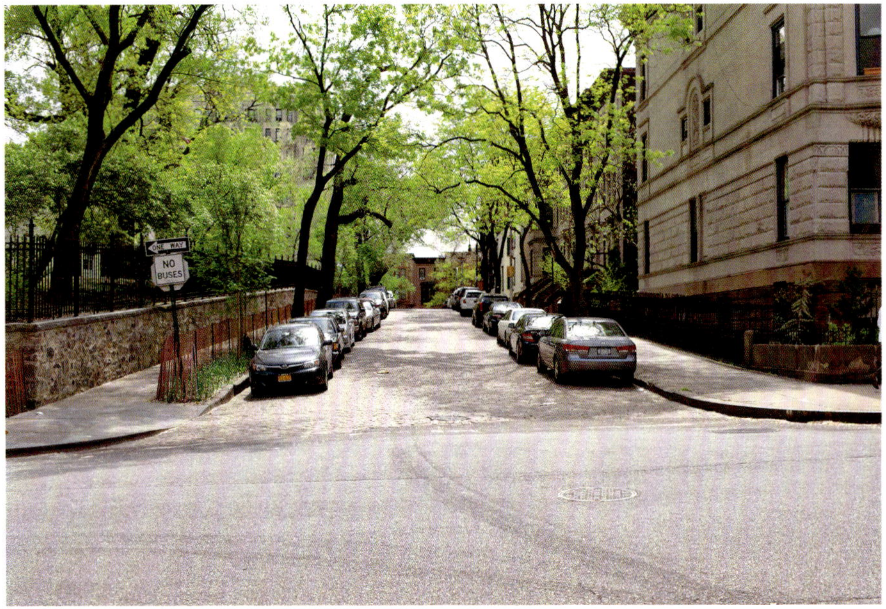

19

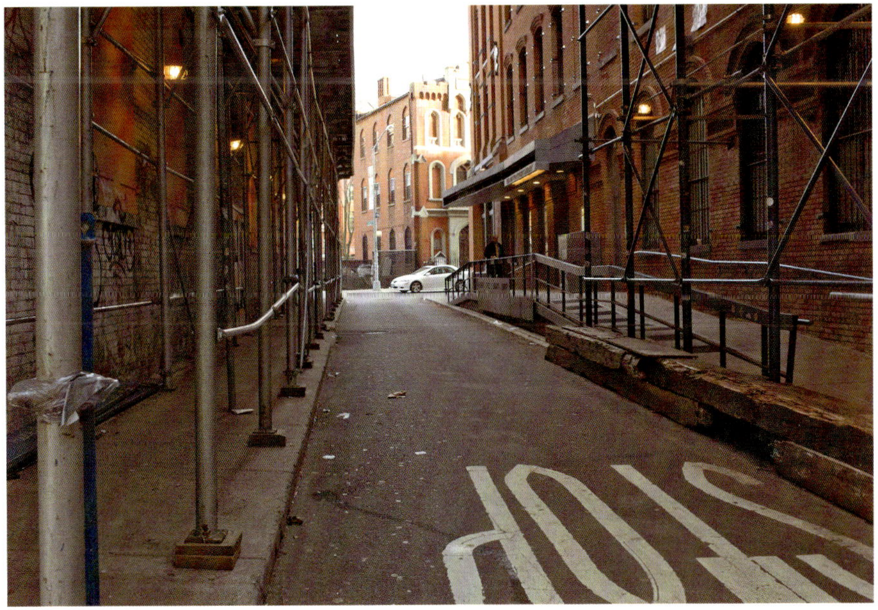

20

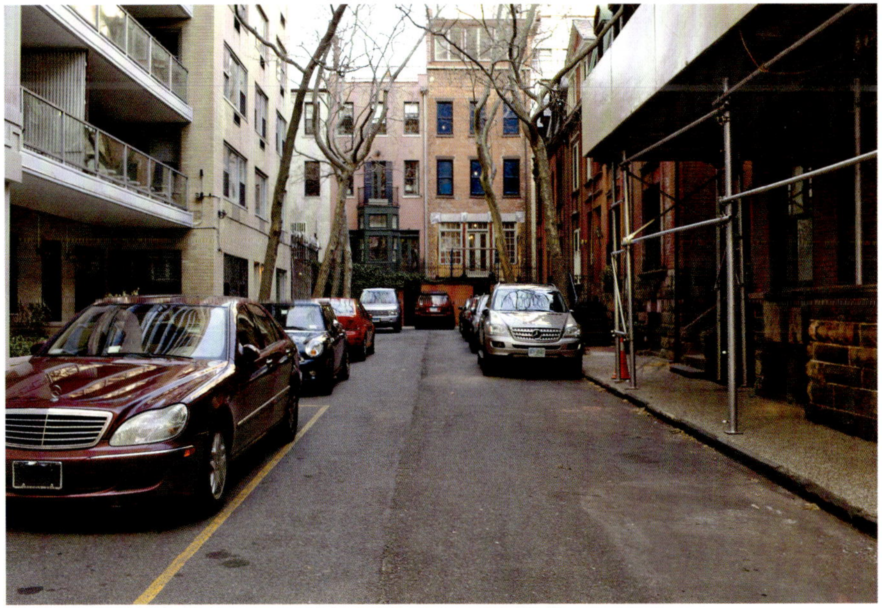

21

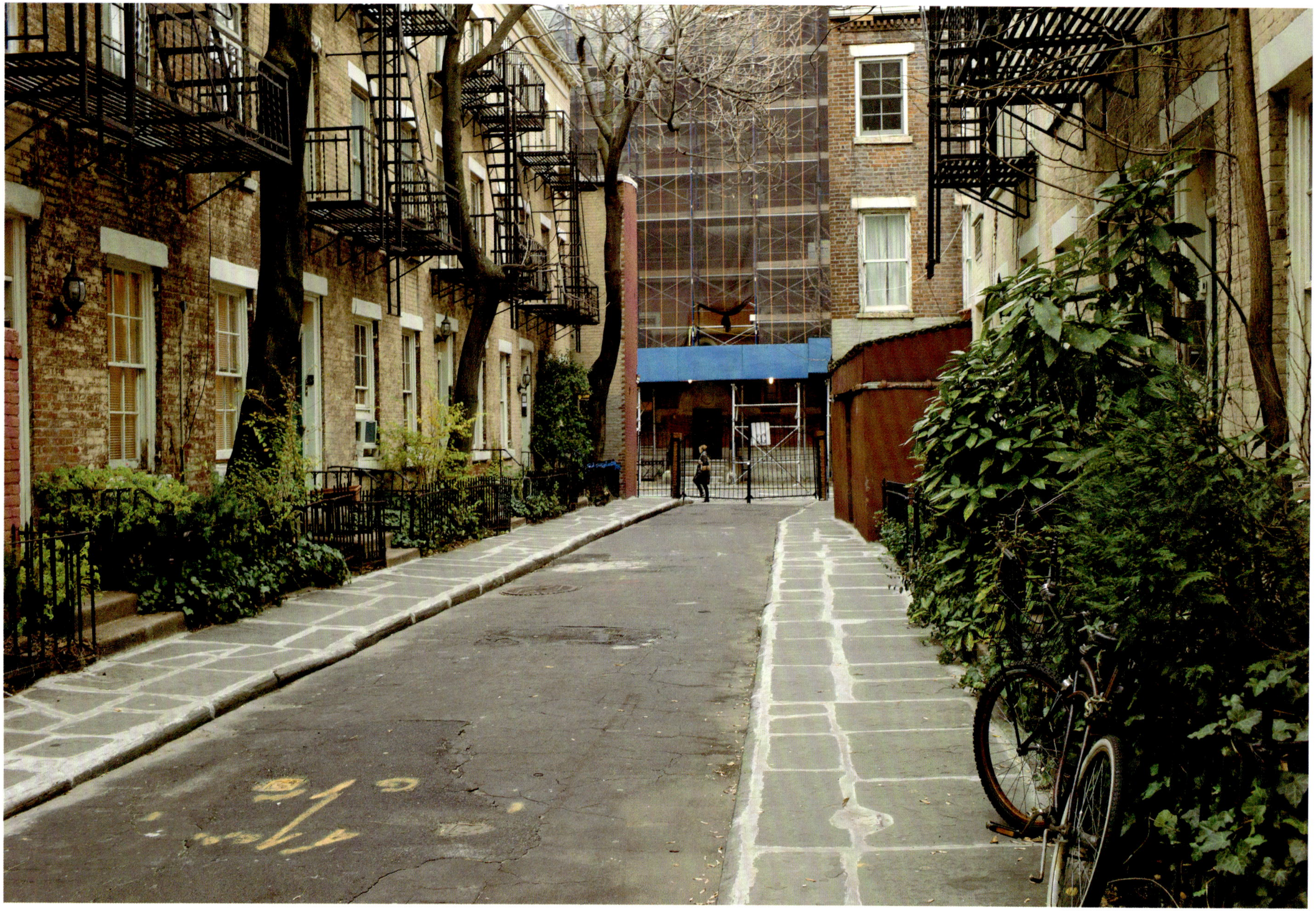

22

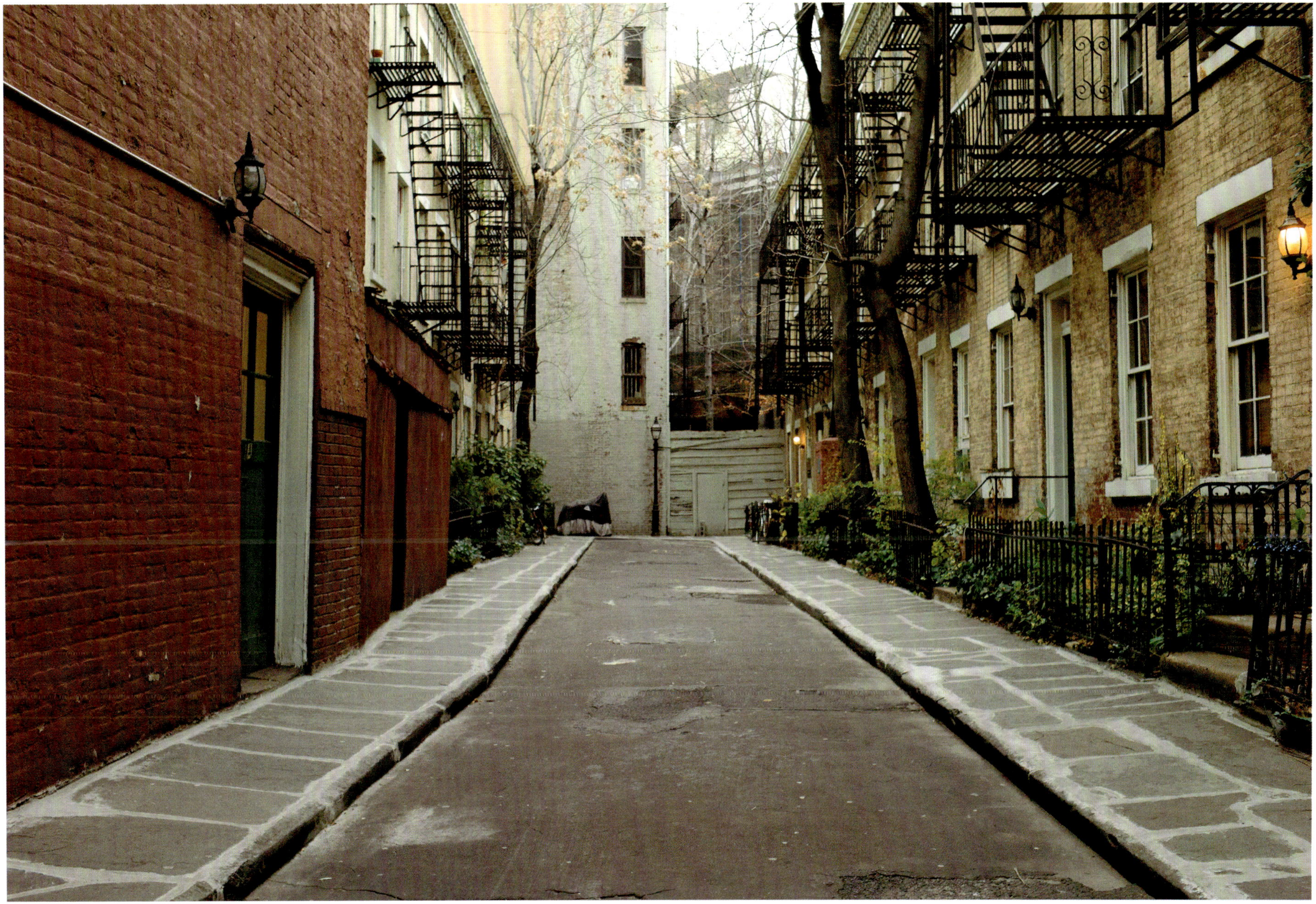

23

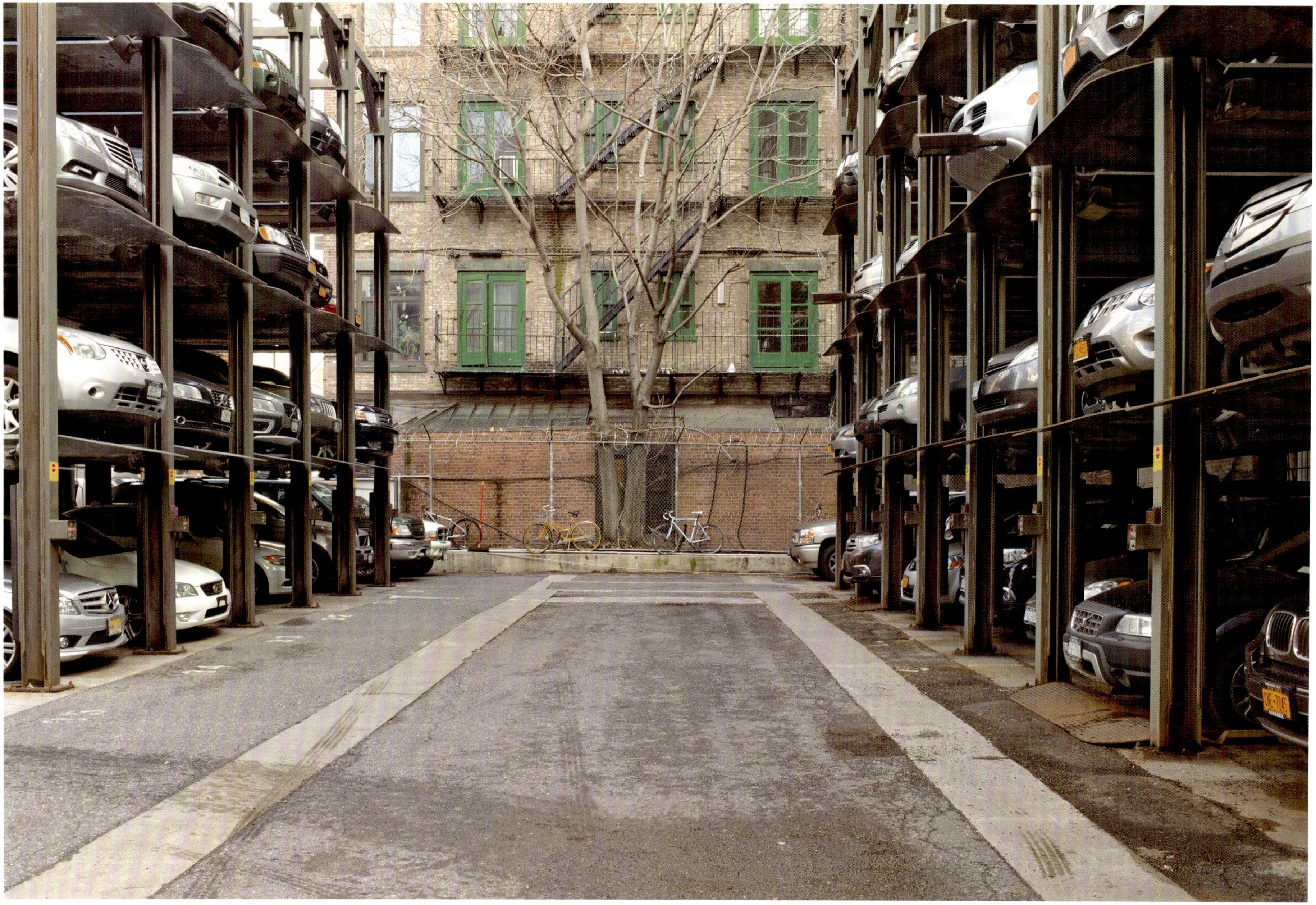

PARKING LOTS

Even in a place as dependent on mass transportation as Manhattan, parking lots still take up an inordinate amount of valuable space. There are over 1100 parking facilities in Manhattan. In particularly dense areas lifts have been installed to allow for multi-level storage. These concentrations of asphalt and metal create heat islands and hardscape where more green spaces are needed. Drivers also take over sidewalks, blocking what little space is left for pedestrians.

Zoned parking minimums, requiring builders to include parking in their buildings, helped create this problem and also increase building costs. Instead of adding more apartments, room must be made for specific quotas of cars. This relic of an earlier zoning philosophy that designed the city around car travel is now under review, to some degree. And many transit advocates hope these parking minimums can be eliminated entirely. Congestion only increases and serious effort will be required to prevent the city from choking on cars.

1 East Village
2 Hell's Kitchen
3 Garment District
4 West Village
5 Financial District
6 Kips Bay
7 Tribeca
8 West Village
9 Chelsea
10 Chinatown
11 SoHo
12 Garment District
13 Tribeca
14 Chelsea
15 Chelsea
16 East Harlem
17 Lower East Side
18 Midtown
19 SoHo
20 Flatiron
21 Kips Bay
22 South Street Seaport
23 Chelsea

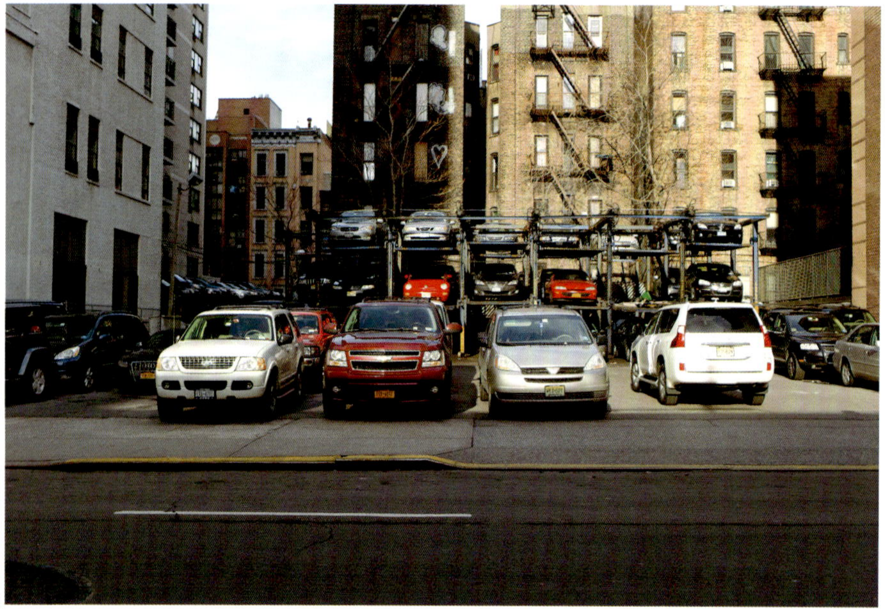

2

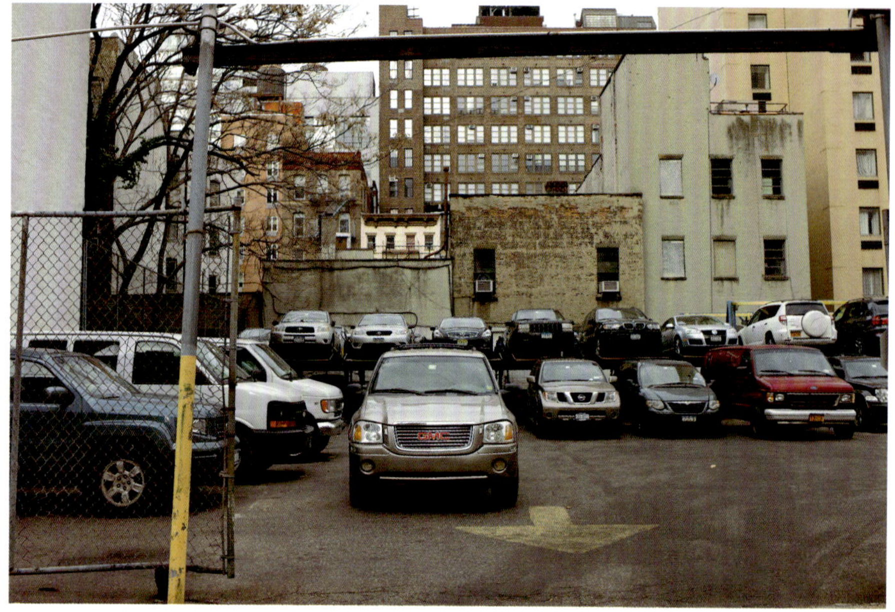

3

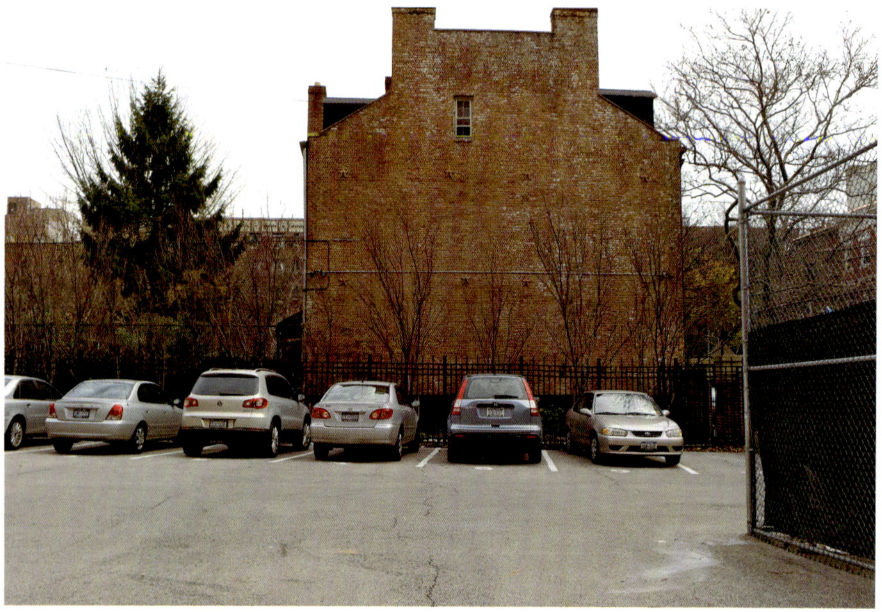

4

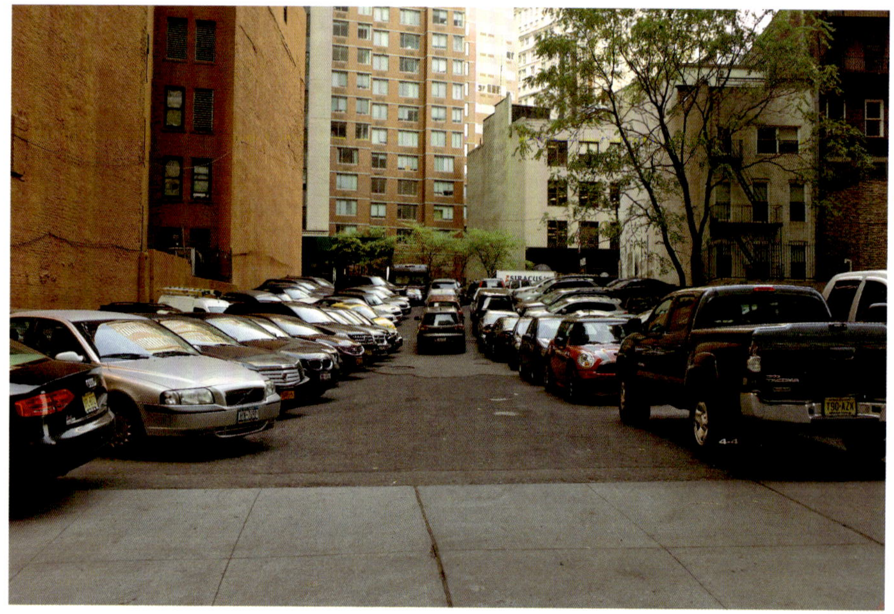

5

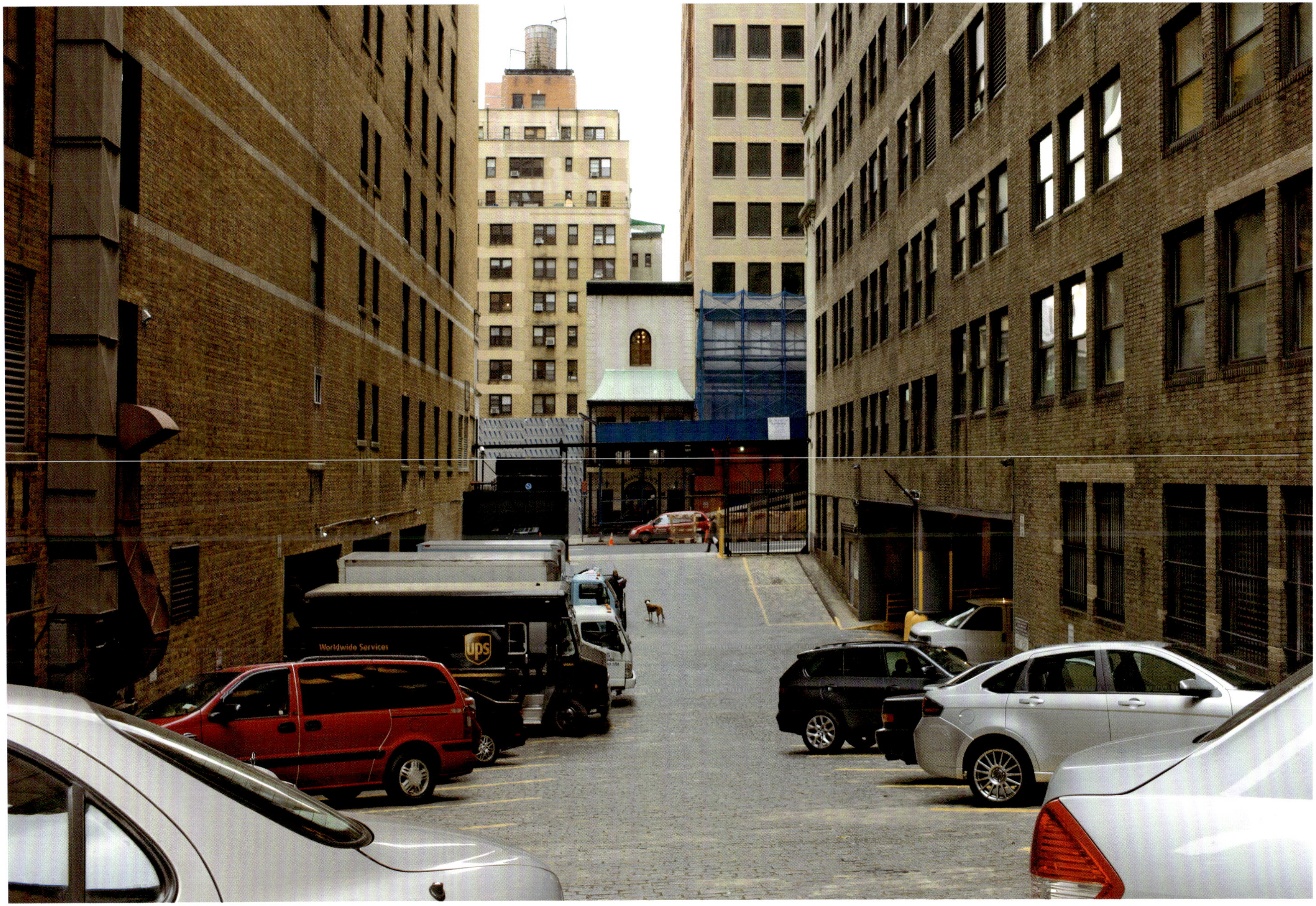

6

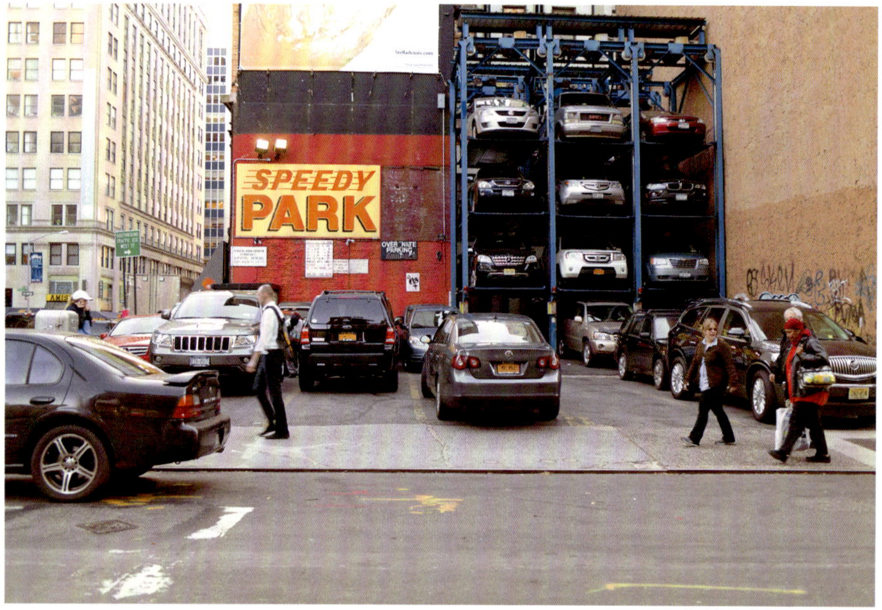
SPEEDY
PARK
Secaucus Junction
Low monthly rates
888-parkfast
parkfast.com
Edison
PARK
FAST
212·storage
OPEN 24 HOURS

7

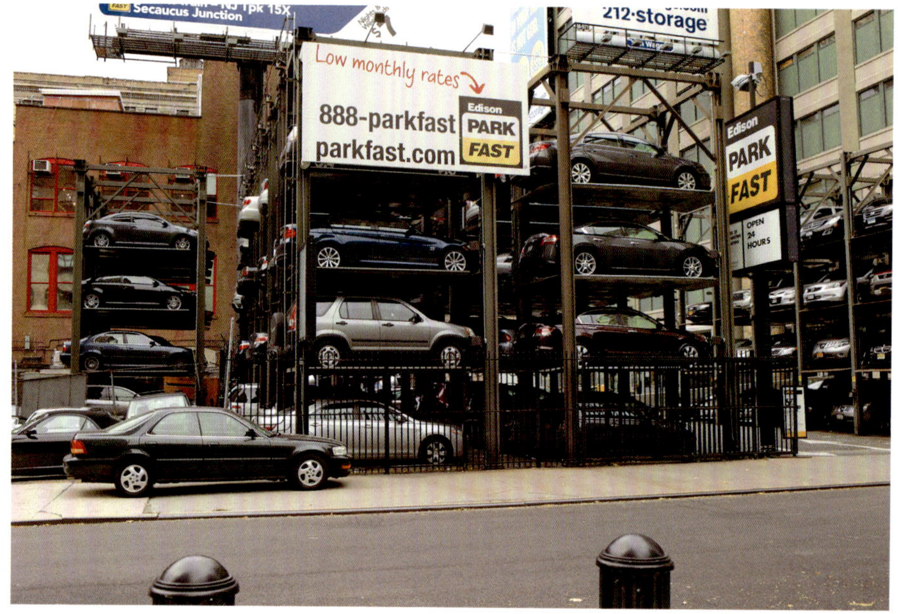

8

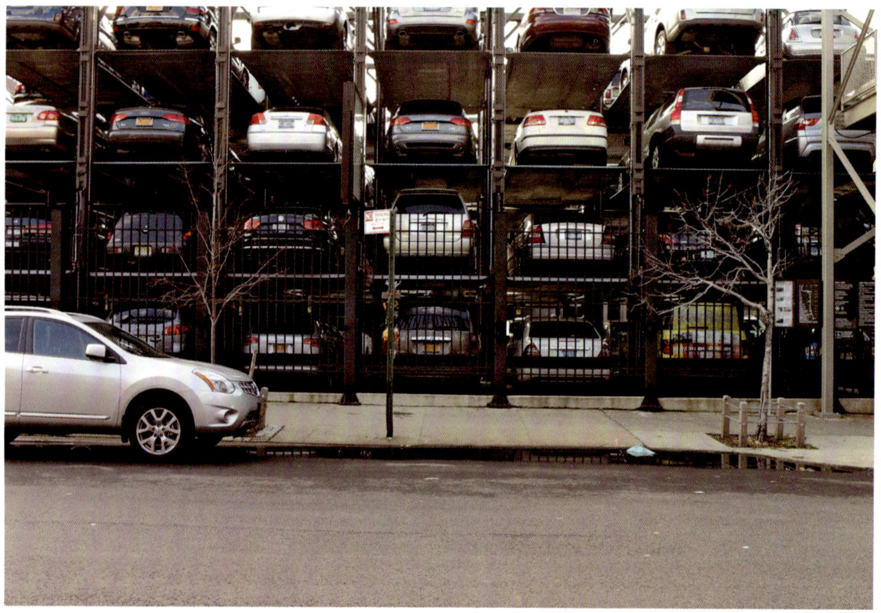

9

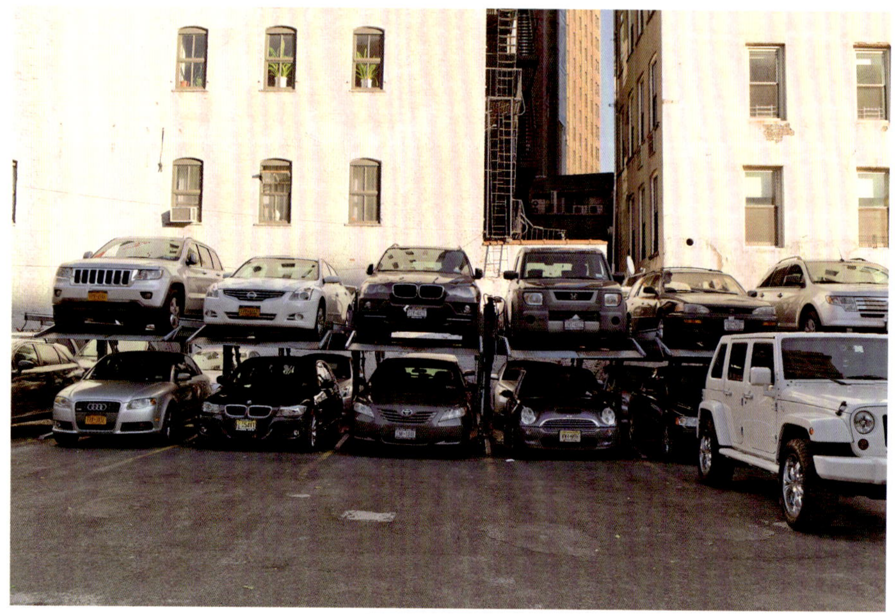

10

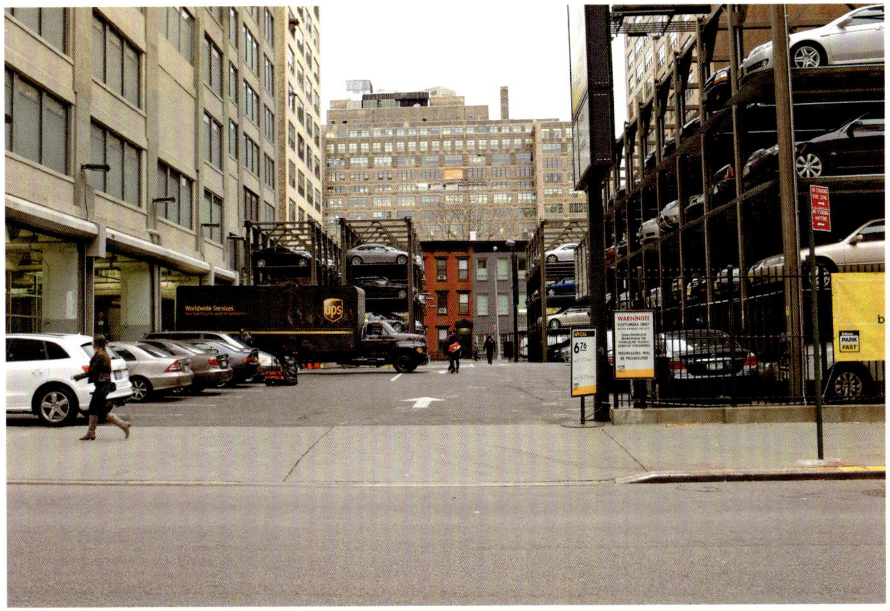

11

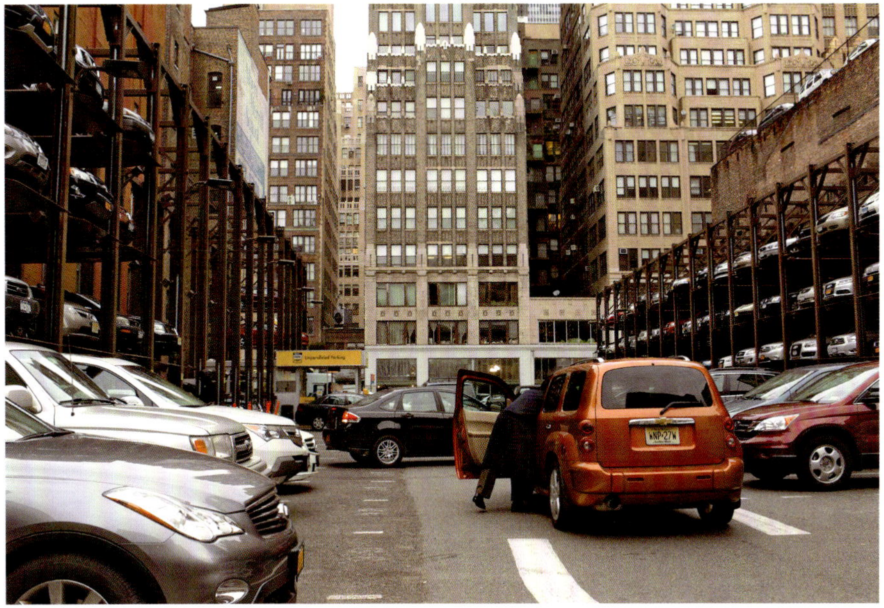

12

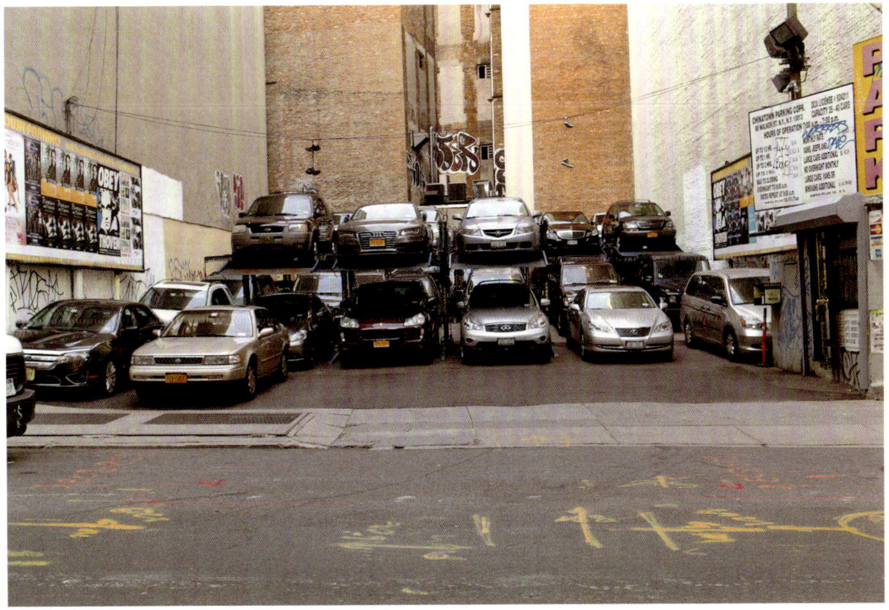

13

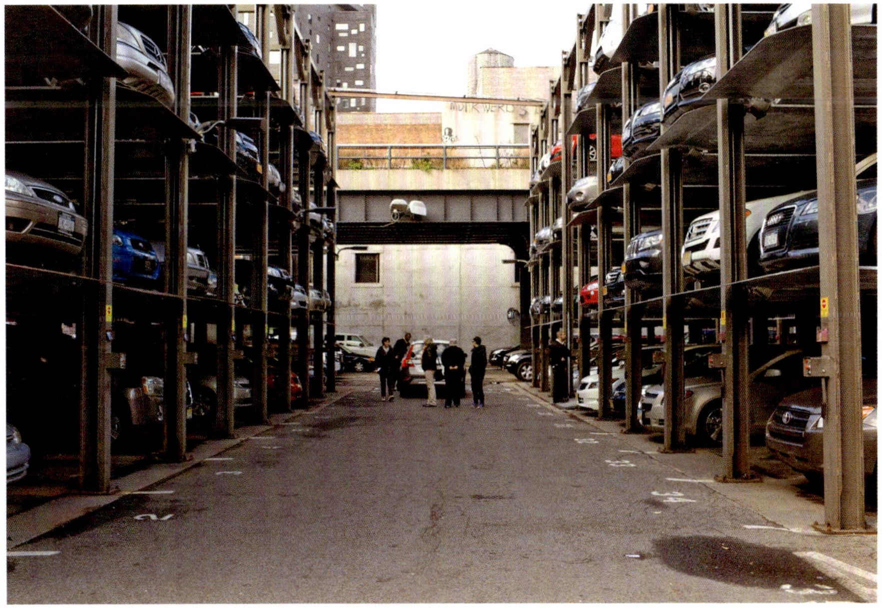

14

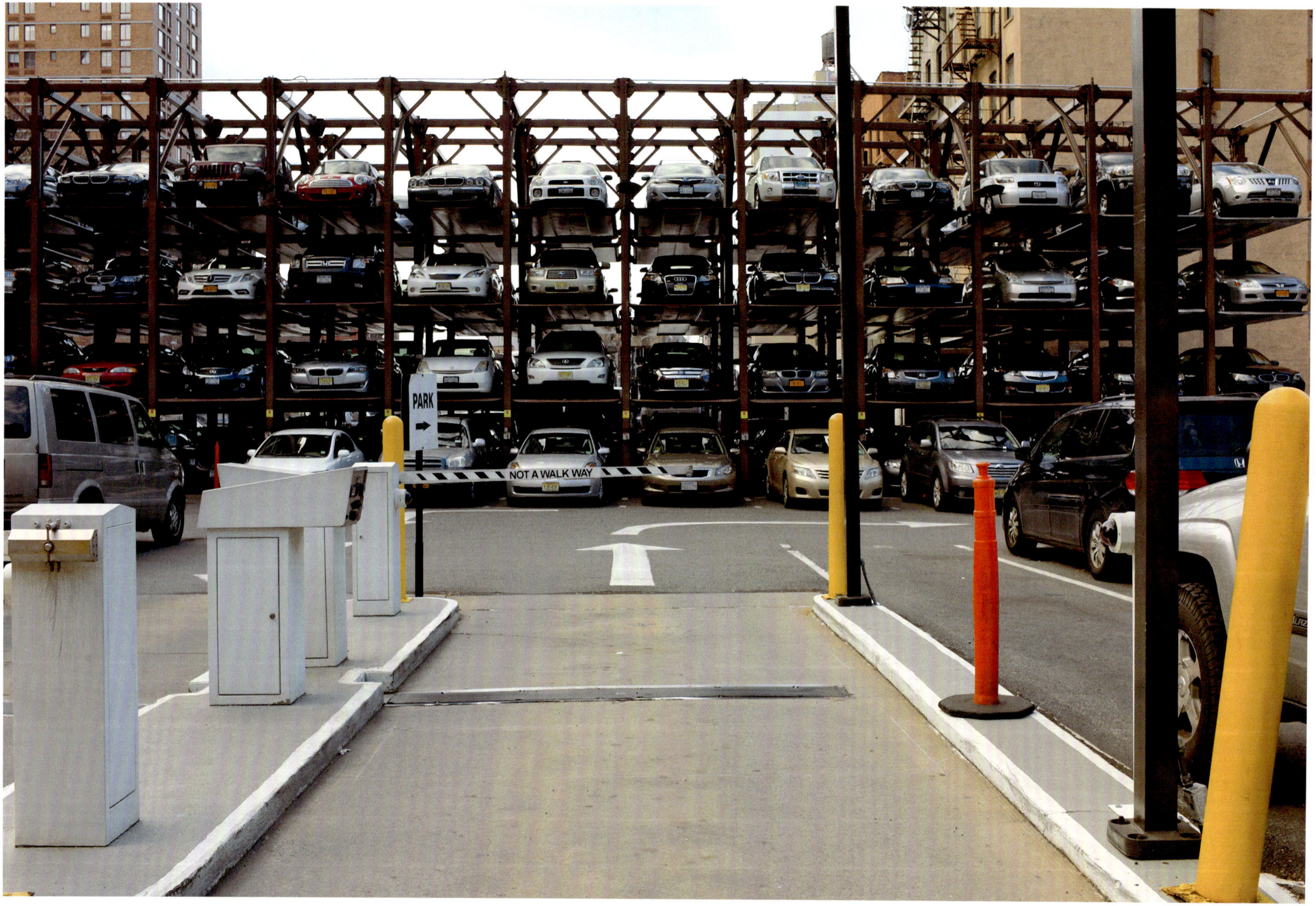

15

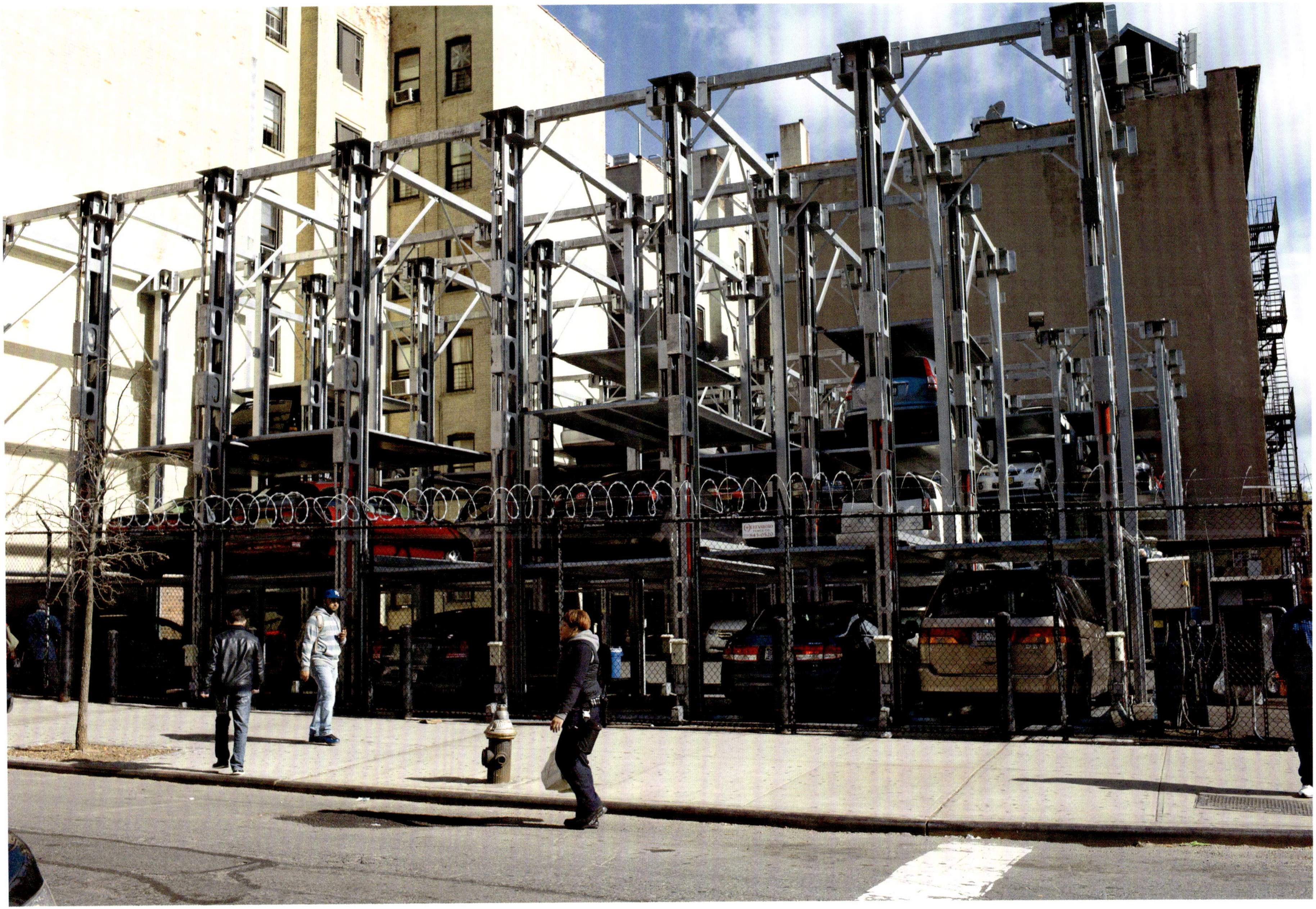

157

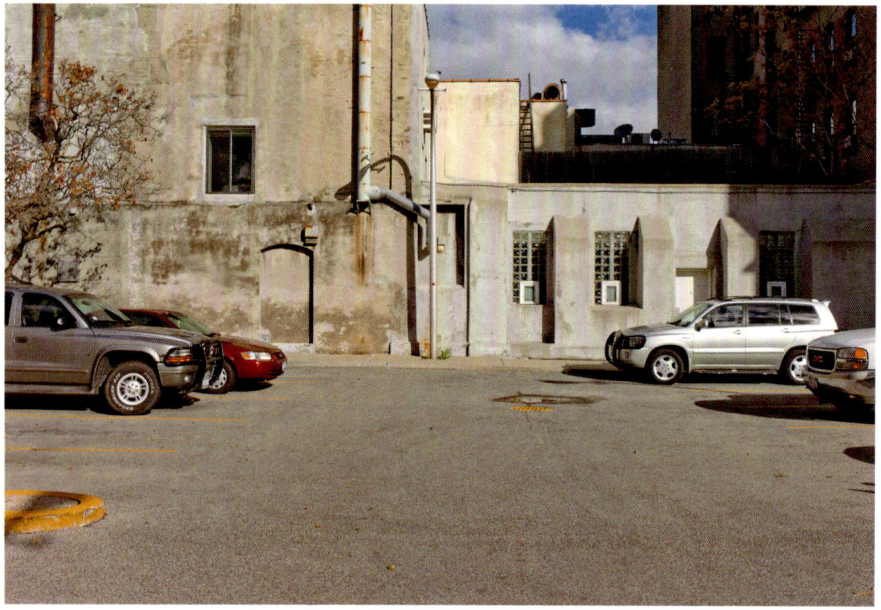

17

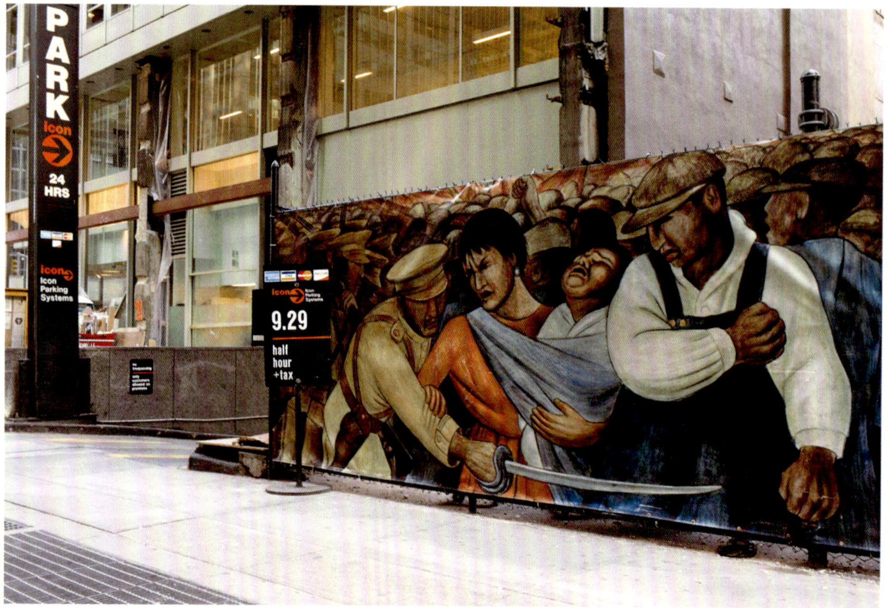
PARK
icon
24 HRS
icon
Icon Parking Systems
9.29
half hour +tax

18

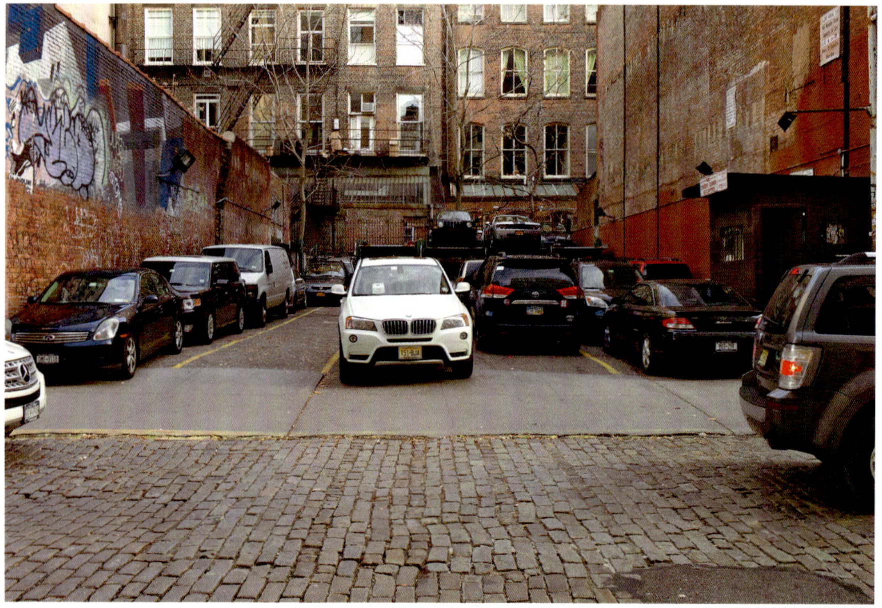

19

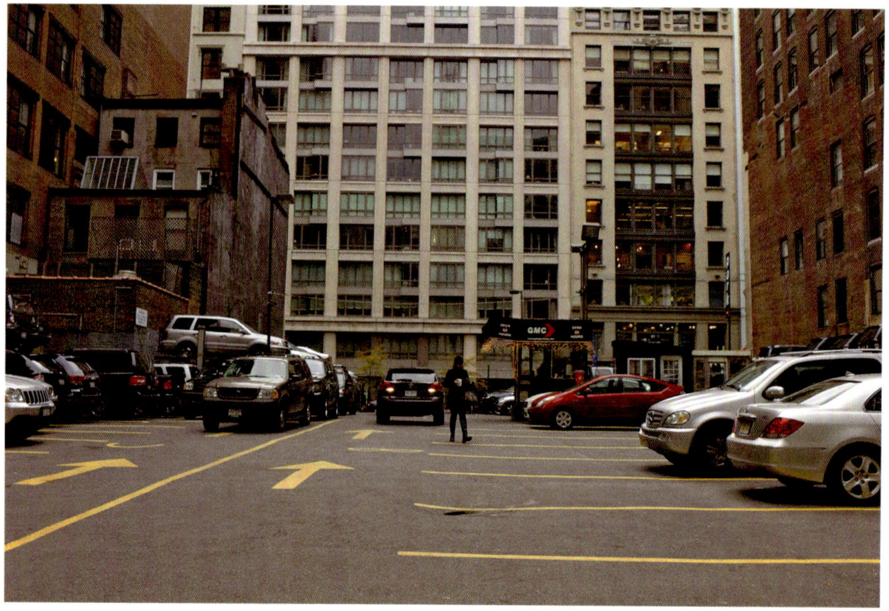
GMC

20

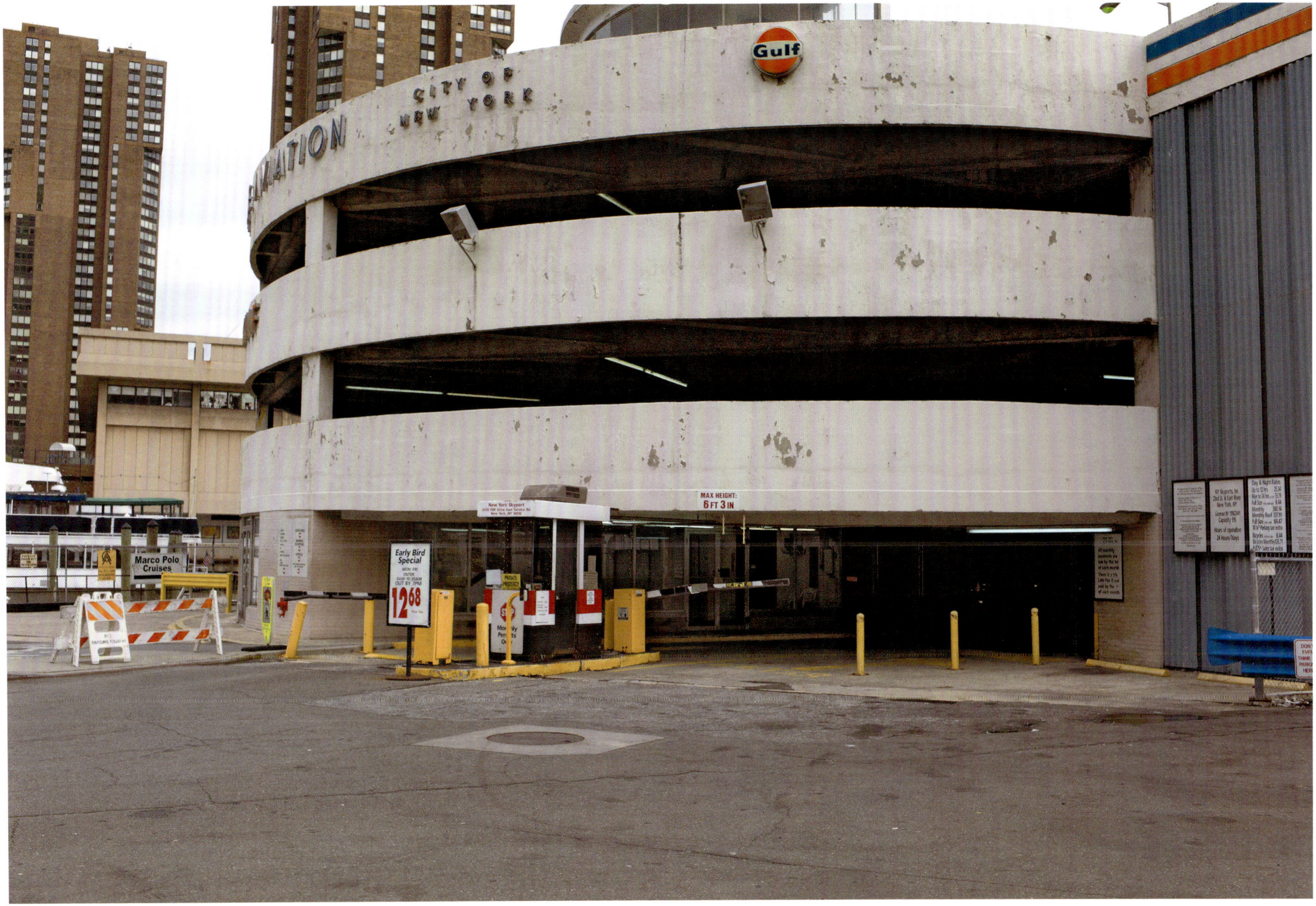
CITY OF
NEW YORK
Gulf
MAX HEIGHT:
6 FT 3 IN
Early Bird
Special
12.68
Marco Polo
Cruises

21

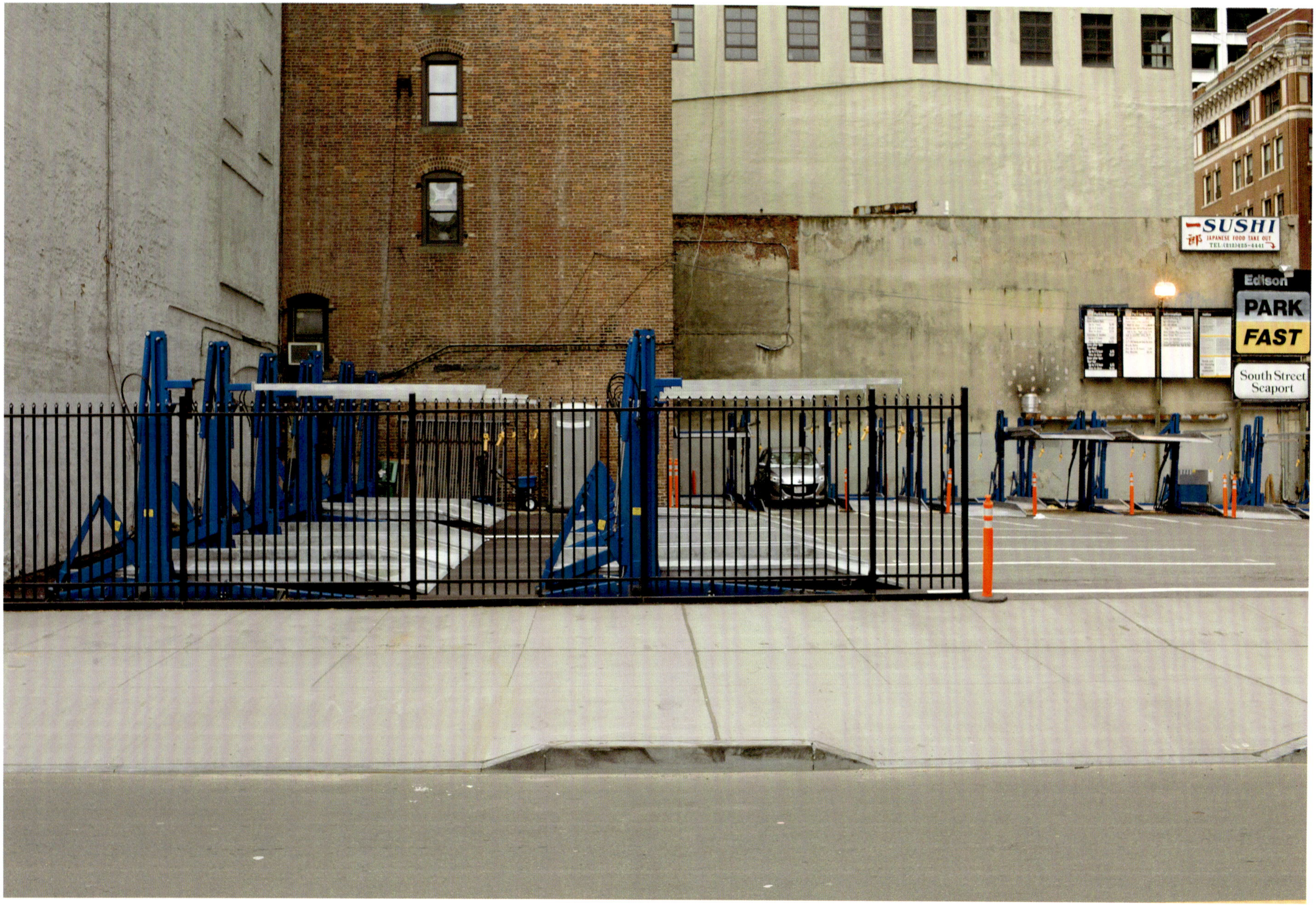
SUSHI
JAPANESE FOOD TAKE OUT
Edison
PARK
FAST
South Street
Seaport

22

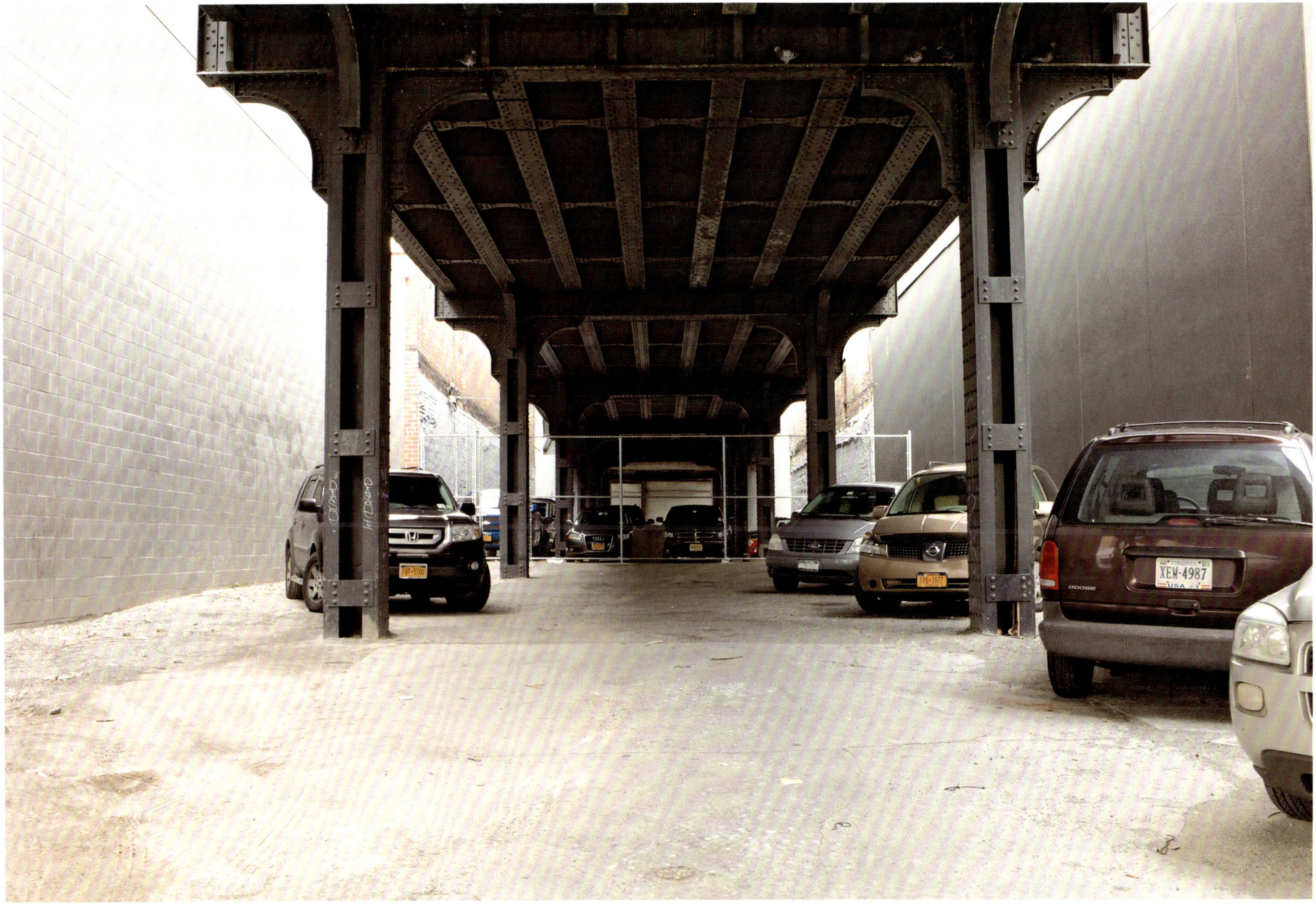

23

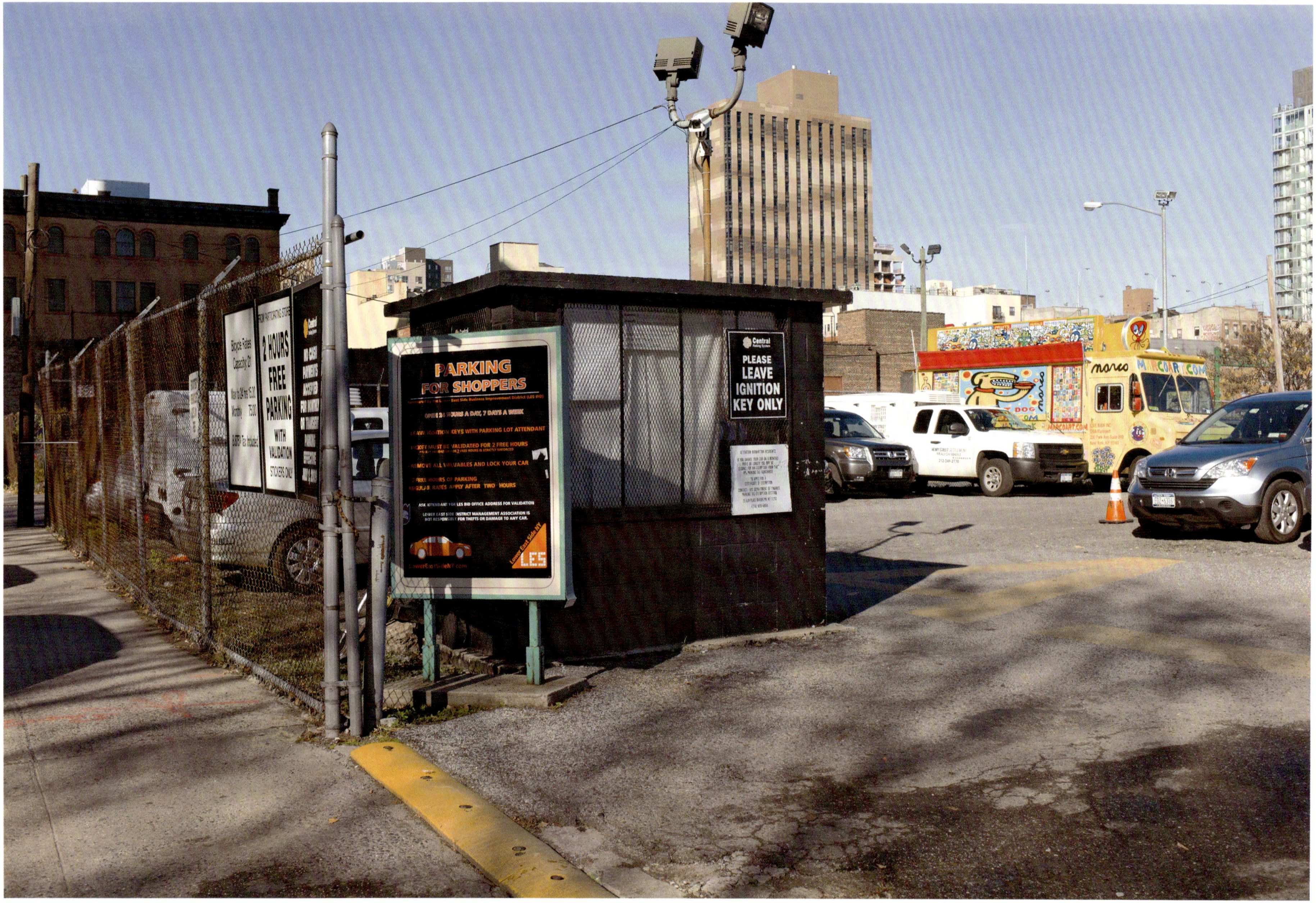
Bicycle Rates
Capacity: 21
2 HOURS
FREE
PARKING
WITH
VALIDATION
STICKERS ONLY
NO CASH
PARKING
FOR SHOPPERS
VALIDATED FOR 2 FREE HOURS
AND LOCK YOUR CAR
APPLY AFTER TWO HOURS
ASK ATTENDANT FOR LES BID OFFICE ADDRESS FOR VALIDATION
FOR THEFTS OR DAMAGE TO ANY CAR.
Lower East Side NY
LES
Central
PLEASE
LEAVE
IGNITION
KEY ONLY

PARKING SHEDS

In many cities parking lots have no attendants; while these sheds are not exclusive to New York, no other city has so many. Many of the family-owned and older sheds still have a home-built feel to them; they can resemble log cabins or farm buildings cobbled together out of plywood or sheet metal or whatever variety of handy scraps.

The sheds belonging to the largest parking lot chains tend to be more generic-looking, and are prefabricated or otherwise of higher quality construction. Whatever the methods and materials, they are often (but not always) heated and air-conditioned, some large enough to sleep in, but others so small one can only work standing.

1 Lower East Side
2 Tribeca
3 Tribeca
4 Chelsea
5 SoHo
6 Lower East Side
7 Hudson Square
8 Lower East Side
9 Midtown West
10 NoHo
11 East Village
12 West Village
13 Chelsea
14 Kips Bay
15 Lower East Side
16 South Street Seaport
17 Flatiron
18 Lower East Side
19 Gramercy Park
20 Chelsea
21 Chelsea
22 Chelsea
23 South Street Seaport
24 Inwood
25 South Street Seaport
26 Chelsea
27 Hell's Kitchen
28 Chelsea
29 Hell's Kitchen
30 Flatiron
31 Chelsea
32 Hell's Kitchen
33 SoHo
34 NoLiTa
35 SoHo
36 SoHo
37 Cooper Square

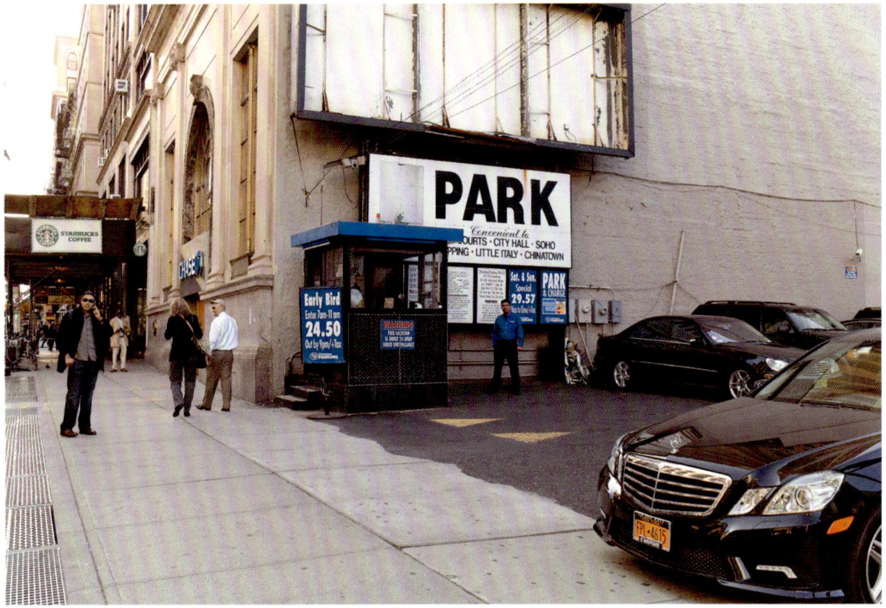
STARBUCKS COFFEE
PARK
Early Bird
24.50
PARK

2

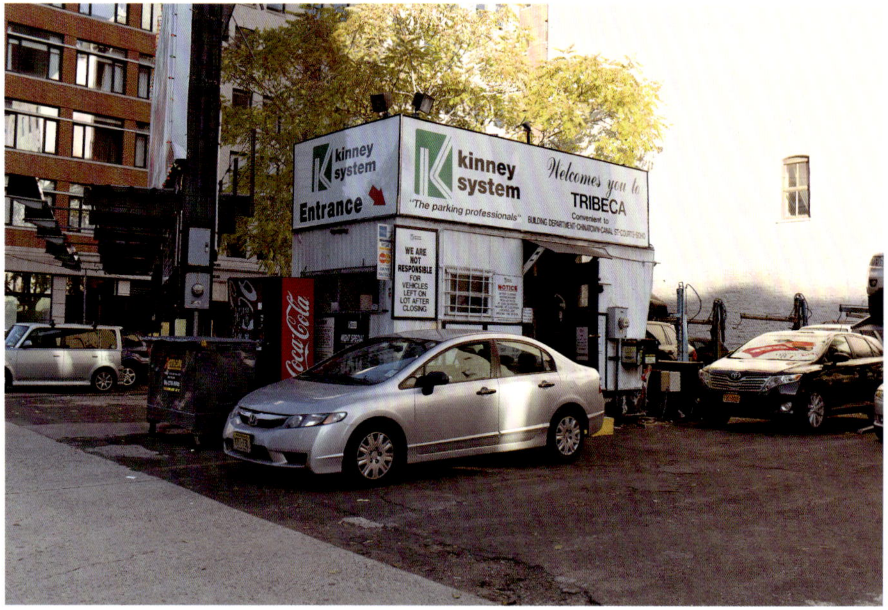
kinney system
Entrance
kinney system
"The parking professionals"
Welcomes you to
TRIBECA
WE ARE NOT RESPONSIBLE FOR VEHICLES LEFT ON LOT AFTER CLOSING
Coca-Cola

3

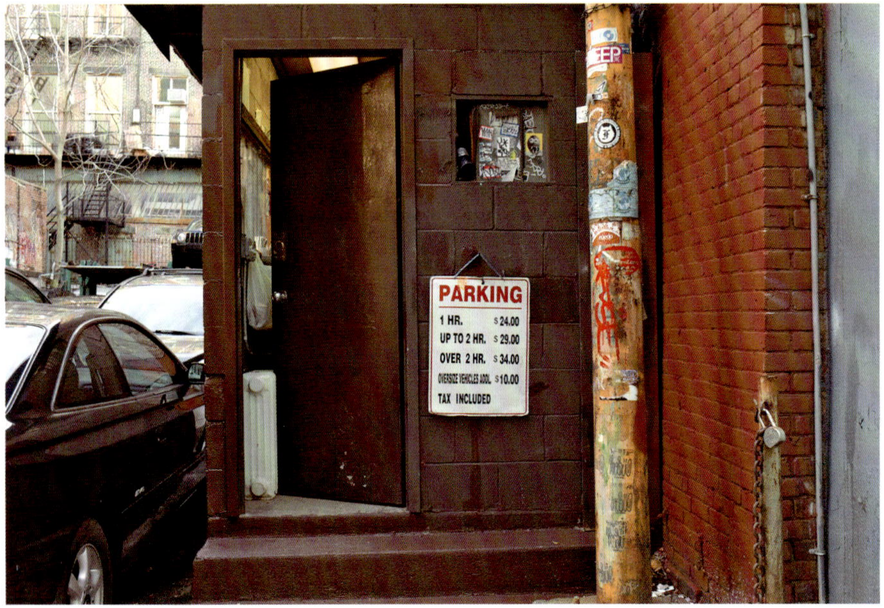
PARKING
1 HR. $24.00
UP TO 2 HR. $29.00
OVER 2 HR. $34.00
OVERSIZE VEHICLES ADDL. $10.00
TAX INCLUDED

4

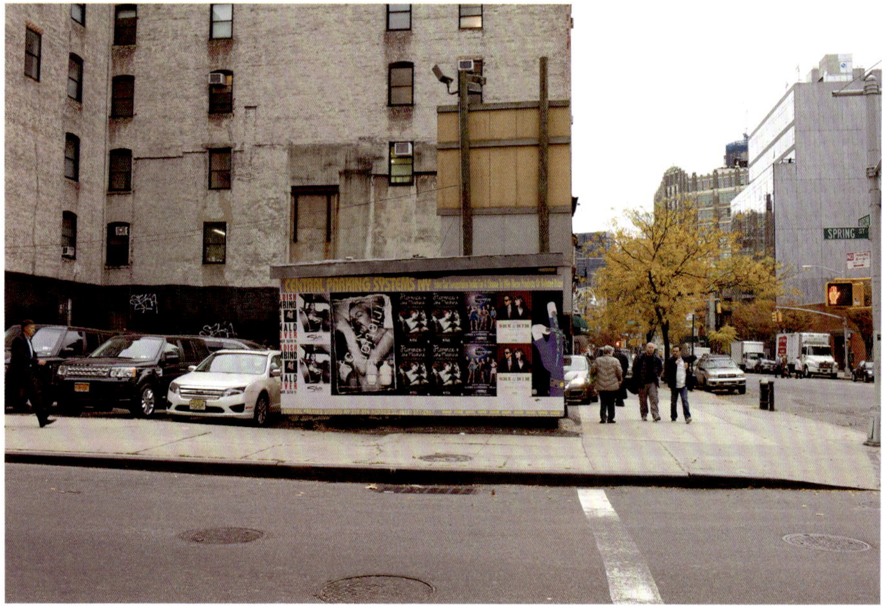
CENTRAL PARKING SYSTEMS NY
SPRING ST

5

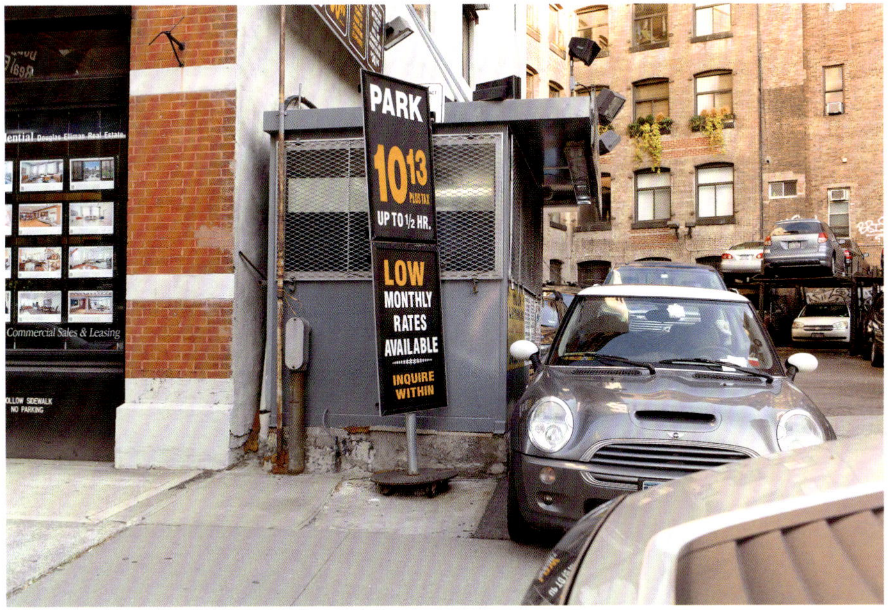
PARK
10 13 PLUS TAX
UP TO 1/2 HR.
LOW MONTHLY RATES AVAILABLE
INQUIRE WITHIN
Commercial Sales & Leasing

6

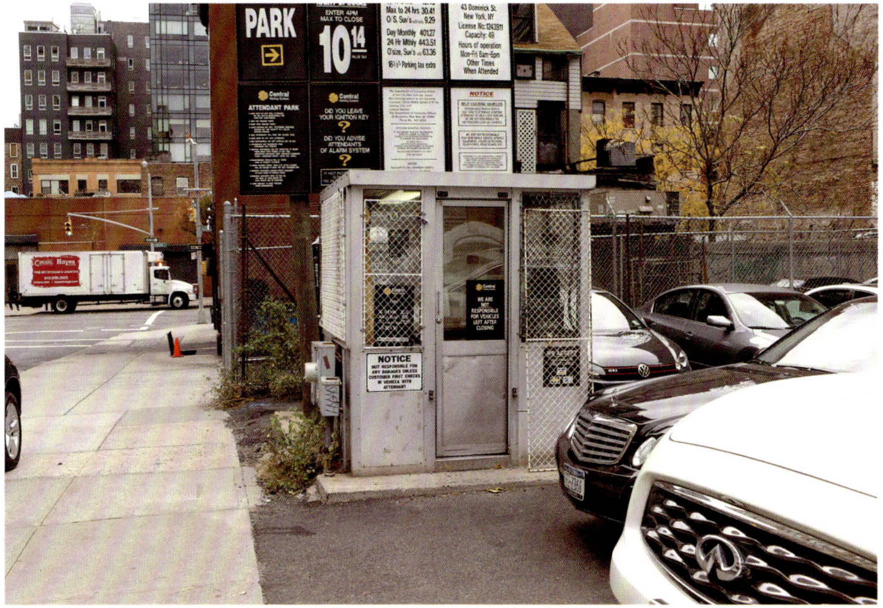
PARK
10 14
ATTENDANT PARK
NOTICE

7

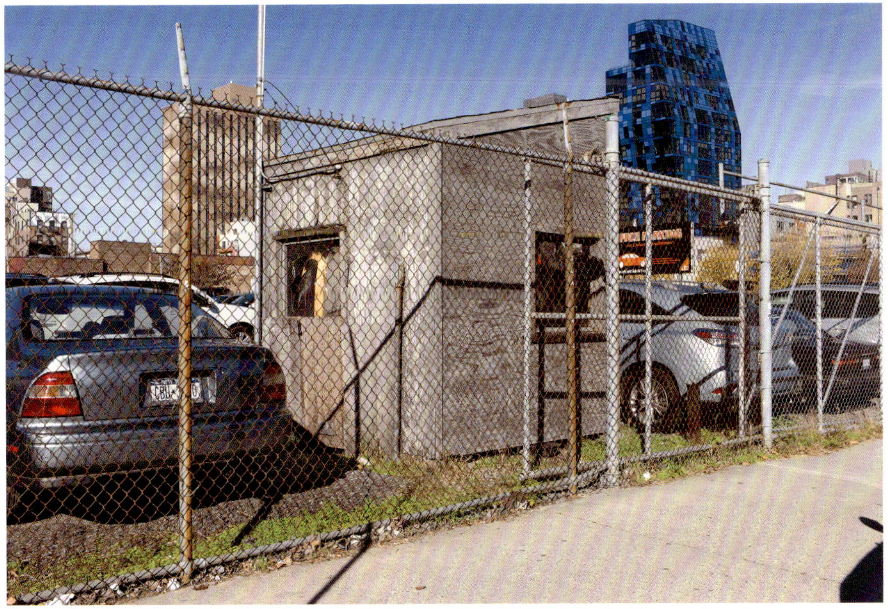

8

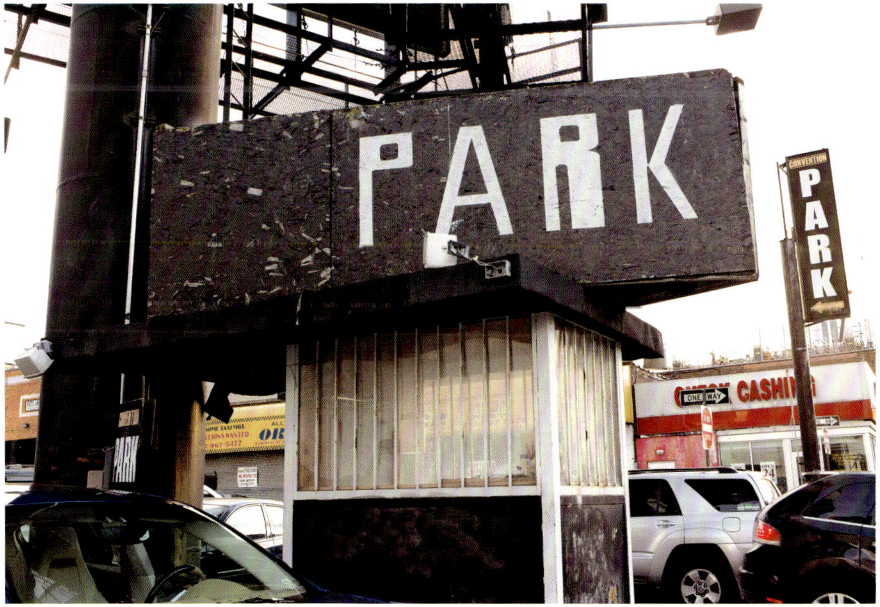
PARK
PARK
ONE WAY

9

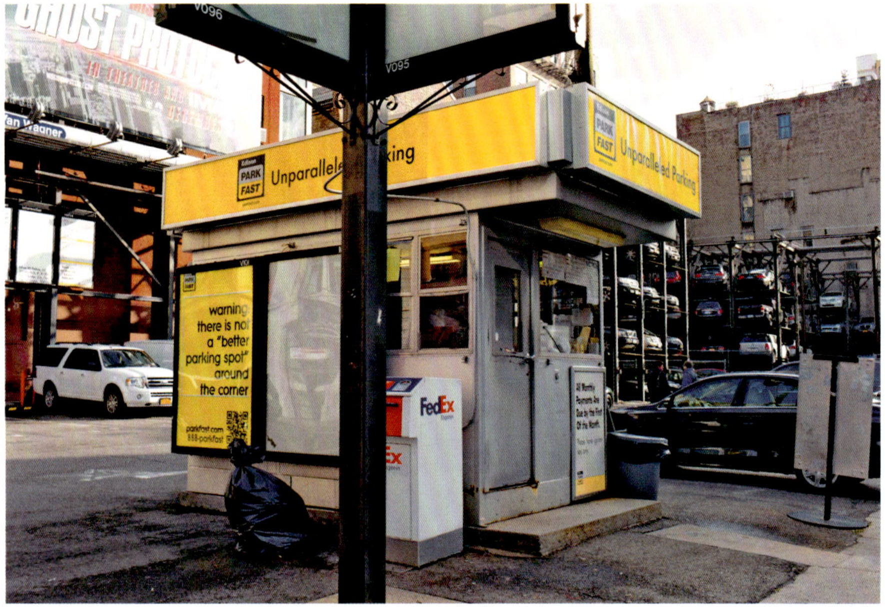
PARK FAST
Unparalleled Parking
warning
there is no
a "better
parking spot"
around
the corner
FedEx

10

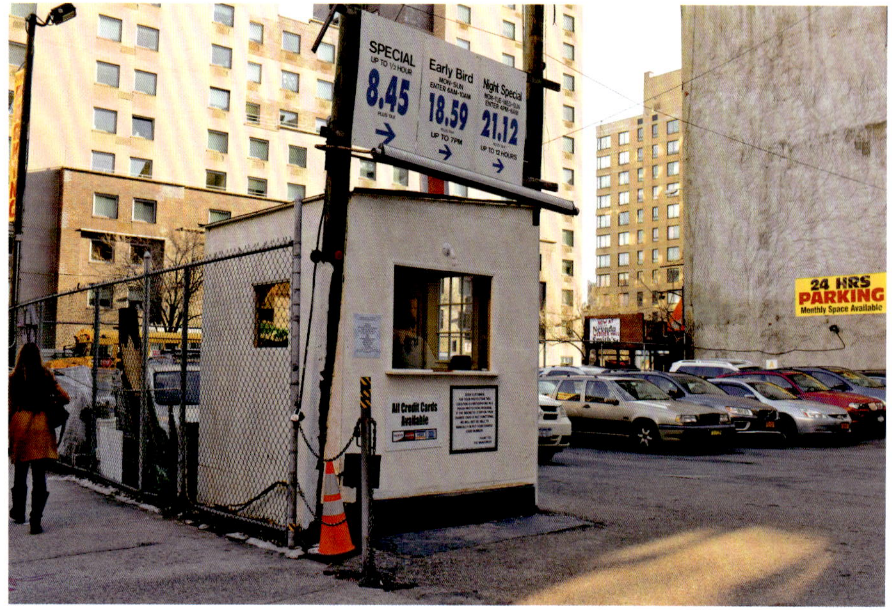
SPECIAL
UP TO 1/2 HOUR
8.45
Early Bird
18.59
Night Special
21.12
UP TO 12 HOURS
24 HRS
PARKING
Monthly Space Available
All Credit Cards
Available

11

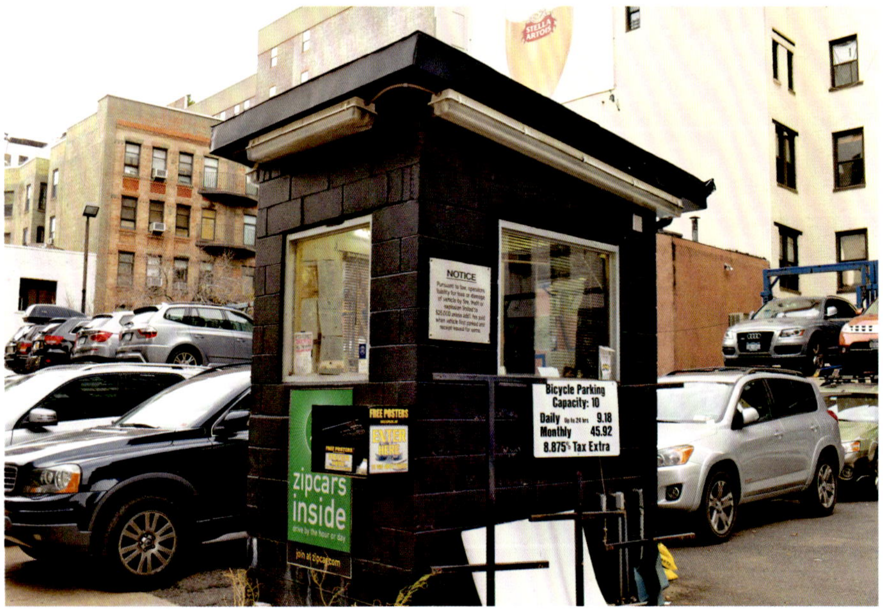
NOTICE
Bicycle Parking
Capacity: 10
Daily 9.18
Monthly 45.92
8.875% Tax Extra
FREE POSTERS
zipcars
inside

12

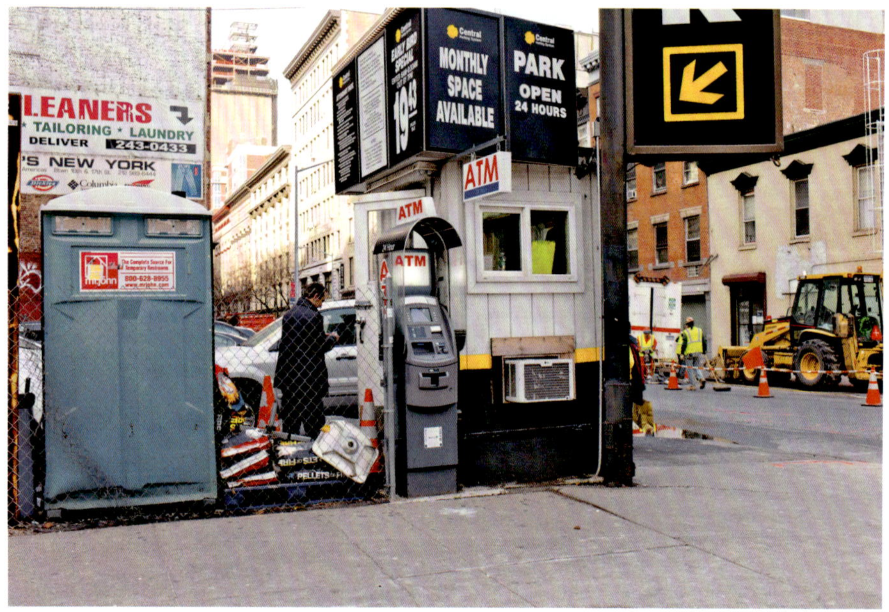
LEANERS
TAILORING * LAUNDRY
DELIVER 243-0433
'S NEW YORK
MONTHLY
SPACE
AVAILABLE
PARK
OPEN
24 HOURS
ATM

13

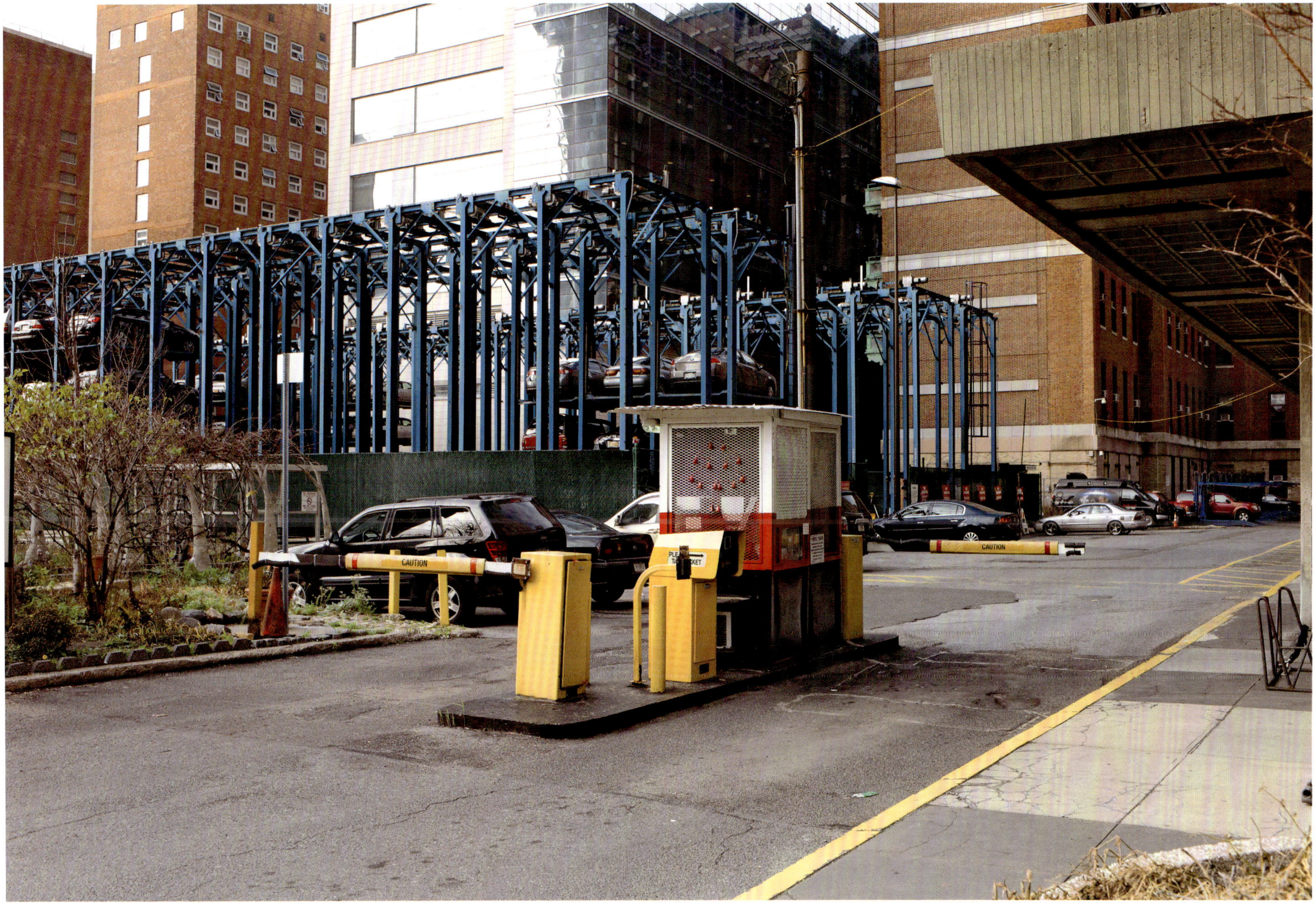
CAUTION
CAUTION

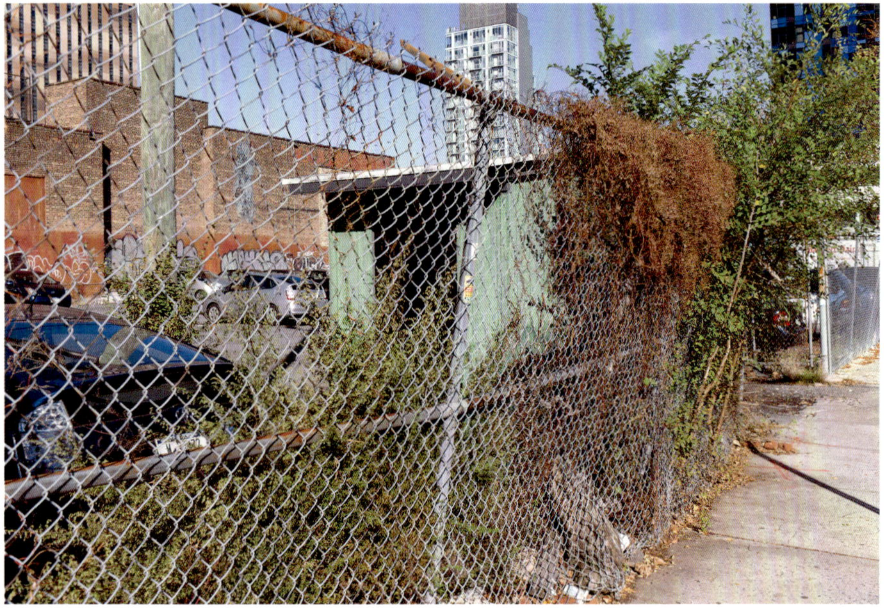

15

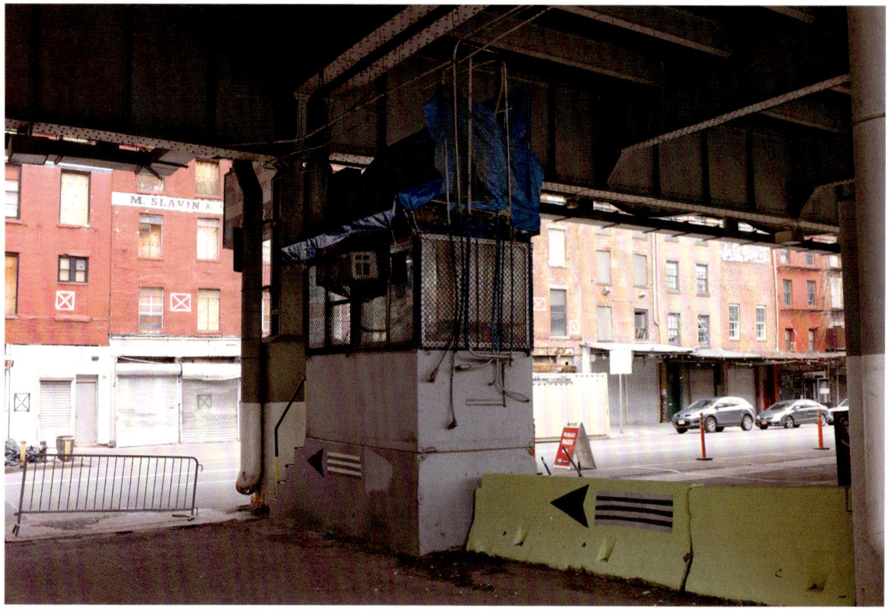

16

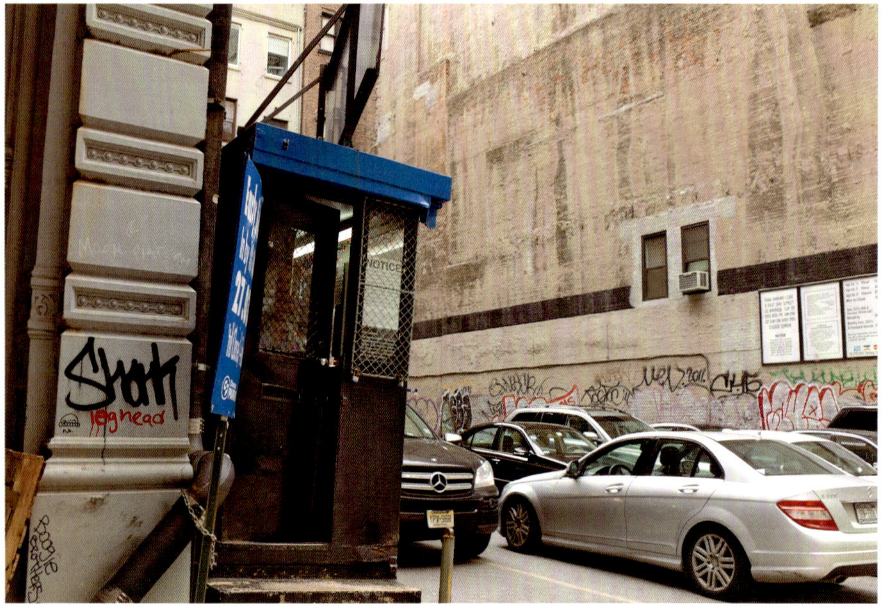

17

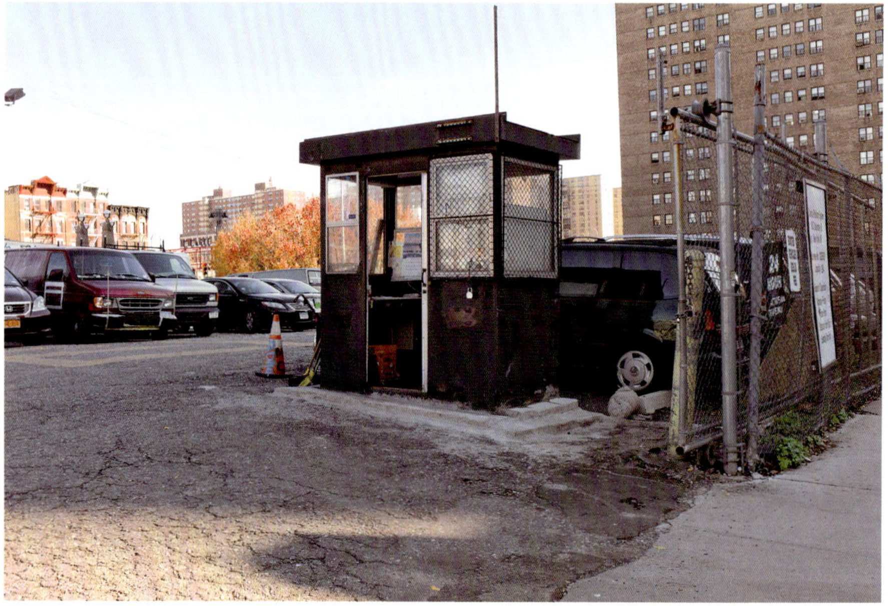

18

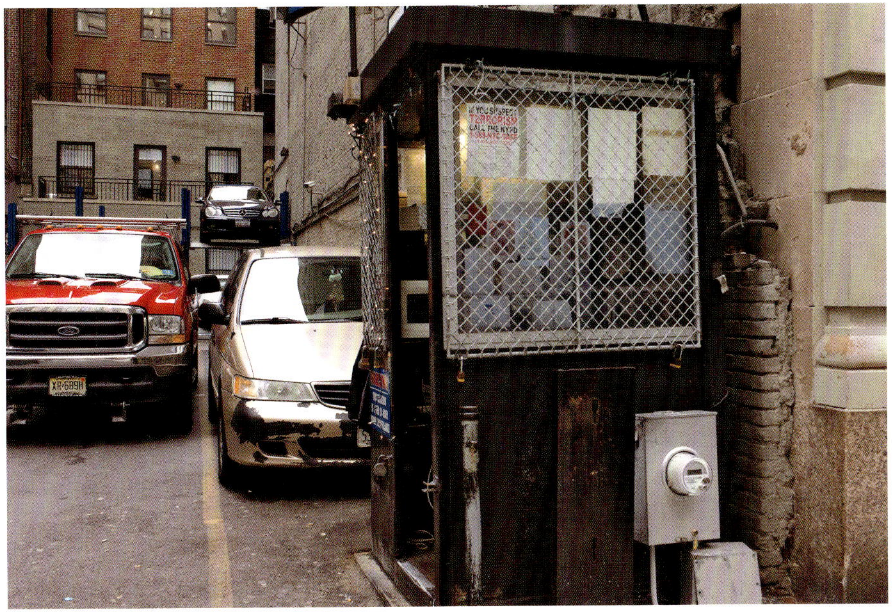

19

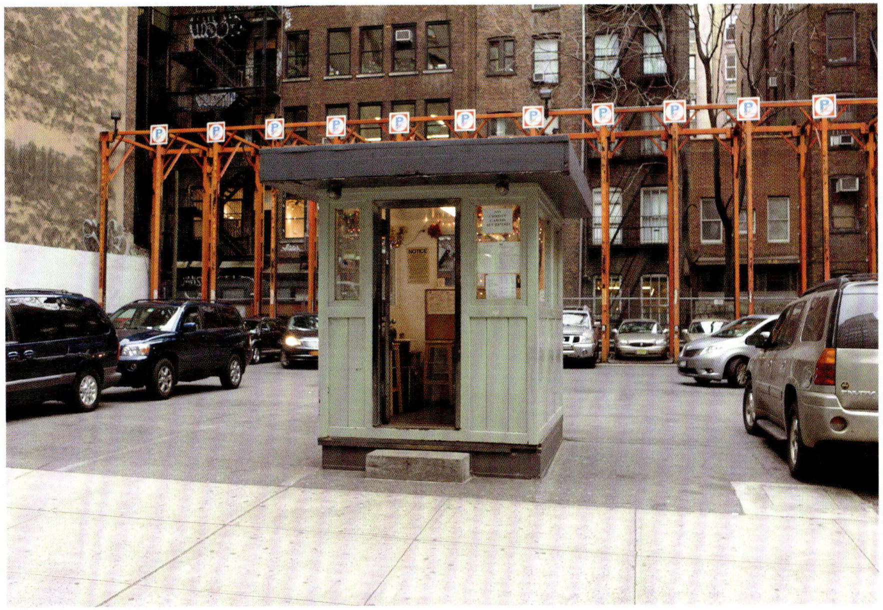

20

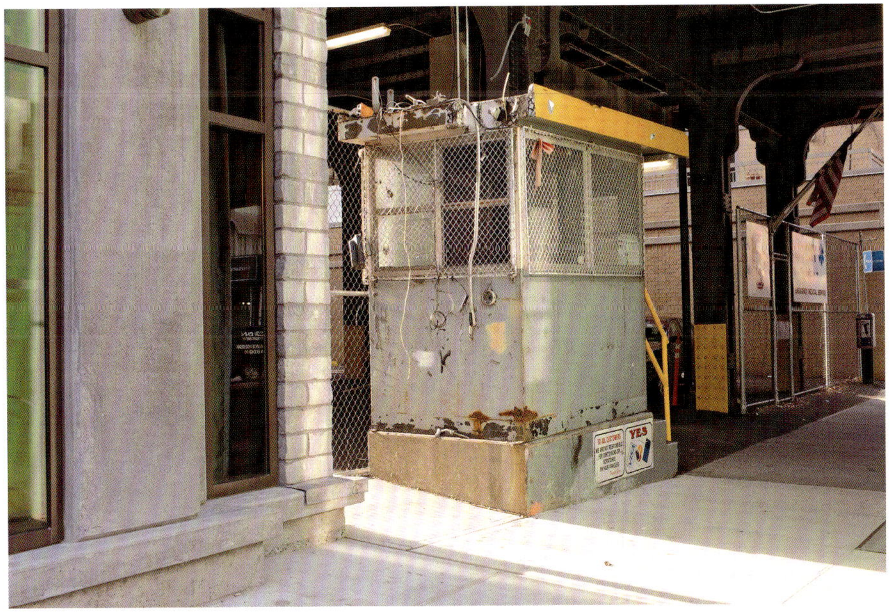

21

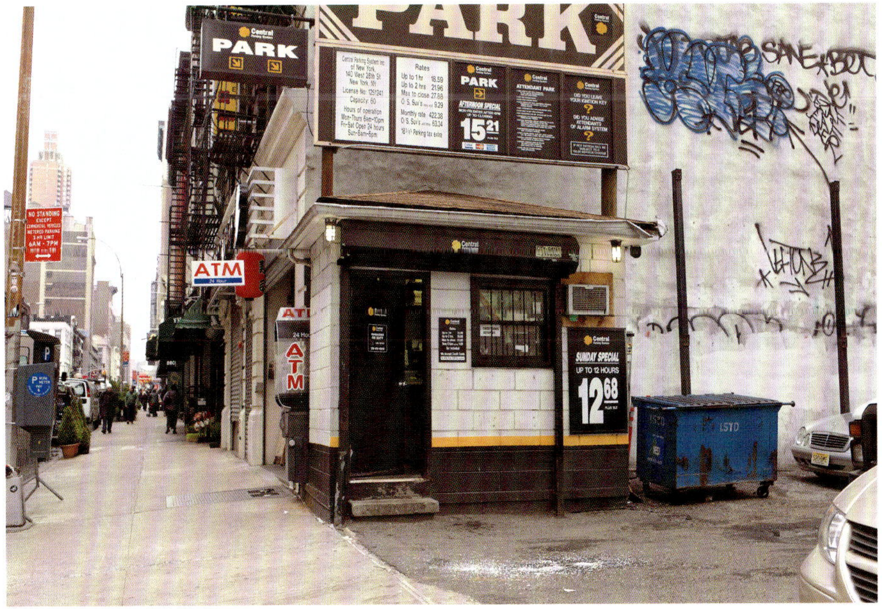

22

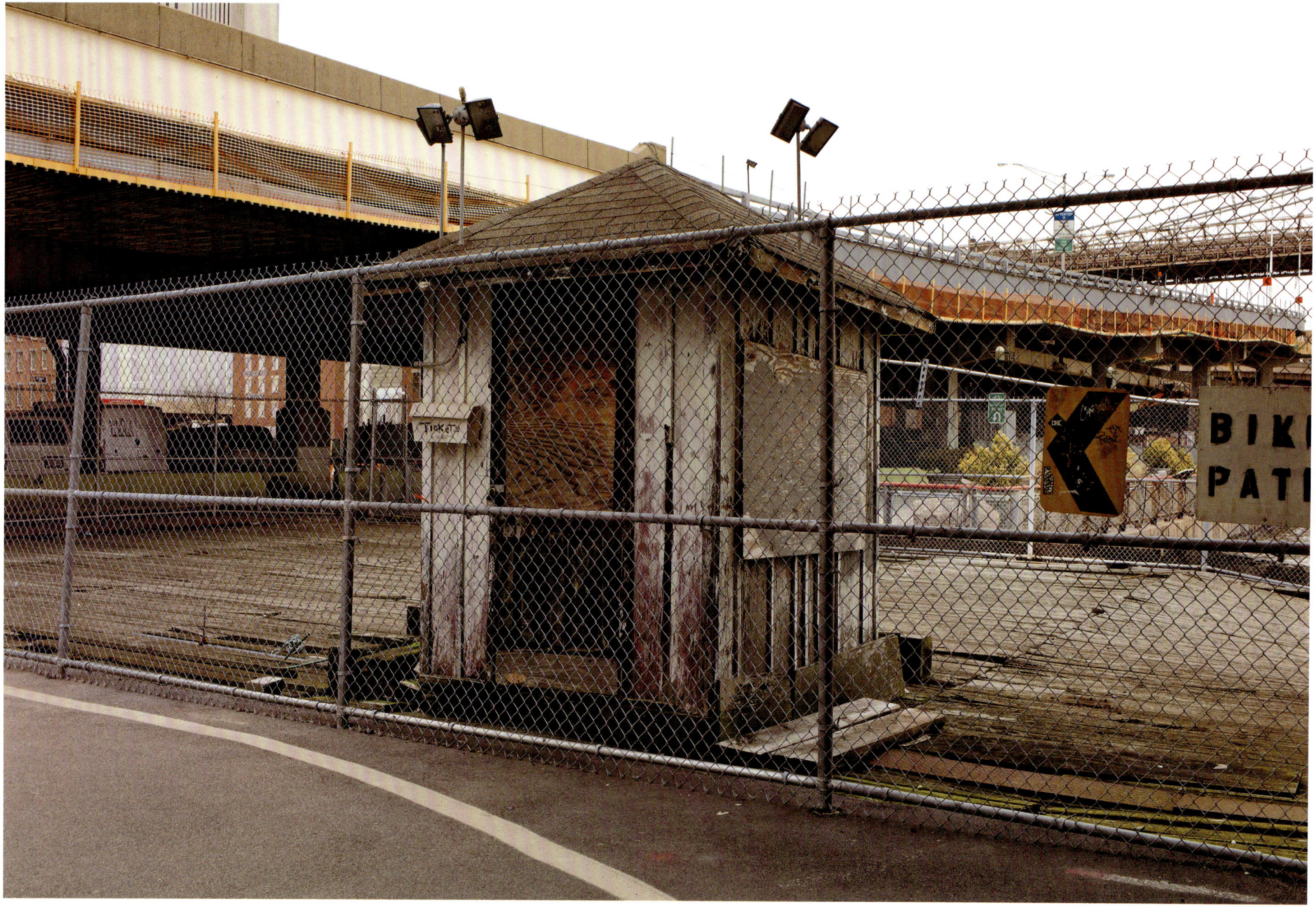

23

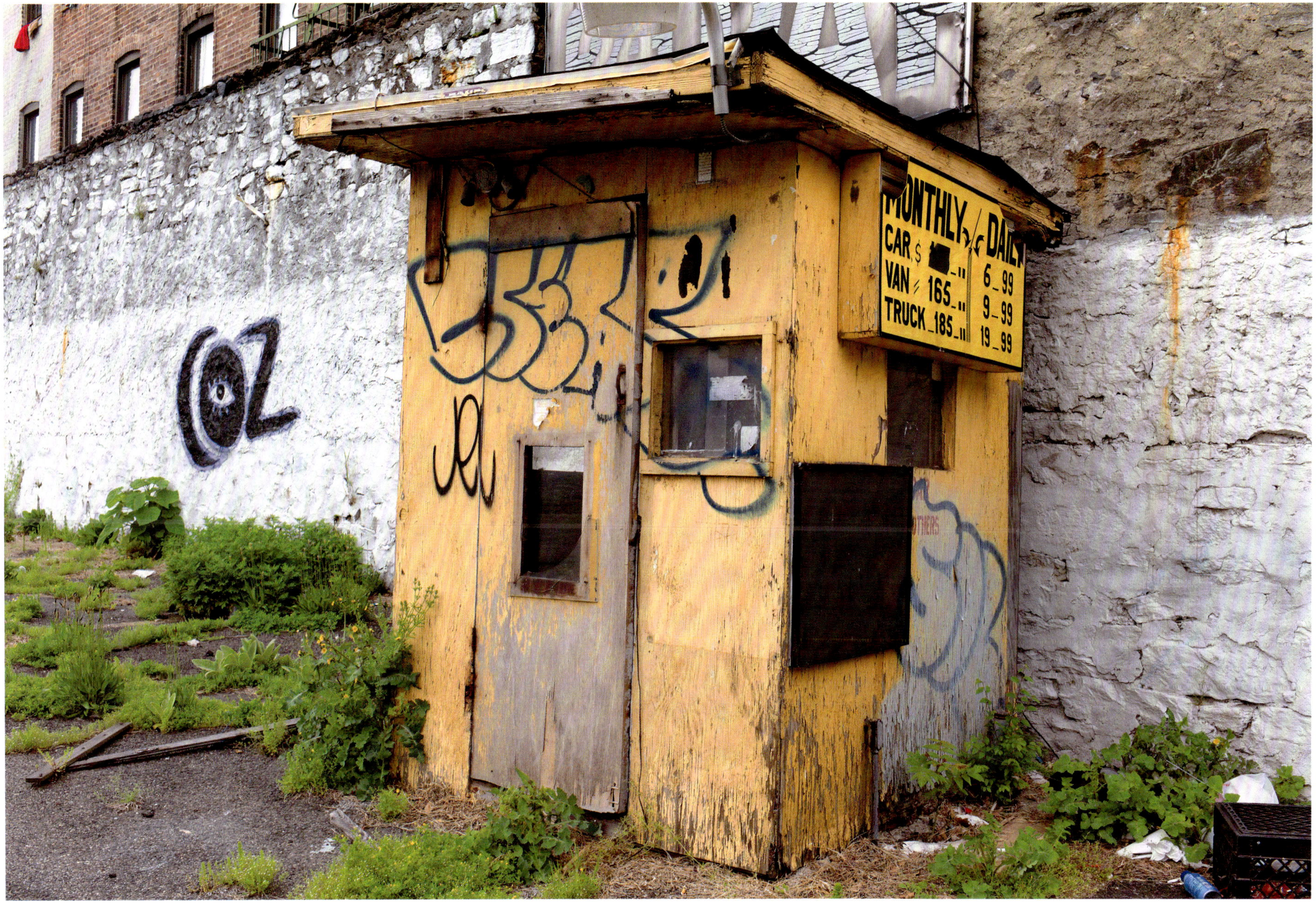

171

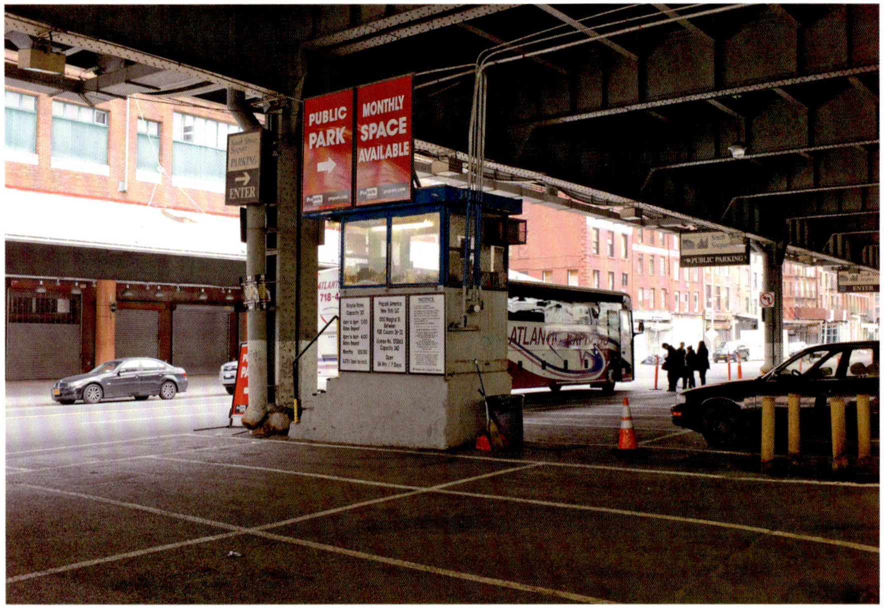
PUBLIC
PARK
MONTHLY
SPACE
AVAILABLE
ENTER
PUBLIC PARKING

25

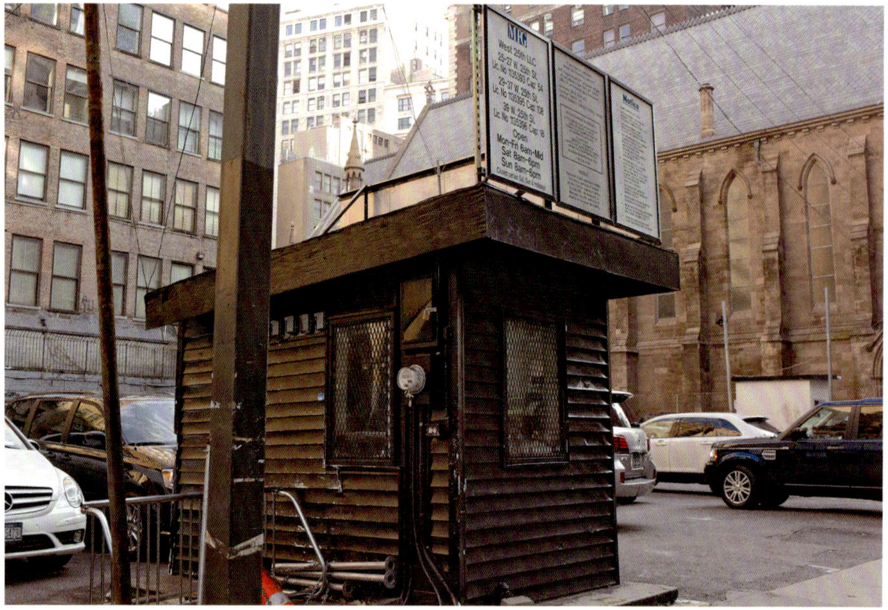

26

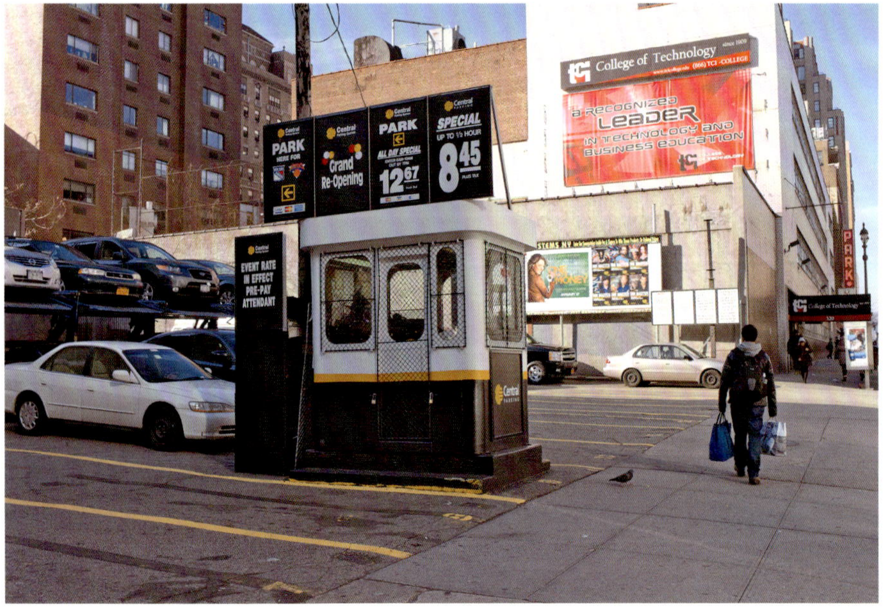
College of Technology
A RECOGNIZED LEADER
IN TECHNOLOGY AND
BUSINESS EDUCATION
PARK
Grand
Re-Opening
PARK
SPECIAL
UP TO 1/2 HOUR
8.45
EVENT RATE
IN EFFECT
PRE-PAY
ATTENDANT
PARK

27

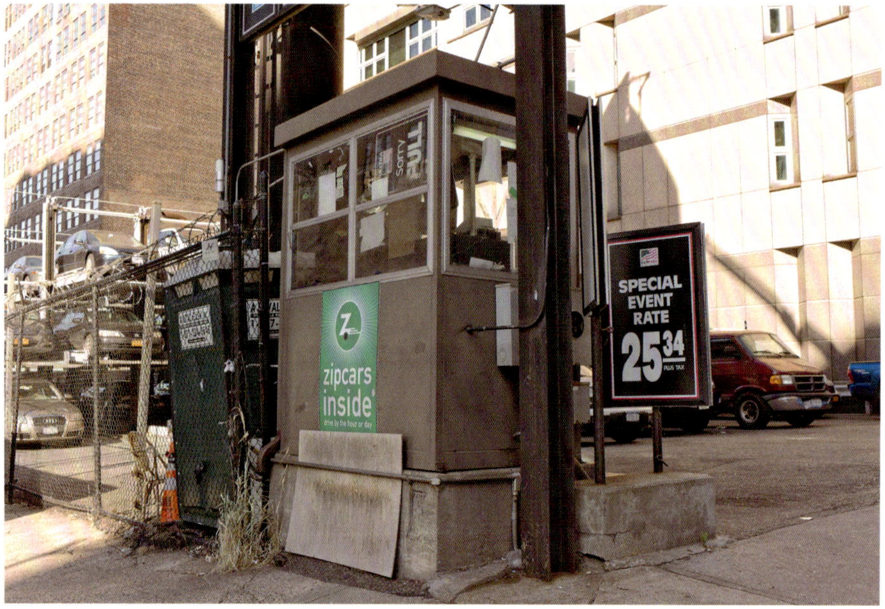
zipcars
inside
SPECIAL
EVENT
RATE
25.34

28

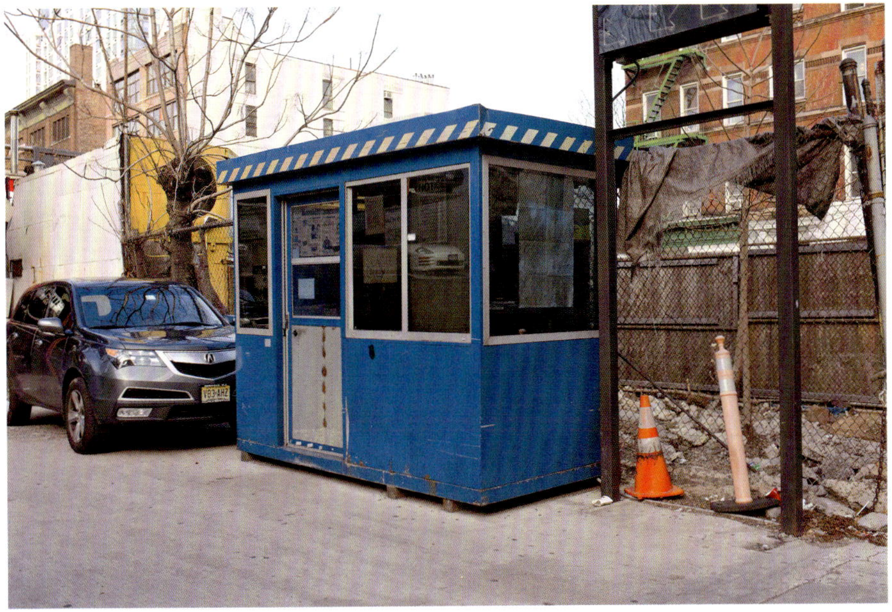

29

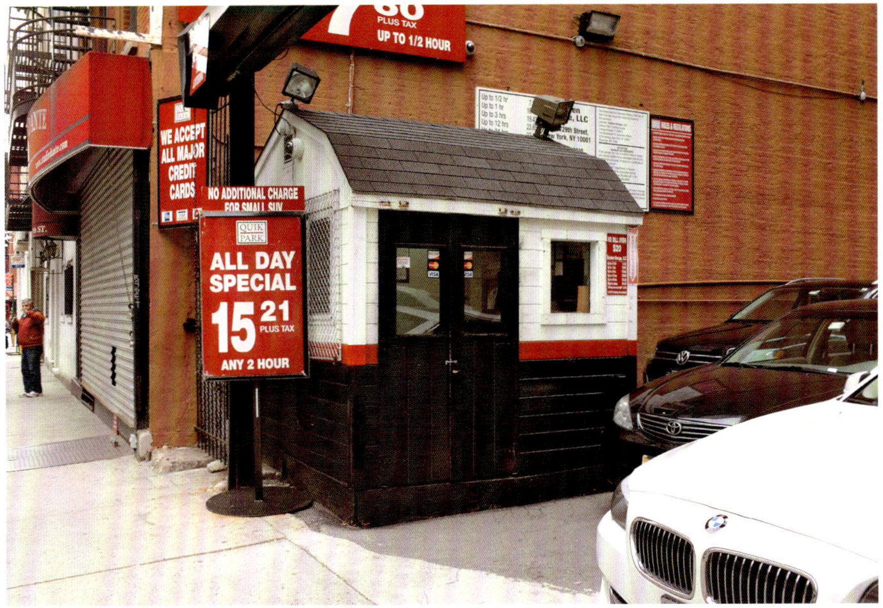
PLUS TAX
UP TO 1/2 HOUR
WE ACCEPT ALL MAJOR CREDIT CARDS
NO ADDITIONAL CHARGE FOR SMALL SUV
QUIK PARK
ALL DAY SPECIAL
15 21 PLUS TAX
ANY 2 HOUR

30

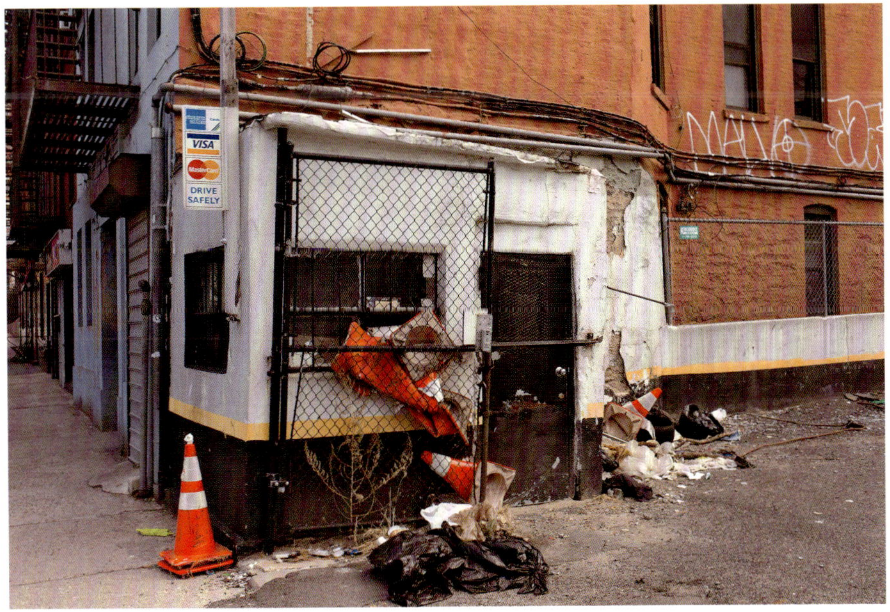
VISA
DRIVE SAFELY

31

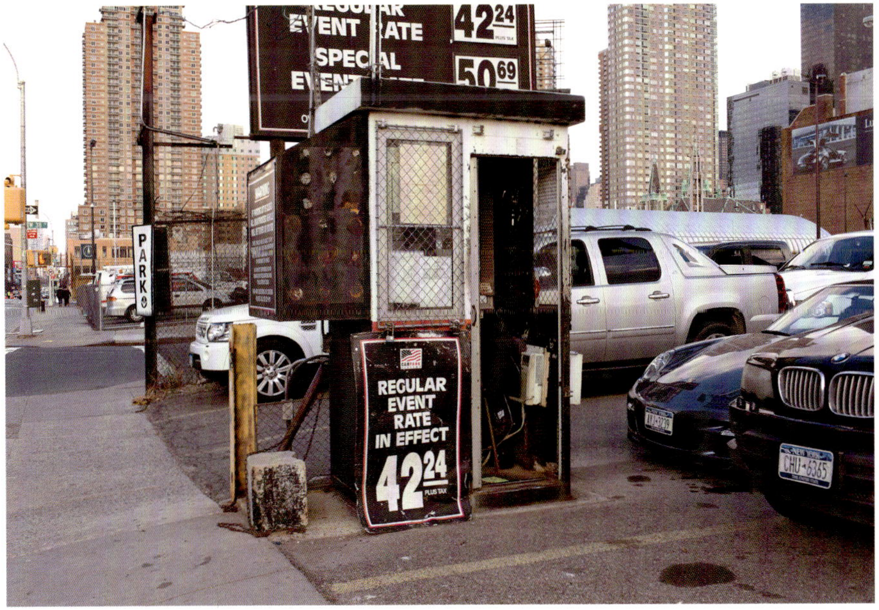
EVENT RATE
42 24
50 69
PARK
REGULAR EVENT RATE IN EFFECT
42 24

32

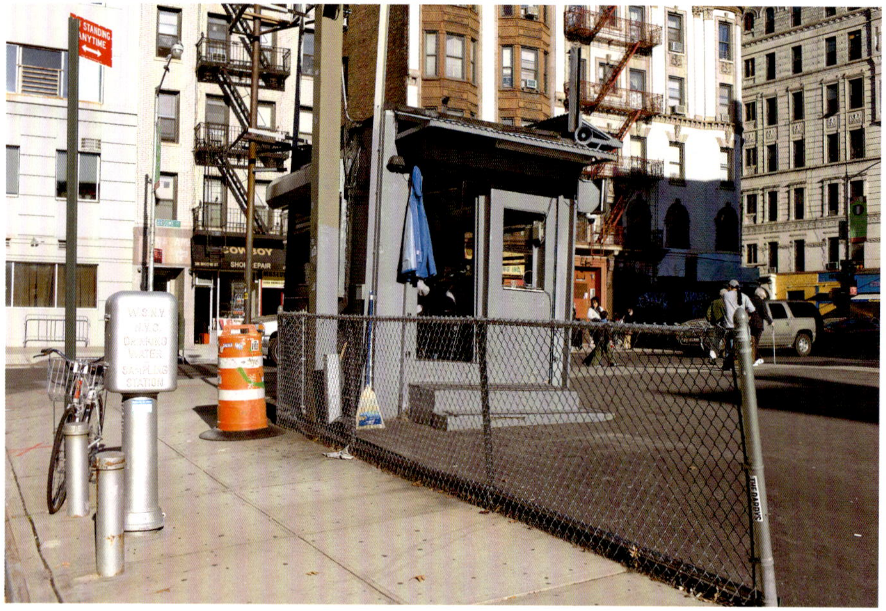

33

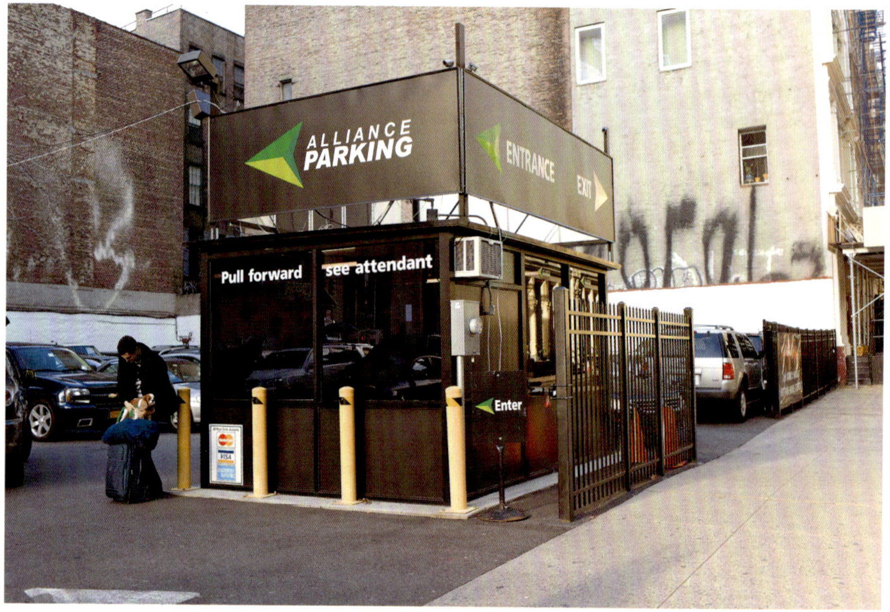
ALLIANCE
PARKING
ENTRANCE
EXIT
Pull forward
see attendant
Enter

34

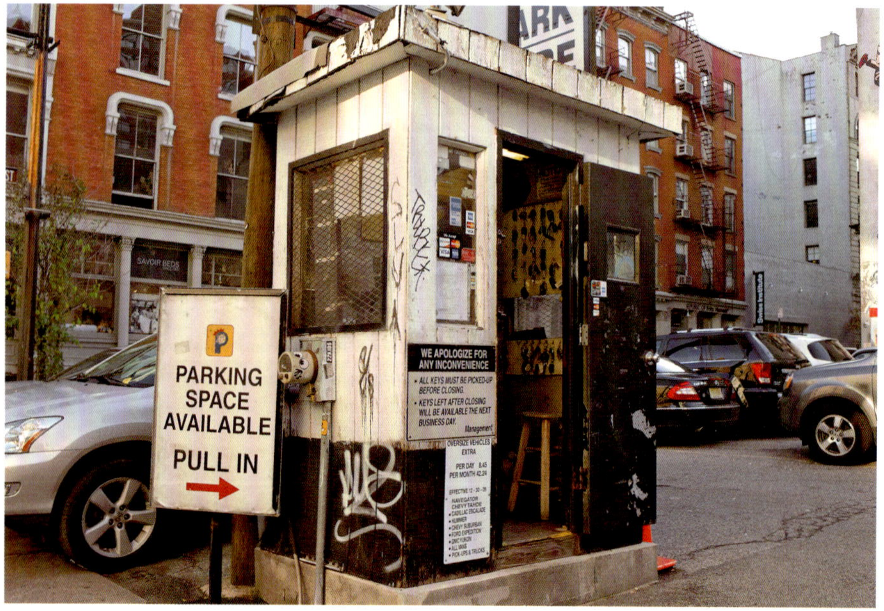
PARKING
SPACE
AVAILABLE
PULL IN
WE APOLOGIZE FOR
ANY INCONVENIENCE

35

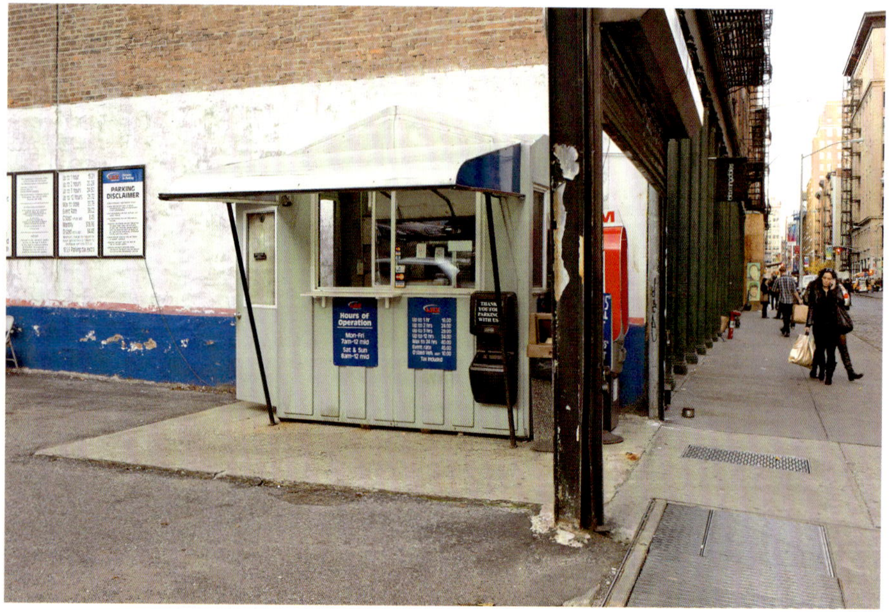
PARKING
DISCLAIMER
Hours of
Operation

36

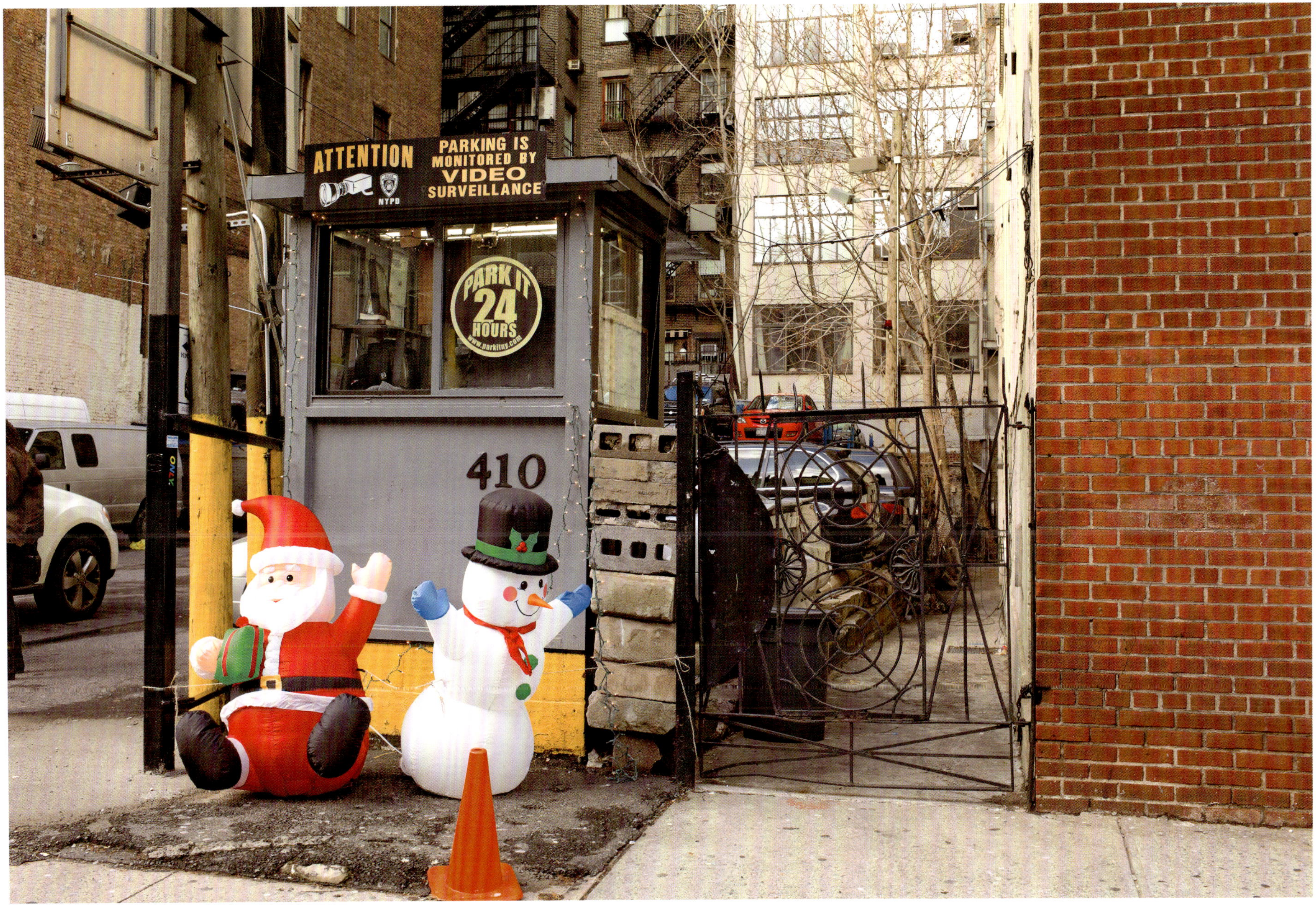
ATTENTION
NYPD
PARKING IS MONITORED BY VIDEO SURVEILLANCE
PARK IT 24 HOURS
www.parkitny.com
410

37

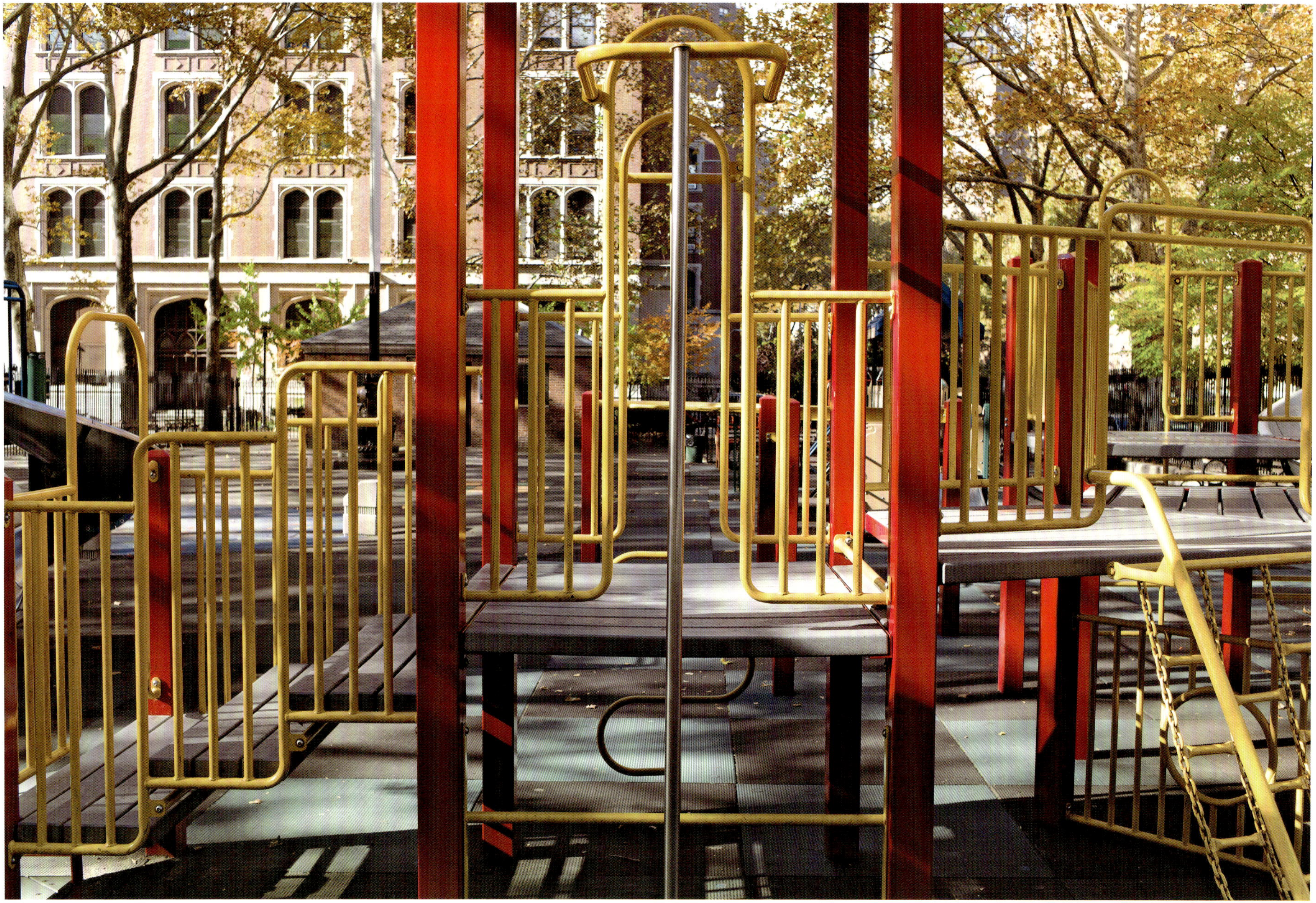

1

PLAYGROUNDS

The Parks Department opened the first playground in Seward Park in 1903; there are nearly 250 throughout Manhattan now. Most of the playgrounds in New York have been upgraded in recent years. Gone are the seesaws and monkey bars, replaced by more colorful, somewhat friendlier-looking structures to climb in or around, many with soft surfaces to fall on. Some reflect their neighborhood contexts, with models of bridges or ships, others with animal sculptures and fountains. Most are still geared to the city's youngest residents, but a few have facilities for grown-ups too.

There's been a movement over the last several years to turn many schoolyards, often used as parking lots, into places for children, creating some of the city's newest playgrounds. Some are so small as to seem like an afterthought, whereas others are elaborately themed.

1 Two Bridges
2 Lower East Side
3 Union Square
4 Chelsea
5 Midtown East
6 Upper West Side
7 Chelsea
8 East Village
9 Lower East Side
10 Lower East Side
11 Chelsea
12 Chelsea
13 Lower East Side
14 Lower East Side
15 South Street Seaport
16 Lower East Side
17 Gramercy Park
18 Upper West Side
19 Harlem
20 Harlem
21 East Harlem
22 Battery Park City
23 Lower East Side
24 Lower East Side
25 Chelsea
26 Hell's Kitchen
27 Hell's Kitchen
28 Chelsea
29 Hell's Kitchen
30 Hell's Kitchen
31 Hell's Kitchen
32 West Village
33 Harlem
34 Upper East Side
35 Lower East Side
36 East Harlem

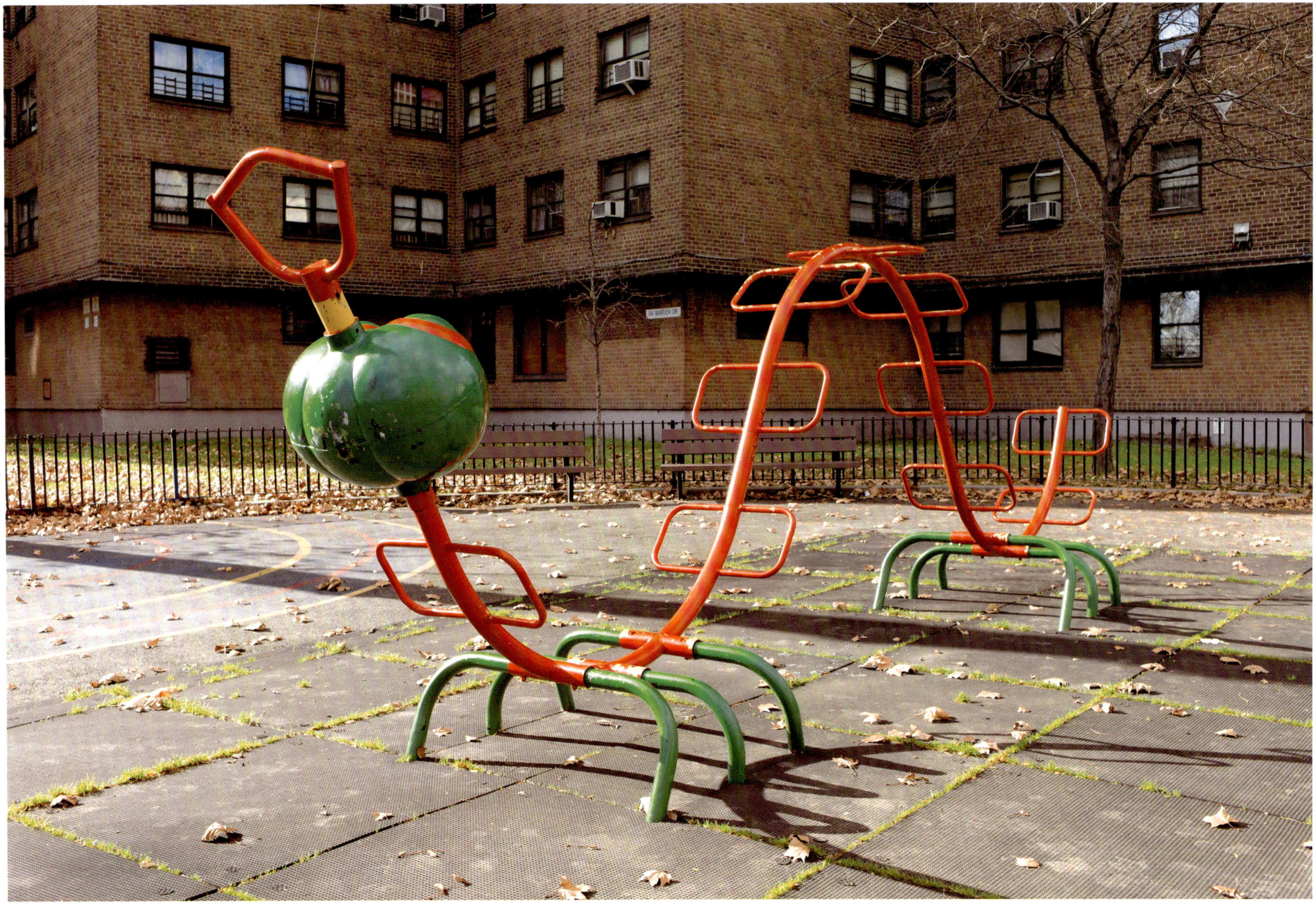

2

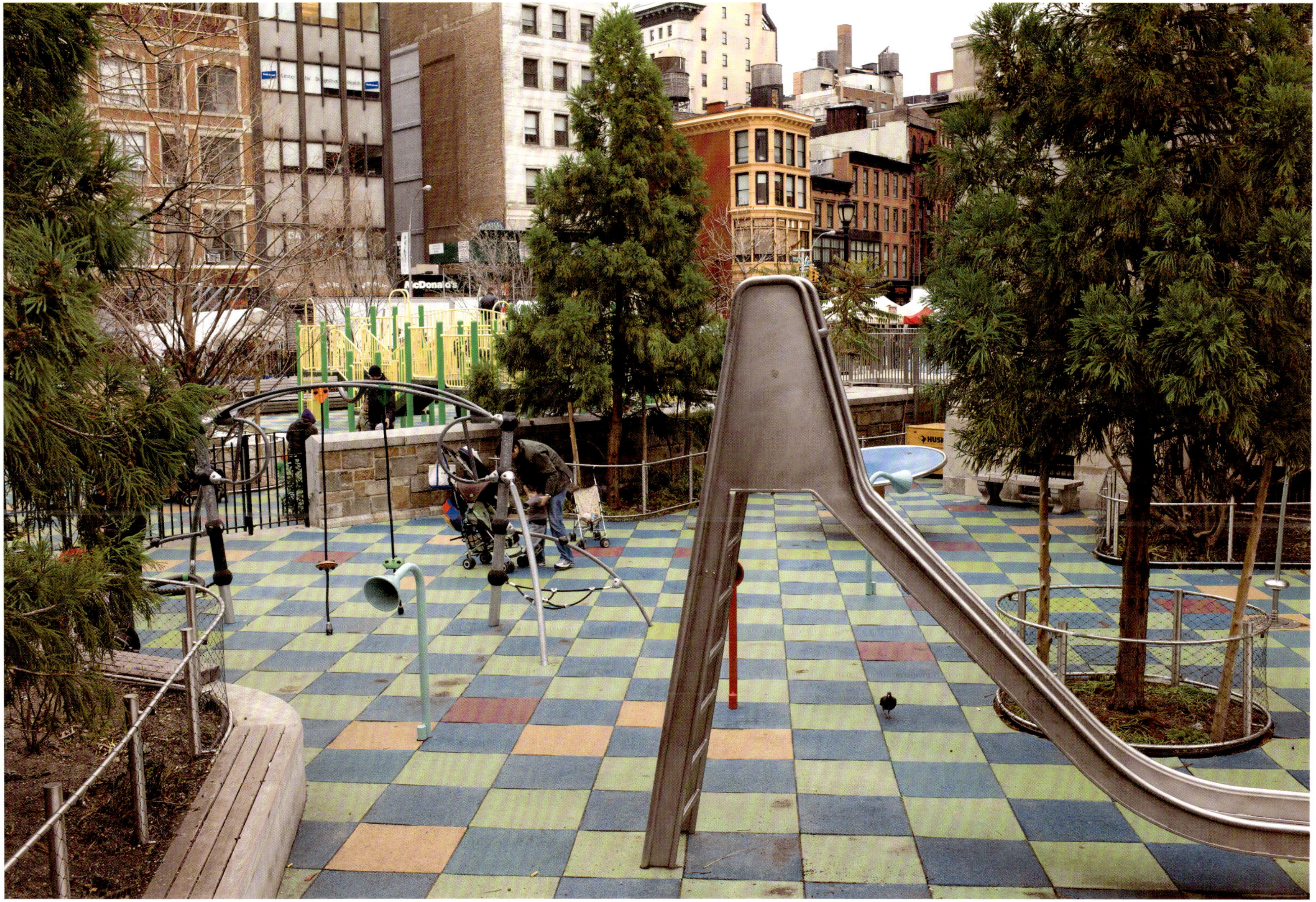

3

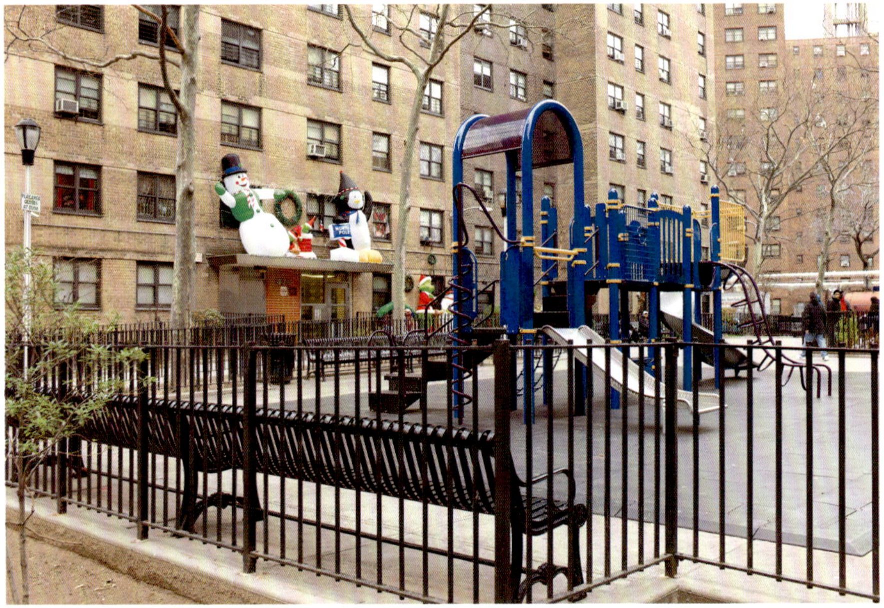

4

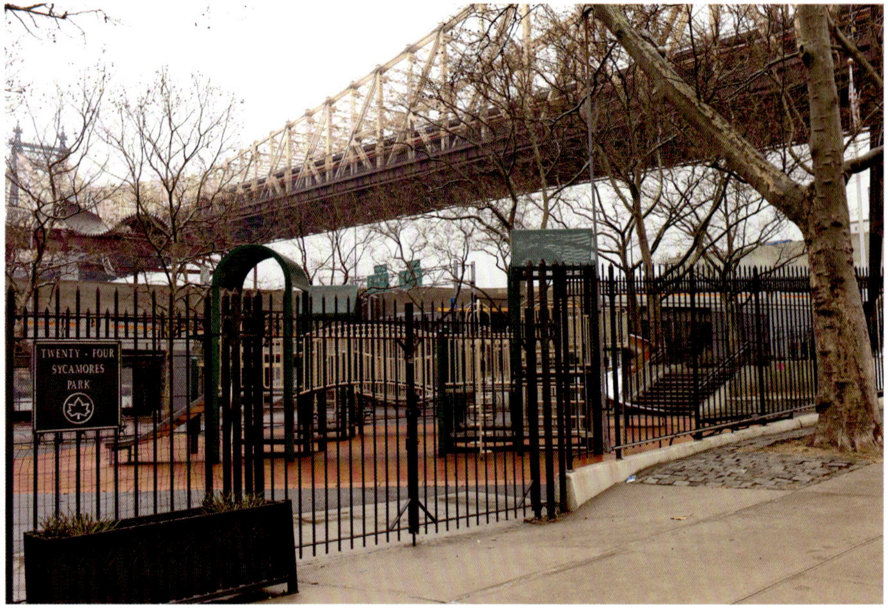

5

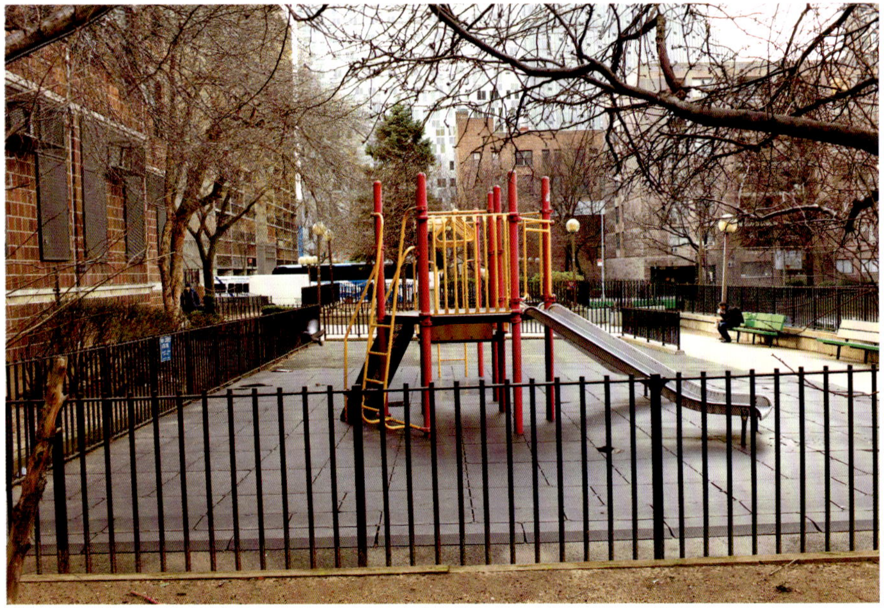

6

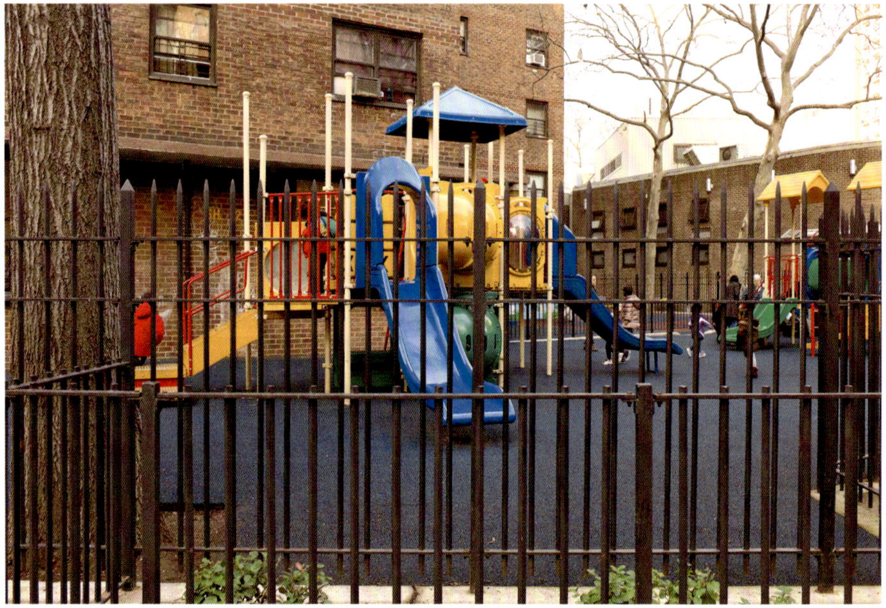

7

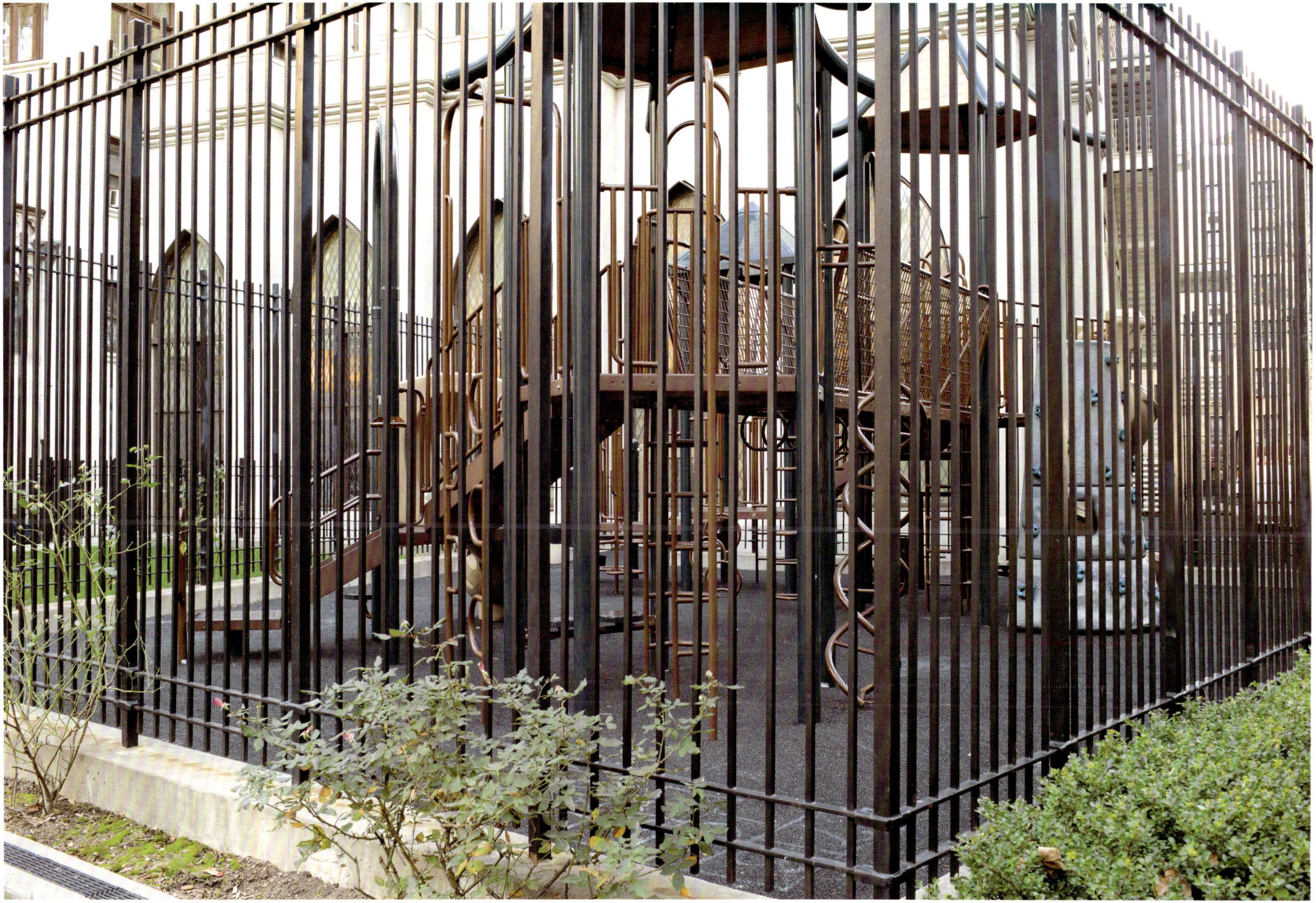

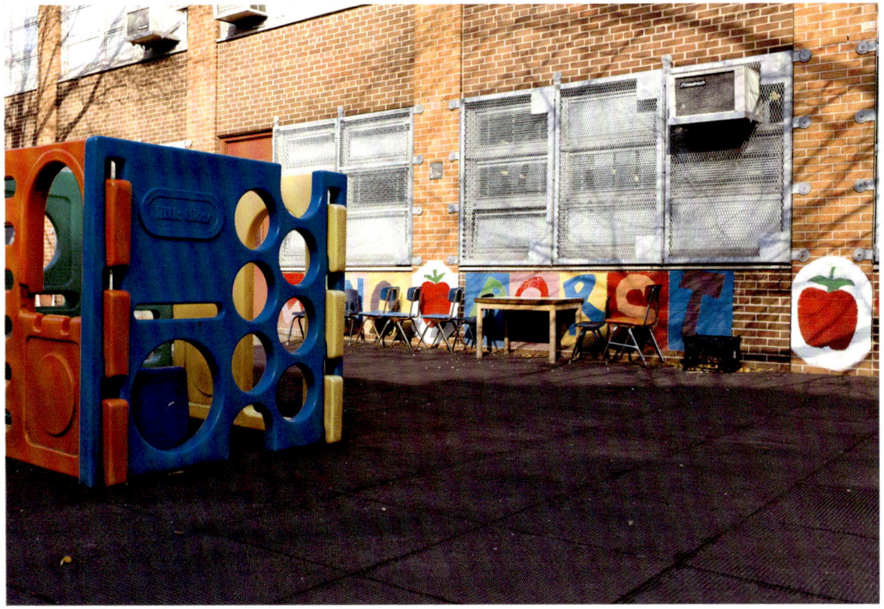

9

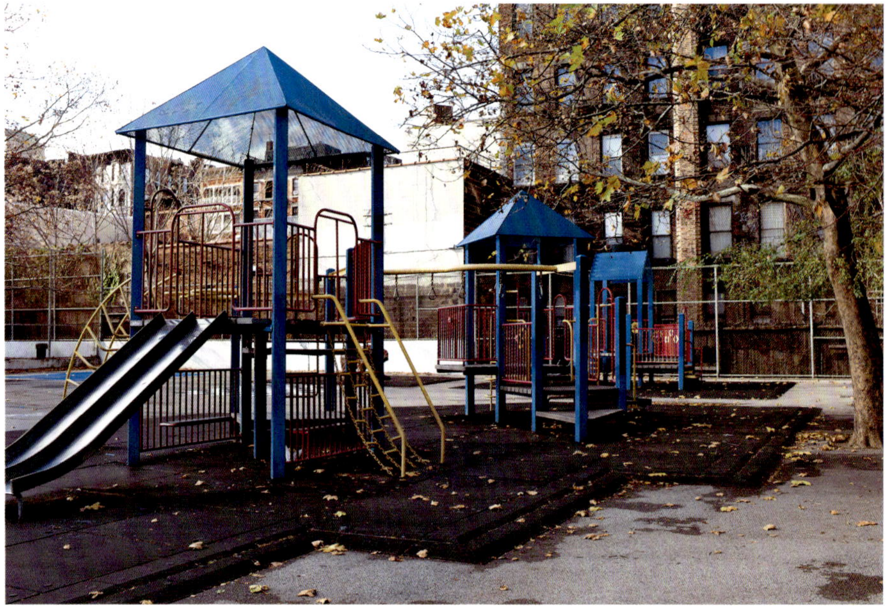

10

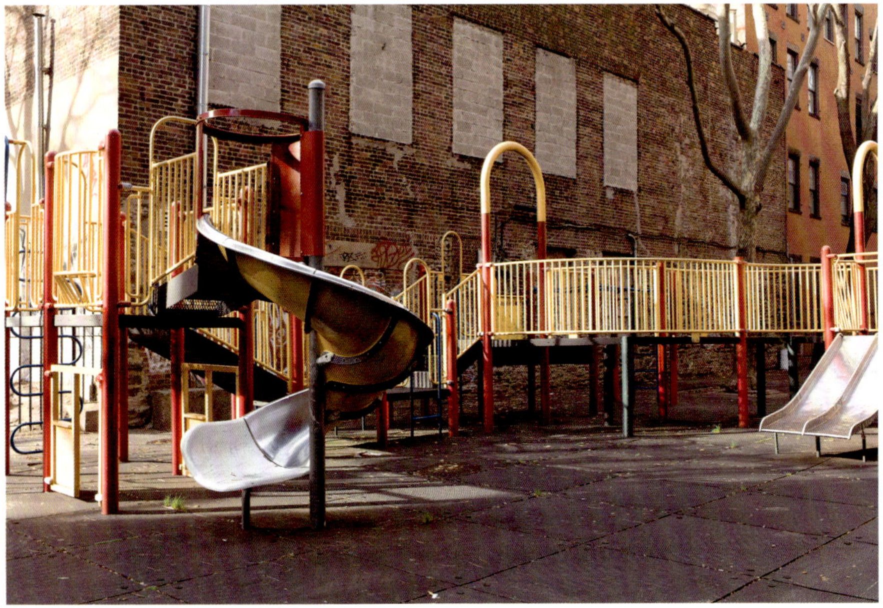

11

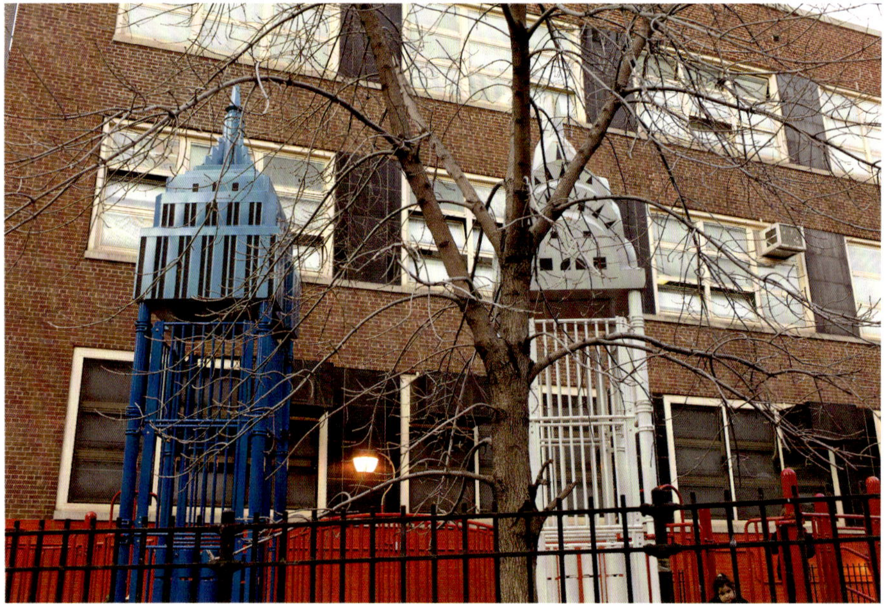

12

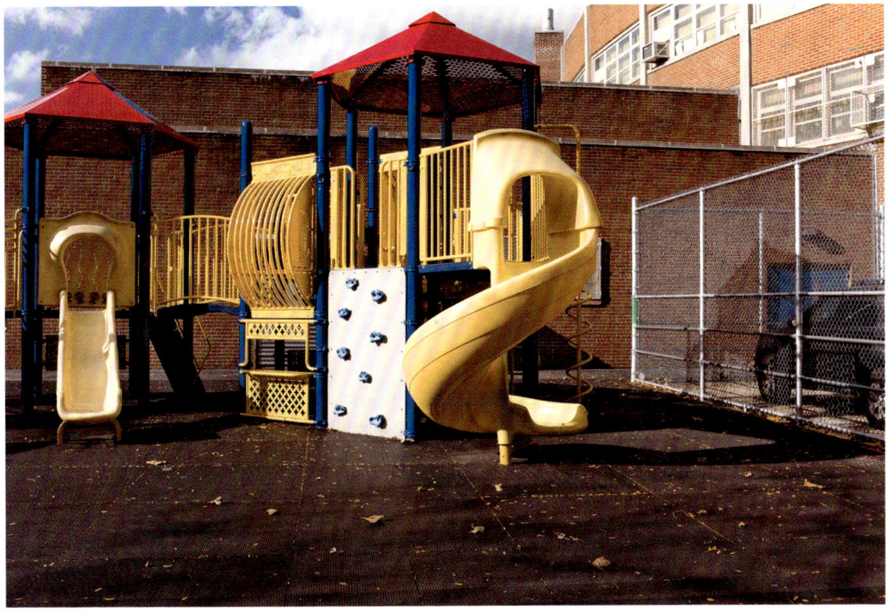

13

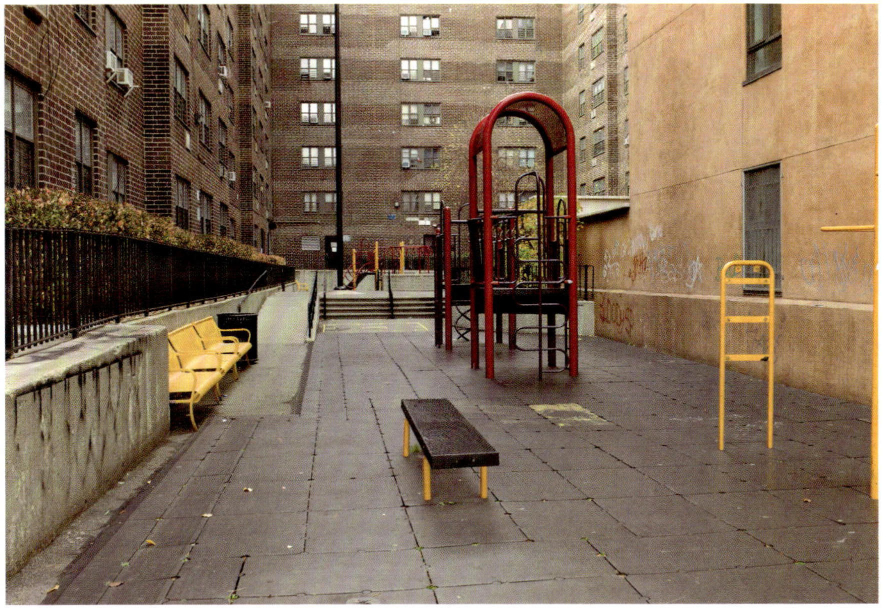

14

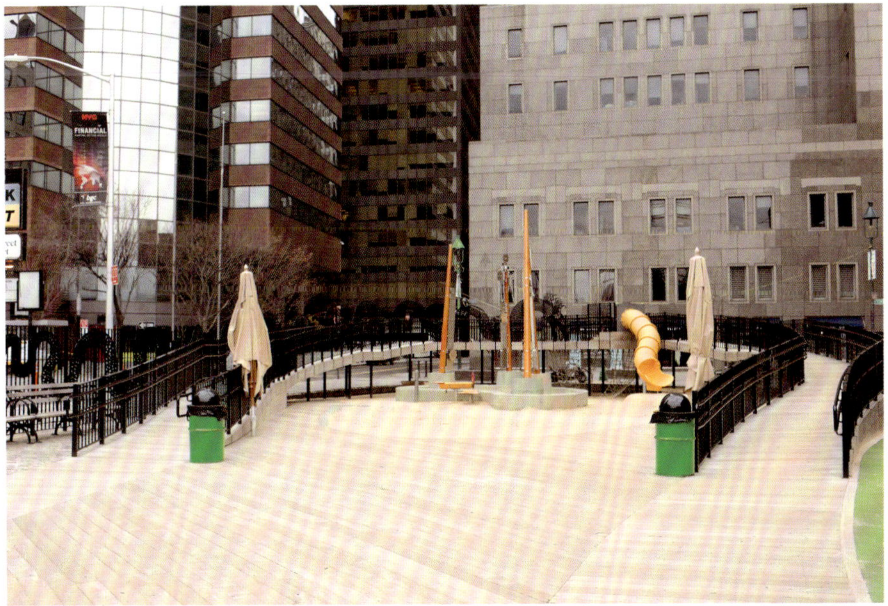

15

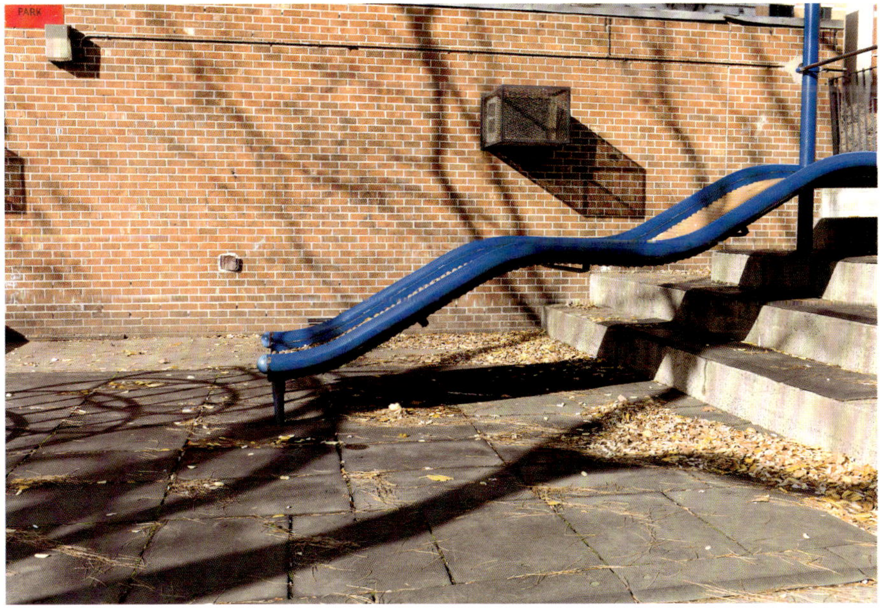

16

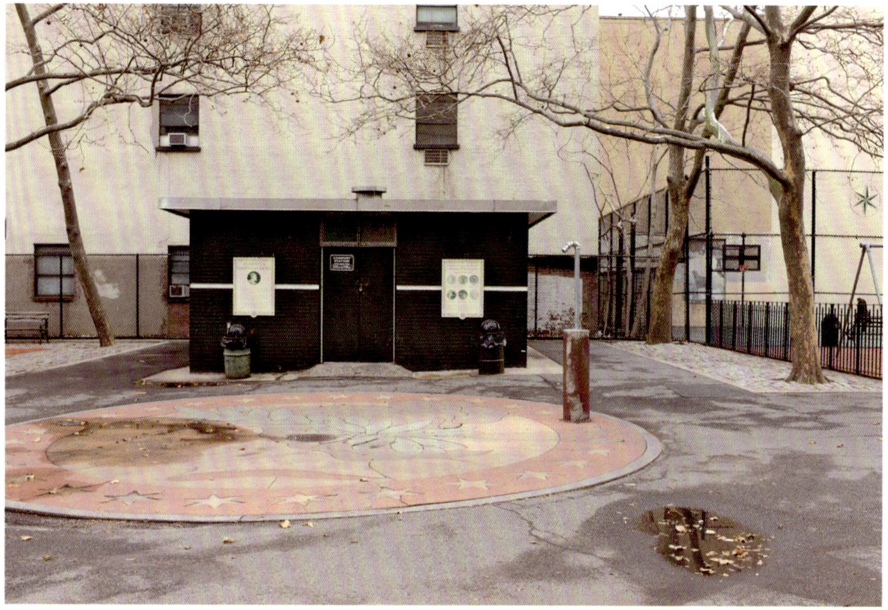

17

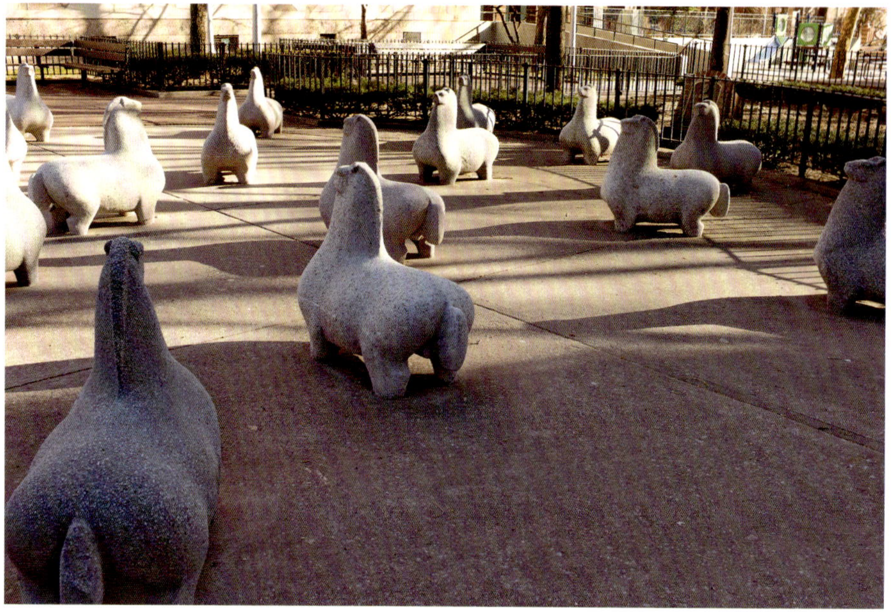

18

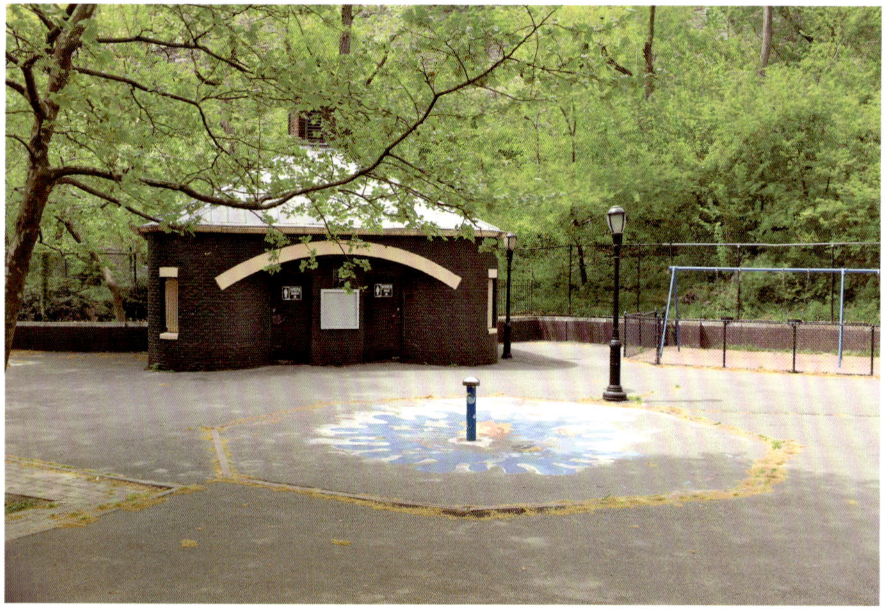

19

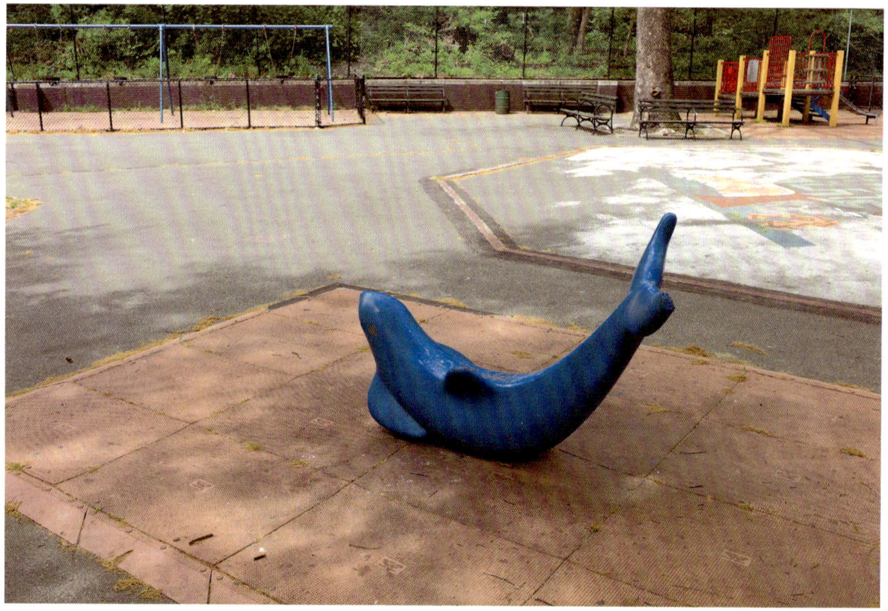

20

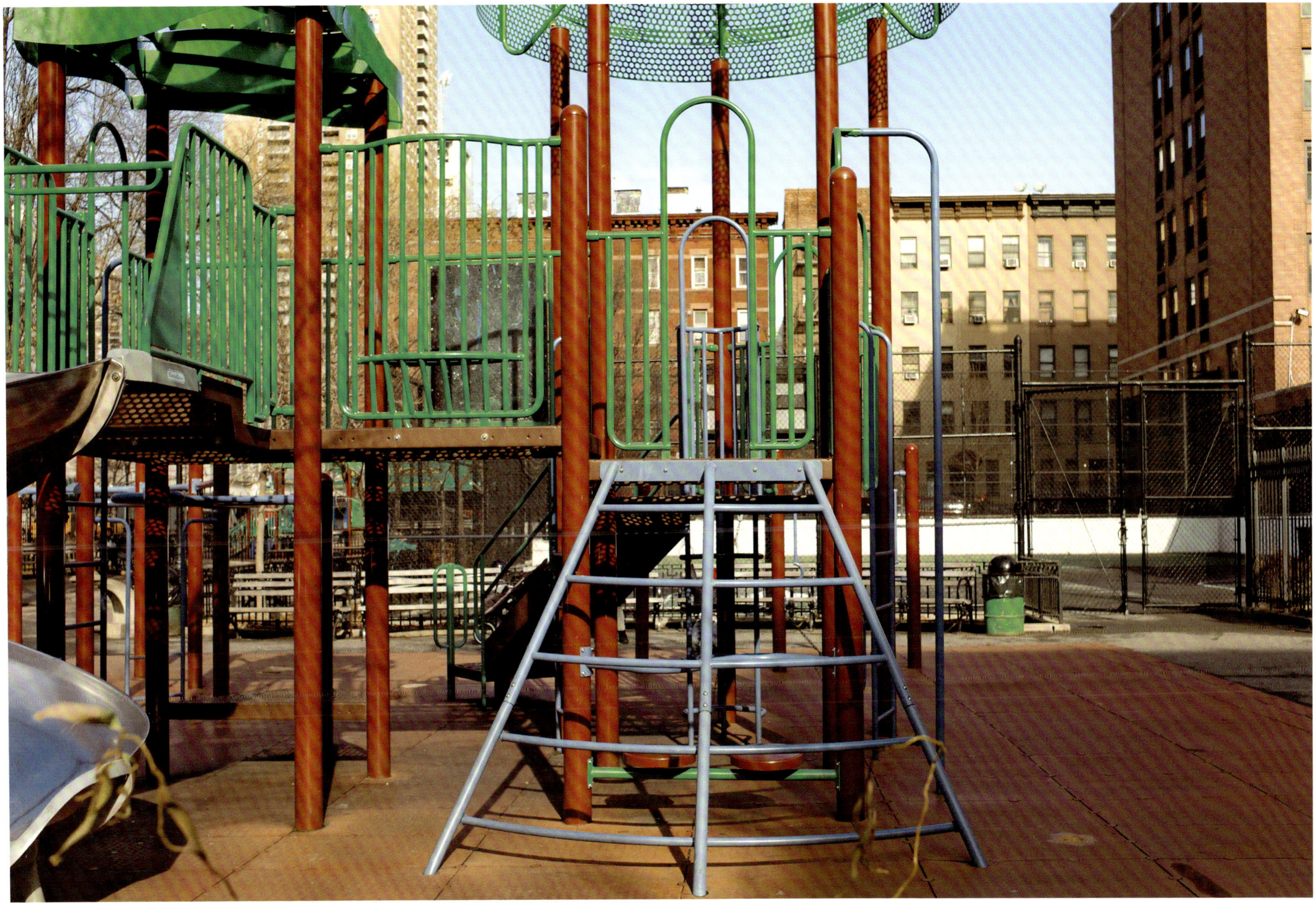

21

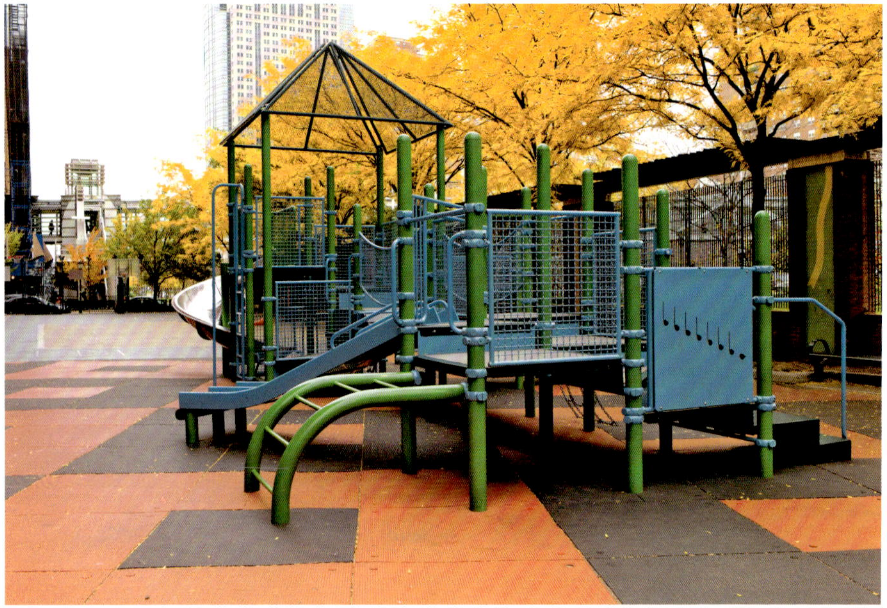

22

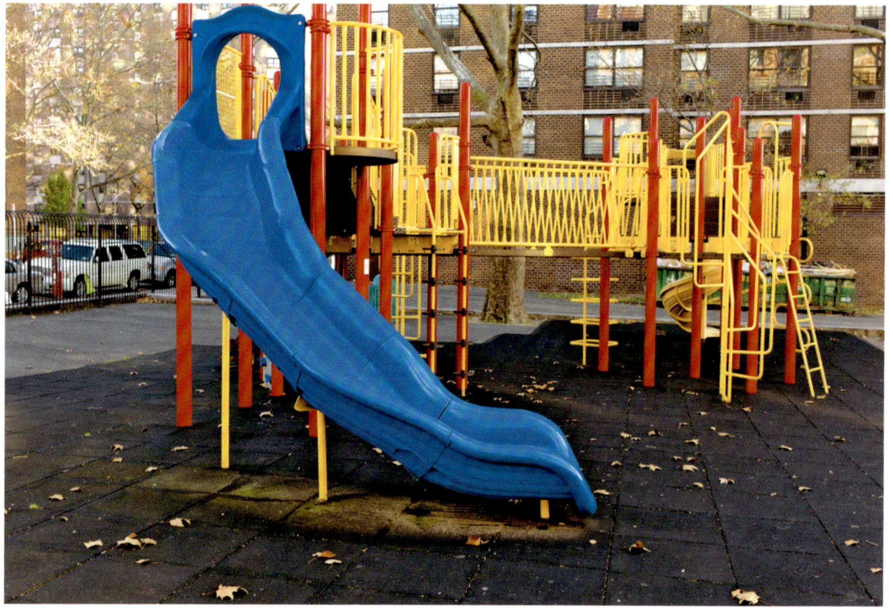

23

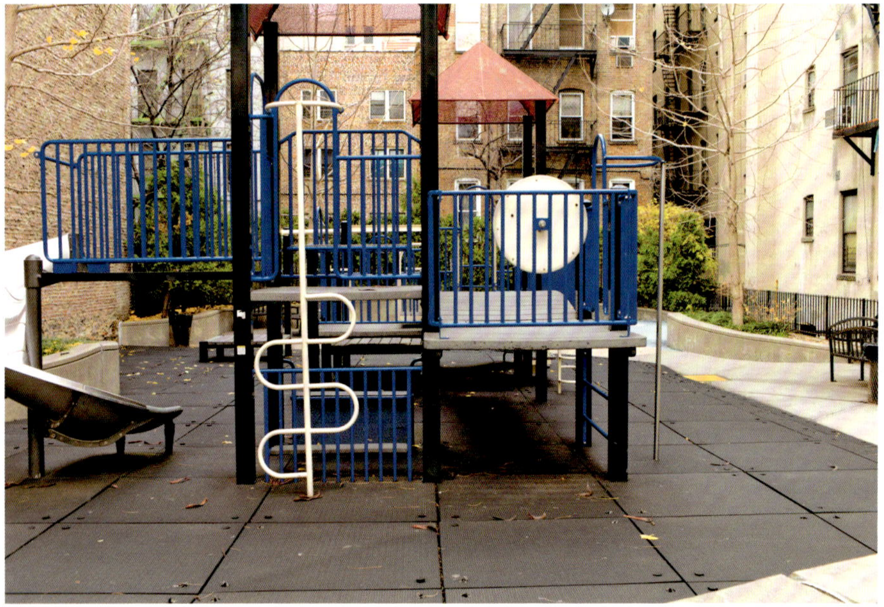

24

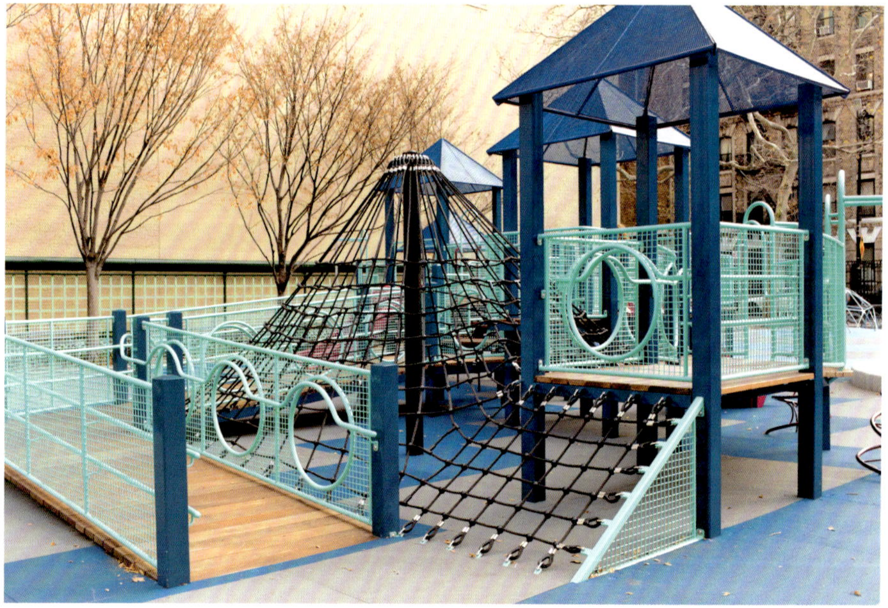

25

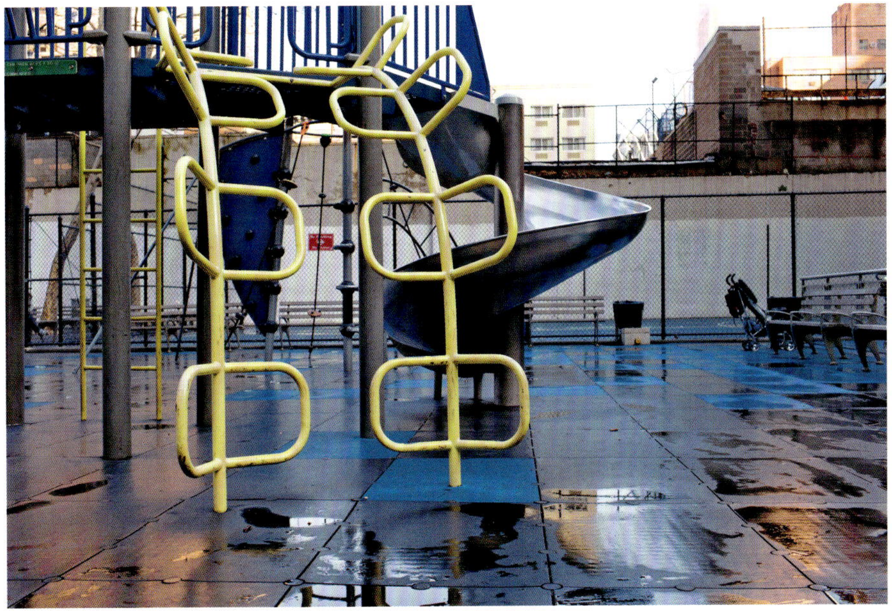

26

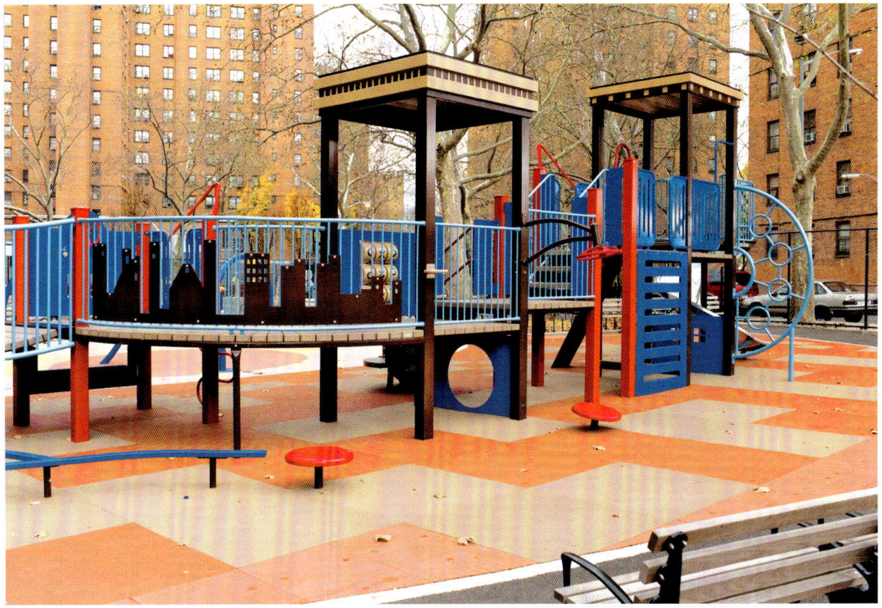

27

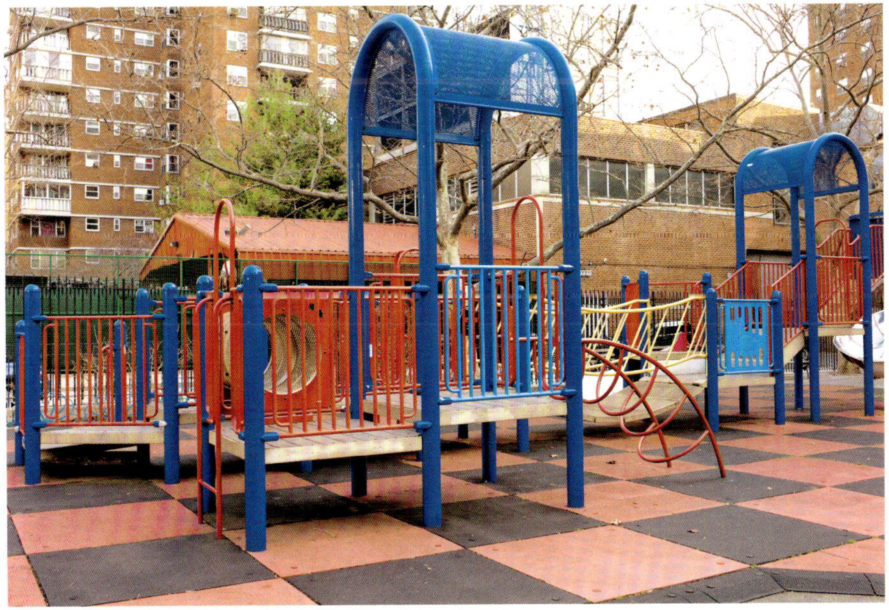

28

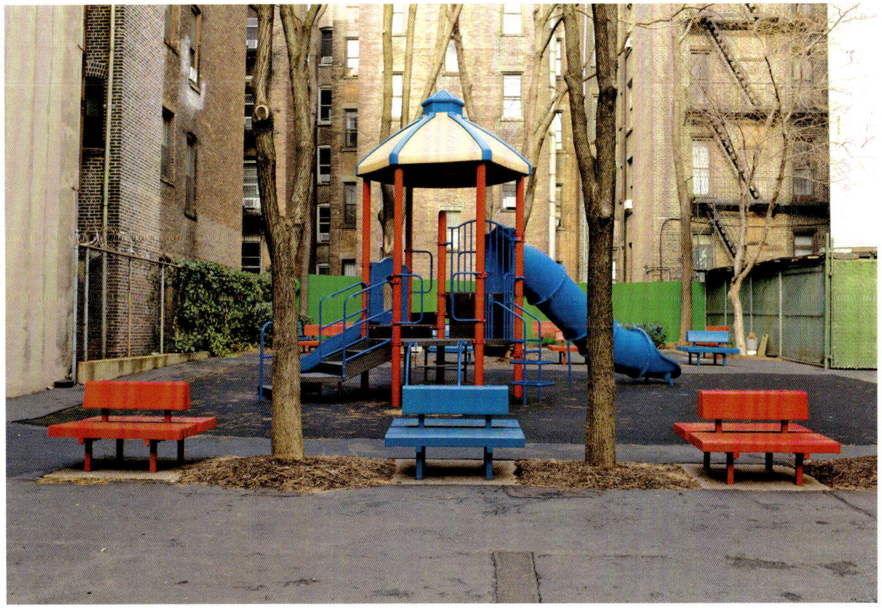

29

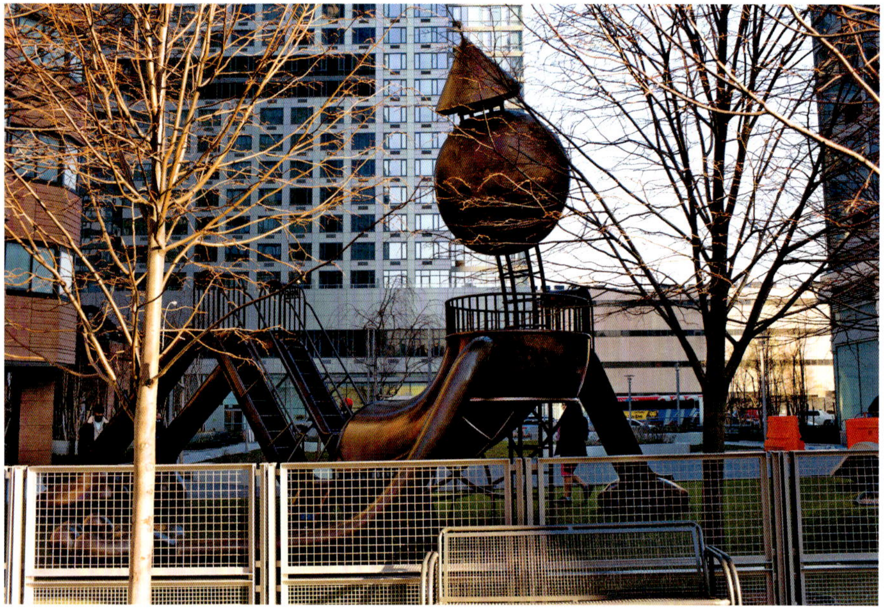

30

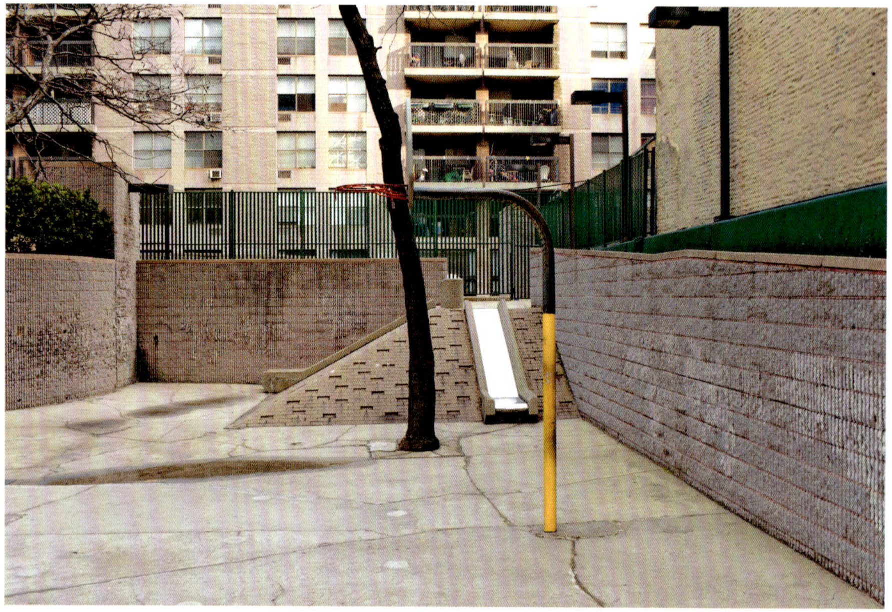

31

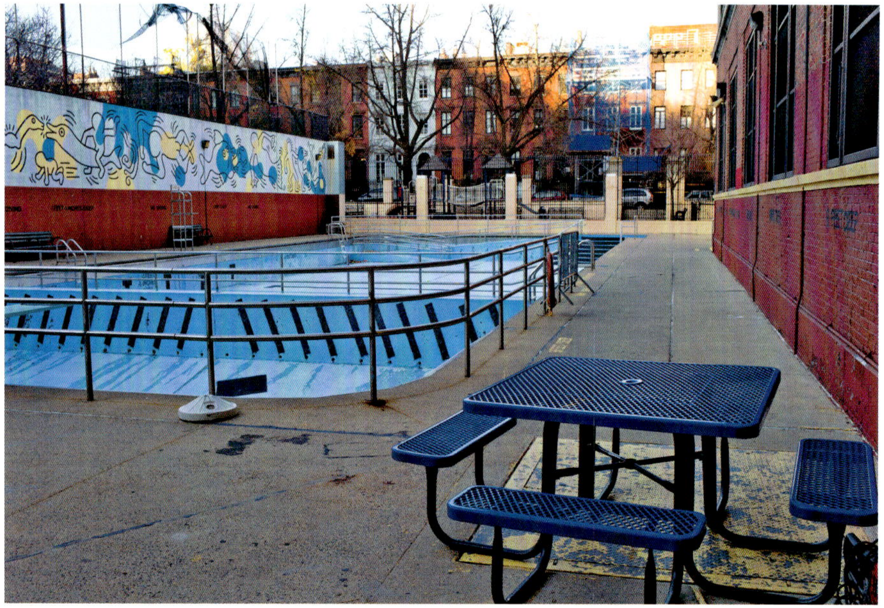

32

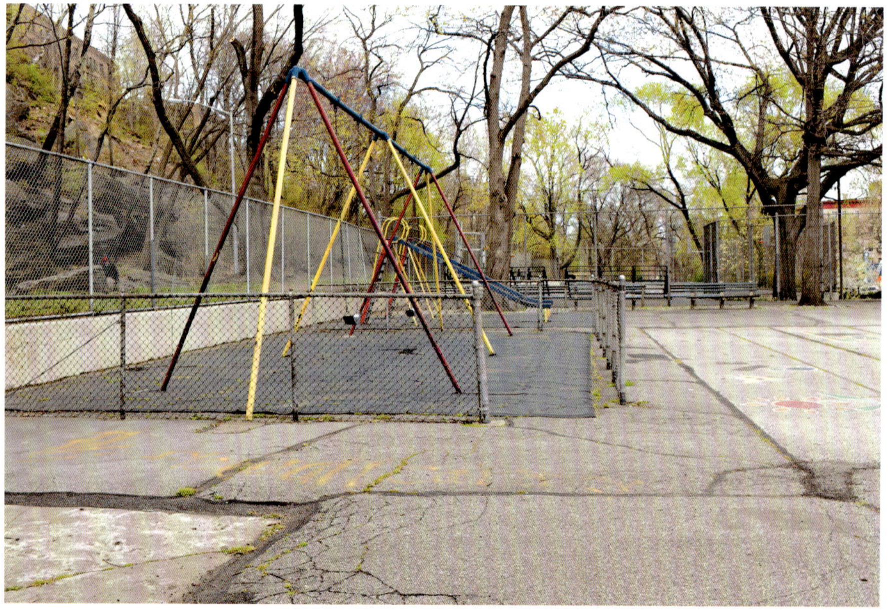

33

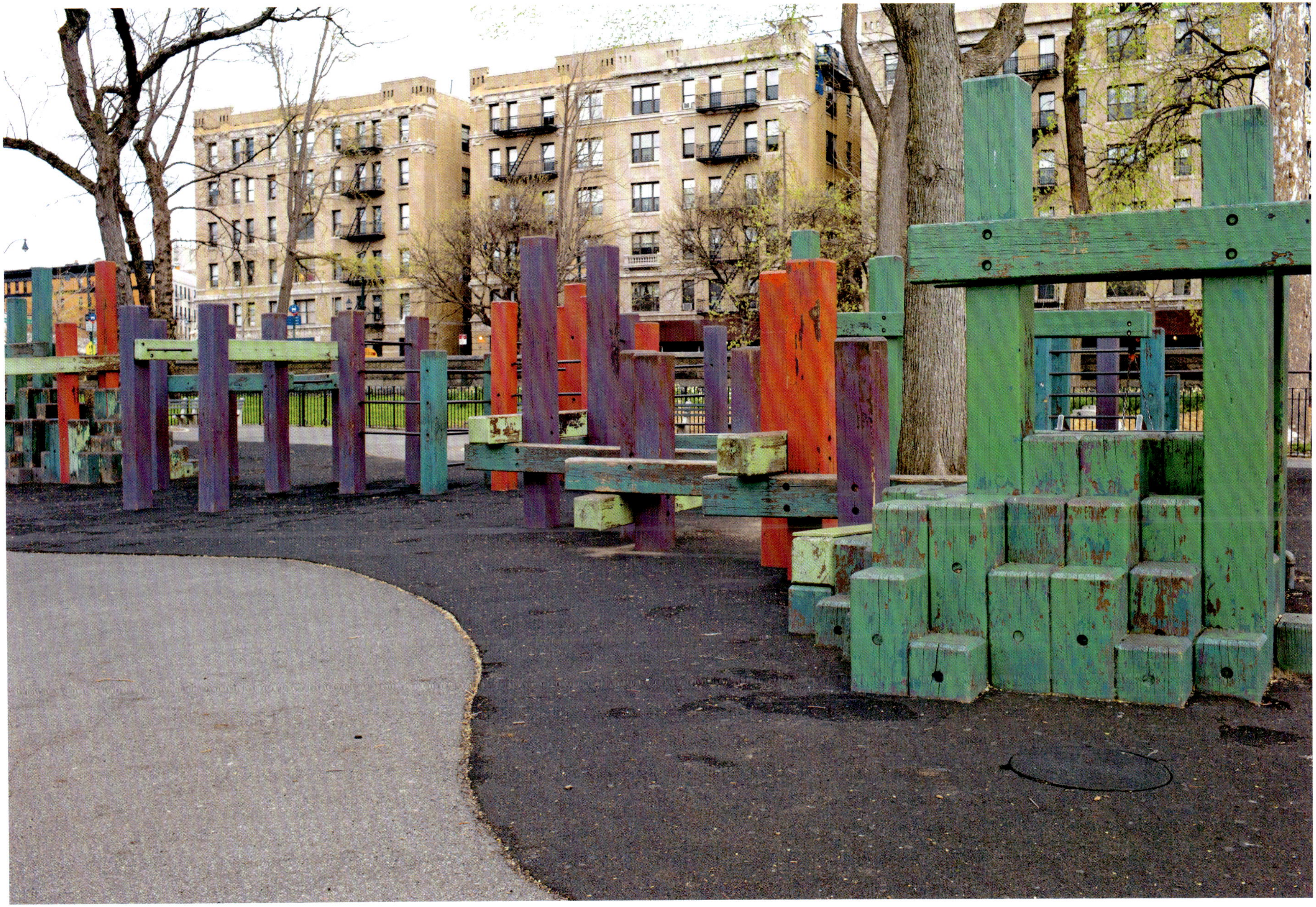

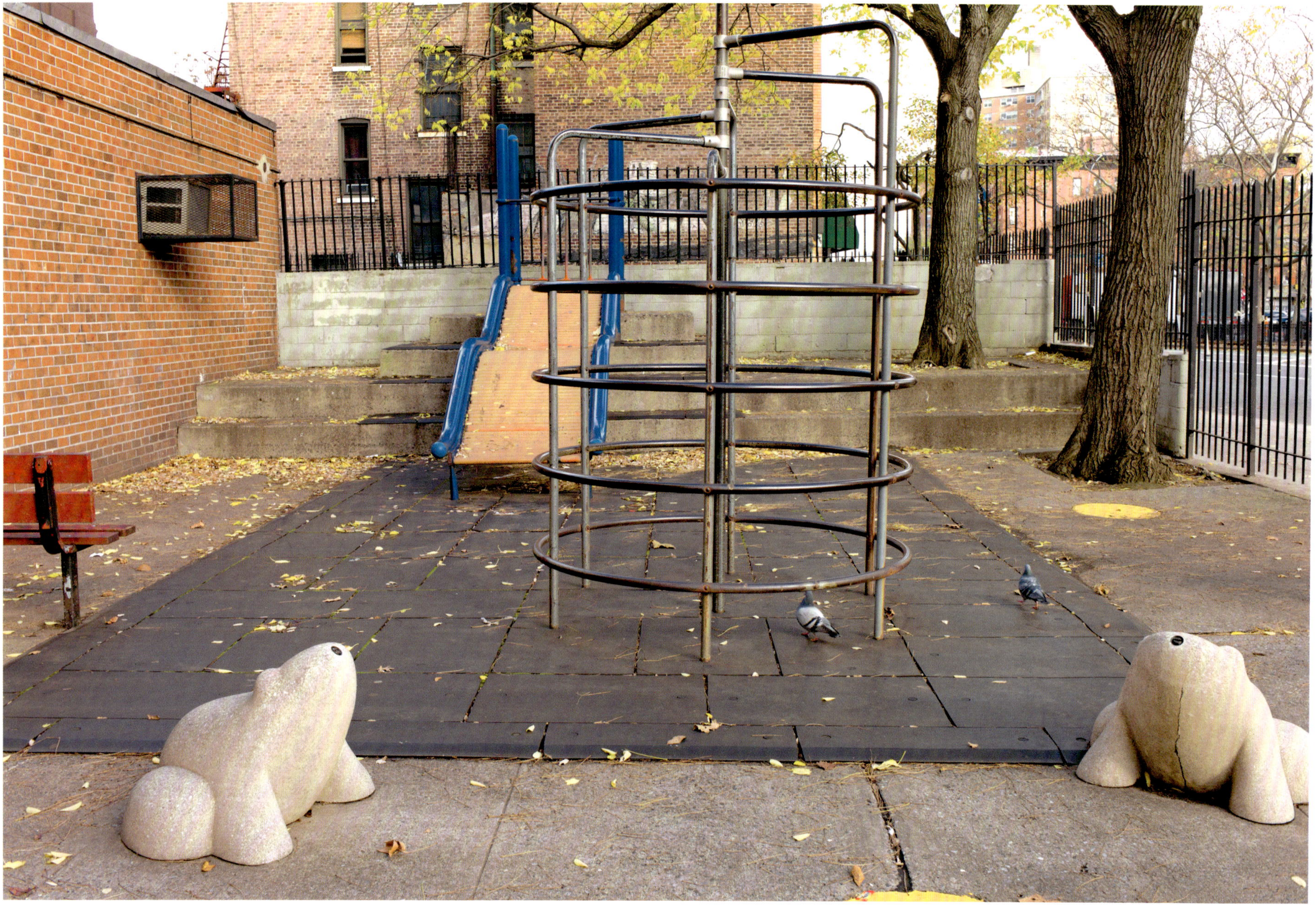

35

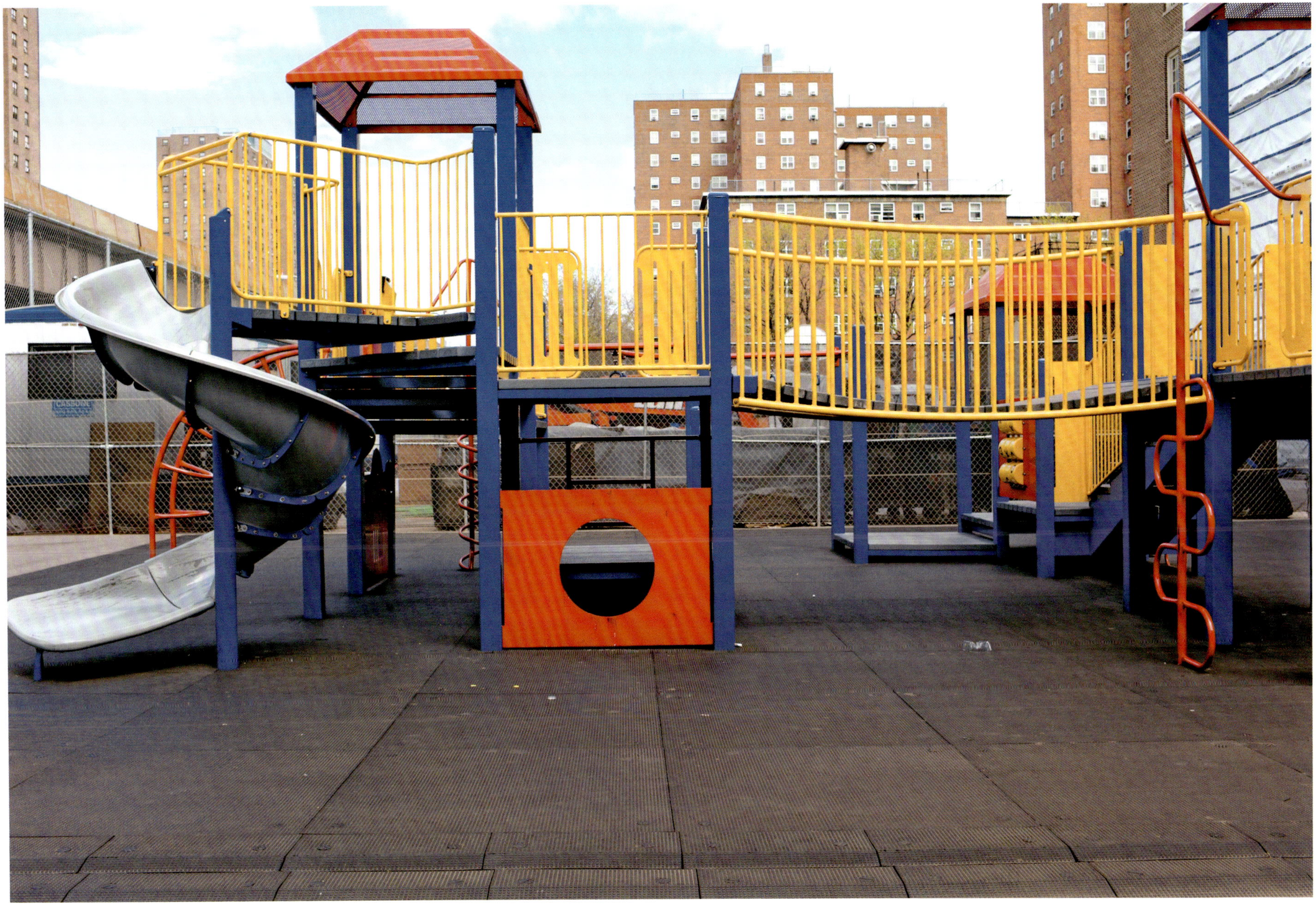

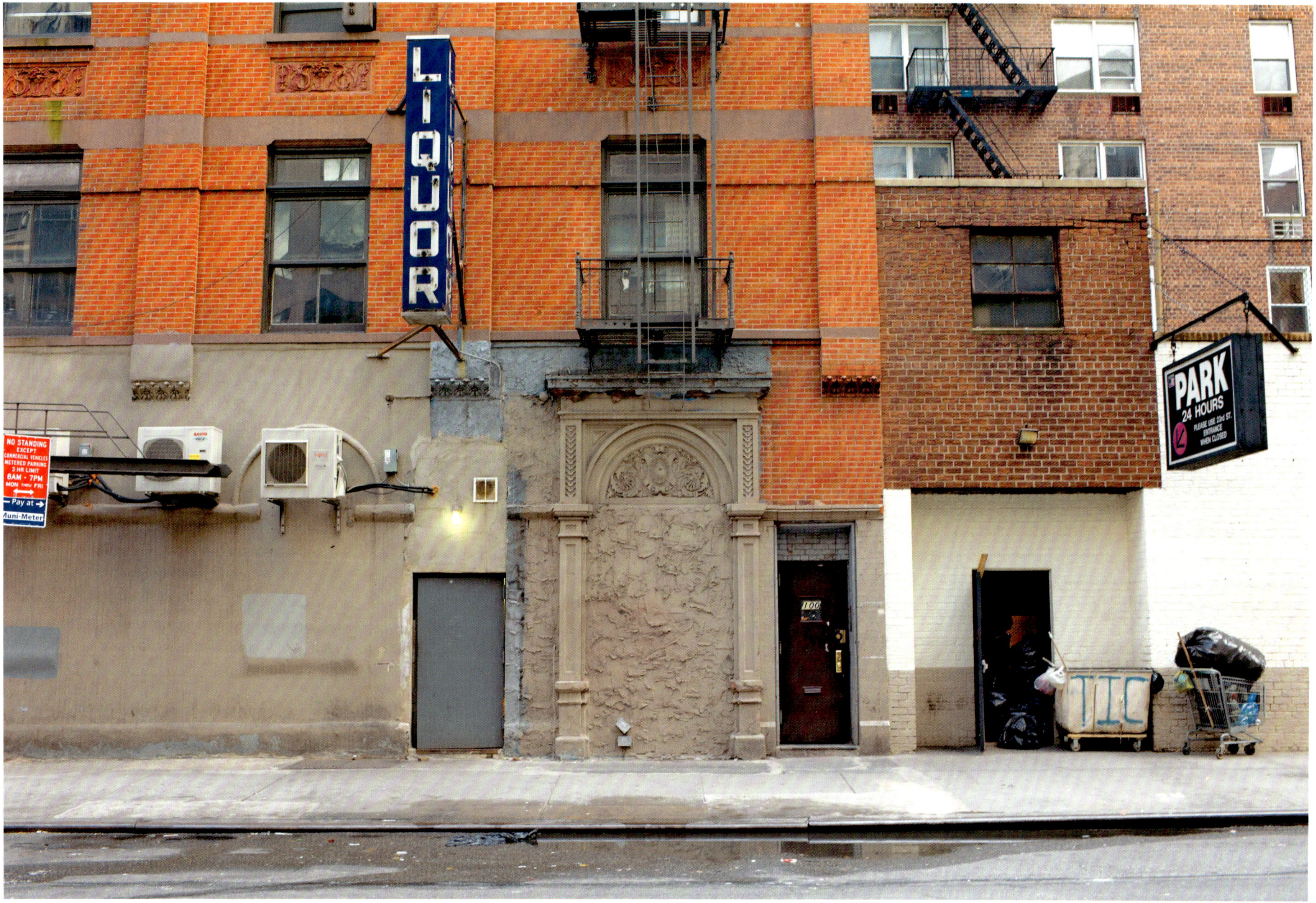
LIQUOR
PARK
24 HOURS
NO STANDING
Pay at
TIC

RELICS

So much of New York is constantly turning over—destroyed and rebuilt, covered up, or otherwise replaced—that it is always surprising to come across something old that has either been preserved or forgotten, often in isolation from the urban context evolving around it. If it's not in the way, we tend to leave it alone. New storefronts that cover old facades often leave parts visible, or sometimes owners decide to remove a latter-day layer and restore what is underneath.

Every once in a while something interesting is uncovered in a renovation process and then preserved: burial grounds, murals, tile designs, clocks, wooden water pipes. Buildings that were parts of the original elevated train system still stand, signs from long-gone businesses peek out from behind or floating above new ones. Old wooden houses survive between newer apartments that surely tried to push them out, and for a variety of reasons a structure from an earlier era can remain right in the middle of new development that completely surrounds it.

1 Financial District
2 Financial District
3 Hamilton Heights
4 SoHo
5 Washington Heights
6 Hamilton Heights
7 Little Italy
8 Herald Square
9 Chinatown
10 Herald Square
11 Harlem
12 Hudson Heights
13 Harlem
14 Fort George
15 Harlem
16 East Village
17 Washington Heights
18 Chelsea
19 Chelsea
20 West Village
21 Manhattanville
22 Gramercy Park
23 East Harlem
24 Upper East Side
25 Hamilton Heights

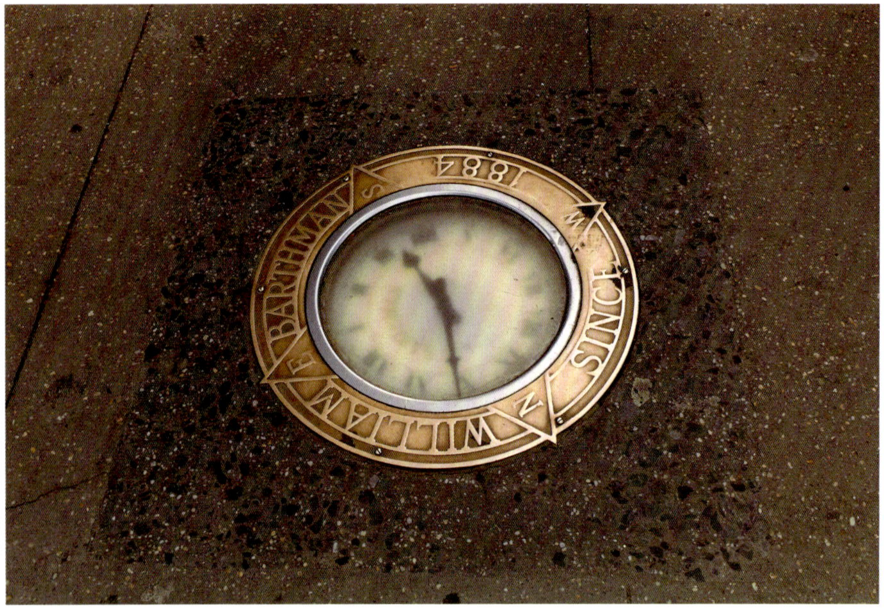

2

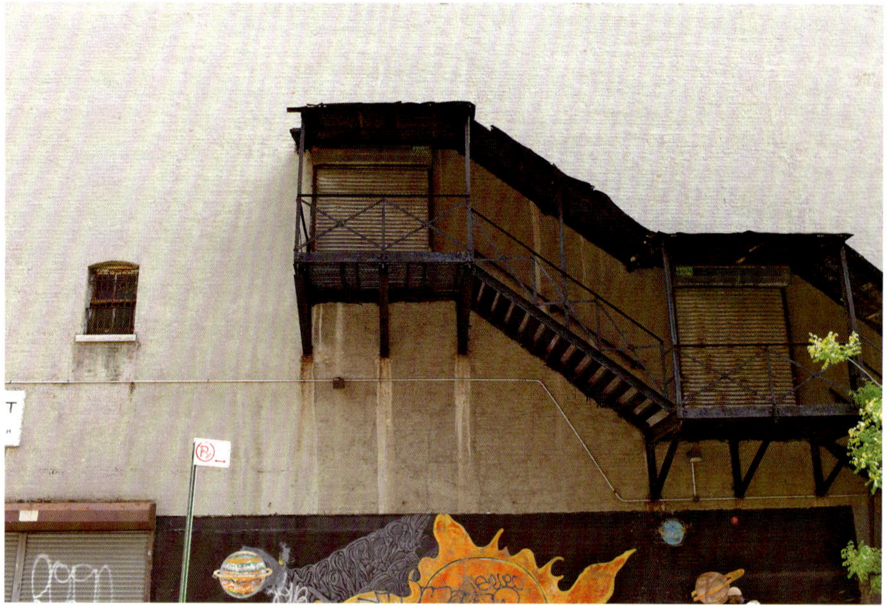

3

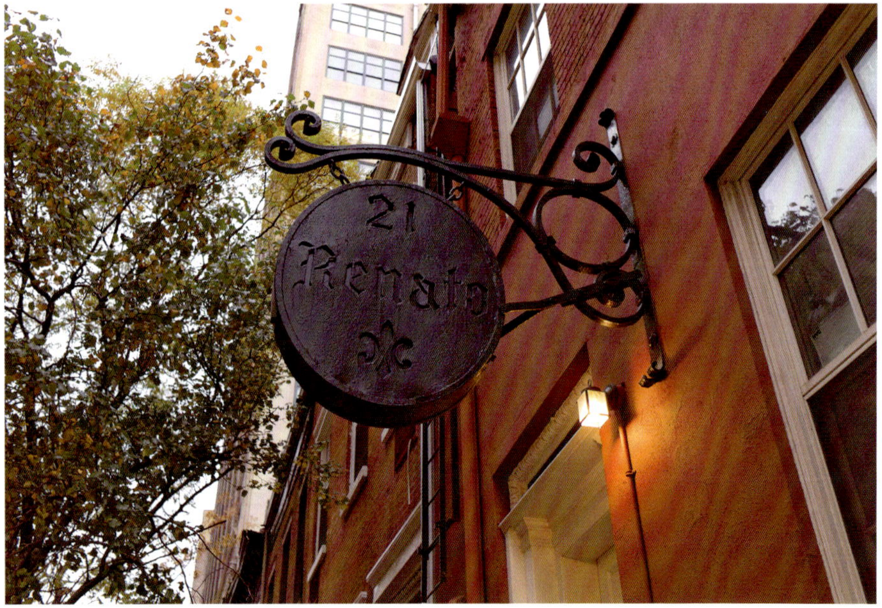

4

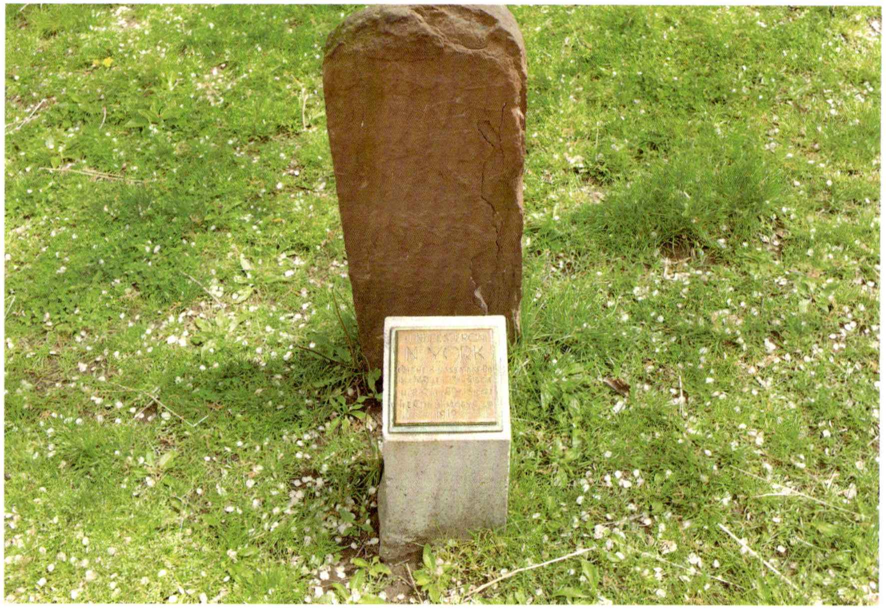

5

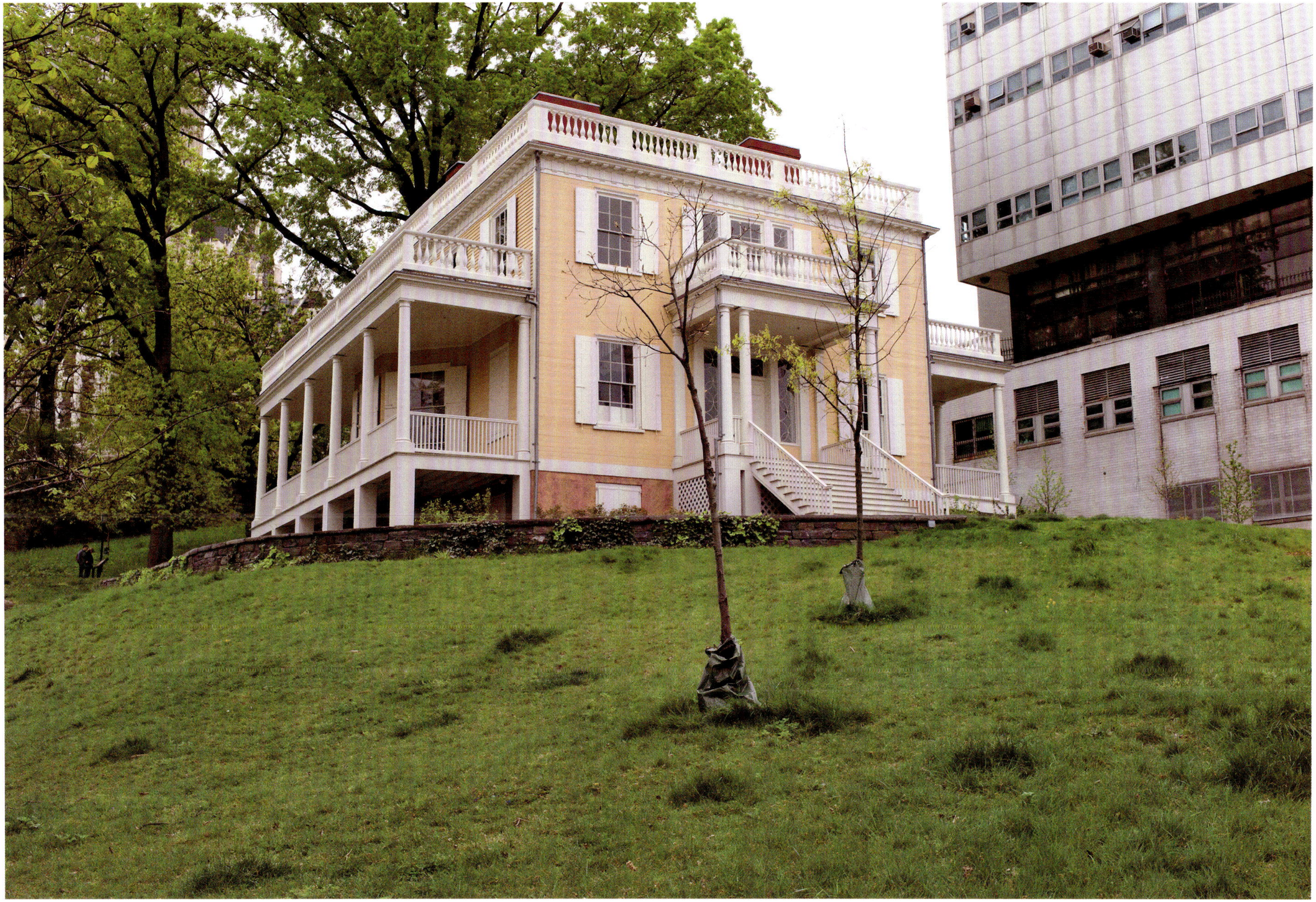

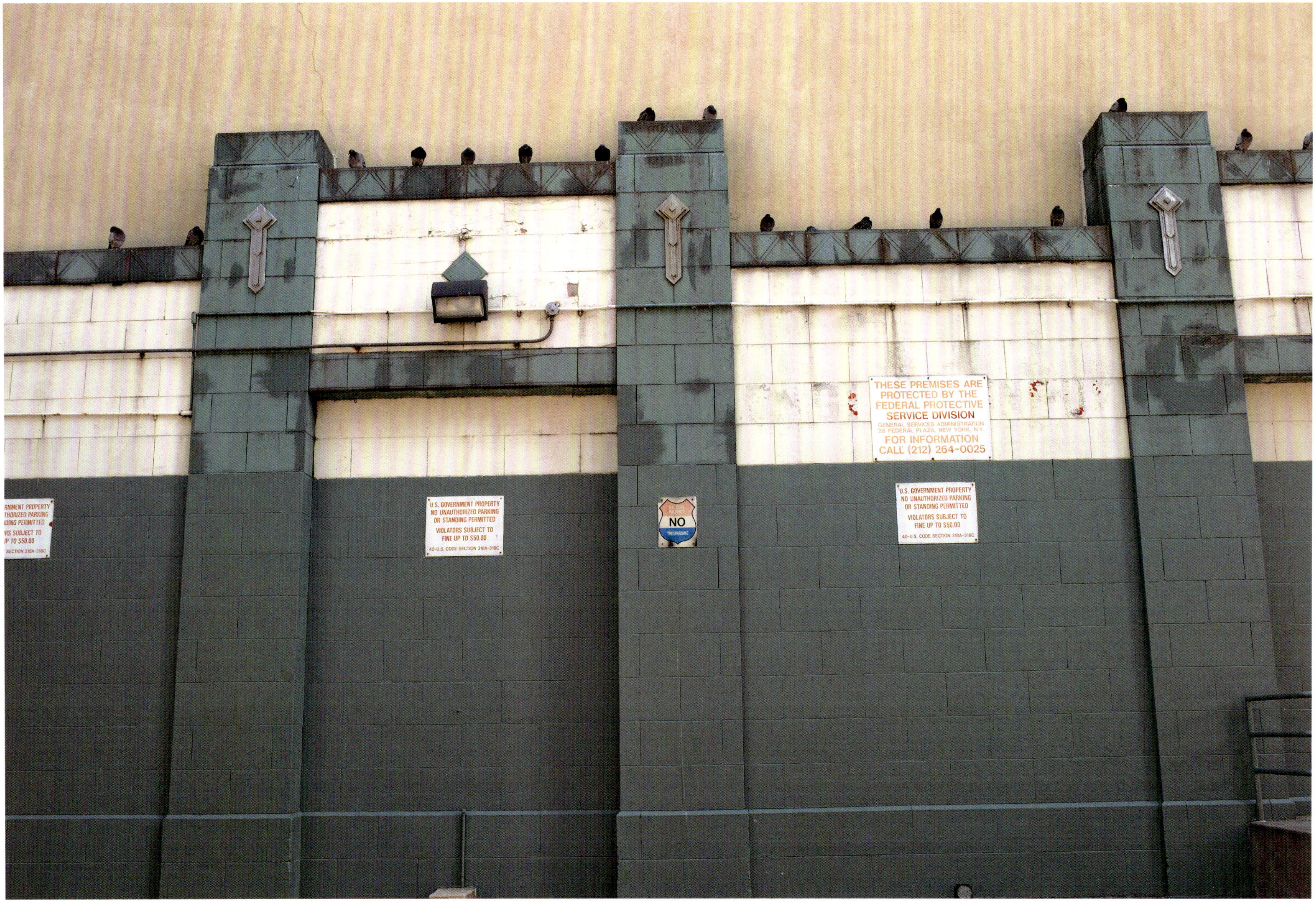
U.S. GOVERNMENT PROPERTY
NO UNAUTHORIZED PARKING
OR STANDING PERMITTED
VIOLATORS SUBJECT TO
FINE UP TO $50.00
40-U.S. CODE SECTION 318A-318C
NO
THESE PREMISES ARE
PROTECTED BY THE
FEDERAL PROTECTIVE
SERVICE DIVISION
GENERAL SERVICES ADMINISTRATION
26 FEDERAL PLAZA, NEW YORK, N.Y.
FOR INFORMATION
CALL (212) 264-0025
U.S. GOVERNMENT PROPERTY
NO UNAUTHORIZED PARKING
OR STANDING PERMITTED
VIOLATORS SUBJECT TO
FINE UP TO $50.00
40-U.S. CODE SECTION 318A-318C

7

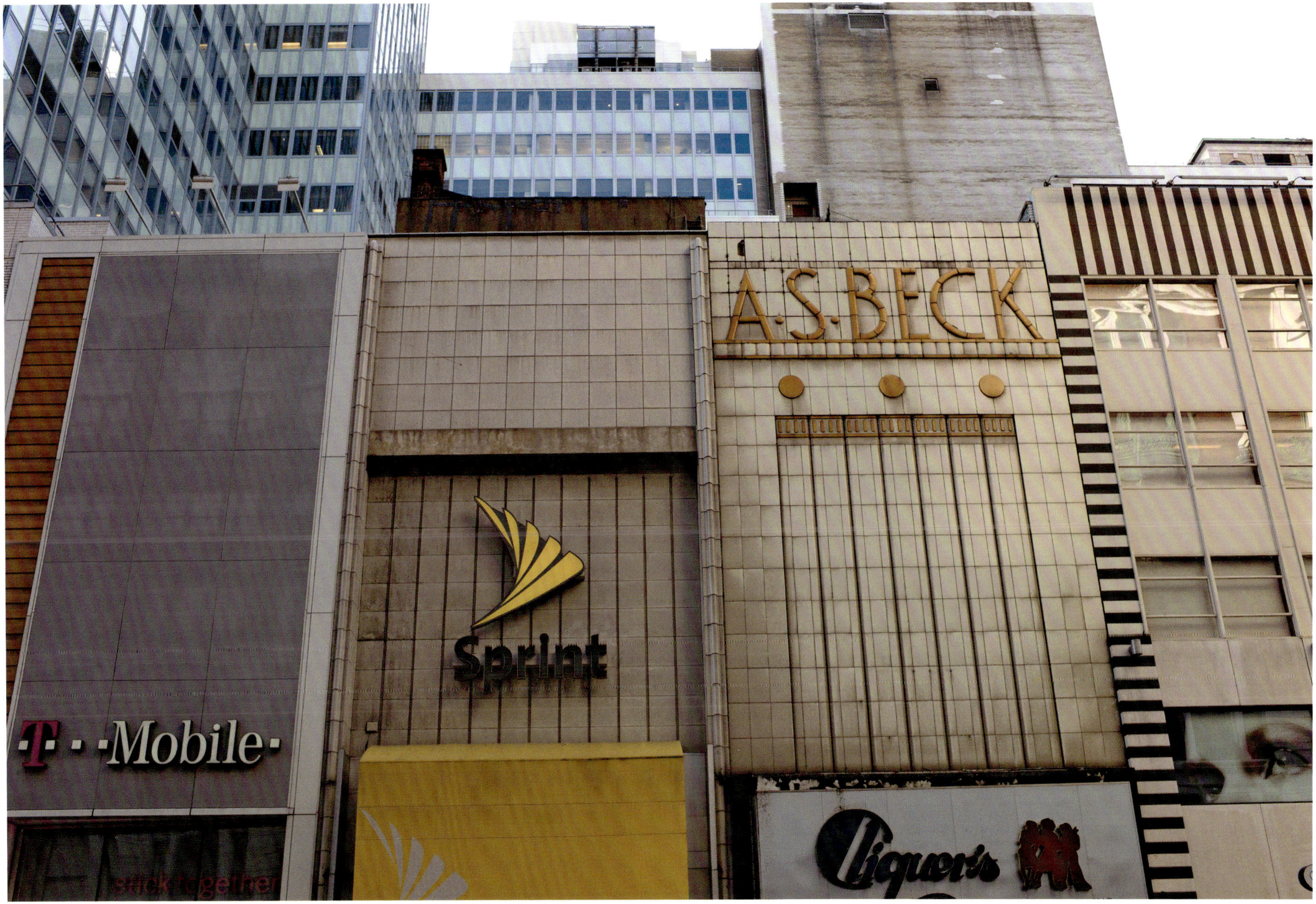
A·S·BECK
Sprint
T · ·Mobile·

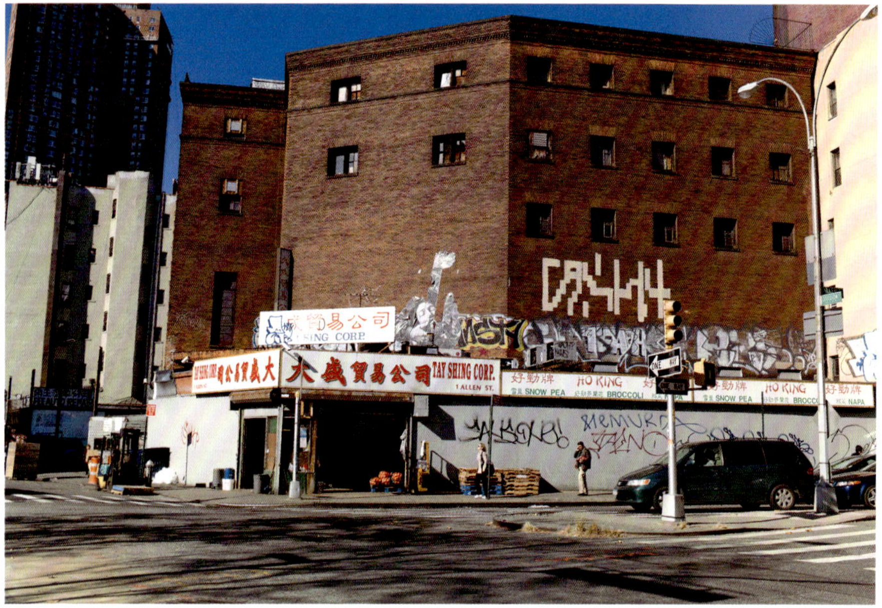
大盛貿易公司
TAY SHING CORP.
1 ALLEN ST.
HO KING
SNOW PEA
BROCCOLI

9

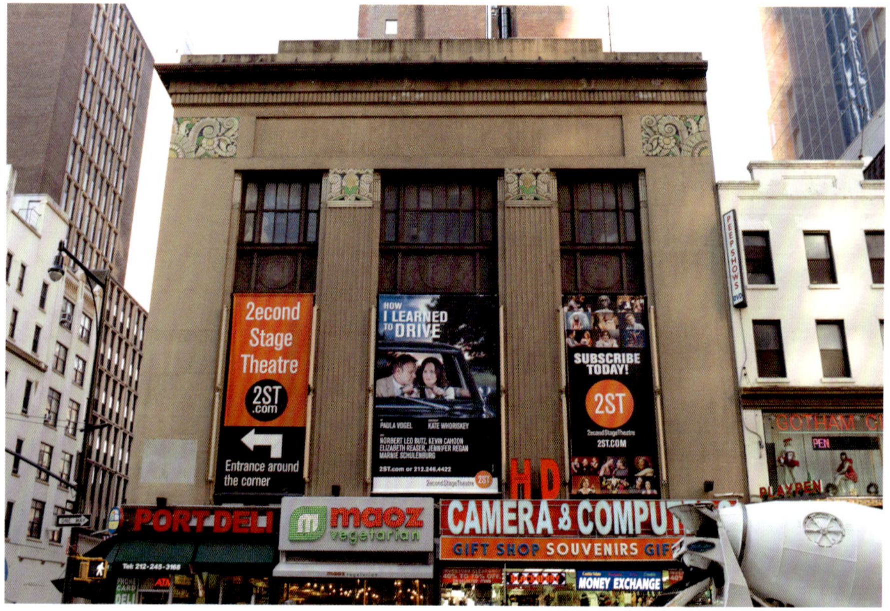
2econd Stage Theatre
2ST .com
Entrance around the corner
HOW I LEARNED TO DRIVE
SUBSCRIBE TODAY!
2ST
PORT DELI
maoz vegetarian
CAMERA & COMPUT
GIFT SHOP SOUVENIRS GIF
MONEY EXCHANGE

10

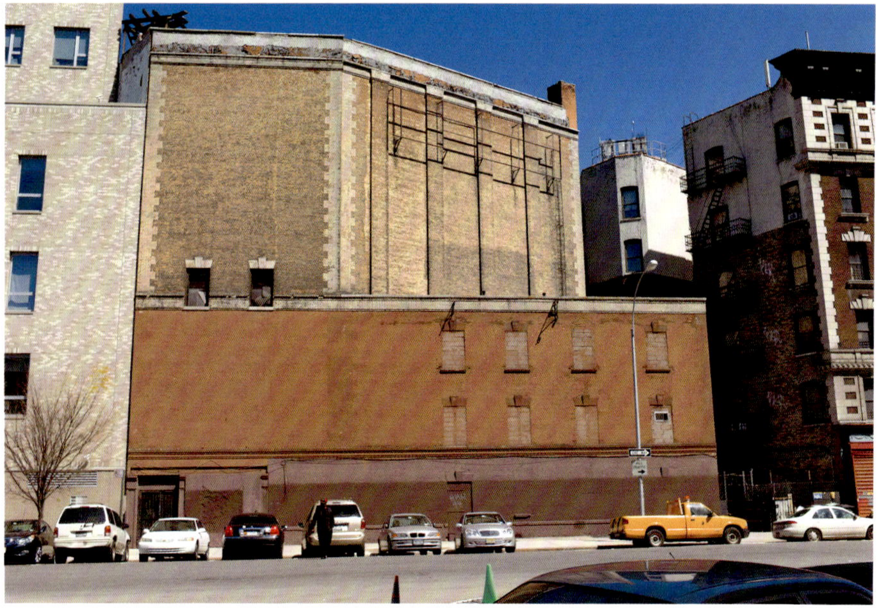

11

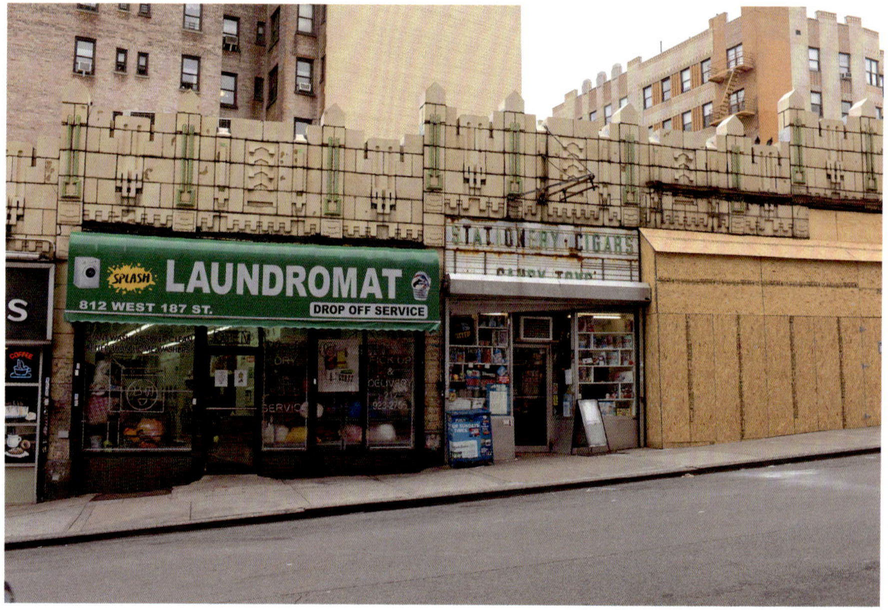
SPLASH
LAUNDROMAT
812 WEST 187 ST.
DROP OFF SERVICE

12

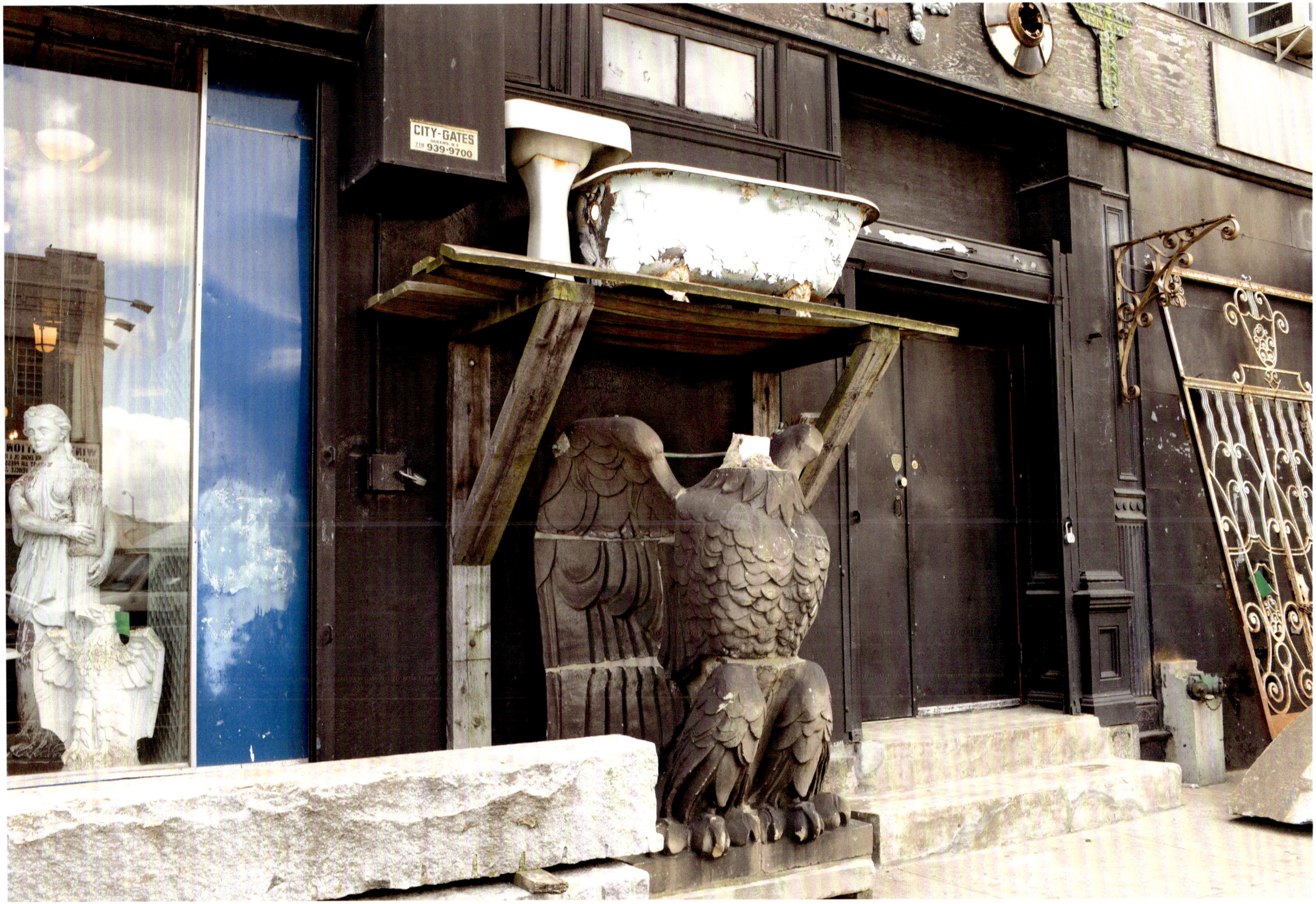

13

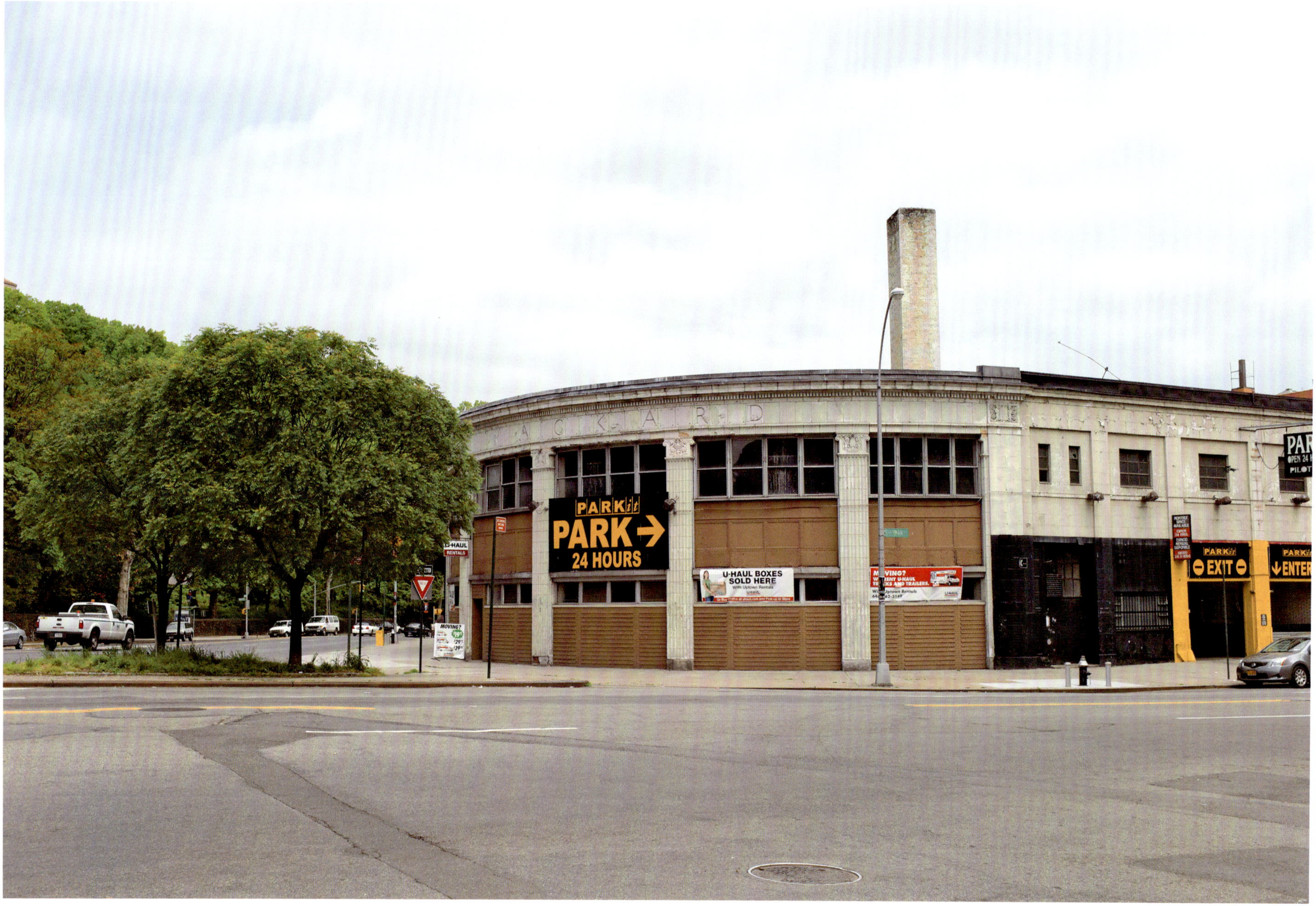

14

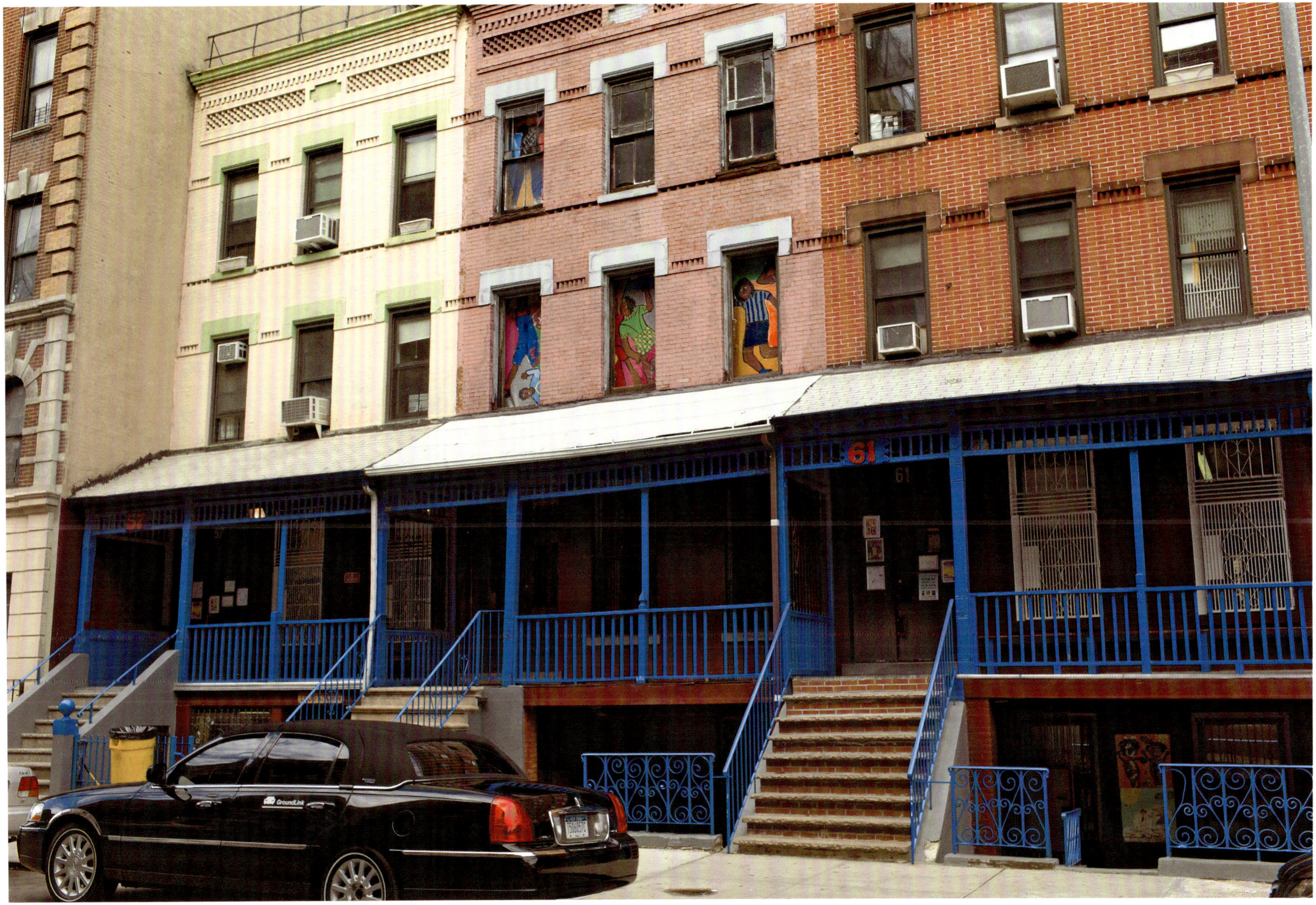

15

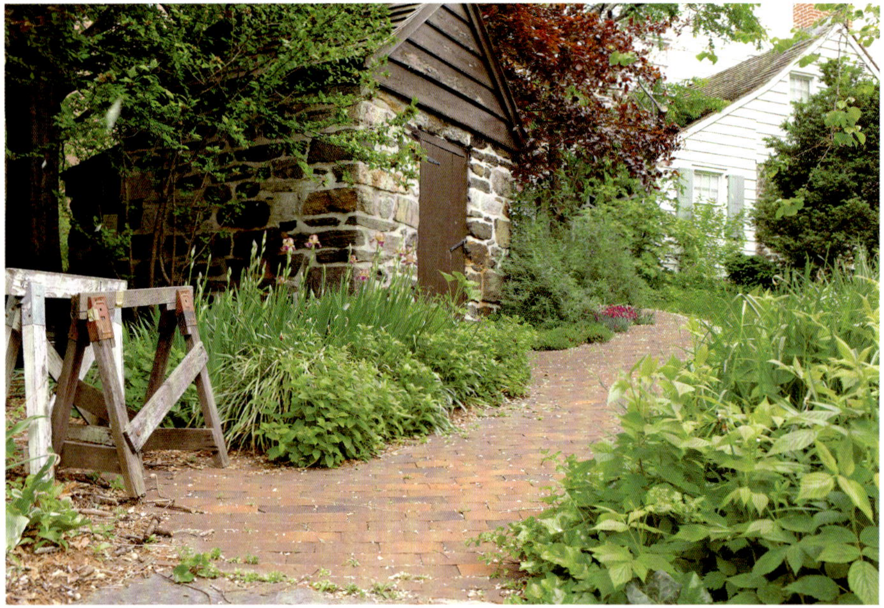

16

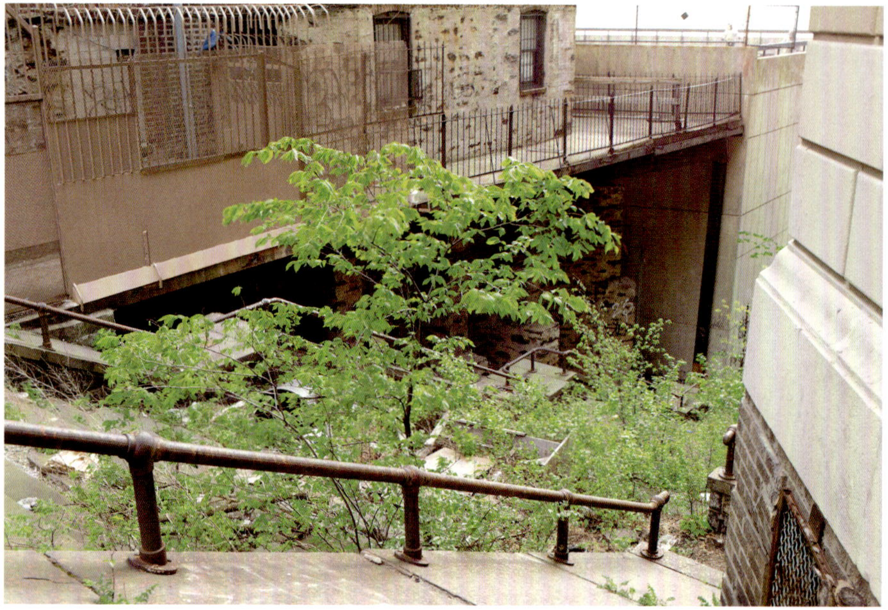

17

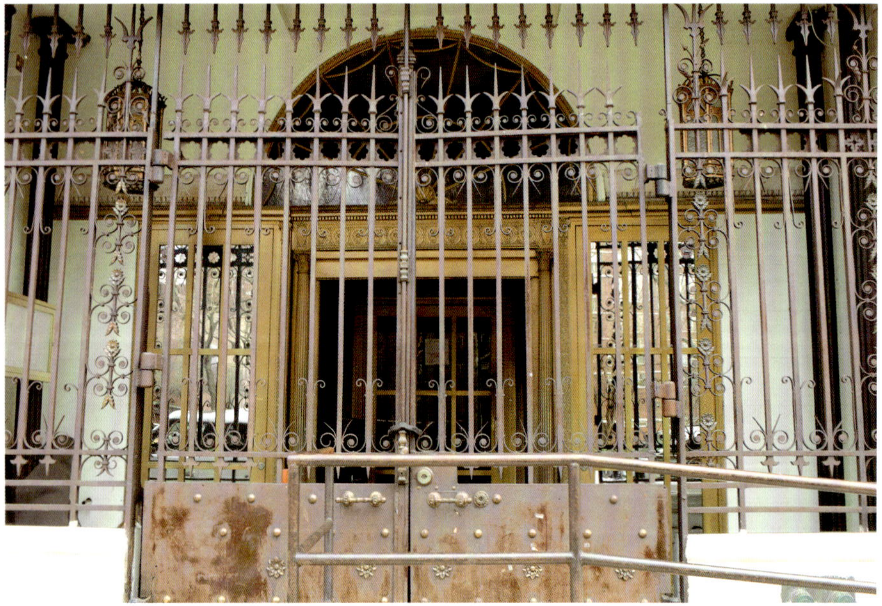

18

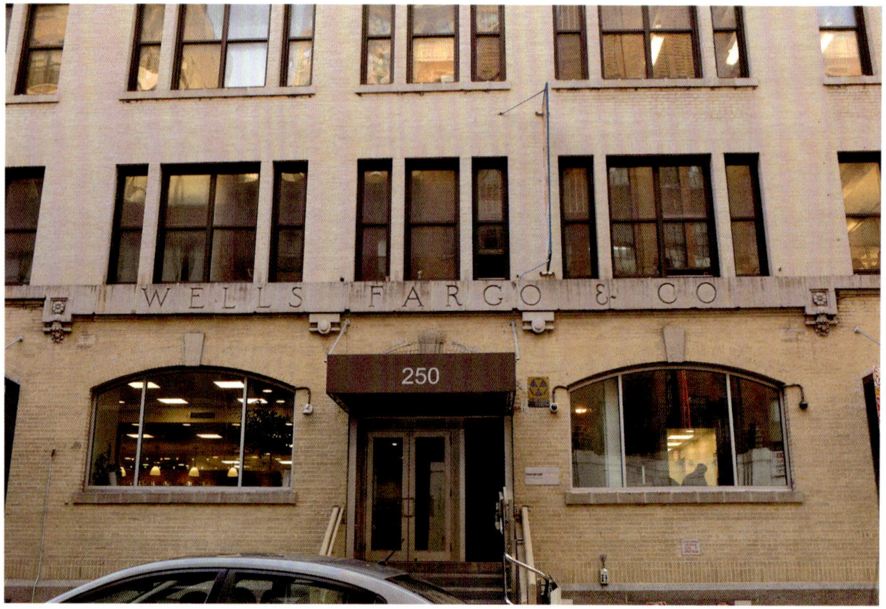

19

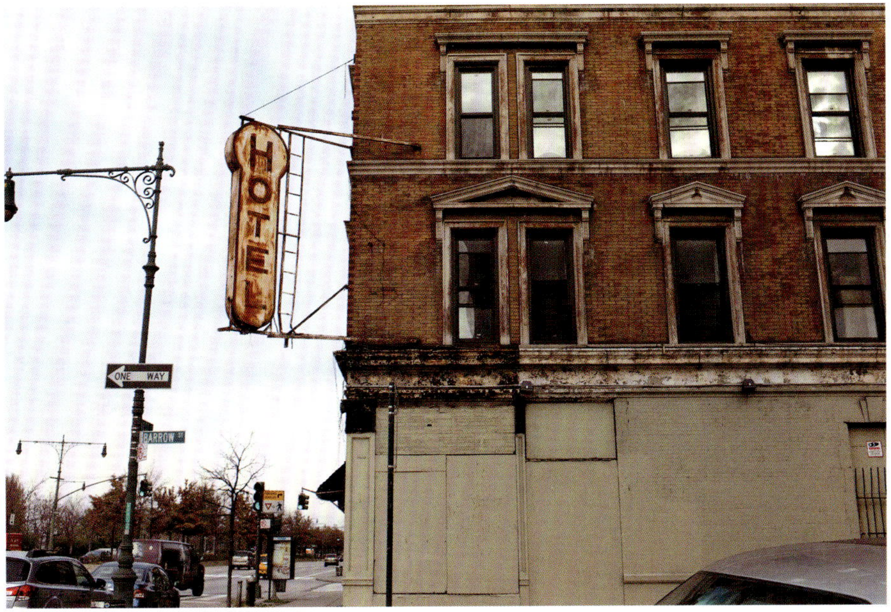

20

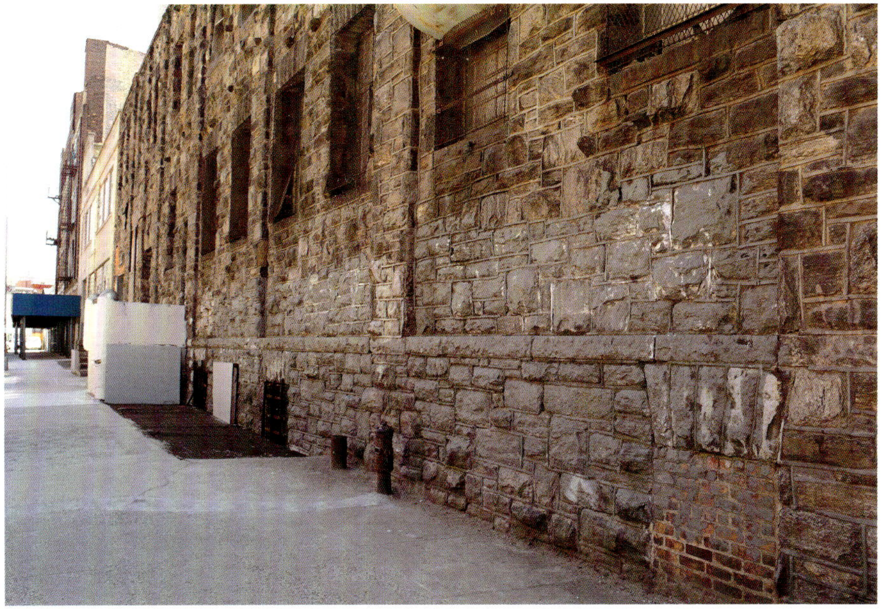

21

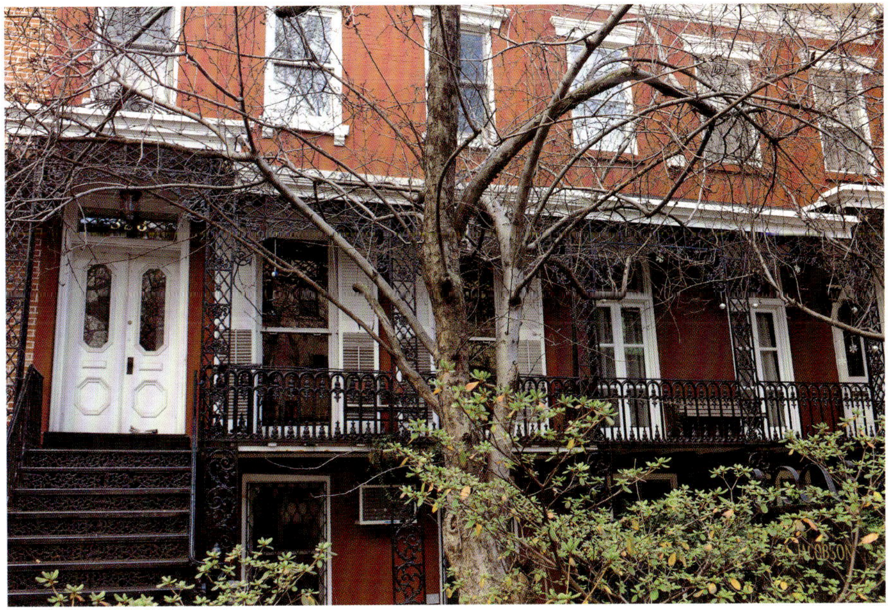

22

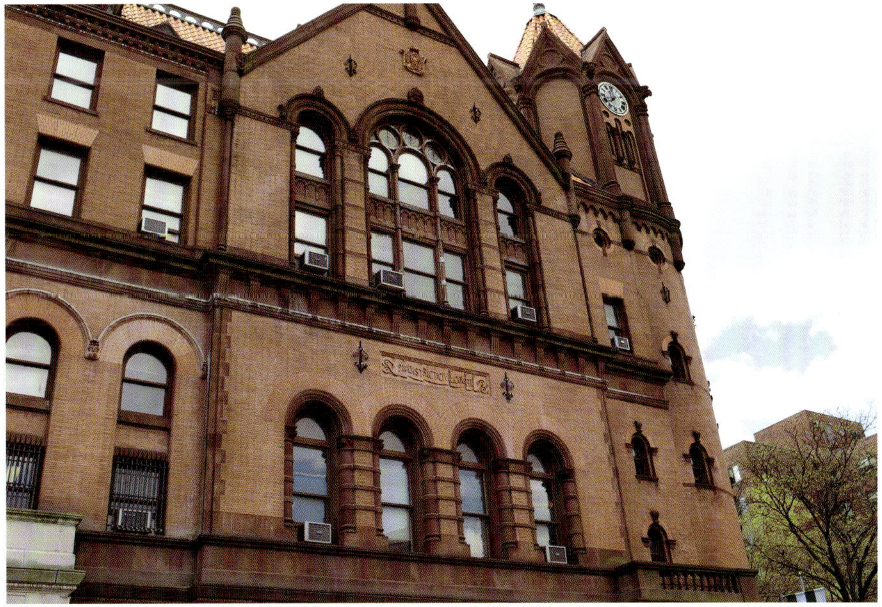

23

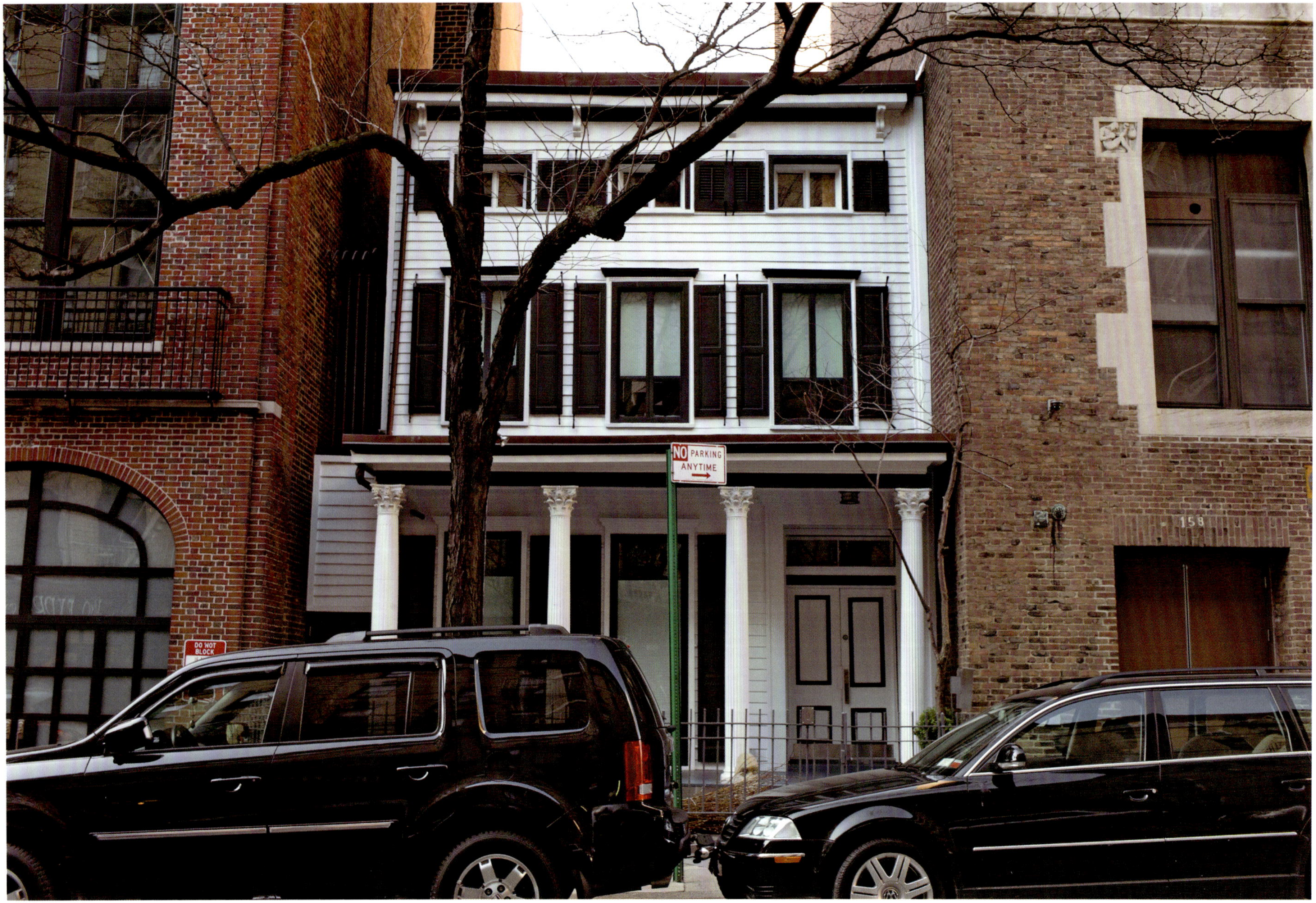

24

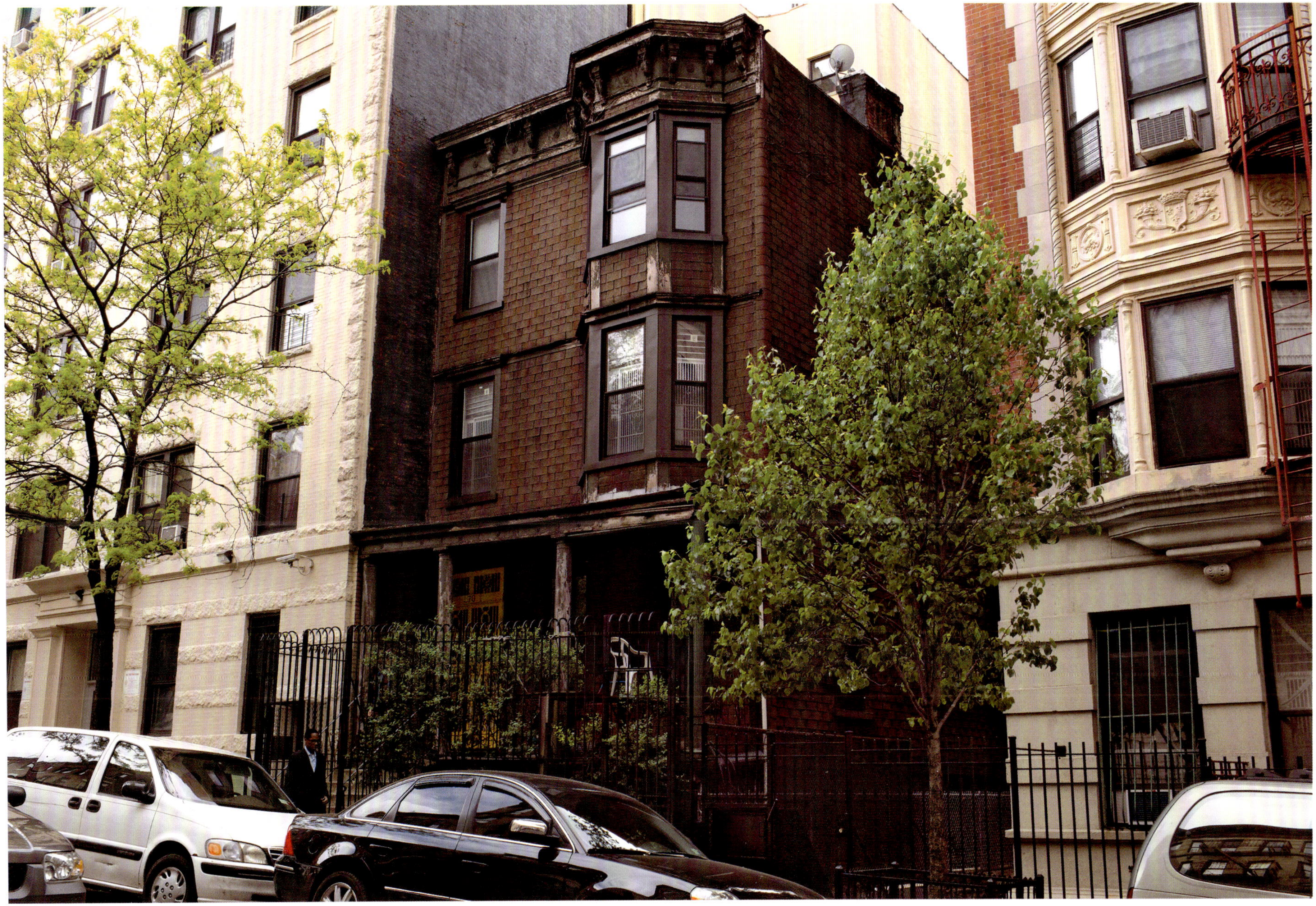

25

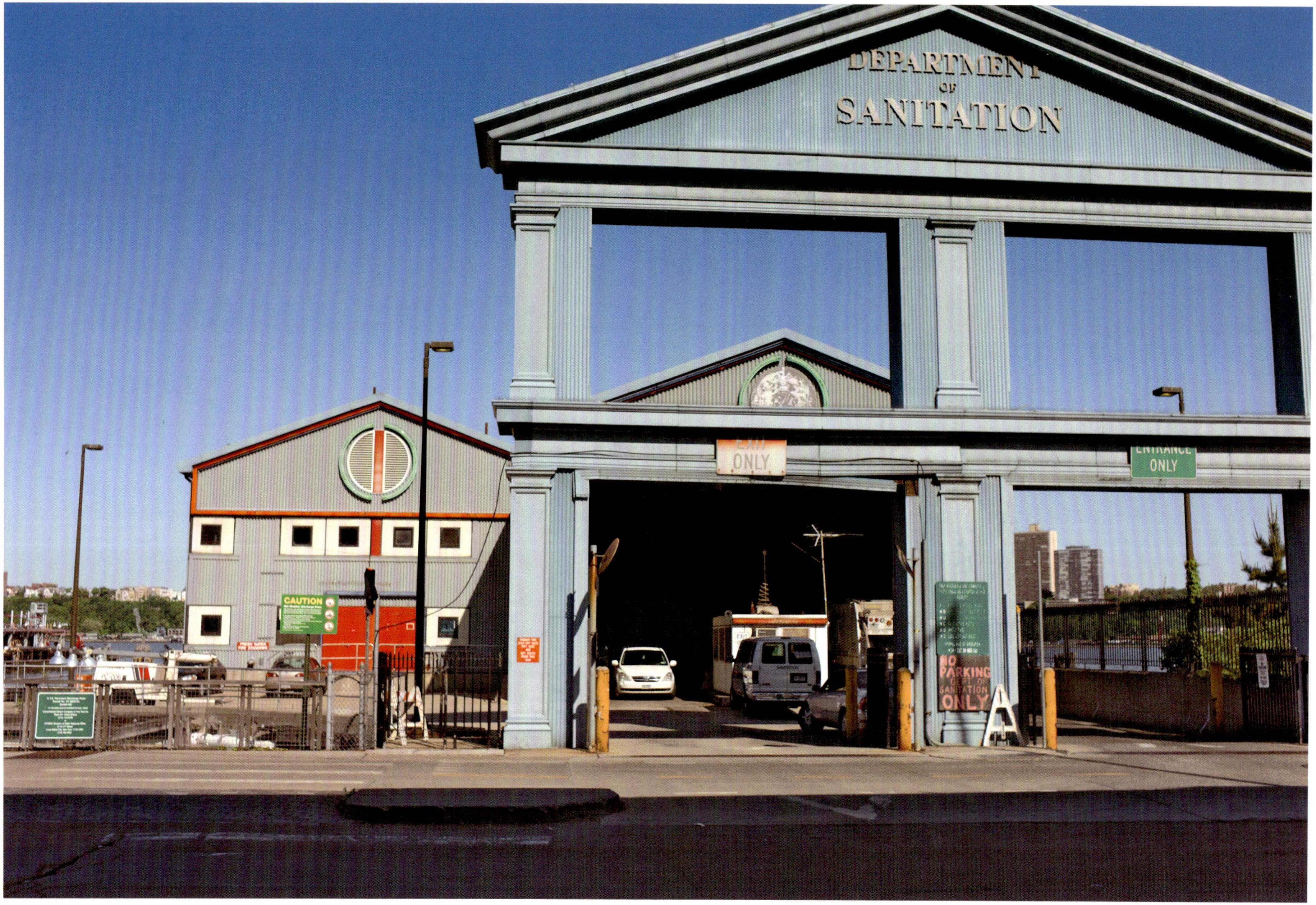
DEPARTMENT
OF
SANITATION
ONLY
ENTRANCE
ONLY
CAUTION
NO
PARKING
DEPT OF
SANITATION
ONLY

SANITATION

During the city's rapid growth in the nineteenth century, street trash was regarded as an insurmountable problem. After numerous disease outbreaks and general frustration with the problem, George Waring was appointed to solve the seemingly intractable problem in 1895, creating the Department of Sanitation much as we know it today. The heroes of the day were sanitation workers clad in white, collecting garbage and sweeping all the streets of the city, wealthy neighborhoods and poor ones alike. Very soon the city became walkable, and eminently more livable, again.

Today New Yorkers make even more trash, and, unfortunately, it cannot all be recycled (and much of what can be, isn't). So we collect it and bring it to places far afield from the center of the city. In the nineteenth century garbage was also routinely dumped in New York Harbor. Then the city began shipping it out further, into the ocean. Now after decades-long clean-up efforts, most of it is shipped to other states. Some of the organic waste is sent to composters on Long Island, mirroring the process of 100 years ago, when New York sent horse manure to Long Island so that the farmers who fed the city could return it to the soil.

Only a few of the city's sanitation waste transfer facilities are in Manhattan, including one station on the West Side. The newest transfer station is on the Upper East Side, but it was not yet built at the time of my walk.

1 Hell's Kitchen
2 Hell's Kitchen
3 Lower East Side
4 Upper West Side
5 Harlem
6 Inwood

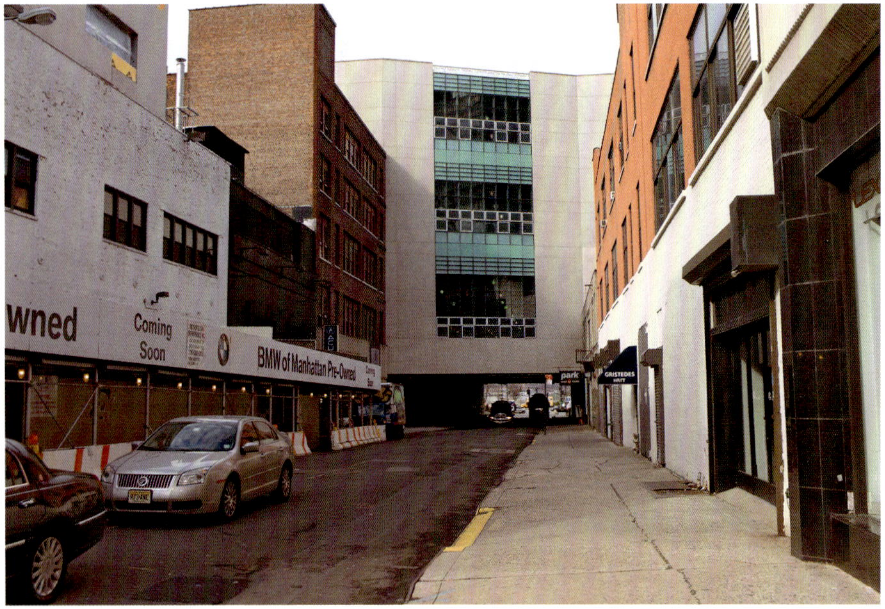

2

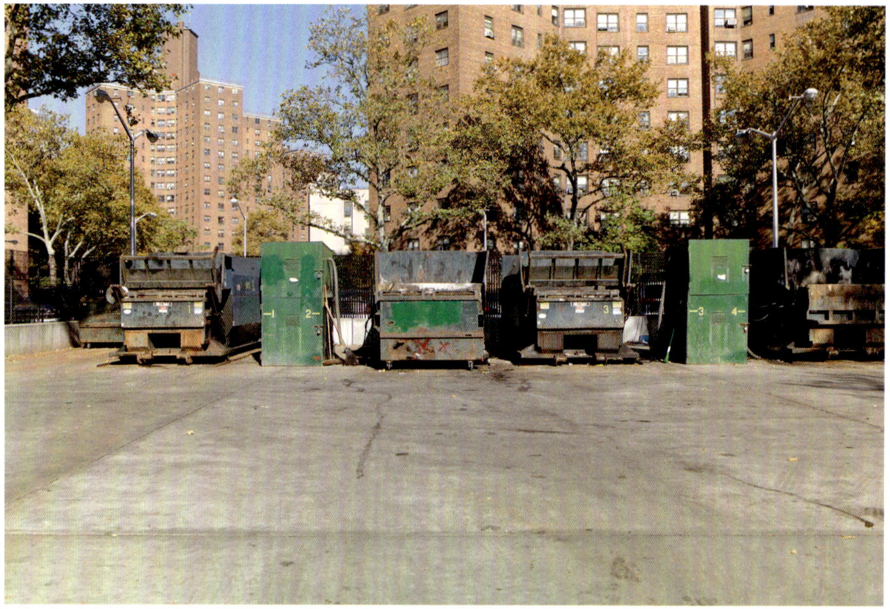

3

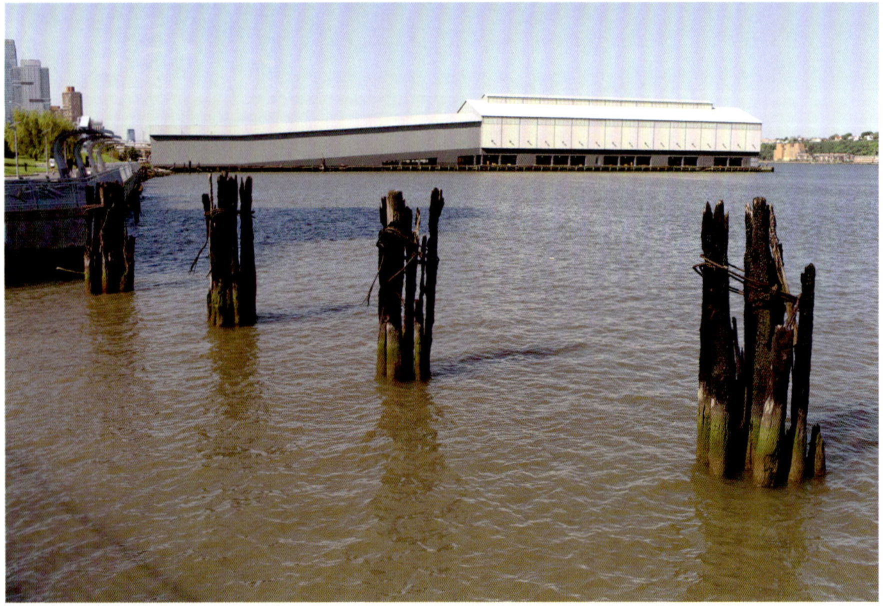

4

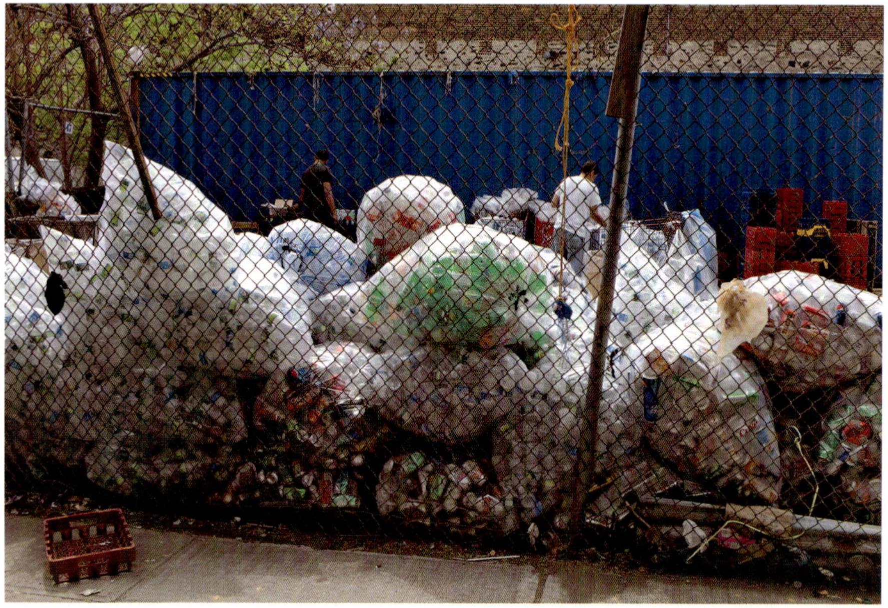

5

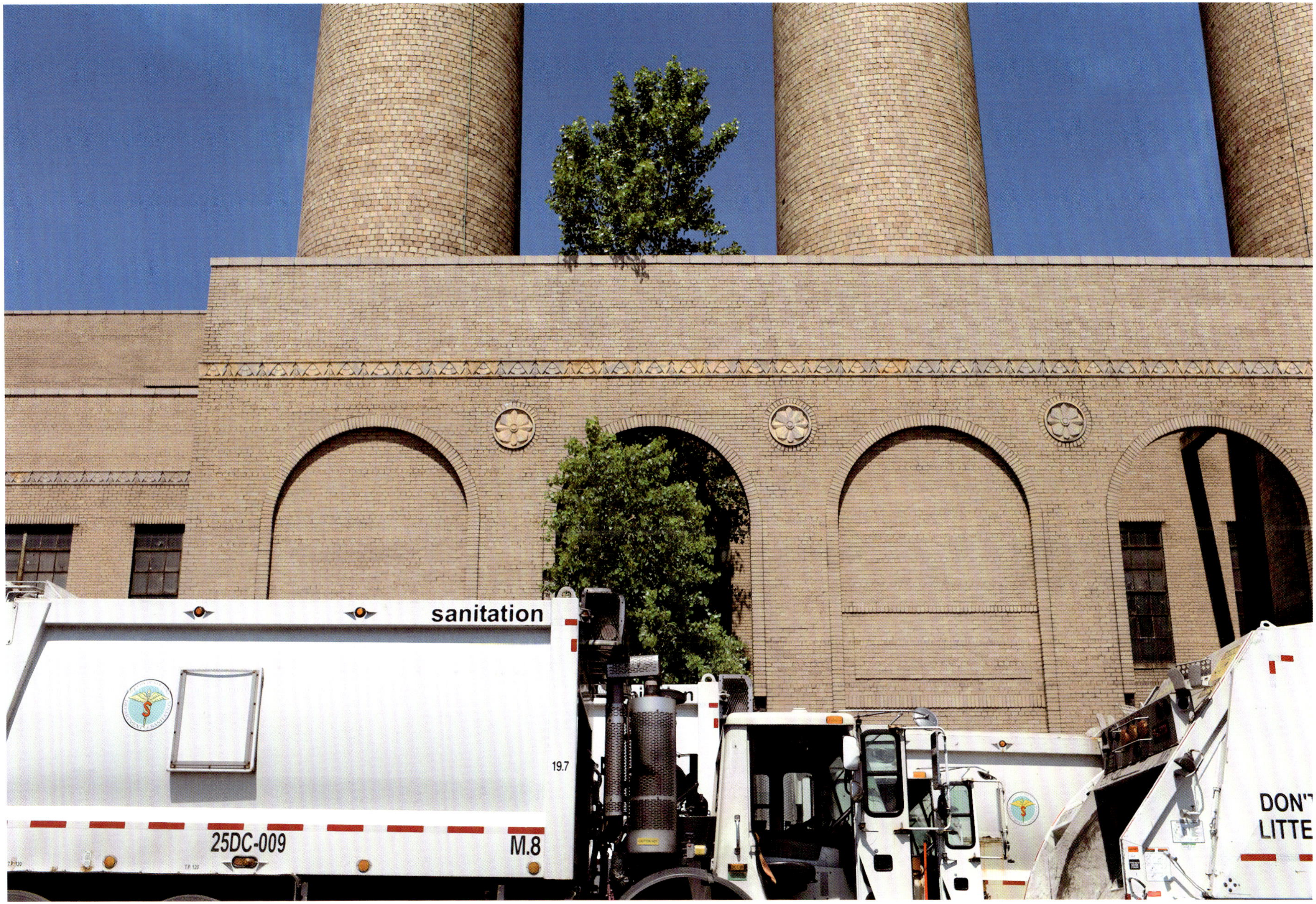

6

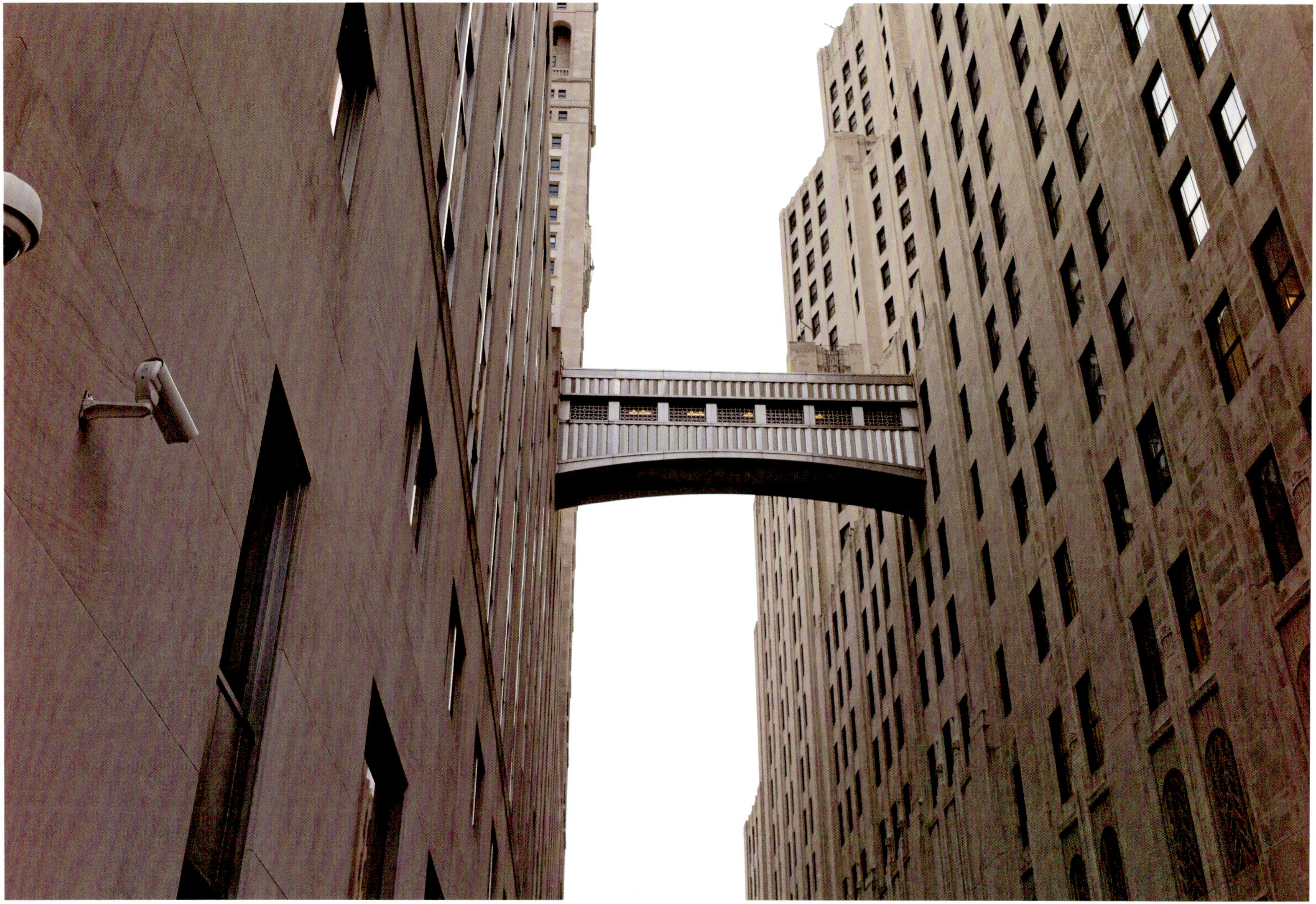

SKYBRIDGES

Skybridges seem to come from another age—either from long ago or perhaps the future. They tend to proliferate on hospitals, which can grow over long periods and then need to connect in a way that allows for patients to be wheeled between older wards and newer ones. But they appear on other kinds of buildings as well, connecting different parts of factories and offices.

One bridge connects federal district court to detention facilities. A few appear to be more about stabilizing structure than transit. Several beautiful art deco examples can be found near the High Line, in former Nabisco Company buildings. A structure further south on Staple Street is one of the oldest, and unusual in its asymmetricality. Newer ones usually look slapped on, with a few exceptions, like the modern example that crosses the Henry Hudson Parkway at Columbia University Medical Center. The skybridge at Chelsea Market used to separate a unit of NYPD Narcotics from an office of the DEA, but now connects one division of the vast New York Googleplex to another on 10th Avenue.

Some cities in colder climates systematically create ways for the public to never go outside, but in New York most of the bridges are private spaces, just for employees.

1 Madison Square
2 Financial District
3 Tribeca
4 Herald Square
5 Chelsea
6 City Hall
7 Washington Heights
8 East Harlem
9 Washington Heights
10 Morningside Heights
11 Upper East Side
12 Stuyvesant Square
13 Chelsea
14 Morningside Heights
15 Morningside Heights
16 Chelsea

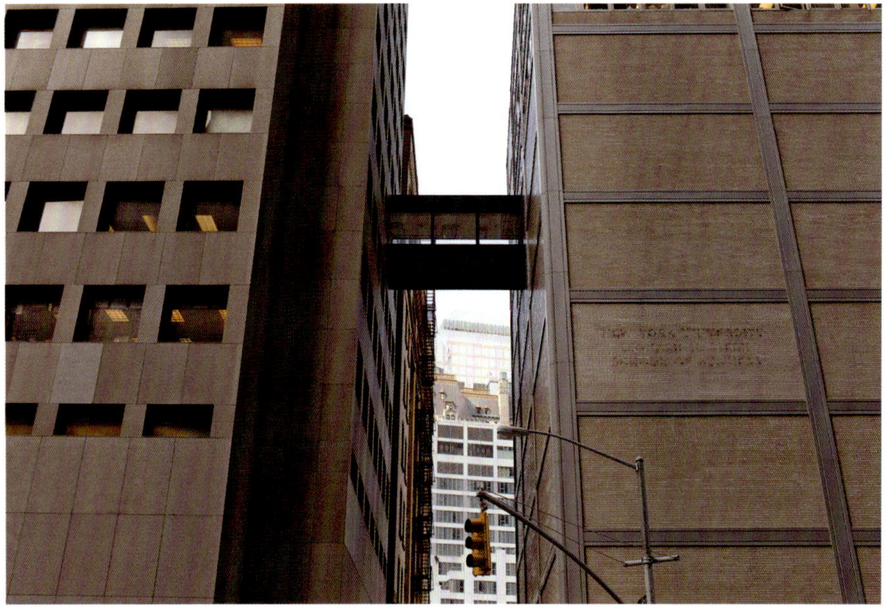

2

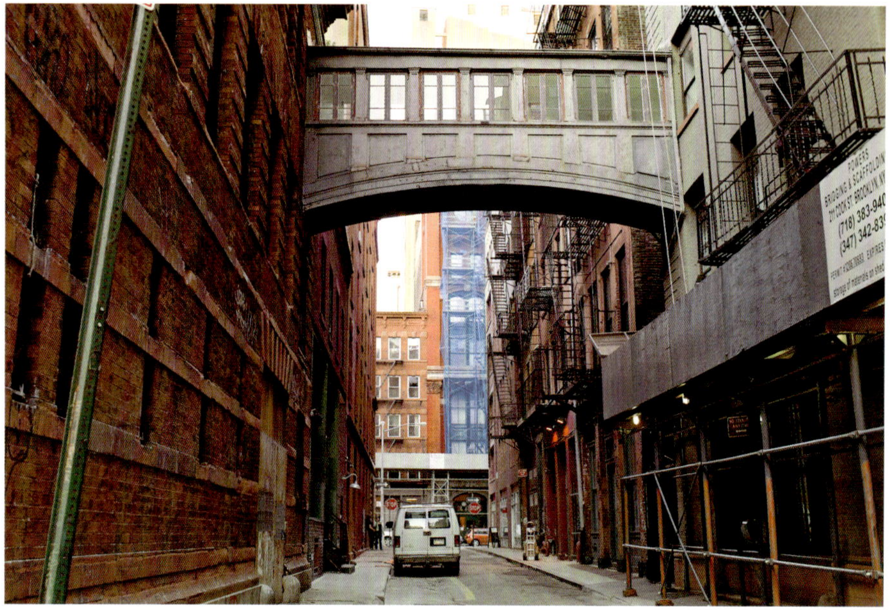

3

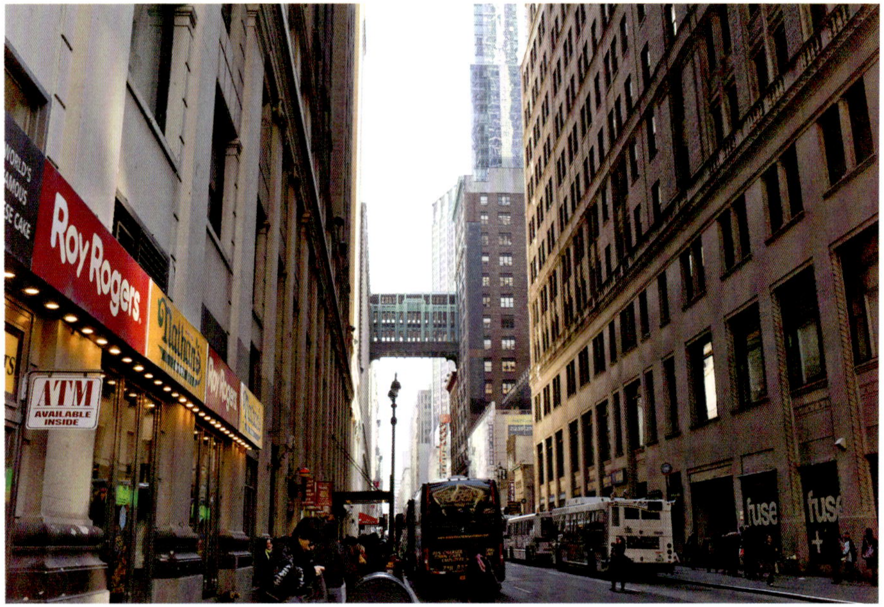
Roy Rogers
ATM
AVAILABLE INSIDE
fuse

4

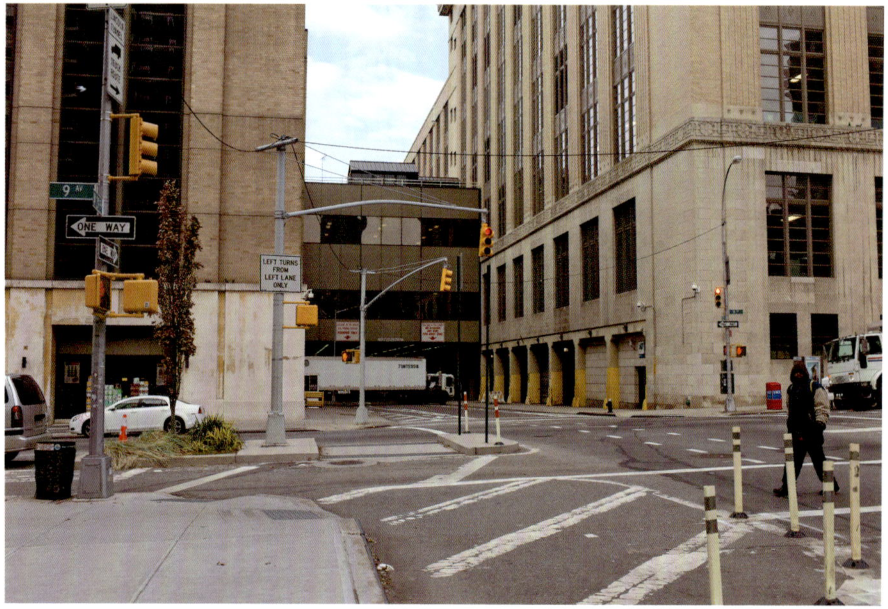
ONE WAY
LEFT TURNS FROM LEFT LANE ONLY

5

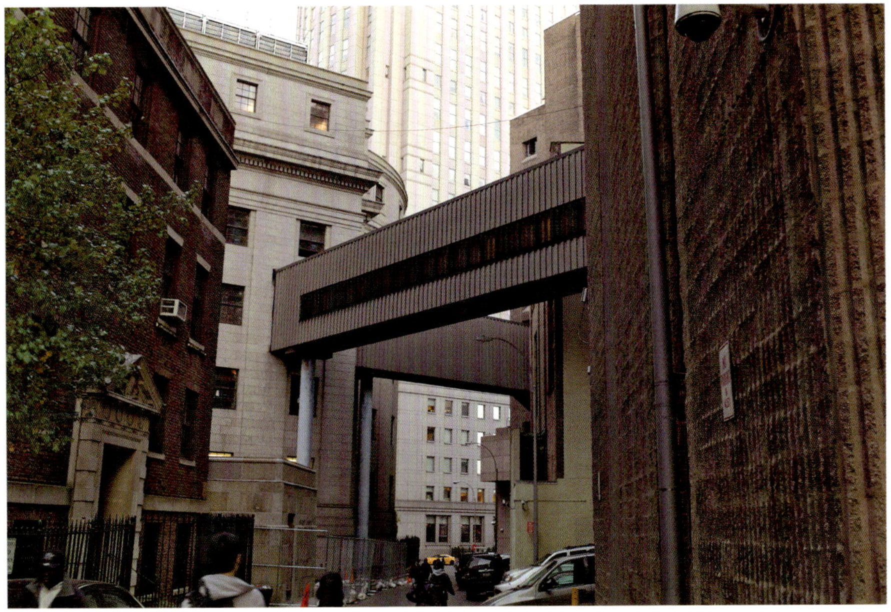
6

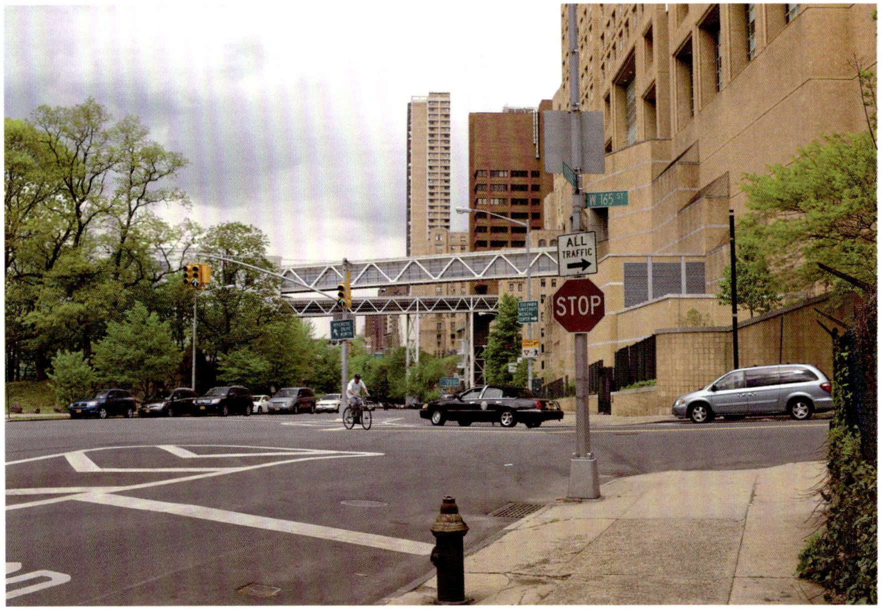

7

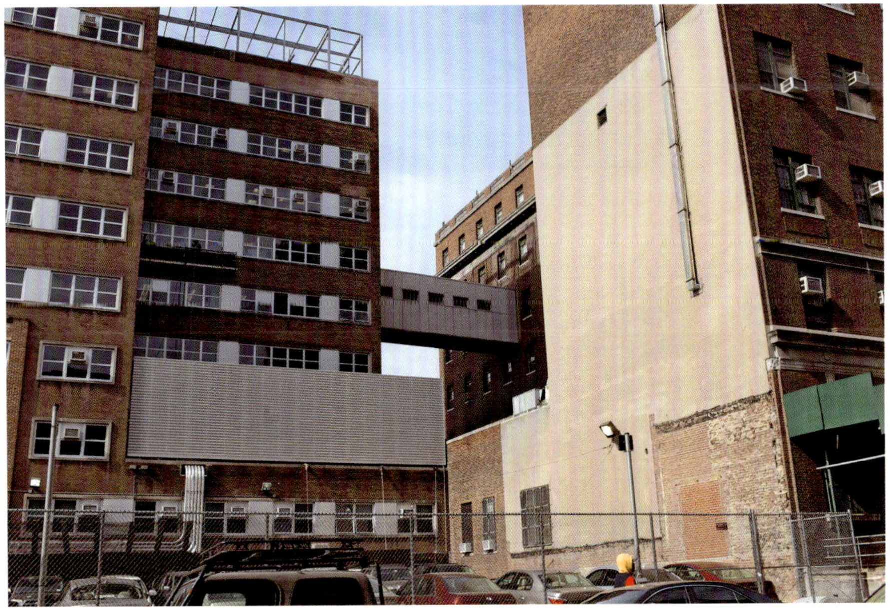
8

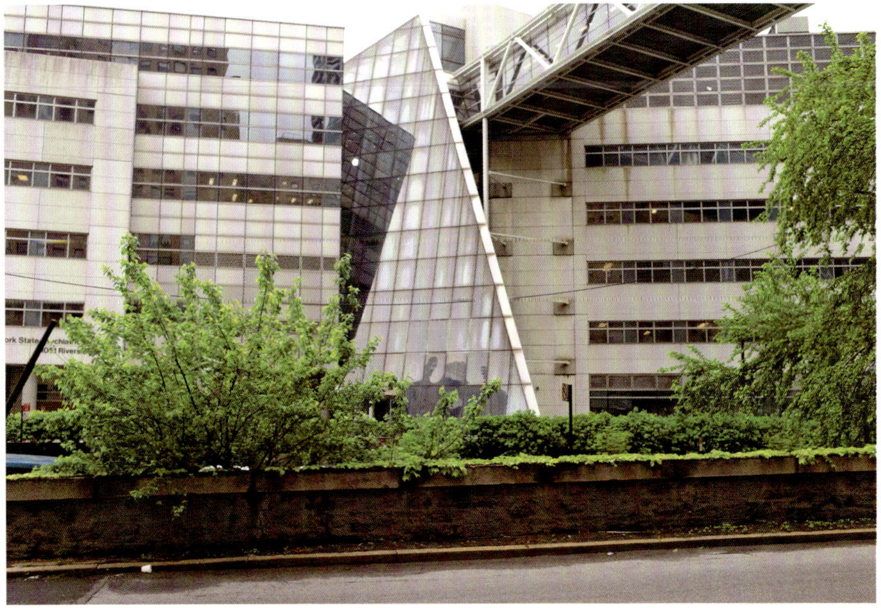
9

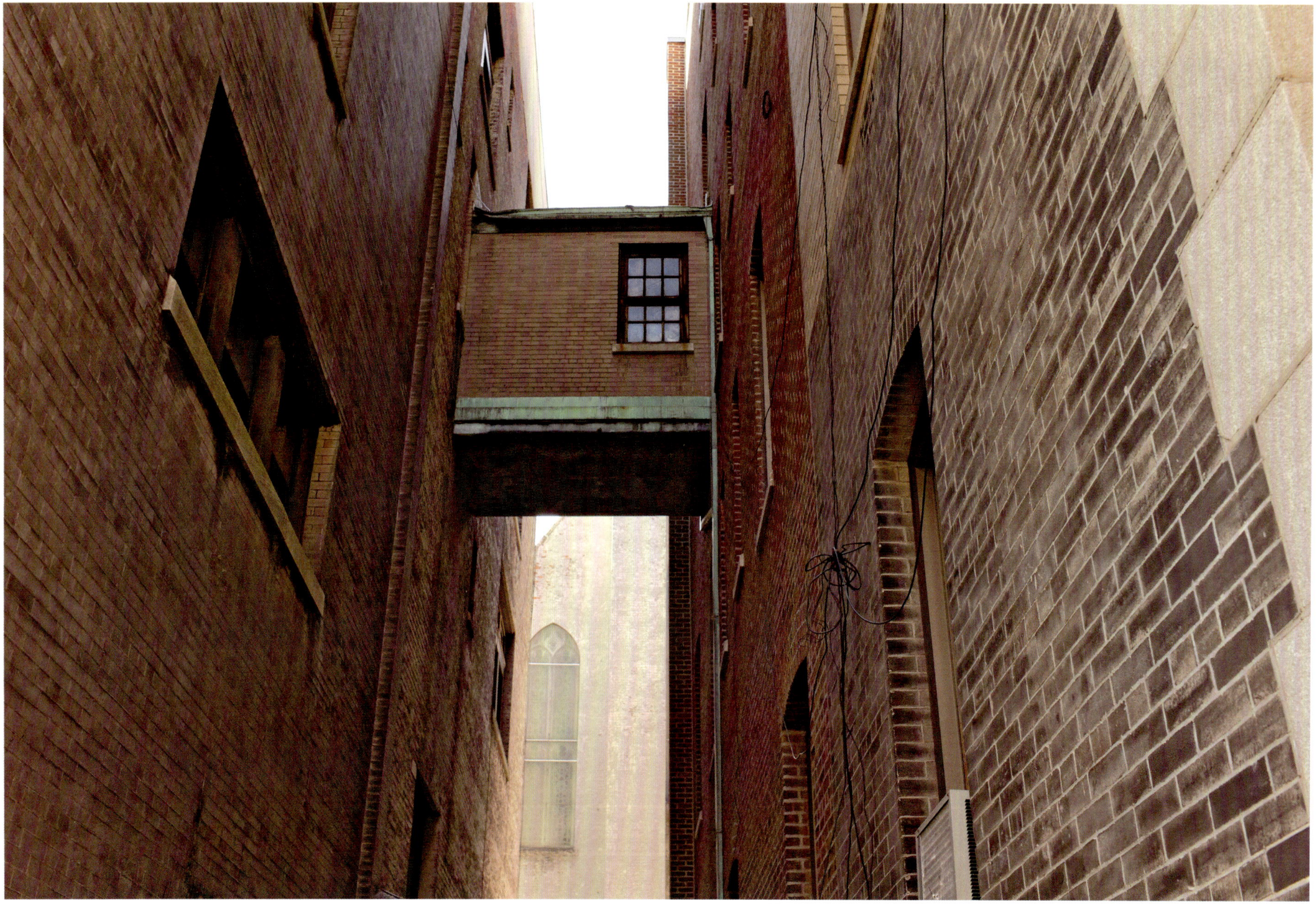

10

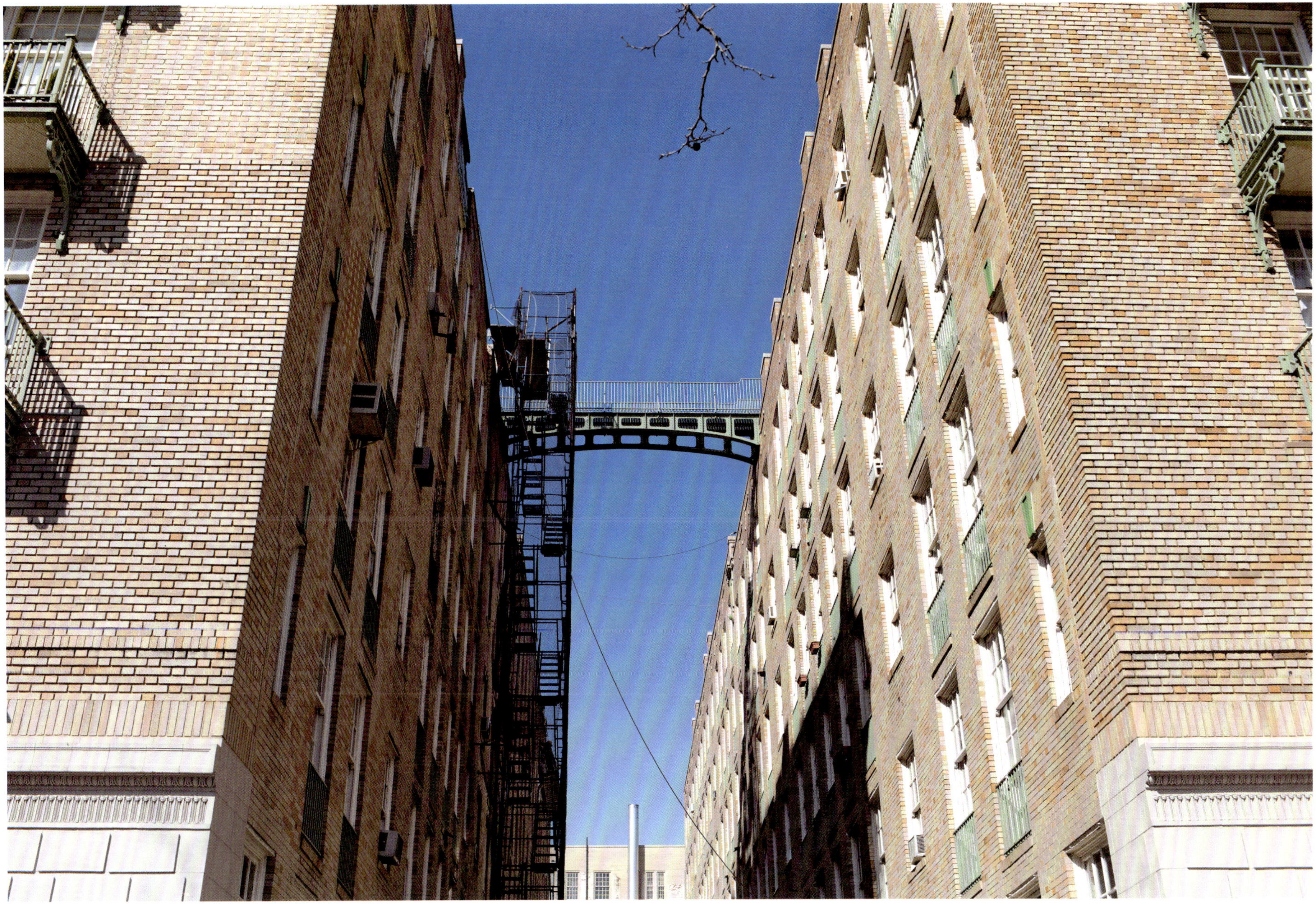

11

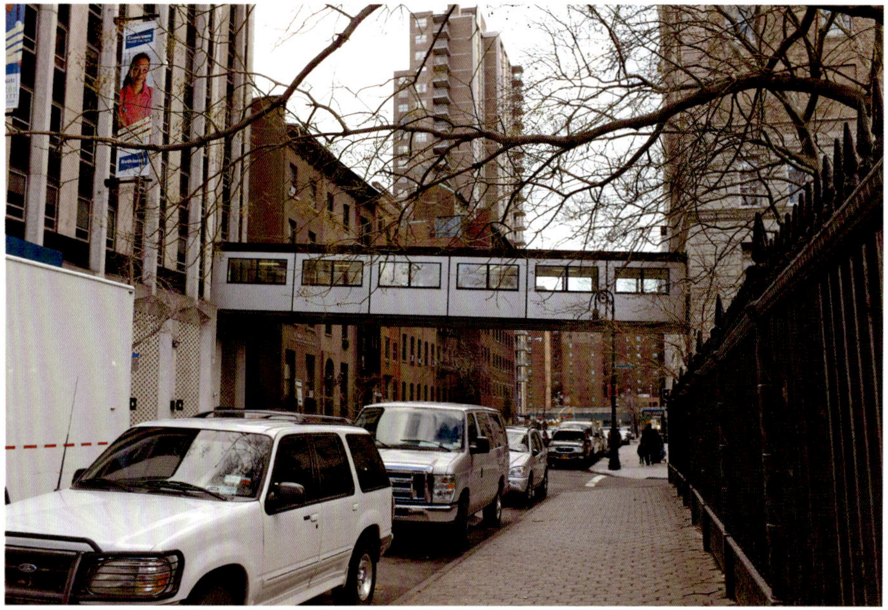

12

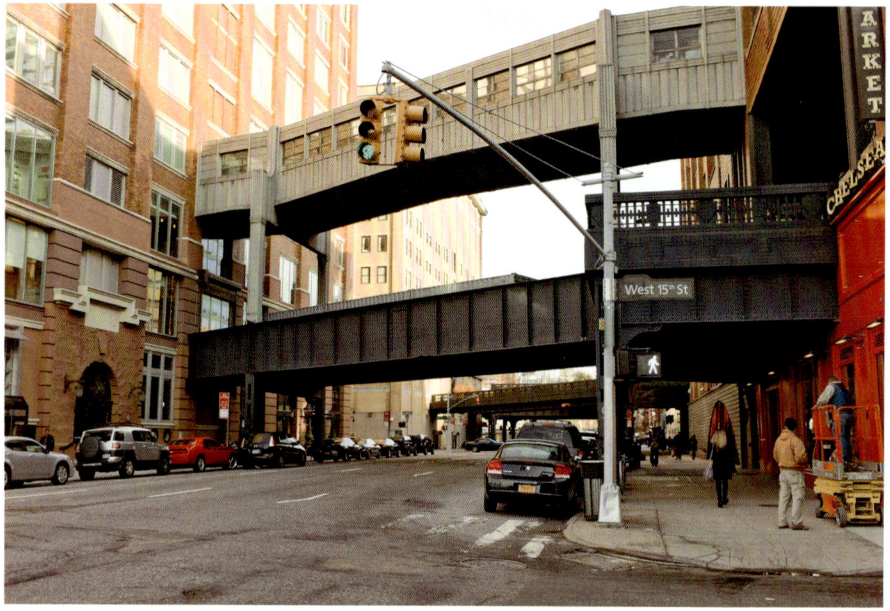

13

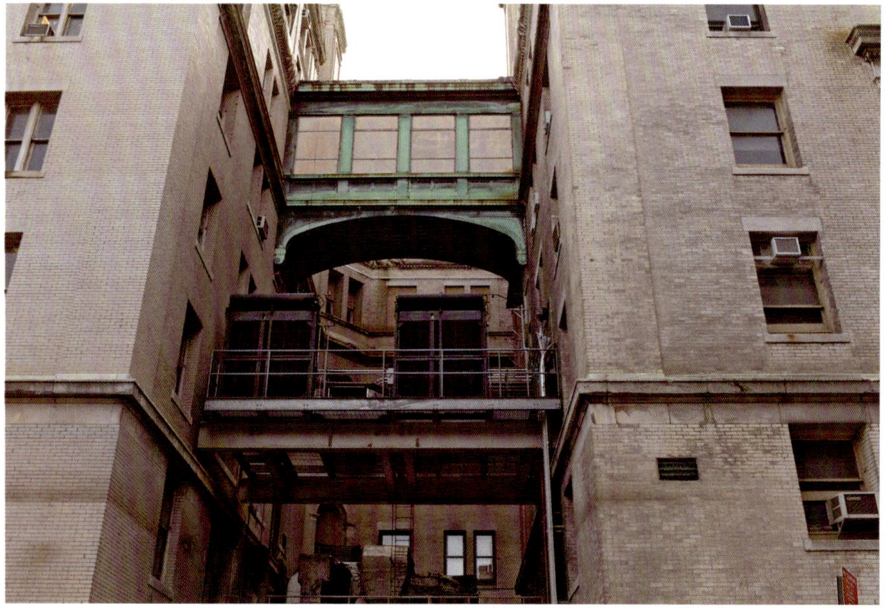

14

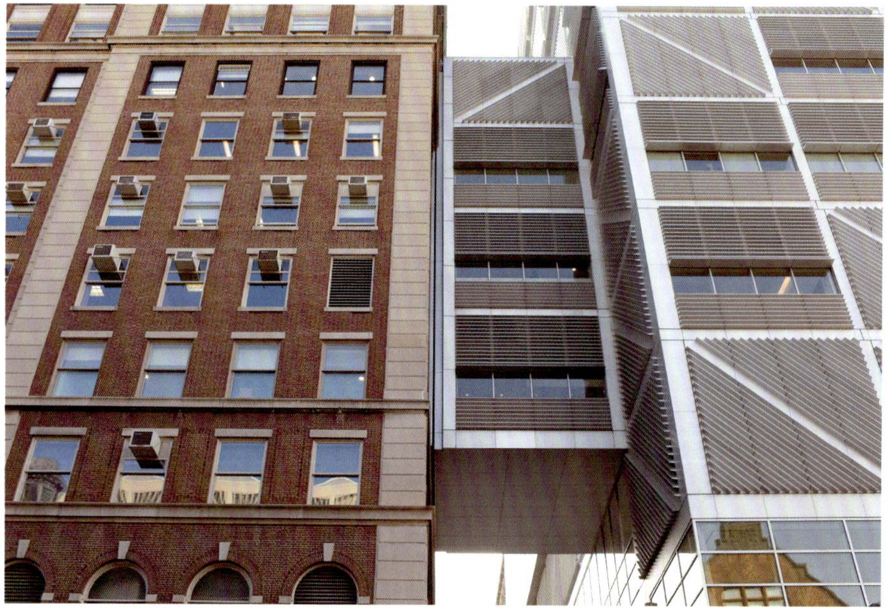

15

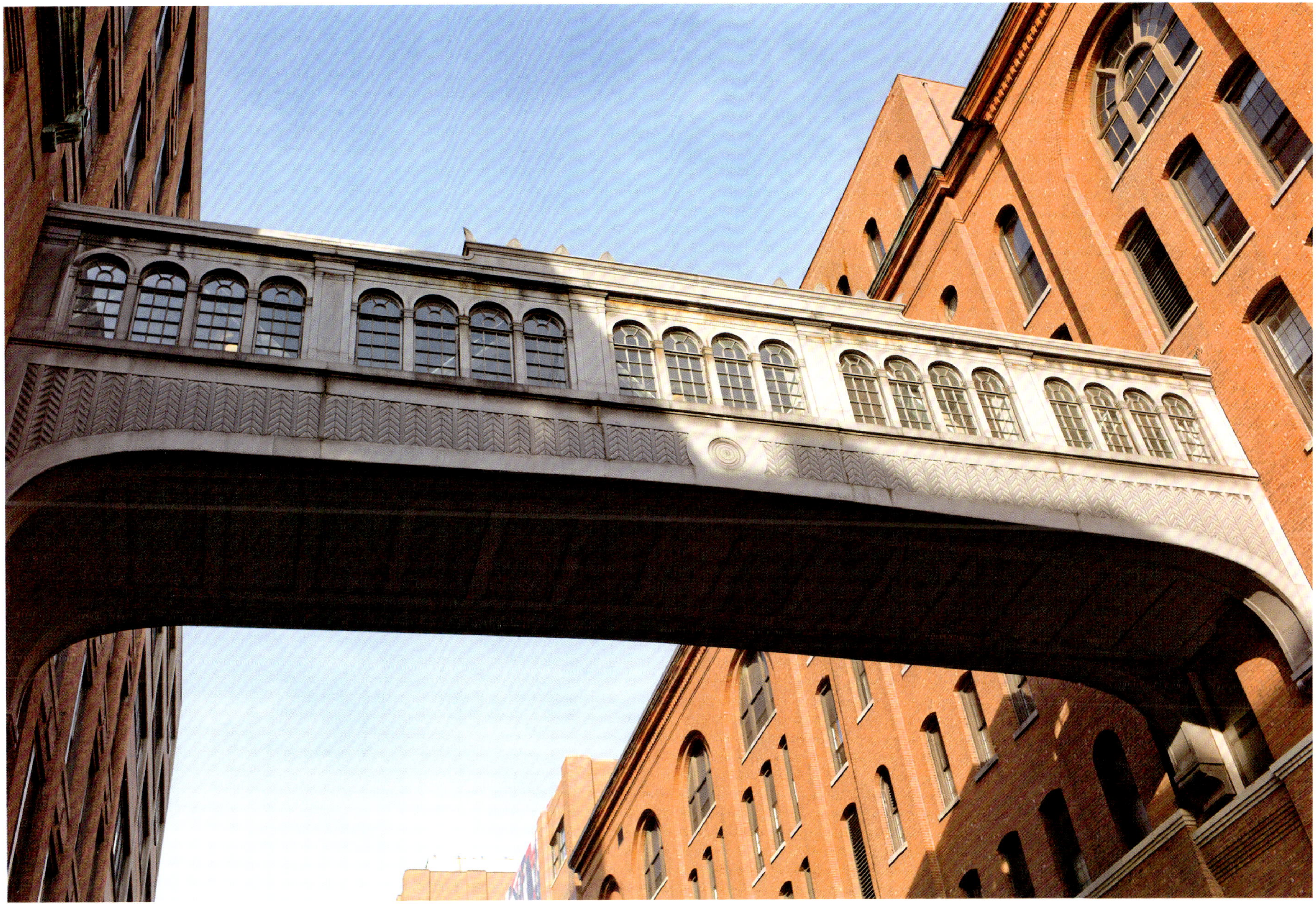

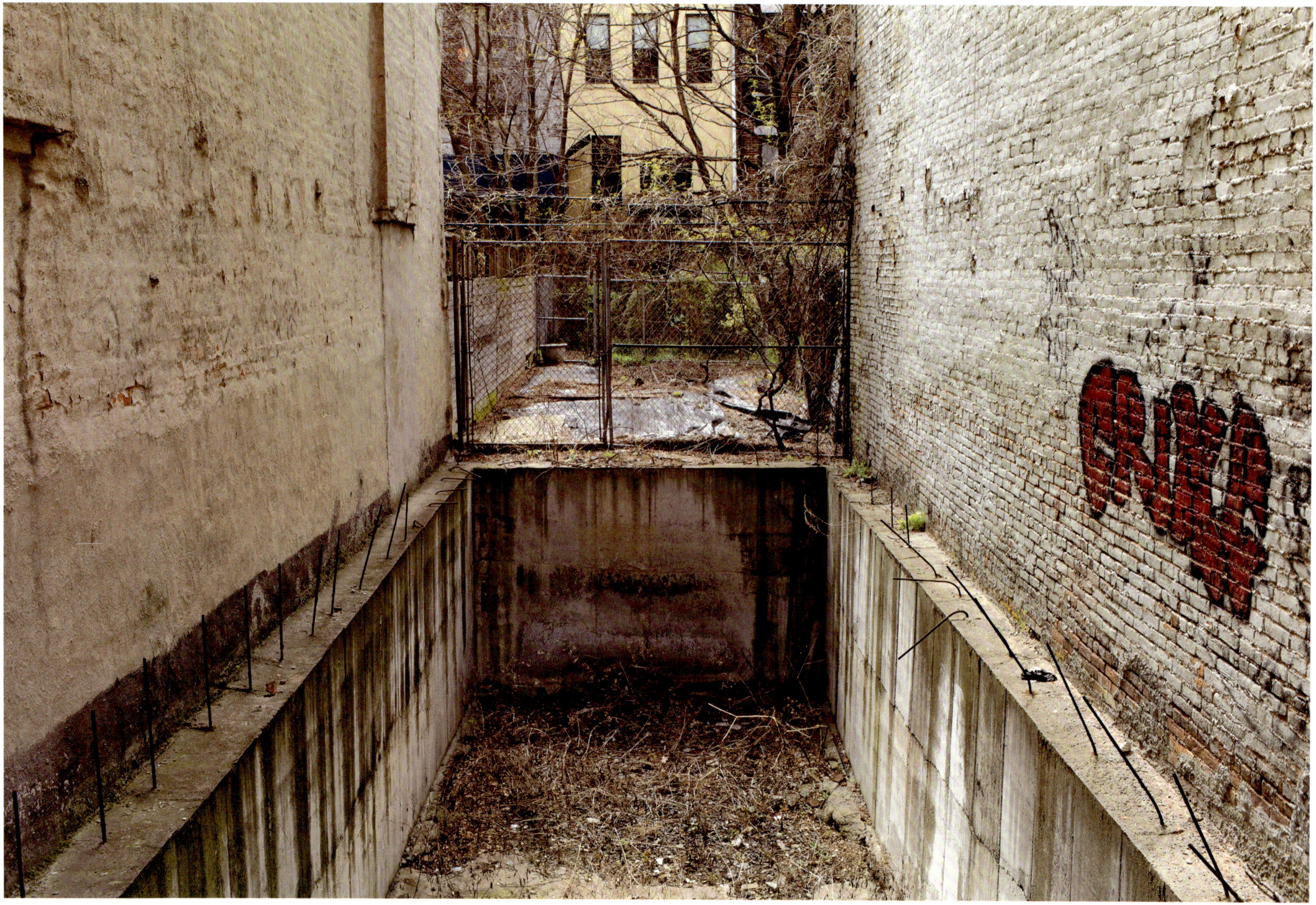

VACANT SPACES

Manhattan is extremely dense, yet openings constantly appear within the grid. Often fleeting, they allow new city views that will soon pass, vistas that would otherwise only exist in speculative architectural renderings.

This project began with a plan to photograph the empty spaces with a small camera and then go back with a large format camera at quieter times. But many of these spaces were encased within plywood walls, or behind fences, making photography with a tripod impossible. Many of these pictures were made through tiny holes in walls, or chain link fences, so the views here do not necessarily represent what a casual walker might see (except if he or she were particularly curious).

The painter Willem de Kooning used to do this type of dedicated looking on walks he took when he lived downtown, and titled one of his paintings *Excavation*, possibly inspired by what he saw. These spaces are like archaeological sites, revealing many layers in the life of the city.

1 East Harlem
2 Hell's Kitchen
3 World Trade Center
4 Hamilton Heights
5 Inwood
6 Harlem
7 Hamilton Heights
8 Harlem
9 Harlem
10 Harlem
11 Harlem
12 East Harlem
13 Chelsea
14 Tribeca
15 West Village
16 The Battery
17 Lower East Side
18 SoHo
19 East Harlem
20 Financial District
21 Financial District
22 Financial District
23 Tribeca
24 SoHo
25 Soho
26 SoHo
27 Lower East Side
28 Chinatown
29 SoHo
30 East Village
31 SoHo
32 East Village
33 Union Square
34 East Village
35 East Village
36 Chelsea
37 West Village
38 Harlem
39 East Village
40 Chelsea
41 Chelsea
42 Madison Square
43 Harlem
44 Gramercy Park
45 Chelsea
46 Hell's Kitchen
47 Hudson Yards
48 Garment District
49 Flatiron
50 Murray Hill
51 Midtown
52 Tudor City
53 Tudor City
54 World Trade Center
55 Hell's Kitchen
56 Midtown East
57 Midtown
58 Manhattanville
59 Upper West Side
60 City Hall
61 Midtown

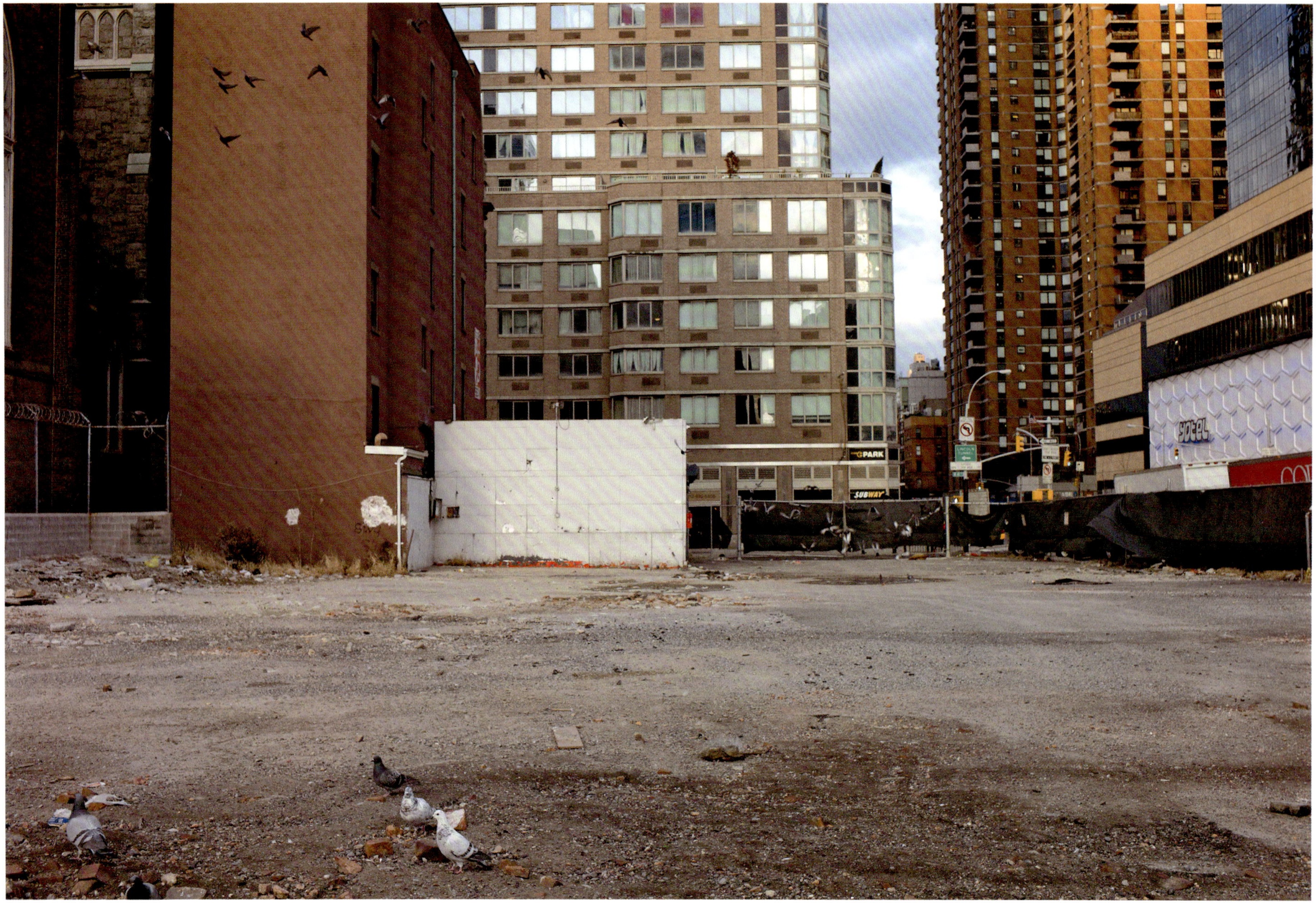

2

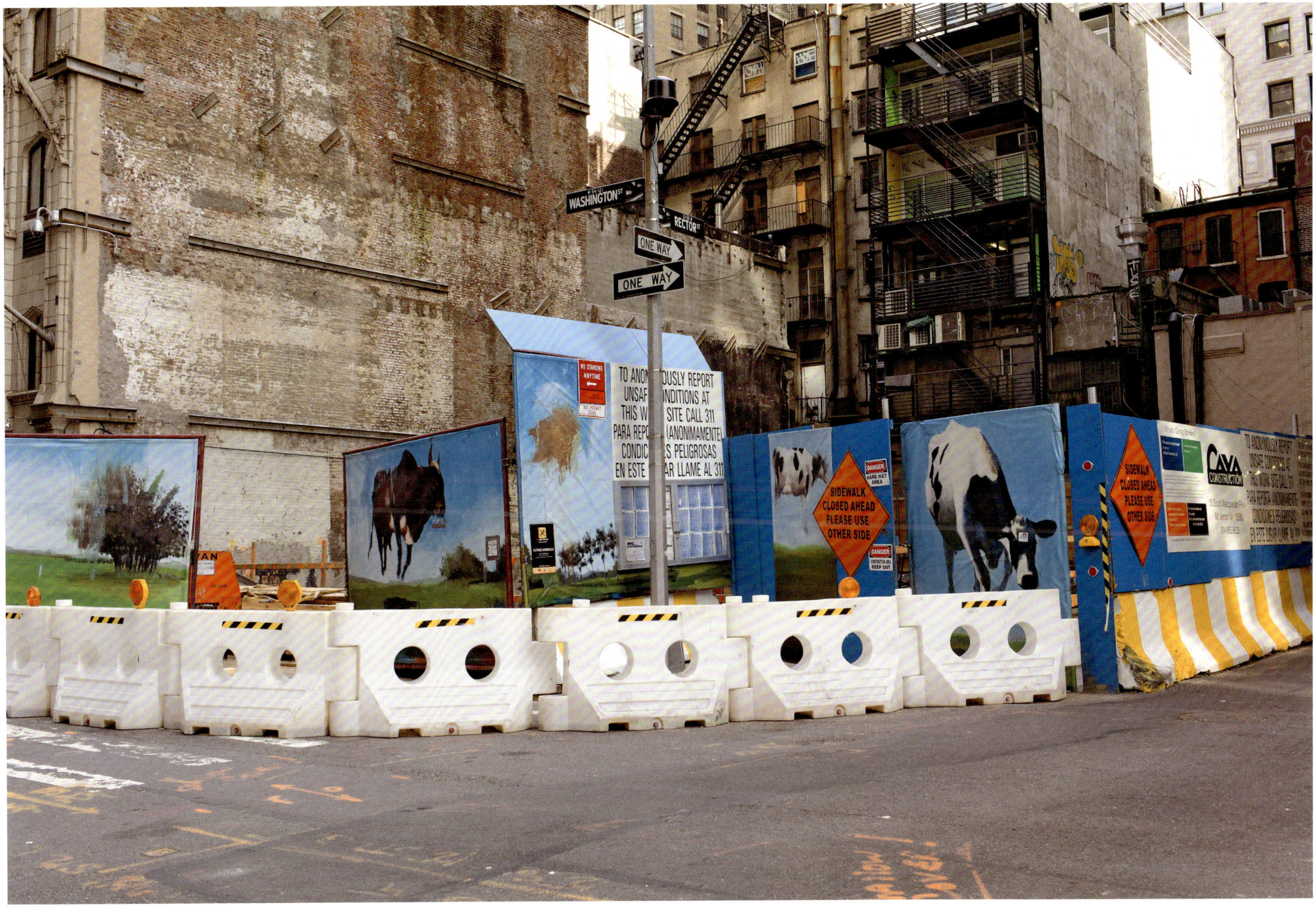
WASHINGTON ST
RECTOR ST
ONE WAY
ONE WAY
NO STANDING ANYTIME
SIDEWALK CLOSED AHEAD PLEASE USE OTHER SIDE
DANGER HARD HAT AREA
SIDEWALK CLOSED AHEAD PLEASE USE OTHER SIDE
CAVA CONSTRUCTION

3

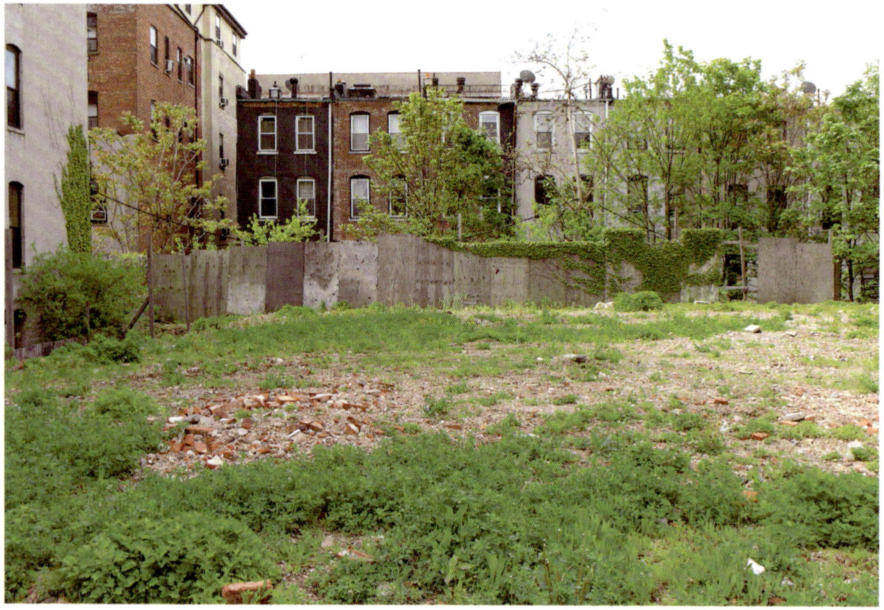

4

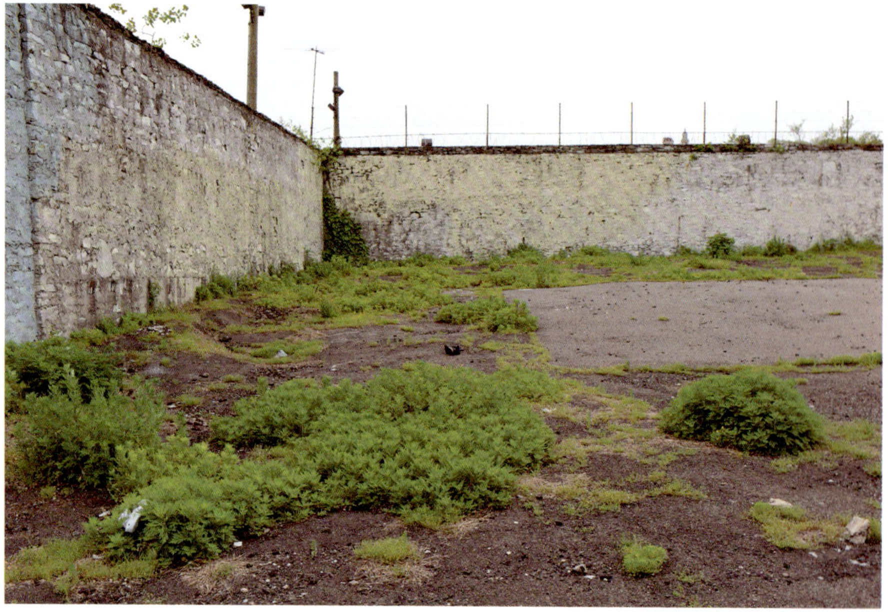

5

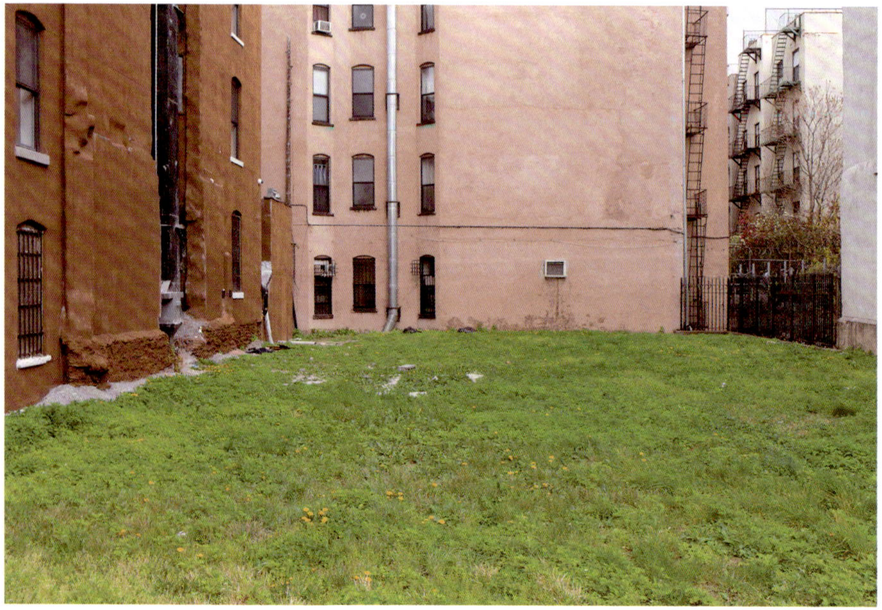

6

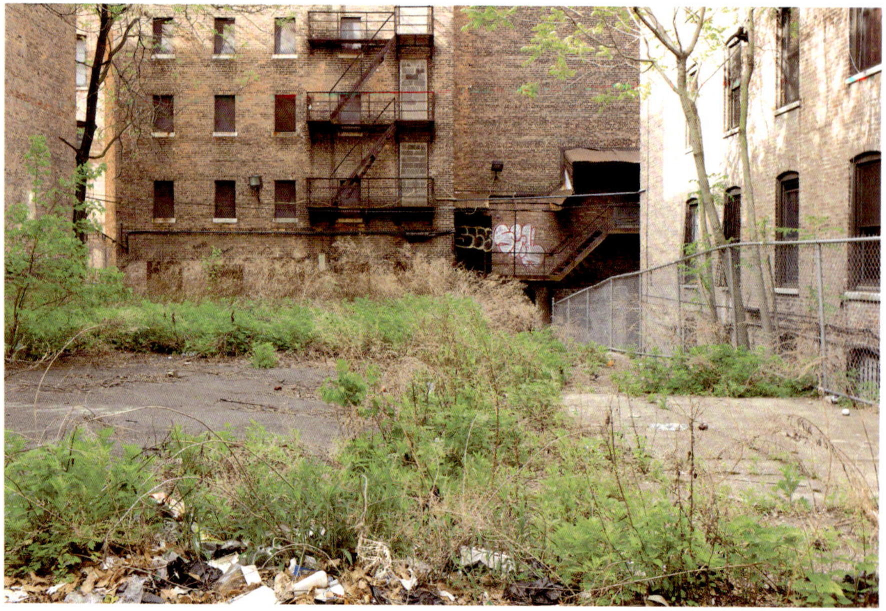

7

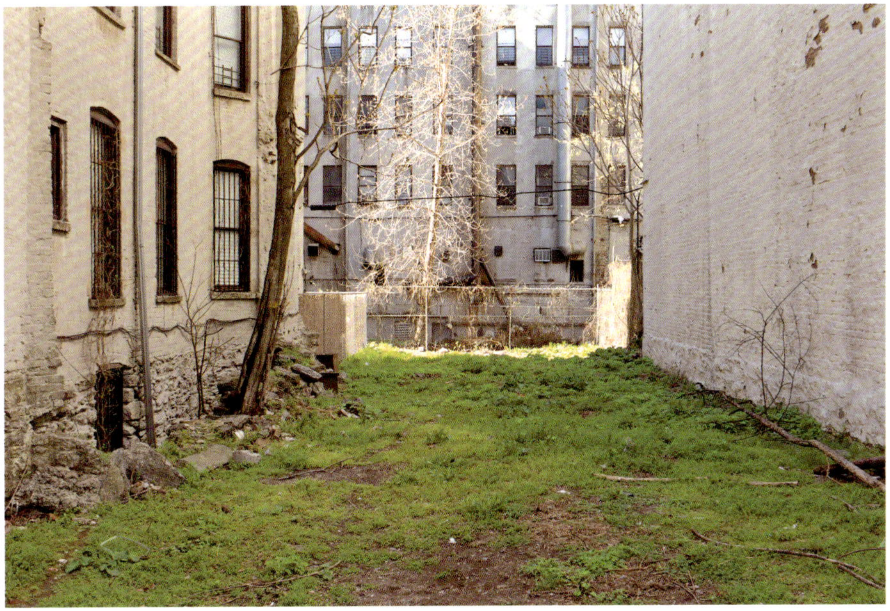

8

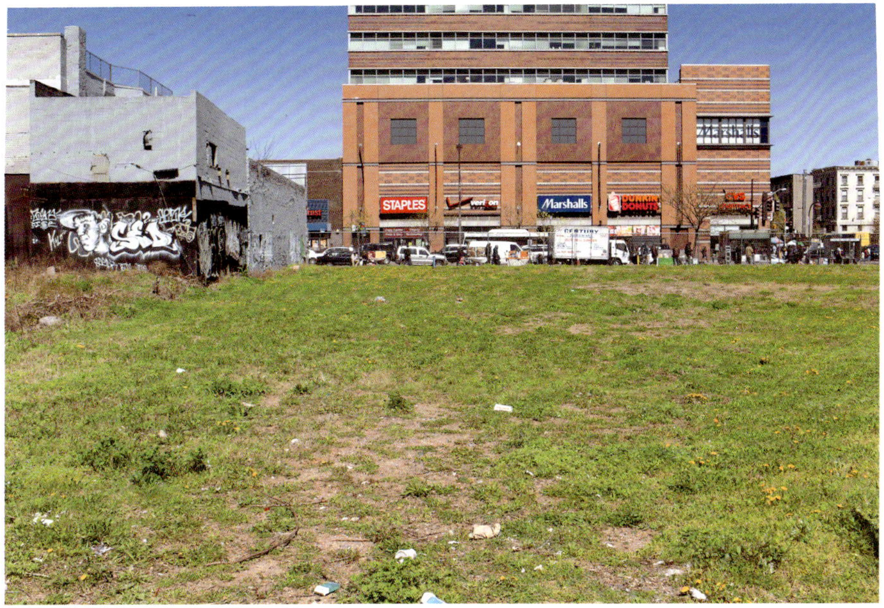

9

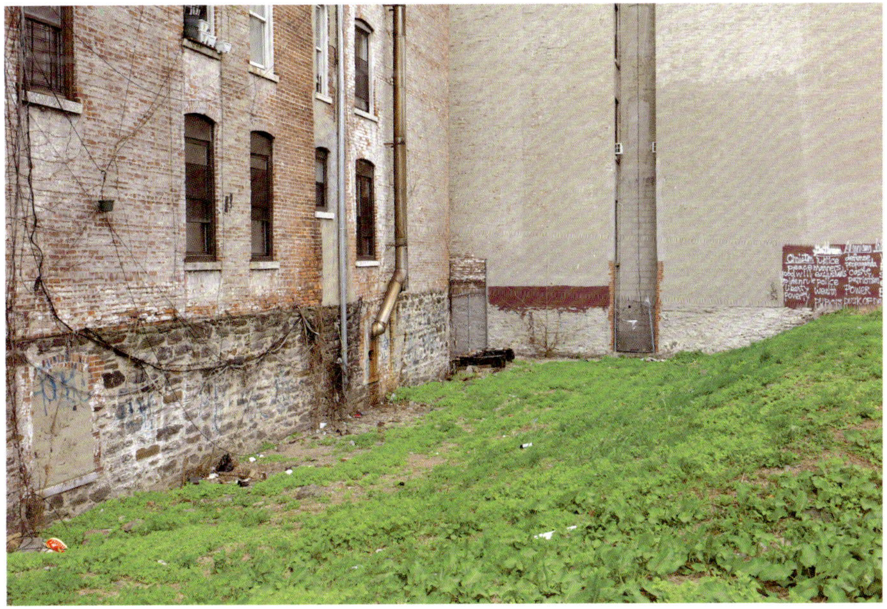

10

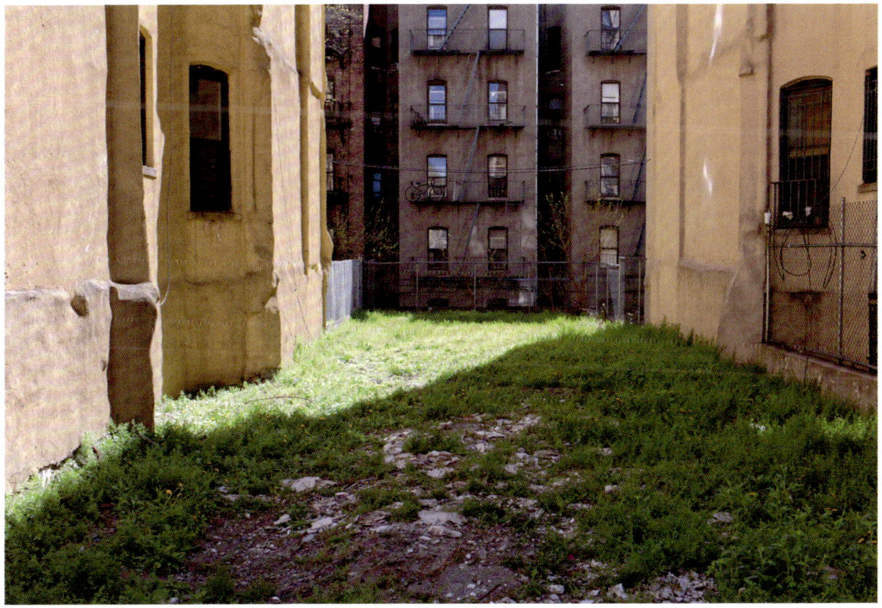

11

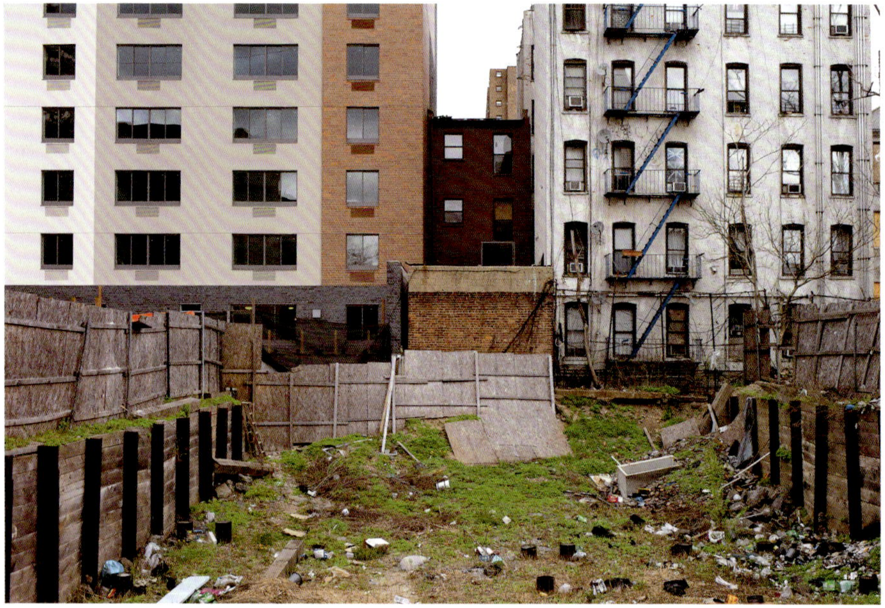

12

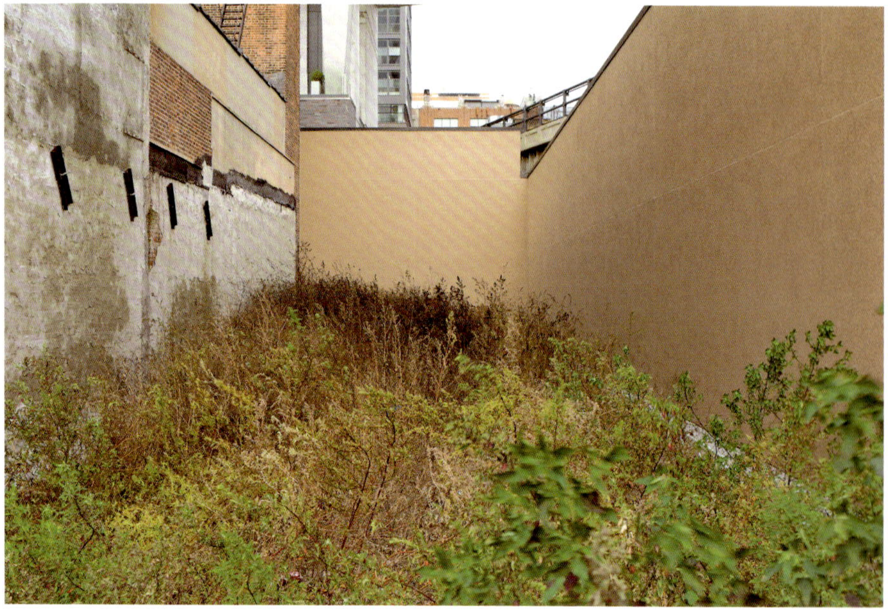

13

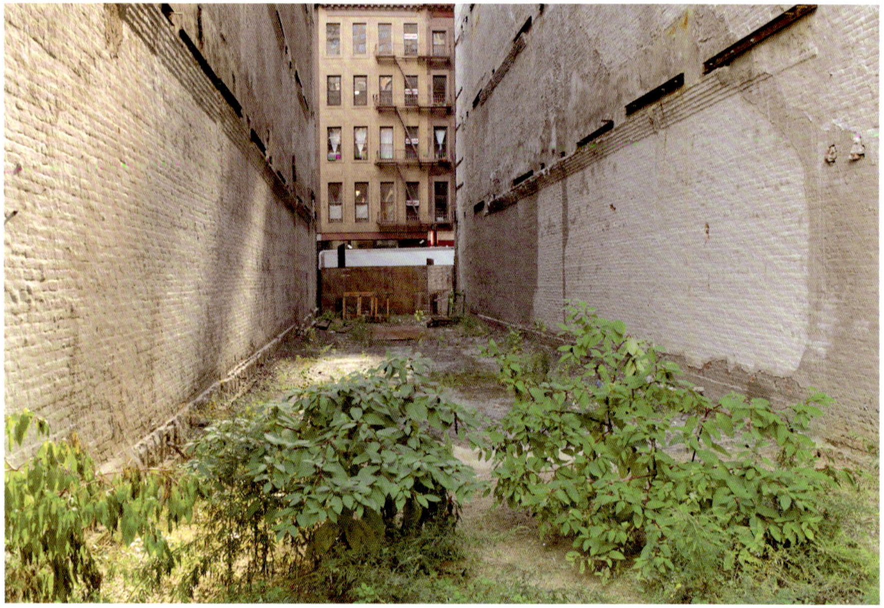

14

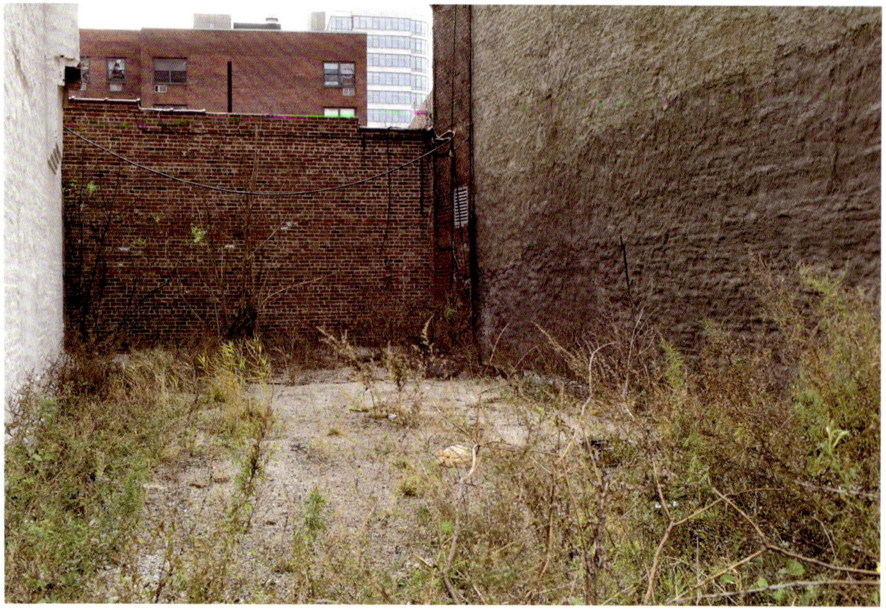

15

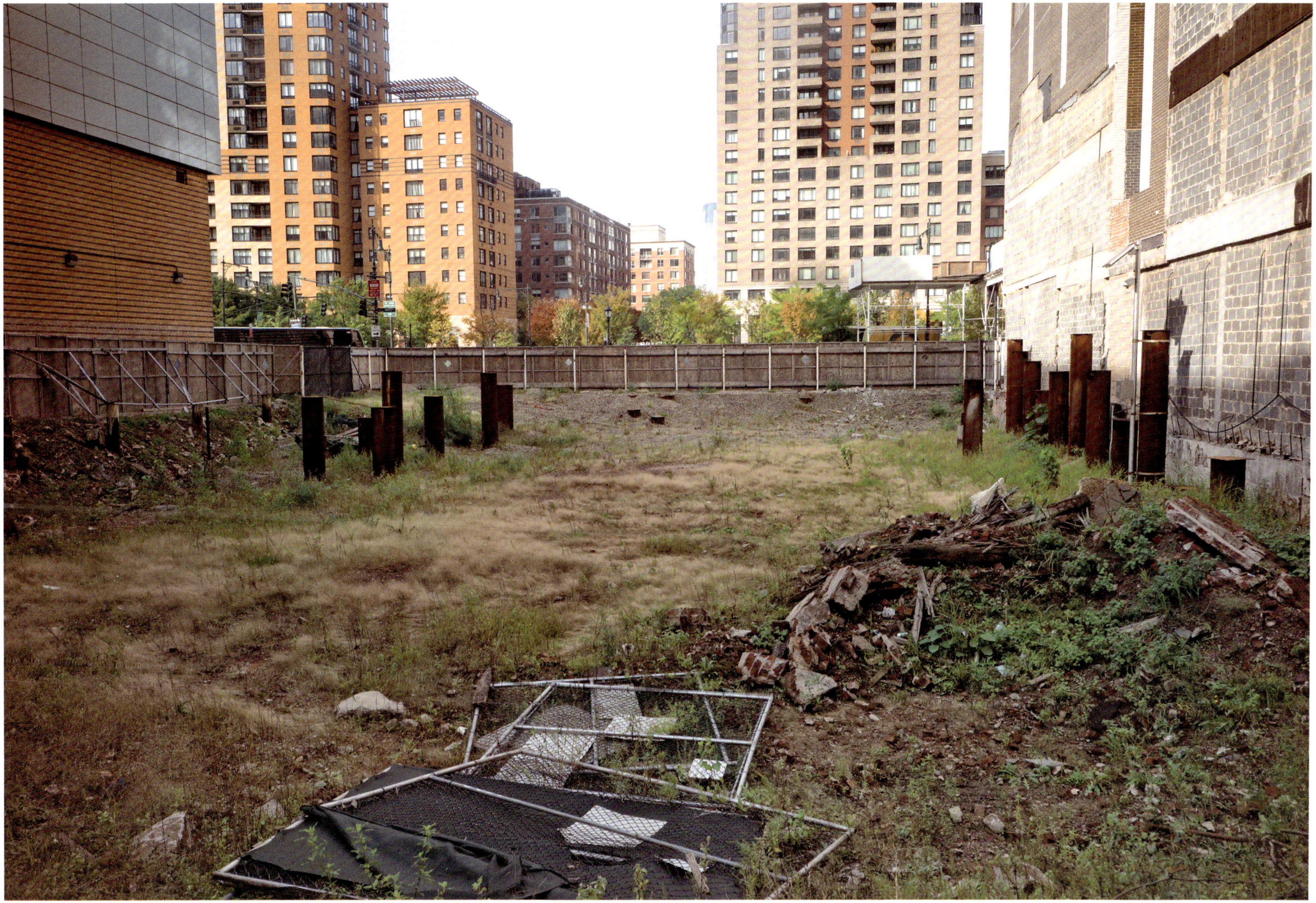

225

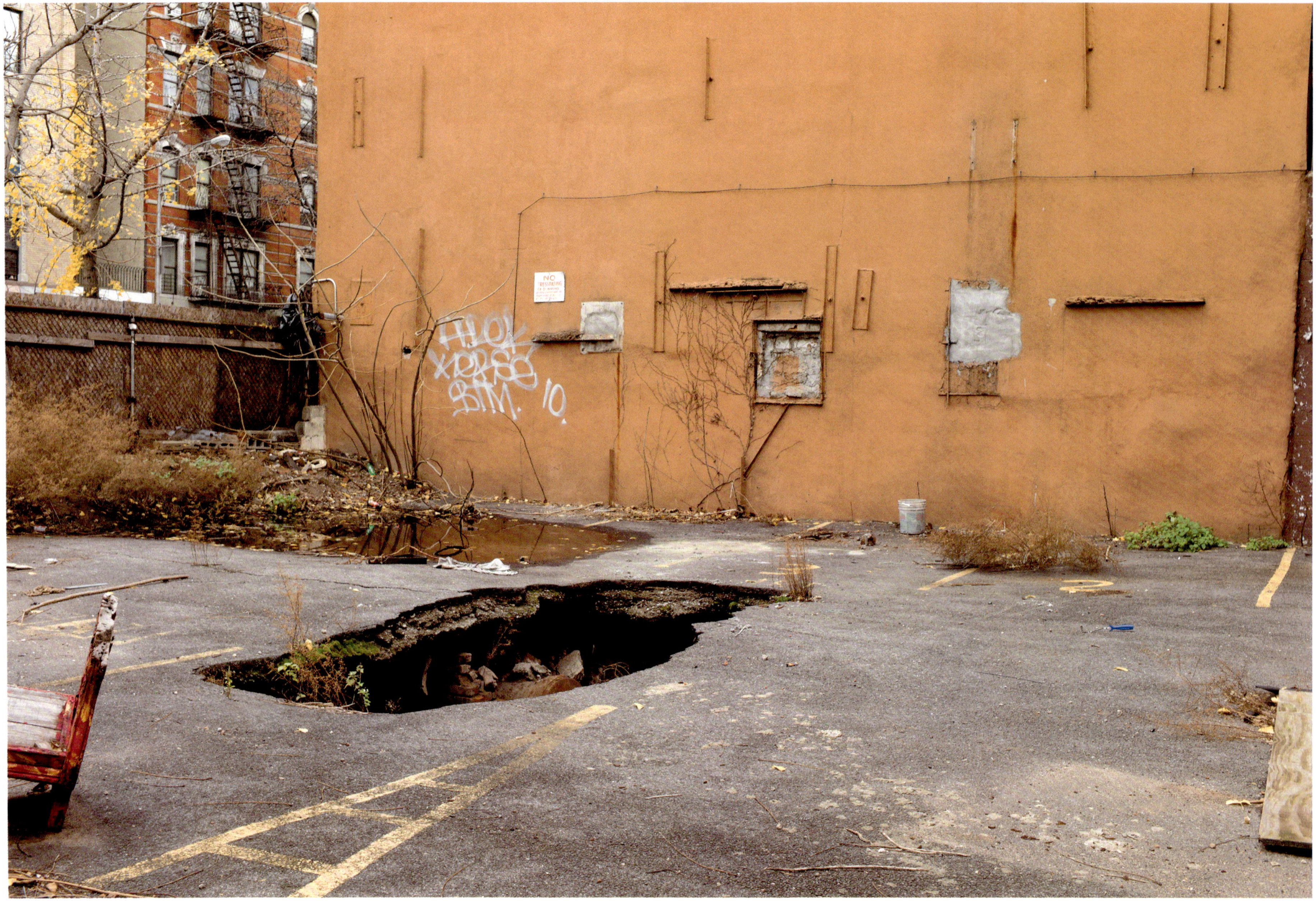

17

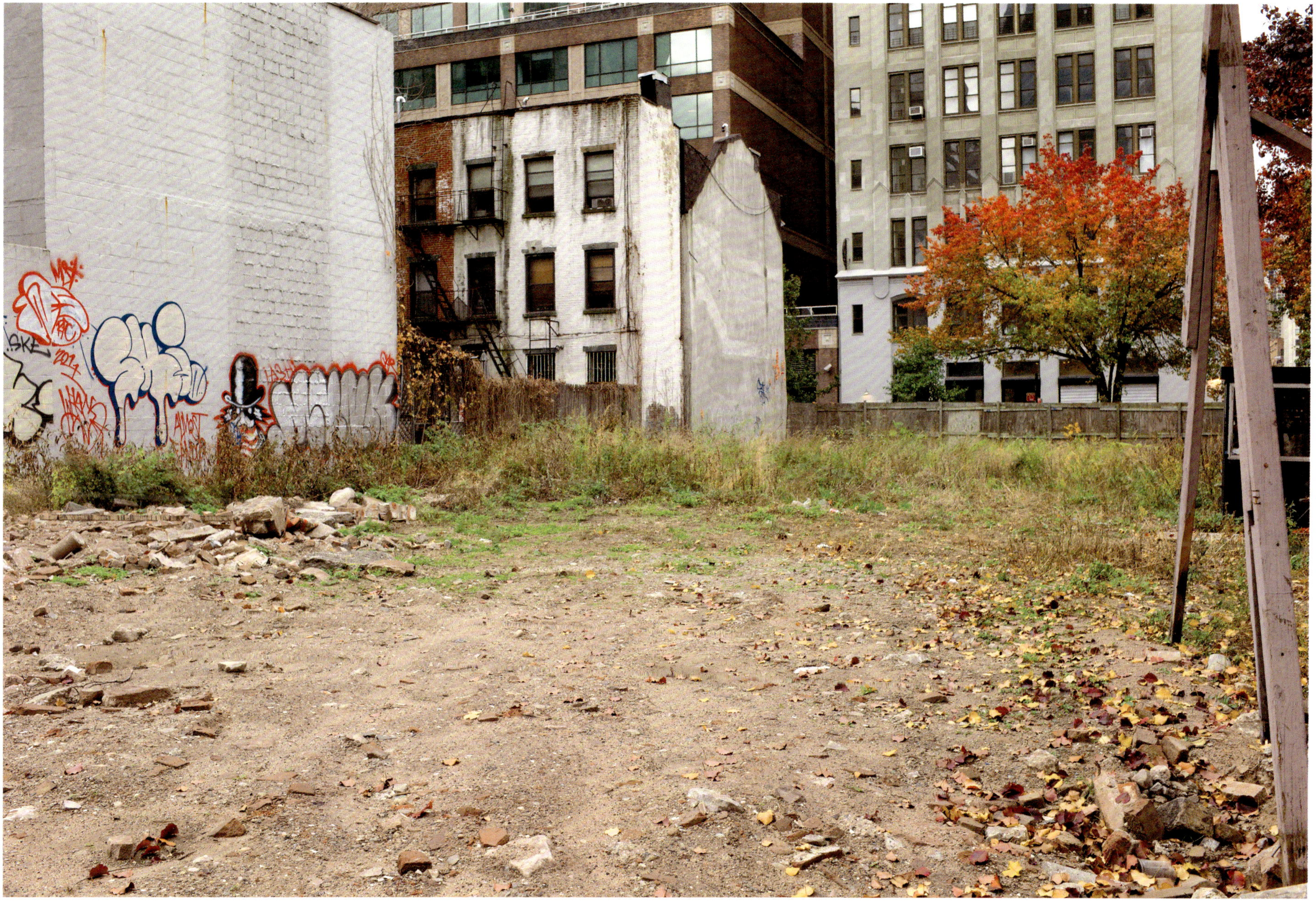

227

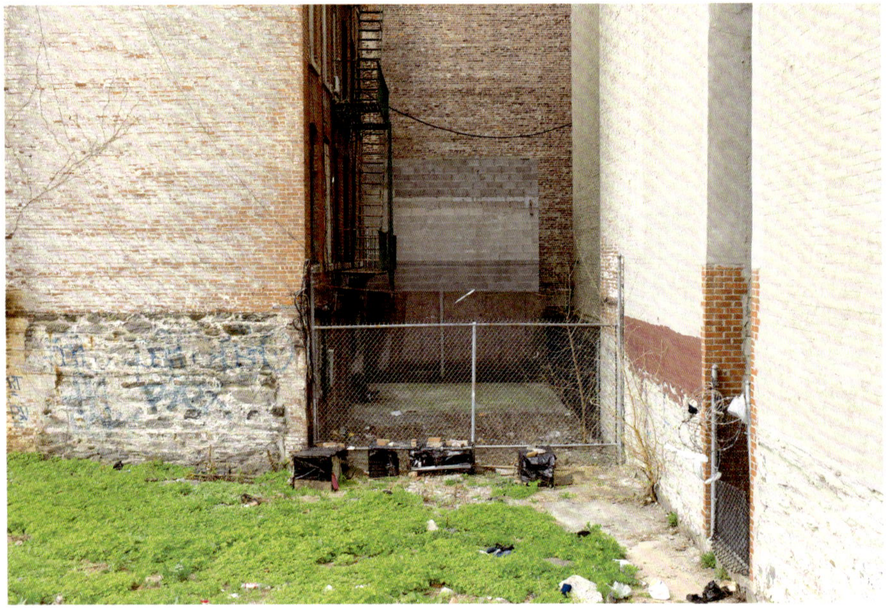

19

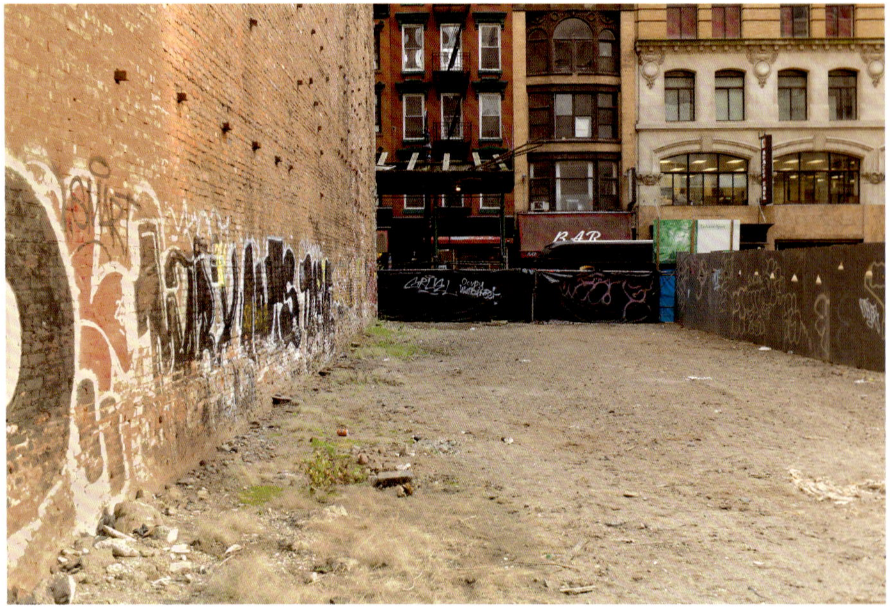

20

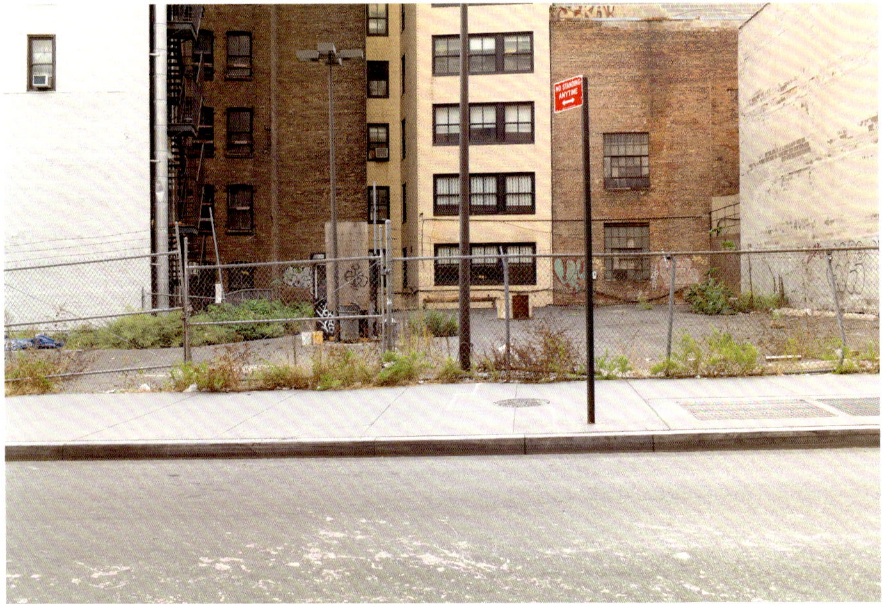

21

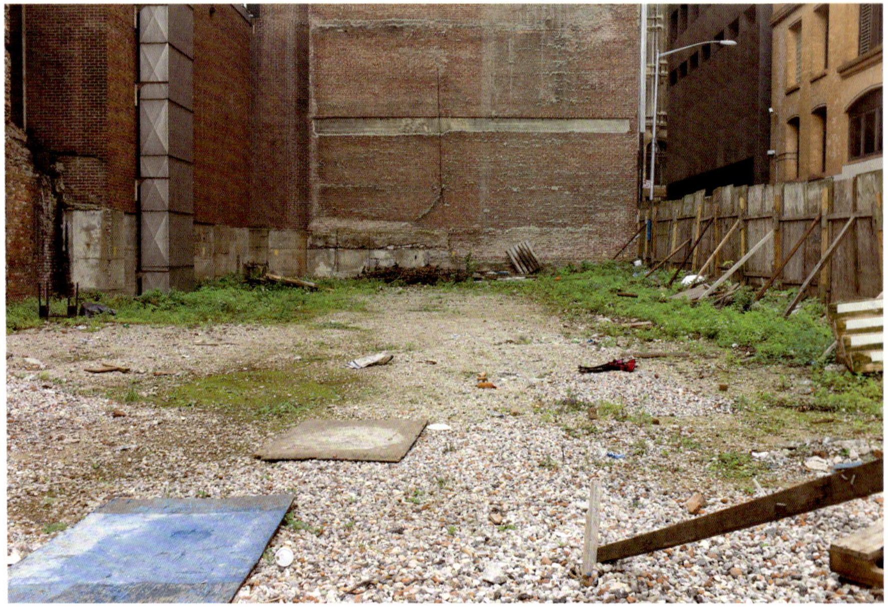

22

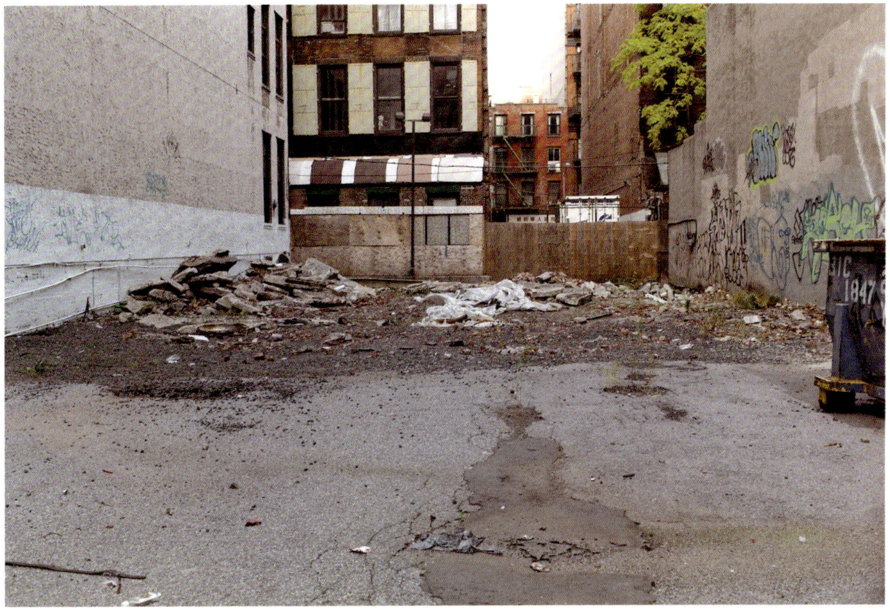

23

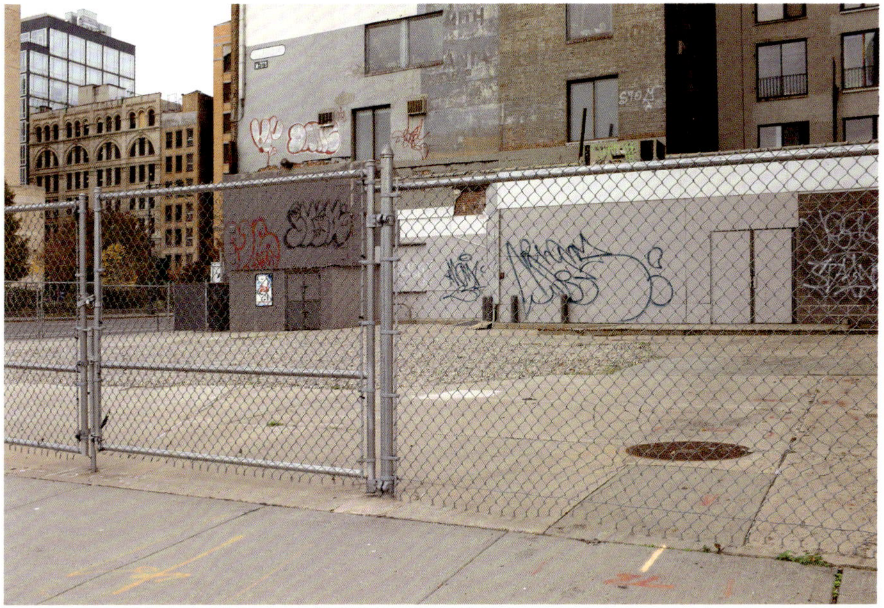

24

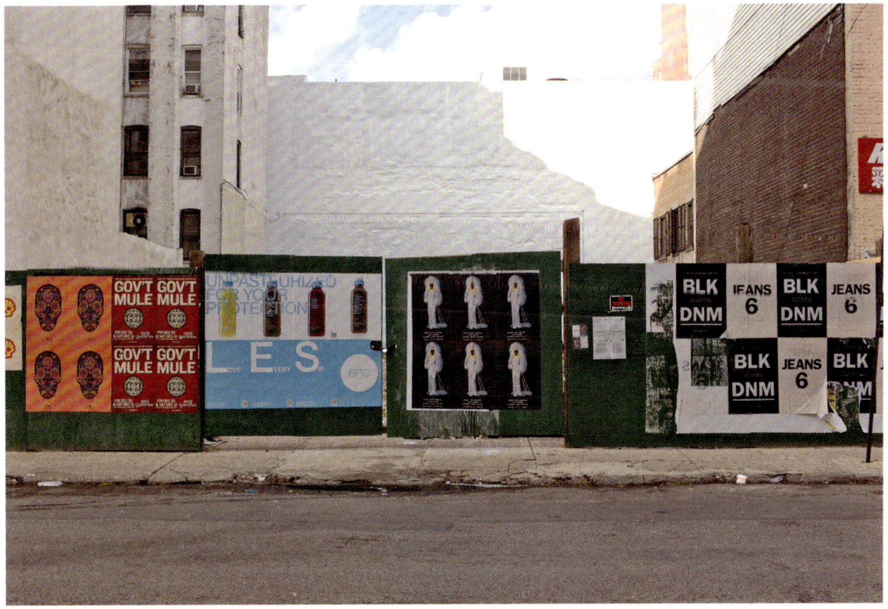
GOV'T GOV'T
MULE MULE
GOV'T GOV'T
MULE MULE
L.E.S.
BLK
DNM
JEANS
6
BLK
DNM
JEANS
6

25

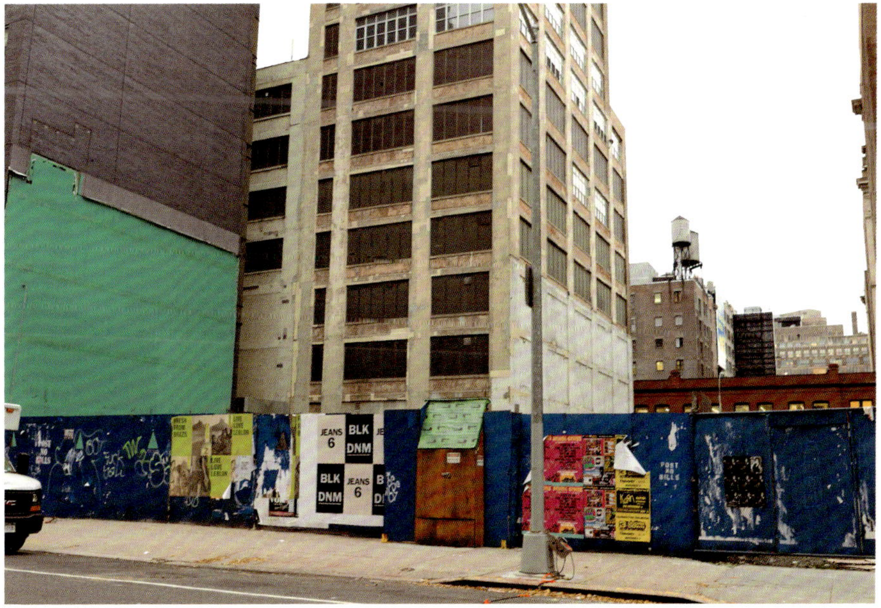
JEANS
6
BLK
DNM
BLK
DNM
JEANS
6

26

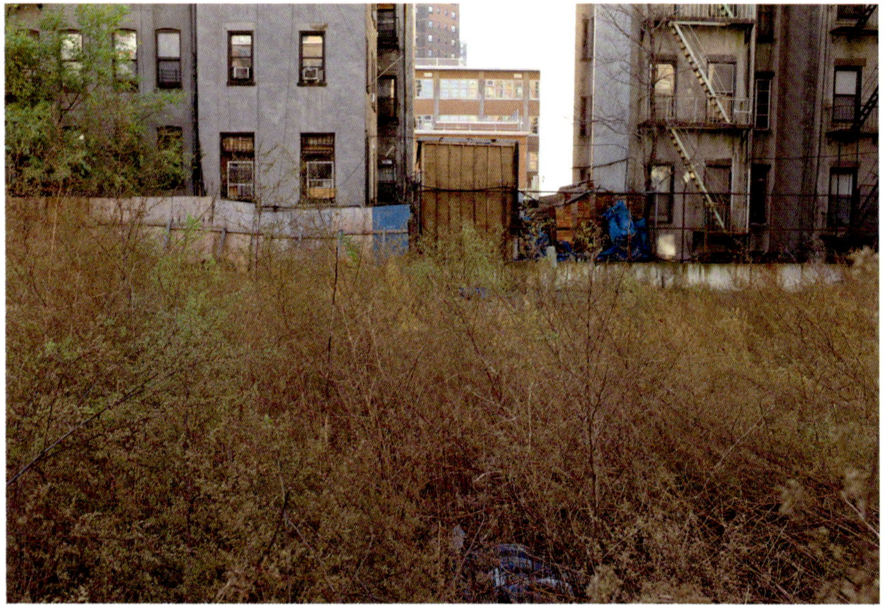
27

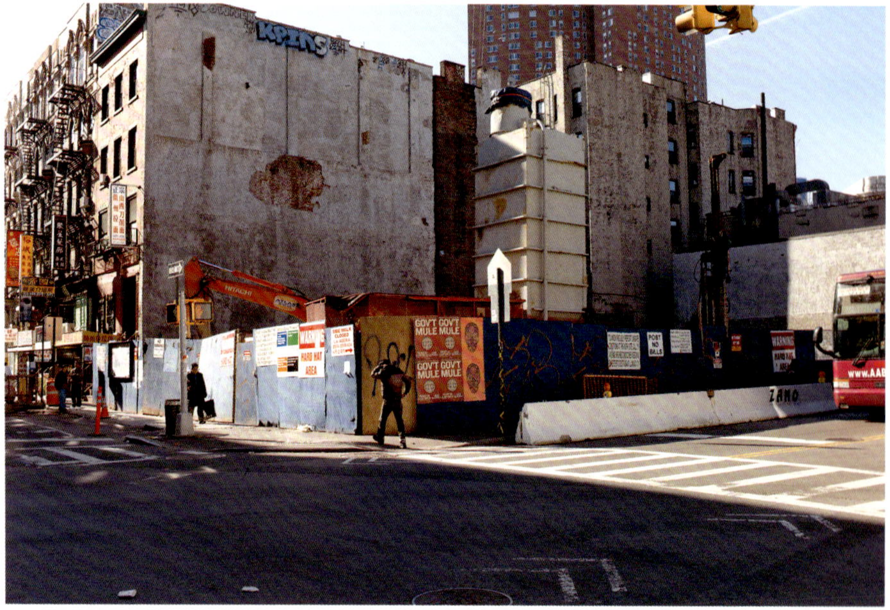
28

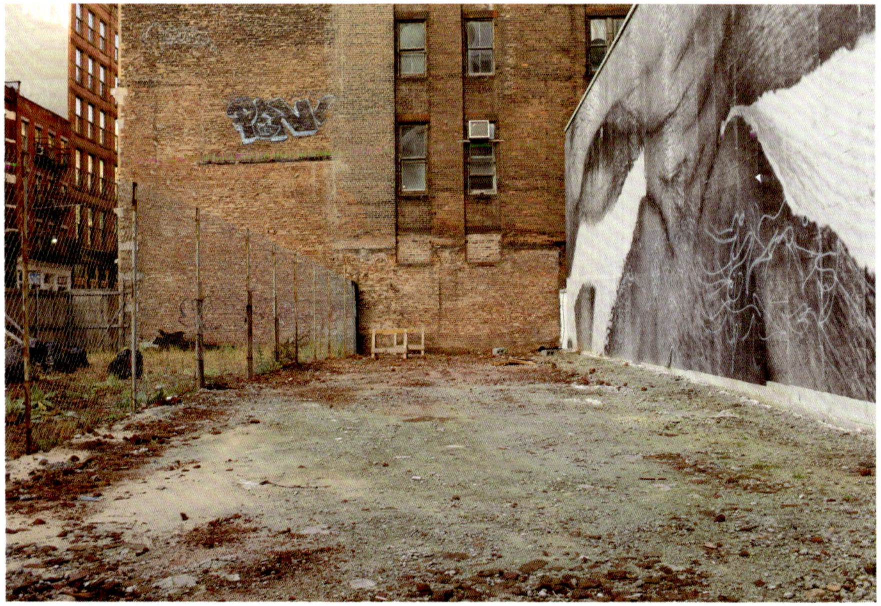
29

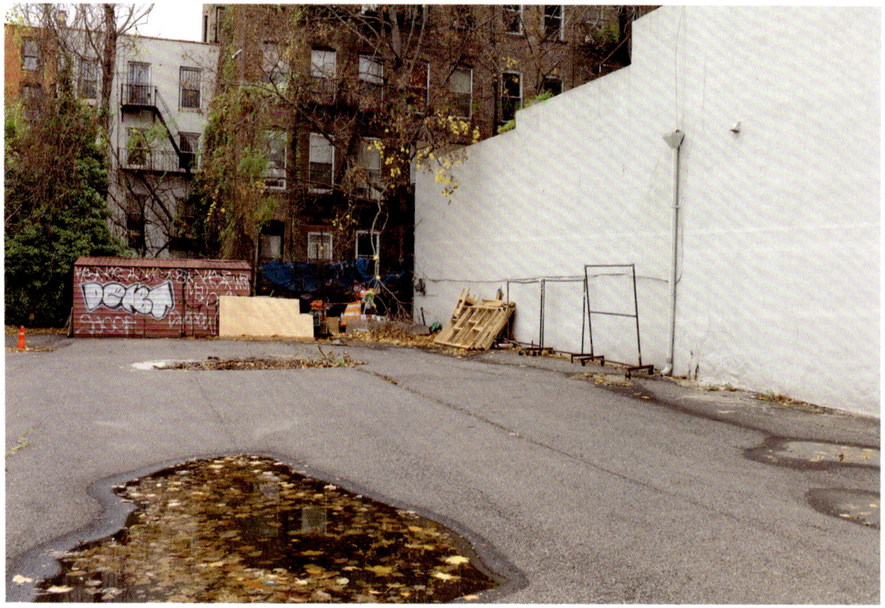
30

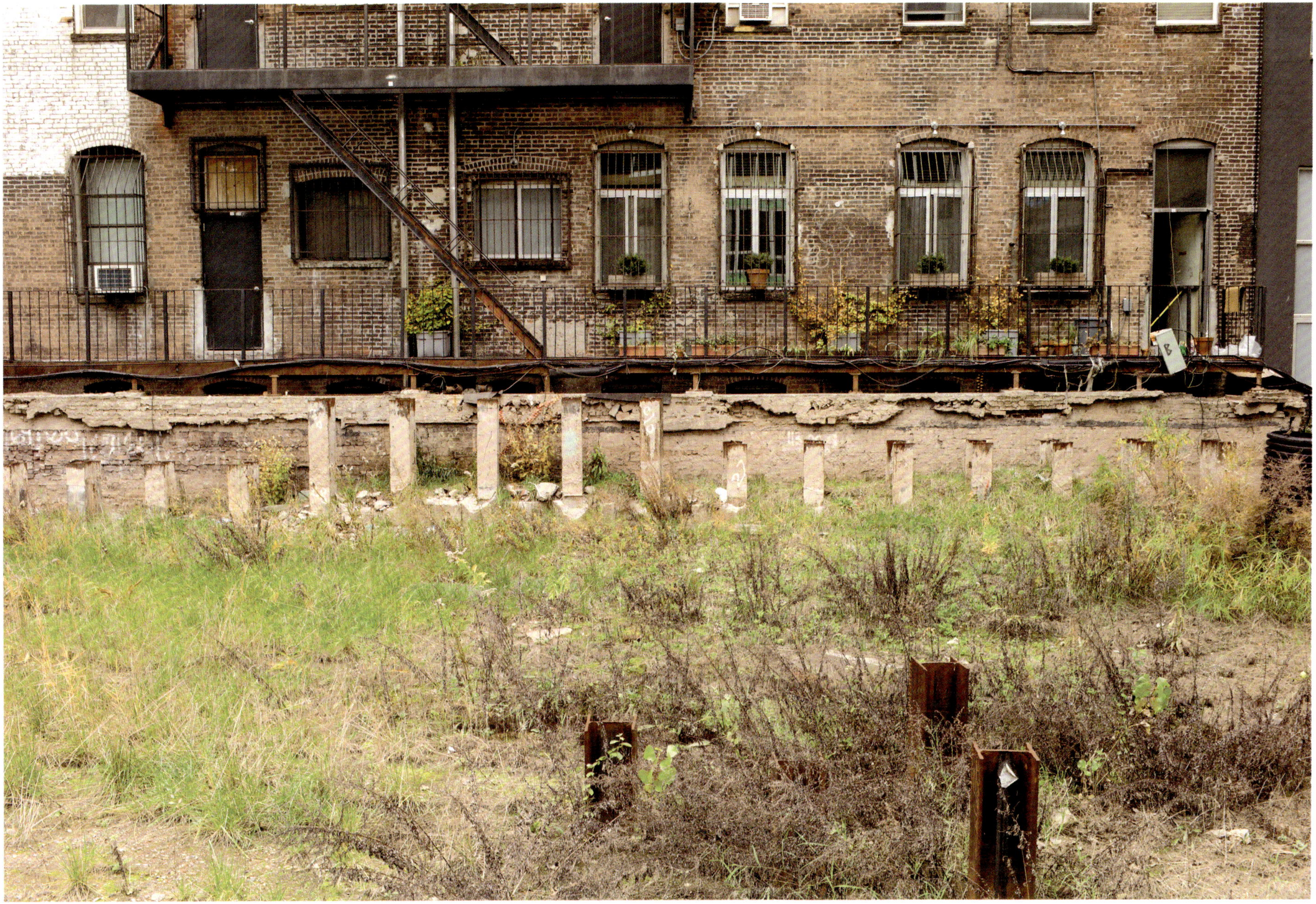

31

232

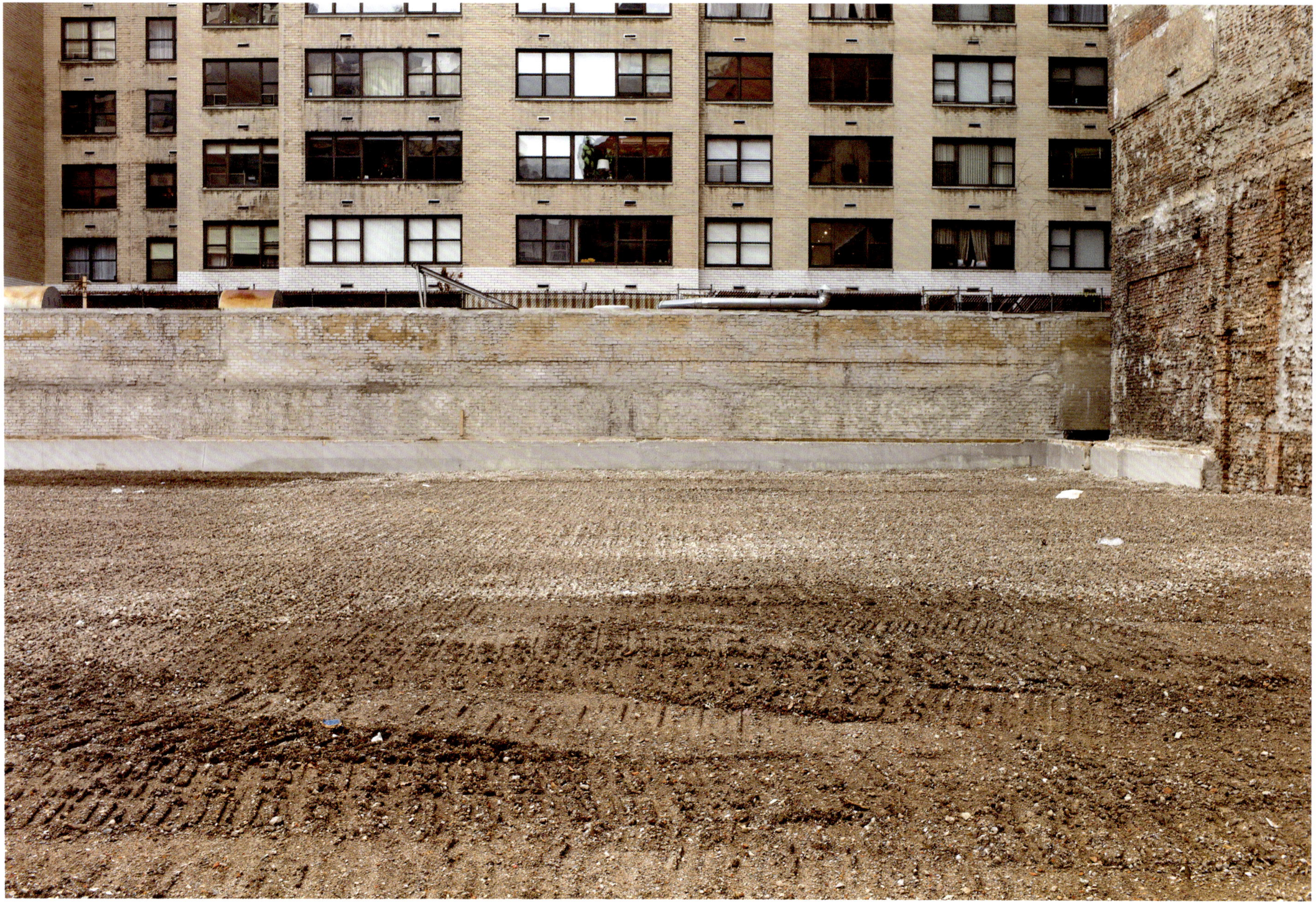

32

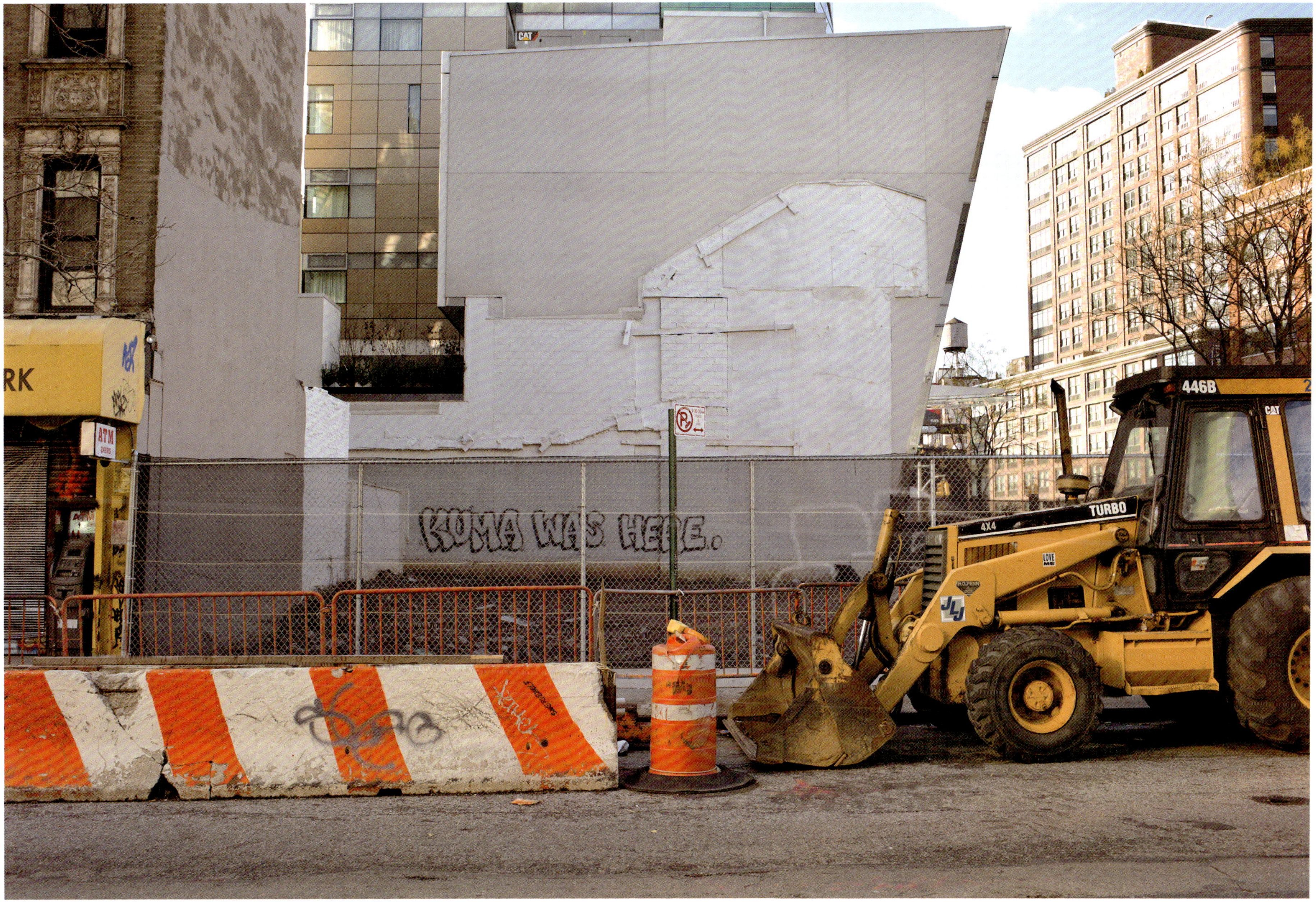
KOMA WAS HERE.
ATM
TURBO
446B
4X4
CAT

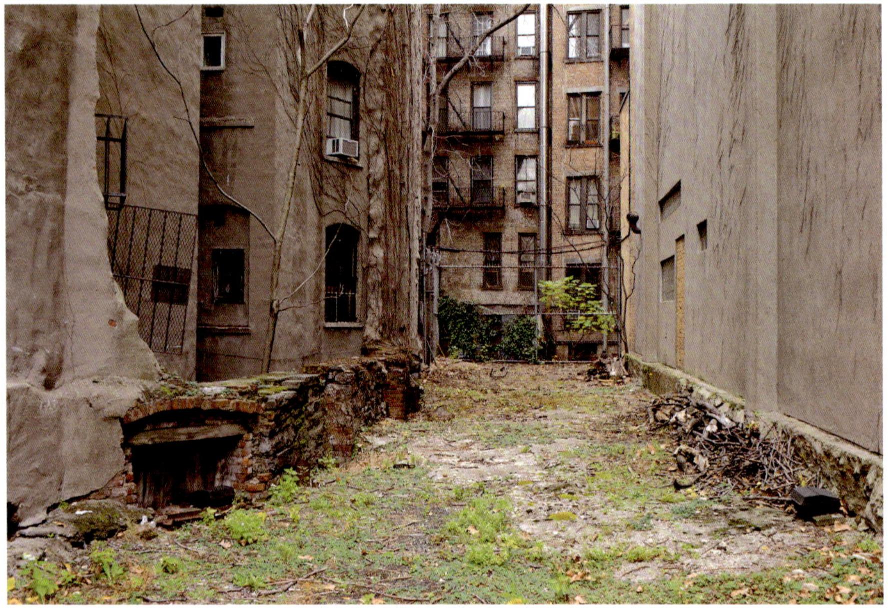

34

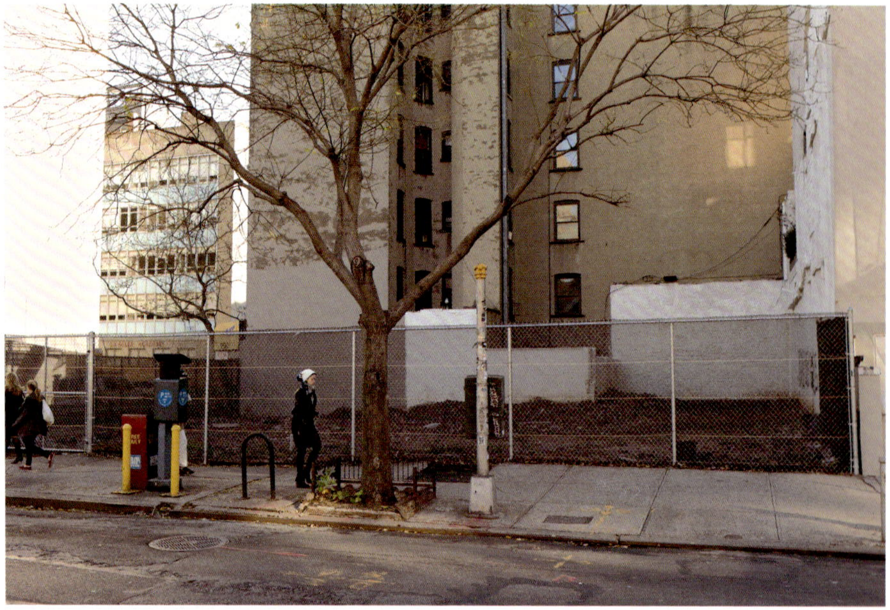

35

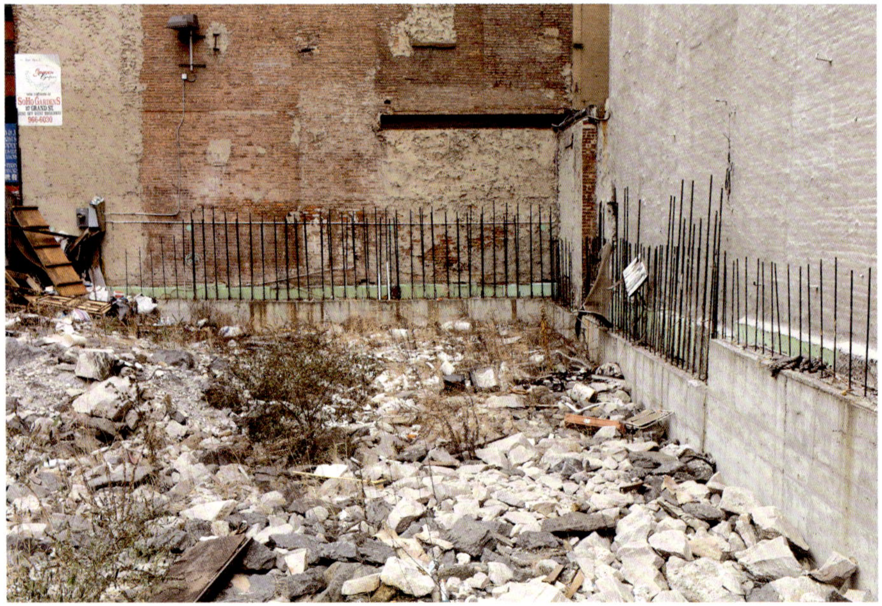

36

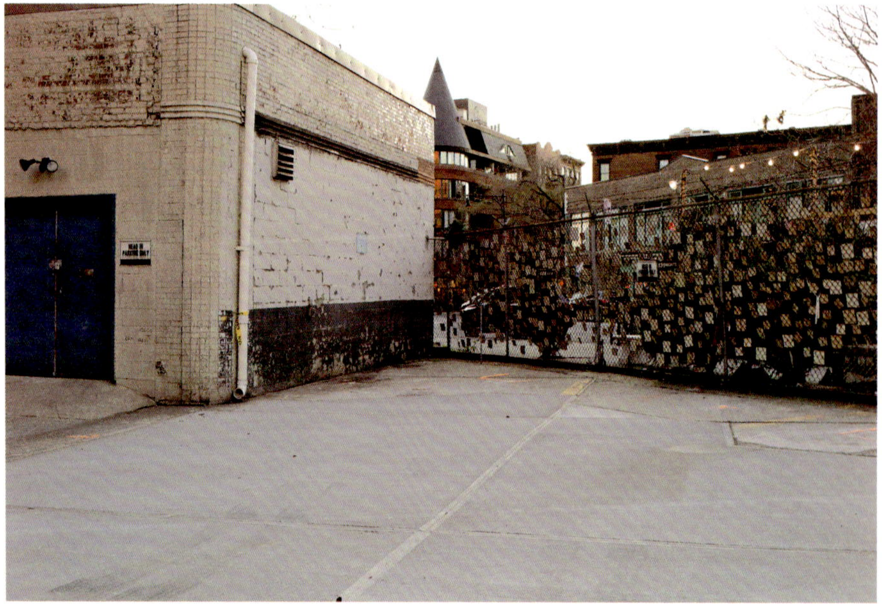

37

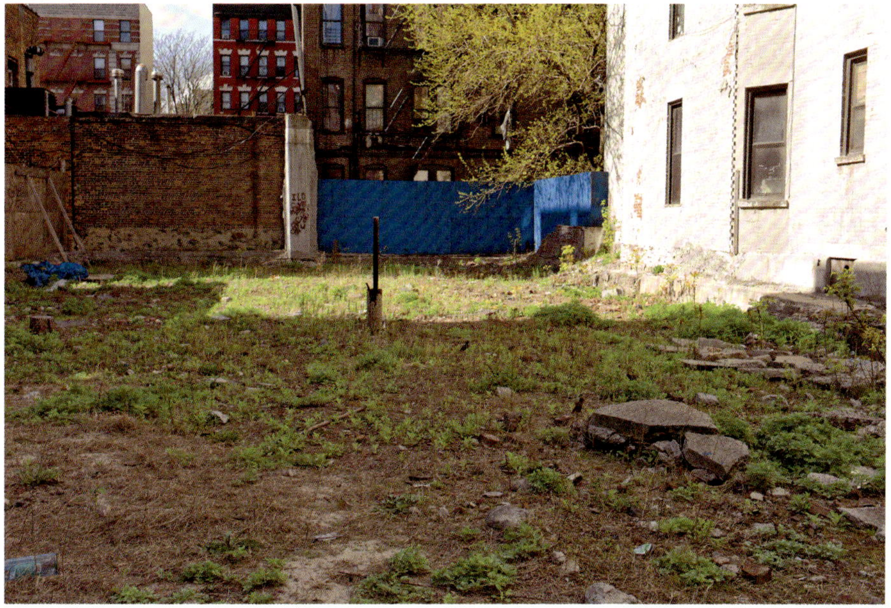

38

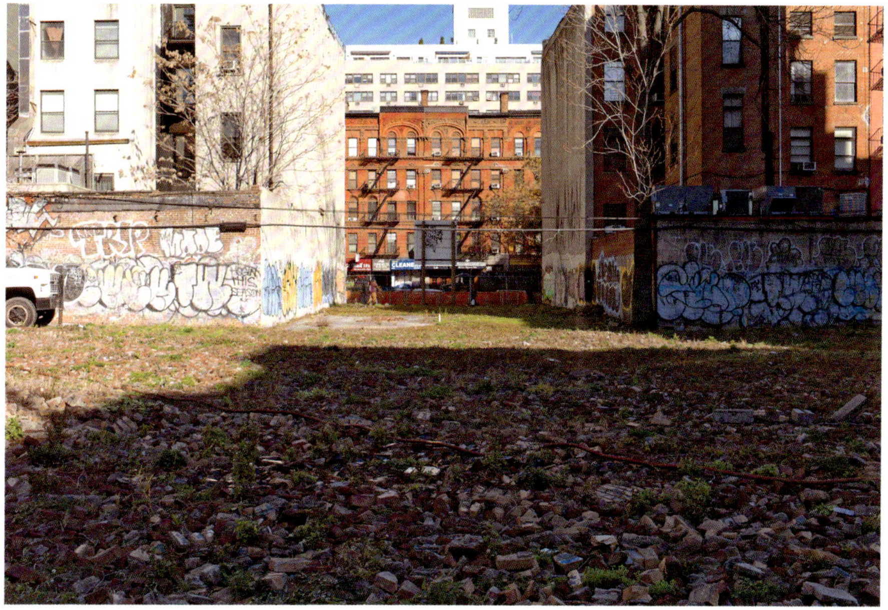

39

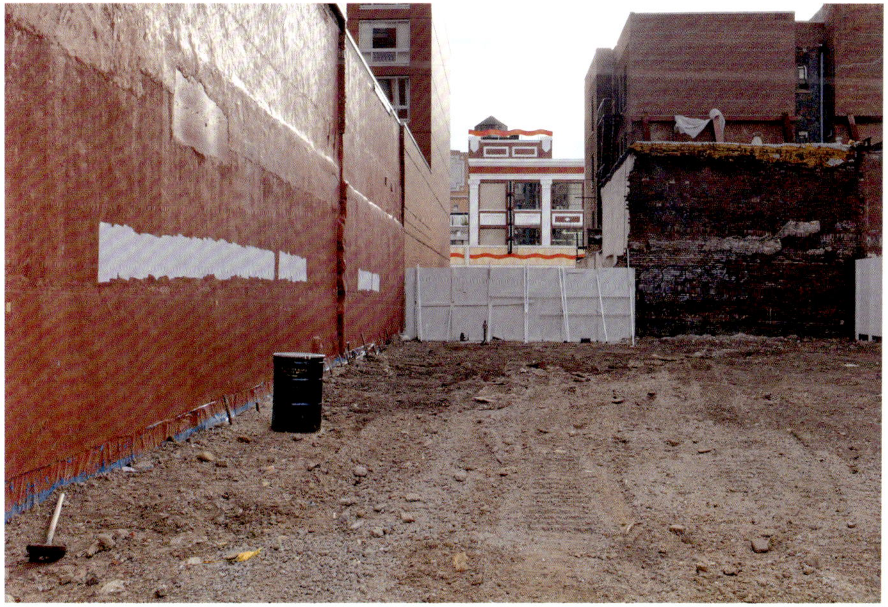

40

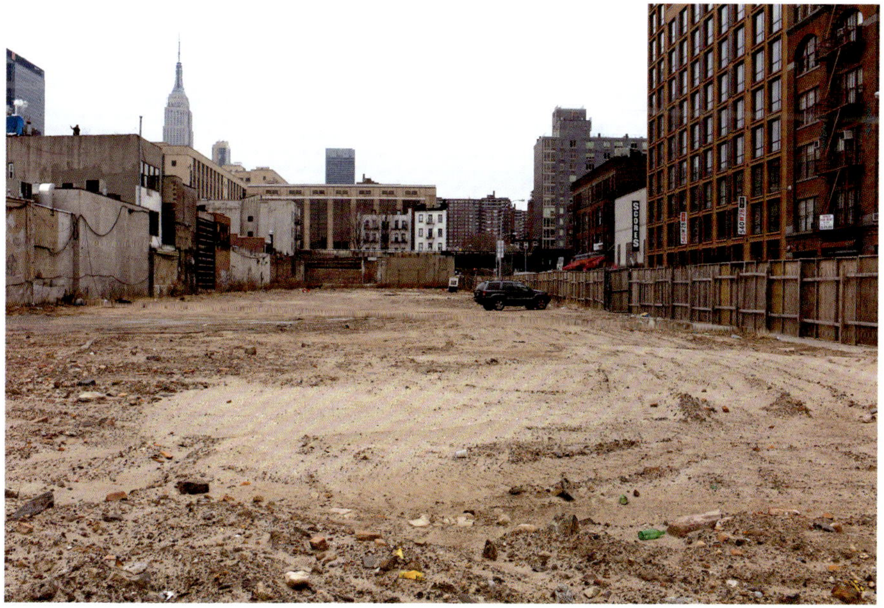

41

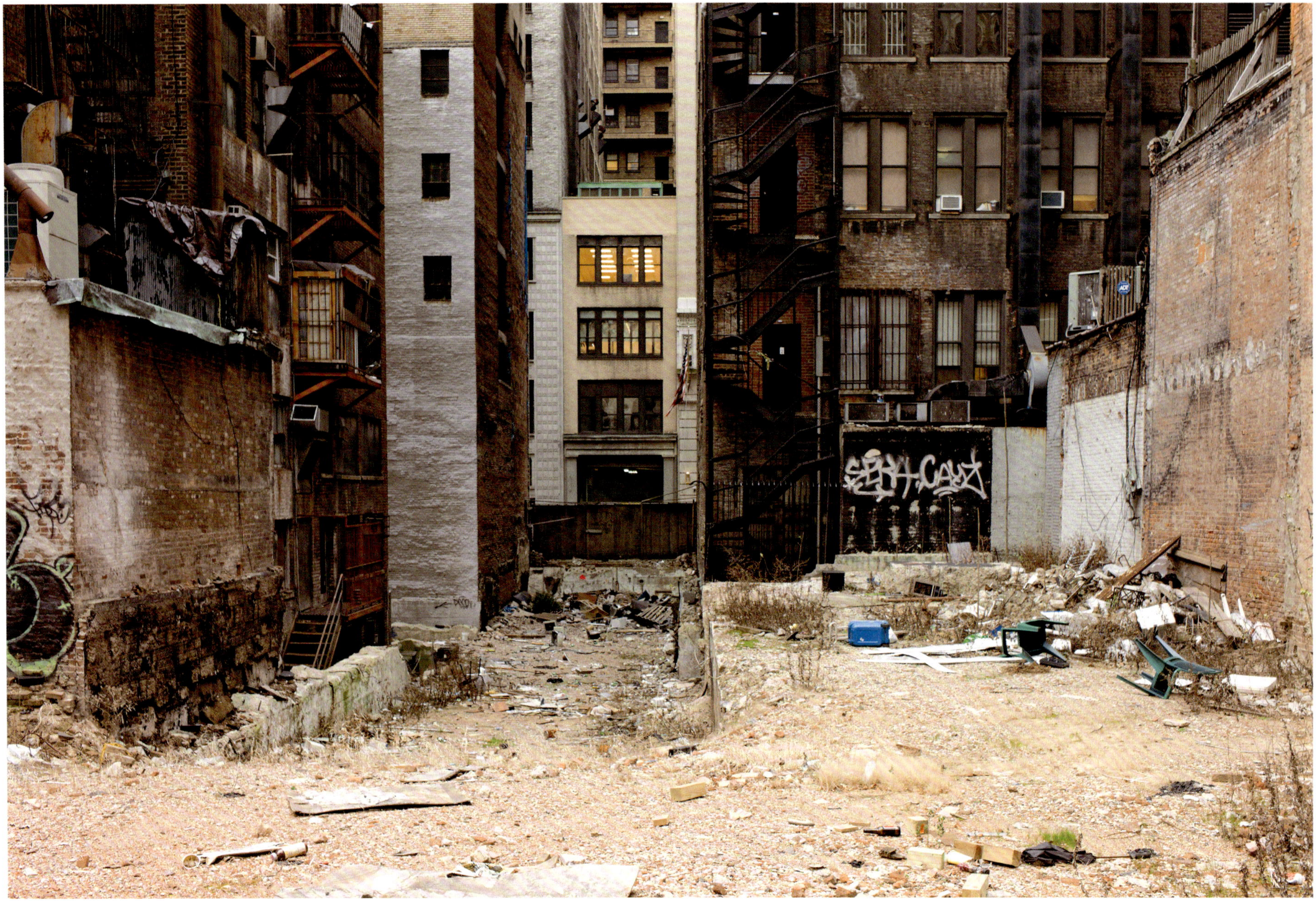

42

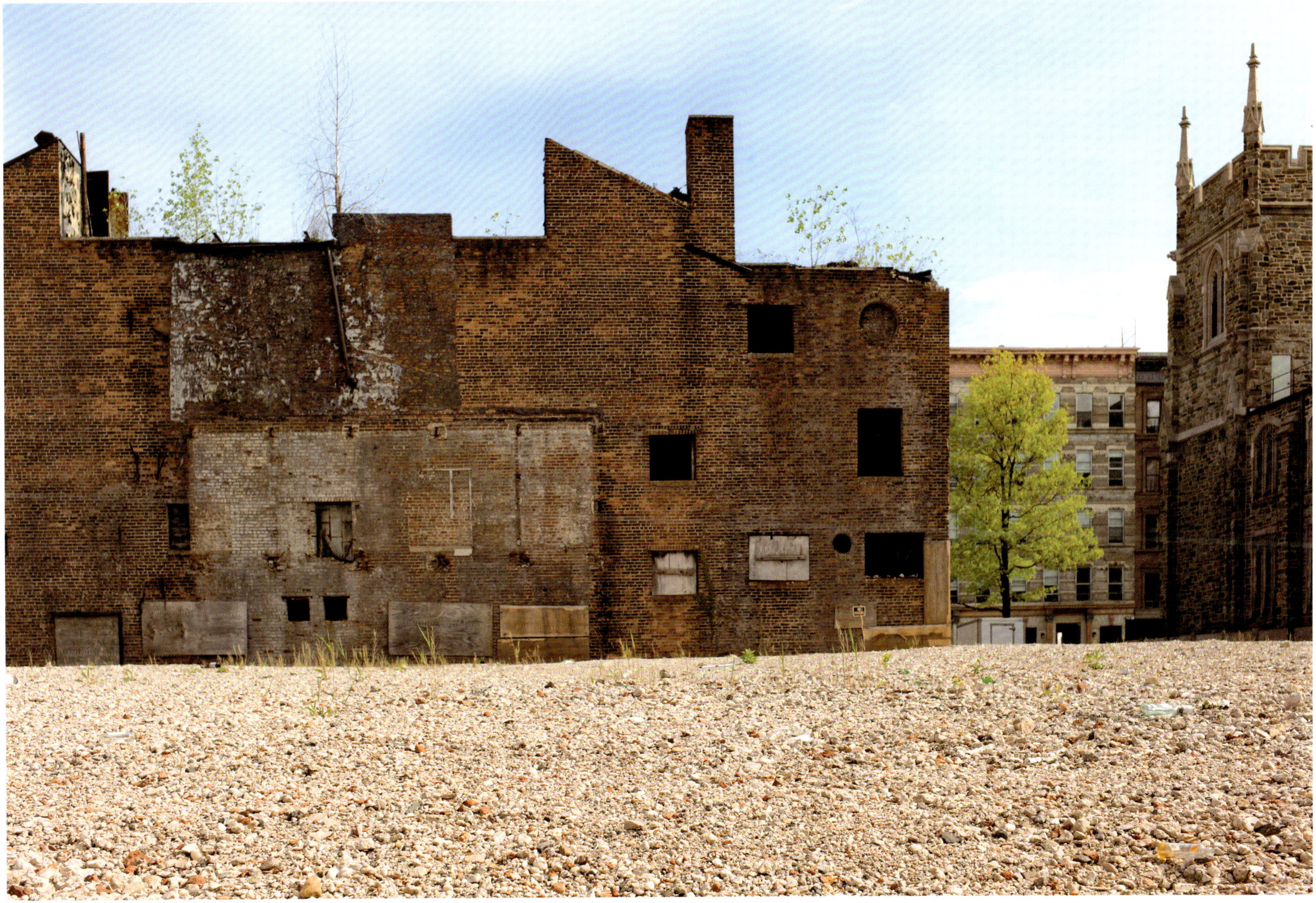

43

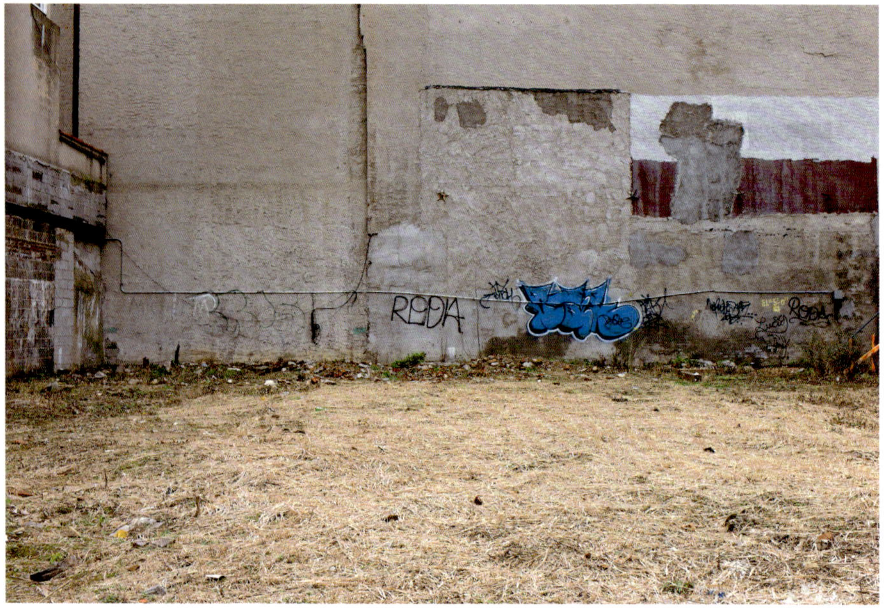

44

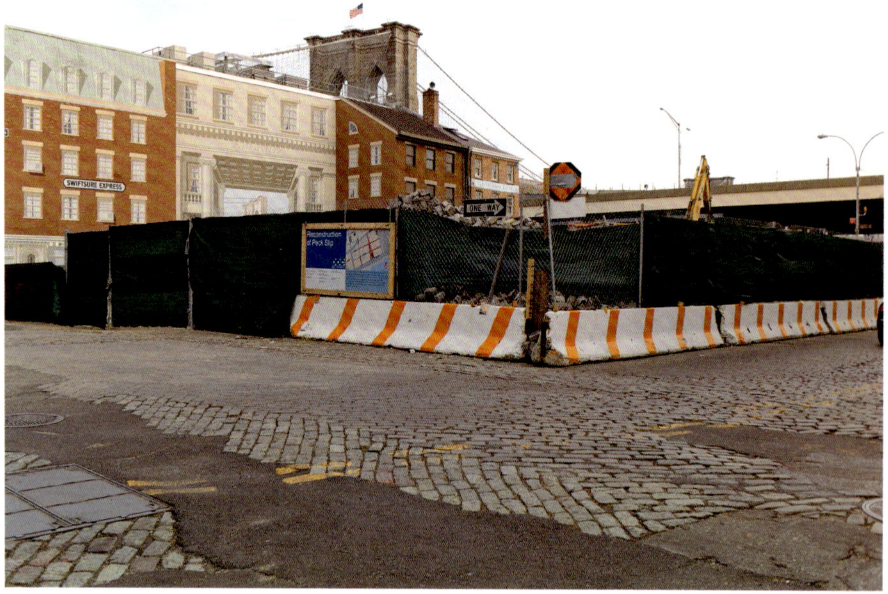

45

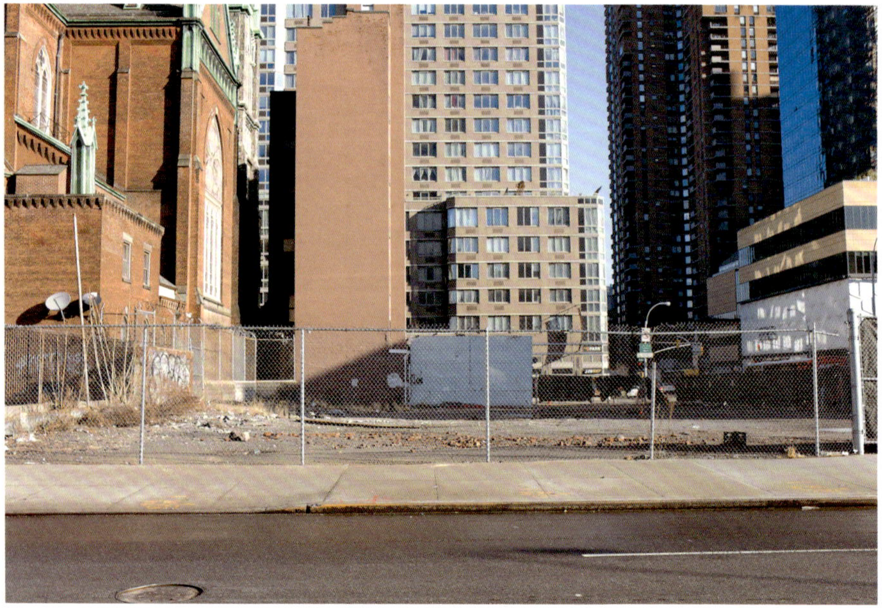

46

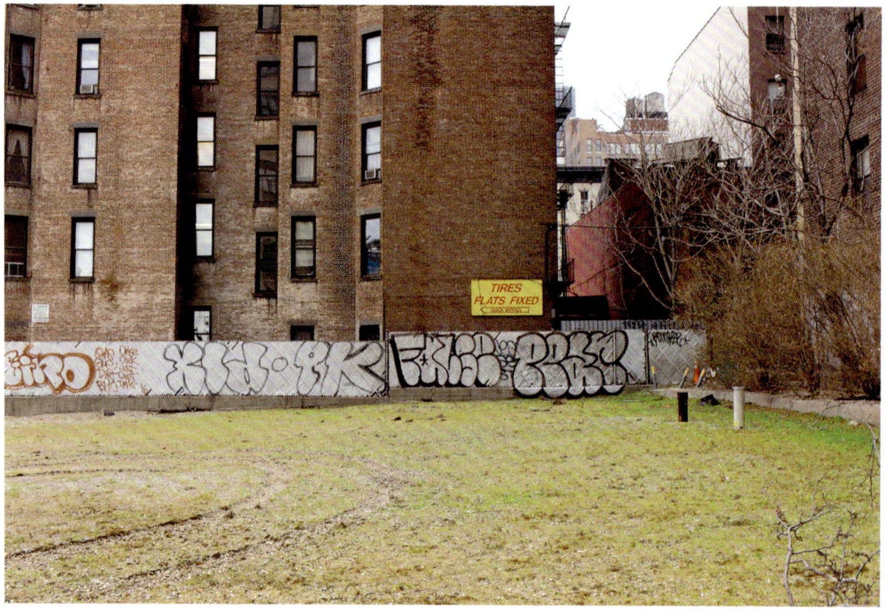

47

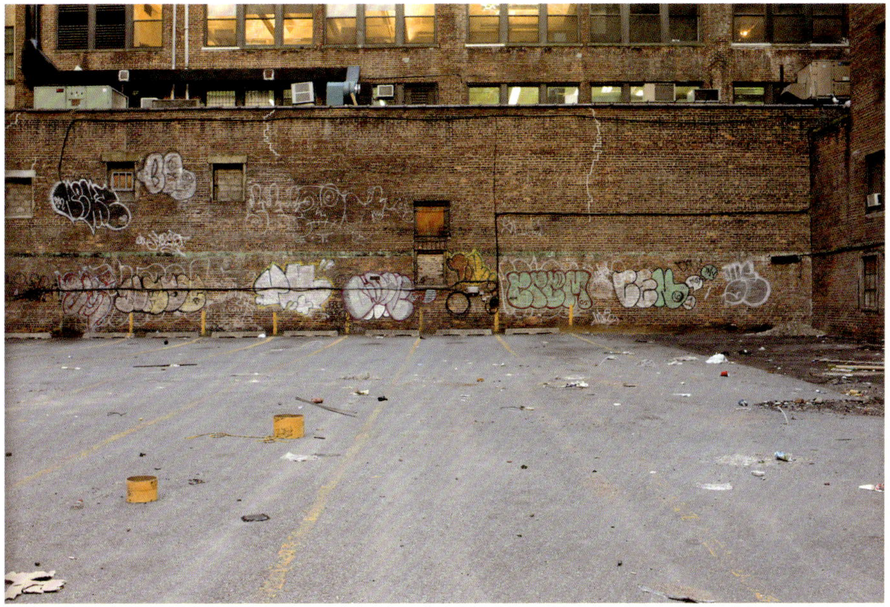

48

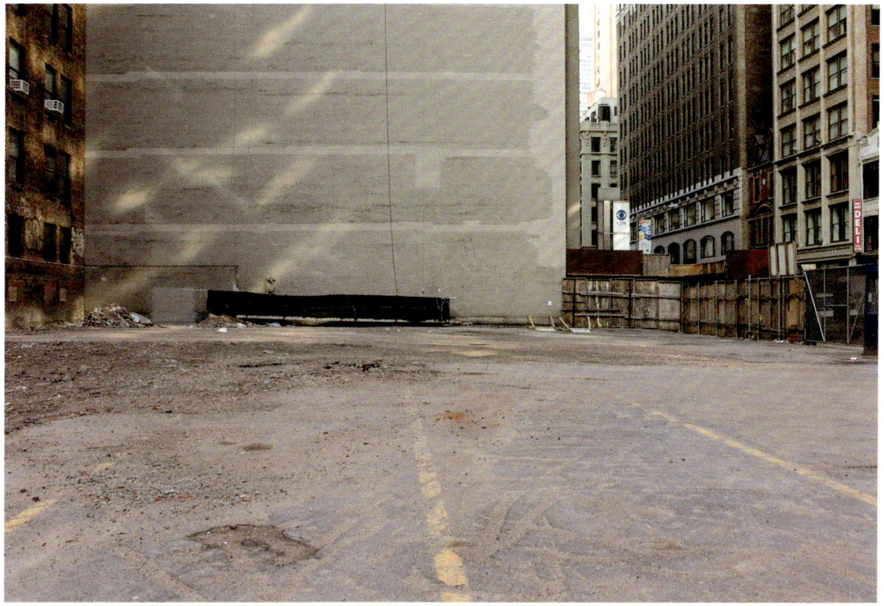

49

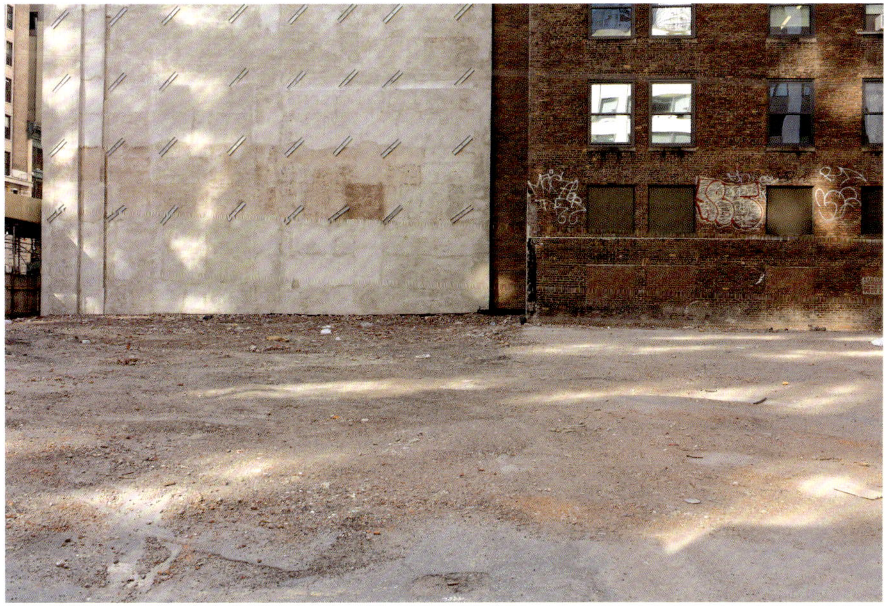

50

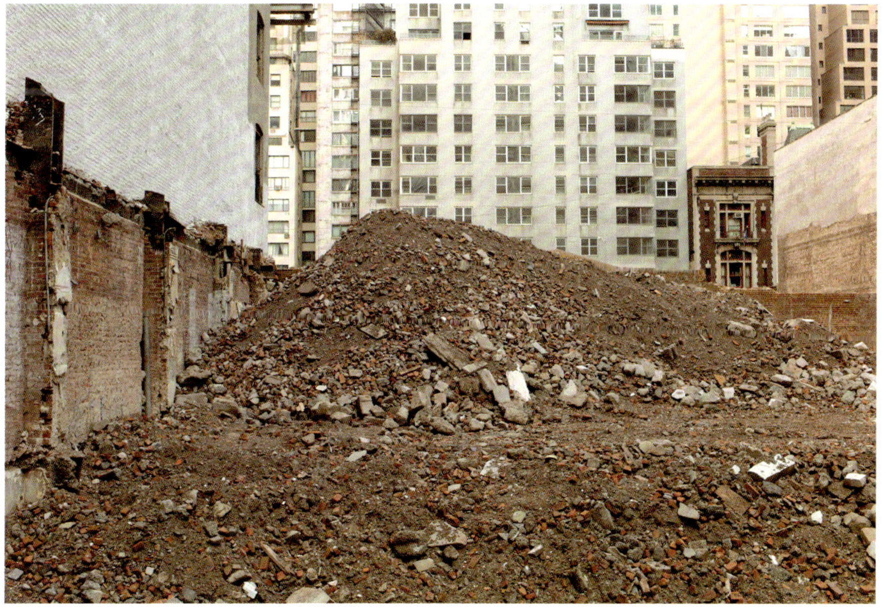

51

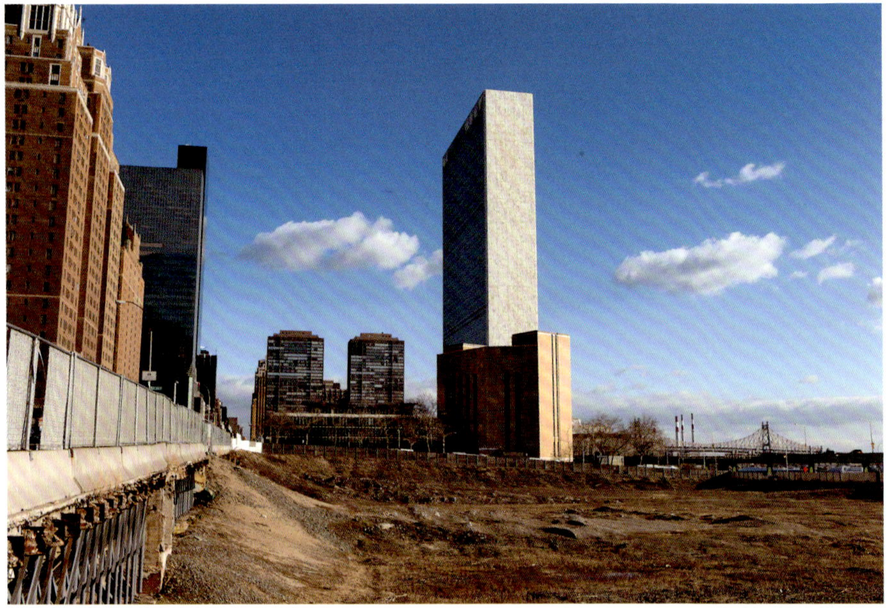

52

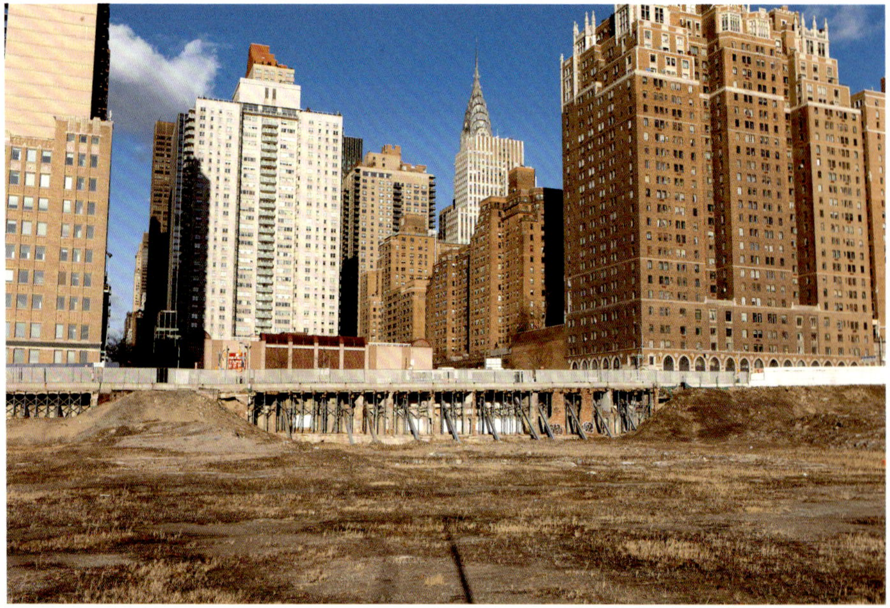

53

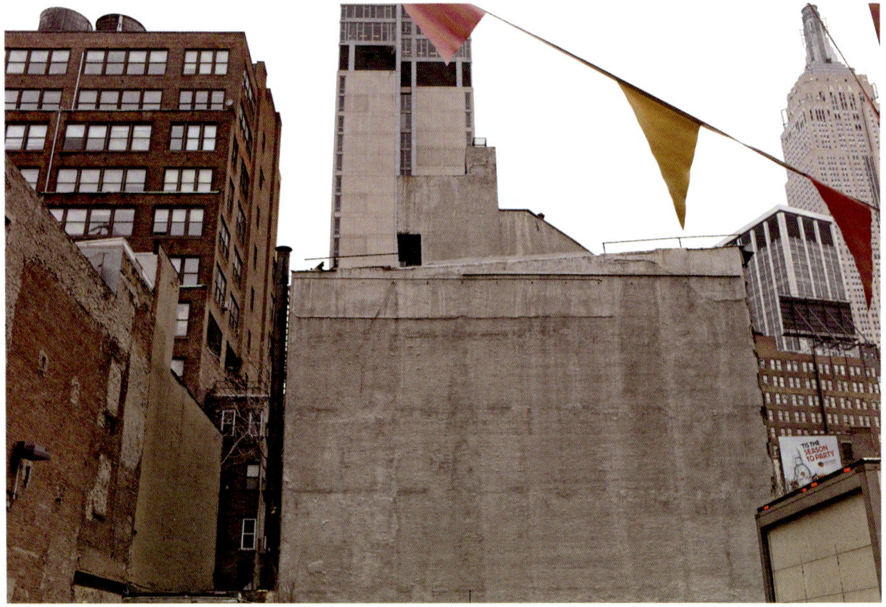

54

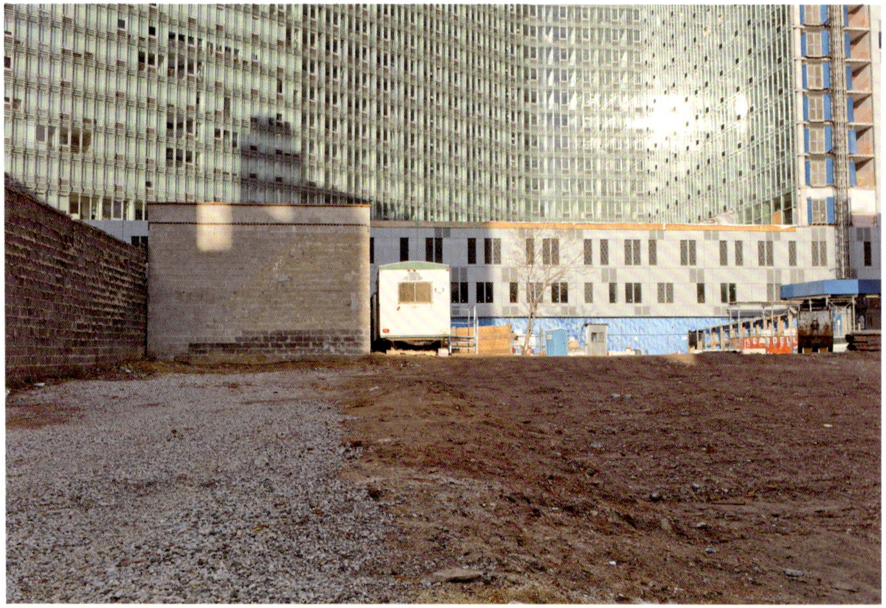

55

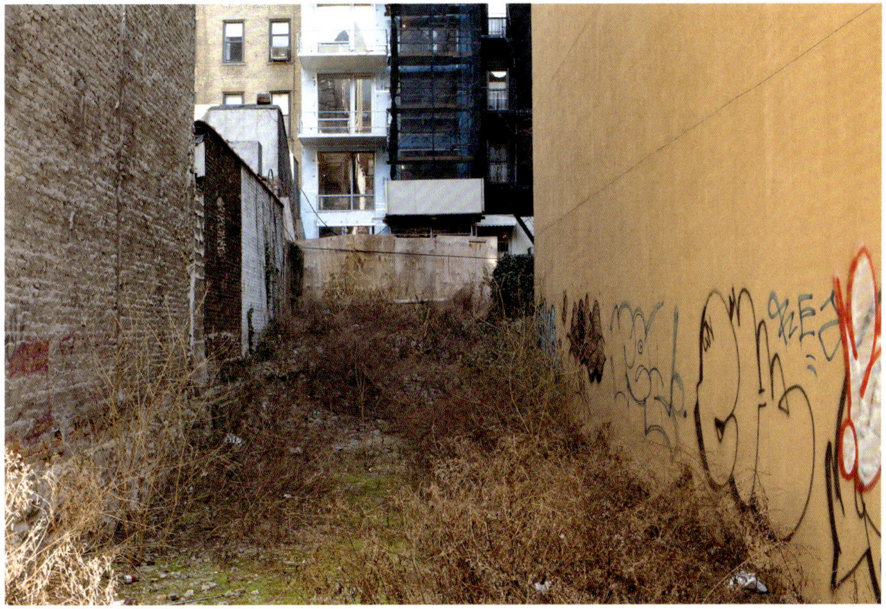

56

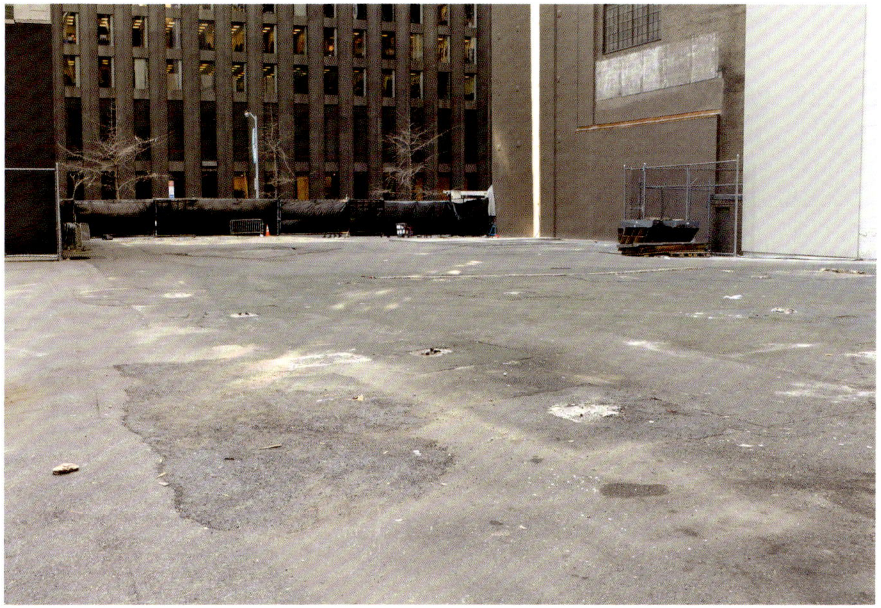

57

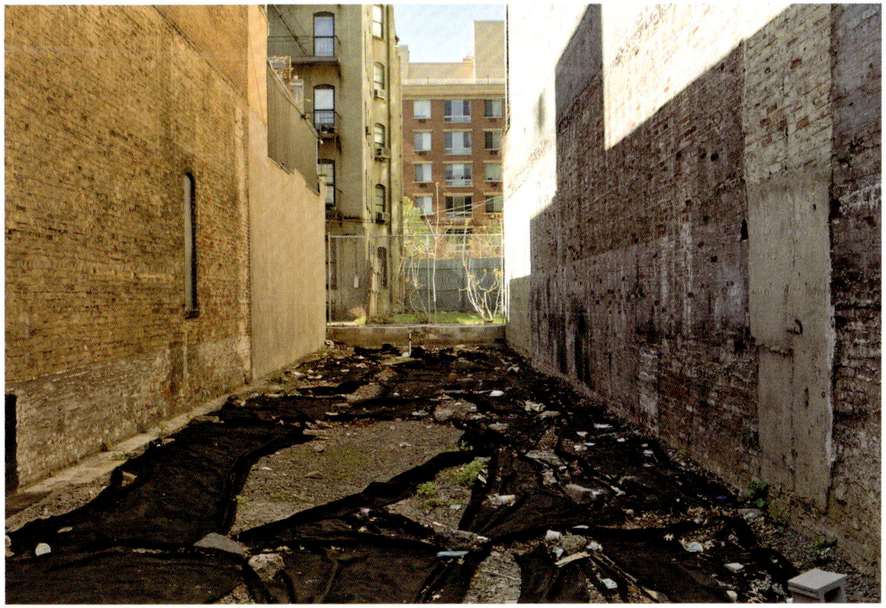

58

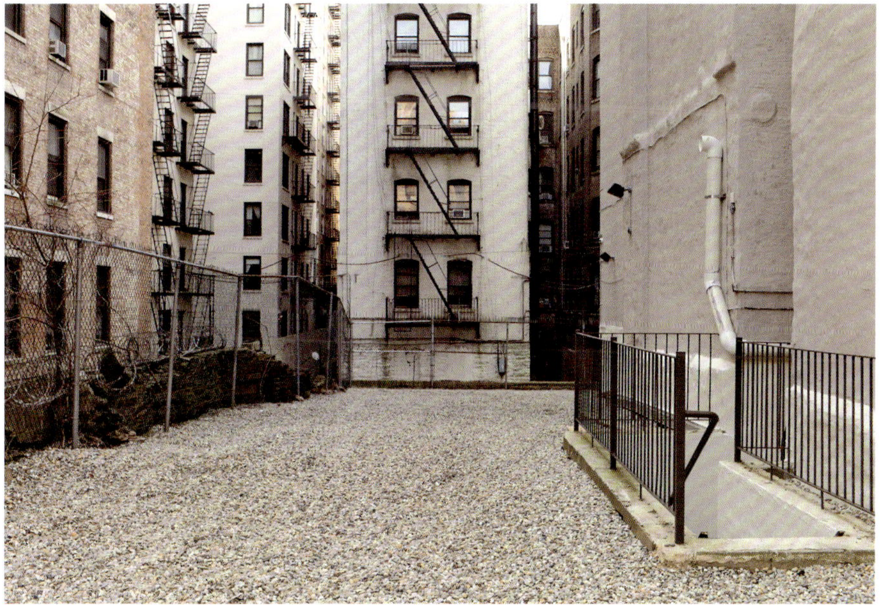

59

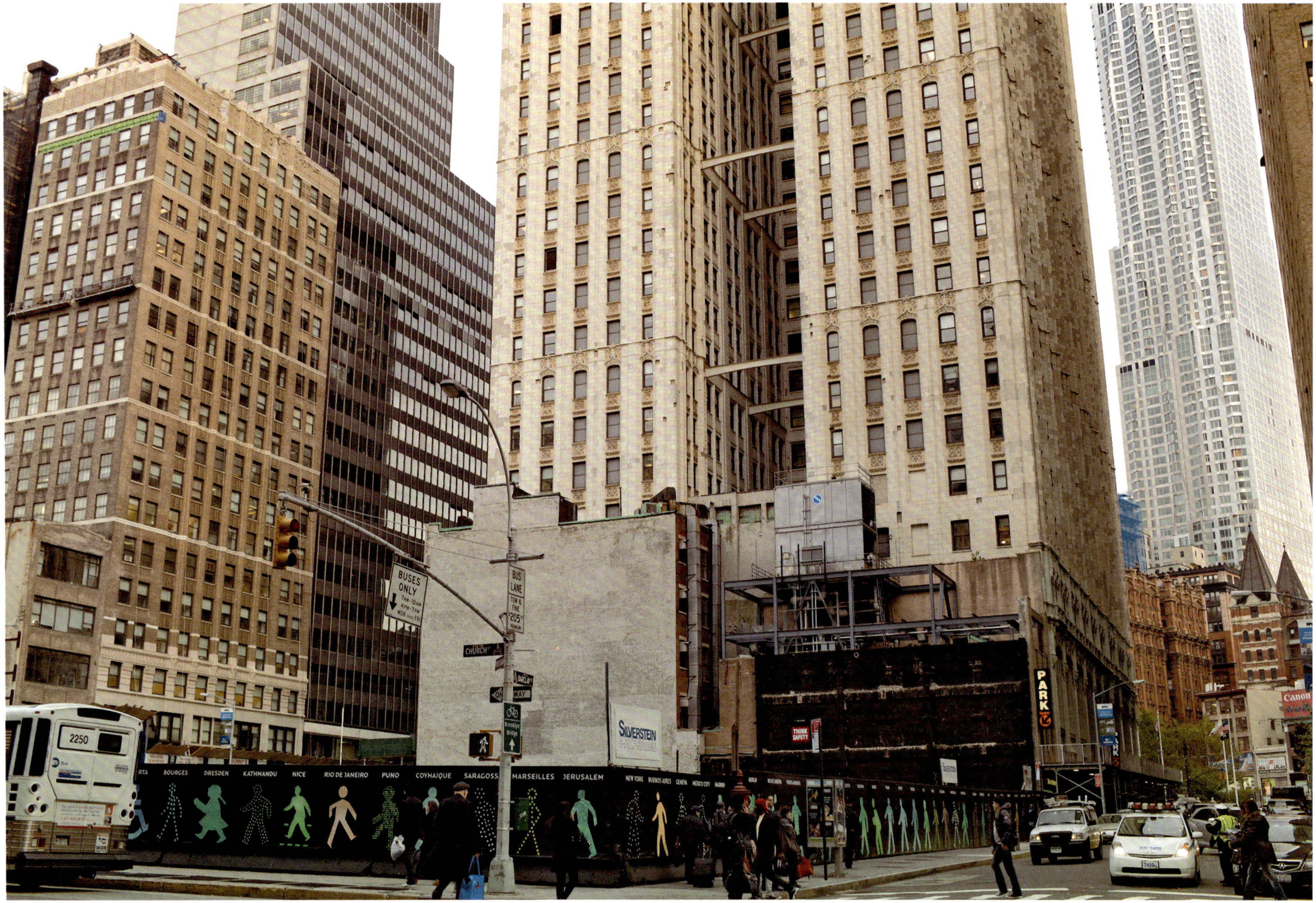
BUSES ONLY
BUS LANE
CHURCH ST
2250
SILVERSTEIN
PARK
THINK SAFETY
Brooklyn Bridge
BOURGES
DRESDEN
KATHMANDU
NICE
RIO DE JANEIRO
PUNO
COYHAIQUE
MARSEILLES
JERUSALEM
NEW YORK
BUENOS AIRES
GENEVA
MEXICO CITY
MADRID
Canon

60

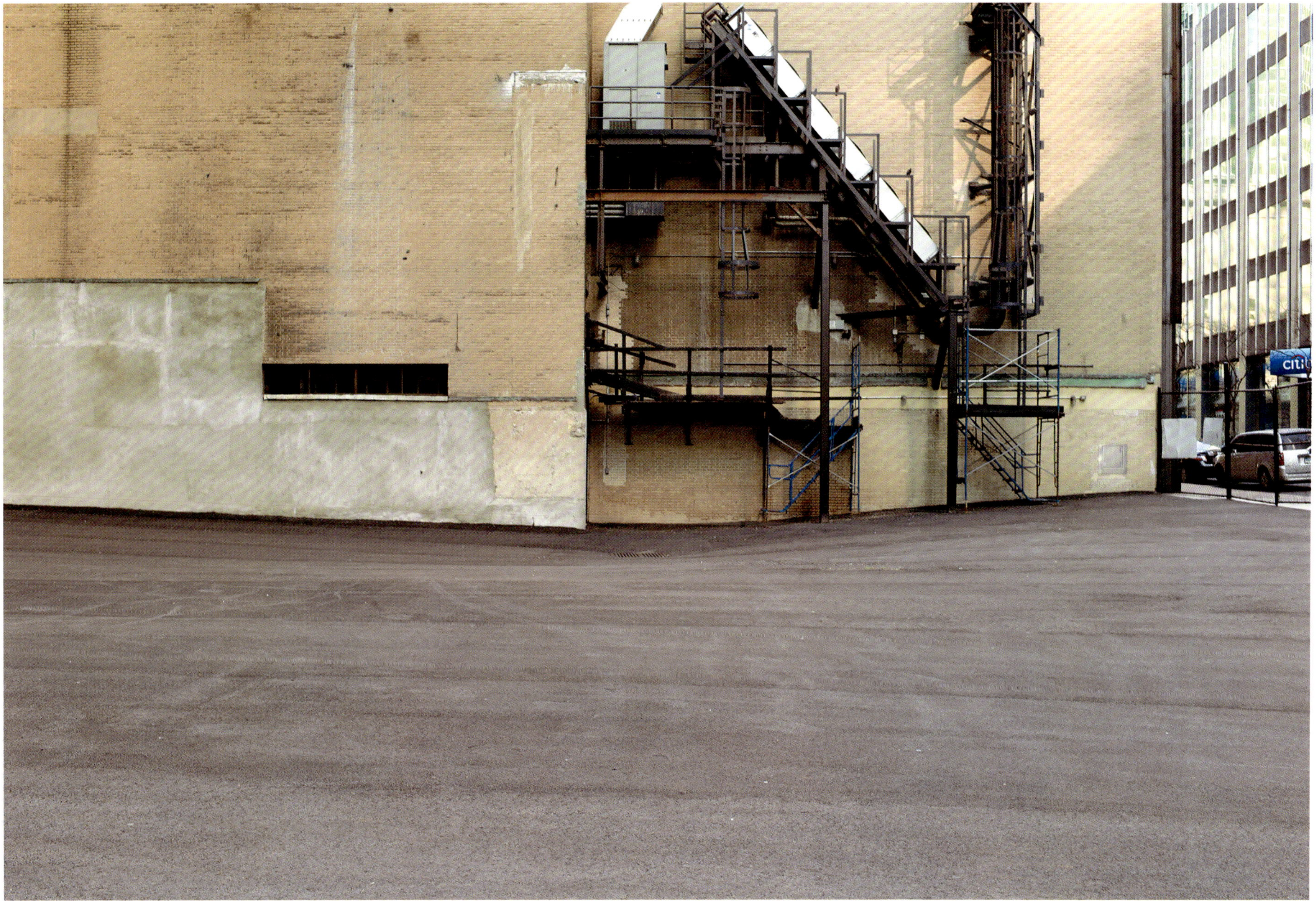

61

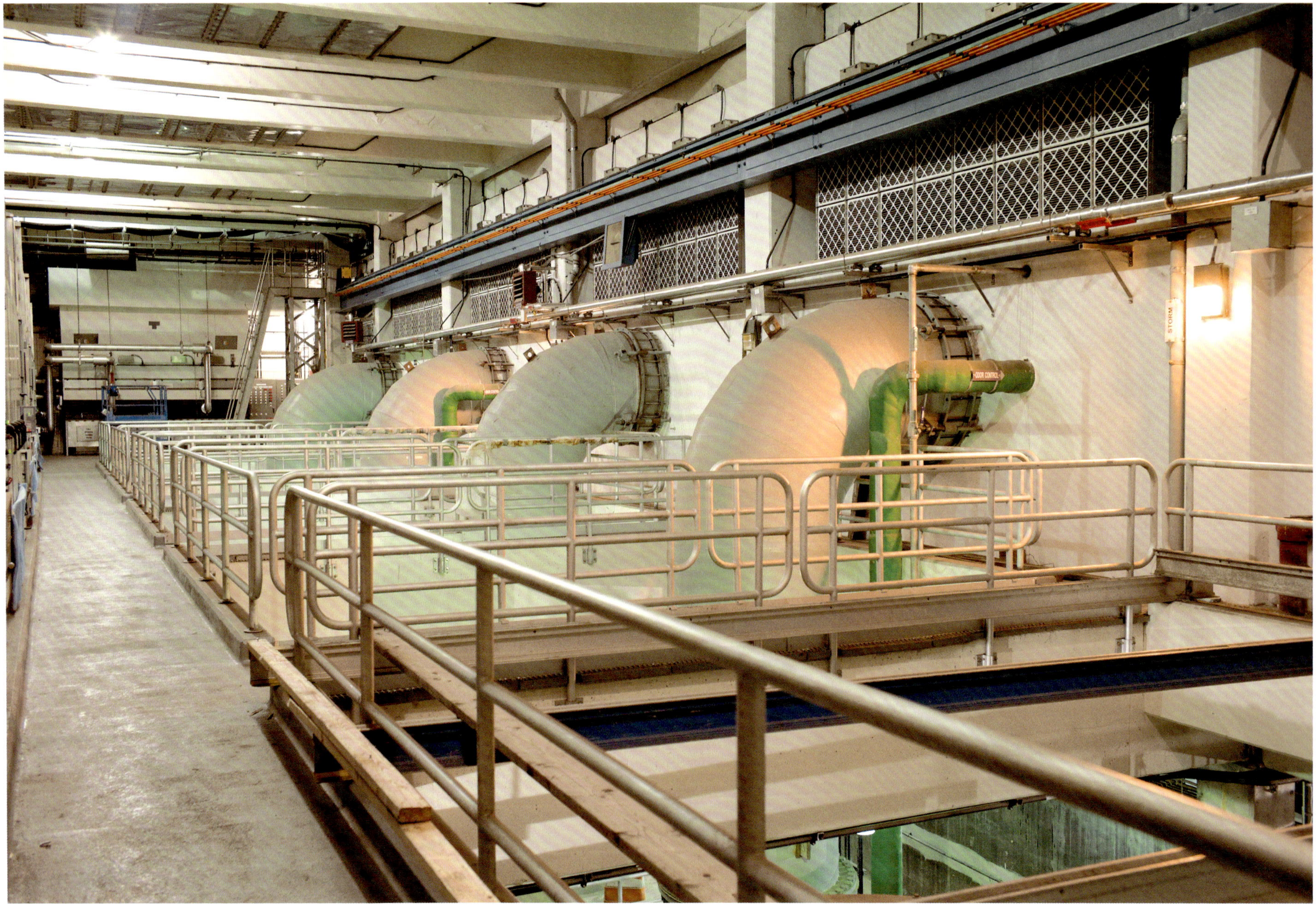

1

WASTEWATER TREATMENT

There is only one wastewater treatment plant on Manhattan Island (two others are located on Wards Island and Newtown Creek). The North River plant on the Hudson includes a park above it, a result of community protests about the odor (which was still strong at first after the park was built, but are now somewhat improved). Before this plant opened, billions of gallons of raw sewage poured into the river annually. This can still happen, to a lesser degree, almost every time it rains, since New York has a combined sewage and stormwater system. The capacity of the plant's tanks and processors is insufficient to handle the extra water from precipitation, so during and after a rain raw sewage outflows to the river. Other ways to mitigate this problem exist, including rainwater collection and daylighting of underground streams, but have not been utilized very much.

I took a side trip to Newtown Creek Wastewater Treatment Plant in Brooklyn, the city's newest and most advanced; four huge steel egg-shaped digesters give the facility its distinctive profile. And while this was a detour for me, all of Lower Manhattan's sewage runs through here, an important reminder that many of Manhattan's needs are filled by facilities in the other boroughs.

1 Newtown Creek
2 Newtown Creek
3 Newtown Creek
4 Newtown Creek
5 Washington Heights
6 Washington Heights
7 Newtown Creek

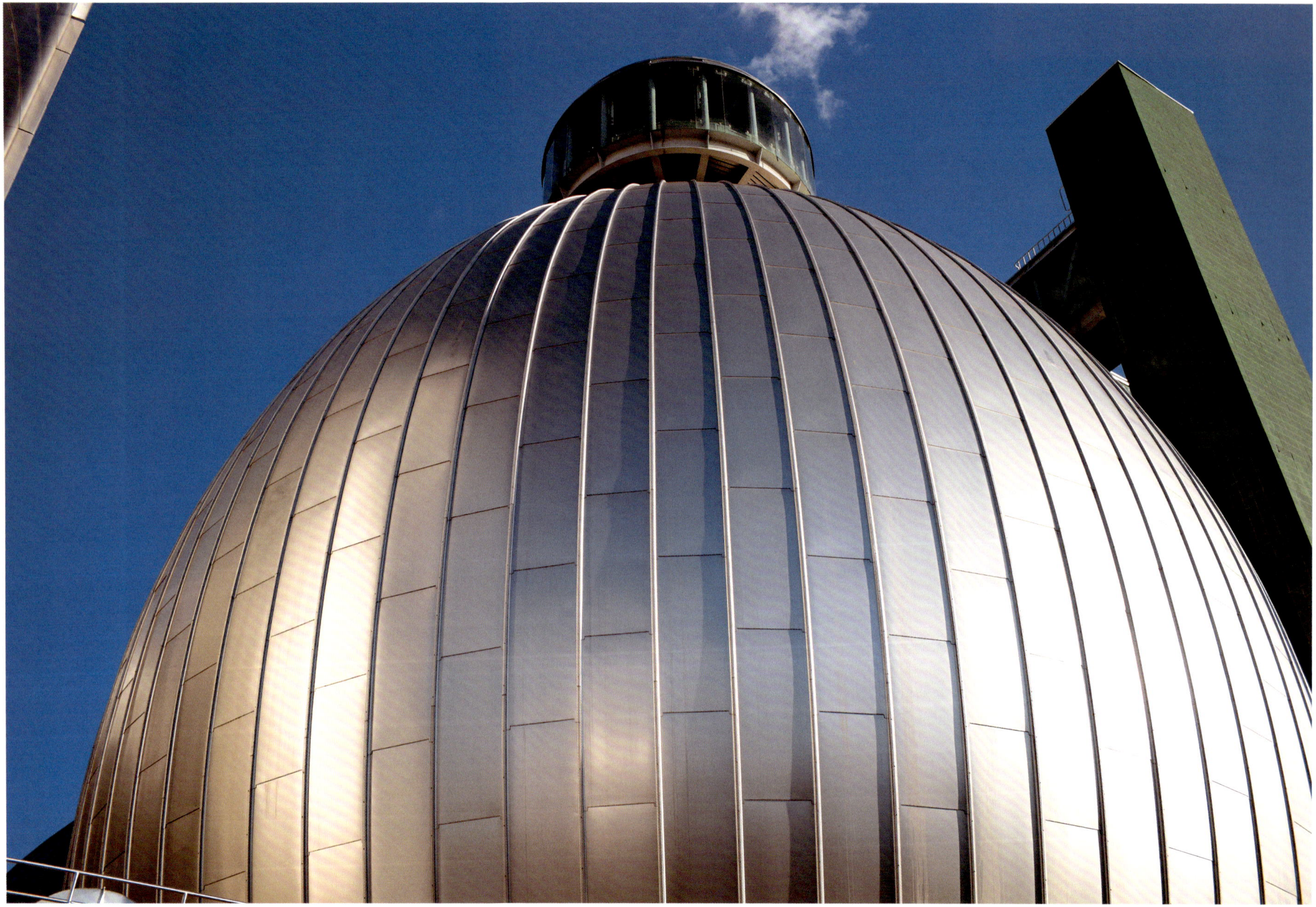

2

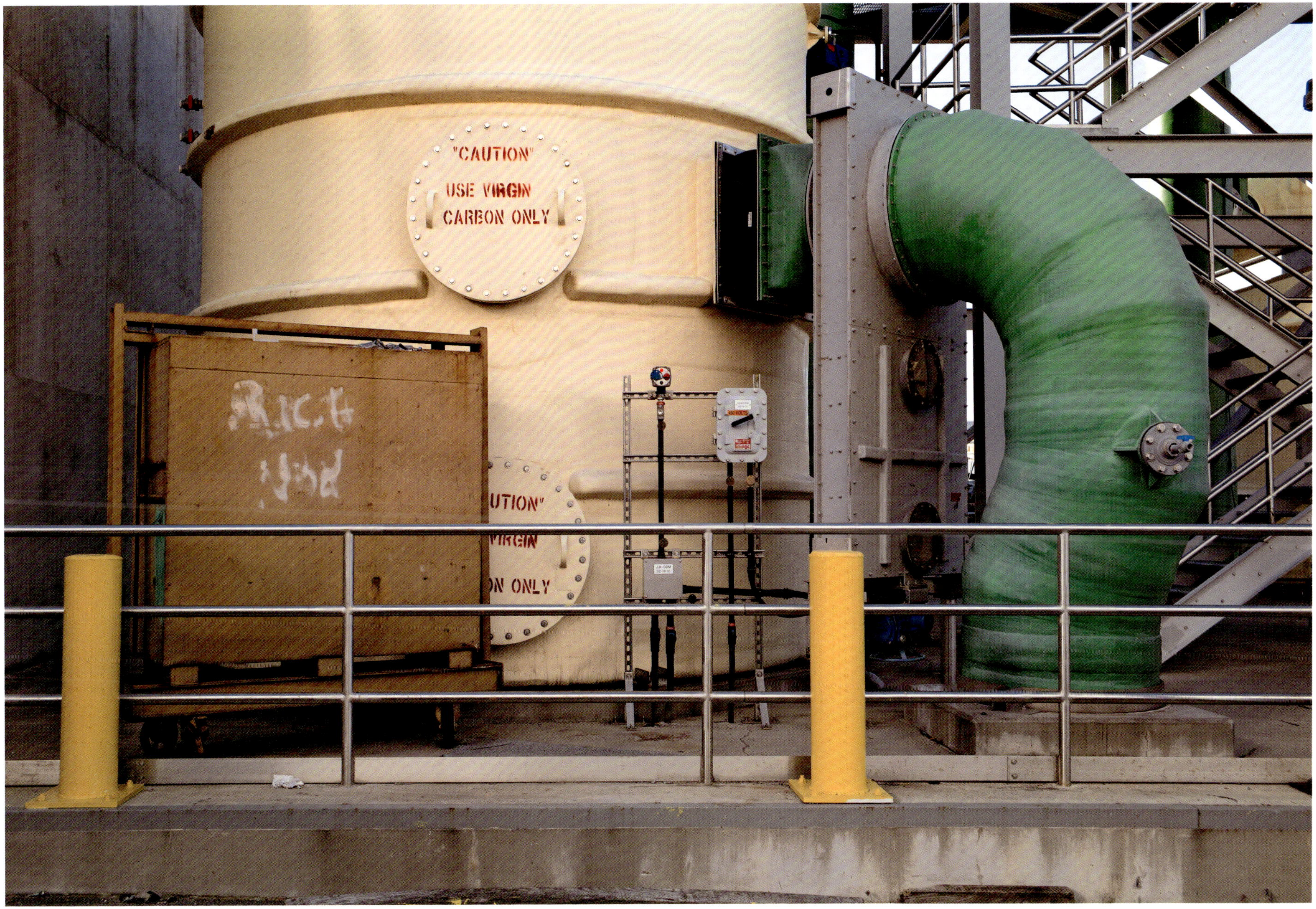

3

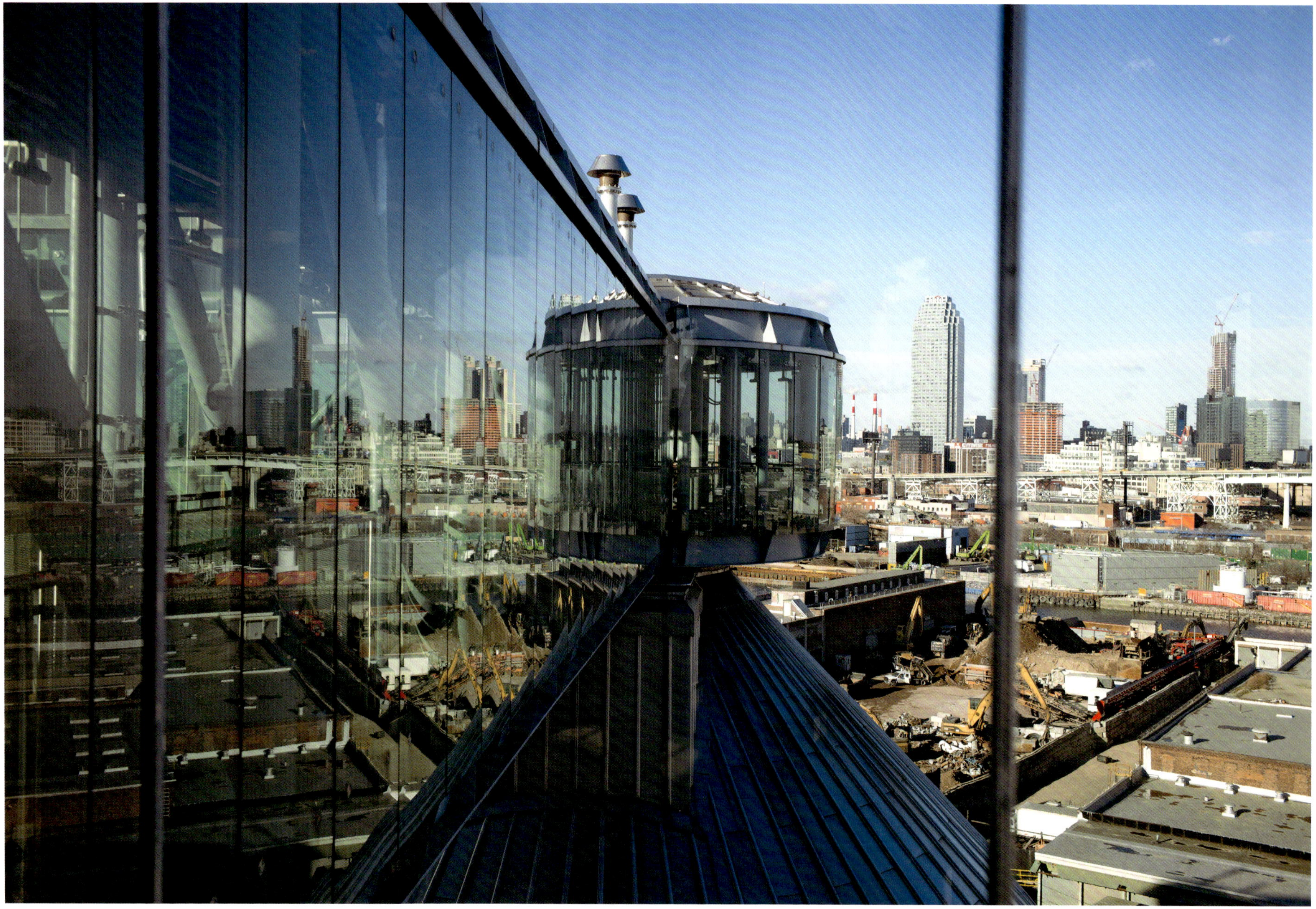

4

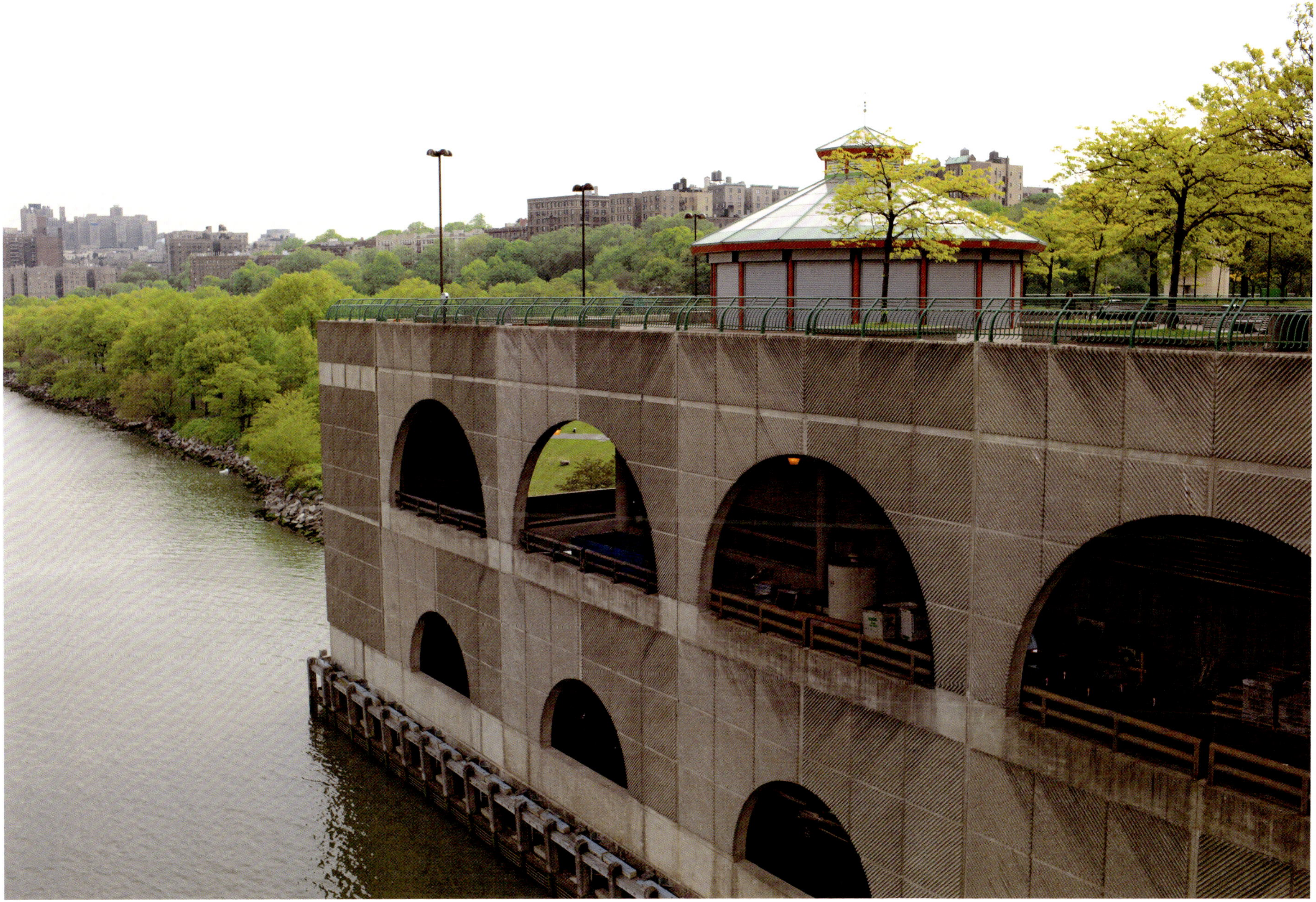

5

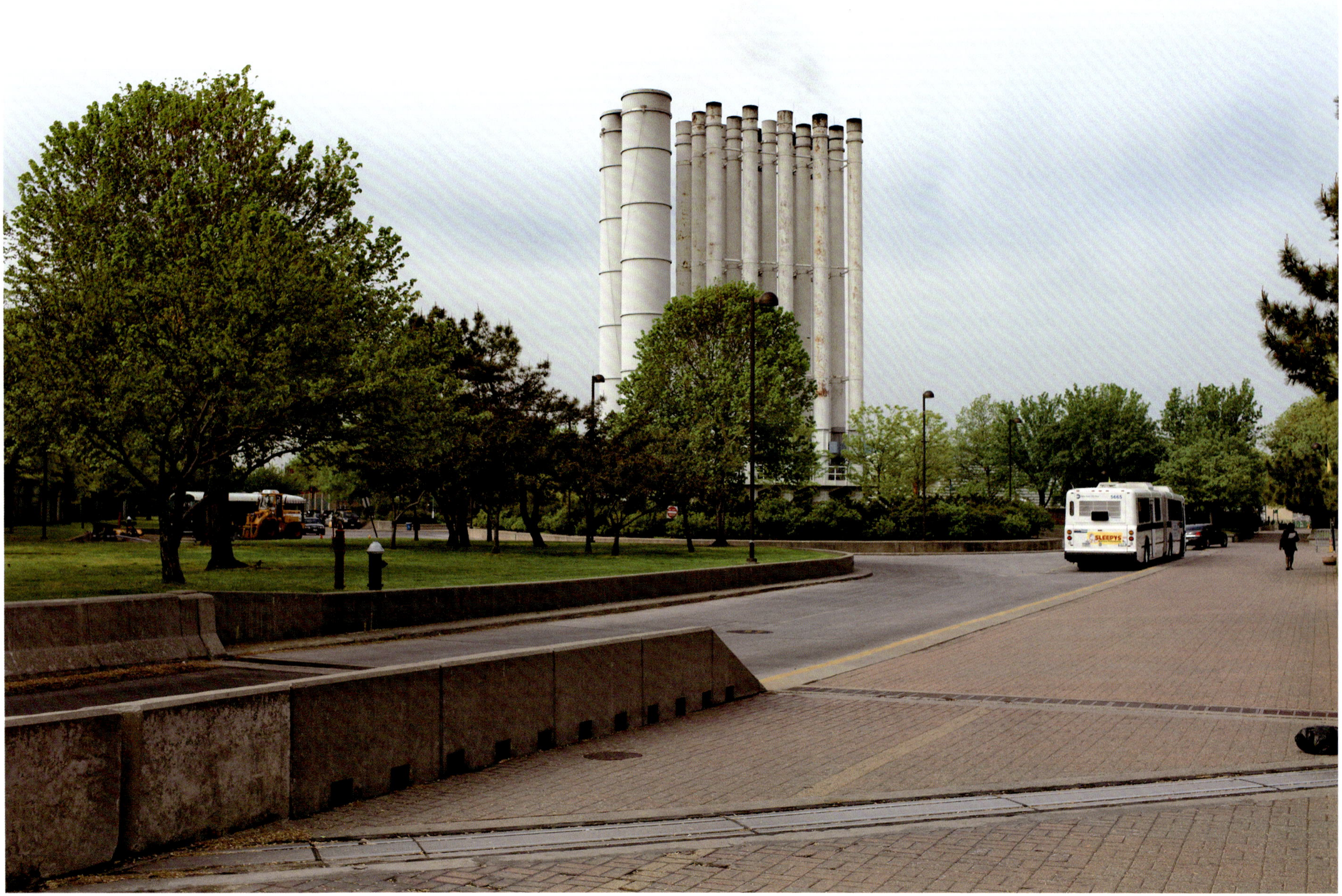

6

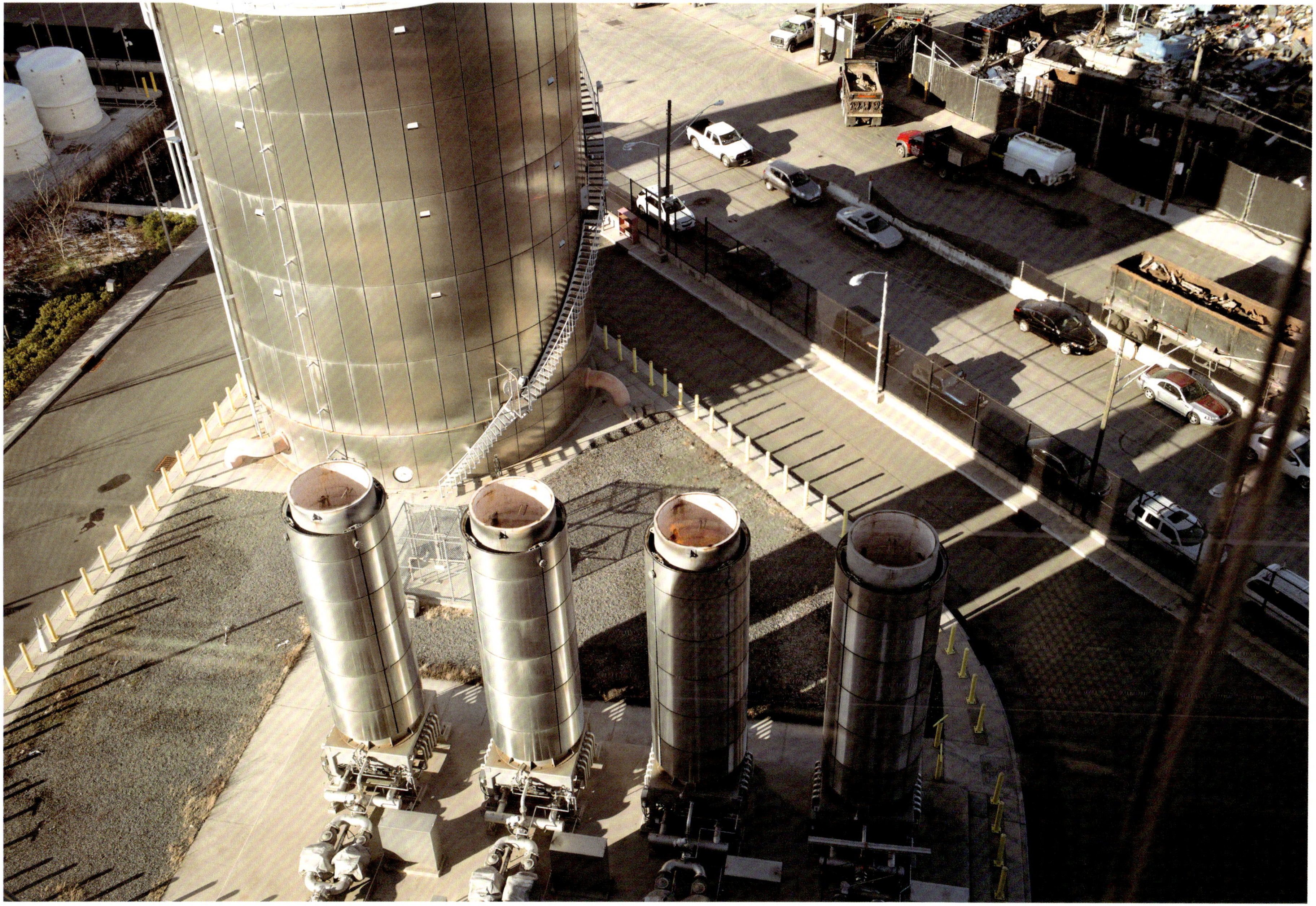

251

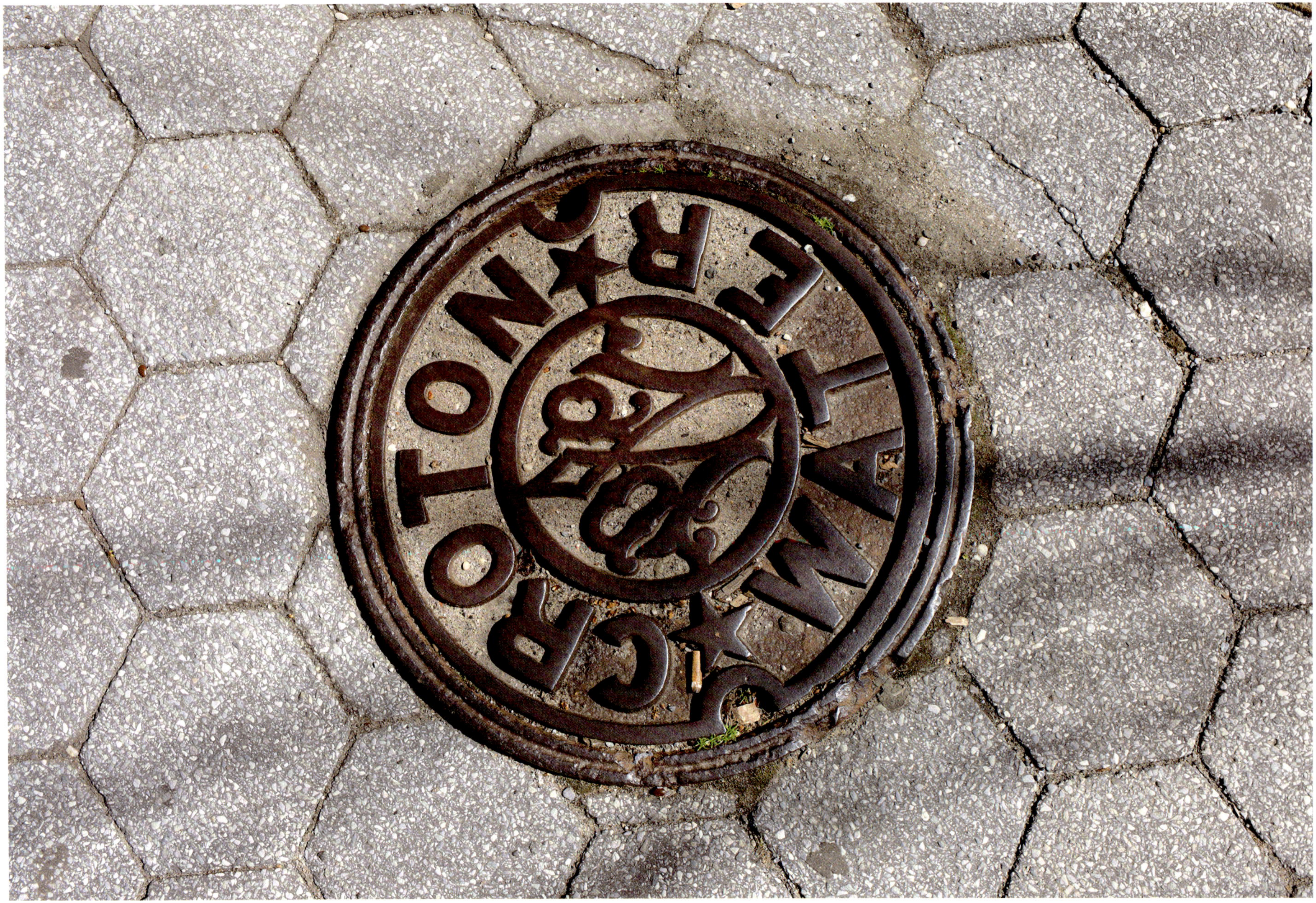
CROTON ★ WATER ★

WATER SUPPLY

The Croton Water Supply System, the city's first reliable water source, was completed in 1842. It was projected to be sufficient for decades but the city has been building new reservoirs and aqueducts ever since. Two main tunnels—one finished in 1918 and the second in 1936—have distributed water throughout the city; construction of a third has been underway since 1970, and in 2019 is almost complete. The new tunnel will allow for more regular maintenance of its older counterparts.

I photographed much of the subterranean system for two previous books. On this walk I photographed many of the aboveground signs of the underground system. Most of them are unremarkable and go unnoticed, but they point to a vast, complex, and nearly invisible underground network that brings clean water to the entire city. The new City Tunnel No. 3 sites are more easily spotted, since most have distinctive stainless steel ventilation towers. Tunnel No. 1 shaft sites are often small stone buildings, or occasionally an unmarked door in a wall. And others are just metal plates or manhole covers in the sidewalk.

1 Central Park
2 Sugar Hill
3 Upper East Side
4 Kips Bay
5 Central Park
6 Hamilton Heights
7 Highbridge Park
8 Sugar Hill
9 Central Park
10 Manhattanville
11 Highbridge Park
12 Chinatown
13 Central Park
14 Central Park
15 Rockefeller Center
16 Bryant Park
17 Madison Square
18 Cooper Square
19 Lower East Side
20 Central Park
21 Central Park
22 Highbridge Park
23 Highbridge Park
24 Sugar Hill
25 Central Park
26 Central Park

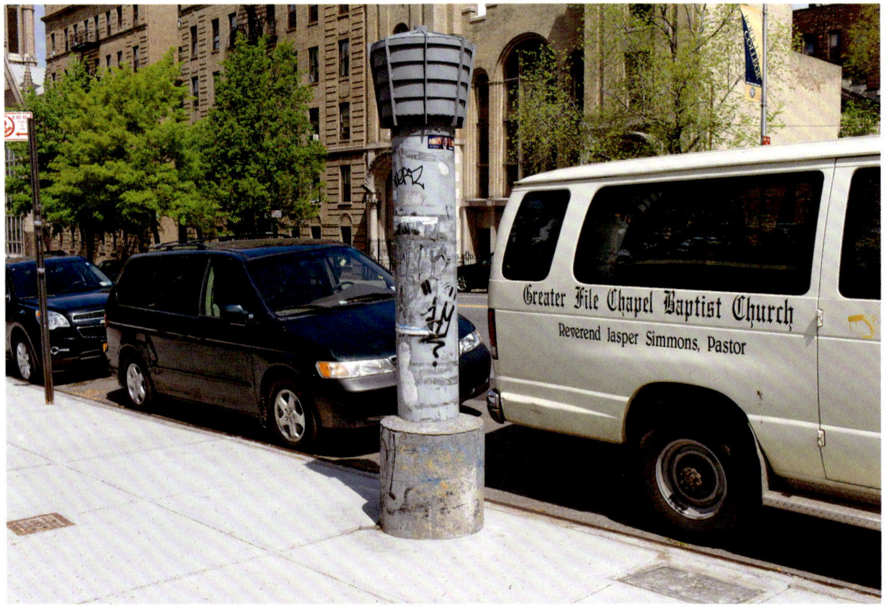
Greater File Chapel Baptist Church
Reverend Jasper Simmons, Pastor

2

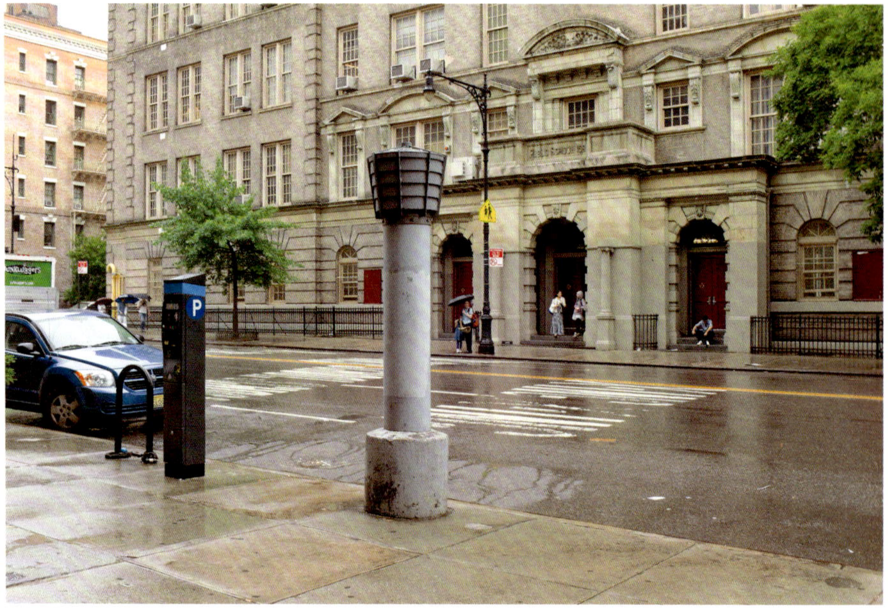
P

3

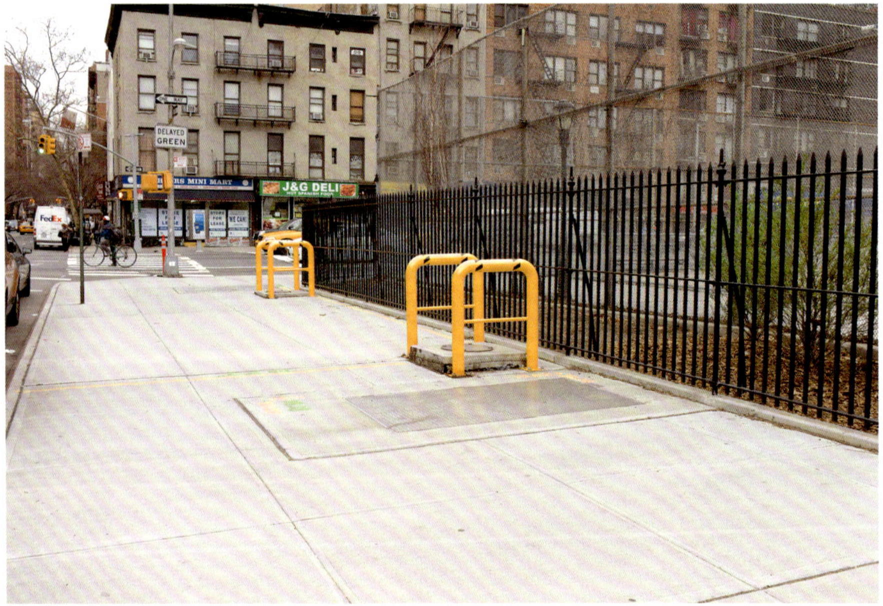
DELAYED GREEN
J&G DELI

4

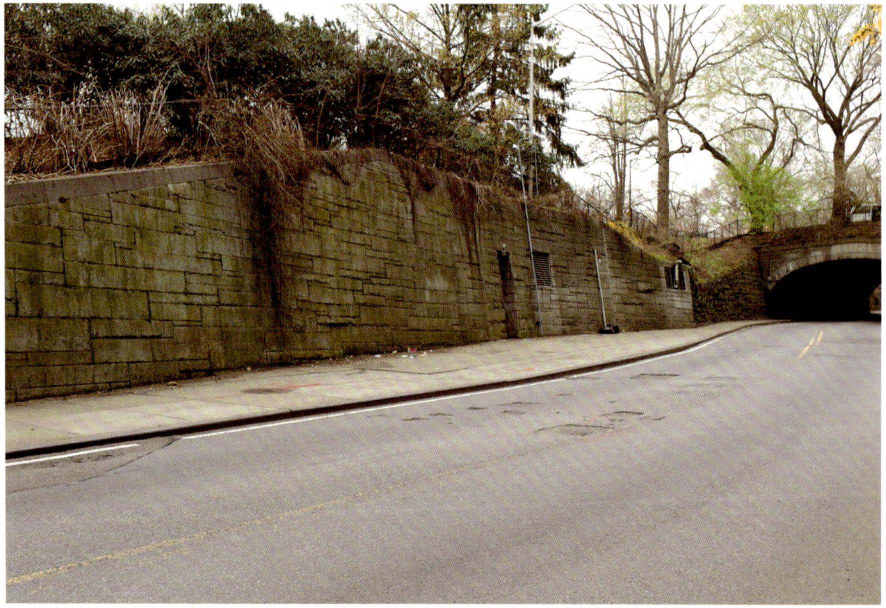

5

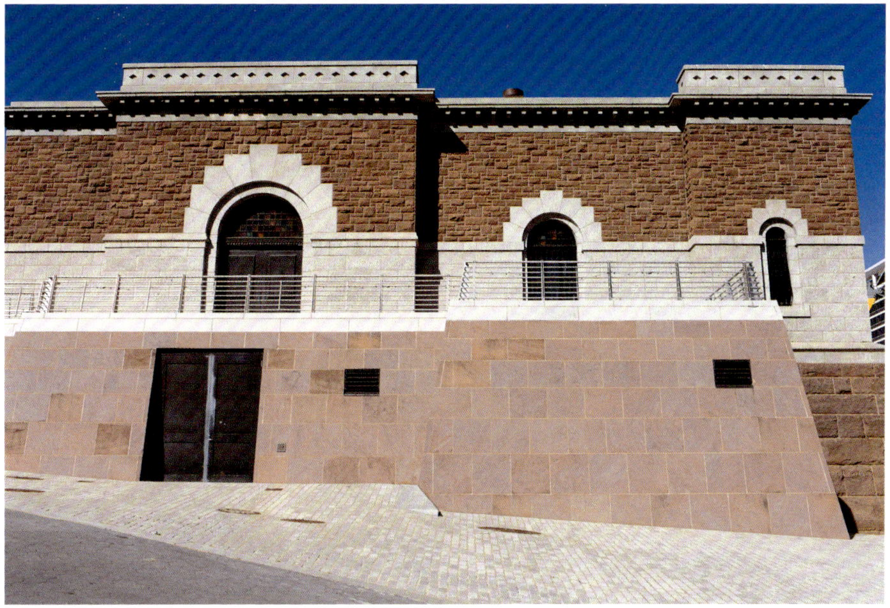
6

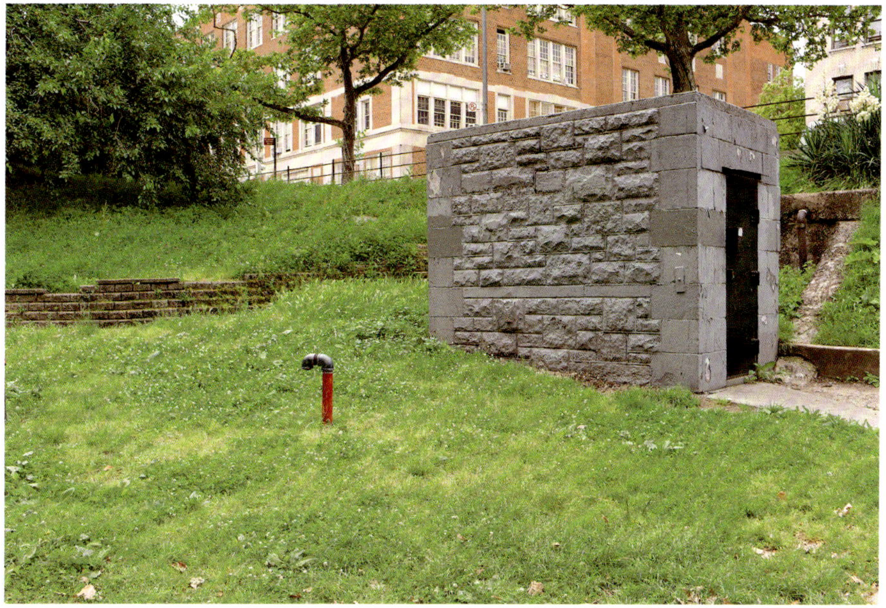
7

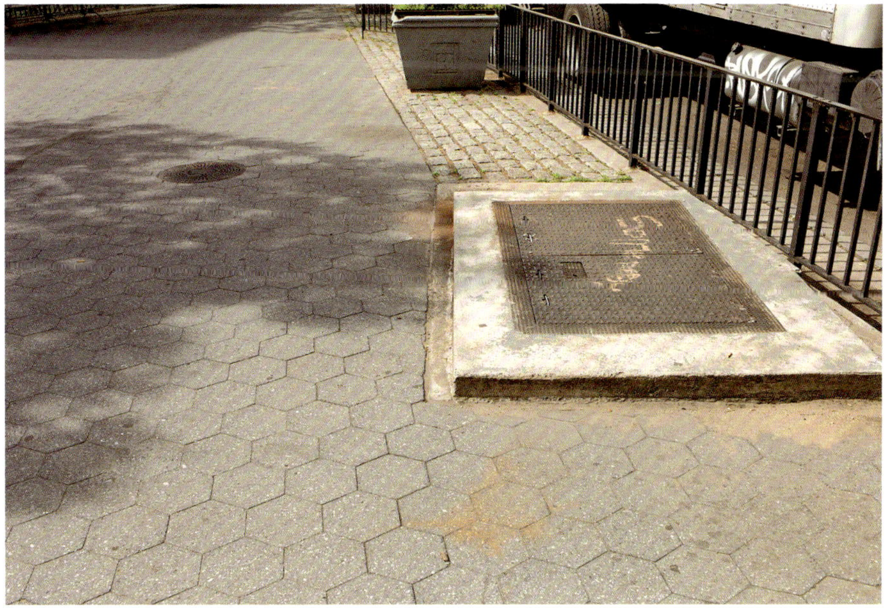
8

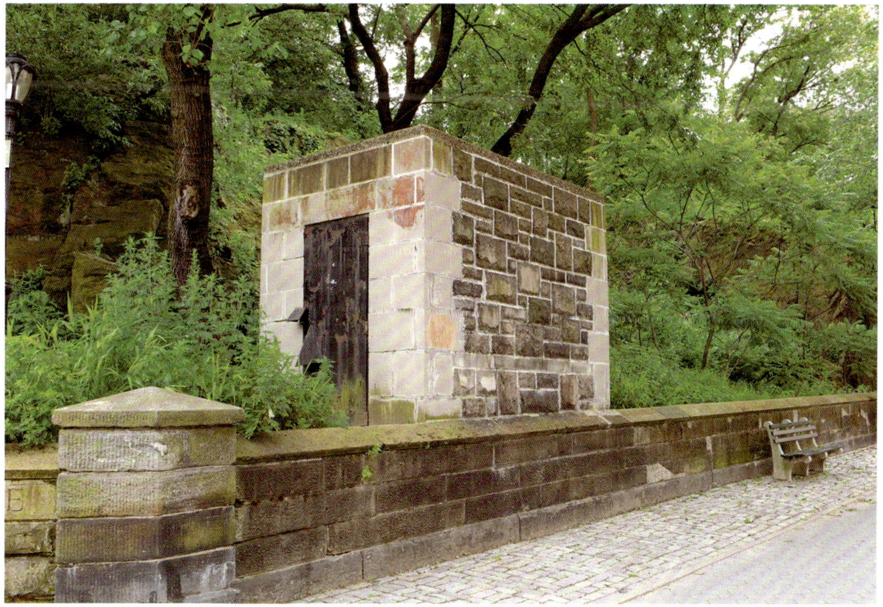
9

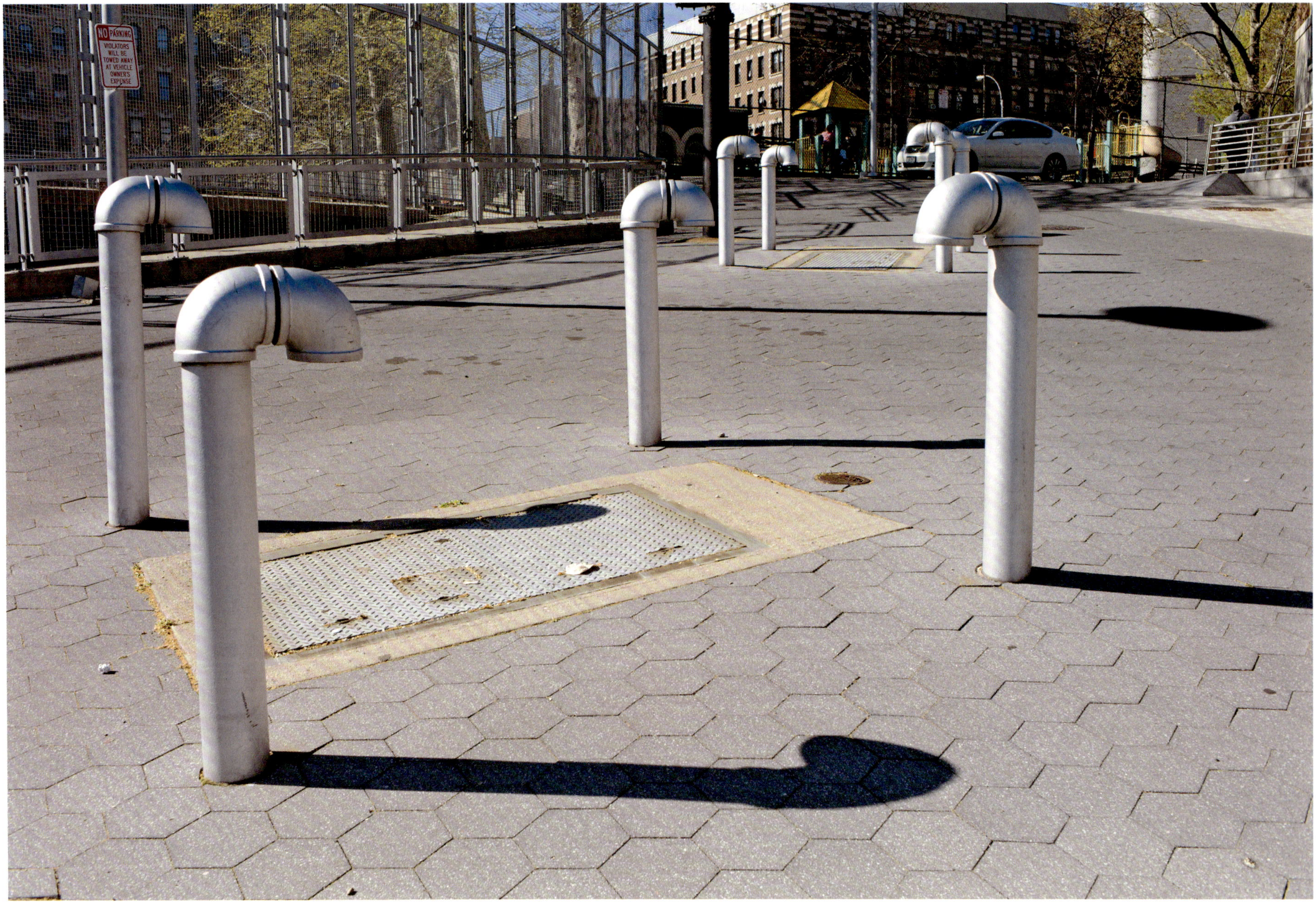
NO PARKING
VIOLATORS
WILL BE
TOWED AWAY
AT VEHICLE
OWNER'S
EXPENSE

10

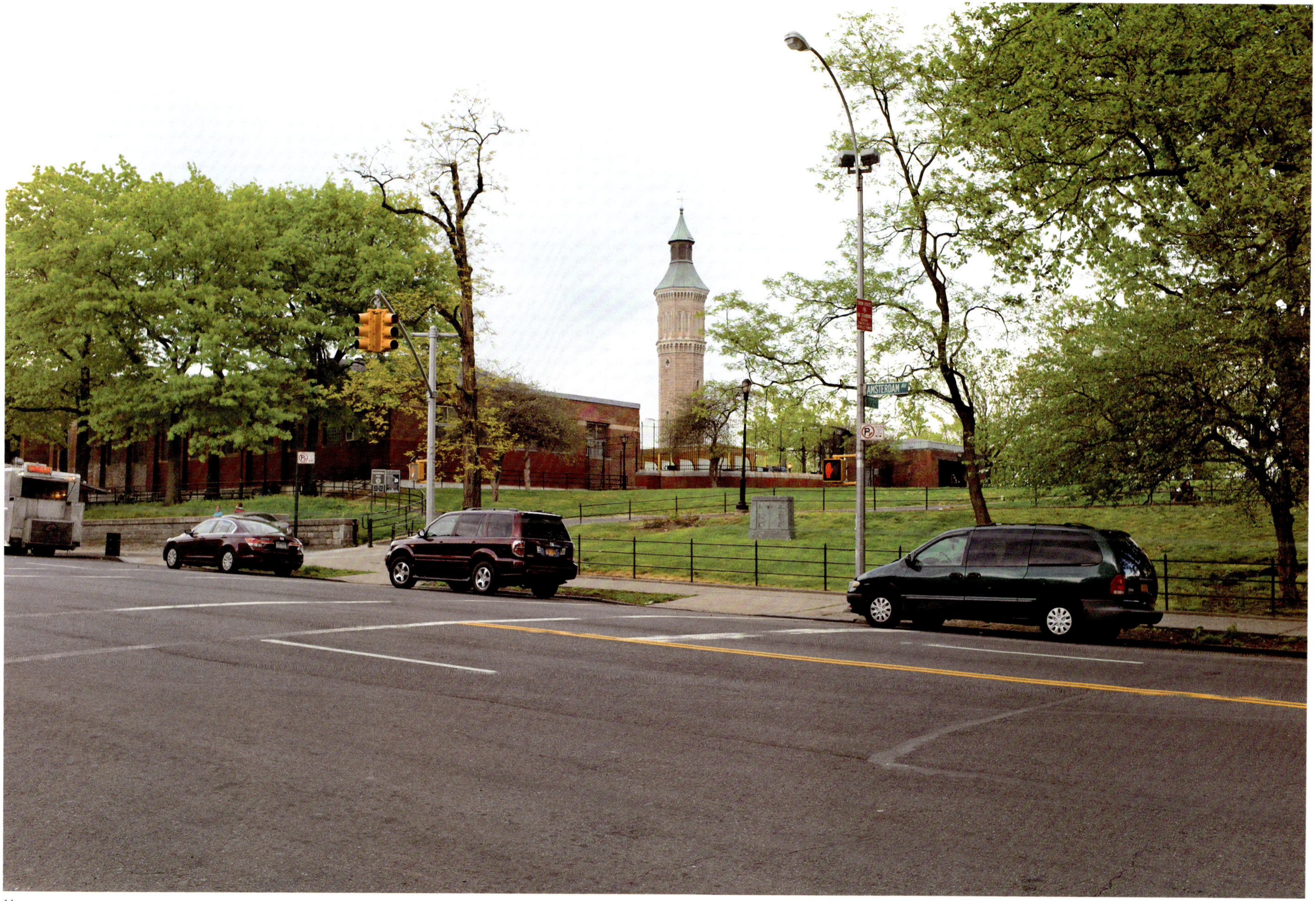

11

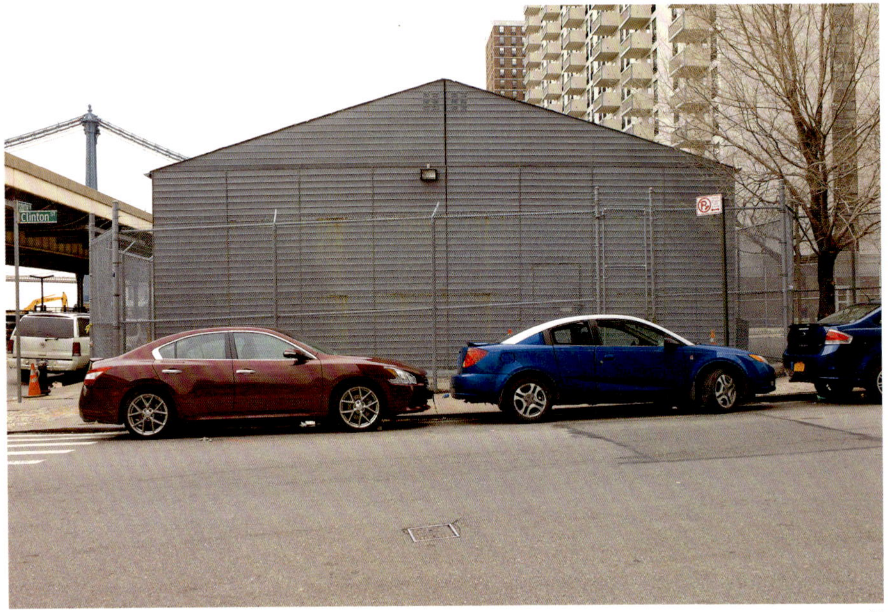

12

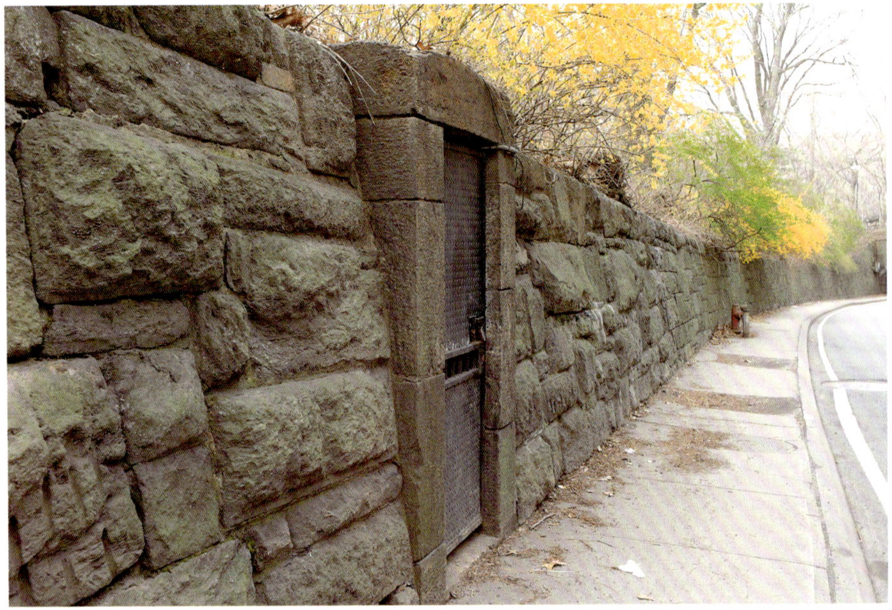

13

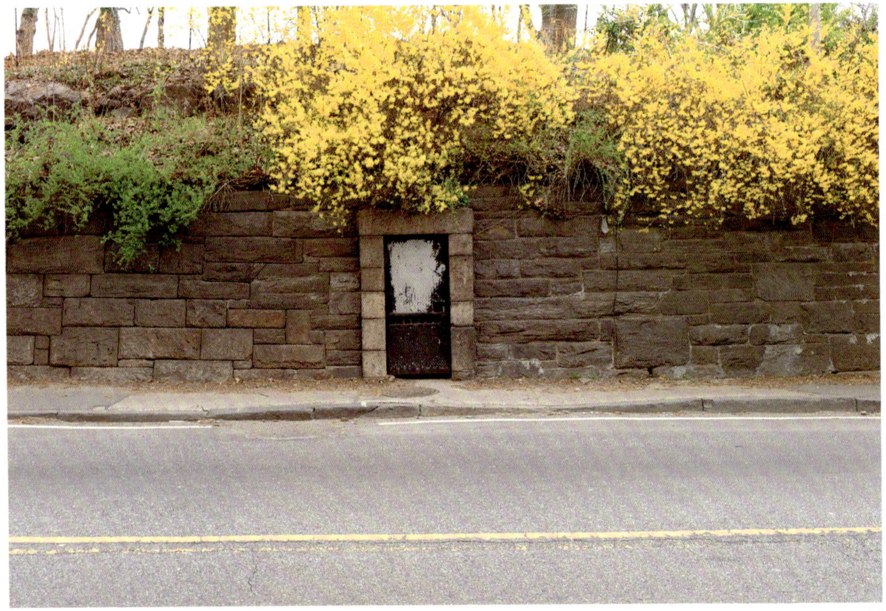

14

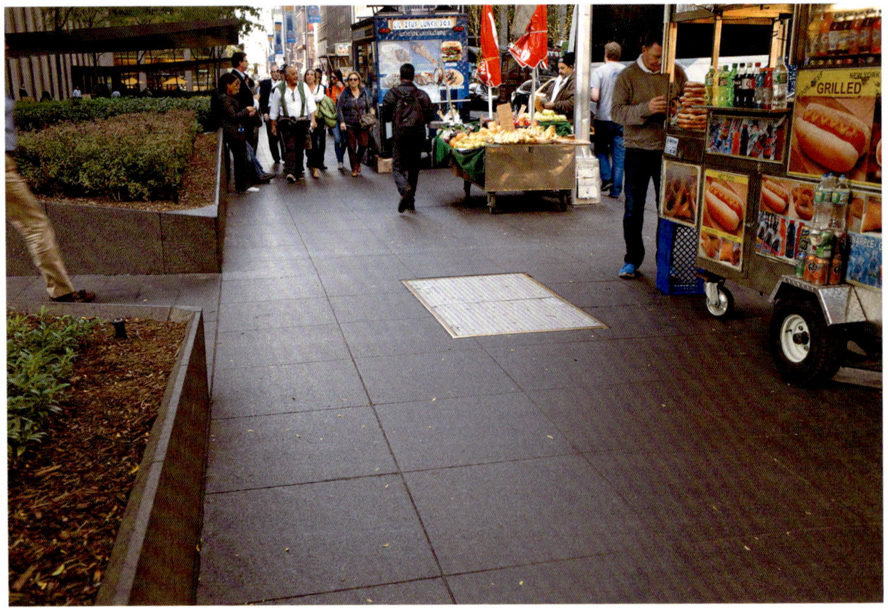

15

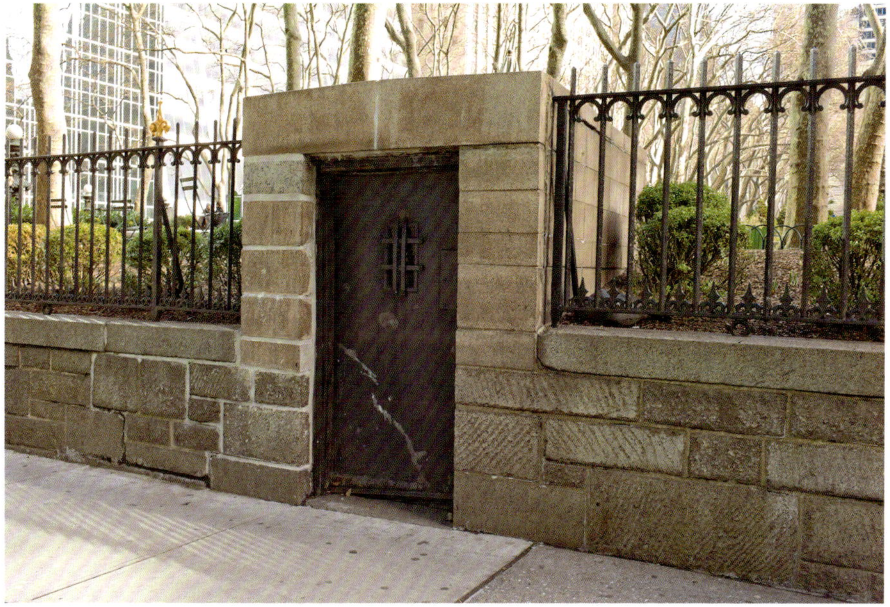

16

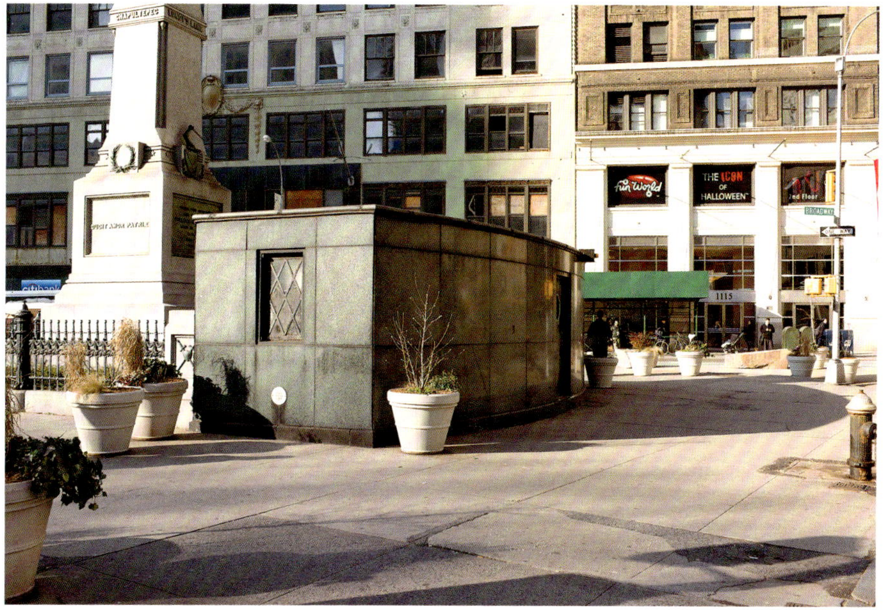
THE ICON
OF
HALLOWEEN
1115

17

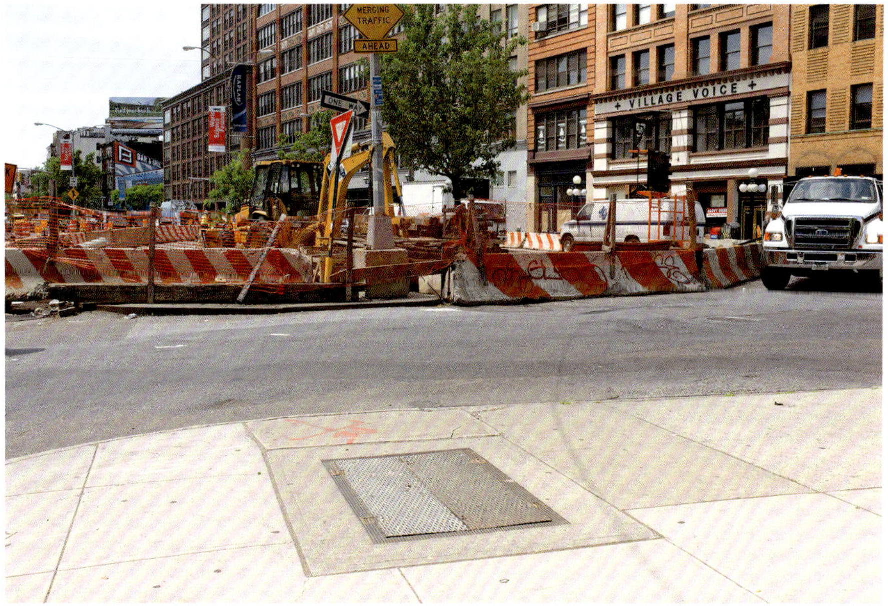
MERGING
TRAFFIC
AHEAD
+ VILLAGE VOICE +

18

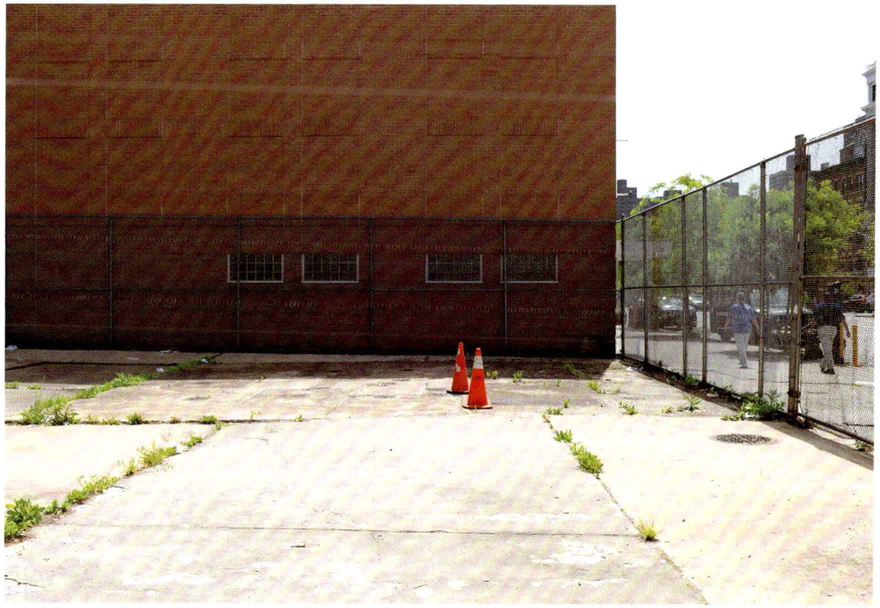

19

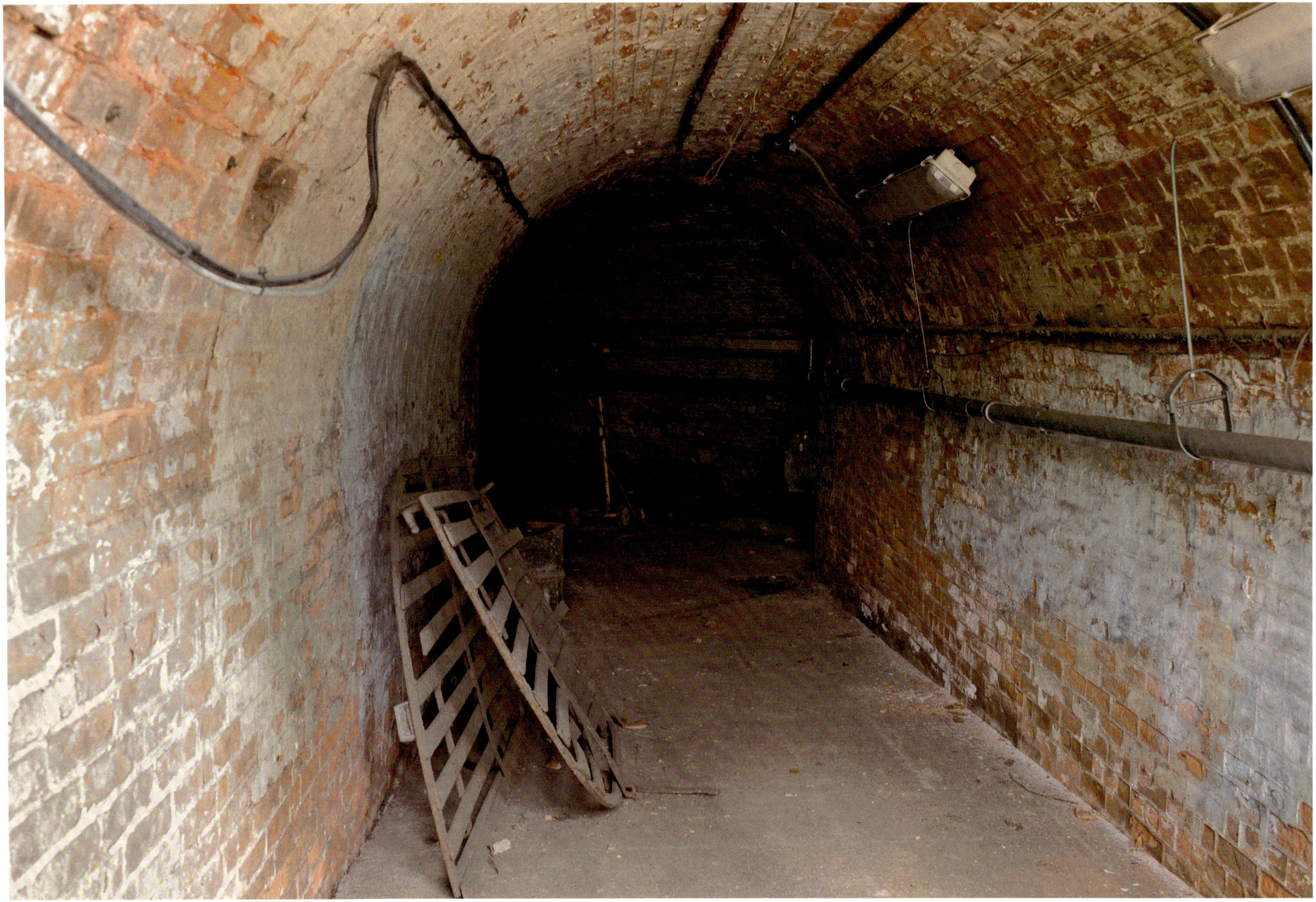

20

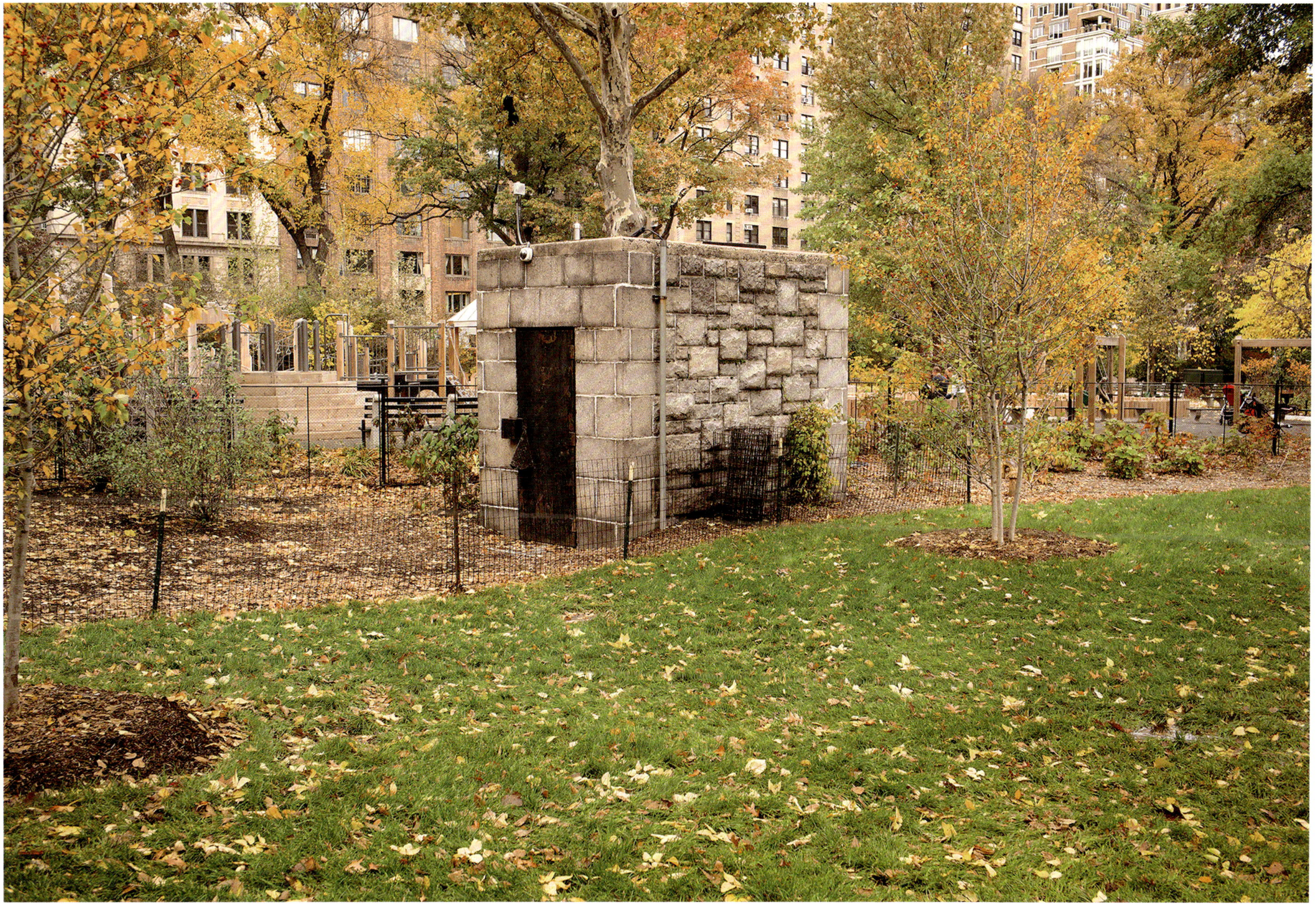

21

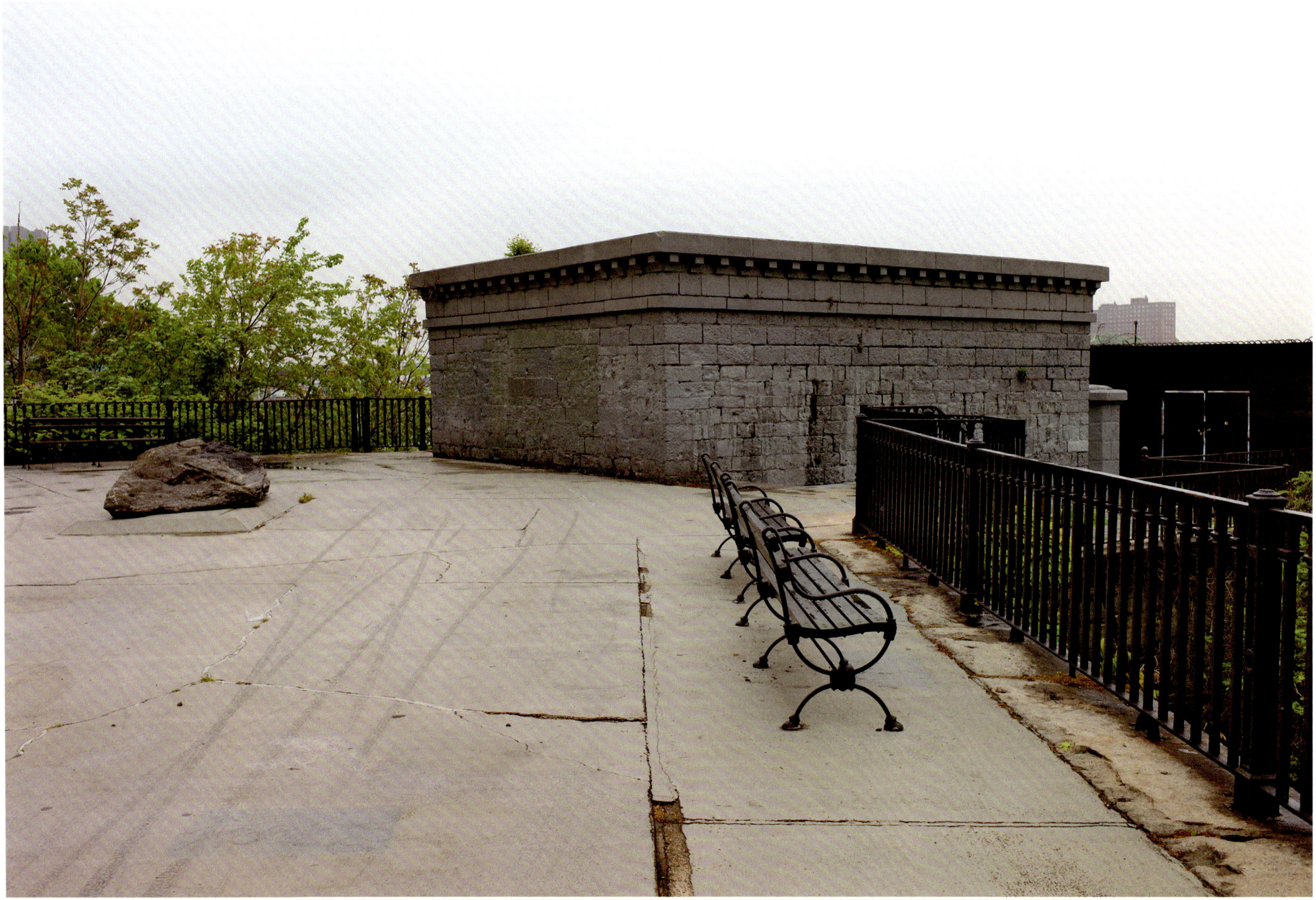

22

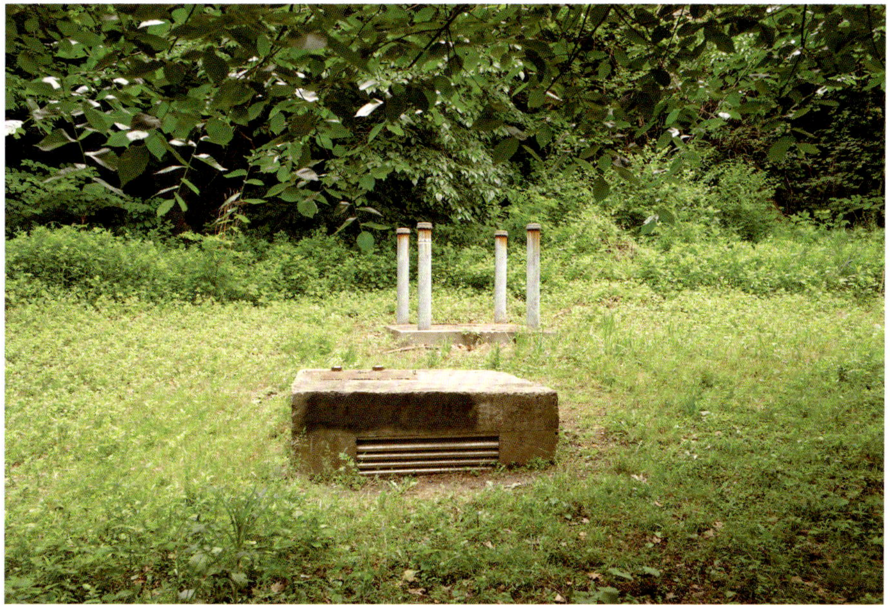
23

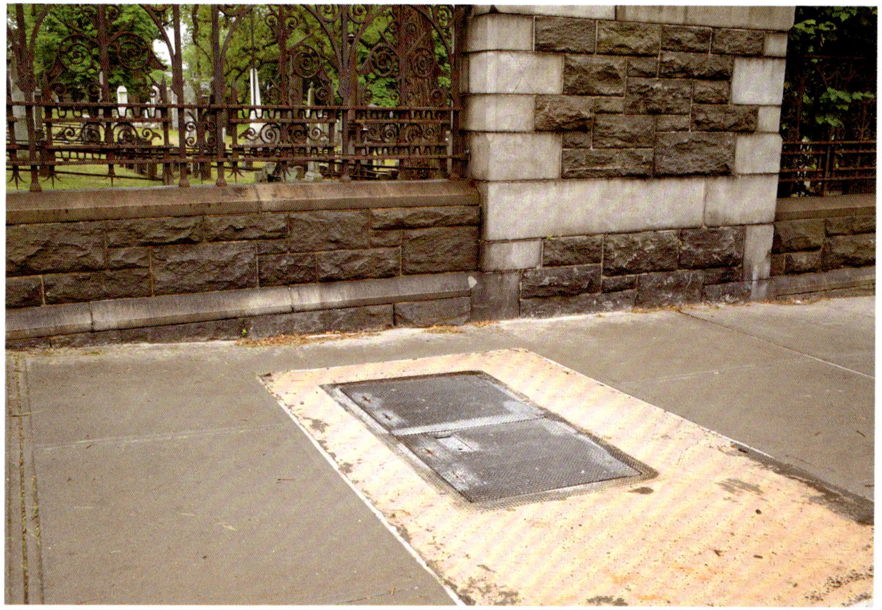
24

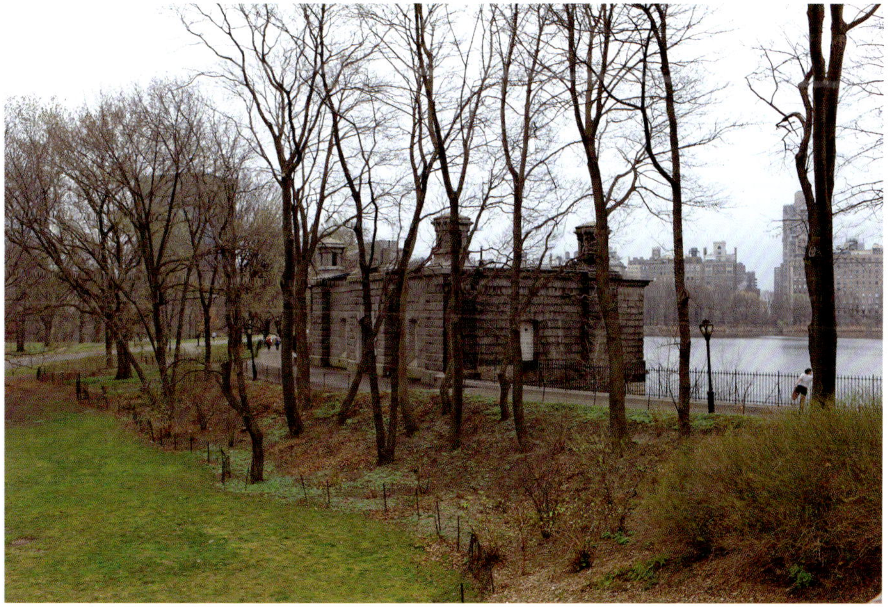
25

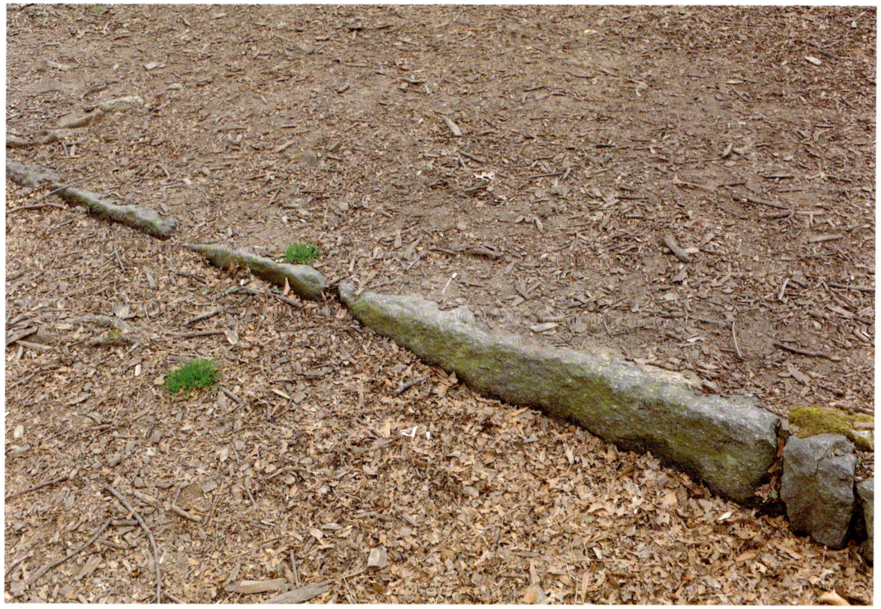
26

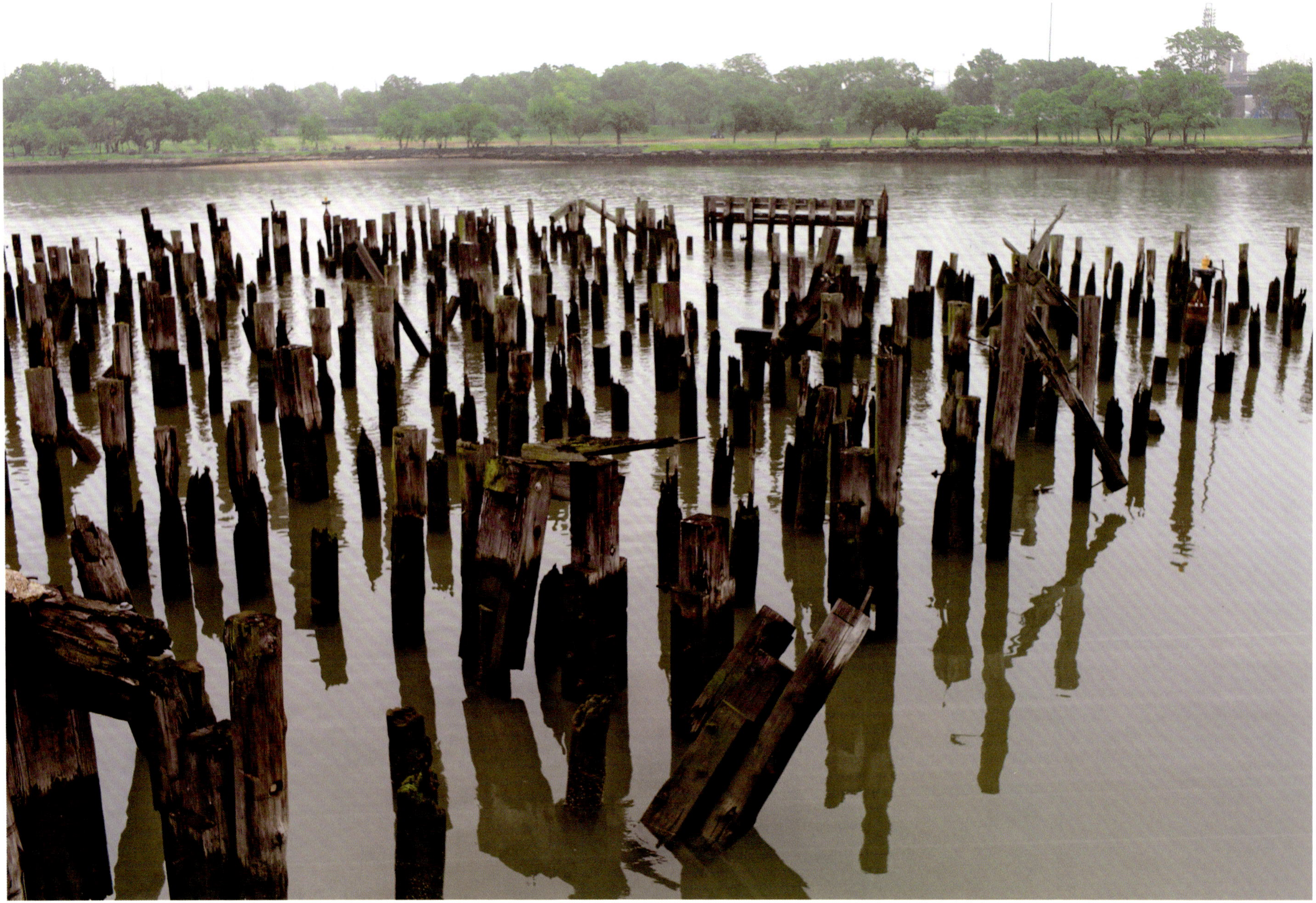

WATERFRONT

New York's waterfront was a major financial engine of the city from the very beginning. Piers for freight, the fishing industry, long distance travelers, and commuters have dominated the space. The shoreline was greatly expanded with fill—whether garbage, "clean" fill from construction sites, torn-down buildings and forts, and even stone from New England. As maritime commerce expanded, piers were extended further out into the river to accommodate ever larger ships. In the 1930s the expansion of Riverside Park changed the Upper West Side as the shoreline was extended with fill from tunnel excavation. Battery Park City is largely built on fill from the original World Trade Center excavation.

New borough-linking bridges largely supplanted the passenger-ferry industry and most commercial goods shipped to the region from overseas are now received at New Jersey's container ports. After many redevelopment battles, some still ongoing, the waterfront is now more accessible to the public. The West Side is home to the busiest bicycle path in the country. But this new access comes with other repercussions: after Superstorm Sandy the areas of worst flooding largely coincided with the artificial extensions of Manhattan created since the seventeenth century. There are plans for resilient parks, but also an explosion of new building in areas that will surely flood again.

1 East Harlem
2 The Battery
3 Financial District
4 Battery Park City
5 Upper West Side
6 Tribeca
7 West Village
8 West Village
9 Washington Heights
10 Stuyvesant Town
11 Sutton Place
12 Upper West Side
13 South Street Seaport
14 South Street Seaport
15 Two Bridges
16 Chelsea
17 Inwood
18 Stuyvesant Town
19 East Harlem
20 Roosevelt Island
21 Hell's Kitchen
22 Inwood
23 Washington Heights
24 Washington Heights
25 Two Bridges
26 Upper West Side
27 Washington Heights
28 Washington Heights
29 Inwood
30 Midtown West
31 Upper West Side

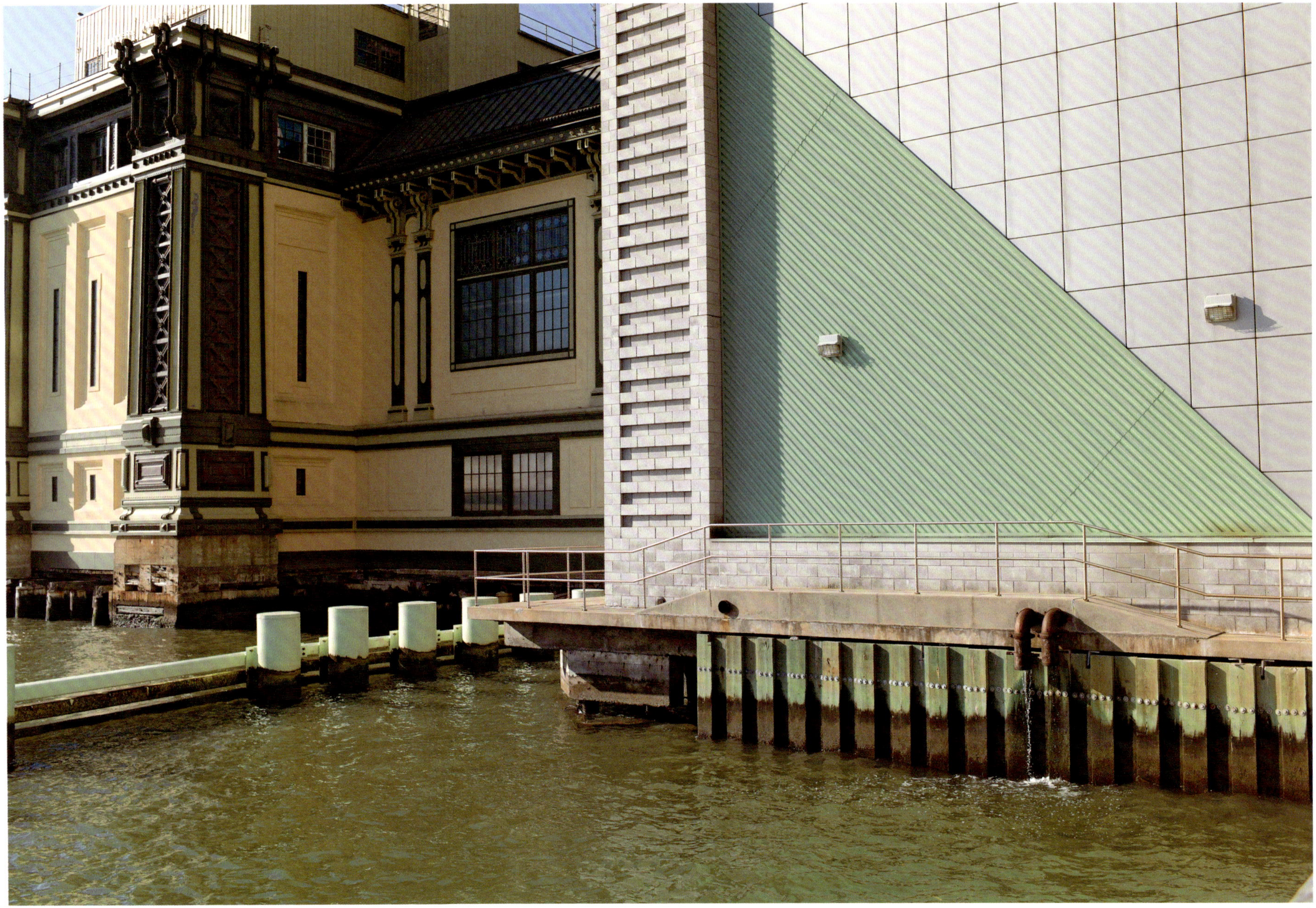

2

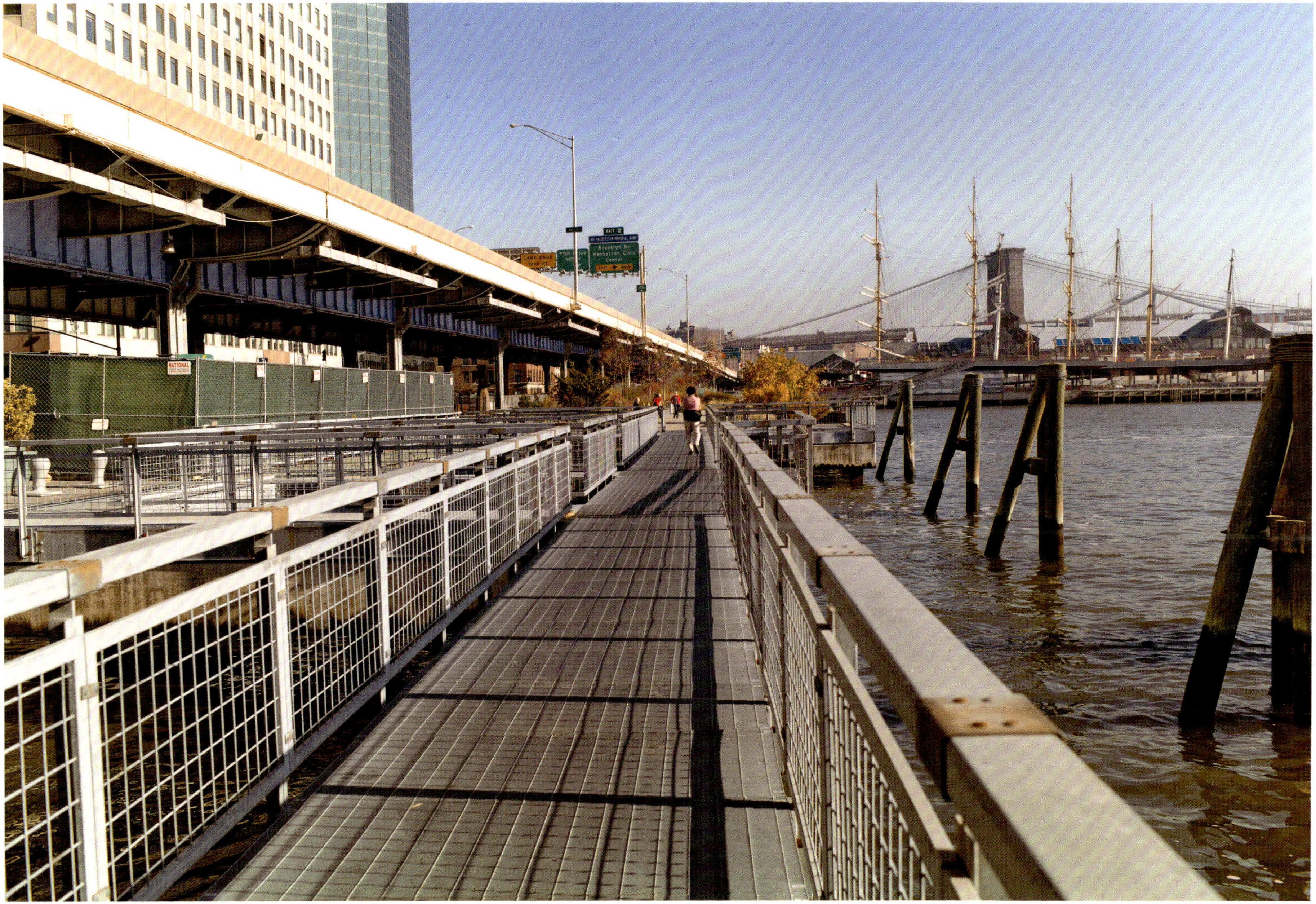
EXIT 2
Brooklyn Br
Manhattan Civic
Center
EXIT ONLY
LANE ENDS
1200 FT
FDR
NATIONAL

3

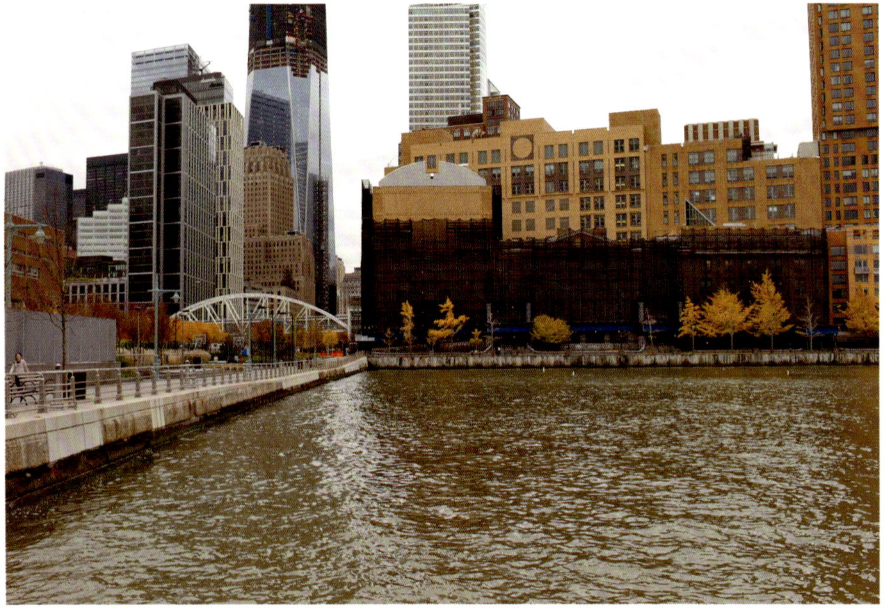

4

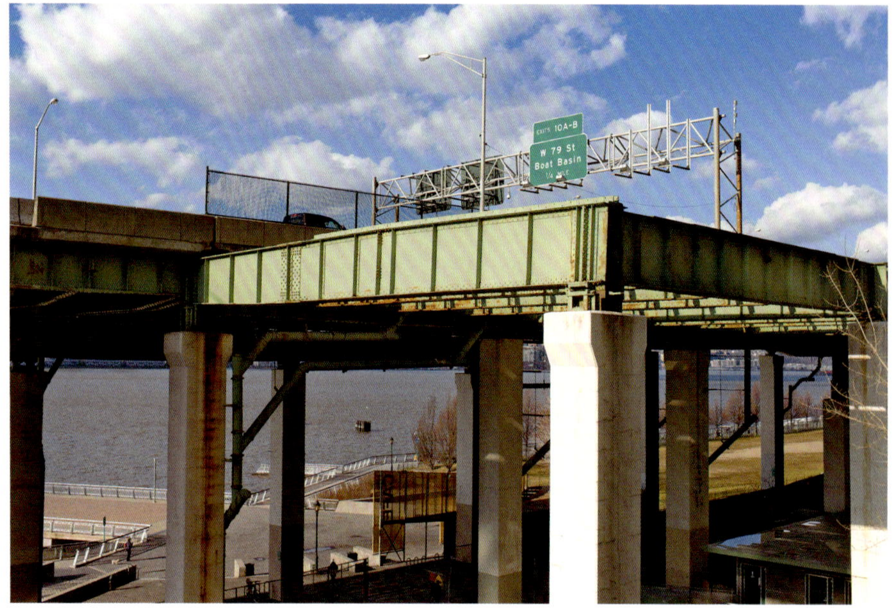

5

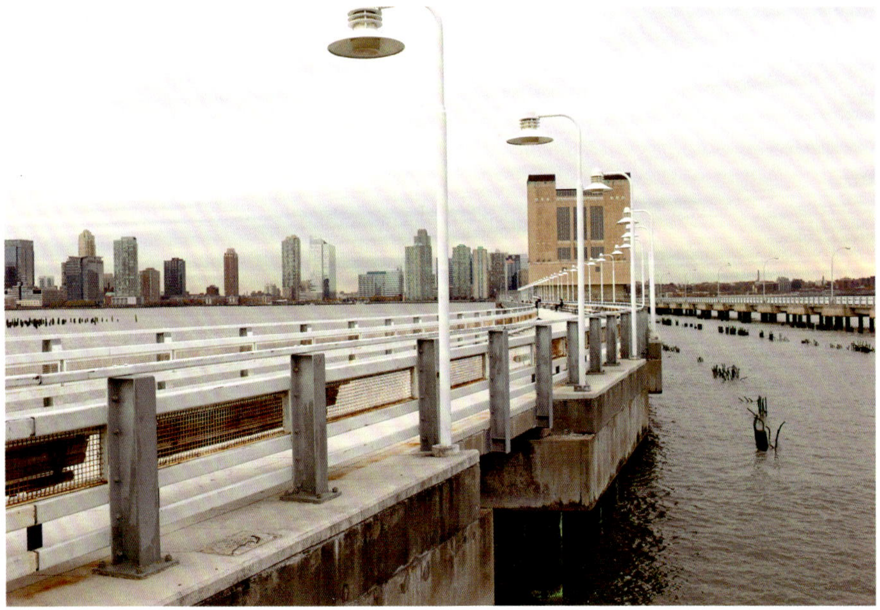

6

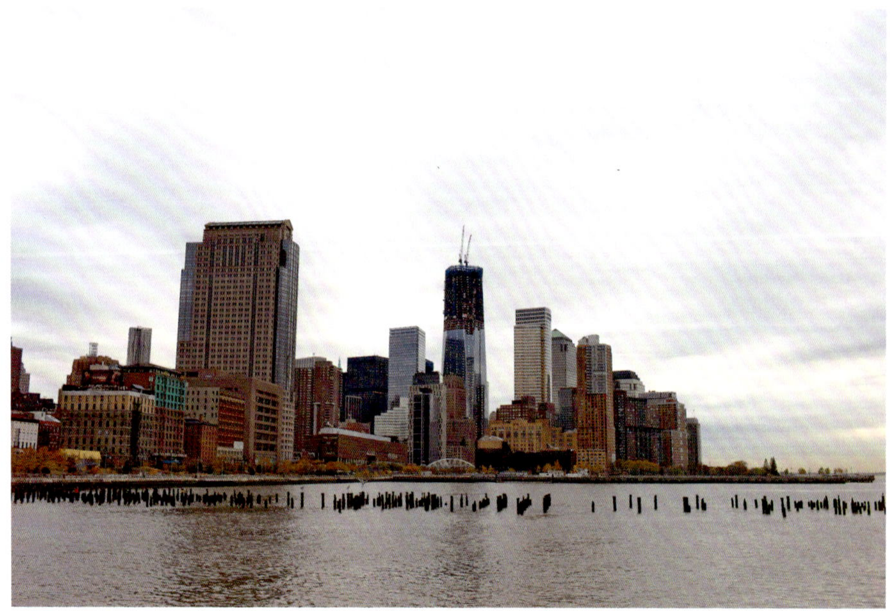

7

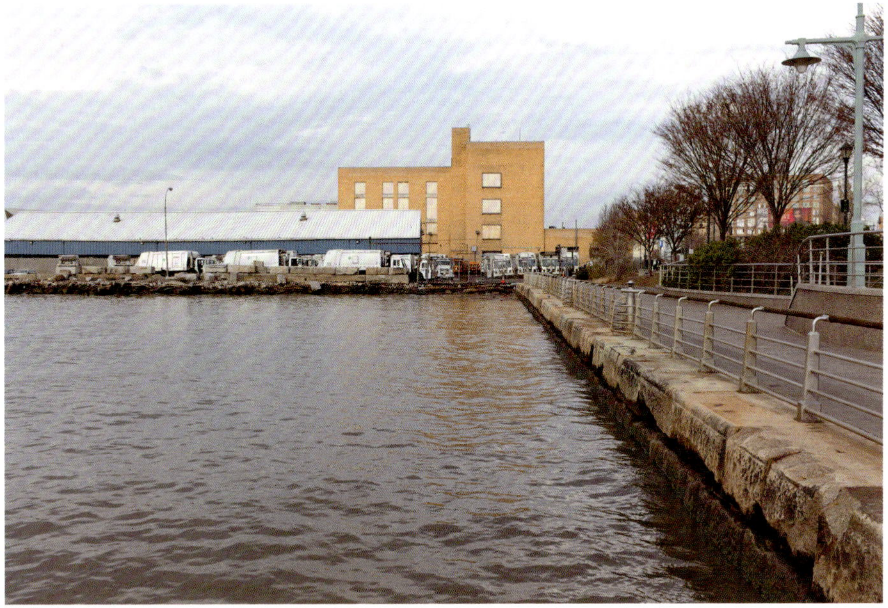
8

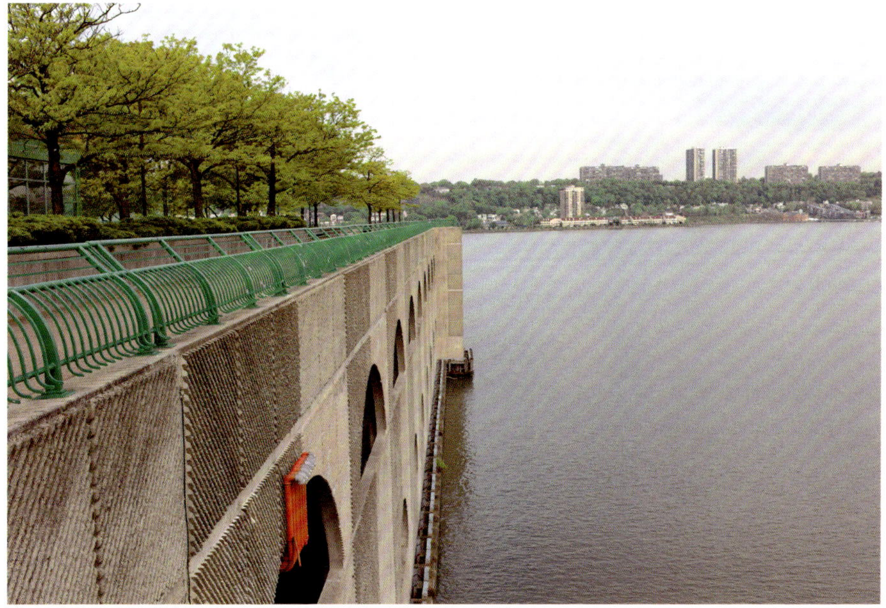
9

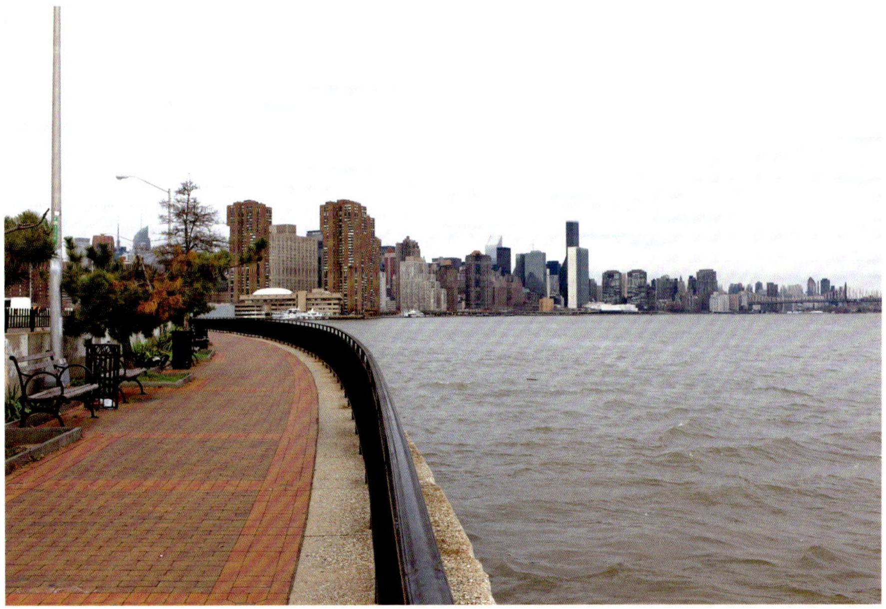
10

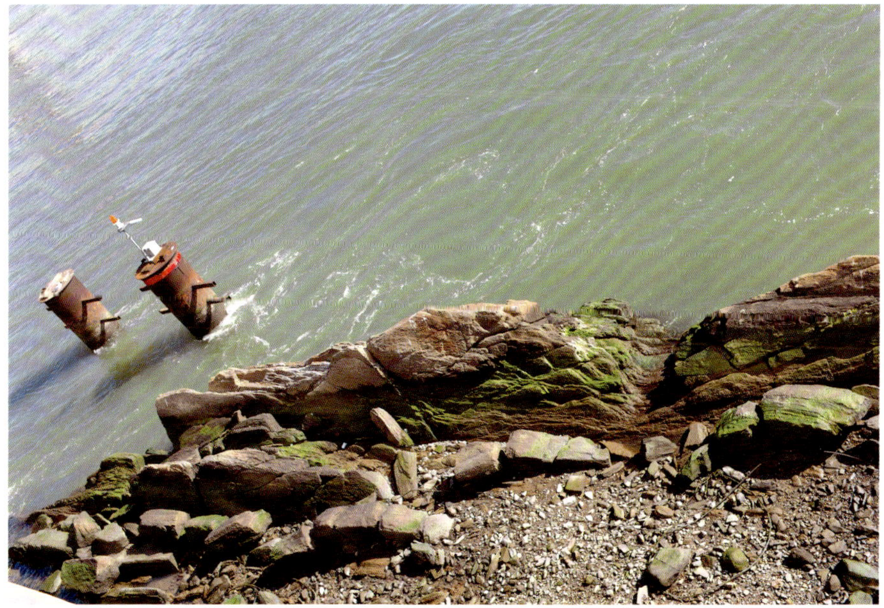
11

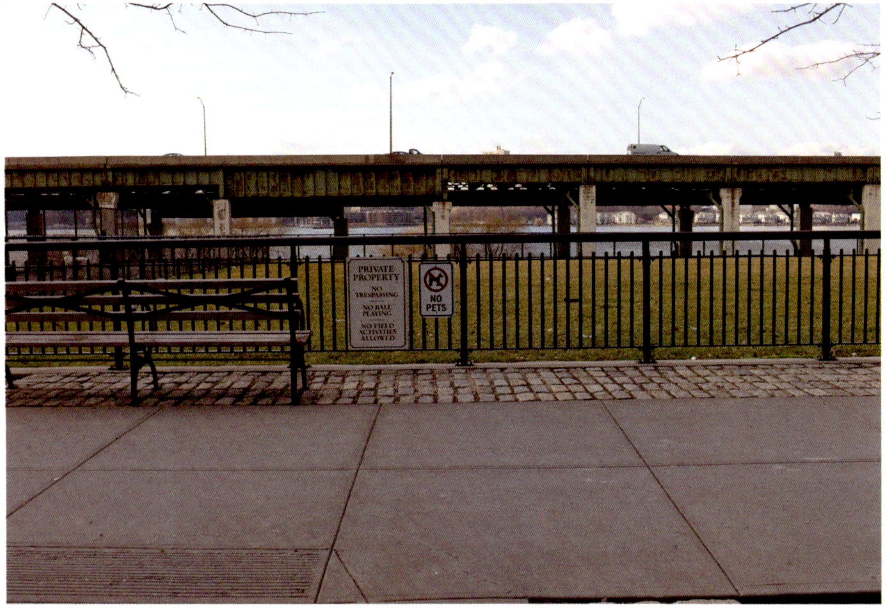

12

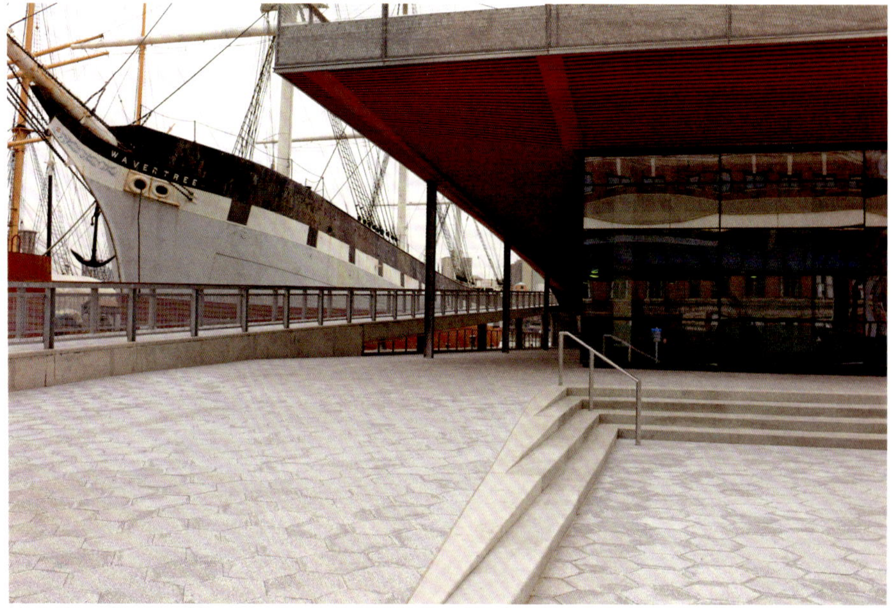

13

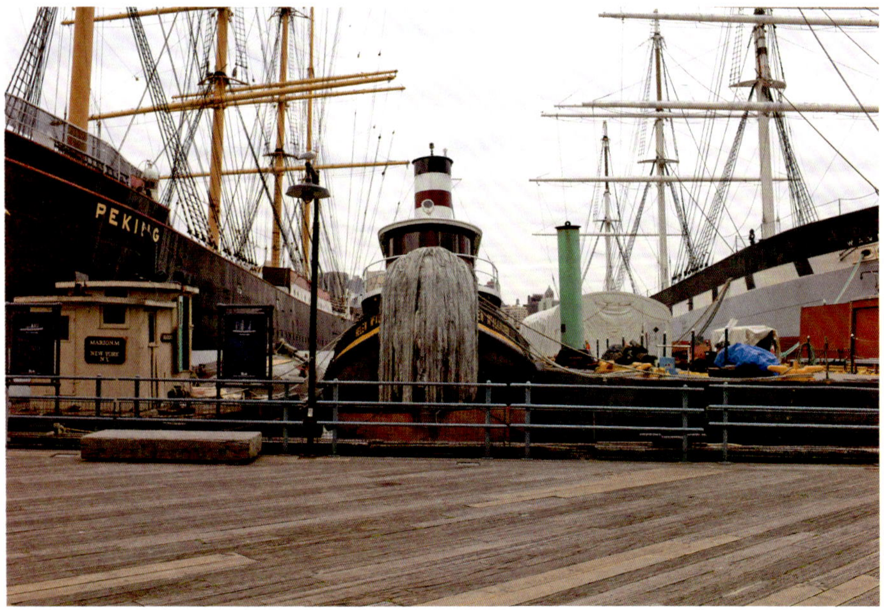

14

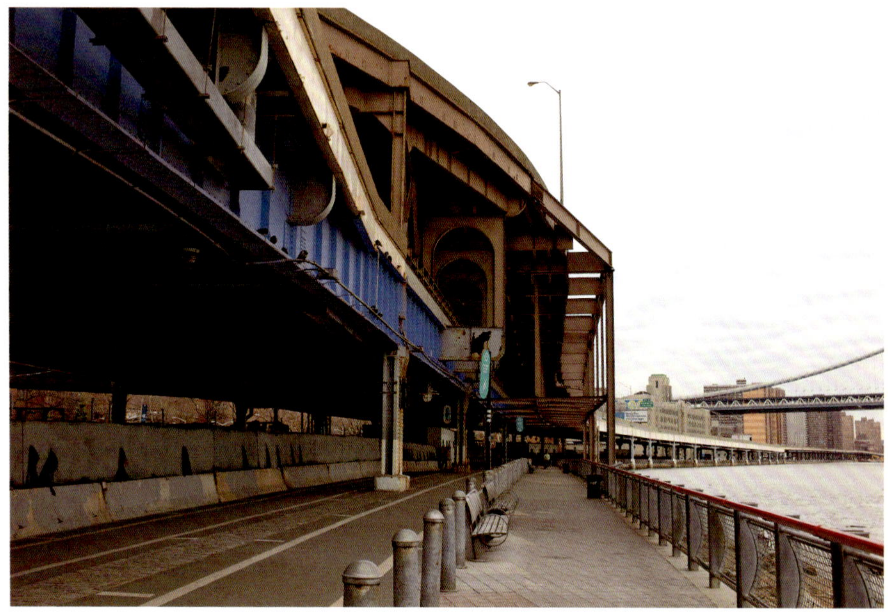

15

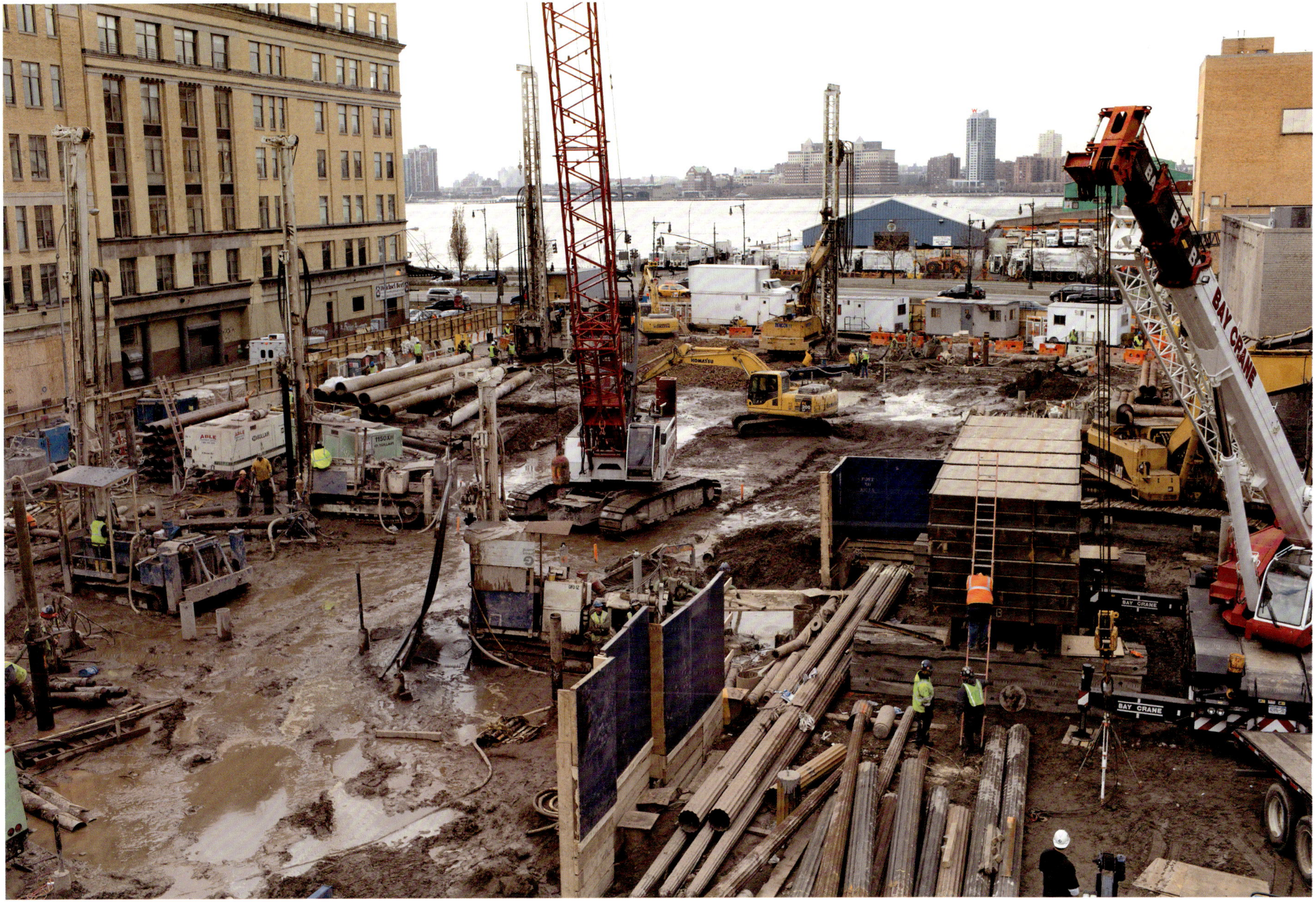
BAY CRANE

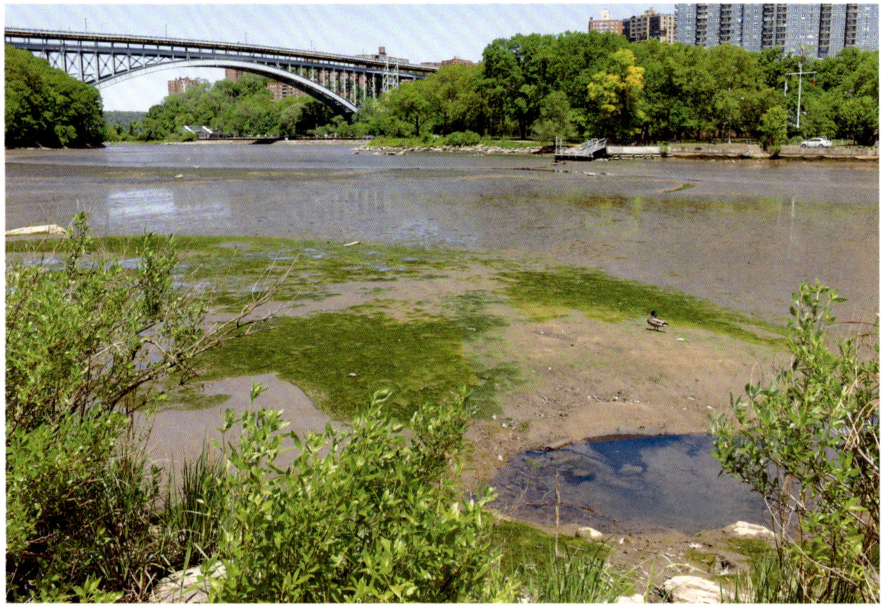

17

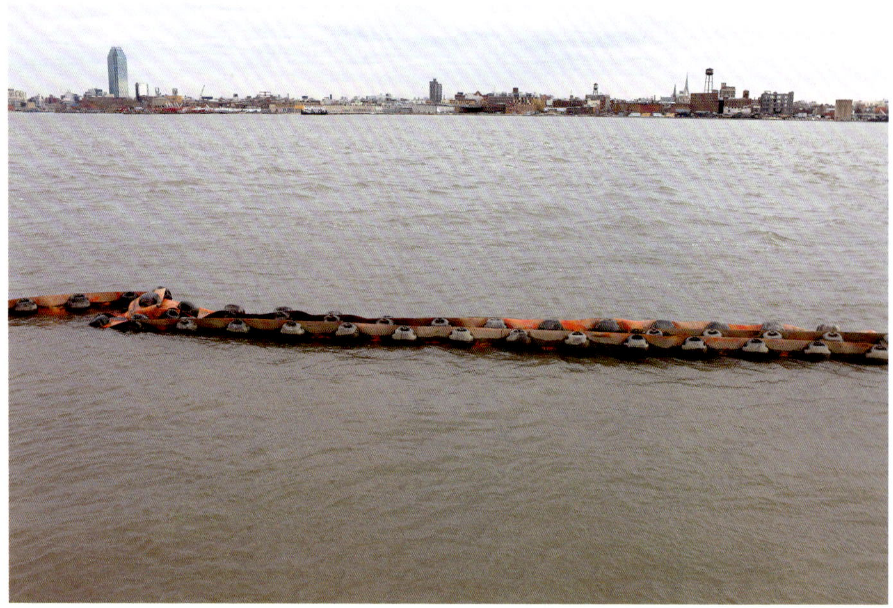

18

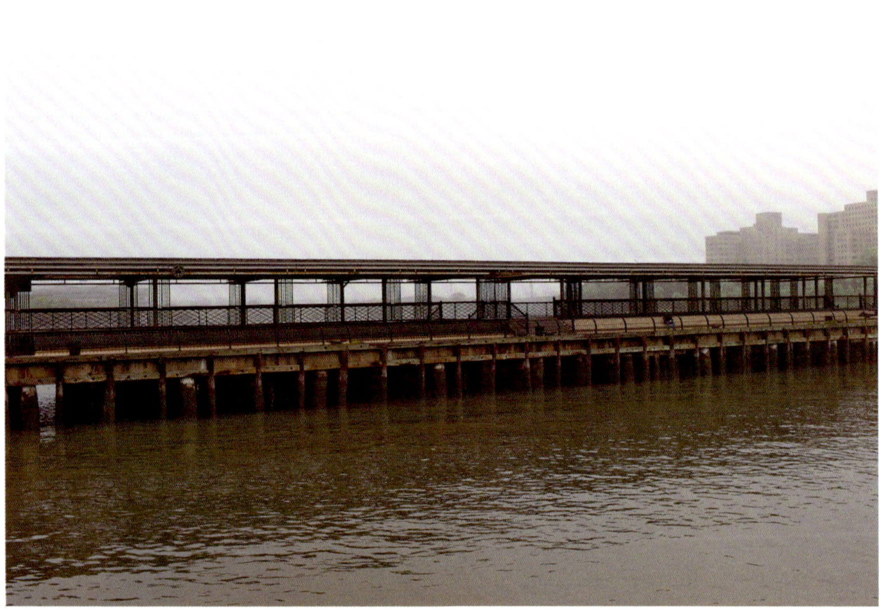

19

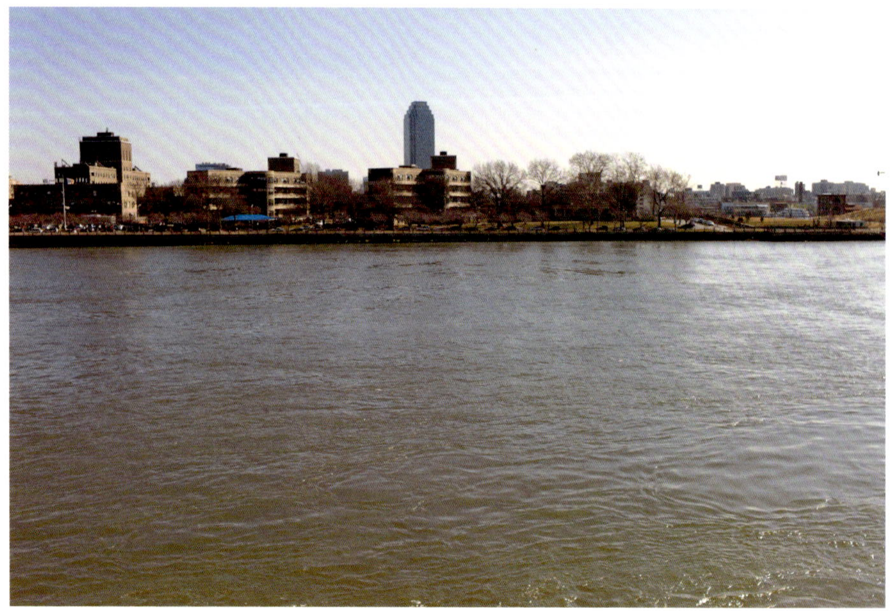

20

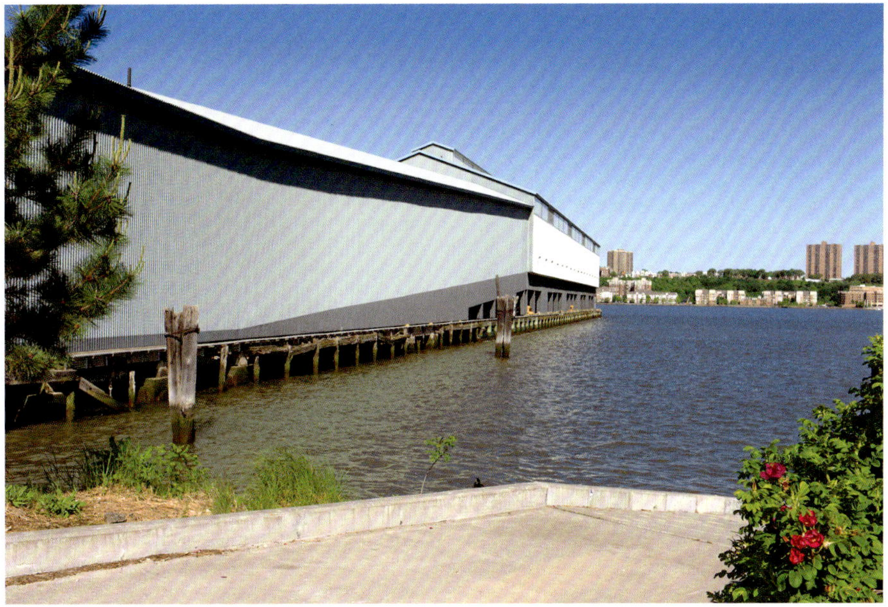
21

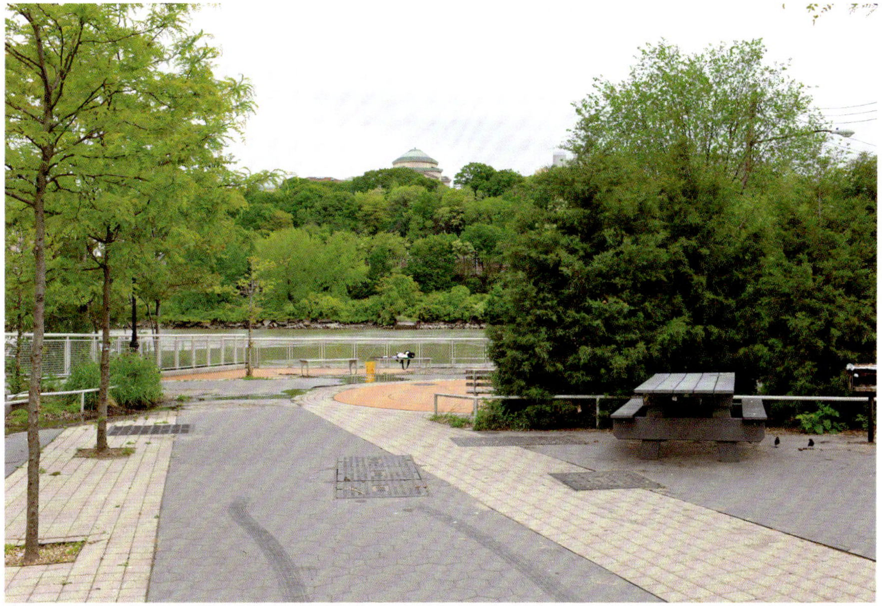
22

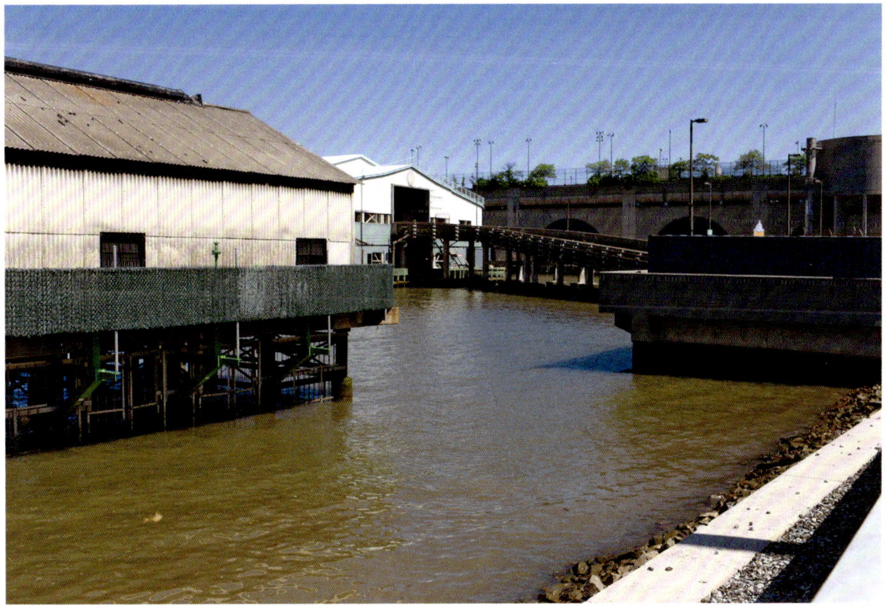
23

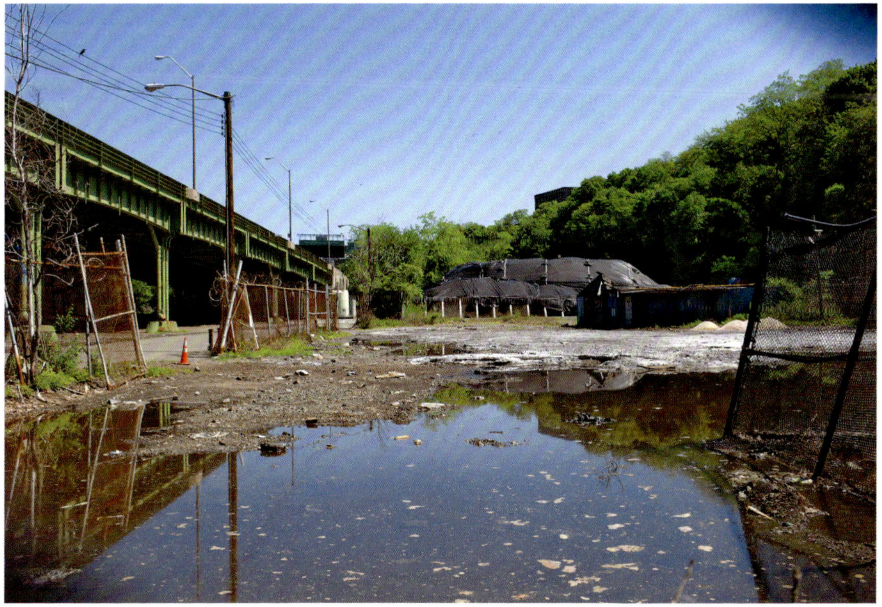
24

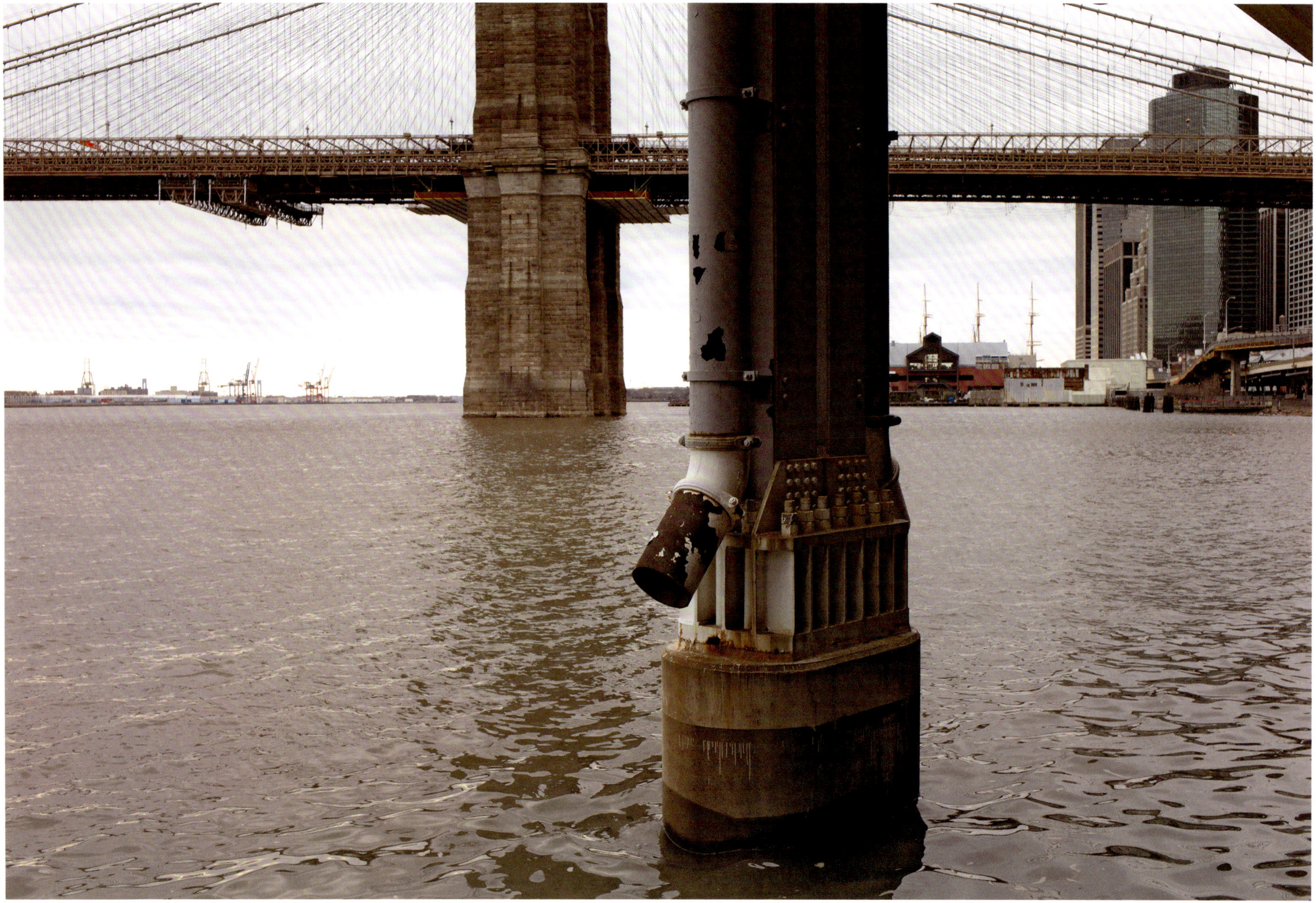

25

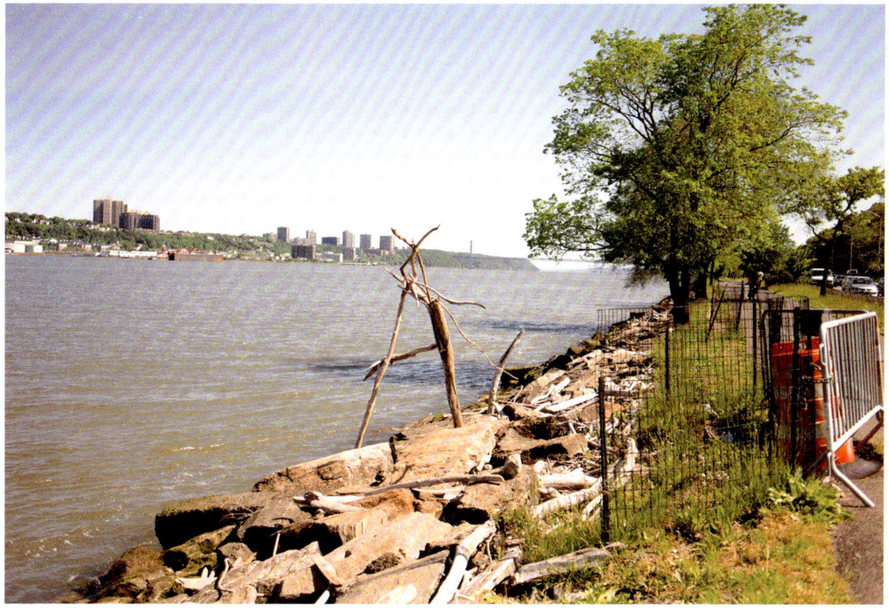
26

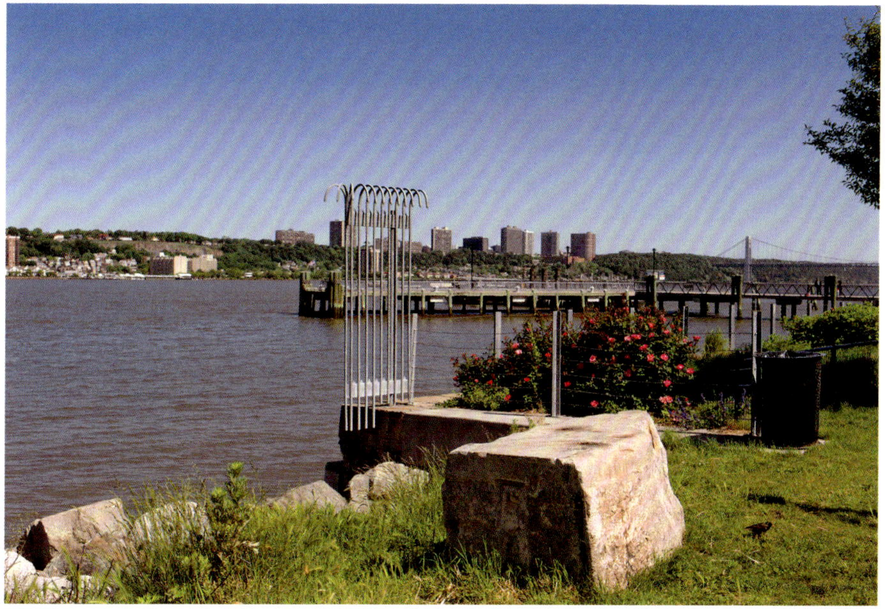
27

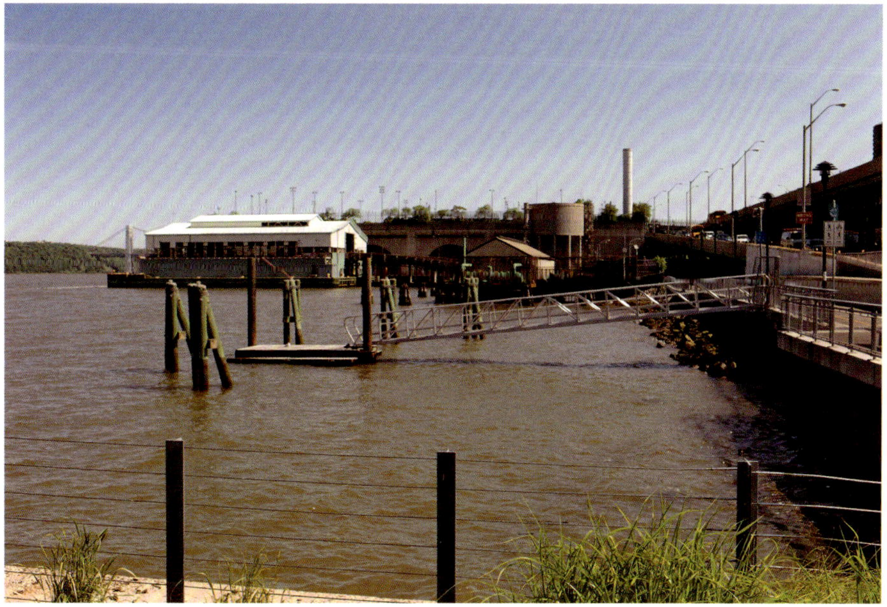
28

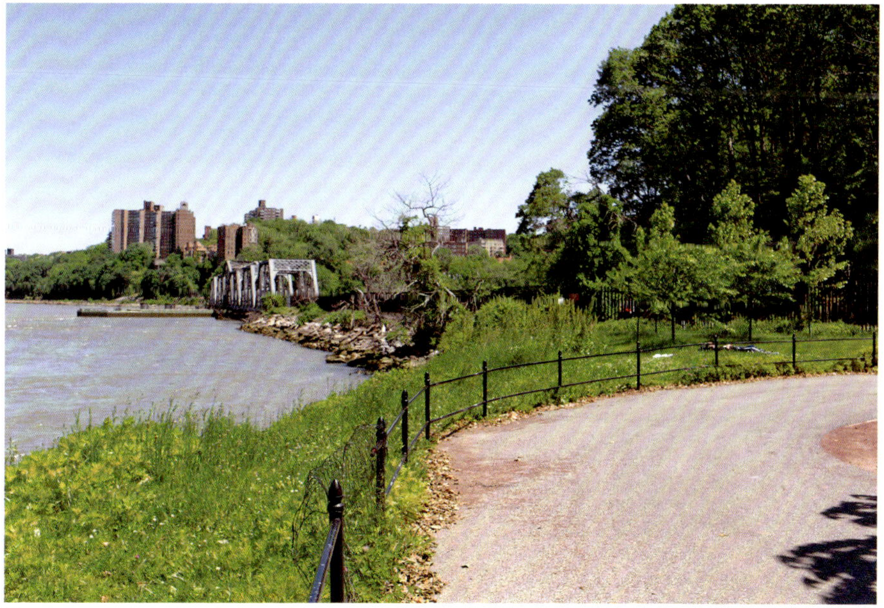
29

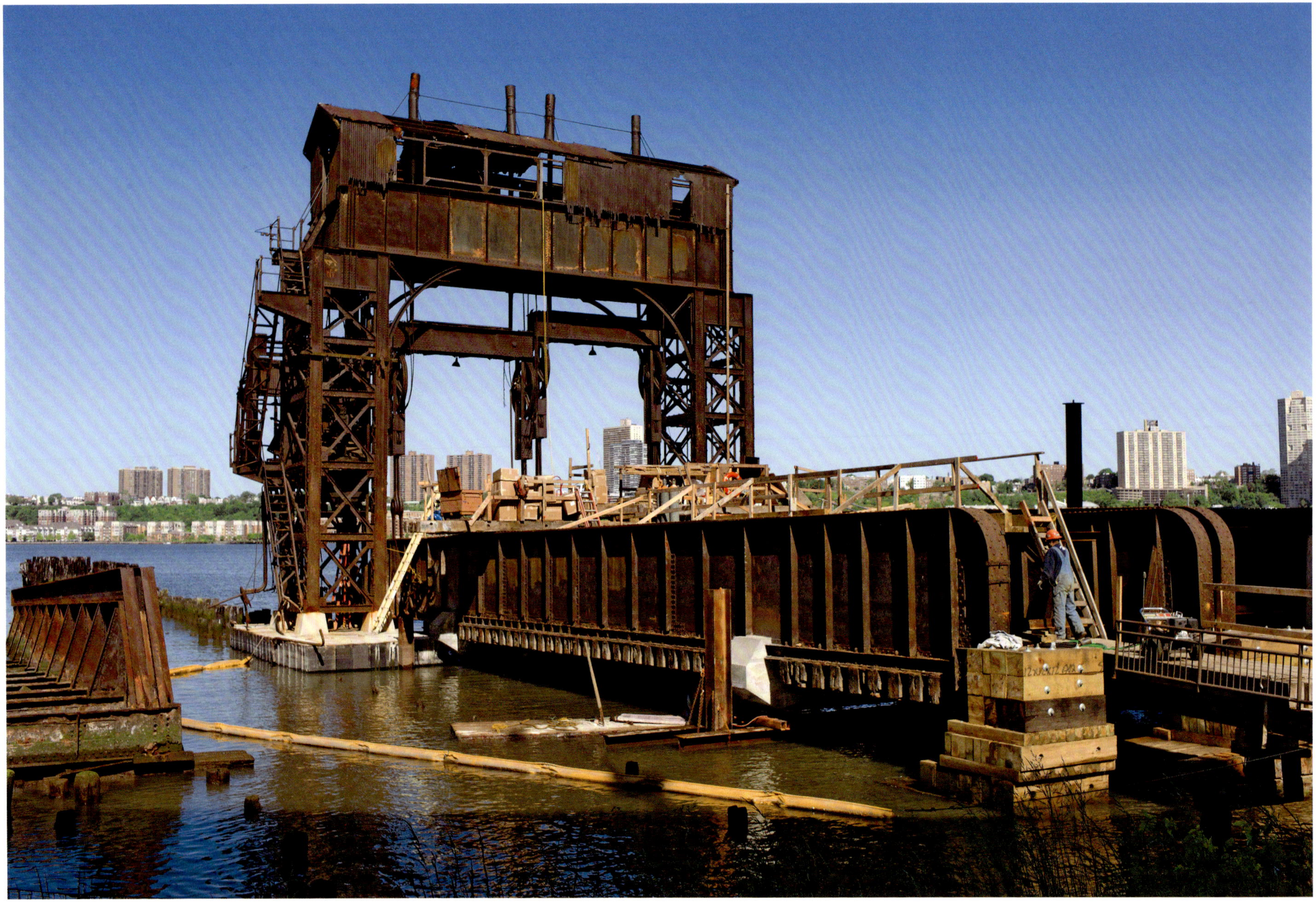

30

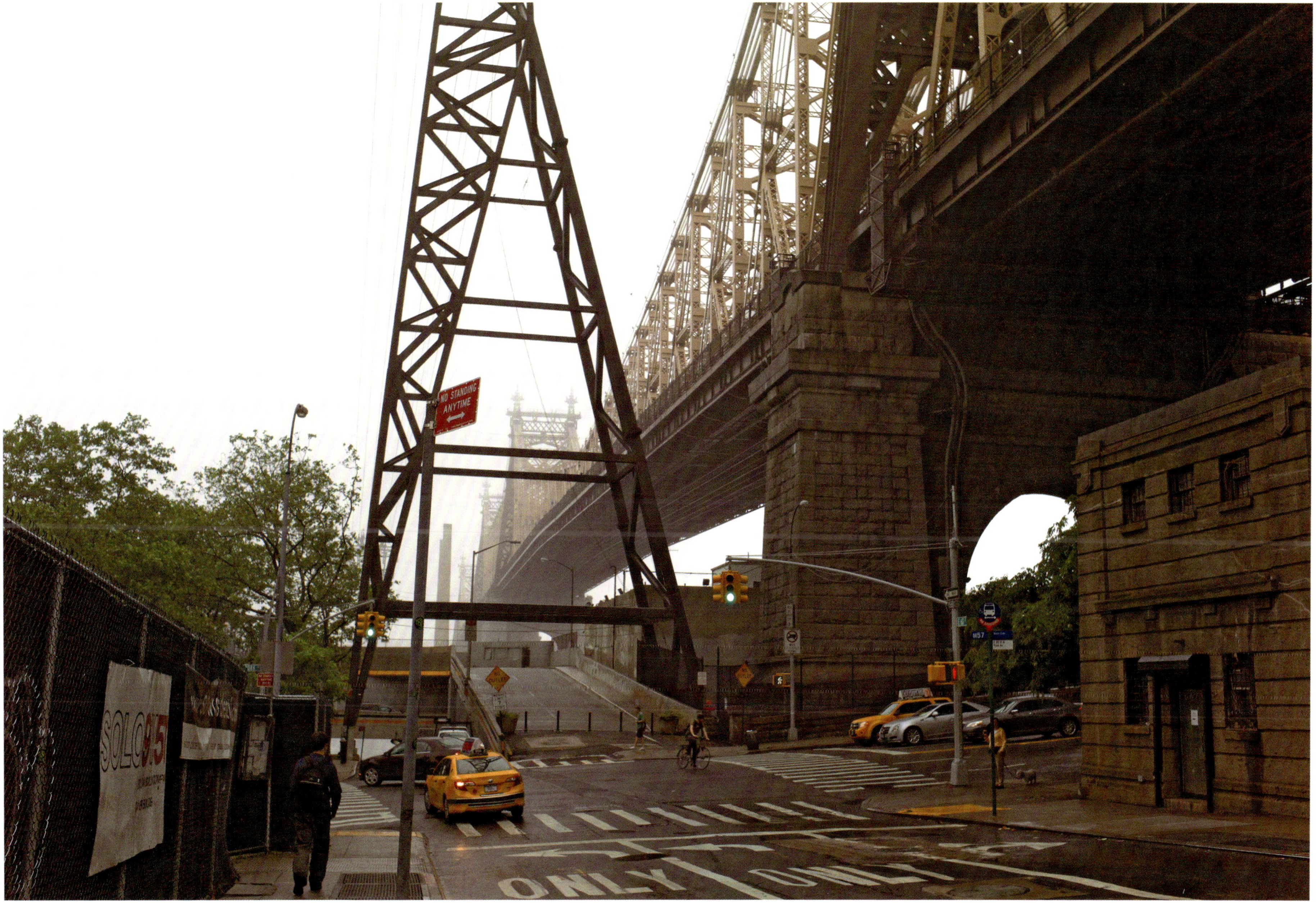

31

Stanley Greenberg is a Brooklyn-based photographer and author of numerous books, including *Invisible New York: The Hidden Infrastructure of the City* (1998), *Waterworks: A Photographic Journey Through New York's Hidden Water System* (2003), *Architecture Under Construction* (2010), and *Time Machines* (2011). His photographs are held in prominent collections, including the Metropolitan Museum of Art, the Whitney Museum of American Art, the New York Public Library, the Yale University Art Gallery, and the Los Angeles County Museum of Art, among others. Greenberg has received a fellowship from the John Simon Guggenheim Foundation, as well as grants from the Alfred P. Sloan Foundation, the National Endowment for the Arts, the New York Foundation for the Arts, and the New York State Council on the Arts. www.stanleygreenberg.org

Karrie Jacobs is a professional observer of the man-made landscape. She writes regularly for *Architect* and Curbed, and is a faculty member at the School of Visual Arts' MA program in Design Research, Writing, and Criticism, where she teaches students how to understand and interpret the design-rich environment all around them. She was the founding editor-in-chief of *Dwell* and the founding executive editor of Benetton's *Colors.* She is the author of *The Perfect $100,000 House* (2006) and coauthor of *Angry Graphics* (1992).

ACKNOWLEDGMENTS

Thanks to Alan Rapp at The Monacelli Press for acquiring and seeing *Codex New York* through to publication, Michael Vagnetti for all his production help, Karrie Jacobs for explaining the project, and to Phil Kovacevich for designing a beautiful book.

Along the way many friends helped out: Riva Blumenfeld, Richard Carboni, Michael Cetera, Greg Conniff, Heather Cristol, Rosalie Genevro, Tom Gitterman, Jon Gold, Elizabeth Goldstein, Mark Hellerman, Dennis Hrehowsik, John Levy, Tod Lippy, John Maggiotto, Mariana Mogilevich, John Shapiro, John Trotter, and Victoria Westhead.

As always, Lynn Yellen and Lena Greenberg made the entire adventure possible.

Photographs and texts © 2019 Stanley Greenberg
Foreword © 2019 Karrie Jacobs

All rights reserved. No part of this book may be reproduced, stored in a retrieval system, or transmitted in any form, by any means, including mechanical, electric, photocopying, recording or otherwise, without the prior written permission of the publisher.

Library of Congress Control Number: 2018967625

ISBN 978-1-58093-522-7

10 9 8 7 6 5 4 3 2 1

Printed in China

Design by Phil Kovacevich

The Monacelli Press
6 West 18th Street
New York, New York 10011

www.monacellipress.com